The Palgrave Handbook of Race and Ethn
Inequalities in Education

Also by A. Gary Dworkin

NEW INTERNATIONAL HANDBOOK OF RESEARCH ON TEACHERS AND TEACHING (*co-author*)

GIVING UP ON SCHOOLS: Student Dropouts and Teacher Burnouts (*co-author*)

HISPANICS IN HOUSTON AND HARRIS COUNTY: 1519–1986 (*co-editor*)

TEACHER BURNOUT IN THE PUBLIC SCHOOLS: Structural Causes and Consequences for Children

FEMALE REVOLT: Women's Movements in World and Historical Perspective (*co-author*)

WHEN TEACHERS GIVE UP: Teacher Burnout, Teacher Turnover, and Their Impact on Children

THE MINORITY REPORT: An Introduction to Race, Ethnic, Gender Relations (*co-author*)

THE BLENDING OF RACES: Identity and Marginality in World Perspective (*co-editor*)

The Palgrave Handbook of Race and Ethnic Inequalities in Education

Edited by

Peter A. J. Stevens
Ghent University, Belgium

and

A. Gary Dworkin
University of Houston, USA

First published 2014 by
PALGRAVE MACMILLAN

Palgrave Macmillan in the UK is an imprint of Macmillan Publishers Limited,
registered in England, company number 785998, of Houndmills, Basingstoke,
Hampshire RG21 6XS.

Palgrave Macmillan in the US is a division of St Martin's Press LLC,
175 Fifth Avenue, New York, NY 10010.

Palgrave Macmillan is the global academic imprint of the above companies
and has companies and representatives throughout the world.

Palgrave® and Macmillan® are registered trademarks in the United States,
the United Kingdom, Europe and other countries.

ISBN 978–0–230–30428–4

This book is printed on paper suitable for recycling and made from fully
managed and sustained forest sources. Logging, pulping and manufacturing
processes are expected to conform to the environmental regulations of the
country of origin.

A catalogue record for this book is available from the British Library.

A catalog record for this book is available from the Library of Congress.

Typeset by MPS Limited, Chennai, India.

To Dr Rosalind J. Dworkin, my wife, best friend, and frequent co-author

A.G.D.

To Alexia, for your inspiration and love and the dreams we make come true

P.A.J.S.

Contents

List of Figures

List of Tables

Preface and Acknowledgments

In the spring of 2010, Peter Stevens initiated a series of email conversations with Gary Dworkin about the development of a handbook that addressed research on racial and ethnic inequality in education around the world. Stevens had recently published two journal articles on research traditions in the UK and the Netherlands on the Handbook's topic, while Dworkin had written 11 books on various aspects of inequality, including race, ethnicity, and gender. These conversations culminated in a proposal to produce the present Palgrave Handbook. During the International Sociological Association's XVII World Congress of Sociology, held in Gothenburg, Sweden in the summer of 2010, the editors recruited several of the contributors to the project. After the conference additional contributors were recruited with the result that the Handbook represents the first systematic review of how sociologists have studied the relationship between race/ethnicity and educational inequality in 18 different national contexts: Argentina, Australia, Austria, Belgium, Brazil, Canada, China, Cyprus, Finland, France, Germany, Ireland, Japan, Russia, South Africa, the Netherlands, the UK, and the USA. Through the use of a similar methodology developed by Stevens in his key journal articles the contributors critically review the relevant literature over the past 30 years.

Each of the contributors was provided with a model that replicated the methodology developed by Stevens, thereby permitting the editors to develop a typology that summarizes the findings reported cross-nationally. The final chapter of this Handbook contains that typology and specifies trends and future directions for the study of racial and ethnic inequality in education that the reader could use in studying nations not included in the current Handbook. While the contributors tended to focus their analyses on research published in English over the past 30 years, the Handbook includes considerable literature published earlier and in other languages when such research helped to clarify issues or to inform the more current state of the field.

Every effort was made by the editors to include a broad swath of countries in this Handbook, with the result that works for all continents are included in the final product. Countries included represent those where the key minority groups are indigenous peoples or peoples brought into the country because of slavery, as well as those countries where the minority groups are refugees either from former colonies or from political and economic upheavals in their own countries. Examples of the latter include European countries that once had colonies or have experienced the migration of peoples following the turbulent eras during the collapse of the Soviet Union, the break-up of Yugoslavia, and the chaos of Somalia. The nations presented in this Handbook include many that are wrestling with issues of multiculturalism and some that have adopted that policy as part of their national agenda. Other nations included in the Handbook have adopted a policy that ignores the cultural heritages of different minority populations, assuming that all peoples in their countries are citizens in common and share in the pervasive national culture. Both the multicultural and the assimilationist strategies have numerous implications and create numerous issues of concern. The final chapter of this Handbook addresses some of the issues of either national strategy.

It is entirely appropriate that a handbook addressing research on racial and ethnic inequality in education is published at this time. Scholars, educators, and national political actors are currently addressing the extent to which the world has met the conclusion of the timetable for the attainment of the United Nations' Millennium Development Goals first proposed in 1999. By 2015 two goals that are relevant to the Handbook should have been attained. Goal number two calls for universal primary education, while goal number three calls for gender equity and the empowerment of women. Within the next two years the nations of the world, in order to attain the goals, must ensure that no racial or ethnic group should be denied access to at least a primary education and that educational opportunities should not be restricted only to male children. Sadly, the goals, while approaching some level of fruition in much of the world, will not be met universally within the next two years. Some of the nations discussed in the Handbook face the deadline even though the editors did not include the most impoverished of nations in the project. One hundred per cent literacy has been attained by only some of the nations in this Handbook and not by even the richest of them. It would have been preferred that some of the most disadvantaged nations could have been included in this Handbook. However, such disadvantages also mean that those nations have been unable to afford the kind of research tradition that could be reported here. In other instances, the study of racial and ethnic inequality in education might be met with some level of official oppression and hence not available to scholars. Nevertheless, the 18 countries presented in this Handbook do present a broad perspective on educational inequality and an array of insights that can be used to study yet other countries.

Finally, we would like to thank Palgrave and their outstanding team for supporting and assisting us with so much patience throughout the whole process.

A. Gary Dworkin
Peter A. J. Stevens
June 2013

Notes on Contributors

Nigel Brooke is an associate professor in the Faculty of Education, Federal University of Minas Gerais, Brazil. A member of the Educational Evaluation and Measurement Group, he obtained his PhD in Development Studies from the University of Sussex, UK. Prior activities include nine years with the Ford Foundation's Rio de Janeiro office, first as Program Officer for Education and then as representative, and ten years as researcher, educational planner, and education policy advisor for the state government of Minas Gerais. Current activities include the coordination of a follow-up study to the GERES project, a longitudinal study of 20,000 elementary school children, and advisory work with the federal government and state and municipal secretariats of education in the field of educational evaluation. Publications cover the themes of educational quality, educational decentralization, educational evaluation and accountability and, most recently, the history of education reform. Contact email address: n.brooke@terra.com.br.

Hua-Yu Sebastian Cherng is a joint PhD candidate in sociology and education policy at the University of Pennsylvania. His research interests include gender and ethnic differences in education and ethnic identification in China, as well as the social lives of racial/ethnic and immigrant adolescents and cultural and social capital transfers between adolescent friends in the United States. Recent papers include articles in the *American Education Research Journal* (with Jessica McCrory Calarco and Grace Kao), *Teachers College Record* (with Kristin Turney and Grace Kao), and the *Oxford Review of Education* (with Emily Hannum and Xuehui An). His dissertation uses a nationally representative sample of US high school sophomores to investigate patterns of social interaction and isolation from peers, teachers, and parents among racial/ethnic minority and immigrant adolescents. He can be contacted through his personal webpage (sites.google.com/site/hscherng) or at cherng@gse.upenn.edu.

Silvina Cimolai is an associate professor and researcher at the Pedagogic University of the Buenos Aires Province in Argentina. She is currently the director of a research project funded by the National Agency for the Scientific and Technological Promotion on the research practices carried out by academics in the intersections of psychology and education in Argentina. She is also a researcher at the research program 'School, Difference, and Inclusion' at the National University of Quilmes. Her research interests have been focused on psycho-educational problems and on the production of knowledge in education. Contact email address: silcimolai@gmail.com.

Noel Clycq is a postdoctoral researcher and coordinator in the FP7-project 'Reducing Early School Leaving in Europe', at the CeMIS, at the University of Antwerp. Noel's research interests cover the areas of ethnic and gender relations and identity constructions, power differences and stratification in the domain of education, integration and the family. His expertise lies in qualitative research methods. His past and current research focuses on: identity construction in the family, ethnicity and cultural diversity and educational inequality, early school leaving, processes of stigmatization in schools, and the appreciation of community funds of knowledge such as supplementary education. All this is located within a theoretical framework taking power differences as a starting point. His work has been published in journals in the field of education, sociology, and gender, including *British Educational Research Journal*, the *Sociological Review* and the *European Journal of Women's Studies*. Noel coordinated a large-scale project on educational trajectories of (immigrant) youth funded by the Government Agency for Innovation by Science and Technology. Contact email address: noel.clycq@ua.ac.be.

Gill Crozier is professor of education and director of the Centre for Educational Research in Equalities, Policy and Pedagogy in the School of Education, University of Roehampton, UK. She is a sociologist of education and has researched and written extensively on parents, families, and school relationships. Her work is underpinned by a deep concern for equalities and social justice and is informed by the analysis of race, class, and gender and the ways these social locations and identities intersect and impact on life chances. Other specific areas of her work include: issues relating to young people, access to and participation in higher education, education policy, and the socio-cultural influences upon identity formation and learner experiences. She has published extensively on these issues. Her research studies include: 'The Socio-Cultural and Learning Experiences of Working Class Students in Higher Education'; 'Identities, Educational Choices and the White Urban Middle Classes'; 'Parents, Children and the School Experience: Asian Families' Perspectives'. Contact email address: g.crozier@roehampton.ac.uk.

Maurice Crul is professor of sociology at the Free University in Amsterdam and the Erasmus University of Rotterdam. His research interests include the areas of education and labor market among children of immigrants in a cross-European and transatlantic perspective. His past and current research focuses on the effect of national and local institutional arrangements in education and the labor market on school, and labor market careers of children of immigrants. He has been a guest editor of special issues in journals including *International Migration Review, Ethnic and Racial Studies, Journal of Ethnic and Migration Studies*, and *Teachers' College Records*. He is the co-author of several books, including *Superdiversity: A New Vision on Integration* (2013), *The Changing Face of World*

Cities (2012), and *The European Second Generation Compared* (2012). He coordinated the TIES project (http://www.tiesproject.eu), a survey project on the second generation in eight European countries and is currently coordinating the ELITES project (http://www.elitesproject.eu/), looking at the upcoming elite among the second generation in Europe. Contact email address: crul@fsw.eur.nl.

Natalino Neves da Silva received his undergraduate and master's degrees in education from the Federal University of Minas Gerais where he is currently a doctoral student. He also teaches Sociology and Anthropology of Education, Childhood in Brazil, and Philosophical Studies: Epistemologies of Education on the teacher training program run by the Faculty of Education of the State University of Minas Gerais. His research area is the sociology of education with a focus on educational inequalities related to race/ethnicity. He has also carried out studies on youth and non-formal education. Contact email address: natalgerais@yahoo.com.br.

Leokadia M. Drobizheva is chief scientific researcher, head of the Research Center for Interethnic Relations at the Russian Academy of Science (RAS) Institute of Sociology, and professor at the Higher School for Economics and the Russian State Humanitarian University. Between 2005 and 2012 she was the chief editor of the Kennan Institute Bulletin in Moscow. Now she heads the Committee for Ethnic Sociology at the Russian Society of Sociologists. She is also a member of the RF President's Council on Interethnic Relations. Professor Drobizheva studies ethnic and civic identity, interethnic identity, disparities of ethnic groups, isolationism and discrimination, and works on problems of ethnic nationalism. She is the author of ten books and over 300 articles. Her books include *Social Problems of Interethnic Relations in the Post-Soviet Space* (2003) and *Ethnicity in the Socio-Political Space of the Russian Federation* (2013). She supervised projects studying nationalisms in the republics of the Russian Federation, social and cultural distances, disparities of ethnic groups, and ethnic and civil identities. Contact email address: drobizheva@yandex.ru.

A. Gary Dworkin is professor of sociology, co-founder of the Sociology of Education Research Group, and former chair of the Department of Sociology, University of Houston, USA. Currently, he is president of Research Committee 04 (Sociology of Education) of the International Sociological Association. He served on the Council of the Sociology of Education section of the American Sociological Association and as president of the Southwestern Sociological Association. His publications include 11 books and numerous articles on teacher burnout, student drop-out behavior, minority–majority relations, gender roles, and on school accountability. His publications on the *No Child Left Behind Act* appeared in the journal *Sociology of Education*, in a special issue of the *International Journal of Contemporary Sociology*, and in several book chapters. He wrote with J. Lorence on the effects of retention-in-grade

(The Brookings Institution, Washington, DC). He and Rosalind J. Dworkin published three editions of *The Minority Report* (3rd edition by Wadsworth, 1999), a book on race, ethnic, and gender relations. Along with L. J. Saha, Dworkin edited *The International Handbook of Research on Teachers and Teaching* (2009). Contact email address: gdworkin@central.uh.edu.

Shaheeda Essack is acting director of the Directorate: Private Higher Education Institutions at the National Department of Higher Education and Training in South Africa. Shaheeda's work experience includes secondary school teaching, adult basic education and training, and academic development in higher education. Her research interests cover the following areas: student/staff/curriculum development in higher education; peer mentoring and educational development in the context of a transforming society; and policy development and implementation in higher education in post-apartheid SA. Her work has been presented at EARLI conferences and published in journals such as *Interactive Discourse* and *Sociopedia.isa*. She is also a senior research associate in the Department of Sociology at the University of Johannesburg. Her current research focuses on the transition of marginalized learners from secondary school to post-school education and training institutions and the challenges they experience in the context of a transforming post-apartheid society. Contact email address: essack.s@dhet.

Daniel Faas is head of the Department of Sociology and member of the University Council at Trinity College Dublin. His research interests are in the sociology of migration with specific emphasis on the intersection of migration and education. His work focuses on youth identities in relation to immigrant integration, national identity, multiculturalism and social cohesion in Europe, diversity management in educational sites and work places, as well as curriculum design and development. He is the author of *Negotiating Political Identities: Multiethnic Schools and Youth in Europe* (2010). His work has been published in high-impact journals in the fields of sociology, education, and ethnic studies, including the *British Journal of Sociology*, *British Educational Research Journal* and *Ethnicities*. He is a winner of the Provost's Teaching Award at Trinity College Dublin, and recipient of the European Sociological Association award for best journal article. He was Marie Curie Research Fellow at the Hellenic Foundation for European and Foreign Policy in Athens, and Fulbright-Schuman Fellow in the Department of Sociology at the University of California, Berkeley. Contact email address: daniel.faas@tcd.ie.

Rachael Fionda is the academic director of the Swan Training Institute in Dublin. Her initial interest in educational inequality stemmed from her research into language rights in bilingual areas. She spent some time in Italy's autonomous South Tyrol region and conducted research on the bilingual school system for her MPhil. After time as a lecturer at the Universität Innsbruck, Fionda began her PhD research with the Trinity Immigration Initiative, a multi-disciplinary research project on diversity, integration, and policy. Working under Professor David Little, her research addressed the integration of migrant students in Irish second-level education. The project employed qualitative research methodologies conducted in school settings, targeting focus groups of educators and students via semi-structured interviews and in-depth case-studies. As a result of the project, she has spoken at a variety of conferences and has published a handful of articles and book chapters. She is currently participating in action research in the field of applied linguistics while working with worldwide students in the private sector of her current workplace. Contact email address: fiondar@tcd.ie.

Paul, Fripp is an undergraduate student pursuing studies in philosophy and sociology, with the intention of pursing a graduate degree in the near future. He holds a Bachelor of Commerce with Honours from the University of British Columbia and is a member of the Institute of Chartered Accountants of British Columbia. Paul has worked in public practice as an auditor for eight years, through which he obtained extensive experience performing quantitative analyses and testing the economic systems within regional and multi-national corporations with asset bases of up to $1.5 billion. This diverse training facilitates Paul's interdisciplinary approach to the study of social inequality. He focuses in particular on the complex interconnections between economic institutions, systemic processes, and the reproduction of inequalities. Contact email address: pfripp@live.com.

Hélène Frohard-Dourlent is a doctoral student in sociology at the University of British Columbia. She is a graduate of Université de Paris 3-Sorbonne Nouvelle (BA) and the University of British Columbia (MA). Her research foci are education, gender, sexuality, and race/ethnicity, with particular interest in discourse analysis and critical media analysis. Her dissertation examines the experiences of school staff (administrators, counselors, teachers, and support staff) who have worked with trans and gender-fluid youth in British Columbia. She is also connected to the Stigma and Resilience Among Vulnerable Youth Centre at UBC as well as Safety Nets for Gender Variant Children and Youth at Simon Fraser University. Her work has been published in the *Journal of LGBT Youth, Sexualities*, as well as the *Canadian Journal of Higher Education*. She continues to be active in local LGBTQ youth organizations to help improve learning environments for all youth. Contact email address: katherine.lyon@live.ca.

Ingrid Gogolin is full professor of international comparative and intercultural education research at University of Hamburg. Her research interests cover the following areas: consequences of migration for education; international comparison of education systems and their historical and contemporary approaches to diversity. Her work has been published in high-ranking educational research journals, including *European Educational Research Journal, British Educational Research Journal*, and the *Zeitschrift für Erziehungswissenschaft*. She is the coordinator of the Center for Research and Support of Migrant Children and Youth (FöRMIG, www.foermig.uni-hamburg.de) at the University of Hamburg, as well as co-coordinator of the Research Center of Excellence 'Linguistic Diversity Management in Urban Areas' (LiMA, www.lima.uni-hamburg.de). Her current research is focused on longitudinal development of migrant children's multilingual performance and on the design and evaluation of supportive educational models for multilingual, multicultural schools. Contact email address: gogolin@uni-hamburg.de.

Luiz Alberto Gonçalves is an associate professor, teaching Research Methodology at the Faculties of Education and Medicine of the Federal University of Minas Gerais. He also teaches Epistemology and Education in the doctoral program in education. His research and publications are on the sociology of education with a focus on educational inequalities based on race/ethnicity, studies of contemporary youth and religious culture, and violence in school. He was a member of the scientific committee of the European Observatory on School Violence. He was also technical and scientific advisor to the Sao Paulo Research Foundation and the Carlos Chagas Foundation. He is currently coordinator of the International Postgraduate Program, collaboration between the Federal University of Minas Gerais and the Eleventh of November University (Angola). Contact email address: laog5@oi.com.br.

Neil Guppy is professor and head of sociology at the University of British Columbia. He was Associate Dean (Students) from 1996 to 1999 and Associate Vice-President (Academic Programs) at UBC from 1999 to 2004. He is a graduate of Queen's University (BA/BPHE) and the University of Waterloo (MSc/PhD, 1981). He has published several books, including *Education in Canada* (1998, with Scott Davies), *The Schooled Society* (2013, 3rd edition, with Scott Davies), and *Successful Surveys* (2008, 4th edition, with George Gray). Recently he has published work in the *American Sociological Review* and *International Migration Review* on public opinion and immigration, in *Sociological Forum* on cultural capital and job search/attainment, and in *Canadian Public Policy* on science policy in Canada (Innovation). His research interests include social inequality (especially class, ethnicity, and gender), work and occupations, and education. At UBC he has received both a University Killam Teaching Prize and a University Killam Research Prize. Contact email address: neil.guppy@ubc.ca.

Emily Hannum is an associate professor of sociology and education and chair of the Graduate Group in Sociology at the University of Pennsylvania. Her research interests include education, global development, gender and ethnic stratification, poverty, and child welfare. She is a principal investigator on the Gansu Survey of Children and Families, a collaborative, longitudinal study of children in rural northwest China that seeks to illuminate sources of upward mobility among children living in some of China's poorest communities, and is a member of a new international research project on social and economic welfare in China's western minority regions. Currently, she is a co-editor of the journal *Comparative Education Review*, and she serves on the international advisory board for the China General Social Survey. Recent papers include 'Poverty and Proximate Barriers to Learning: Vision Deficiencies, Vision Correction and Educational Outcomes in Rural Northwest China' (with Yuping Zhang, 2012, *World Development*) and 'Why Are Returns to Education Higher for Women than for Men in Urban China?' (with Yuping Zhang and Meiyan Wang, forthcoming, *China Quarterly*). She can be contacted at hannumem@soc.upenn.edu.

Päivi M. Harinen is a lecturer in sociology at the Faculty of Social Sciences and Business Studies, University of Eastern Finland, and adjunct professor in sociology of education at the Department of Educational Sciences, University of Tampere, Finland. Her research interests cover issues dealing with young people's societal membership positions when scrutinized through the attributes of age, gender, ethnicity, socio-economic indicators, and domicile. Harinen has also conducted research concerning racism and other forms of discrimination among the youth who represent different minorities (ethnic, sexual, religious, handicapped etc.). School and leisure surroundings as meaningful social spaces for the youth have framed the main contexts for her analyses. Her work has been published in national and international outlets, including the *Journal of Leisure Studies*. Harinen is currently leading two research projects: 'Alternative Sports as Youth Cultural Forms' and 'Contexts for Diaspora Citizenship: Somali Immigrants in Finland and in the US' Contact email address: paivi.harinen@uef.fi.

Barbara Herzog-Punzenberger is chair of the research program on multilinguality, interculturality, and mobility at the Federal Institute for Research in Education, Innovation, and Development of the Austrian School System BIFIE. Her research interests cover the areas of sociology of education, ethnic relations and minorities, political philosophy, and mixed methods research. She has been leading the Austrian part of the EU comparative study of the second generation TIES at the Austrian Academy of Sciences and was a member of the EU network of excellence in migration research IMISCOE. She is standing expert of the EU Fundamental Rights Agency and member of the EU network on policy development in the field of migrant education SIRIUS. She taught at the University of Vienna, the University of Economics in Vienna, the University of Hannover, and the University of Salzburg. She is particularly interested in the governance of education systems in societies of immigration and has been lecturing at the OECD, Metropolis Canada and Metropolis International, Kennedy School of Government at Harvard University, and the Open Society Institute. Contact email address: b.herzog-punzenberger@bifie.at.

Duncan Hindle is currently a special adviser to the minister of agriculture, forestry and fisheries in South Africa. He was previously the director general of education in South Africa from 2004 to 2010. A teacher by profession, he has taught mathematics at primary and secondary schools, educational technology at a teacher training college, and sociology of education at the University of Natal in Durban. His research interests focused on policy contestations in education during the transition from apartheid to democracy. His work has been published in various journals and books. He also served as president of the South African Democratic Teachers Union (SADTU), the largest teachers' union in South Africa, before joining government in 1996. Contact email address: hindle@mweb.co.za.

Mathieu Ichou is a PhD student in sociology at Sciences Po. His doctoral research focuses on the academic trajectories of children of immigrants in France and the UK. His broader research interests include sociology of education, migration and ethnicity, social stratification and inequality, comparative sociology, and quantitative and mixed methodology. His work has been published by high-profile academic presses and journals, including Stanford University Press, *Oxford Review of Education* and *Revue Française de Sociologie*. He has presented his research at numerous international conferences including the American Sociological Association Annual Meeting, the International Sociological Association RC 28 Meeting, and the European Consortium for Sociological Research Annual Conference. Ichou is also affiliated with the Center for Research in Economics and Statistics (CREST) and the National Institute for Demographic Studies (INED). He was a junior visiting scholar at Nuffield College (University of Oxford) in 2010–2011. Contact email address: mathieu.ichou@sciencespo.fr.

David L. Konstantinovskiy is head of the Department of Sociology of Education, Science and Culture at the Institute of Sociology, Russian Academy of Sciences. He is also professor of the Russian Presidential Academy of National Economy and Public Administration. His research interests cover the areas of sociology of education, sociology of youth, and social prognosis. His main past and current research focuses on social inequality in education and social mobility and particularly on: the dynamics of social processes from the Soviet period till the present time; the differentiation of educational institutions; impact of social changes; and methodological issues in social research. He has conducted more than 20 research projects in Russia and other countries. His works have been published in various journals including *European Journal of Education,* has been translated into English and published in *Russian Education and Society.* Contact email address: dav.konstant@gmail.com.

Ruth N. López Turley is an associate professor of sociology at Rice University. She is the director of the Houston Education Research Consortium (HERC), a research partnership between Rice and HISD that aims to close the socio-economic gaps in achievement and attainment, and she is the associate director of the Kinder Institute for Urban Research. She has a BA from Stanford University and an MA and PhD from Harvard University, where she was a doctoral fellow at the Kennedy School of Government's Multidisciplinary Program in Inequality and Social Policy. She was previously a National Academy of Education Postdoctoral Fellow and was on the faculty at the University of Wisconsin, Madison, where she was an affiliate of the Wisconsin Center for Education Research. She recently served on the National Research Council. Contact email address: turley@rice.edu.

Chunping Lu is an associate professor at the School of Social Development and Public Administration at Northwest Normal University. Director of the Ethnic Minority Women Study's Center in Northwest Normal University, her research interests cover Chinese NGOs, sociology of organization, sociology of education, and social work. She is currently conducting a research project funded by the China National Social Science Foundation, which focuses on the development and management of NGOs in ethnic minority areas of Northwest China. She is the author of *The Socialization of People's Mediation Organization in China's Transformation.* Contact email address: luchunping@nwnu.edu.cn.

Katherine A. Lyon is a PhD student in sociology at the University of British Columbia and a recipient of the Joseph-Armand Bombardier Graduate Scholarship provided by the Social Sciences and Humanities Research Council of Canada. Her research interests include gender, sexuality, education, and social inequality, with a particular focus on the historical construction of Canadian sex education curricula. Katherine received her MA in Sociology and the Collaborative Program in Women's and Gender Studies from the University of Toronto. Her MA thesis explored how common-law gay and lesbian couples in Toronto, Ontario negotiate and experience their access to the institution of marriage (legal in the province since 2003). At University of Toronto Katherine was a junior fellow of Massey College and a recipient of the C.B. McPherson Graduate Admissions Award, the Dean's Students Initiative Fund, and the Ontario Graduate Scholarship. Contact email address: katherine.lyon@live.ca.

Analía Inés Meo is a full-time researcher at the Consejo Nacional de Investigaciones Científicas y Técnicas (University of Buenos Aires, Argentina). Her research interests include the areas of sociology of education and qualitative and collaborative research methods. Her past and current research focuses on: social class, gender and educational inequality, teachers' professional identities, school segregation, and educational policy processes. She has published articles in academic journals such as the *British Journal of Sociology of Education*, the *International Journal of Qualitative Methods* and the *Revista de Metodología de Ciencias Sociales*. She has also (co-)written numerous book chapters and co-authored the book *La voz de los otros: el uso de la entrevista en la investigación social*. She was a postgraduate fellow of the Department of Sociology at the University of Warwick, a post-doctoral fellow and visiting research associate at the London Institute of Education, and part-time lecturer at the University of Buenos Aires. Her current research focuses on educational policy process and teachers' work identities in the educational system of Buenos Aires. Contact email address: analiameo@conicet.gov.ar.

Kaori H. Okano is professor of Asian studies at the Faculty of Humanities and Social Sciences, La Trobe University, Melbourne. Kaori researches on education and social inequality (class, gender, and ethnicity), multiculturalism and transnationalism in education, indigenous education, and is undertaking a longitudinal ethnographic study of growing up. Her focus is Japan and Asia. Books include *Minorities and Education in Multicultural Japan: An Interactive Perspective* (ed. with R. Tsuneyoshi and S. Boocock, 2011), *Handbook of Asian Education* (ed. with Y. Zhao et al., 2011), *Young Women in Japan: Transitions to Adulthood* (2009), *Language and Schools in Asia* (ed., 2006), *Education in Contemporary Japan* (with M. Tsuchiya, 1999), and *School to Work Transition in Japan* (1993). Contact email address: k.okano@latrobe.edu.au.

Andrea V. Pérez is a PhD candidate at the Latin American Faculty of Social Sciences (FLACSO) Argentina. She is associate professor and researcher of the National University of Quilmes and the Pedagogical University, Buenos Aires Province, Argentina. She is also the director of the Centre for Disability of National University of Quilmes. Her research interests cover the areas of pedagogy, philosophy, and cultural diversity. Her previous research focused on the educational experiences of Bolivian immigrant children in Argentine schools. Her current research focuses on pedagogy's discourses on otherness, legal frameworks governing education, and social regulations. Contact email address: aperez@unq.edu.ar.

M'hammed Sabour is professor of sociology of knowledge and culture at the University of Eastern Finland. His main fields of research and teaching are higher education, intellectuals, cultural globalization, racism, cultural discrimination, and ethnic minorities. During the last two decades he has been supervising numerous studies on exclusion and inclusion of minorities in school, society, and labor market. Due to his research work in helping immigrant integration he has been nominated officially as goodwill ambassador by ETNO (Finland) since 2004. He is the managing editor of *International Journal of Contemporary Sociology*. Publications include 'Socio-cultural Exclusion and Self-Exclusion of Foreigners in Finland: The Case of Joensuu', in P. Littlewood et al. (Eds) *Social Exclusion* and 'The Impact of Globalisation on the Mission of the University', in Joseph Zajda (Ed.) *International Handbook of Globalisation and Education Policy Research*. Contact email address: mhammed.sabour@uef.fi.

Lawrence J. Saha is professor of sociology at the Research School of Social Sciences, Australian National University. He is former head of the Department of Sociology, and former Dean (Faculty of Arts). He has published widely in the fields of comparative education, education and national development, student aspirations and expectations, and political socialization among youth. He was editor of *The International Encyclopedia of the Sociology of Education* (1997) and co-authored *The Untested Accusation: Principals, Research Knowledge and Policy-Making in Schools* (2002). He was co-editor of the two-volume *International Handbook of Research on Teachers and Teaching* (2009), *Youth Participation in Politics* (2007), and *Nation-Building, Identity and Citizenship Education* (2009). He is currently editor of *Social Psychology of Education: An International Journal* and is also a vice-president of the Research Committee of Sociology of Education, International Sociological Association. Contact email address: Lawrence.Saha@ anu.edu.au.

Tanja Salem is a PhD student in the Faculty of Education, Psychology and Human Movement, Department of Education, University of Hamburg. Her research interests include the consequences of migration for education, linguistic diversity/language development, and language education in pre- and primary schools in multilingual contexts. Salem is research assistant at the Center for Research and Support of Migrant Children and Youth (FöRMIG, www.foermig.uni-hamburg.de) at the University of Hamburg. She is a fellow of the Research and Study Program on Education in Early Childhood at the Robert Bosch Stiftung. Her current research focuses on cooperation of preschool and primary school teachers regarding the language education of (multilingual) children at the transition from pre- to primary school. Contact email address: tanja.salem@uni-hamburg.de.

Philipp Schnell is a post-doctoral researcher at the Department of Sociology, University of Vienna, and affiliated researcher at the Swiss Forum for Migration and Population Studies. He further serves as a lecture at the University of Vienna and Salzburg. He received his PhD from the University of Amsterdam in 2012. He has been a visiting scholar at the Institute for Migration and Ethnic Studies, University of Amsterdam and at the Institut National D'Études Démographiques in Paris. His past and current research interests cover migration and ethnicity, social inequality, social mobility, urban studies and comparative sociology. His work has been published in journals in the field of education, sociology, and urban studies, including *Annals of the American Academy of Political and Social Sciences, Education Inquiry* and *Polish Sociological Review*. His current research focuses on the educational mobility of second-generation Turks in cross-national perspective. Contact email address: philipp. schnell@univie.ac.at.

Marieke W. Slootman is a PhD student at the Amsterdam Institute for Social Science Research (AISSR) and the Institute for Migration and Ethnic Studies (IMES) at the University of Amsterdam. She graduated *cum laude* in political science/gender studies at the University of Amsterdam in 2005. Her research interests are ethnic and religious minorities, ethnic and national identification, integration, gender, social mobility, and social and cultural capital. In previous projects, she studied processes of individual radicalization and deradicalization at IMES. Her current research focuses on second-generation immigrants, and particularly on the social mobility and ethnic and national identifications among highly educated Turkish and Moroccan Dutch. Contact email address: m.w.slootman@uva.nl.

Spyros Spyrou holds a PhD in social anthropology from Binghamton University. He is the director of the Center for the Study of Childhood and Adolescence and an associate professor of anthropology and sociology at the European University, Cyprus. In 2012 he was a visiting professor in the Department of Anthropology at the University of Vienna. Currently, he serves as the president of the International Childhood and Youth Research Network and as the executive secretary of the 'Commission on Children, Youth, and Childhood' of the International Union of Anthropological and Ethnological Sciences. He is a member of the editorial boards of *Childhoods Today*, the *Wheelock International Journal of Children, Families, and Social Change*, and *Journal of the Institute for Educational Research* as well as a member of the advisory board of *Children and Society*. He has published widely in international peer-reviewed journals on a variety of issues related to childhood, education, nationalism, ethnicity, identity construction, and methodology. He is currently pursuing research on children and borders and on constructions of motherhood and babyhood. Contact email address: s.spyrou@euc.ac.cy.

Peter A. J. Stevens is assistant professor in qualitative research methodology at the Faculty of Political and Social Sciences, Ghent University. His research interests include the areas of race and ethnic relations, sociology of education, and mixed methods research. His past and current research focuses on: race/ethnicity and educational inequality, processes of tracking/streaming in schools, and the contextual development, management, and consequences of experiences of racism. His work has been published in journals in the field of education, sociology, and race/ethnicity, including *Review of Educational Research*, *Sociology of Education* and *Ethnic and Racial Studies*. He was a research assistant at the Department of Sociology, Ghent University, post-doctoral research officer at the London Institute of Education (UK), post-doctoral fellow of the Scientific Research Foundation Flanders (FWO) and part-time lecturer at the European University of Cyprus and the University of Nicosia. His current research focuses on the development, management, and effects of racism in schools in divided communities (Belgium and Cyprus). Contact email address: peter.stevens@ugent.be.

Christiane Timmerman is research professor at the University of Antwerp where she also teaches anthropology. She is also director of the Interdisciplinary Research Centre on Migration and Intercultural Studies (CeMIS). She is coordinator of several international research projects; i.e. the EU FP7 projects: EUMAGINE 'Imagining Europe from the Outside' and RESL.EU 'Reducing Early School Leaving in the EU', the IWT Flanders project BET YOU 'School Careers of Children with and without an Immigrant Background'. She is also a member of the board of directors of the European IMISCOE Research Network on International Migration, Integration, and Social Cohesion. Her publications focus on international migration, ethnicity, gender, education, and multiculturalism. Until 2012 she was also director of academic affairs of the Academic Centre St-Ignatius Antwerp (UCSIA). Contact email address: christiane.timmerman@ua.ac.be.

Mieke Van Houtte is head of the Research Group CuDOS, at the Department of Sociology at Ghent University, Belgium. Her research interests cover diverse topics within the sociology of education, particularly the effects of structural and compositional school features on several outcomes for pupils and teachers. Her work has been published in *Journal of Curriculum Studies*, *Journal of Educational Research*, *Oxford Review of Education*, *School Effectiveness and School Improvement*, *Sociology of Education* and *American Educational Research Journal*. She is currently the president of the Flemish Sociological Association and a member of the board of the network Sociology of Education of the European Sociological Association. Contact email address: Mieke.VanHoutte@UGent.be.

Lore Van Praag is a PhD fellow of the Scientific Research Foundation Flanders (FWO) at the Department of Sociology, Ghent University and member of the research group CuDOS. Her past research project focused on gendered community effects on mental health outcomes. Currently, her research interests include interethnic relations in school, processes of tracking/streaming, discrimination, educational achievement, social support, educational policies, grounded theory, and ethnography. In her doctorate, she focuses on the success determinants of ethnic minority students in secondary education in Flanders, considering structural characteristics of educational systems and society, migration settlement of ethnic communities and interactions between students, teachers, and significant others. Contact email address: LoreVanPraag@UGent.be.

Agnès van Zanten is senior research professor at the Centre Nationale de la Recherche Scientifique (CNRS) and Sciences Po working at the Observatoire Sociologique du Changement. Her research focuses on social and ethnic inequalities, school internal dynamics and competition, processes of institutional channeling, global, national and local policies, social class and parental educational practices and school choices, elite education and widening participation policies in elite education. She has published widely in high-ranking sociological and educational journals and has also written more than 15 authored and edited books including *L'Ecole de la periphery: Ségrégation et scolarité en banlieue* (2nd edition, 2012), *Choisir son école: Stratégies familiales et mediations locales* (2009), and *Sociologie de l'école* (with M. Duru-Bellat and A. Colin, 4th edition, 2012). She is currently preparing one authored and one edited book, as well as several articles, on elite education and working on three projects concerning students' transition to higher education, the educational strategies of teachers as parents, and the changing management and roles of private schools. Contact email address: agnes.vanzanten@sciences-po.fr.

Marios Vryonides is an associate professor of sociology at the European University Cyprus since 2007. He obtained his PhD from the Institute of Education, University of London in 2003. From 2004 until 2009 he was visiting lecturer at the Institute of Education. He has taught at Anglia Polytechnic University (2001–2003) and the University of the Aegean (2004–2007). Since 2008 he has acted as Cyprus' national coordinator of the European Social Survey. Among the funded projects he has recently successfully completed is an EU-funded project titled 'Children's Voices: Exploring Interethnic Violence and Children's Rights in the School Environment' (2011–2012). He has published widely on sociological and educational issues in international peer-reviewed journals and is the co-editor of *The Politics of Education: Challenging Multiculturalism* (2012). He is currently the secretary of the Research Committee on Sociology of Education (RC04) of the International Sociological Association (2010–2014). His research interests focus on contemporary sociological theory, sociology of education, and the theories of cultural and social capital. Contact email address: M.Vryonides@euc.ac.cy.

1

Introduction to the Handbook
Comparative Sociological Perspectives on Racial and Ethnic Inequality in Education

Peter A. J. Stevens and A. Gary Dworkin

This book brings together more than 30 years of sociological research on the relationship between race/ethnicity and educational inequality carried out in 18 national contexts.

The development of this was inspired by two earlier reviews from Stevens and colleagues on the relationship between race/ethnicity and educational inequality in England (Stevens 2007) and the Netherlands (Stevens et al. 2011). In conducting these reviews it became apparent that England and the Netherlands can fall back on rich traditions of research on this topic, but also that both bodies of literature are characterized by a focus on very different research questions and/or theoretical and methodological approaches. In addition, and somewhat in contradiction to what can be expected from a global, academic research community, scholars working in England and the Netherlands were mainly stimulated by national policy and research debates in developing and carrying out particular areas of research and less so by research conducted outside their national boundaries. The lack of mutual consideration and international cross-fertilization of research between these two (and other) countries, the abundance of research on race and ethnic inequalities in education, and the lack of recent, more systematic and comprehensive reviews of literature in this area called for efforts to further investigate how different national contexts develop particular research traditions and findings and how they can learn from each other in further developing our knowledge of the relationship between race/ethnicity and educational inequality.

This book builds on the two reviews published earlier by Stevens and colleagues in two ways. First, it expands the scope of these reviews by presenting the findings of research carried out on the relationship between race and ethnic inequality in 18 different national contexts, including updated reviews of the articles written by Stevens and colleagues. These 18 countries are purposively selected to cover a broad range of socio-economic and educational contexts and geographical regions throughout the world, including reviews of research in Africa (South Africa), Asia (China and Japan), Australia, Europe (Austria, Belgium, Cyprus, England, Finland, France, Germany, Ireland, and the Netherlands), Euro-Asia (Russia), North America (the USA and Canada) and South America (Argentina and Brazil).

While the Anglo-Saxon countries included in this Handbook are well recognized in terms of the amount and importance of research carried out in relationship to race and ethnic inequalities in education, this is far less the case for the other countries included. This can in part be explained by the observation that research in these countries is often not written in English and/or does not find its way to high profile academic outlets. As a result, an important achievement of this book is that it offers a platform for this non-English research to be accessed and acknowledged by an English-speaking academic community. In so doing, this Handbook pays tribute to and recognizes the importance of the work conducted by many scholars throughout the world in developing knowledge on the relationship between race/ethnicity and educational inequality worldwide.

Second, each of the contributions included in this edited book follows the same methodology in carrying out the review and structure in presenting the findings. Hence, while each national review can be read and stands on its own, the similarities in terms of methodology and structure between the chapters allow the reader to better compare the development of knowledge on the relationship between race/ethnic inequalities between different countries. More specifically, all chapters are similar in that they:

(a) Offer a brief introduction of the characteristics of the educational system, the main migration processes and developments in terms of social policy in relationship to ethnic and racial inequality. This allows readers to better contextualize the findings of each review.
(b) Are primarily concerned with identifying and critically reviewing the key research traditions that developed between 1980 and 2012 within their national context in relationship to research on race and ethnic inequalities in education. In line with Stevens (2007: 148), a research tradition is defined as: 'a set of studies developed over a certain period of time, which explore the relationship between educational inequality and race/ethnicity in a similar way by focusing on similar research questions, units of analysis, or social processes and use a similar set of research methods to achieve this goal'.
(c) Are explicit about the employed sampling procedures, or which criteria of inclusion and databases were employed in developing a sample of literature to be reviewed, with the primary goal to be as comprehensive as possible. This transparency in terms of employed sampling frame helps the reader to better evaluate the focus and scope of the review.

Whilst the international scope of the contributions and the similarities in terms of structure and methodology between the chapters contribute to the uniqueness of this Handbook and its relevance to the field, certain limitations need to be pointed out in advance. First, while most of the chapters in this Handbook are highly successful in offering a truly comprehensive review of the research literature that developed in their respective countries, there is unavoidably some variation between the chapters in terms of how comprehensive the reviews aim to be. Due to limitations in resources and/or the vast amount of literature written on this topic, some chapters necessarily restrict their focus on a smaller number of research traditions (e.g. chapters on the USA and Finland) and particular types of (for instance, secondary) schooling (e.g. chapters on Ireland and the Netherlands). Furthermore, as it took over two years to develop this Handbook, some chapters focus on the period 1980–2010, while others also cover research carried out more recently.

Secondly, in developing our conclusions, we as editors decided against writing a fully integrative review, that is one that aims to bring together all the findings that emerged out of these studies into a single text and advises on future directions for research in each of the key research traditions and national contexts. As space limitations simply do not allow for such a review, the conclusions summarize some of the key characteristics of each national review (see, for example, the overview grid included in the concluding chapter) and point to main gaps in the literature. In so doing, this Handbook does not only aim to map out how researchers have explained and studied race and ethnic inequalities in education and how future research can build on this, but it also functions as the most complete and comprehensive sourcebook to date on this topic, effectively allowing readers to carry out their own integrative reviews on particular topics by reading the conclusions of this Handbook and critically summarizing particular sections of chapters.

However, despite these shortcomings, we are adamant that this Handbook offers a wealth of relevant information to students, researchers, social policy makers, and activists interested in the relationship between race and ethnicity and educational inequalities. We hope that this book will encourage readers to investigate questions concerning inequality in education and society more generally from an international point of view, and consider the rich bodies of literature developed on this topic worldwide.

The focus on racial and ethnic inequality in education which is central to this Handbook reflects a significant concern of the Sociology of Education Research Committee (known as RC04) of the International Sociological Association. The ISA, which was formally established in 1949, holds a charter from UNESCO and counts among its membership sociologists from 167 nations. As a professional organization, ISA holds membership in the International Council of Science. Its central office is in Madrid, Spain.

RC04 has addressed issues of educational equity and access at most of the ISA's World Congresses and Forums held around the world since the RC's inception in 1971, then under the leadership of Pierre Bourdieu as president. Distinguished sociologists of education have held office in RC04, including Basil Bernstein, Margaret Archer, Jaap Dronkers, Carlos Alberto Torres, Jeanne Ballantine, and Ari Antikainen. The editors and several of the contributors to this handbook are current members and even officers of RC04. In fact, some of the chapters in this Handbook originated as papers delivered at the 2010 World Congress of Sociology in Gotheburg, Sweden and the 2012 Second Forum of Sociology in Buenos Aires, Argentina.

References

Stevens, Peter A. J. 2007 Researching Race/Ethnicity and Educational Inequality in English Secondary Schools: A Critical Review of the Research Literature between 1980 and 2005. *Review of Educational Research* 77 (2): 147–185.

Stevens, Peter A. J., Noel Clycq, Christiane Timmerman, and Mieke Van Houtte. 2011 Researching Race/Ethnicity and Educational Inequality in the Netherlands: A Critical Review of the Research Literature between 1980 and 2008. *British Educational Research Journal* 37 (1): 5–43.

2
Argentina
Mapping Ethnic and Educational Inequalities in an Uncharted Territory. Argentinean Research Traditions, Their Contributions and Challenges

Analía Inés Meo, Silvina Cimolai, and Andrea Pérez

2.1 Introduction

Despite the existence of indigenous people and immigrants, Argentina has until recently denied, silenced, and marginalized socio-cultural differences and particularities. Up until the 1980s, a homogenizing cultural paradigm permeated educational policies and it is only recently that cultural and linguistic differences and diversity have been legally and culturally acknowledged. From the 1980s onwards, 'diversity' and 'difference' have entered into the educational policy agenda, triggered by the globalization of these concerns as well as the recognition of prior indigenous struggles demanding their rights. For instance, in 2006, the Education Law created a new type of education: 'intercultural and bilingual education', which was targeted at indigenous communities.

Concerns surrounding 'cultural differences' have been unfolding into complex socio-economic and political scenarios that have impacted on the structuration of the field of knowledge production in education and the configuration of research traditions. The last three decades have witnessed dramatic political changes: the return of democracy and its consolidation, the deepening and dismissal of neoliberal economic reforms, the shrinking and growth of the state's role and intervention, and severe socio-economic crises such as those triggered by the hyperinflation of 1989 and the bankruptcy of the financial system in 2001, followed by a period of economic prosperity. These social, economic, and political fluctuations have affected the boundaries, levels of autonomy, and power relations between players and research agendas in the field of educational knowledge.

This chapter maps research traditions examining ethnic and educational inequalities in basic education in Argentina from the 1980s up to 2010. The lack of any previous similar analyses implies a considerable challenge and one which has involved acknowledging not only the history of the education system but also the nature of the recent developments in the field of educational knowledge production. This chapter offers a typology of research traditions, which are

5

described via a set of studies that have addressed specific research themes or topics, and have deployed similar theoretical tools and methodological strategies (Stevens 2007; Stevens et al. 2011). Boundaries between traditions are not clear and tend to overlap; however, each revolves around specific educational research concerns involving indigenous people and/or immigrants.

This chapter is organized into four main sections. The first section presents basic information regarding social and educational policies targeted at indigenous people and immigrants both before and during the period under analysis. It also depicts the current socio-demographic situation of these groups. Moreover, it offers key data on the Argentine education system, such as structure, governance, participation of the state and private sector, and recent democratizing trends of basic schooling. The second section presents the methodological strategy deployed to make 'visible' what previous studies have neglected. It describes a set of systematic and flexible criteria used for searching, identifying, and sampling research on ethnic and educational inequalities in Argentina. The following sections explore the identified five research traditions in turn: 'mapping educational access', 'intercultural educational policies', 'language conflict and schooling', 'difference and diversity', and 'school texts as a means of othering'. After summarizing the key findings of this chapter, the last section identifies potential territories to be charted by these expanding, rich, and promising research traditions.

2.1.1   The Argentinean education system

In Argentina, education is compulsory from age 5 to 17/18 (Law, 26.206)[1] and encompasses at least 12 school years (one for early childhood, six or seven for primary education and five or six years for secondary schooling). Primary education should offer an integrated basic and common education, whereas secondary schooling is composed of two different cycles: (i) the basic and common cycle, and (ii) the oriented cycle which includes different specializations related to knowledge and the social and working world. Primary schooling became almost universal in the 1990s, and secondary schooling has rapidly grown from a net school rate of 32% in 1970 to an estimated 81.4% in 2009 (Rivas et al. 2010; SITEAL 2011).[2] Similarly to other Latin American and African countries, if pupils do not achieve the expected educational standards for primary or secondary education, then they have to repeat the school year.

There are no centralized entrance exams or final general exams on completion of either level, and pupils cannot be allocated to different types of schools or internal tracks within a school according to their educational achievement. Access to non-university institutions and to state universities is open: this means that any secondary school graduate is able tao enroll in any degree without any further entrance requirement (Figure 2.1).

Up until the 1960s, the Argentinean education system was highly centralized and monopolist (Narodowski and Andrada 2001). By the mid-1990s, provincial

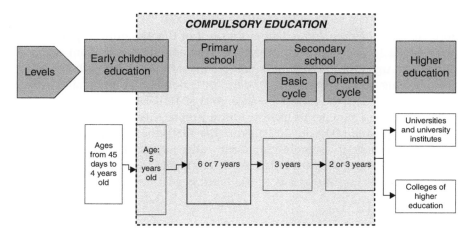

Figure 2.1 Structure of the Argentinean national education system (Law 26.206)

Note: The Argentinean national education system consists of four levels (early childhood education, primary school, secondary school and higher education) and eight types (modalididades) (organizational and/or curricular options of common education within one or more educational levels). The intercultural and bilingual education is one of them.

authorities directly funded, managed, staffed, and supervised state primary, secondary, and tertiary education, whilst the National Ministry of Education monitored the educational system by producing and evaluating data concerning educational quality and by giving financial and technical support to compensate for inequalities between regions or social groups (López 2002; Palamidessi et al. 2007). From the mid-1990s the national government started to gather data from schools, students, and educational achievement (National Annual Census of Schools and Students and Educational Standards Assessment Survey (*Operativo Nacional de Evaluación Educativa*)).

Regarding the participation of the public/state and private sectors in education, the educational transformation of the 1990s continued a process which started during the 1950s and which deepened in the 2000s: the increase of the private sector's powers and coverage. In 2010, around 50% of pupils enrolled in primary and secondary education were in state schools (DiNIECE 2010) and there is evidence of socio-economic segregation between types of school sectors (Rivas et al. 2010).

2.1.2 Immigration to Argentina

Since the middle of the 19th century, specialist literature has identified different migratory patterns interwoven with wider socio-economic process that transcend national boundaries (Devoto 2003; Mármora 2002).[3] Up to the mid-19th century, the majority of immigrants were mainly from European origins (Italy and Spain). Poverty, wars, racism, and/or religious/ideological intolerance forced them to flee to Argentina (Oteiza et al. 2000). At the beginning of the 20th century, they represented almost a third of the Argentinean population (see Figure 2.2). The World Wars, the 1930 crisis, and the concomitant aggravation of the Argentinean economic situation dramatically changed this trend in the following decades (Devoto 2003). By 2001, non-border immigrants represented only 1.7% of the total population (603,824) (INDEC 2001).

Border country immigrants have historically represented around 2% or 3% of the total population (Devoto 2003). From the 1950s the decrease of European immigration made them more visible and easier targets of racism: they were not perceived or defined as 'immigrants' by the media and lay discourses. They were labeled as *'cabecitas negras'* (little black heads), a derogatory term that

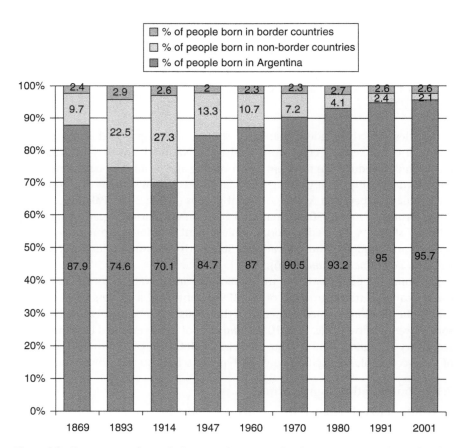

Figure 2.2 Percentage of people born in Argentina, border countries, and non-border countries 1869–2001

Source: our elaboration based on the National Population Census data.

referred to people migrating to urban areas attracted by the industrialization process that took place at that time. In the public opinion, border country immigrants and Argentinean rural migrants were perceived as belonging to the same underprivileged social class and racially produced as 'black' (Grimson 2006). In 2001, border country immigrants represented 2.6% of the population (923,496) (INDEC 2001).

Non-border and border immigrants have historically settled in the central region of the country (city of Buenos Aires and the metropolitan area of the province of Buenos Aires), and in the provinces of Patagonia (such as Santa Cruz, Río Negro, Neuquén, Chubut, and Tierra del Fuego). In 2001, in terms of nationalities, immigrants from American countries represented the largest group, followed by European (mainly from Italy and Spain) and Asian countries (largely from Korea). The great majority of American immigrants come from border countries and Peru (Cerrutti 2009).

Immigrant pupils are a poorly studied group. Available statistics focus on border countries immigration. Cerrutti (2009), using data from the *Encuesta Complementaria de Migraciones Internacionales 2002/2003*, states that enrollment rates of immigrant children diminished after the age of 14 and varied highly across nationalities.

2.1.3 Indigenous people in Argentina

Historically, there have been few official data sources recording the existence of indigenous communities in Argentina.[4] Ethnic groups have been misrecognized as such by the national and provincial states until the 1980s. The National Population Census 2001 was the first one that included questions to identify people who consider themselves or someone else in their households as indigenous.[5] In 2004, a special survey (*Encuesta Complementaria de Pueblos Indígenas (ECPI)*) was carried out to gather information about a representative sample of indigenous households. It identified 30 indigenous communities. The four largest are the Mapuche, Toba, Kolla, and Wichí. According to this survey, in 2004, 600,329 people considered themselves or at least one of their antecessors indigenous. They represented 1.7% of the total country population. In terms of their geographical location, the majority of the indigenous communities were in the Northwest region (mainly based in the provinces of Jujuy and Salta).

Regarding educational information of these groups, students in bilingual and intercultural education represented 0.5% of the total number of students enrolled in common kindergarten, primary, and secondary schooling in 2010 (Alonso et al. 2011). Schools are classified by the central government as 'indigenous' and 'non-indigenous' schools. The former should provide BIE and should be made up of a majority of indigenous students (50% or more). Following general demographic patterns, the majority of these schools are in the Northern and Southern provinces. In terms of the students' educational trajectories, indigenous pupils in primary schools have high levels of repetition (25.4%) during the first school years. This trend decreases in the seventh grade (5.7%) due to mainly high levels of drop out (28%) (Alonso et al. 2011).[6] Regarding indigenous secondary schooling, the repetition rate is lower than that of pupils from rural state schools.[7] For instance, for the eighth grade, while the repetition rate is 13.5% for pupils in rural schools, it is 8.6% for indigenous pupils (Alonso et al. 2011). Analysts suggest that this lower level of repetition could be explained by the high levels of drop out of the indigenous pupils compared to non-indigenous pupils.

2.1.4   Educational policies: From homogenization to partial recognition of difference

Up to the 1980s, the education system played a key role in the cultural assimilation and in the denial of linguistic and cultural differences of indigenous people and European immigrants (Quijada 2003). Central aspects of the educational policy have been the *'castellanización'* of its population (the inculcation through schooling of Spanish as the legitimate language), and the teaching of Argentinean national history (as the shared past of a wider community) (Acuña 2010). The institutional assumption that all children spoke Spanish, together with the symbolic and physical invisibility of indigenous communities and their social marginalization, has been part and parcel of the discursive production of Argentina as being a by-product of European immigration. Argentina has been defined as a 'melting pot' and Argentinean people as 'coming from the boats' (Quijada 2003). This metaphor contributed to the definition of Argentina as different from the rest of Latin American countries and comparable to white European countries, producing it as a white 'imagined community' (Anderson 1993).

With regard to indigenous communities, from the 1980s onwards, 'diversity', 'interculturalism', and 'multiculturalism' (amongst other concepts) became pivotal notions in educational, academic, and policy debates. In this new scenario – triggered by global concerns around these issues and by historical political struggles in Latin America and Argentina – indigenous groups, their ethnic identities, and cultural differences started to be recognized. For example, during the 1980s, the city of Buenos Aires, Salta, Misiones, Río Negro, Formosa, and Jujuy introduced different types of legislation recognizing them as political actors. At national level, in 1985, the National Law 23.302 declared that the state should respond to indigenous communities' needs and cultural specificities, and should promote their socio-economic participation. In 1994, the new Argentinean National Constitution not only recognized the ethnic and cultural pre-existence of the Argentinean indigenous communities, but also established that the state had to respect indigenous people's right to bilingual and intercultural education.

Educational policies were deeply shaped by this wider legal rights agenda. For instance, the Federal Law of Education (1993)[8] promoted more freedom to develop curricular content at provincial and school levels in order to reflect regional, provincial, and local particularities. This paved the way to the development of indigenous curriculum in different jurisdictions. This law also expressed the need to implement provincial programs oriented to the 'rescue' and strengthening of indigenous language and cultures. In addition to this, at the end of the 1990s, the national government executed various educational programs targeted at improving schooling and promoting curricular innovation in indigenous schools. In 1999, for the first time, national kindergarten and basic general education indigenous teaching titles were created. In 2006, the new Education Law 26.206 created the educational type 'intercultural and bilingual education' for kindergarten, primary, and secondary schooling. It aims to accomplish the constitutional right of indigenous communities to receive education that 'contributes to preserve and strengthen their cultural patterns, languages, vision, and ethnic identity' (Education Law 26.206: Art. 52, our translation).

The historical production of official statistics concerning immigrants and indigenous people reflects the uneven interest of the state in these groups. As mentioned above, while population censuses had gathered basic socio-demographic and educational information on immigrants since 1869, indigenous people as ethnic groups remained statistically 'invisible' until the 2000s when the central government intensified the production of quantitative information on immigrants and indigenous people. With regards to educational statistics, although the National Annual Educational Census (*Relevamiento Anual*) has gathered basic information on schools, teachers and students since 1996, including the number and nationality of foreign students, it only started collecting data on the numbers of indigenous students in 2007.

The methodological and analytical sections will show how the misrecognition of immigrants and indigenous people by the state (whether at policy or data information production level) has strongly influenced the ways in which knowledge about ethnicity and educational inequalities have been produced.

2.2   Methodology

While some reviews of educational research focus on the context of Argentina (such as Milstein et al. (2007) on educational anthropology; Llomovate (1992) and Paviglianiti (1989) on educational research; and Palamidessi et al. (2007) on the history of the educational research field), this is the first study to (systematically) review research on race and ethnic inequalities in education in Argentina. As such, it maps 'what is out there', identifying highlights and tracing boundaries of a very complex and dynamic scenario. The aim of this exercise imposes limits to our own analysis: issues that have been neglected in the existent literature will only appear marginally in our final section as potential future research endeavors. In developing a comprehensive review of research and in considering time and resource constraints, and access and availability of literature, this study employs the following parameters in sampling literature for review: (i) Argentinean studies with a broadly sociological approach, including studies primarily classified as anthropological and educational studies; (ii) research conducted between 1980 and 2010; (iii) analyses on basic and compulsory education; and (iv) different types of scholarly productions: books, peer-reviewed journal articles, and official reports.

The traditional low structuration of the sub-field of sociology of education in the country, as well as the marginal attention paid to ethnicity and education,[9] has demanded that this study includes other academic fields (anthropology and education sciences), and their questions, methods, and contributions. In Argentina, since the 1980s the newly born field of educational anthropology has played a fundamental role in the development of studies on ethnicity and education, looking at developing critical interpretations of school life, and providing useful insights on topics related to socio-cultural diversity and social inequalities (Achilli 2001; Milstein et al. 2007).

Due to the history of the education research field in Argentina (which has until very recently promoted the publication of outputs only academic journals in Spanish) (Palamidessi et al. 2007), articles were searched for in education, anthropology, and sociology journals written in Spanish indexed in the most reputable academic journal database in Argentina (produced by the *Centro Argentino de Investigación Científica y Tecnológica* (CAICyT)) and in Latin America (called LATINDEX and created by an international network of academic organizations from Latin America, the Caribbean, Spain, and Portugal).[10] This initial search led to the identification of ten academic education journals. However, interviews with key researchers led to the detection of three more well-known journals that have yet to be indexed. Every issue of these journals was searched; 12 out of the 13 journals were initiated during the 1990s (n=7) or after 2000 (n=5) and only one in the late 1980s. A total of 2268 articles were checked and only 22 papers were focused on ethnicity and educational inequalities. Six anthropology (1088 articles) and nine sociology or social sciences (632 articles) journals were also checked[11] and these publications encompassed only four relevant articles.

Due to the low number of articles identified in this first stage, the search needed to be widened to include other academic journals in sociology, education, and anthropology, and other publication types, such as books and government reports. Relevant Argentinean centralized catalogues or databases did not exist when this review was carried out. Searches were performed in selected libraries in the city of Buenos Aires and also in the province of Buenos Aires together with academic browsers (such as Google Scholar) on the internet. Key producers of educational research in each discipline were identified, such as publishing companies, national universities, think tanks, non-governmental organizations (NGOs), and central and provincial governmental agencies. Previous research on knowledge production in education, and informal interviews with key figures in the field also led to the identification of relevant publications (such as books) and a wide range of organizations and academics involved in the production of potentially relevant studies. Using this information, a multi-layered strategy was deployed to obtain further research outputs, ranging from requests to individual academics from different national universities for copies of their work and to research departments of provincial educational authorities, to visiting a wide range of institutional websites. This approach allowed the results from the first search to be enriched.

After identifying around 300 publications that seemed to fall under the general search criteria, a sampling strategy was deployed in order to produce a database with relevant research outputs. To achieve this, the relevance of each publication was assessed by identifying its aims, key findings, and date of publication. This resulted in a database containing 175 publications, including books, book chapters, journal articles, and reports. Although conference proceedings were excluded from the database, we finally decided to include a few papers of this kind due to their unique and relevant character.

To analyze this set of publications, more detailed information regarding each one was gathered, such as its objectives, theoretical and methodological strategy, population described (indigenous and/or immigrants), level of education (initial, primary, or secondary), area (urban or rural), region of the country, key findings, and institutional affiliation of the author/s. With this data, commonalities and differences were identified across the publications. This allowed significant aspects of each tradition to be defined and difference or nuances within them to be recognized.

The summaries of these articles, books, and reports were analyzed and included in different provisional research traditions according to their research questions, methodological strategy, and theoretical approaches. With these preliminary analyses completed, one matrix per research tradition was constructed and this included key data such as target population, area, educational level, methodological strategy, theoretical approaches, and key findings. The majority of the identified publications were from the 2000s, with a large group having been published in the 1990s and only a minority from the 1980s.

The composition of the assembled database also reflects the historical development of the education knowledge field in Argentina. In other words, research on ethnicity and educational inequalities follows the general developmental trends of this complex multi-disciplinary academic field. As mentioned above, the state's and academics' interest on ethnicity is recent and marginal. Since the return of democracy in 1983, the field of educational knowledge has undergone major transformations that have impacted on the nature and scope of research on ethnicity and educational inequalities. While at the beginning of the 1980s insufficient and poorly trained staff, lack of funding, and severe organizational difficulties were key features of the research institutions (Palamidessi et al. 2007), recent changes in the national science and technology policies as well as the growth of research activity in general have positively influenced knowledge production (Palamidessi et al. 2007; Pérez Lindo 2005). All of this, together with the rapid expansion and consolidation of regional catalogues, academic journals, and collective research outputs (SPU 2008), and a slow but steady trend to tightened peer review processes (via self-regulation and indexing), is leading to a more dynamic and self-regulated educational research field, which has boosted the rhythm of growth and the quality of the studies on ethnicity and education.

2.3   Research on ethnicity and educational inequality in Argentina

Having described the methodological strategy and some aspects of the field of educational knowledge, the research traditions 'mapping the educational access', 'intercultural educational policies', 'language conflict and schooling', 'difference and diversity', and 'school texts as means of "othering"' will now be examined in turn.

2.3.1   Mapping the educational access of indigenous and immigrant students: An emerging tradition

This emerging body of research mainly depicts the levels of educational access attained by indigenous people and immigrants by examining quantitative data. These reports have mostly been produced by experts working within government agencies or international organizations. The type of knowledge produced is descriptive and oriented towards policy decision-making. These analyses do not usually engage with any theoretical discussions.

Compared with other research traditions, fewer studies were identified in this group and most of them were produced from 2000 onwards. The late and under-developed statistical information and datasets by government agencies and/or NGOs explains the weakness and slow development of this research strand. Put more succinctly, the availability of data restricts the types of questions researchers can formulate. These reports explicitly acknowledge the limitations of the existing data sources in producing more complex analyses of the educational situation of these groups. During the 1980s and 1990s, the reasons for so few reports were due not only to the underdevelopment of official data but also to the lack of a tradition of using resources from research to inform policy decision-making in education (Hernández 1988; Paviglianiti 1989).

While only three of the reports present data collected from the whole country (Alonso et al. 2007; Cerrutti 2009; UNICEF 2009),[12] the remainder focus on particular regions. Some of the analyses consider the situation of these groups across different levels of the education system (Alonso et al. 2007; Catalá et al. 2009; Cerrutti 2009; Costarelli 2008), while several examine only primary education (for example Fulco 1980; Moscato 1996; Padawer et al. 2010).

Indigenous groups have been the focus of much attention. Reports using secondary data sources have examined the coverage and types (public or private) of schools with indigenous students, as well as indigenous people's literacy levels, geographical distribution, and types of ethnic groups (Alonso et al. 2007; Avellaneda 2001; Costarelli 2008; Fischman 1993; Fulco 1980; Ministerio de Educación de Corrientes 2008; UNICEF 2009). Some of the reports have been produced to inform the development of intercultural and bilingual education schools.

These analyses demonstrate the unequal access and permanence of indigenous groups in the educational system (Cid and Paz 2004; Fischman 1993; UNICEF 2009). For instance, a recent UNICEF study[13] (2009) asserts that at the national level, the vast majority of indigenous children aged between 5 and 14 years do attend primary school, a figure which is similar to national trends. However, in the case of the Mbyá Guaraní and Wichí communities, the enrollment rate of this age group is significantly lower (UNICEF 2009). Moreover, school enrollment rate of Mbyá Guaraní and Wichí girls and boys between 15 and 19 years was significantly lower than national trends. In this age group, more than half had not completed primary education. Despite this grim scenario, the entrance age for primary education for girls and boys has been lowered over time.

Studies that generated their own data are limited to small areas of the country. These have been undertaken to produce useful data for improving the educational situation of the indigenous population in the region analyzed. In so doing, they utilize surveys as the privileged data collection technique. For example, the Ministry of Education in the province of Corrientes in 2007 (Ministerio de Educación de Corrientes 2008) conducted a survey to determine head teachers', teachers' and students' attitudes towards the use of indigenous language in schools.

With respect to foreign students and immigrants, few reports could be identified. Two studies were carried out in the city of Buenos Aires and measured the number of foreigners enrolled at each educational level according to their nationality and geographical distribution within the city, and the evolution of immigrant students' enrollment rate over the last decade (Catalá et al. 2009; Padawer et al. 2010). Padawer et al. (2010), for instance, showed an increase in the number of foreign students enrolled in state primary schools in this city during the period 2000–2008. At a national level, Cerrutti's report (2009) showed that the enrollment rate of foreign students is almost 100% for primary education but it dramatically decreases for secondary and higher education to around 50%.

The majority of the analyses are descriptive, with the study of Cid and Paz (2004) being an exception to this trend and the only one identified that generates explicative models based on the concept of discrimination, defined as unequal treatment under similar conditions. The study explored determining factors of educational achievement with a focus on ethnic differences. Regression models were used to identify educational exclusion processes based on discrimination towards the indigenous population in Salta. The authors compared the indigenous and non-indigenous population in order to establish whether there was discrimination experienced by the former group that could not be explained by other variables, such as poverty. They focused their attention on 'school attendance' and 'educational achievement' and argued that there was evidence of discrimination towards students who lived in households with at least one indigenous person. The data showed that young indigenous people had to overcome more difficulties in order to attend school and to continue their education than their non-indigenous counterparts.

In sum, this research tradition focuses on describing educational access attained by indigenous people and immigrants, mainly using quantitative data. The introduction of new quantitative data-gathering instruments has promoted its recent expansion. Studies are generally carried out by government agencies and international organizations and tend to be used for policy decision-making purposes.

2.3.2 Intercultural educational policies

This rich research tradition focuses on the educational policies targeted at mainly indigenous people in Argentina from the inception of the nation-state onwards. Only a few studies focus on policies targeted at immigrant people (see Barbero and Roldán 1987; Citrinovitz 1991). It has grown notably during the last decade and it comprises qualitative analyses mainly carried out by anthropologists. Many studies have been commissioned by national or provincial governments and NGOs as part of the BIE policy development (see Arce 2007; Cervera et al. 2010; Hernández and Kleinerman 1999; MECT 2004; Novaro 2004; Wallis 2010). Others have been funded by academic organizations (Hirsch 2010; Hirsch and Serrudo 2010; Serrudo 2010).

The research conducted, on the one hand, has examined policy texts or documents (such as national educational laws, educational programs, and teachers' work statutes) and, on the other hand, has scrutinized the ways in which different individual and collective actors (such as provincial governments, teachers, and indigenous communities) interpret, redefine and resist them in different socio-economic, cultural, and linguistic contexts.

The first strand of research is focused on studies that analyze policy texts and interpret them as the outcomes of complex interpretative processes stemming from social, economic, and cultural struggles between different social groups (see for instance Barbero and Roldán 1987; Díaz and Alonso 2004; Hecht 2007; Hecht and Szulc 2006; Hirsch and Serrudo 2010; Serrudo 2010). Many focus on policy documents produced by the national and provincial states (see Alonso and Díaz 2004a; Bella 2007; Bordegaray and Novaro 2004; Falaschi et al. 2005; Hecht 2007, 2010; Hecht and Szulc 2006; Lanusse 2004; Serrudo 2010). Only a few pay any attention to other 'producers' of educational documents. For example, Nicoletti (2002/2003) examined an educational document written by a key missionary within the Salesian congregation of the Catholic church, and Alonso and Díaz (2004b) produced an educational document together with the Mapuche community from Neuquén.

The majority of the analyses in this strand focus on two sets of educational policy documents: those produced by the central government at the end of the 19th century, and those introduced mainly from the 1980s onwards by the national and provincial governments. Bilingual and intercultural education (BIE) policies have been the center of many analysts' attention (Briones 2004; Hirsch and Serrudo 2010; Lanusse 2004; Serrudo 2010). The term 'BIE policies' refers to a wide range of educational policies targeted at indigenous children and young people from the 1980s onwards. An example of this type of policy research is the study of Serrudo (2010) on the legal frameworks that regulate the recruitment and training of indigenous teachers in different provinces. She scrutinized different sets of policy documents produced by the governments of the provinces of Formosa, Chaco, and Salta. The author argued that each provincial state has deployed different policies towards the inclusion and training of indigenous teachers and each has a different scope, pace of implementation, and level of support. Moreover, this seems to foster different degrees of professionalization among indigenous teachers.

The great majority of the studies agree in identifying two major types of educational policies: the so-called 'homogenizing' (*homogeneizadoras*) and the 'focalized' (*focalizadas*) policies (see Achilli 2001; García and Paladino 2007; Hecht 2007; Soria 2009). While, as presented in previous sections, the former misrecognizes indigenous people, the latter both recognizes but reifies sociocultural difference. Analysts have critically examined focalized educational policies which emerged during the 1990s, considering them as part of a wider process of recognition of ethnic and linguistic diversity, that, paradoxically, contributed to a non-critical celebration of cultural difference in schools, its reification, othering, and decoupling from social inequalities (Bella 2007; Bordegaray and Novaro 2004; Hecht 2007; Soria 2009). Few researchers have also highlighted the negative effects the decentralization of the education system had on the focalized policies of BIE. Despite the optimistic official rhetoric highlighting its positive effects on the appreciation of regional and local demands, decentralization promoted greater inequalities between provinces and, in particular, weakened the poorest which were the ones with the highest numbers of indigenous people (Hecht 2006).

With regards to immigrants, only Barbero and Roldán (1987) examined the educational policies towards immigrants in the 'foundational period' of the nation (1880–1910). They clearly demonstrated the central role of the state and the concomitant displacement of the Catholic church from the educational policy-making process. This lack of attention to immigrants corresponds to the persistence of a 'homogenizing' approach, which permeated social, cultural, and educational policies directed towards this group (Domenech 2003). Unlike indigenous communities, immigrants (unless they were poor) have not become the target of specific policies that construct them as a distinctive group in need of specific educational policies.

A second strand of research within this tradition encompasses those studies which explore the ways in which educational policies targeted at indigenous people have been implemented, interpreted, and/or resisted by different actors in diverse socio-cultural and linguistic contexts (see Aguirre 2010; Arce 2007; Bertella 2006; Carozzi 1983; Cebolla de Badie 2005; Cervera et al. 2010; Gómez Otero 2001; Hernández and Kleinerman 1999; Lanusse 2004; Novaro 2004; Rodríguez de Anca 2004; Szulc 2009; Zidarich 2010). Analyses have been concerned with improving indigenous children's education (Acuña 2010; Hirsch 2010). Although the vast majority of such studies were produced during the 2000s, some foundational research was carried out during the 1980s, such as that by Grimsditch et al. (1987) which examined the aspirations and needs of indigenous and Creole women from rural areas in Formosa. This study investigated the cultural transmission model of this community and focused on what they knew, how they learnt and what they would like to learn in the future.

The great majority of these analyses are descriptive. Analyses that engage with theoretical discussions define the scope and nature of intercultural education, sometimes against other perspectives of social differences such as biculturalism and multiculturalism (Alonso and Díaz 2004b, 2004c; Arce 2007; Bertella 2006; Briones 2004; Enriz 2010; Hirsch 2010; Novaro 2004; Rodríguez de Anca 2004; Zidarich 2010). These concepts operate as an analytical yardstick against which different experiences can then be critically examined.

The methodological strategy of this research strand is mainly qualitative. Although the majority of the publications do not include detailed information about how evidence has been gathered, ethnographies of communities and schools, individual and group interviews, participant observations of training courses, documentary analysis, and participatory methods such as workshops have all been used. Few studies include references to quantitative data on BIE experiences (see Bertella 2006; MECT 2004) and several authors make no reference to the year in which they have carried out their research.[14]

Research mainly gravitates around the analysis of how BIE policies targeted at indigenous people have been implemented in different provinces, communities, and schools,[15] and how different school actors, such as policy-makers, indigenous and non-indigenous teachers, teachers' unions, and indigenous communities, have interpreted them. The focus has been on 'how' these policies operate. The study of the National Ministry of Education, Culture and Technology (MECT 2004) illustrates key aspects of this approach. The document '*Sistematización de experiencias de EIB*' (MECT 2004) presented a collection of 107 narratives depicting rural and urban educational experiences, mainly from schools but also from universities, teaching training institutes, and NGOs, at the beginning of the 2000s. These experiences addressed linguistic and cultural diversity. The national government gathered this information in order to map and strengthen these experiences, disseminate their work and achievements, and identify pros and cons with the aim of developing wider national state policies. Common features across the collected experiences were identified, such as (i) problems in delineating adequate pedagogic strategies in order to address interculturalism in schools; (ii) the need to develop teachers' training material; (iii) the lack of clear guidelines and/or knowledge regarding the implementation of BIE experiences in some jurisdictions; (iv) serious difficulties when including families and communities; and (v) school actors' lack of knowledge regarding indigenous cultures and their teaching and learning styles.

The majority of the studies highlighted obstacles, gaps, and contradictions between the principles and practices of BIE, and made (implicit or explicit) policy recommendations. For instance, research has highlighted the need: (i) to develop non-indigenous teachers' socio-cultural awareness of indigenous cultures across BIE experiences (Carozzi 1983; Cebolla de Badie 2005; MECT 2004); (ii) to raise the status of indigenous teachers' pedagogic role in schools (Zidarich 2010); (iii) to promote indigenous and non-indigenous teachers' training (Cervera et al. 2010; MECT 2004; Serrudo 2010); (iv) to develop alternative pedagogies that recognize cultural differences (Bertella 2006; Cebolla de Badie 2005; Gómez Otero 2001; MECT 2004; Novaro 2004); (v) to redefine indigenous teachers' pedagogic role without restricting it to translation (Bertella 2006; Zidarich 2010); and (vi) to improve indigenous teachers' working conditions in terms of salaries and job stability (Arce 2007).

Various studies also present the achievements of BIE experiences. Hirsh (2010) for instance, argued that bilingualism and interculturalism (although in different ways) have favored school retention in one rural and one urban Guarani communities in Salta with different levels of predominance of indigenous language. Arce (2007) claimed that BIE has promoted the participation of indigenous teachers (*Auxiliar Docente Indígena*) in their schools and communities, fostered community participation and demands, and improved indigenous teachers' working conditions and access to training.

This research tradition provides evidence that BIE policies have been developed at dissimilar rates and have implied different degrees of indigenous communities' participation (Díaz et al. 2010; Wallis 2010). Wallis (2010), for example, showed that the implementation of BIE in Salta has been very difficult to achieve due to its divorce from the ways in which Wichí communities understand education and knowledge production. Moreover, the author asserts that this disconnection is also reflected in the fact that schools have misrecognized the negative impact that formal schooling has on Wichí culture.

In sum, this research tradition examines the educational policies directed towards mainly indigenous people and has two principal strands. While the first is focused on the analysis of policy texts, the second strand comprises the analysis of how educational policies have been implemented and how different school actors have interpreted them.

2.3.3   Language conflict and schooling

This is a small but growing research tradition, where studies are guided by wider concerns originating from 'linguistic anthropology', 'sociolinguistics' and the 'sociology of language'. These perspectives emerged in the aftermath of World War II and have focused on language use and its implicit and complex rules rather than on its formal structuration (Unamuno 1995).

In Argentina, researchers have used a sociolinguistic perspective to study schooling from the mid-1990s onwards (see for instance Acuña 2001, 2005, 2010; Armatto de Welti 2005, 2008; Bigot 2007a, 2007b; Gandulfo 2007a, 2007b; Hecht 2006, 2010). This research tradition interprets schooling as one, albeit central, sociolinguistic scenario, where conflicts, exchanges, and power relations around the use of language/s take place (Acuña 2001, 2010; Bigot 2007a). It examines different aspects of schooling such as teachers' and families' views and the linguistic aspects of educational policy *vis a vis* the sociolinguistic situation of indigenous communities and to a lesser extent, of immigrant students. According to Milstein et al. (2007), this research strand interprets communicational problems of certain indigenous and poor rural pupils as part and parcel of wider conflictive relationships between diverse linguistic codes and socialization processes. In so doing, this tradition provides evidence that, despite recent reforms towards bilingual and intercultural education, schooling remains a site of cultural and linguistic domination of indigenous people and their communities or immigrants.

The majority of these studies are interested in examining the vitality of languages and their relationships with the complex production of ethnic identities in linguistic contact zones. Only a few studies directly explore the relationships between language vitality and learning (Acuña 2001, 2010; Armatto de

Welti 2005, 2008; Unamuno 1994). Some analyses focused on the relationship between language and school failure for children living in bilingual Spanish-Guarani contexts (Gandulfo 2007a, 2007b; Armatto de Welti 2005, 2008; Unamuno 1992, 1994).

Research is mainly ethnographic. Only a few have also drawn on sociological quantitative methods such as interviews or surveys to gather information on socio-cultural and linguistic aspects (see Bigot 2007b; Unamuno 1992). Several were undertaken in rural communities in different provinces with relatively high proportions of indigenous communities, such as Salta, Corrientes, Misiones, Formosa, Neuquén, and Chaco. Other analyses looked at deprived urban areas (*áreas urbano-marginales*) in the provinces of Buenos Aires and Rosario (see, for instance, Armatto de Welti 2005; Bigot 2007b; Messineo and Hecht 2007; Unamuno 1992, 1994).

Analyses mainly scrutinize indigenous people and their communities (Acuña 2001, 2005, 2010; Bigot 2007a, 2007b; Hecht 2006, 2010). Primary schooling was the main focus of attention[16] and research has been conducted by individual researchers and interdisciplinary teams. In general, this has been linked to the development of educational interventions such as teachers' training courses and school texts (Armatto de Welti 2008).

Unamuno's (1992) and Acuña's (2001, 2010) studies illustrate how learning and educational failure has been examined in this research tradition. Unamuno (1992) analyzed the social representation of Argentina as a monolingual country which is promoted by schools receiving bilingual immigrant children from a slum in the agglomeration of Greater Buenos Aires. The majority of pupils came from Paraguay and spoke Guaraní and Spanish. Interviews were conducted with female and male household heads and with children attending primary schools. Unamuno argued that linguistic conflict is associated with educational failure, mainly due the asymmetrical prestige of the languages used in school and at home, rather than the communicational competence of socially excluded children. Linguistic differences were ignored by teachers who viewed these children as '*villeros*', or slum-dwellers. Acuña (2010) argued that the educational failure of indigenous children, which surpasses that of non-indigenous people, is the result of teachers' misrecognition of the distance between their linguistic type of Spanish and the linguistic situation of indigenous pupils, which varies greatly in different regions of the country. This analysis provides evidence of how this distance is interpreted as a deficit, rather than as a linguistic difference that needs to be addressed in order to guarantee access to school knowledge.

In sum, this research tradition offers a rich perspective to unpack the relationships between language, power, and schooling. Furthermore, it offers insights on the ways in which educational inequalities are produced on a daily basis in linguistic contact zones.

2.3.4   'Difference' and 'diversity': Perspectives and identities

This research tradition addresses the social construction of cultural difference in the education system. With regards to main research questions, the majority of the studies have mapped how the 'other' is viewed, produced, perceived, judged, and represented at schools (see for instance Achilli 1996; García 2010; Sinisi 2000). Few researchers have explored how identity is produced by indigenous and non-indigenous people's silence and denial of intercultural differences (Heras Monner Sans 2002). Some examinations have scrutinized the discontinuities between the schools' and children's interpretative frameworks to unpack school failure, which has included interactional and communicational styles, use of language, learning styles, and conceptions surrounding knowledge production (Borton et al. 2010; Borzone and Rosemberg 2000; Cardin 2003; Novaro et al. 2008).

Teachers' perspectives have often been the focus of attention (for example, Montesinos and Pallma 1999; Montesinos et al. 1999; Sinisi 1999). Some studies also examine the views of parents, teaching students, indigenous leaders, and professionals from interdisciplinary teams working in schools (see Heras Monner Sans 2002; Holstein 1999; Margulis and Lewin 1999; Novaro et al. 2008; Pérez 2008; Sagastizabal 2006). Few researchers have focused on pupils' perspectives (Holstein 1999) and many contrast the views of different school actors (Borton et al. 2010; Domenech 2004; Neufeld and Thisted 1999; Pérez 2008; Sagastizabal 2006). Social discourses such as the official curricula (Bigot 2010; Heras Monner Sans 2002; Montesinos et al. 1999), national and international legal frameworks (such as national laws and the National Constitution, and resolutions of international NGOs such as the UN) (Bigot 2010; Martínez 2008), and newspaper articles (Bigot 2010; Montesinos et al. 1999) have been scrutinized.

In relation to the ethnic groups examined, several studies have focused on the production of cultural difference of discrete ethnic groups: indigenous people (Bigot 2010; García 2010; Soria 2010) or immigrants (Castiglione 2007; Crosa Pottilli et al. 2009; Ghiglino and Lorenzo 1999; Margulis and Lewin 1999; Malegaríe 2009). However, other researchers have examined how different minority groups are 'othered' in schools, such as immigrants, mainly from other Latin American countries and their descendants; national migrants; indigenous groups; and poor people (Domenech 2004; Feldsberg 2004; Holstein 1999; Montesinos 2005; Neufeld and Thisted 1999; Sagastizabal 2006; Sinisi 1999, 2000). According to these authors, rather than compartments, these groups need to be interpreted as social positions that can be occupied simultaneously, as in the case of poor immigrant children. Authors have argued that despite particularities, these diverse groups are construed as 'different', inferior, and subordinate by the daily, mainly unconscious, deployment of symbolic and material practices of 'othering'.[17] Only a few studies compare the situation of immigrants and indigenous pupils in schools (see Domenech 2004; Novaro et al. 2008).

Participant observations, interviews of different types, and document analysis have been the main research techniques for this tradition. Some researchers have deployed participatory methods of data collection and analysis (Heras and Holstein 2004; Sagastizabal 2000) and have argued that researchers and research participants have co-produced knowledge together. Numerous researchers have developed theoretical tools, diagnoses, and pedagogic interventions in order to address the complexity of diversity (Achilli 1996; Heras and Holstein 2004). The great majority of the analyses focused on state primary schools (see Borton et al. 2010; Feldsberg 2004; Novaro 2009; Pérez 2008; Sagastizabal 2006).

Analyses, although from different theoretical standpoints, have argued that representations and practices surrounding socio-cultural diversity and difference in schools are not produced in a vacuum. They are part and parcel of wider 'symbolic and material configurations' (Montesinos and Pallma 1999), 'socio-cultural matrixes' (Achilli 1996), socio-cultural fields (Margulis and Lewin 1999), and intercultural relationships (Heras and Holstein 2004; Neufeld and Thisted 1999). From this perspective, schools are unique sites for understanding and challenging discrimination, racism, and stigmatization of minority groups, including immigrants and indigenous people. These examinations interpret schools as a cultural sub-field with relative autonomy. Exploring connections and differences between school actors' perspectives and practices, and other discursive and social arenas, together with enlightening the particularities of the former, has been a central task of this research strand.

In this research tradition, numerous studies have examined the processes of inferiorization, stigmatization, and discrimination of immigrant and/or indigenous children from a constructivist perspective, recognizing their historical, situated, and relational nature. Different theoretical perspectives and concepts have been deployed. Several researchers labeled the objects of their study as 'perspectives', 'images', 'prejudices', 'beliefs', 'ideas', 'judgments', and/or 'representations', without making explicit their theoretical grounds (see Pérez 2008; Sagastizabal 2006). In many cases, definitions of these terms are lacking.

One particularly rich group of studies use the concept of 'social representation' to explore school actors' perspectives and views (see Borton et al. 2010; Crosa Pottilli et al. 2009; Malegaríe 2009; Neufeld and Thisted 1999). Although there are theoretical nuances amongst these analyses, this concept refers to social actors' interpretative templates and their practical knowledge. Sociological and anthropological studies have also used it. Among the former, Crosa Pottilli et al. (2009) compared primary and secondary school teachers and young people's discriminatory social representations of immigrants (*extranjeros*). Researchers performed semi-structured and in-depth interviews, and held focus groups with teachers and young people aged 18 to 30 from 2001–2008 in the metropolitan area of Buenos Aires. The authors argued that teachers' and young peoples' social representations concerning a selection of nations including Bolivia, Peru, Chile, Germany, Ukraine, Italy, Korea, and Spain, are extrapolated to their nationals. In this manner, research partici-pants associated 'rich nations' with 'desirable people', and 'poor nations' with 'unwanted people' (Crosa Pottilli et al. 2009). The authors assumed that this hierarchy permeates people's actions and strategies, which in turn contributes to the legitimation of the 'hegemonic moral code'.

Other analysts have engaged with the concepts of racism and neo-racism as defined by Balibar, Menéndez, and/or Wieviorka (see for example Bigot 2010; Crosa Pottilli et al. 2009; Margulis and Lewin 1999). During the 1990s, these studies found similar social and cultural trends regarding immigration. Comparable to the situation in Europe, a 'racism of crisis' emerged which was accompanied by an active search for a scapegoat to be identified and blamed for social problems such as unemployment and poverty. Immigrants became visible social categories that were expected to assume negative behaviors and features. This 'new racism' refers to a new type of discrimination based on the cultural traits of a group, such as language, religion, traditions, and habits, rather than on biological differences. This requires that the 'other' be rejected due to its values and culture. Bigot (2010), for instance, compared current international and national legal frameworks against discrimination with how Toba people from the community Los Pumitas in Rosario city experience racism. Following Wieviorka, Bigot argued that her concept of 'indigenous discrimination', defined as attitudes, discourses, and practices that suppose mistreatment of people for belonging to indigenous groups, is a form of neo-racism, which is denounced by indigenous leaders as the key reason for their children's educational failure. Another illustration of this type of research is Margulis' and Lewin's (1999) study. They described in their study how (i) rac-ism and discrimination take place in schools and in the school system, and (ii) the school and its actors contribute to or mitigate discrimination against immigrants. These studies offer evidence of schools', teachers' and children's racist practices. Similarly to numerous other studies, this analysis showed how teachers establish a hierarchy amongst different ethnic groups, locating at its top those that are 'like us', the 'normal', and classifying immigrant children and families according to racist and ethnocentric values.

Drawing heuristic tools mainly from anthropology but also sociology, it mainly investigates how representations and practices around 'difference' and 'diversity' contribute to the production of social inequalities of various social groups. This tradition traces how 'difference' is produced and defined, and how it is intertwined with identity-making processes.

2.3.5   School texts as a means of 'othering'

This research tradition contributes to exploring the ways in which school textbooks and handbooks (*textos* and *manuales escolares*) have defined cultural difference in Argentina. The majority of the studies have analyzed how indigenous people have been discursively produced in school textbooks (Artieda 2002, 2005, 2006; Artieda et al. 2009; Nicoletti 2006; Novaro 2003). Several analyses have looked at the portrayal of immigrants (Alloatti 2008; Devoto 1993; Zelaya de Nader and Suayter de Iñigo 1990) and a few have focused their attention on how the image of Argentina and its national identity has been produced by defining different types of outsiders or 'others' (Cucuzza 2007; Romero 2004). Although several studies were carried out in the 1980s, the majority of these analyses were performed during the last decade.

Primary and basic education has been the main focus of analysis (Alloatti 2008; Artieda 2002, 2005; Artieda et al. 2009; Novaro 2003; Zelaya de Nader and Suayter de Iñigo 1990), with just a few examining secondary education (Devoto 1993; Romero 2004). Only a minority have looked at other types of educational texts, such as curriculum documents, school notebooks, and educational policies (Díaz and Rodríguez de Anca 2004; Fischman 1993; Montesinos 2005). Few researchers have examined texts alongside other data sources such as interviews (Artieda et al. 2009; Novaro 2003).

Researchers have examined textbooks edited by a diverse range of institutions, such as the national government up to the decentralization of primary education in the late 1970s and secondary schooling in the early 1990s, provincial governments following the abandonment of the role by the central government, the Catholic church in the origins of the nation-state and in specific regions of the country, private publishing companies and NGOs, and individual schools following the educational reform of the 1990s and the concomitant proliferation of different school text producers.

Although this body of research looks at different periods of Argentinean history, the great majority of the analyses have examined textbooks during the emergence and consolidation of the national education system,[18] whether as a stand-alone period or from a comparative perspective. Many researchers have adopted a historical perspective and have traced continuities and discontinuities between different periods. In general, the so-called 'foundational period', which we have referred to as the early period of the hegemony of the cultural homogenization, has been taken as the baseline (Novaro 2003; Romero 2004). Artieda (2007) and Artieda and colleagues (2009), for instance, compared the symbolic construction of the relationships between ethnic groups in this 'foundational period' with other crucial historical moments, such as Peronism, the last military dictatorship, and the 1980s onwards, with the return of democracy and the discursive dominance of 'cultural diversity' and multiculturalism.

School texts have been interpreted as 'discourses' (Artieda 2005, 2006, 2007), 'devices' (Nicoletti 2006), 'state's representations' (Nicoletti 2002/2003), 'means of formal socialization' or 'ideological containers' (Zelaya de Nader and Suayter de Iñigo 1990), 'curriculum in act' (Romero 2004), and 'means for subjectivity production' (Artieda and Rosso 2009). Despite the theoretical nuances, this research body assumes that textbooks are part of wider social representations which are enmeshed in particular social, economic, cultural, and political contexts. Moreover, these analyses assume that textbooks are important tools to produce legitimate meanings and representations of the past and present. Via this view, school discourses play a key role in the production and reproduction of socio-political and symbolic domination of indigenous people and/or immigrants. Their findings point to striking continuities between the 'foundational period' up to the late 1970s and the coexistence of contradictory discourses around cultural difference from the 1980s onwards, a mixture of cultural 'sediments' and new and emerging ways to define difference.

Artieda (2006), one of the most prolific authors in thisarea, illustrates this tradition. She examined basic education school texts from two periods: the last military dictatorship (1976–1983) and from the return of democracy (1983) onwards. With regards to the last dictatorship, the author identified the emergence of a religious and moral discourse, which was utilized to explain the relationship between indigenous people and 'society'. While the role of the state in the 'homogenization' of indigenous communities is misrecognized, their evangelization is highlighted. Following the return of democracy, these discourses disappeared from school texts. Narratives concerned with the evangelization of indigenous people were displaced by the centrality of the past and present role of the state. Unlike the school texts of the dictatorship, school texts used in democratic times have started to explore the asymmetrical relationship between indigenous and non-indigenous people, as well as the history of their suffering and oppression.

In sum, this research tradition has identified different ways of 'othering' indigenous people and immigrants by: (i) making them invisible; (ii) asserting the qualities of 'being Argentinean' and demarcating its virtues, qualities, and common history and future; (iii) 'othering' those who did not comply with these criteria; and (iv) recognizing and celebrating cultural difference, although on many occasions in contradictory ways. These discursive identity-making mechanisms have had a different centrality over time. While the production of a white Argentinean masculine nation and the parallel 'othering' of indigenous people and/or immigrants was dominant up until the end of the 1970s, the recognition of cultural difference, in particular in the case of indigenous people, together with the persistence of essentialist, apolitical, and ahistorical perspectives was a feature of the period which began in the 1980s with the return of the democracy and the introduction of a multicultural educational agenda. To date, there are no studies examining school texts in the period initiated by the new national law in 2006.

2.4 Discussion and final remarks

Despite their particularities, the five research traditions reviewed above share a common interpretative matrix to unpack key aspects of the relationships between ethnic groups and education. On the one hand, they all agreed in identifying a dominant homogenizing paradigm in education since the inception of the Argentinean nation-state and the early 1980s. This paradigm involved a cultural assimilation approach and implied the denial and marginalization of cultural and linguist differences of a variety of immigrant and indigenous groups. On the other hand, from the 1980s onwards, researchers coincided in recognizing a new period where key educational policies revolved around cultural differences and diversity. Moreover, all of them evidenced both continuity with and break from previous essentialist and ahistorical conceptions about cultural difference. They offer clues about how social, policy, and educational discourses contribute to disadvantage some minority ethnic groups' educational experiences and schooling.

Few researchers asked questions about ethnic and educational inequalities during the 1980s. The 1990s witnessed a considerable increase and from 2000s onwards these different research strands have blossomed. This growth reflects the centrality that cultural difference, diversity, and multiculturalism have had in shaping the cultural and educational agenda (both at policy and school levels). State educational policies have been strongly influenced what has been researched. In particular, the emergence of national, provincial and local bilingual and intercultural education initiatives have configured a fertile ground for researchers to look at. Educational anthropology has had a significant influence in the development of this research field. Unlike other national research traditions, sociologists of education have played a marginal role in asking difficult questions about ethnicity and compulsory schooling.

The majority of the research traditions have predominantly looked at indigenous people and their educational experiences. The 'intercultural educational policies' tradition, for instance, have focused on how BIE policies largely targeted at indigenous pupils have been interpreted by different policy and social actors. The 'school text tradition', on the other hand, has unfolded how school texts portray mainly indigenous communities in different historical periods. The quantitative research tradition has also mainly looked at indigenous groups. The exceptions are the 'socio-cultural tradition' and the 'sociolinguistic' one, which look at both immigrants and indigenous people.

Qualitative research is dominant in the majority of the research traditions. Policy-making, teachers' and students views, language conflict, and discursive production of cultural difference have been scrutinized using interviews of different types, participant observations, ethnographies, and document and discourse analysis. The views and perspectives of school actors (mainly teachers) have been at the center of attention. Only few analyses have examined children's and young people's voices. Only one tradition revolves around quantitative research methods. This set of research largely uses secondary data sources. Up to the 2000s, statistical information about indigenous pupils at national level was nonexistent. This seems to explain the recent (although slow) increase of work in this research area. On the other hand, despite the availability of general educational information about immigrants, educational researchers have tended – with few exceptions – to overlook the use of secondary data sources to examine the levels of educational participation of different immigrant groups.

Several research traditions unpack how certain aspects of (largely primary) schooling operate to discriminate against certain groups of students. The 'school text' and the 'difference and diversity'[19] traditions investigate how different types of discourses contribute to the 'othering' of certain minority ethnic groups. The 'sociolinguistic' tradition focuses on how language conflict is linked to the production or dissolution of ethnic identities and, in some cases, to learning. 'Intercultural educational policies' studies look at how BIE has been interpreted by policy texts and by different school and non-school actors (in particular, teachers). They show that is necessary to look at local contexts to recognize the diversity of BIE policies. Moreover, researchers identified different types of challenges that these initiatives imply for the provincial education system and the schools. The nature, scope, and challenges of indigenous teachers have been at the center of attention.

Research addressing the social construction of cultural difference in the education system is by far the strongest research tradition in Argentina within the field of ethnicity/race inequalities in education. Around 40% of the publications included in our database were clustered in this tradition. Research on BIE policies is a growing and promising field, although in general it has not yet taken full advantage of all the conceptual frameworks involved in policy studies. The 'school text' and the 'sociolinguistic' traditions comprise fewer publications. However, they have clearer research questions, designs, and conceptual frameworks than other traditions. Finally, as we pointed out earlier, quantitative approaches examining immigrants and indigenous education, is the smallest tradition in number and a slowly emerging field of study.

Charting this complex territory allows us to identify some challenges and potential areas for further research and collaboration. First, the new educational policy scenario, with its combination of universal and focalized policy approaches targeted at indigenous people, together with the raising of the school leaving age, configure new challenges. The majority of the reviewed studies examined ethnic and educational inequalities up to the Education Law of 2006. The new social, economic, and educational scenario will demand both revisiting of 'old issues' and the formulation of new research questions. For instance, studies will need to pay more attention to how the new BIE type of education is being implemented. Moreover, future research would benefit by examining indigenous and immigrants' experiences at secondary schooling. Second, research traditions could benefit from engaging with wider sociological concerns around gender, social class, and ethnicity. In particular, looking at how schools promote the inclusion or exclusion of ethnic minority groups with different levels of economic, social, cultural, and linguistic capital would contribute to a more nuanced understanding of the production of, reproduction, and challenge to educational inequalities. Although Argentinean research strands offer significant clues, they have not yet engaged with sociological theories that may contribute to enrich current understandings. In particular, 'whiteness studies' could offer a fruitful lens to unpack racism in the education system. Third, it would be fruitful if future studies unpack the reasons behind educational failure of indigenous and immigrant students. Available quantitative data sources have impeded this type of approach. However, qualitative approaches could offer a richer understanding of some minority ethnic students' educational engagement. Studies within the sociolinguistic tradition are already working in this direction. Fourth, it would be valuable if future research examines children's and young people's views and perspectives. Educational anthropologists have started to do so (although not yet to unpack ethnic and educational inequalities). Fifth, studies would benefit from making visible the role that researchers' relationships with research subjects have in the production of knowledge. With some exceptions, this issue has been overlooked. Sixth, it seems that more attention should be paid to the schooling of immigrants. Some studies have mainly focused on border country immigrants, misrecognizing national groups such as the Peruvians and Koreans. Finally, future research needs to reflect on the power of academic knowledge to reify socio-cultural differences, and on the risk of imposing its categorizations on the phenomena under study. In this sense, the promotion of collective and individual reflexive accounts on how we produce knowledge on ethnic and educational inequalities is paramount.

Notes

The authors thank the National Council of Scientific and Technical Research of Argentina (CONICET), the research program 'School, Difference and Inclusion' of the National University of Quilmes (UNQ), and the Pedagogical University of the Buenos Aires Province (UNIPE) for their financial support. The authors acknowledge the assistance provided by the National Teachers Library (BNM), National Centre of Educational Information and Documentation (CeNIDE), Documentation Centre of the Gino Germani Research Institute, National Library of Argentina, Laura Manzo Library (UNQ), Enzo Faletto Library (FLACSO), and National University of Lujan Library. They also appreciate the collaboration provided by the journals *Claroscuro*, *Avá*, and *Publicar*.

The authors especially thank different people who – in different ways – helped us to identify and obtain publications and clues to unpack the complexities of the Argentinean field: Laura Artieda, Yamila Liva, Diana Milstein, Ignacio Mancini, Margot Bigot, Ricardo Baquero, Lorena Lentini, Mirta Mantilla, Cecilia Carreras, Vanesa Romualdo, Emilio Tenti Fanfani, Néstor López, Fernanda Saforcada, Valeria Dabenigno, Liliana Sinisi,

Gabriela Novaro, Cecilia Veleda, María Paula Montesinos, Stella Maris García, Berta E. Llorente, Jason Beech, Diego Pereyra, Mariela Goldberg, Gladys Massé, Lloyd Hill, Carola Goldberg, Ana Carolina Hecht, Virginia Unamuno, and Axel Rivas. Finally, the authors also thank Javier García Fronti, Hugo Gallardo, Patricio Álvarez, Silvina Tomé, Fabiana Cappello, Alejandra Serial, and Karina Pérez for their collaboration at different stages of this research.

1. The current structure of the national education system consists of four levels (early childhood education, primary, secondary, higher education) and eight 'types' (*modalidades*) amongst which is the intercultural and bilingual education (Education Law 26.206: Art. 17).
2. Primary schooling has been compulsory since 1884 (Law 1420), whilst lower secondary schooling and the last school year of kindergarten school became compulsory in 1993 (Federal Law of Education 24.195). The new Education Law 26.206 passed in 2006, increased the school leaving age by making upper secondary education compulsory.
3. Only in the 19th century did immigration start to be systematically recorded (Devoto 2003).
4. For information about the past of indigenous communities see *Gobierno de la República Argentina* (2011).
5. The only survey that previously gathered information at a national level on indigenous people was the National Indigenous Census in 1965–1968.
6. In primary schooling, the general repetition rate is 5.18% and the drop-out rate is 1.16%.
7. For the period 2008–2009, the general repetition rate at secondary schooling was 12.18% for the basic cycle and 7.73% for the oriented one (Alonso et al. 2011).
8. This law restructured the organization and governance of the national education system (the pillars of which were established in 1884 by the Law 1420).
9. Studies on socio-economic inequalities and schools' daily lives in changing contexts have been at the center of the interest of sociology of education.
10. At the beginning of the study, we also searched for key words (such as education, school, inequality, race, ethnicity and Argentina) in international databases such as Sociological Abstracts, ERIC, and Web of Knowledge. However, as expected, these catalogues of mainly English-language academic journals did not contain any relevant articles.
11. In some cases it was not possible to check the complete collection.
12. The report of Cerrutti (2009) is a general characterization of the immigrant population. Only selected sections are focused on the educational situation of this population.
13. This study analyzed data from the ECPI.
14. The lack of detailed methodological information is more common in chapters of books. The wider target audience could explain this tendency.
15. Only one study (Citrinovitz 1991) examined educational policies targeted (bilingual literacy) at immigrants in frontier schools in order to determine the reasons behind their educational failure.
16. Only Armatto de Welti (2008) studies kindergarten schooling.
17. Some authors have also compared the situation of these groups with that of special education needs pupils: Sinisi (1999); Skliar (2005); Padawer et al. (2010).
18. Alloatti (2008) argued that during the second half of the 19th century, primary education school texts started to be published in Argentina. School textbooks and school acts were crucial aspects in the production of a 'national identity'.
19. In this paper, this tradition has been entitled "Difference and diversity: perspectives and identities".

References

Achilli, E. (1996) *Práctica docente y diversidad sociocultural* (Rosario: Homo Sapiens).

Achilli, E. (2001) 'Antropología y políticas educativas interculturales (notas sobre nuestro quehacer en contextos de desigualdad social)', *Claroscuro. Revista del Centro de Estudios sobre Diversidad cultural de la Universidad Nacional de Rosario*, I, 1, 57–74.

Acuña, L. (2001) 'De la castellanización a la educación intercultural bilingüe: sobre la atención de la diversidad lingüística en la Argentina', *Revista Nebrija de Lingüística Aplicada a la Enseñanza de Lenguas*, 6, 90–98, http://www.nebrija.com/revista-linguistica/revista_6/articulos_n6/biblioteca_1.pdf, date accessed 11 September 2011.

Acuña, L. (2005) 'Los chicos mismos te enseñan: bilingüismo en la educación intercultural bilingüe' in Tissera De Molina, A. and Zigarán, J. (eds) *Lenguas, educación y culturas* (Salta: CEPIHA/Departamento de Lenguas Modernas de la Facultad de Humanidades de la Universidad Nacional de Salta).

Acuña, L. (2010) 'Lenguas propias y lenguas prestadas en la EIB' in Hirsch, S. and Serrudo, A. (eds) *Educación intercultural bilingüe en Argentina. Identidades, lenguas y protagonistas* (Buenos Aires: Novedades Educativas).

Aguirre, D. (2010) 'Educación intercultural bilingüe en el ámbito ranquel' in Castel, V. and Cubo De Severino, L. (eds) *La renovación de la palabra en el bicentenario de la Argentina. Los colores de la mirada lingüística* (Mendoza: Editorial FFyL, UNCuyo).

Alloatti, N. (2008) 'Las representaciones sobre inmigrantes en los primeros libros de lectura argentinos (1880–1930)', *Biblioteca Virtual, Sociedad Argentina de Historia de la Educación*, Documento 53, http://www.sahe.org.ar/pdf/sahe053.pdf, date accessed 11 September 2011.

Alonso, G. and Díaz, R. (2004a) 'Los "usos" de la diversidad cultural aplicadas a la exclusión' in Díaz, R. and Alonso, G. (eds) *Construcción de espacios interculturales* (Buenos Aires: Miño y Dávila).

Alonso, G. and Díaz, R. (2004b) 'Documento para el debate: Educación intercultural: alcances y desafíos' in Díaz, R. and Alonso, G. (eds) *Construcción de espacios interculturales* (Buenos Aires: Miño y Dávila).

Alonso, G. and Díaz, R. (2004c) 'Integración e interculturalidad en épocas de globalización' in Díaz, R. and Alonso, G. (eds) *Construcción de espacios interculturales* (Buenos Aires: Miño y Dávila).

Alonso, M. L., Díaz, M. B. and Goicochea, M. (2007) *Las escuelas que reciben a alumnos indígenas. Un aporte a la Educación Intercultural Bilingüe* (Buenos Aires: DiNIECE, Ministerio de Educación de la Nación. Argentina).

Alonso, M. L., Falcone, J., Baruzzi, G., Basualdo, M., Masautis, A., Albergucci, L. and Chamut, L. (2011) *La educación argentina en cifras* (Buenos Aires: DiNIECE, Ministerio de Educación de la Nación. Argentina).

Anderson, B. (1993) *Comunidades Imaginadas. Reflexiones sobre el origen y la difusión del nacionalismo* (México: Fondo de Cultura Económica).

Arce, H. (2007) 'Mboe´akuéry Mbyareköpy ("Maestro en Cultura Mbya"). Experiencias de Educación Intercultural Bilingüe en Misiones (Argentina)' in García, S. M. and Paladino, M. (eds) *Educación escolar indígena. Investigaciones antropológicas en Brasil y Argentina* (Buenos Aires: Antropofagia).

Armatto De Welti, Z. (2005) *La escuela: situación de contacto multilingüe-intercultural* (Rosario: Humanidades y Arte Ediciones).

Armatto De Welti, Z. (2008) 'Estrategias para el enriquecimiento mutuo entre los sujetos escolares en situaciones de contacto lingüístico-cultural', *Revista de la Escuela de Antropología*, XIV, 151–160.

Artieda, T. (2002) 'Los pueblos aborígenes en el curriculum y en los libros de texto de la escuela primaria durante el primer peronismo (1946–1955)', *Historia de la Educación, Anuario*, Sociedad Argentina de Historia de la Educación, 4, 113–136.

Artieda, T. (2005) 'Los discursos escolares sobre los indígenas. Continuidades y rupturas a fines del siglo XX', *Educación, Lenguaje y Sociedad*, III, 3, 59–74.

Artieda, T. (2006) 'Lecturas escolares sobre los indígenas en dictadura y en democracia (1976–2000)' in Kaufmann, C. (ed.) *Dictadura y educación. Los textos escolares en la historia argentina reciente* (Buenos Aires: Miño y Dávila/UNER).

Artieda, T. (2007) 'La invención de la identidad nacional a través de los libros de lectura (1880–1930). O de cómo manipular identidades a través del discurso escolar' in AA.VV. (ed.) *Interfaces metodológicas na História da Educação* (Fortaleza: UFC Edições).

Artieda, T. and Rosso, L. (2009) 'Pedagogía para indígenas del Chaco, a fines del siglo XIX y principios del XX. La asimilación "dulce" por vía de la educación y del trabajo' in Ascolani, A. (ed.) *El sistema educativo en Argentina. Civilidad, derechos y autonomía, dilemas de su desarrollo histórico* (Rosario: Laborde Editor).

Artieda, T., Rosso, L. and Ramírez, I. (2009) 'De "salvajes en extinción" a autores de textos. La producción de textos como expresión de conflictos interétnicos' in Artieda, T. (ed.) *Los otros en los textos escolares. Conflictos en la construcción de imágenes de nación* (Luján: Universidad Nacional de Luján).

Avellaneda, J. (2001) 'Área de Educación Aborigen Bilingüe e Intercultural', *Horizonte: revista de información educativa*. Chaco: Ministerio de Educación, Cultura, Ciencia y Tecnología. IV, 11, 17–18.

Barbero, M. I. and Roldán, D. (1987) 'Inmigración y educación (1880–1910). ¿La escuela como agente de integración?', *Cuadernos de historia regional*, Universidad Nacional de Luján, 3, 9, 72–86.

Bella, R. (2007) 'La cuestión aborigen en la escuela. Análisis de la cuestión en la Ley Federal de Educación', *Antes de Ayer. Área de Educación de la Escuela de Gobierno de la Universidad Torcuato Di Tella. Infancia en red*, http://www.educared.org/c/document_library/get_file?p_l_id=12484004&folderId=12484098&name=DLFE-20614.pdf, date accessed 11 September 2011.

Bertella, M. L. (2006) 'Diversidad sociocultural y pobreza: desafíos de la educación intercultural', *Claroscuro. Revista del Centro de Estudios sobre Diversidad cultural de la Universidad Nacional de Rosario*, V, 5, 157–172.

Bigot, M. (2007a) *Los aborígenes 'qom' en Rosario. Contacto lingüístico-cultural, bilingüismo, diglosia y vitalidad etnolingüística en grupos aborígenes 'qom' (tobas) asentados en Rosario* (Rosario: UNR Editora).

Bigot, M. (2007b) 'Cuestionarios para el análisis de vitalidad etnolingüística y discriminación indígenas en contextos de contacto lingüístico-sociocultural', *Papeles de Trabajo. Centro de Estudios Interdisciplinarios en Etnolingüística y Antropología Socio-Cultural*, 15, 165–194, http://www.scielo.org.ar/scielo.php?script=sci_issues&pid=1852-4508&lng=es&nrm=iso, date accessed 12 June 2011.

Bigot, M. (2010) 'Discriminación indígena. Los indígenas qom de los Pumitas', *Papeles de trabajo. Centro de Estudios Interdisciplinarios en Etnolingüística y Antropología Socio-Cultural*, 19, http://www.scielo.org.ar/scielo.php?script=sci_issues&pid=1852-4508&lng=es&nrm=iso, date accessed 12 June 2011.

Bordegaray, D. and Novaro, G. (2004) 'Diversidad y desigualdad en las políticas de Estado. Reflexiones a propósito del proyecto de educación intercultural bilingüe en el Ministerio de Educación', *Cuadernos de Antropología Social*, 19, 101–119.

Borton, L., Enriz, N., García Palacios, M. and Hecht, A. C. (2010) 'Una aproximación a las representaciones del niño indígena como sujeto de aprendizaje' in Hirsch, S. and

Serrudo, A. (eds) *La Educación Intercultural Bilingüe en Argentina: identidades, lenguas y protagonistas* (Buenos Aires: Novedades Educativas).

Borzone De Manrique, A. M. and Rosemberg, R. (2000) *Leer y escribir entre dos culturas* (Buenos Aires: Aique).

Briones, C. (2004) 'Del dicho al hecho. Poniendo la interculturalidad en sus varios contextos' in Díaz, R. and Alonso, G. (eds) *Construcción de espacios interculturales* (Buenos Aires: Miño y Dávila).

Cardin, L. (2003) 'Educación y relaciones de poder en una comunidad toba del Chaco argentino', *Estudios Atacameños*, 25, 117–127, http://redalyc.uaemex.mx/src/inicio/ArtPdfRed.jsp?iCve=31502507#, date accessed 12 June 2011.

Carozzi, M. J. (1983) 'Algo bueno en educación para aborígenes', *Mundo Nuevo*, 5, 5 41–44.

Castiglione, C. (2007) 'Inmigración y escuela media. El caso de la inmigración coreana y su inserción en la escuela pública', *Claroscuro. Revista del Centro de Estudios sobre Diversidad cultural de la Universidad Nacional de Rosario*, VI, 6, 259–287.

Catalá, S., Coler, M., Lara, L. and Susini, S. (2009) 'Matrícula extranjera en la Ciudad de Buenos Aires período 2000–2008', *Informes temáticos de la Dirección de Investigación y Estadística del Ministerio de Educación del Gobierno de la Ciudad de Buenos Aires*. (Buenos Aires: Ministerio de Educación del Gobierno de la Ciudad de Buenos Aires).

Cebolla De Badie, M. (2005) 'Docentes y niños: Jurua Kuery e indios. Breve reseña sobre la situación de las escuelas aborígenes bilingües-biculturales en la provincia de Misiones, Argentina', *AIBR: Revista de Antropología Iberoamericana*, 41, http://redalyc.uaemex.mx/src/inicio/ArtPdfRed.jsp?iCve=62304109, date accessed 21 September 2011.

Cerrutti, M. (2009) *Diagnóstico de las poblaciones de inmigrantes en la Argentina. Serie de Documentos de la Dirección Nacional de Población.* (Ciudad de Buenos Aires: Dirección Nacional de Población. Secretaría de Interior. Ministerio del Interior. Argentina).

Cervera Novo, J. P., Corbato, G., Hecht, A. C., Losada, S., Pais, G., Petz, I. and Schmidt, M. (2010) 'Educación Intercultural Bilingüe en el chaco salteño. Reflexiones sobre la capacitación de auxiliares bilingües y la producción de textos multilingües' in Hirsch, S. and Serrudo, A. (eds) *La educación intercultural bilingüe en Argentina: identidades, lenguas y protagonistas* (Buenos Aires: Novedades Educativas).

Cid, J. C. and Paz, J. (2004) 'Pobreza, educación y discriminación. Los aborígenes en Salta', *Anales Asociación Argentina de Economía Política*. Anales Buenos Aires 2004, http://www.aaep.org.ar/anales/works/works2004/CIDYPAZ.pdf, date accessed 21 June 2011.

Citrinovitz, E. (1991) 'La alfabetización en zonas fronterizas bilingües: lineamientos pedagógicos, práctica docente y aprendizaje', *Propuesta Educativa*, FLACSO, 3, 5, 79–83.

Costarelli, J. M. (2008) *Informe Área de Educación Aborigen Bilingüe e Intercultural* (Chaco: Ministerio de Educación, Cultura, Ciencia y Tecnología).

Crosa Pottilli, J., Silberstein, Y. and Tavernelli, P. (2009) 'De la jerarquización de las naciones a la clasificación de sujetos: representaciones que perpetúan un orden exclusor' in Cohen, N. (ed.) *Representaciones de la diversidad: trabajo, escuela y juventud* (Buenos Aires: Ediciones cooperativas).

Cucuzza, H. R. (2007) *Yo argentino. La construcción de la Nación en los libros escolares (1873–1930)* (Buenos Aires: Miño y Dávila).

Devoto, F. (1993) 'Idea de nación, inmigración y "cuestión social" en la historiografía académica y en los libros de texto de Argentina (1912–1974)', *Propuesta educativa*, FLACSO, 5, 8, 19–27.

Devoto, F. (2003) *Historia de la inmigración en la Argentina* (Buenos Aires: Sudamericana).

Díaz, R. and Alonso, G. (2004) *Construcción de espacios interculturales* (Buenos Aires: Miño y Dávila).

Díaz, R. and Rodriguez De Anca, A. (2004) 'La interculturalidad en debate. Apropiaciones teóricas y políticas para una educación desafiante', *Astrolabio*. Centro de Estudios Avanzados de la Universidad Nacional de Córdoba, 1, http://www.astrolabio.unc.edu. ar/articulos/multiculturalismo/articulos/diasanca.php, date accessed 5 June 2011.

Díaz, R., Rodríguez De Anca, A. And Villarreal, J. (2010) 'Caminos interculturales y educación: aportes al debate desde la Provincia de Neuquén' in Hirsch, S. and Serrudo, A. (eds) *Educación intercultural bilingüe en Argentina. Identidades, lenguas y protagonistas* (Buenos Aires: Novedades Educativas).

Diniece (2010) *Anuario Estadístico Educativo 2010*. Red Federal de Información Educativa. (Buenos Aires: DiNIECE, Ministerio de Educación de la Nación. Argentina).

Domenech, E. (2003) 'La otredad y el espejismo de la integración. Reflexiones sobre la escuela multicultural en Argentina', *Noticias de Arqueología y Antropología: Educación y Antropología II (Número temático sobre multiculturalismo y educación)*. CDROM.

Domenech, E. (2004) 'Etnicidad e inmigración ¿Hacia nuevos modos de integración en el espacio escolar?', *Astrolabio*. Centro de Estudios Avanzados de la Universidad Nacional de Córdoba, 1, http://www.astrolabio.unc.edu.ar/articulos/multiculturalismo/articulos/ domenech.php, date accessed 5 June 2011.

Enriz, N. (2010) 'Un sueño blanco: reflexiones sobre la educación Mbyá Guaraní en Argentina', *Amazônica-Revista de Antropologia*, 2, 1, 28–44.

Falaschi, C., Sanchez, F. and Szulc, A. (2005) 'Políticas indigenistas en Neuquén: pasado y presente' in Briones, C. (ed.) *Cartografías Argentinas. Políticas indigenistas y formaciones provinciales de alteridad* (Buenos Aires: Antropofagia).

Feldsberg, R. (2004) 'La influencia del contexto sociocultural en la escolarización: estudio de población boliviana en escuelas públicas de la ciudad de Buenos Aires' in Elichiry, N. (ed.) *Aprendizaje de niños y maestros: hacia la construcción del sujeto educativo* (Buenos Aires: Manantial).

Fischman, G. (1993) 'Educación y etnicidad. Socialización escolar y relaciones interétnicas' in Hernández, I. (ed.) *La Identidad Enmascarada: Los Mapuches de los Toldos* (Buenos Aires: EUDEBA).

Fulco, M. (1980) 'Población aborigen y deserción escolar. Una investigación en progreso', *Revista Deserción Escolar*, 1, 1, 29–36.

Gandulfo, C. (2007a) *Entiendo pero no hablo. El guaraní 'acorrentinado' en una escuela rural: usos y significaciones* (Buenos Aires: Antropofagia).

Gandulfo, C. (2007b) 'Un proceso de reflexividad compartido: el caso de una maestra bilingüe de una escuela rural en Corrientes, Argentina' in García, S. M. and. Paladino, M. (eds) *Educación escolar indígena. Investigaciones antropológicas en Brasil y Argentina* (Buenos Aires: Antropofagia).

García, S. M. and Paladino, M. (2007) *Educación escolar indígena: investigaciones antropológicas en Brasil y Argentina* (Buenos Aires: Antropofagia).

García, S. M. (2010) ' "Me da miedo cuando grita". Indígenas Qom en escuelas urbanas. La Plata. Argentina', *Currículo sem Fronteiras*, 10, 1, 49–60.

Ghiglino, J. and Lorenzo, M. (1999) 'Miradas de los docentes acerca de la diversidad sociocultural' in Neufeld, M. R. and Thisted, J. (eds) *De eso no se habla … Los usos de la diversidad sociocultural en la escuela* (Buenos Aires: EUDEBA).

Gobierno De La República Argentina (2011) *Acerca de la Argentina. Pueblos Originarios*, http://www.argentina.gov.ar/argentina/portal/paginas.dhtml?pagina=181, date accessed 10 October 2011.

Gómez Otero, J. (2001) 'Educación intercultural y bilingüe en escuelas con población aborigen: una experiencia inicial en la provincia del Chubut', *Colección*. Pontificia Universidad Católica Argentina, 11, 251–266.

Grimsditch De Marchesotti, J. E., Sorín De Starna, A. L. and Corbalán, M. A. (1987) *Educación para la mujer que vive en la comunidad rural o en poblaciones de escasa densidad demográfica: mujeres criollas y aborígenes, diagnóstico de situación* (Buenos Aires: Ministerio de Educación y Justicia. Argentina).

Grimson, A. (2006) 'Nuevas xenofobias, nuevas políticas étnicas en Argentina' in Grimson, A. and Jelin, E. (eds) *Migraciones regionales hacia la Argentina. Diferencias, desigualdades y derechos* (Buenos Aires: Prometeo).

Hecht, A. C. (2006) 'De la familia wichí a la escuela intercultural bilingüe: procesos de apropiación, resistencia y negociación (Formosa, Argentina)', *Cuadernos Interculturales*, 4, 6, 93–113.

Hecht, A. C. (2007) 'Pueblos indígenas y escuela. Políticas homogeneizadoras y políticas focalizadas en la Educación Argentina', *Políticas Educativas*. Campinas: Revista del Programa de Políticas Educativas del Núcleo Educación para la Integración de la Asociación de Universidades Grupo Montevideo, UNICAMP, Brasil, 1, 1, 183–194.

Hecht, A. C. (2010) 'Encrucijadas entre las políticas educativas y el mantenimiento de las lenguas indígenas', *Espaço Ameríndio*, 4, 1, 92–116.

Hecht, A. C. and Szulc, A. (2006) 'Los niños indígenas como destinatarios de proyectos educativos específicos en Argentina', *Qinasay. Revista de Educación Intercultural Bilingüe*, 4, 4, 45–66.

Heras Monner Sans, A. I. (2002) 'Acerca de las relaciones interculturales: un presente-ausente tenso', *Scripta Ethnologica*, XXIV, 24, 149–172.

Heras, A. I. and Holstein, A. (2004) 'Herramientas para comprender la diversidad en la escuela y la comunidad', *Cuadernos de la Facultad de Humanidades y Ciencias Sociales*, 22, 79–99.

Hernández, A. M. and Kleinerman, N. (1999) 'Apoyo a escuelas bilingües-interculturales de comunidad aborigen', *Forum*, 1, 1, 71–74.

Hernández, I. (1988) 'Identidad indígena y educación', *Desarrollo Económico*, 28,109, 121–137.

Hirsch, S. (2010) 'Pensando la Educación Intercultural Bilingüe en contextos pluriétnicos y plurilingüísticos' in Hirsch, S. and Serrudo, A. (eds) *Educación intercultural bilingüe en Argentina. Identidades, lenguas y protagonistas* (Buenos Aires: Novedades Educativas).

Hirsch, S. and Serrudo, A. (2010) 'La educación de comunidades indígenas de la Argentina: de la integración a la Educación Intercultural Bilingüe' in Hirsch, S. and Serrudo, A. (eds) *Educación intercultural bilingüe en Argentina. Identidades, lenguas y protagonistas* (Buenos Aires: Novedades Educativas).

Holstein, A. (1999) 'La experiencia de la diversidad en los grupos escolares' in Neufeld, M. R. and Thisted, J. (eds) *De eso no se habla ... Los usos de la diversidad sociocultural en la escuela* (Buenos Aires: EUDEBA).

INDEC (2001) Censo Nacional de Población, Hogares y Viviendas del año 2001. Buenos Aires: Instituto Nacional de Estadísticas y Censos, http://www.indec.gov.ar/, date accessed 1 October 2011.

Lanusse, P. (2004) 'La cuestión indígena en educación: algunas consideraciones sobre la educación intercultural y bilingüe en el proyecto ANEPA' in Díaz, R. and Alonso, G. (eds) *Construcción de espacios interculturales* (Buenos Aires: Miño y Dávila).

Llomovate, S. (1992) 'La investigación educativa en Argentina', *Propuesta educativa*, FLACSO, 4, 6, 92–102.

López, N. (2002) *Estrategias sistémicas de atención a la deserción, la repitencia y la sobreedad en escuelas de contextos desfavorecidos. Un balance de los años 90s en la Argentina* (Buenos Aires: IIPE-UNESCO).

Malegaríe, J. (2009) 'El binomio nativos migrantes' in Cohen, N. (ed.) *Representaciones de la diversidad: trabajo, escuela y juventud* (Buenos Aires: Ediciones cooperativas).

Margulis, M. and Lewin, H. (1999) 'Escuela y discriminación social' in Margulis, M. and Urresti, M. (eds) *La segregación negada. Cultura y discriminación social* (Buenos Aires: Biblos).

Mármora, L. (2002) *Las políticas de migraciones internacionales* (Buenos Aires: Paidós).

Martínez, M. E. (2008) 'La noción de "diversidad" en los documentos educativos de los noventas y en las perspectivas de los docentes', *Políticas Educativas*. Campinas: Revista del Programa de Políticas Educativas del Núcleo Educación para la Integración de la Asociación de Universidades Grupo Montevideo, UNICAMP, Brasil, 1, 1, 13–26.

Mect (2004) *Educación intercultural bilingüe en Argentina. Sistematización de experiencias* (Buenos Aires: Ministerio de Educación, Ciencia y Tecnología. Argentina).

Messineo, C. and Hecht, A. C. (2007) 'Bilingüismo, socialización e identidad en comunidades indígena', *Anales de la educación común*, 3, 138–143.

Milstein, D., Fernández, M. I., García, M. A., García, S. M. and Paladino, M. (2007) 'Panorama de la Antropología y la Educación escolar en la Argentina 1982–2006', *Anuario de Estudios en Antropología Social – 2006*, 77–96.

Ministerio De Educación De Corrientes (2008) *Programa Intercultural Bilingüe Guaraní/Español – Programa Intercultural Bilingüe de Escuelas de Frontera* (Corrientes: Ministerio de Educación de la Provincia de Corrientes).

Montesinos, M. P. (2005) 'En torno a la diversidad sociocultural. Algunas relaciones posibles entre migraciones, estado, sociedad y educación en Argentina' in Domenech, E. (ed.) *Migraciones, identidad y política en Argentina* (Córdoba: Centro de Estudios Avanzados de la Universidad Nacional de Córdoba).

Montesinos, M. P. and Pallma, S. (1999) 'Contextos urbanos e instituciones escolares. Los usos del espacio y la construcción de la diferencia' in Neufeld, M. R. and Thisted, J. (eds) *De eso no se habla ... Los usos de la diversidad sociocultural en la escuela* (Buenos Aires: EUDEBA).

Montesinos, M. P., Pallma, S. and Sinisi, L. (1999) 'La diversidad cultural en la mira. Un análisis desde la Antropología y la Educación', *Revista Publicar en Antropología*, VII, 8, 149–169.

Moscato, P. (1996) 'Problemática de la educación bilingüe y el nivel de bilingüismo de los alumnos', *Revista IRICE*, 10, 37–46.

Narodowski, M. and Andrada, M. (2001) 'The privatization of education in Argentina', *Education Policy*, 16, 6, 585–595.

Neufeld, M. R. and Thisted, J. (1999) 'El 'crisol de razas' hecho trizas: ciudadanía, exclusión y sufrimiento' in Neufeld, M. R. and Thisted, J. (eds) *De eso no se habla ... Los usos de la diversidad sociocultural en la escuela* (Buenos Aires: EUDEBA).

Nicoletti, M. A. (2002/2003) 'Derecho a ser educados: conceptos sobre educación y evangelización para los indígenas de la Patagonia a través del escrito inédito de un misionero salesianos', *Historia de la Educación, Anuario*, Sociedad Argentina de Historia de la Educación, 4, 137–158.

Nicoletti, M. A. (2006) 'Los indígenas de la Patagonia en los libros de texto de la congregación salesiana: la construcción de otros internos (1900–1930)', *Historia de la Educación. Anuario*, Sociedad Argentina de Historia de la Educación, 7, 182–207.

Novaro, G. (2003) '"Indios", "Aborígenes" y "Pueblos originarios". Sobre el cambio de conceptos y la continuidad de las concepciones escolares', *Educación, lenguaje y sociedad*, I, 1, 199–219, http://www.biblioteca.unlpam.edu.ar/pubpdf/ieles/n01a13novaro.pdf, date accessed 10 June 2011.

Novaro, G. (2004) 'Pueblos indígenas y escuela. Avances y obstáculos para el desarrollo de un enfoque intercultural' in Ministerio De Educación Ciencia Y Tecnología (ed.)

Educación Intercultural Bilingüe en Argentina: sistematización de experiencias (Buenos Aires: Ministerio de Educación, Ciencia y Tecnología. Argentina).

Novaro, G. (2009) 'Palabras desoídas – palabras silenciadas – palabras traducidas: voces y silencios de niños bolivianos en escuelas de Buenos Aires', *Educação Revista do Centro de Educação UFSM*, 34, 47–64.

Novaro, G., Borton, L., Diez, M. L. and Hecht, A. C. (2008) 'Sonidos del silencio, voces silenciadas. Niños indígenas y migrantes en escuelas de Buenos Aires', *Revista Mexicana de Investigación Educativa*, 13, 173–201.

Oteiza, E., Novick, S. and Aruj, R. (2000) *Inmigración y discriminación. Políticas y discursos* (Buenos Aires: Prometeo).

Padawer, A. C., Pitton, E., Di Pietro, S. C., Migliavacca, A., Medela, P. and Tófalo, A. (2010) 'La enseñanza primaria en contextos de desigualdad social y diversidad sociocultural Estudio sobre políticas de atención al fracaso escolar en escuelas de educación común', *Informes de Investigación de la Dirección de Investigación y Estadística del Ministerio de Educación del GCBA* (Buenos Aires: Ministerio de Educación del Gobierno de la Ciudad de Buenos Aires).

Palamidessi, M., Suasnábar, C. and Galarza, D. E. (2007) *Educación, conocimiento y política: Argentina, 1983–2003* (Buenos Aires: Manantial).

Paviglianiti, M. (1989) *Diagnóstico de la administración central de la educación* (Buenos Aires: Ministerio de Educación de la Nación).

Pérez, A. (2008) 'Procesos de identificación y distinción en escuelas del conurbano bonaerense', *Question. Revista Especializada en Periodismo y Comunicación (UNLP)*, 1, 18, http://www.perio.unlp.edu.ar/ojs/index.php/question/article/view/601/512, date accessed 13 June 2011.

Pérez Lindo, A. (2005) *Políticas de investigación en las universidades argentinas* (Caracas: IESALC).

Quijada, M. (2003) '¿ "Hijos de los barcos" o diversidad invisibilizada? La articulación de la población indígena en la construcción nacional argentina (siglo XIX)', *Historia Mexicana*, 2, 469–510.

Rivas, A., Vera, A. and Bezem, P. (2010) *Radiografía de la educación argentina* (Buenos Aires: Fundación CIPPEC; Fundación Arcor; Fundación Roberto Noble).

Rodríguez De Anca, A. (2004) 'Disputas acerca del discurso escolar de la diferencia' in Díaz, R. and Alonso, G. (eds) *Construcción de espacios interculturales* (Buenos Aires: Miño y Dávila).

Romero, L. A. C. (2004) *La Argentina en la escuela. La idea de nación en los textos escolares* (Buenos Aires: Siglo XXI).

Sagastizabal, M. A. (2000) 'Hacia una realidad concreta' in Sagastizabal, M. A. (ed.) *Diversidad cultural y fracaso escolar. Educación intercultural: de la teoría a la práctica* (Buenos Aires: Novedades Educativas).

Sagastizabal, M. A. (2006) 'La multiculturalidad en el sistema educativo' in Sagastizabal, M. A. (ed.) *Aprender y enseñar en contextos complejos. Multiculturalidad, diversidad y fragmentación* (Buenos Aires: Novedades Educativas).

Serrudo, A. (2010) 'Indígenas en la escuela: representaciones y tensiones acerca de los docentes indígenas bilingües en argentina' in Hirsch, S. and Serrudo, A. (eds) *La Educación Intercultural Bilingüe en Argentina. Identidades, lenguas y protagonistas* (Buenos Aires: Novedades Educativas).

Sinisi, L. (1999) 'La relación nosotros-otros en espacios escolares "multiculturales". Estigma, estereotipo y racialización' in Neufeld, M. R. and Thisted, J. (eds) *De eso no se habla ... Los usos de la diversidad sociocultural en la escuela* (Buenos Aires: EUDEBA).

Sinisi, L. (2000) 'Las representaciones docentes en torno a la diversidad sociocultural: un análisis sobre escuelas urbanas y diferencia' in Magendzo, A. and Donoso, P. (eds)

Cuando a uno lo molestan ... Un acercamiento a la discriminación en la escuela (Santiago de Chile: LOM Ediciones).

Siteal (2011) *Argentina. Perfiles de países* (Ciudad de Buenos Aires: Sistema de Información de Tendencias Educativas en América Latina), http://www.siteal.iipe-oei.org/sites/default/files/perfil_argentina.pdf, date accessed 10 September 2011.

Skliar, C. (2005) 'Poner en tela de juicio la normalidad, no la anormalidad. Argumentos a falta de argumentos con relación a las diferencias en educación' in Vain, P. and Rosato, A. (eds) *La construcción social de la normalidad* (Buenos Aires: Novedades Educativas).

Soria, S. (2009) 'Discursos sobre "indios" en la escuela: un caso de investigación para la intervención', *Praxis Educativa*, 13, 106–114.

Soria, S. (2010) 'Interculturalidad y Educación en Argentina: Los alcances del "reconocimiento"', *Andamios. Revista de Investigación Social*, 7, 167–184.

Spu (2008) *Indicadores científico-tecnológicos de Universidades Nacionales. 1998–2006.* Programa de Incentivos a Docentes-Investigadores (Buenos Aires: Secretaría de Políticas Universitarias. Ministerio de Educación de la Nación. Argentina).

Stevens, P. (2007) 'Researching Race/Ethnicity and Educational Inequality in English Secondary Schools: A Critical Review of the Research Literature between 1980 and 2005', *Review of Educational Research*, 77, 147–185.

Stevens, P., Clycq, N., Timmerman, C. and Van Houtte, M. (2011) 'Researching Race/Ethnicity and Educational Inequality in the Netherlands: A Critical Review of the Research Literature between 1980 and 2008', *British Educational Research Journal*, 37, 5–43.

Szulc, A. (2009) 'Becoming "Neuquino" in Mapuzugun: Teaching Mapuche Language and Culture in the Province of Neuquen, Argentina', *Anthropology and Education Quarterly*, 40, 129–149.

Unamuno, V. (1992) 'Conflicto lingüístico y fracaso escolar. El guaraní y el español en un barrio marginal del Gran Buenos Aires' in *Actas de las Primeras Jornadas de Lingüística Aborigen* (Buenos Aires: EUDEBA).

Unamuno, V. (1994) 'Hacia una descripción del proceso de sustitución de la lengua guaraní en un barrio marginal del Gran Buenos Aires. Algunas consideraciones' in *Actas de las Segundas Jornadas de Lingüística Aborigen* (Buenos Aires: EUDEBA).

Unamuno, V. (1995) 'Diversidad Lingüística y rendimiento escolar', *Textos de didáctica de la lengua y la literatura*, 6, 19–28.

UNICEF (2009) *Los pueblos indígenas en Argentina y el derecho a la educación. Situación socioeducativa de niños, niñas y adolescentes de comunidades rurales wichí y mbyá guaraní* (Buenos Aires: Fondo de las Naciones Unidas para la Infancia (UNICEF)).

Wallis, C. (2010) 'Discurso y realidad de la EIB en comunidades wichí del Pilcomayo, Salta: ¿Es factible la interculturalidad en la escuela pública?' in Hirsch, S. and Serrudo, A. (eds) *Educación intercultural bilingüe en Argentina. Identidades, lenguas y protagonistas* (Buenos Aires: Novedades Educativas).

Zelaya De Nader, H. and Suayter De Iñigo, M. (1990) 'La inmigración en los libros de lectura: 1900–1940', *Propuesta Educativa*, FLACSO, 2, 2, 96–99.

Zidarich, M. (2010) 'Pareja vulnerable si la hay: docente originario y docente no originario' in Hirsch, S. and Serrudo, A. (eds) *La educación Intercultural Bilingüe en Argentina. Identidades, lenguas y protagonistas* (Buenos Aires: Novedades Educativas).

3
Australia

Lawrence J. Saha

3.1 Introduction

The purpose of this chapter is to critically review the Australian research literature which focuses on the relationship between race and ethnicity, education, and social inequality. The chapter is limited to research between 1980 and 2010 and with few exceptions is limited to secondary schools. The chapter begins with an introduction to the national context within which research on this topic in Australia takes place. Here it is essential to recognize the importance of immigration and immigration policy, particularly since World War II, as that explains both the source and numbers of immigrants who arrived in Australia and the extent to which research was directed to their settlement experiences and attainments. Alongside that of migration, a separate treatment of indigenous Australians is also provided, as their profile regarding education and inequality represents a different set of sociological variables and processes. The literature is presented within the context of different research traditions which guide the investigations. These research traditions include both theoretical and methodological perspectives which guide the research, and the many policy-related programs which have affected the salience of racial and ethnic research questions.

3.1.1 Education in Australia

In order to understand the relationship between immigration and education in Australia, it is important to understand the education system itself. Prior to federation in 1901, when six separate colonies came together to form the Commonwealth of Australia, each colony had developed its own educational system. Although there were variations in the evolution of education in each colony during the 19th century, beginning in 1872 with Victoria and continuing until 1893 with Western Australia, all the colonies passed education acts whereby the colony provided education to its citizens which was 'free, compulsory and secular'. However what was, and continues to be important, is that when federation occurred, many powers were transferred to the federal government, but the powers over education remained with the states. Thus, to this day there are variations in educational structures between the states, and the control of education falls within the authority of each state government. Although the differences in structure are minor, it remains the case that the experience of school students varies between states. These differences and similarities between the states and the territories can be seen in Figure 3.1.

The important similarities between the states are the common level of compulsory education, which is to Grade 10, roughly for youth of 15 to 16 years

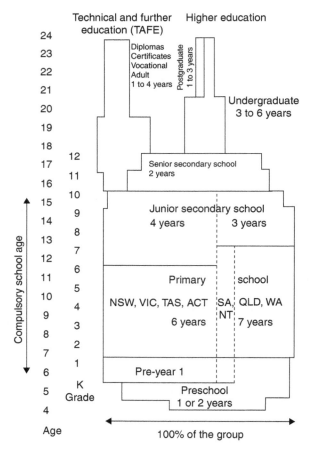

Figure 3.1   Australia: Structure of the formal education system
Note: Key (from left to right): NSW = New South Wales, Vic = Victoria, Tas = Tasmania, ACT = Australian Capital Territory, SA = South Australia, NT = Northern Territory, Qld = Queensland, WA = Western Australia.
Source: McKenzie, 1994, p. 417.

of age. There are variations in years of starting preschool and kindergarten. In addition, there are variations in cut-off points which separate primary from secondary schooling, and for Tasmania and the Australian Capital Territory, Years 11 and 12 are separated into senior secondary colleges in which students are given greater independence and the ability to begin specialization.

What is most important in the educational structures for our concern is that each state and territory can pass its own legislation regarding educational policy. Thus, for example, in 2008, the Northern Territory decided to abandon its bilingual education policy for some schools, thereby bringing to an end the possibility of indigenous children being able to study part of each school day in their native language. Similarly, in New South Wales, the state government policy for education for refugees was an initiative of that state alone. A further example is that the state of New South Wales introduced, in 2010, a policy to extend compulsory schooling to age 17, in spite of the implications for some ethnic groups (Reid and Young, 2012).

Although there are trends whereby the Australian federal government is increasing its influence over education in the states and territories, mainly though funding and the push for a unified national curriculum, the legacy of the colonies continues to exist in Australian schooling. This structural arrangement does have real and potential implications for the educational experience of all migrants, refugees, and the indigenous Australians.

Another unique feature of education in Australia is the growing private sector. In 2010, 71% of primary and secondary schools in Australia were government schools. Of the 29% non-government schools, 63% were Catholic and 37% were independent. In terms of total student enrollments, 66% were in government schools, 20% in Catholic schools, and 14% in independent schools. Between 2000 and 2010, enrollments increased in Catholic and independent schools by 11% and 37% respectively, while government schools increased by only 1.3% (Australian Bureau of Statistics 2013a). During the period of the six colonies, many schools were private and were denominationally linked. However, with the passage of the Education Acts in the late 19th century, the only schools to receive funding were the colonial government schools, and this continued after federation. Private schools existed, but with little or no assistance from the state or federal governments. In recent years, in the interest of equity, the Commonwealth has begun to provide funding for private schools on a need basis. This binary system does have implications for the school experience of migrant students and indigenous students, as they are not equally represented throughout the educational system, and many of Australia's highest performing schools are in the private sector which tends to be dominated by Anglo-Australian students.

Given the above, Australia does strive to maintain as equitable an education system as possible. As has happened in many other countries, especially in

Europe and North America, the introduction of standard high-stakes testing and accountability measures have been adopted, although with some modification. Every year since 2008, standardized tests in literacy and numeracy are administered in Grades 3, 5, 7, and 9. The National Assessment Program – Literacy and Numeracy (known as NAPLAN) provides the basis for assessing every school in the country according to reading, writing, language conventions (spelling, grammar, and punctuation), and numeracy. The results of these tests for Australia's almost 9500 schools are made publically available on the internet at a website known as My School (Australian Curriculum and Reporting Authority (ACARA), 2012). A profile is provided for each school, which includes the percentage of students whose language background is other than English, and the percentage of students of indigenous origin. Although a low ranking on the four NAPLAN scores does not draw punitive consequences as in some parts of the United States, the public availability of school performance represents a form of transparency and accountability.

Australia also participates in the Programme for International Student Assessment (PISA) of the OECD. The results and rankings of Australia with respect to the various assessment tests receive high national visibility and debate. In recent years, a longitudinal study, funded by the federal government, known as the Longitudinal Study of Australian Youth (LSAY), has been built into the PISA tests so that a growing body of data is becoming available for more sophisticated and longitudinal analyses of Australian education. The performance of migrants and indigenous students are included in these data.

Overall, recent developments in education in Australia have been very much influenced by global trends, particularly with respect to monitoring, assessing, and maintaining transparency and accountability in the performance of schools. The development of educational policy has a unique cultural and structural form, given the characteristics of the system described above, but at the same time it reflects the influence of outside institutional and globalized pressures which have become a large part of the wider educational world (Rizvi and Lindgard, 2010).

3.1.2   Migration in Australia

There are two major groupings when one discusses race/ethnic issues in Australian society, namely those of the indigenous people and the migrants. The indigenous people are normally divided into the Aborigines and Torres Strait Islanders because of the social structural and cultural differences between them. They are not normally regarded as 'migrants', as they have been the inhabitants of the Australian continent for at least 40,000 years. On the other hand, apart from the origins of the first colonizers from the United Kingdom and Ireland, ethnic minorities in the form of 'migrants' did not occur in any sizeable number until after World War II, when a large-scale program for migrants began, many of whom were displaced war refugees. In fact, it was only in 1945 that the first Commonwealth Department of Immigration was established, and since then more than seven million people have come to Australia as permanent migrants. In 1945 Australia's population was a little more than seven million, by September 2011 it was 22.69 million, and in April 2013 it officially passed 23 million. Of this growth, many were migrants.

Migration to Australia during this 65-plus year span was not evenly distributed, nor was it the result of specific demand. During this period there were numerous government policies and international agreements about the amount, and from where, this migration would occur. Although not officially espoused in government documents, Australia had, from colonial times, a 'white Australia policy' which effectively reduced the number of immigrants from non-Anglo-Saxon or non-European backgrounds. In fact, one of the first acts of the new Australian Parliament in 1901 was to enact the Immigration Restriction Act (Jupp, 2002). This is perhaps why, prior to the 1970s, migrants were assumed to more or less 'assimilate' into Australian society with relative ease. According to Martin (1978) migrants 'were to become more like us'. If migrants encountered any problems in schools or the workforce, it was because 'their main problem is that they can't speak English' (cited in Foster, 1990, p. 227). However since 1979 when 'multiculturalism' was formally adopted by the Australian government, migrants were recognized as distinct minority groups who had the right to maintain their own languages and cultures (Australian Ethnic Affairs Council, 1981). At the same time, migrants began to arrive in small numbers from Asian and other countries. In addition, another form of migration occurred in April 1976, with the arrival of the first 'boat people' from Vietnam following the conclusion of the war in that country. This phenomenon has continued to occur sporadically, involving many countries of origin, to the present day, and remains a social and political issue, with educational challenges.

3.1.3   Multiculturalism in Australia

The events that had a profound effect on the experience of all migrants in Australia occurred just prior to 1980. The two major documents which set the stage for a new era of migrant and minority conditions were the Galbally Report (*Review of Post-Arrival Programs and Services for Migrants. Migrant Services and Programs*, 1978) and the McNamara Report (*Report of the Committee on Multicultural Education, Education for a Multicultural Society*, 1979). The first of these has been called a 'watershed' in Australia's ethnic relations policy, because it moved away from the idea of migrants as 'assimilable', or if they could not, as 'people with problems', and it moved toward a multicultural policy whereby the preservation of ethnic languages and practices was seen as a benefit to Australian society (Foster, 1990, pp. 228–229). The second of these reports, the McNamara Report, focused on education as the main driving force in implementing multiculturalism. In schools, the promotion of the awareness and understandings between cultures was to take place both in the formal curriculum as well as in the informal curriculum. Various other agencies, such as the Standing Committee for Multicultural Education and the Curriculum Development Centre, incorporated the policy of multiculturalism in their work, particularly in the development of language programs and other multicultural activities in government schools, and also the establishment of ethnic schools.

The ethnic schools functioned independently of the formal education system, and met in the evenings or weekends. Their purpose was to maintain the language, culture, and identity of children of ethnic parents while growing up in Australia (Kringas and Lewins, 1981; Smolicz, 1984). Once established, ethnic schools, with assistance from local governments, became a mainstay of multiculturalism in Australia. Although Australia-wide figures are difficult to obtain, by 2010 in the state of South Australia, for example, there were 198 funded ethnic schools with a total enrollment of 6899 students (Government of South Australia, 2010, p. 21).

Thus by 1980 the stage was set for four decades of multicultural education in Australia's schools, which had a profound effect on the educational performance and attainments of migrant groups and indigenous Australians. However there continues to be much discussion about Australia's multicultural policy, and particularly the theory underlying it, the policy itself, and its practice in schools (Rizvi, 1987). Indeed, the policy was virtually 'closed down' during the late 1990s and early part of the 21st century with the absorption of the Department of Multicultural Affairs into other government departments. It has been suggested by some that multicultural education in Australia has been too 'culturalist' and sometimes 'victimizes' and 'problematizes' different cultural values and norms (Leeman and Reid, 2006; Keddie et al., 2013). Indeed, the policy of multiculturalism has been related to Australia's immigration policy, sometimes referred to as the 'Ethnic Movement', with the consequence of adding a welfare and status dimension to tolerance and understanding. Thus, rather than integration, multiculturalism and subsequent immigration policies have been seen by some as producing 'ethnic separatism', and with subsequent costs to the federal and state governments for the maintenance of migrant and ethnic services. Indeed, it has been argued that rather than multiculturalism and ethnic difference, Australia might have been better served by a policy to promote a new Australian identity (Birrell, 1995). Nevertheless, multiculturalism remains to this day an official government policy, and it is frequently endorsed to promote tolerance and understanding between cultures, as well as multicultural activities in schools.

It is with this social and political backdrop that the relationship between ethnicity, race, and educational inequality in Australian must be understood.

3.2   Methodology

Literature on race and ethnicity in Australia is extensive. Hardly any aspect of migrant and minority experience has been ignored in a wealth of material about migrants. This material ranges from the journalistic, autobiographical, and anecdotal to, of course, academic. Within the academic sphere, the research has cut across almost all disciplines. The literature on migrant schooling occurs primarily within educational research and therefore emanates from departments of education. In this respect 'sociological' studies on ethnicity and education appear in a variety of journals and types of publications. The searches for research findings to be included in this review covered a wide range of sources, including Proquest and the Australian Education Index (AEI). The latter, which is published by the Australian Council for Education Research, is the most comprehensive and sophisticated source for identifying research on all aspects of Australian education. The AEI includes the scanning of over 200 Australian journals and a total of 500 Australian and international journals in the search for Australian educational research studies. The index also includes books, conference proceedings, technical reports, theses, and legislation. The index includes more than 130,000 entries relating to Australian educational research, policy, and practice. It covers the period from 1979 to the present.

The criteria for selecting research for inclusion in this review were as follows: (i) the literature had to focus on Australian education; (ii) the literature had to have a sociological perspective, taken broadly, and focus on educational inequality and race/ethnicity; (iii) the research should focus primarily on secondary education; and (iv) the journals should be restricted to those which are peer reviewed. Using these criteria, the literature search identified 27 key articles, of which nine focused on educational inequality among Aborigines and Torres Strait Islanders. Thus this highly selective set of research studies represents the work of key sociologists of education in Australia who focus on race and ethnicity and educational inequality. In addition, other literature has been included, such as journal articles and books, which are closely related to the topic. These are intended to contextualize and to enrich the empirical research studies. As such, this review provides perhaps the most reliable picture of this aspect of inequality in Australian education between the years 1980 and 2010.

3.3   History of the research

There is a long history of sociological research on migrant educational attainment. In 1971, eight years before the policy of multiculturalism was officially introduced, Smolicz and Wiseman (1971) acknowledged that 'there is more or less tacit pressure put upon migrants, but more especially on their children, to shed their cultural skins' (p. 3). This observation is even more apparent in a statement made by a state minister of education who, in the mid-1960s, explained:

> we deliberately refrain from collecting any statistics in regard to school pupils from overseas. Once they are enrolled in school they are, from our point of view, Australian children. (Cited in Smolicz, 1987, p. 318)

This comment probably was driven by the changes in migration patterns in Australia following World War II. As Smolicz and Wiseman (1971) noted, in 1947 immediately following the war, one in five Australians was a migrant. However in that year, of the 700,000 non-Australian-born about 75% were British-born. By 1970 the number of non-Australian-born had risen to 2.2 million, of which less than half were British-born. Thus over the 23-year period there occurred a large number of mostly European migrants who were either displaced persons from the war, or migrant workers who had been brought to Australia to work on major post-war projects, such as the Snowy Mountains hydro-electric scheme. These latter waves of migrants were from linguistic and cultural backgrounds which were European and not Anglo-Saxon. Thus the attention to language and cultural differences, and their effects, came to the forefront of the migrant 'problems'.

Because of the rapidity and size of this post-war migration, a large body of research occurred from the late 1950s to the 1980s, which is where this review begins. There were many researchers who made valuable contributions in this early stage of understanding the issues of educating migrant children, particularly given the assimilationist assumptions and expectations that were held about the European migrants at that time. Remember that this research was done before multiculturalism became a federal policy. Surveys of that research literature can be found in Sturman (1985) and Smolicz (1987), and some of the themes of that period continue in this review.

In addition to the content or themes of the research, attention is given to the methodologies and research designs used by the researchers. The categories used here are quantitative, qualitative, case studies, and mixed methods, Sometimes it is not easy to categorize these methodologies in a clear manner, but the purpose is to appreciate the extent to which the findings of a particular study can be generalized across a population, or whether it provides us with a deeper (and some would say 'richer') understanding of the experiences of migrant children in a new cultural environment.

3.4   Review of research

This review is divided into four ethnic and racial groups which form the target populations: (i) early European migrants, (ii) Asian migrants, (iii) refugee or humanitarian migrants, and (iv) indigenous Australians. The discussion attempts to identify and cluster the research into themes which share a common subject and goal, for example family factors, or language deficit, and so on. Each section has a short conclusion, before the final discussion and conclusion of the review as a whole.

3.4.1 The early studies of European migrants

It is ironic that following the adoption of multiculturalism, early studies of inequalities in educational attainment and subsequent careers did not focus on ethnic differences at all. It was during this period that attention was directed to school types and the importance of a number of background sociological variables. A good example of a study which covered the transition into our period of interest is that conducted by Carpenter (1985a, 1985b). Carpenter followed a sample of Queensland Year 12 students in 26 schools over a period of four years, from 1978 to 1982 and was able to demonstrate that both school type (government, Catholic and independent) and sex streaming (single-sex and co-educational) had independent effects on academic attainment, defined as retention or staying longer in the education system.

With respect to type of school, Carpenter found that contrary to public perception, of those students still in school in Year 12, those in government schools performed just as well, if not better, than students in independent schools, and about the same as students in Catholic schools. More importantly, he found that academic performance was primarily a function of four sociological variables, namely mother's occupation, father's occupation, the study of science in the final three years of high school, and friends' higher educational plans. Carpenter's methods were straightforward in the first of his reports of his project in that he used cross-tabulations and weighted percentages. His results seem to have been based on a sample of around 1100 students, although this figure varied from table to table. The use of weighted percentages allowed Carpenter to confirm the findings using simple cross-tabulations.

Carpenter's study of girls in single-sex and co-educational schools (Carpenter, 1985a) was based on 503 girls in the longitudinal sample, and they were divided into girls attending co-educational (428) and single-sex (75) schools. The number of sociological variables was expanded, and included the mother's occupational status, the student's academic self- concept, and whether the student lived in the capital city as compared to the rest of the state. Cross-tabulations and regression were used to investigate the relationships. The findings did not allow a straightforward assessment of advantages for either type of schooling. For example, girls in government schools were advantaged because they were more likely to receive teacher encouragement regarding their achievement. Conversely, girls in private schools were more likely to take science courses, which in turn gave them an advantage in academic achievement. However, just as in the first of Carpenter's study, the ethnic background of the students was not taken into account. Nevertheless the approach by Carpenter in this study laid the foundation for later studies of the importance of ethnicity in explaining educational inequalities.

3.4.1.1   Social psychological and family factors

Some early studies not only adopted a sociological perspective, but also included social psychological variables, such as parental satisfaction with school, and also parental aspirations for their children. The shift to aspirations, both of parents and students, was grounded on the assumption that these social psychological dispositions are related to later educational and occupational outcomes, and not mere flights of fancy (Martin and Mead, 1979). A later review of the relationship of the aspiration variable of parents and students with long-term educational and occupational outcomes ranged from correlations of .42 to .62 (Saha, 1997), which indicates that Marjoribanks's design, as discussed below, was well founded.

Marjoribanks (1980) rejected the deficit model which had been so popular in the 1960s and 1970s in examining educational inequalities among children, and argued that schools and families were of more importance. He also regarded the transmission of cultural capital as a primary mechanism whereby the family is partly responsible for the educational inequalities among children.

In the beginning of the multiculturalism period, Marjoribanks reported on what was probably one of the most methodologically sophisticated sociological studies of the achievements of children from ethnic families. Using the concept of 'ethclass' (a combination of ethnicity and social status), Marjoribanks drew samples of Anglo-Australian (250), British (120), Greek (170), Southern Italian (120), and Yugoslavian (50) families. The four non-Australian groups represented the largest ethnic groups in Australia at the time of his study.

Using multiple regression procedures, Marjoribanks found that independent variables such as parental aspirations, achievement orientations, press for English, individualistic value orientations, and press for independence, did differ between the ethnic groups and were related to academic performance. As Majoribanks concludes, 'for non-Anglo children being taught in English-speaking contexts, low press for English, high press for dependence, and collectivistic value orientations may act as environmental obstacles restricting high parental aspirations, and in the case of Greek and Yugoslavian families, moderate achievement orientations, from being translated into successful children's academic performance' (p. 62). In a subsequent study, Marjoribanks (1991) limited his analysis only to Anglo-Australian, Greek and Southern Italian families and, using discriminant analysis, he found that two discriminant functions differentiated between the three groups. In effect he found that Anglo-Australian families were more likely than both the Greek and Southern Italian families to manifest a stronger press for English, greater press for independence, and an individualistic orientation. On the other hand, the Greek families were more likely than the Italian to manifest a greater press for English and a more collectivistic orientation than the Southern Italian families (p. 88).

A common policy concern emanating from the early work of Marjoribanks was the importance of the English language for academic success in Australian schools. This concern was consistent with that of the Galbally Report which recommended 'new multicultural and English language programmes' (Galbally, 1978, p. 40, cited in Marjoribanks, 1980). During this period there was considerable research and policy development on the educational performance of migrant children, in particular their apparent lower achievement orientations. In effect, Marjoribanks's findings pointed to the family environment, and its cultural context (or what he called their environment group profiles) as a major explanatory variable for the lower academic performance of migrant children throughout the 1960s and 1980s. In particular, parental aspirations for their children were seen as a major part of that family environment (Marjoribanks, 1984).

In his subsequent research Marjoribanks (1984) was able to differentiate between the migrant backgrounds with high and low levels of 'environmental press' on children regarding long-term aspirations. What is particularly interesting is that some migrant families had higher levels of aspirations for their children than parents of Anglo-Australian children. In effect, Marjoribanks found that the children of Greek origin perceived their parents to have higher educational aspirations for them than did the Anglo-Australian and the Italian children. Importantly, he saw this as an area of possible intervention from teachers. As he stated: 'There is a challenge for teachers, therefore to create school contexts that will assist in reducing social group differences in the educational and occupational aspirations of adolescents' (Marjoribanks, 1984, p. 171).

During a number of years Marjoribanks continued to explore this direction of research, as long as the major composition of Australian migrant children remained the same. With the use of multivariate analytic strategies, his early research focused on social psychological dimensions of attainment. The cumulative contribution of his studies was in the better understanding of the factors which were found to affect the aspirations of young Australians, be they Anglo-Australian or migrant children. Perhaps more importantly, he identified key aspects of the family environment, in particular what he called 'environmental press', to explain the effect of ethnicity on school-related outcomes.

Marjoribanks later expanded his earlier studies by incorporating the notion of family human capital, parenting style, parents' aspirations and parent practices on student cognitive outcomes, which consisted of performance in mathematics, word knowledge, and word comprehension, as measured in standardized tests constructed by the Australian Council for Educational Research (Marjoribanks, 1996a). His sample was composed of 800 sixth grade students from government and Catholic schools in South Australia. The ethnic groups included were

Anglo-Australian, English, Greek, and Southern Italian. Overall, the Anglo-Australian students and the English students had higher levels of all family environment variables, including independence-oriented parenting styles, and these were important in explaining the higher levels of student cognitive performance. Marjoribanks concluded that family environment factors, rather than any other factors, were responsible for the lower performance of migrant children, or at least those from the migrant backgrounds that he studied. In this respect, the focus of his approach differed considerably from the earlier studies in the 1960s and 1970s especially, which focused on the lack of proficiency in the English language as the major cause of migrant student problems.

Because of the research findings from the family-oriented studies of Marjoribanks and his colleagues, policy implications which emanated from this body of knowledge pointed to further research. This research needed to focus on factors which explain how family environments might become more consistent with the demands of schooling in a culturally different environment, and promote school success. In this regard, he also acknowledged those family environments which may be oppositional in nature, that is unwilling to adapt, or what he calls 'involuntary' minority groups.

> What is required now are studies of ethnic group variations of young adolescents' school outcomes that involve voluntary and involuntary minority groups and that include refined family models that examine both the parents' and young adolescents' perceptions of those environments. [...] If such analyses were undertaken, then parents and teachers would have a greater understanding of those manipulable environment variables that account for differences in young adolescents' performances in school. (Marjoribanks, 1996a, pp. 356–357)

Additional research on European migrants during this period is consistent with the general findings of Marjoribanks, but added two further dimensions to understanding the educational and occupational ambitions of ethnic students, namely gender and academic versus vocational education plans. In a representative sample study of 2153 secondary school students from 125 schools in the capital cities, who were planning to leave at the end of the year, Saha (1985) was interested in how occupational aspirations and expectations affected the plan to pursue further academic education, or vocational education, and early schooling leaving. The focus was less on family press and more on the student's socio-economic background and own preferences. Grouping students into Australian, United Kingdom, and European, and replicating analyses for each group, Saha found that ethnicity was not related to the choice of vocational education and early leaving. Furthermore he found that the ambitions were strongly related to remaining in school through Year 12 for all groups, including United Kingdom and European. In other words, it was the socio-economic status which made the difference and not ethnicity. However what was also interesting, is that of all the groups, the male Europeans had the highest aspirations while females from all groups had the lowest. These findings were confirmed in a more elaborate study of educational plans, where the male migrant students had the highest occupational plans, and these in turn most strongly affected educational plans (Saha, 1987).

In conclusion, these studies strongly concentrated on the social psychological dimensions of educational plans and attainments. The general findings were that migrant students, for the most part, were as ambitious as Australian students, and for migrant males, even more so. However in those cases where migrant students did not achieve as highly, it was generally due to the family-related factors.

3.4.1.2   Structural family factors

Subsequent research in this quantitative tradition continued to build on the social psychological orientation of Marjoribanks and others. However, researchers also have since begun to consider structural as well as cultural/family variables. Bowden and Doughney (2010) did exactly this in their online study of 2189 students from 80 secondary schools, both government and private, in the western corridor of Melbourne. The researchers chose this area because of its diversity in ethnic groups. They operationalized 'structural' as the socio-economic status of the student's home background. Their dependent variables were the aspirations and expectations of the students after leaving school. Bowden and Doughney were particularly interested in the interplay between socio-economic status and ethnicity, and they incorporated a wide range of theoretical perspectives in their research, in particular those of Pierre Bourdieu, for the notion of 'cultural capital', and Raymond Boudon, for his notion of decision pathways, modified by socio-economic status. Bowden and Doughney had 62 different countries represented in their 2006–2007 survey, measured by country of birth of student or parents. What they found was that, of the most recently arrived non-English-speaking migrants, those from Africa, Asia and the Middle East had the highest aspirations for higher education attainment. The weakest aspirations were among students 'who were, or their parents were, born in Oceania (principally New Zealand and the Pacific Islands), followed by Australia'. (Bowden and Doughney, 2010, p. 122). However, unlike Marjoribanks and others years before, they found no difference between the non-English and English-speaking students in perceived parental support. However they attributed the non-English and English differences in educational aspirations to differences in socio-economic status. In particular, they found that low socio-economic status English-speaking students had the lowest level of aspiration for higher education, thus partly explaining the ethnic differences.

The Bowden and Doughney study is particularly important since it captures in part the changing nature of migration to Australia. Unlike Marjoribanks, Smolicz, and the early researchers into the educational experiences of migrant students in Australia, Bowden and Doughney could incorporate more recent migrants into their study by focusing on the western corridor of Melbourne, in particular migrants from Africa, Asia and the Middle East. They found these migrant aspirations to be very high. Clearly the landscape of migrant education in Australian was already changing by the 2000s.

One characteristic of the above studies is that they tend to aggregate migrant categories to a greater or lesser degree. They are also all quantitative and in the political arithmetic tradition. They also are consistent in that migrant children, with some exceptions, do pretty well in school, and where they do not, the explanation can be found in some deficit, either in the English language or some aspect of family background. To this extent, they endorse the 'ethnic success' thesis which was espoused by Bullivant (1988) and Birrell (1995; Birrell and Seitz, 1986) during this period. Bullivant and Birrell argued that European migrants shared many of the values of the Australians before migration, and therefore, apart from language, their children were able to adapt reasonably well to the values of Australian schooling. This conclusion was supported in a recent study by Marks (2010) who found, using the 1995 cohort of the LSAY study, that migrant students from an English-speaking background, such as Hong Kong and India, actually do better than Australian students throughout their schooling. He attributed this to 'more positive attitudes to their school-work, more homework and, more importantly, a more strategic selection of sub-jects' (p. 151). They also recognized that education is the 'key to life chances'.

However, Windle (2004) argued that the tendency to aggregate ethnic cat-egories by many quantitative researchers has masked some ethnic groups' fail-ures to achieve in education. Drawing on quantitative data of Turkish migrants, and comparing them with other, mainly Asian, students, Windle argued that their difficulties in school stem from far more complex factors than nor-mally included in earlier migrant studies. He argued for a more disaggregated approach to the study of migrant education experiences.

The vastly differing school experiences of Australia's current heterogene-ous mix of labour migrants, refugees, fee-paying overseas students, skilled professionals and business migrants, demand of future research attention to specific conditions of arrival and differential demands made by educational systems. (Windle, 2004, p. 283)

From the above, it is clear that there were some limitations in the aggregation of migrant categories in the quantitative studies, and pockets of migrant fail-ure might not have been so apparent. Nevertheless, the large body of data and knowledge about migrant children in schools made a major contribution during that period of research on the factors which contributed to migrant student ambitions and achievements in schools.

3.4.2   The studies of Asian migrants

One of the major shifts in migration trends in Australia has been the increase in Asian migrants. Between 1976 and 2001, the proportion of the Australian population who were born in Asia rose from 1.1% to 5.5%. Looked at another way, among the 'recent' migrants to Australia between 2000 and 2010, 10.3% were from China, 2.3% from Malaysia, 2% from South Korea, and 1.7% from Vietnam, for a total of 16.3%. This is more than the 14.5% from the United Kingdom, or the 13.2% from India. Given the extensive research on the presumed high achievement orientation of Asian students compared to that of Western students, particularly with respect to the importance of effort rather than ability, one would expect the educational ambitions and attainments of Asian migrant students to differ considerably from that found among European migrant children. This is in line with the research of McInerney (2006), who found that Asian students in Australia had higher levels of achievement motivation than Australian students. However results from the Third International Mathematics and Science Study (TIMSS) suggests that students across all countries, including the Chinese, share views about the importance of hard work for mathematics attainment (Leung, 2002).

Martin and Hau (2010), in their comparative study of samples of Hong Kong and Australian students, found that there were no differences in the kind of achievement motivation, but there were differences in degree. In effect, the Australian students reported higher levels of 'adaptive' achievement motivation (planning, task management, and persistence), and lower levels of 'maladaptive' achievement motivation (self-handicapping, and disengagement). In contrast, Asian students have been found to have higher standards and a desire for self-perfection, and feel shame and guilt when they fail to attain these goals (Li, 2002, 2005). It would seem, therefore, that comparisons between Asian and Australian students in educational achievement attainments are more complex than have been assumed.

The documentation of these similarities and differences between Asian and Australian students forms a backdrop to understanding the academic performance of Asian migrant students in Australia. Tan and Yates (2011) argue that the primary cause of the effort that Asian students give to their studies lies in their Confucian cultural heritage. Students from countries such as China, Taiwan, Singapore, Hong Kong, Japan, and Korea share the values of hard work and filial piety which is deeply embedded in Confucian teaching. Therefore it is as much their cultural background, as it is the characteristics of their family environment, which explain the high expectations, the determination, and the perfectionism which typify the educational engagement and achievement of Asian students.

However, Tan and Yates also argue that these values create a highly stressful environment for Asian students which dominates their schooling and also the attainment of a high status job. Other studies, such as that by Ho and Yip in Singapore (2003) have documented the extent to which students considered education to be 'the most stressful aspect of school life' and that they were 'least satisfied with the grades they had received' (pp. 390–391). The study by Tan and Yates on Singaporean students confirmed the extent to which their sample of Asian students felt subjected to the high expectations of their teachers, their parents, and themselves, and that they experienced high levels of stress as a result.

The characteristics of migrant Asian students in Australia were confirmed by a qualitative study by Matthews (2002). Focusing on interviews with female Asian students in a co-educational Australian state school she argued that the 'pro-school conformity of Asian-Australian young women sets them in a problematic and precarious relationship to the material and symbolic processes of racialization' (p. 194). Matthews accepts the cultural argument which explains the high attainments of Asian migrant students, but she points out that while this might bring about 'ethnic success', it also brings with it racialization and, in the case of Asian females, sexualization. She argues as follows:

> stereotypes and practices of racialization and sexualisation sustain pro-school culture and Asian female group associations. While they have the effect of securing Asian female educational success, they are also problematic because they limit girls' educational possibilities and employment opportunities. (Matthews, 2002, p. 194)

Ironically, it is the very value system, and its pressure for achievement, which brings about a form of 'new racism' which accentuates 'difference' and thus brings with it forms of disparagement.

Once again, it is useful to recall ethnic success theory (Bullivant, 1988) which is based on the notion that educational success can be explained by the consistency between student cultural values and those espoused by the school. It can therefore be assumed, for example, that the success of Asian students in Australian schools is due to the consistency of their values (which Tan and Yates would call 'Confucian' values) and some of the values adhered to in schools. Examples of these values are hard work, respect for teachers, self-discipline, motivation, deference and politeness, a desire for perfection, and not questioning the teacher. These are typically Asian values, and not the same as identified in the research of European migrants. The main problem that Matthews finds with this theory is that Asian students in Australia are not a culturally homogeneous category, and that the category 'Asian' 'conceals national, cultural and "racial" distinctions, and does not refer to the same categories of people in Australia' (p. 195).

Nevertheless, as a label Matthews argues that it may be advantageous because being 'Asian' means being smart and pro-school, and thus provides an advantage with regard to academic success. Teachers expect Asian students to be 'smart, passive and polite', and they therefore give them more attention and are 'favored' in many ways, including tolerance from the teacher regarding lateness or other 'off-task' behaviors. However, as Matthews notes, Asian students, especially female students, may not receive help when they need it because they are assumed to be 'smart'. Thus the label 'Asian' may have disadvantages. This form of disadvantage is augmented by Australian students who respond to the 'Asian' label with a subtle form of racism, involving harassment and exclusion, especially toward Asian female students.

There is yet little systematic data which has tested, or could test the arguments made by Matthews. As Sweetnam (2003) has noted, test scores by ethnicity are not routinely compared in Australia (unlike in the United States) because 'improvement of student achievement is not an apparent motivation in Australia' (p. 209). However what Matthews has demonstrated with her qualitative data is that the stereotypes of 'being smart' and 'being motivated' are not the advantage that culture theorists assume, and that these stereotypes can bring about negative consequences of racism.

Research on Asian migrant students in Australian schools is far less developed than that of the European migrants. This may be due to their more recent arrival, or perhaps the fact that they have not been identified as 'problematic' in their educational experience and performance. However Matthews argues, like Windle did earlier regarding European migrants, that Asian students need to be disaggregated in research. This is necessary to examine the national, cultural, and 'racial' distinctions which may in fact mask differences in the educational experiences and outcomes of students of Asian origin in Australia.

3.4.3   Studies of refugee migrants

The study of 'refugee' or 'humanitarian' migrants is a variation of the study of migrants generally, since they represent movements from one country to another on a permanent basis. However in Australia they do differ in that they have not come through the normal recruitment or selection system as do other migrants in Australia, and nor do they come from the same countries. Since World War II, Australia has been a country of refuge with a total of 750,000 people from many different countries having arrived in response to global resettlement and humanitarian needs (Australian Government, 2011). In the early years, most of the refugees were from Europe as a result of the war. However during the 1970s many refugees arrived as 'boat people' from Vietnam as a result of the war there, and starting in 1998, the waves of refugees increasingly arrived from Africa and the Asia/Pacific region. From 2003 to 2005, 70% of refugee arrivals came from Africa, and in 2009–2010, approximately 32% of all visas granted on a humanitarian basis were to people affected by conflicts in the Middle East and South West Asia (Australian Bureau of Statistics, 2012).

Australia's immigration program consists of two components: (1) Immigration Program for skilled and family migrants, and (2) Humanitarian Program for refugees and others in refugee-like situations (Australian Bureau of Statistics, 2012).

Taylor (2008) is an example of a researcher who has been concerned with refugees from Africa, who have been considered to have 'greater settlement needs than people from previous source regions' (cited in Department of Immigration and Cultural Affairs, 2006). One of these needs was access to an education system which would respond to students who had 'lower levels of English proficiency [and] lower levels of literacy in their own languages' (p. 58). Taylor argued that three factors have worked against the full settlement of African refugees: (i) a climate of fear among Australians toward asylum seekers and refugees, (ii) a move away of the country from the policy of multiculturalism, and (iii) the neoliberal policy trends which have resulted in a reduction of funding for schools.

In a small study of government policies toward refugees in Brisbane, as reflected in websites, Taylor found that refugee education was rarely mentioned and was virtually 'invisible' or conflated with other issues, such as policies regarding English as a second language (ESL) or 'students at risk', with the result that the education of refugee children was 'left to chance' (Taylor, 2008). From the analysis of data based on semi-structured interviews with 11 community-sector and 14 ESL teachers, Taylor concluded that only the Brisbane Catholic schools, and not the government schools, had developed a policy for the support of refugee students.

In addition to the 'left to chance' status of the education of refugees, Fozdar and Torezani (2008) found, in their study of 150 refugees, which included Yugoslavs, Middle-Easterners, and Africans, that in spite of feeling discriminated against, these refugee migrants felt generally a sense of well-being and were satisfied with life in their new country, and perhaps only mild disappointment but no serious dissatisfaction. Although Fozdar and Torezani's study was primarily concerned with perceptions of negative life events related to employment, one could ask whether there are implications for the experience of refugee children in Australian schools. Fozdar and Torezani did point out that refugees place value on opportunities for their children, and therefore their sense of well-being might have been due not to their own negative discriminatory experiences, but in the hope and expectation that life would be ultimately better for their children, compared to where they came from (Fozdar and Torezani, 2008, p. 54).

Studies of the actual achievement of recent refugee students are not yet available, although there is research on the experiences that these students have in Australian schools. Using interviews and focus groups, Cassity (2007) studied 65 African refugee students from Sudan, the country which constituted 47% of humanitarian refugees allowed into Australia in 2003–2004. There were 2775 admissions in that year, but this had increased to 5654 in 2004–2005. Other countries represented in the admissions at this time were Ethiopia, Congo, Somalia, Sierra Leone, Liberia, Burundi, and Rwanda. Many of the refugee students had experienced considerable trauma due to violence and conflict in their home countries. The students who were studied were in three government schools in Western Sydney, and were making the transition from their home country with little education or interrupted education, and poor English language skills.

According to Cassity, 'the NSW [New South Wales] school system is not working for recently arrived African children' (p. 92). Various programs were in place to assist the students in her sample, for example the Intensive English Course (IEC) and the Young Africans in School Project (YASP). However the immense gap between the preparedness of the African refugee students, and their traumatized condition, were such that few were succeeding. For many refugee students, schooling in Australia was seen as directed towards 'coping up', or catching up for lost time, for the periods when they were not in school because of conflicts or refugee flight (p. 101). Furthermore, even though they perceived themselves to be in a new and 'safe' country, the trauma of past experiences continued to interfere with their return to schooling through memory distractions and loss of concentration. Many of these concerns are reported in greater detail in the earlier report by Cassity and Gow (2006).

The findings of Cassity and Gow are similar to another study in Victoria. Brown, Miller and Mitchell (2006) interviewed in depth eight Sudanese refugee students in two schools and found that they had experienced significant gaps in their schooling before coming to Australia. As the largest African refugee group in the schools, the Sudanese students represent '… an extremely high risk group, which faces great challenges in terms of adaptation to the school system, acculturation, social adaptation, English language learning, and eventual academic success' (p. 150). Brown and her colleagues identify one of the main problems for the Sudanese students is learning the 'highly specific form of English' that is used in Australian classrooms. Furthermore, oral fluency in English is not sufficient for academic study. The students themselves identified their discomfort with subject-specific language (for example, biology and science generally), cultural knowledge about Australia, various teaching approaches such as group activity, and the use of textbooks. The researchers found that the students had high aspirations, but their career aspirations sometimes were based on misunderstandings of Australian society. Brown and her colleagues conclude that new strategies are needed, mainly in the form of more teachers, more help with English in specific subjects, peer support from one's own culture, and time to learn before coming to school.

From the above, it is apparent that there has been sufficient concern about the difficulties in the education for refugees, and in particular their lack of knowledge in English among researchers and education authorities. Nevertheless it has been argued that their education has been 'left to chance' (Sidhu and Taylor, 2007). For the most part, efforts to remedy this disadvantage have taken the form of ESL teaching, and a study of the language teachers of refugees found that for the most part, they used sound educational practices (Windle and Miller, 2012). However, Windle and Miller (2012) argue that additional attention needs to be directed to the inculcation of 'autonomous learning', or the ability of students to take more control over their own learning. They found that most teachers simply did not have the resources to include this skill in their teaching (p. 328).

The education of recent refugees, although taking place over a ten-year period, continues to be problematic in Australia. Just as with the migrants and refugees following World War II, both the cause and the solution have been seen to be the lack of adequate English. However there is growing awareness that more than English teaching is necessary if the disadvantages of refugee experience and refugee status are to be overcome.

3.4.4   Studies of indigenous Australians

Although Australia is home to many migrant groups whose ancestry can be traced back to early British settlement in the late 18th century, it is also home to one of the ancient cultures of the worlds, namely the Australian Aborigines, who have inhabited the continent for at least 50,000 years. In one sense, Aborigines also were the first migrants, having arrived across a land bridge which then connected the Australian continent with the land masses of South East Asia. The Torres Strait Islanders are another indigenous group who inhabit the far north of Queensland, and who are regarded as distinct from the Aborigines, being culturally and genetically linked with Melanesian peoples. The word 'indigenous' is commonly used to refer to both groups, and this is the way it is used in this section.

The education of Australian Aborigines throughout the 19th and 20th centuries was sporadic. This was, in part, due to the view that the Aborigines would eventually die out, or be absorbed into the dominant white majority. The government policies during this period were motivated primarily to 'smooth the pillow of a dying race', and therefore little was done to promote their education on a large scale. Indeed, it was only in the 1960s that the Aborigines began to be taken seriously as a part of mainstream society, and it was only in 1971 that they were counted as citizens in the official census. Because of their disadvantaged condition regarding health and well-being, relative to indigenous groups in other Western countries, the indigenous Australians are regarded as some of the most disadvantaged (Cooke et al., 2007).

Determining the exact number of Aborigines has always been difficult because of definition. In recent years there has been an increasing propensity for people identifying themselves as Aborigines. Nevertheless, the official figure given by the 2011 Census for those who identify as Aboriginal or Torres Strait Islander is 669,900, which represents 3% of the total Australian population (Australian Bureau of Statistics 2013b). In general, the indigenous population is younger than the rest of the Australian population, due to increasing birth and survival rates. While the state of New South Wales has the largest number of indigenous people (28.7% of the indigenous population), they comprise 31.6% of the total population of the Northern Territory (Australian Human Rights Commission, 2008).

In terms of geographical distribution in 2006, 32% lived in major cities, 21% lived in 'inner regional' areas, 22% in 'outer regional' areas, 10% in 'remote' areas, and 16% in 'very remote' areas. This distribution is important because it explains in part why many young Aboriginal children do not have normal access to educational facilities (Australian Human Rights Commission, 2008).

Over the period from 1980 the retention rate for indigenous children has steadily increased, so that by 2007 the retention rate from Year 7/8 to Year 10 was 91%, and to Year 12 it was 43%. While these figures are far below the figures for non-indigenous Australians, the disparity is lessening. Nevertheless, in 2006 indigenous people aged 15 or older were only half as likely as non-indigenous to have completed Year 12, the figures being 23% compared to 49%. In higher education, the non-indigenous people were four times as likely to have a bachelor degree or above, 21% compared to 5%. So even though the educational status of the indigenous had improved considerably over the years, by 2010 they still lagged far behind the non-indigenous Australians. And the indigenous people living in remote areas were less well off, educationally, than those living in cities, the figures for those completing Year 12 being 22% compared to 31%, but only 14% in very remote areas. (Australian Human Rights Commission, 2008). However in 2012 the number of indigenous students who were staying on to Year 12 reached an 'all time high' to 50% (Australian Bureau of Statistics 2013b). Nevertheless, this is considerably lower than the figure for non-indigenous students, who have a retention rate of around 85%.

Whichever way one examines the data, in spite of improvements in indigenous educational attainment, they not only lag far behind their non-indigenous counterparts, but the differences within the indigenous peoples in differing geographical areas is also great. It should be noted, however, that in some areas of performance, there are no differences between males and females.

The performance of indigenous children in schools has been studied for many years. For a review of research which was conducted in the 1960s and 1970s, see Gale et al. (1987). Here we will examine recent studies and discuss some of the factors which have been regarded as explanations for their low educational attainment.

3.4.4.1   Political arithmetic studies

In spite of the fact that the educational attainments of Australia's indigenous population had been of concern to the country for some time (Long, Frigo, and Batten, 1999), many of the studies on the issue were of a qualitative or case-study nature. Indeed, Bodkin-Andrews, O'Rourke and Craven (2010) commented that many of these studies lacked generalizability and sufficient scope of methodologies to fully investigate the many factors which contributed to the performance of the indigenous children in school. However with the emergence of larger data sets and the ability to meaningfully measure concepts such as self-concept for both indigenous and non-indigenous Australians, a better understanding of the educational disadvantage of indigenous students will be better understood and appropriate interventions to improve their condition might be introduced.

Bodkin-Anderson and colleagues (2010) have noted that self-concept and a stronger sense of self-determination had been found related to studies of indigenous mental health. However they have argued that it is important to progress beyond one-dimensional or global measures of self-concept, to those which differentiate between self-concepts regarding education, family relations, peer relations, and career aspirations, to name just a few. They used this self-concept approach in a study of four high schools (rural and urban) which had at least 10% indigenous students in Years seven to ten, which resulted in 1369 participants. Data were gathered on a range of self-concept measures, as well as school aspiration and school achievement in English and mathematics. They found that indigenous students 'in comparison to non-Indigenous students, displayed significantly lower scores for general self-esteem, mathematics self-concept, verbal self-concept, home educational resources, English grades, and mathematics grades' (p. 289).

Bodkin-Anderson and colleagues (2010) concluded that the self-concept variables had the strongest effect on the educational outcomes for both indigenous and non-indigenous students, although there were variations between the domain-specific concept measures. However the results were sufficiently strong to prompt them to comment that 'no teacher is wasting his or her time in enhancing specific domains of self-concept in order to influence schooling outcomes' (p. 299). They advocated a culturally inclusive pedagogy, and supported Purdie's (2003) observation that 'The challenge for educators is to ensure that schools are places where Indigenous children want to be, where their presence and participation is valued, where they feel successful and where they see value in completing their schooling' (p. 299).

Clearly, in these quantitative studies the concept of self-identity emerges as important for understanding difficulties that indigenous children have in schools. But self-identity regarding education, whether it is positive or negative, is also related to culturally linked practices which take place in the classroom. What are some of these?

3.4.4.2   Cultural studies

As with studies of immigrants, many researchers have seen culture as the main factor which explains the low educational attainment and performance of the indigenous students in Australian schools. Much of this research is a response to greater cultural diversity in schools and universities and represents an effort to understand academic performance issues. (See Omeri et al. (2003), and Ramburuth and Tani (2009) for reviews of both qualitative and quantitative research about culture in the classroom.) In a qualitative study of indigenous students in South Australia, Rahman (2010) found that the attendance, retention, learning, and achievement of indigenous secondary school students were related to 'culturally responsive schooling, culturally responsive pedagogy and cultural safety' (p. 67). Based on interviews with indigenous secondary school students, Rahman noted that, in addition to responsive and supportive teachers, and the encouragement of parents, that teachers 'in particular the way that they relate to students, can significantly impact on student interest in school, their learning engagement and levels of retention, attendance and achievement' (p. 74).

The conclusions regarding the unique effects of culture are mixed. However, in a major report on cultural dimensions and indigenous participation in education, Dockery (2009), for example, argues that traditional Aboriginal cultures are not necessarily a barrier to educational participation and attainment, but may, in fact, be complementary. Using statistical data from the Australian Bureau of Statistics, Dockery demonstrates that the maintenance and respect for traditional Aboriginal culture, and a greater sensitivity on the part of teachers, especially for students from non-remote areas, can have positive effects.

There is a growing body of literature which has tested the dominant cultural deficit theory with quantitative data for progression to university studies for Aboriginal students. For example, even at the university level, White and Fogarty (2000–2001) found, with samples of indigenous and non-indigenous students, that the former tended to hold collective values while the latter espoused individualist values. In addition, and in a similar vein, other studies, such as that by Teasdale and Teasdale (1992), had found that indigenous students tended to be informal and incidental in their learning as part of day-to-day experience, whereas non-indigenous students, with individualist values, tended to more self-directed, independent, and in general more motivated and ambitious. These latter are values more consistent with the Australian schools. Fogarty and White (1994) argued that as a minority group, not sharing the values of the wider society could be a cause for educational disadvantage.

However the same authors replicated their study with a new sample of indigenous and non-indigenous students, and they added a larger number of control variables, including dimensions from Schwartz's Values Survey (1992) (Fogarty and White, 1994). Drawing samples of 202 Aboriginal and 194 non-Aboriginal students in a southern Queensland university, they found significant differences in educational performance, as measured by 'progression rate', that is the ratio of passed courses to total courses attempted. The Aboriginal students had a progression rate of 38.72, compared to 84.83 for the non-Aboriginals. This means that the Aboriginal students passed about four out of ten courses, while the non-Aboriginals passed between eight and nine courses out of every ten that they attempted. The authors also found that the Aboriginal students scored higher on the 'security', 'conformity' and 'tradition' scales, all of which indicated a collectivist orientation. Furthermore they found that the tradition and conformity scales correlated with low progression scores. However, when a regression analysis was conducted, and the variable 'race' was included, the strong relationship between these values disappeared, except for a small effect for conformity. The authors concluded that 'the greater collective orientation of the Aboriginal students...is not a barrier to success in education' (p. 266). They concluded that it was lack of preparation for university which eventually explained their poor performance. This was reflected by the fact that most of the Aborigines had been admitted to university under 'special or alternate entry procedures and had not completed the normal twelve years of schooling prior to university entry' (p. 262). This, they concluded, was a downside of the access and equity policies in Australia which encouraged acceptance of non-traditional students to university. But most importantly, this body of research calls into question the culture and values argument for the low performance of indigenous students in Australian schools. It also emphasizes the importance of effective and high quality education at the primary and secondary levels for the indigenous students, if they are to progress to post-secondary education.

3.4.4.3   *Language studies*

Language maintenance is important for educational success with respect to the indigenous peoples of Australia. There are about 150 languages spoken by the Aborigines and Torres Strait Islander people (Cavallaro, 2005). Although there are some who argue that language maintenance is not important for the integration of the indigenous peoples into Australian society, others argue that language maintenance is important for a wide range of reasons, including group identity, cognitive development, and academic achievement. However, rather than seen as a disadvantage, current research suggests that bilingualism is an advantage. The argument regarding bilingualism among the indigenous Australians is based on the notion that maintaining the native language, alongside English, contributes to self-identity, self-esteem, and self-confidence, and therefore to educational attainment.

The acquisition of English literacy skills is generally seen as a way of getting ahead in contemporary Australian society. Without knowledge of English, it has been argued that indigenous youth will not be able to succeed in contemporary Australian life (Clancy and Simpson, 2002). A number of policies have been enacted regarding the education of Aborigines, beginning with the New South Wales Aboriginal Policy Act (1982). This act advocated that the inclusion of Aboriginal culture in the curriculum would serve both the Aborigines as well as the white majority (Clancy and Simpson, 2002).

A much more broad policy was introduced in 2000 regarding the English literacy of indigenous people, with a focus on improving their English literacy, the *National Indigenous English Literacy and Numeracy Strategy 2000–2004* (2000). This policy was intended to heighten the awareness of those in education of the issues relating to Aboriginal literacy and numeracy.

3.4.4.4 *Training prepared teachers*

In 1986, Marjoribanks and Jordan (1986) did a study of the stereotypes that Anglo-Australian and Aboriginal adolescents had of each other. They found that the stereotype that the Anglo-Australians had of Aborigines 'was unfavourable, uniform, and characterized by an intensity that reflected extreme negative feelings'. On the other hand, the stereotype Aboriginals had of Anglo-Australians 'was particularly favourable and defined by intense positive orientations' (p. 17). This study of differences in stereotyping highlights a major issue in the preparation of teachers for interacting with indigenous students. Partington (2003) advocates having indigenous teachers in indigenous classrooms. The practice of having Aboriginal and Torres Strait Islander teaching aides, he argues, has not been successful. Clancy and Simpson (2002) also note that often teachers of indigenous students are not well equipped, and this leads to misunderstandings by both teacher and student, and contributes to student 'shaming' and a lower self-esteem.

In a study of beginning Australian teachers, Bornholt (2002) found that moderately positive and negative stereotypes toward Aborigines were indeed held. However, she also found that the teachers felt 'worry and guilt with little anger' and that they had 'intentions for positive action' and 'intentions to gain experience with Aboriginal people'. Her conclusion was that the attitudes of Anglo-Australians toward Aborigines were very complex, but that it would be possible to design 'attitude change events' in the process of teacher training, and that these should include contacts to reduce stereotyping.

There is a growing awareness of teachers as part of the problem and the solution of indigenous schooling, and some research such as that of Bornholt on how to better prepare teachers for diversity in the classroom, and particularly for schools with indigenous students identifies possible input into teacher training programs which might improve teacher–student interactions and understandings with indigenous students.

3.4.4.5 *Conclusion*

Educational issues related to Aborigines and Torres Strait Islanders are highly complex. Although until the 1960s, the general view has been that the issues would go away, with the dying out of the indigenous people altogether, or their assimilation into Australian white society. However neither of these have happened. Furthermore, the issues relating to Aboriginal and Torres Strait Islander education performance has become very complex as well, with increasing knowledge about the many factors related to their educational attainment. In this section, based on both quantitative and qualitative studies, social psychological variables, such as social identity and self-efficacy, collectivist cultural orientations, and finally English-language literacy, have been recognized as important factors in explaining why the indigenous Australians have a lower level of educational attainment, compared to white Australian students. In addition, there is growing awareness that the preparation of better-equipped and better-trained teachers, both indigenous and non-indigenous, will further improve the educational achievement and attainment of Australia's indigenous peoples.

3.5   Conclusion: Migrants, refugees, and the indigenous as an Australian educational mosaic

This chapter has attempted to identify and describe the knowledge that we have about the educational experiences and attainments of migrants and racial groups in Australia. We have divided our discussion in terms of the different relevant groups, namely the early British and European migrants, recent migrants mainly from Asia, refugees or involuntary migrants, and Indigenous Australians.

In each group of migrants or racial groups discussed in this chapter we have seen the general evidence which suggests, perhaps with the exception of the Asian migrants, that at least some migrant students do not achieve as well as Anglo-Australian students. However, the evidence also makes it difficult to generalize on a large scale. The migrant and indigenous populations in Australia are extremely diverse. Thus some migrant groups, particularly those from European countries, have tended to do well in schools during the 30-year period covered in this study (for example, see Meade (1981, 1983) and Cahill, et al. (1996)). On the other hand there continues to be evidence that specific migrant groups, and especially refugees, struggle in keeping up with Anglo-Australians. However research has clearly documented that this is not due the lack of ambition and aspirations, as evident in the findings of Smolicz (1987), Marjoribanks (1996b), and others.

In 1965, John Porter, the Canadian sociologist, described the class and power structure in Canada in the context of ethnic stratification as a 'vertical mosaic'. What prompted Porter to use the adjective 'vertical' was the fact that the English and French 'charter groups' in Canada have never been equal, with the English occupying higher social class positions and also holding most positions of power. While this 'vertical' analogy does not seem to fit well within the Australian ethnic and racial landscape, the notion of a 'mosaic' might. While the original Anglo-Australians of British/Irish origin continue to occupy the dominant position in terms of culture, politics, and institutions, it would be difficult to argue that the paths to upward mobility through education are closed to migrants, or to the indigenous people. In spite of the evidence for various impediments to some ethnic groups in schools, as Windle (2004) pointed out, by and large most ethnic groups eventually seem to succeed reasonably well. In fact in some cases, as Marks (2010) pointed out, some do better than the Anglo-Australians.

It would be premature to argue that this review of Australian research has thrown much light on the relative ranking of various ethnic and racial groups both in schooling and subsequent attainments in society. In fact one might make the case that the ethnic and racial landscape, at least in the area of education, is more like a 'horizontal mosaic', in which various categories of ethnic and racial groups struggle side-by-side, and with the Anglo-Australians, to make their way up the educational ladder. The issues which the groups need to confront and conquer in the classroom are varied, ranging, as we have seen, from English-language deficiency, cultural incompatibilities, trauma lack of self-identity and confidence, and most of all social and economic disadvantage. These issues are not in competition with each other, and thus the migrant students and the indigenous students coexist with Anglo-Australian students in a patchwork type of relationship, with educational policies at the federal, state, and territory levels attempting to address issues that will bring about greater equality in schools for all ethnic and racial groups, and greater tolerance and understanding between teachers and students, and between the students themselves. Multiculturalism, as an official policy, may be disputed and debated, and even rejected by some, but the evidence of the research in this review suggests that it continues to guide both policy and practice in Australia's classrooms.

References

Australian Bureau of Statistics. (2012). *Humanitarian Arrivals*. Canberra: Australian Bureau of Statistics.

Australian Bureau of Statistics. (2013a). *Schools, Australia 2012*. Canberra: Australian Bureau of Statistics.

Australian Bureau of Statistics. (2013b). *Estimates of Aboriginal and Torres Strait Islander Australians*, June 2011. Canberra: Australian Bureau of Statistics.

Australian Curriculum and Reporting Authority (ACARA). (2012). *My School*, from http://www.myschool.edu.au/.

Australian Ethnic Affairs Council. (1981). *Perspectives on Multicultural Education*. Canberra: Australian Government Publishing Service.

Australian Government. (2011). *Fact Sheet 60 Australia's Refugee and Humanitarian Program*.

Australian Human Rights Commission. (2008). *A statistical overview of Aboriginal and Torres Strait Islander peoples in Australia: Social Justice Report*.

Birrell, R. (1995). Dynamics of Multiculturalism in Australia. In D. L. Lovell (Ed.), *The Australian Political System*. Melbourne: Longman.

Birrell, R., and Seitz, A. (1986). The Myth of Ethnic Inequality in Australian Education. *Journal of the Australian Population, 3*(1), 52–74.

Bodkin-Andrews, G., O'Rourke, V., and Craven, R. (2010). The Utility of General Self-Esteem and Domain-Specific Self-Concepts: Their Influence on Indigenous and Non-Indigenous Students' Educational Outcomes. *Australian Journal of Education, 54*(3), 277–306.

Bornholt, L. J. (2002). Thoughts, Feelings and Intentions to Learn: Attitudes by Beginning Teachers Towards Aboriginal Peoples. *Social Psychology of Education, 5*(3), 295–309.

Bowden, M. P., and Doughney, J. (2010). Socio-economic Status, Cultural Diversity and the Aspirations of Secondary Students in the Western Suburbs of Melbourne. Australia. *Higher Education, 59*, 115–129.

Brown, J., Miller, J., and Mitchell, J. (2006). Interrupted Schooling and the Acquisition of Literacy: Experiences of Sudanese Refugees in Victorian Secondary Schools. *Australian Journal of Language and Literacy, 29*(2), 150–162.

Bullivant, B. M. (1988). The Ethnic Success Ethic Challenges Conventional Wisdom about Immigrant Disadvantage in Education. *Australian Journal of Education, 32*, 223–243.

Cahill, D., Birchall, G., Fry, I., and Vine, E. (1996). *Immigration and Schooling in the 1990s*. Canberra: Australian Government Publishing Service.

Carpenter, P. (1985a). Single-sex Schooling and Girls' Academic Achievements. *Journal of Sociology, 21*(3), 456–472.

Carpenter, P. (1985b). Type of School and Academic Achievement. *Journal of Sociology, 21*(2), 219–235.

Cassity, E. (2007). Voices Shaping Education: Young African Refugees in Western Sydney high schools. *International Education Journal, 8*(3), 91–104.

Cassity, E., and Gow, G. (2006). *Making Up for Lost Time: Young African Refugees in Western Sydney High Schools*. Sydney: University of Western Sydney.

Cavallaro. (2005). Language Maintenance Revisited: An Australian Perspective. *Bilingual Research Journal, 29*(3), 561–582.

Clancy, S., and Simpson, L. (2002). Literacy Learning for Indigenous Students: Setting a Research Agenda. *The Australian Journal of Language and Literacy, 25*(2), 47–63.

Cooke, M., Mitrou, F., Lawrence, D., Guimond, E., and Beavon, D. (2007). Indigenous Well-Being in Four Countries: An Application of the UNDP's Human Development Index to Indigenous Peoples in Australia, Canada, New Zealand, and the United States. *BMC International Health and Human Rights, 7*(9), 1–39.

Department of Immigration and Cultural Affairs. (2006). Measures to Improve Settlement Outcomes for Humanitarian Entrants. *Discussion Paper*.

Dockery, A. M. (2009). *Cultural Dimensions of Indigenous Participation in Education and Training* (Vol. 2).

Fogarty, F. A., and White, C. (1994). Differences Between Values of Australian Aboriginal and Non-Aboriginal Students. *Journal of Cross-Cultural Psychology, 25*(3), 394–408.

Foster, L. E. (1990). Sociology and Educational Policy. In L. J. Saha and J. P. Keeves (eds), *Schooling and Society in Australia: Sociological Perspectives* (pp. 215–235). Sydney: Australian National University Press.

Fozdar, F., and Torezani, S. (2008). Discrimination and Well-Being: Perceptions of Refugees in Western Australia. *The International Migration Review, 42*(1), 30–63.

Galbally, F. (1978). *Review of Post-Arrival Programs and Services for Migrants. Migrant Services and Programs.* Canberra: Australian Publishing Government Service.

Gale, F., Jordan, D., McGill, G., McNamara, N., and Scott, C. (1987). Aboriginal Education. In J. P. Keeves (Ed.), *Australian Education: Review of Recent Research* (pp. 269–285). Sydney: Allen & Unwin.

Government of South Australia. (2010). *Ethnic Schools Board Annual Report 2009/2010.* Adelaide.

Ho, K. C., and Yip, J. (2003). *YOUTHsg: The State of Youth in Singapore.* Singapore: National Youth Council.

Jupp, J. (2002). *From White Australia to Woomera: The Story of Australian Immigration.* Cambridge: Cambridge University Press.

Keddie, A., Gowlett, C., Mills, M., Monk, S., and Renshaw, P. (2013). Beyond Culturalism: Addressing Issues of Indigenous Disadvantage through Schooling. *The Australian Educational Researcher, 40*(1), 91–108.

Kringas, P., and Lewins, F. W. (1981). *Why Ethnic Schools? Selected Case Studies.* Canberra: Australian National University Press.

Leeman, Y., and Reid, C. (2006). Multi/intercultural Education in Australia and the Netherlands. *Compare, 36*(1), 57–72.

Leung, F. K. (2002). Behind the High Achievement of East Asian Students. *Educational Research and Evaluation, 8*, 87–108.

Li, J. (2002). A Cultural Model of Learning. *Journal of Cross Cultural Psychology, 33*, 248–269.

Li, J. (2005). Mind or Virtue: Western and Chinese Beliefs about Learning. *New Directions in Psychological Science, 14*, 190–194.

Long, M., Frigo, T., and Batten, M. (1999). *Indigenous School to Work Transition.* Canberra: Department of Employment, Education, Training and Youth Affairs.

Marjoribanks, K. (1980). *Ethnic Families and Children's Achievements.* Sydney: George Allen & Unwin.

Marjoribanks, K. (1984). Ethnicity, Family Environment and Adolescents' Aspirations: A Follow-Up Study. *Journal of Educational Research, 77*(3), 166–171.

Marjoribanks, K. (1991). The Relationship of Children's Ethnicity, Gender, and Social Status to Their Family Environments and School-Related Outcomes. *Journal of Social Psychology, 131*(1), 83–91.

Marjoribanks, K. (1996a). Ethnicity, Proximal Family Environment, and Young Adolescents' Cognitive Performance. *Journal of Early Adolescence, 16*(3), 340–359.

Marjoribanks, K. (1996b). Ethnicity, Family Achievement Syndrome, and Adolescents' Aspirations: Rosen's Framework Revisited. *The Journal of Genetic Psychology, 157*(3), 349–359.

Marjoribanks, K., and Jordan, D. (1986). Stereotyping among Aboriginal and Anglo-Australians. *Journal of Cross-Cultural Psychology, 17*(1), 17–28.

Marks, G. (2010). Improvements over the Career of Immigrant Students. *Australian Journal of Education, 54*(2), 134–154.

Martin, A. J., and Hau, K.-T. (2010). Achievement Motivation among Chinese and Australian School Students: Assessing Differences of Kind and Differences of Degree. *International Journal of Testing, 10*, 274–294.

Martin, J. I. (1978). *The Migrant Presence.* Sydney: Allen & Unwin.

Martin, J. I., and Meade, P. (1979). *The Educational Experience of Sydney High School Students (Report No. 1).* Canberra: Australian Government Printing Service.

Matthews, J. (2002). Racialised Schooling: 'Ethnic Success' and Asian-Australian Students. *British Journal of Sociology of Education, 23*(2), 193–207.

McInerney, D. M. (2006). The Motivational Profiles and Perceptions of Schooling of Asian Students in Australia. *Malaysian Journal of Learning and Instruction, 3*, 1–31.

McKenzie, P. (1994). Australia: System of Education. In T. Husén and N. Postlethwaite (eds), *The International Encyclopedia of Education: Second Edition* (Vol. 1, pp. 415–423). Oxford: Pergamon.

Meade, P. (1981). *The Educational Experience of Sydney High School Students (Report No. 2).* Canberra: Australian Government Printing Service.

Meade, P. (1983). *The Educational Experience of Sydney High School Students (Report No. 3).* Canberra: Australian Government Printing Service.

Omeri, A., Malcolm, P., Ahern, M., and Wellington, B. (2003). Meeting the Challenges of Cultural Diversity in the Academic Setting. *Nurse Education in Practice, 3*, 5–22.

Partington, G. (2003). Why Indigenous Issues are an Essential Component of Teacher Education Programs. *Australian Journal of Teacher Education, 27*(2), 39–48.

Porter, J. (1965). *The Vertical Mosaic.* Toronto: The University of Toronto.

Purdie, N. (2003). Positive Self-Identity for Indigenous Students. *Journal of the Aboriginal Studies Association, 12*, 27–33.

Rahman, K. (2010). Addressing the Foundations for Improved Indigenous Secondary Student Outcomes: A South Australian Qualitative Study. *Australian Journal of Indigenous Education, 39*, 65–76.

Ramburuth, P., and Tani, M. (2009). The Impact of Culture on Learning: Exploring Student Perceptions. *Multicultural Education & Technology Journal, 3*(3), 182–195.

Reid, C., and Young, H. (2012). The New Compulsory Schooling Age Policy in NSW, Australia: Ethnicity, Ability and Gender Considerations. *Journal of Educational Policy, 27*(6), 795–814.

Rizvi, F. (1987). *Multiculturalism as an Educational Policy.* Victoria: Deakin University Press.

Rizvi, F., and Lindgard, B. (2010). *Globalizing Educational Policy.* Abingdon, Oxon: Routledge.

Saha, L. J. (1985). The Legitimacy of Early School-Leaving: Occupational Orientations, Vocational Training Plans, and Educational Attainment Among Urban Australian Youth. *Sociology of Education, 58*(October), 228–240.

Saha, L. J. (1987). Tertiary Education or Vocational Training? Alternate Routes to Perceived Occupational Destinations Among Male and Female Urban School Leavers. *Education Research and Perspectives, 14*(2), 49–61.

Saha, L. J. (1997). Aspirations and Expectations of Students. In L. J. Saha (Ed.), *International Encyclopedia of the Sociology of Education* (pp. 512–517). Oxford: Pergamon Press.

Sidhu, R., and Taylor, S. (2007). Educational Provision for Refugee Youth in Australia: Left to Chance? *Journal of Sociology, 43*(3), 283–300.

Smolicz, J. J. (1984). Minority Languages and the Core Values of Culture: Changing Policies and Ethnic Response in Australia. *Journal of Multilingual and Multicultural Development 5*(1), 23–41.

Smolicz, J. J. (1987). Education for a Multicultural Society. In J. P. Keeves (Ed.), *Australian Education: Review of Recent Research* (pp. 316–345). Sydney: Allen & Unwin.

Smolicz, J. J., and Wiseman, R. (1971). European Migrants and Their Children: Interaction, Assimilation, Education. Part 1. *Quarterly Review of Australian Education,* 4(2), 1–42.

Sturman, A. (1985). Immigrant Australians and Education. *Australian Education Review* 22, 1–96.

Sweetnam, L. A. (2003). Lessons on Multicultural Education from Australia and the United States. *The Clearing House, 76*(4), 208–211.

Tan, J. B., and Yates, S. (2011). Academic Expectations as Sources of Stress in Asian Students. *Social Psychology of Education, 14,* 389–407.

Taylor, S. (2008). Schooling and the Settlement of Refugee Young People in Queensland: '… The Challenges are Massive'. *Social Alternatives, 27*(3), 58–65.

Teasdale, G. A., and Teasdale, J. I. (1992). Culture and Curriculum: Dilemmas in the Schooling of Australian Aboriginal Children. In S. Iwawaki, Y. Kashima and K. Leung (eds), *Innovations in Cross-Cultural Psychology* (pp. 442–457). Amsterdam/Lisse: Swets & Zeitlinger.

White, C., and Fogarty, G. J. (2000–2001). Educational Implications of the Values Held by Australian Aboriginal Students. *Journal of College Student Retention, 2*(3), 253–270.

Windle, J. (2004). The Ethnic (Dis)advantage Debate Revisited: Turkish Background Students in Australia. *Journal of Intercultural Studies, 25*(3), 271–286.

Windle, J., and Miller, J. (2012). Approaches to Teaching Low Literacy Refugee-Background Students. *Australian Journal of Language and Literacy, 35*(3), 317–333.

4

Austria

Barbara Herzog-Punzenberger and Philipp Schnell

4.1 Introduction

The goal of this chapter is to describe how researchers in Austria have studied ethnicity and educational inequality between 1980 and 2010 as well as critically assess the reasons for specific research activities and the lack thereof. Even today, Austria still lacks a systematic overview of research in the field of ethnicity/race and educational inequality. This is in direct contrast to countries like the United Kingdom or the Netherlands where a strong interest developed in this particular field of enquiry from the 1980s onwards. Nonetheless, Austrian research on educational inequality has sharply increased parallel to Austria's participation in large-scale studies such as the Programme for International Student Assessment (PISA), Progress in International Reading Literacy Study (PIRLS), and Trends in International Mathematics and Science Study (TIMSS).

This contribution is structured as follows: we first provide background information on the Austrian educational system, main immigration periods and outline the most important developments of social policy between 1980 and 2010. Next, we describe how the data gathering for this literature review was applied. The centerpiece of our review is the analysis of five distinct research traditions on ethnicity/race and educational inequality in Austria: the political arithmetic tradition, the family background tradition, the structures of educational systems tradition, the intercultural education and discrimination tradition, and the multilinguality tradition. We concentrate on their major focuses, methods, findings and implications for debates within this field of inquiry. We conclude by summarizing and critically assessing the research traditions explored and provide suggestions for future research on the relationship between race/ethnicity and educational inequality in Austria.

4.2   National context

This section offers a brief overview of the main characteristics of the Austrian educational system, immigration patterns to Austria after World War II, and the development of relevant policies in this field.

4.2.1   Educational system

Full-time compulsory education in Austria starts at age six and lasts nine years until age 15. Primary education is the most comprehensive phase in the Austrian system, takes four years and is compulsory except for the small percentage selected into special school (*Sonderschule*) for remedial education. Most primary schools (*Volksschule*) operate on a half-day basis. Pupils who are classified by teachers as 'not ready' spend an additional year in preschool. Since 2008, children have to take a German language test 15 months before entering school. If their German is not at the defined level they are provided with German language support in kindergarten (Stanzel-Tischler, 2011). Since 2010, kindergarten attendance is compulsory for the year before schooling begins. These measures were introduced with the aim of having all children begin their schooling with a reasonable level of German language proficiency.

After primary school, at the age of ten, pupils in Austria are streamed into two separate types of school: vocationally (*Hauptschule*) or academically oriented (*AHS-Unterstufe*) lower secondary education. Hauptschule represents the lower tier and is open to everybody after primary school. In contrast, admission to the academically oriented track, which prepares students to continue in upper secondary schools and sit the university entrance certificate 'Matura', depends on marks derived from the last year of primary school. The scale of assessment ranges from 1 (very good) to 5 (inadequate) and only pupils assessed as 'very good' or 'good' in German and mathematics may be admitted to the academic secondary school. Teachers can also give recommendations but these do not have a binding character. Additionally, lower secondary school pupils who are classified as not fit for regular school, in this case Hauptschule, are streamed into special schools where they receive specific support. Besides downward streaming, students have to retake a year in primary and secondary education if they do not meet the demands for that year. In the Austrian educational system, all exams are developed, administered, and evaluated by teachers and have yet to be standardized. The first standardized national exams took place in spring 2012.[1]

Since compulsory education in Austria lasts until age 15, students who finish Hauptschule (and did not repeat a grade) have to attend one year more of school. Those heading for the labor market attend a one-year preparatory class (*Polytechnikum*) before continuing either as an unskilled worker or with an apprenticeship position to become a skilled worker. The apprenticeship system is a combined three-year period, in firm training with one day per week in school. The young adults streamed into the academic track in lower secondary education predominately move on to the upper secondary level (*AHS-Oberstufe*) within the same school. In Austria the majority of youth in the upper secondary level are in vocational education and training (VET) whereas only a minority (around 20% of peers in their age group) is in general academic education. VET consists of three separate paths with varying content and credentials. Among them is the apprenticeship path, which trains young adolescents in a certain profession (four days in an enterprise and one day in school) as mentioned above. The apprenticeship path was, for decades, the main path into adulthood for the male population, albeit with widely varying prestige depending to firms and professions. A parallel path without a position in an enterprise is found in schools with a medium vocational education lasting three years (BMS). Only the higher technical and vocational colleges (BHS) provide access to tertiary education through the 'Matura' diploma. Tertiary education is two tiered, consisting of classical universities and so-called '*Fachhochschulen*'. The former offer university programs while the latter are full-time schools where students can extend and refine their skills with a strong labor-market orientation. Once the entrance certificate 'Matura' is obtained, the student is free to choose their study program and university. Binding entry exams at this point in time only exist for specific study programs, such as medicine and law. In short, until 2012 the Austrian educational system was characterized by non-compulsory preschool education, early selection at age ten and highly stratified secondary education. The proportion of private schools accounted around 10% (Statistik Austria, 2012[2]), the majority of these run by religious congregations. Moreover, participation at the post-secondary/tertiary educational level remains low in Austria compared to other OECD countries (for a graphical overview of the Austrian school-system see Figure 4.1).

4.2.2 Migration to Austria

After the end of World War II, Austria soon experienced labor shortages in specific industrial sectors that required more workers than the domestic labor market could supply. Accordingly, unemployment rates decreased at the end of the 1950s and the recruitment of unskilled labor increased during the 1960s, with a peak during the first years of the 1970s. Official recruitment agreements were signed with Spain (1962), Turkey (1964), and Yugoslavia (1966) (Fassmann and Münz, 1994).[3] Until the break-down of the Eastern bloc in 1989, Austria mostly attracted migrants from Yugoslavia and Turkey. The recruitment period finished in 1973 when the oil price shock cut back the economic boom throughout Europe. From 1975 until 1990, migration to Austria and the employment of foreign workers was regulated (and restricted) by the employment law for foreigners and the residence law. Up to 1990, immigration policy was purely conceived as labor market policy and continued to rest

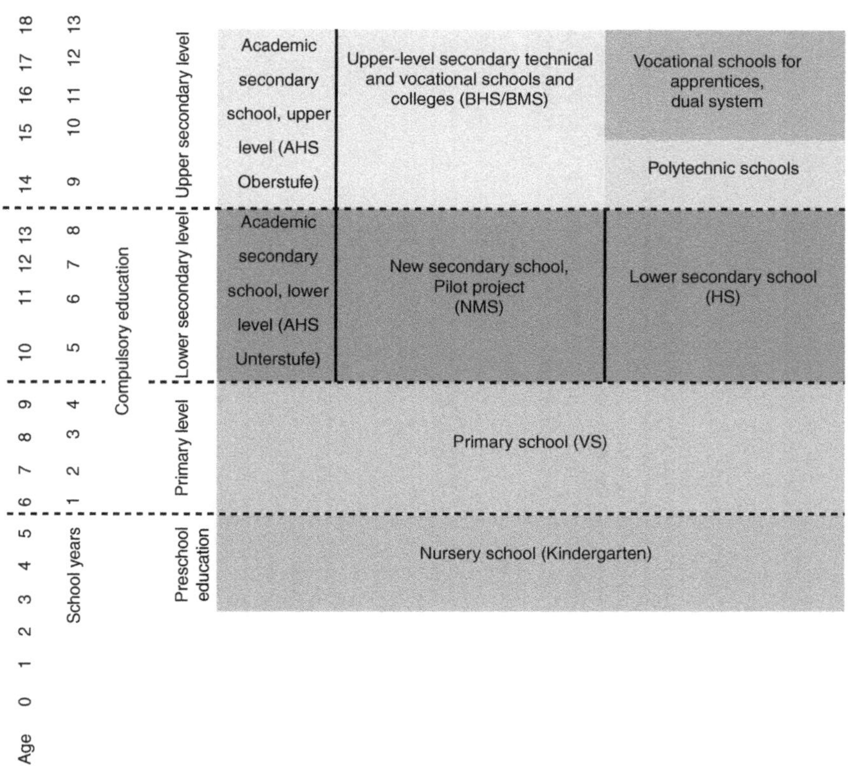

Figure 4.1 The Austrian educational system

on the assumption of the temporary nature of the presence of 'guest workers' (Perchinig and König, 2003).

After the fall of the iron curtain in 1989 and the collapse of Yugoslavia in 1991, an influx of refugees and immigrants reached Austria. The size of the foreign-born population increased from 5% to almost 9% between 1989 and 1993. Austrian politicians reacted by implementing restrictive migration laws which led to a sharp decrease of inflows from 1994 onwards.

In the early 2000s, immigration from other European countries increased (Germany in particular), including Eastern European countries which had joined the European Union in 2004. Recent statistics classify 18.6% of the current Austrian population as persons with a 'migration background' (Bundesministerium für Inneres, 2011). This statistical category contains foreign-born as well as native-born with both parents being either foreign-born or holding foreign citizenship.

Table 4.1 displays the population with a migration background broken down by generation and parents' country of origin. Foreign-born persons represented

Table 4.1 Austrian population with a migration background (2011), by generation and parents' country of origin

	Total population			Migration background				
		Total	% of total population	1st generation	% of total population	2nd generation	% of total population
Total	8,283,000	1,543,000	18.6	1,138,000	13.7	404,565	4.9
				Country of origin parents			
Austria	6,739,947						
Europe (without Austria)	515,374	515,374	6.2	411,891	5.0	103,482	1.2
Non-European	1,027,915	1,027,915	12.4	726,833	8.8	301,083	3.6
Former Yugoslavia	507,090	507,090	6.1	361,042	4.4	146,048	1.8
Turkey	262,974	262,974	3.2	163,914	2.0	99,060	1.2

Note: Definition of migration background and generational status according to Statistics Austria: first generation immigrants are born abroad; second generation immigrants are born in Austria. Both generations have both parents born abroad.
Source: Micro-census 2011 (Statistics Austria). Own calculations.

13.7% of the Austrian population in 2011. Among them, the majority origi-
nates from non-European countries, double the share of those from European
states. Table 4.1 additionally provides the percentages of first generation immigrants from (former) Yugoslavia (6.1%) and Turkey (3.2%), who still represent
two of the largest labor migrant groups in Austria. The predominance of former
Yugoslavian immigrants in the Austrian population is also reflected in the
size of second-generation immigrants with 1.8%, and the second-generation
Turkish population as somewhat smaller, comprising 1.2% of the Austrian population. Compared to other North-Western European countries, the number
of children of immigrants in Austria is still small (5% of the total population).

The classification available is by 'first language', 'first' in this case refers
to the biographical timing of language acquisition.[4] By 2010, 17% of the
total population of pupils in Austria had a first language other than German
(Bundesministerium für Unterricht, Kunst und Kultur (BMUKK), 2011). As
shown in Table 4.2, the proportion has almost doubled within the last 15
years, indicating that children of immigrants are entering schools in steadily
increasing numbers. This trend is reflected to differing extents in different
school types and tracks. In primary schools, the percentage of non-German

Table 4.2 Proportion of students with first language other than German by school type
and across selected years

		1993/1994	2000/2001	2009/2010
Primary school	Volksschulen incl. Vorschule	11.3	14.4	23.2
Lower secondary education	Sonderschulen	18.4	23.3	27.8
	Hauptschulen	10.2	13	20.9
	AHS-Unterstufe allgemeinbildende höhere Schulen	na	7.9	15.2
	Polytechnische Schulen	15.9	12.5	23.2
Upper secondary education	BPS berufsbildende Pflichtschulen	8	5.5	8.8
	BMS berufsbildende mittlere Schulen	4.6	10.7	18.2
	BHS berufsbildende höhere Schulen	3.2	6.6	11.7
	AHS-Oberstufe allgemeinbildende höhere Schulen	na	7.3	12.7
	N (all schools)	100,407	131,494	201,275

Note: Percentages show proportion of non-German mother tongue pupils within each school type.
na=not available.
Source: BMUKK (2011).

mother tongue pupils grew from 11% in 1994 to 23% in 2010 and from the considerably higher level of 18% to 28% in special schools; however, although the percentages of pupils with a first language other than German in academic-oriented educational tracks (BHS and AHS-Oberstufe) has quadrupled, it still lags behind with 12%. As in many metropolitan cities, the situation in Vienna is quite different. The majority is multilingual, so that, on average, monolingual German-speakers are the minority. Notably, the situation is very different among teachers. There are almost no multilingual teachers in Vienna, let alone in the rest of Austria (Sertl, 2009, p. 120).

While migrants and their descendants are sometimes called 'new' minorities, Austria also has a number of 'old' minorities. Following gradual recognition in legal texts, there are now six officially recognized minorities: Carinthian Slovenes, Burgenland Croats, Hungarians, Roma, Czechs and Slovaks. They are less a legacy of the Austro-Hungarian monarchy (all internal migrants had to leave the first Republic of Austria after the Peace Treaty of Saint Germain) as they are a reminder that state borders are artificial lines of separation and that settlement patterns have been mixed concerning linguistic and ethnic diversity. There is no reliable data on the size of the minorities and it appears, given the estimates on language use, that none of these groups exceeds 50,000 people, while some probably comprise less than 10,000 people (Luciak, 2008, p. 46). The 'old' minorities have special rights in Austria to date which are built on either the 1955 State Treaty or the 1976 Ethnic Minorities Act. In school matters, the respective provinces adopted Minority Schools Acts in 1959 (Carinthia) and 1994 (Burgenland) so that instruction in designated primary and secondary schools can be either bilingual or in one of the minority languages of the region. Interestingly enough, the share of students attending these schools or classes is rising, even when teachers report that a majority of the pupils have little or no knowledge of the minority language upon registration (Landesschulrat für Kärnten, 2011, p. 24).

4.2.3   Policy development in the field of education and research

In the field of education and ethnic diversity, the Austrian school system offers – at least since the beginning of the 1990s – three distinct approaches (cf. Luciak and Kahn-Svik, 2008): (a) minority language schooling for autochthonous ethnic minorities, (b) educational provision for migrants, and (c) intercultural education for all pupils. Until the beginning of the 1990s policies towards foreign nationals were characterized by the 'guest worker' idea, which was originally built on the rotation principle, i.e. that migrant workers will stay for one year, and then return home. Therefore, their children, if not ignored by educational politicians, were to be prepared for their return home. As the number of migrant children steadily increased from the 1970s onwards, three measures were applied: (i) support in learning the language of instruction, i.e.

German, (ii) support in learning the mother tongue, (iii) extra-matricular status for those who could not follow instruction in German. The extra-matricular status was meant to protect children for the duration that they could not sufficiently understand the language and comprised a first phase of 12 months with the possibility of prolongation for another 12 months. Additional support in learning German was offered for two to three hours per week on average while legal provisions allowed for 11 hours per week with up to 18 hours in special cases. The implementation of the defined legal provision generally failed due to lack of resources. In 1980/1981 the Viennese school administration reacted to the growing numbers of migrants, who tended to cluster in specific neighborhoods and thus sent their children to the same schools, by installing an alternative model: the accompanying teacher (*Begleitlehrer*). This meant that a second teacher worked with the migrant children in the classroom during regular teaching hours for five to six hours per week often using one of the main migrant languages as the primary teaching language (Bosnian-Croatian-Serbian, Turkish).

From the mid-1970s until 1990, instruction in Serbo-Croatian or Turkish language, history and culture was provided by the two 'sending' countries of the 'guest workers', Yugoslavia and Turkey, for three to five hours per week. Not only textbooks, but also teachers were sent to Austria by the two state administrations. Finally, in 1992, the above mentioned instruments of support in German language learning, mother tongue instruction, and extra-matricular status were regularized in the law together with the new principle of instruction in 'intercultural learning'. Adding onto the 12 existing principles of instruction, such as health, peace, environment, and traffic, 'intercultural learning' became part of the curriculum's general objectives and therefore had to be implemented in the didactic process of each subject (Bundesgesetzblatt II 277/2004). In addition to these major instruments, the ministry occasionally offered new, innovative approaches on a voluntary basis which were often neglected by school administration, headmasters, and teachers.

As neither the German remedial classes (or the alternative form of accompanying multilingual teachers in classrooms) nor the mother tongue courses were compulsory nor guaranteed, their implementation in school was dependent on organizational matters such as the number of children in need. Without any justification, funding for the different forms of support was cut every few years between the mid-1990s and the mid-2000s. Only in 2006/2007 were additional funds for remedial teaching in German made available, with the Ministry of Education being required to biannually apply to the Ministry of Finance for continuation.

At roughly the same time, political measures to improve educational results, especially among children with a first language other than German, have shifted to the period before schooling starts. Not only is kindergarten now compulsory for one year before entering school (age five to six), children must be registered with a school 15 months prior to starting and are evaluated by the headmaster regarding their proficiency in German. Those in need get specific training in German language in kindergarten.

4.3   Methodology

In order to achieve a systematic sampling approach of relevant literature on educational inequality and race/ethnicity between 1980 and 2010 in Austria, this study followed the guidelines developed by Stevens (2007) and Stevens et al. (2011). Five major criteria of inclusion guided the first steps in our review process. First, only literature focusing on Austria as a research context is included. Second, the review investigates studies that primarily research educational inequalities and race/ethnicity within a sociological framework. At the same time, the academic production in Austria has been quite limited and dominated by particular personalities who were also situated in disciplines other than sociology. In fact, as the boundaries between the disciplines are rather blurred in cross-cutting topics such as migration and ethnicity, we include researchers and contributions from neighboring disciplines. Third, this review captures both 'old' and 'new' minorities in Austria, highlighting the importance of the political framework and historic development of group-relationship for the situation of children from ethnic minorities in Austrian schooling. Fourth, we review studies on primary as well as (lower and upper) secondary schooling since research was not differentiated into educational levels. Actually, the transition between primary and secondary level attracted specific attention. Finally, we take peer-reviewed journals, (edited) books, book sections and official reports as primary sources. As secondary sources we additionally consider unpublished but officially available reports that had an impact on educational inequalities and race/ethnicity research in Austria. This strand of publications commissioned by state actors (often labeled as 'grey literature') is of particular importance to better understanding the dynamics in the field. This applies especially for the time periods until the end of the 1990s.

The sampling of specific research contributions consisted of four specific steps: As suggested by Stevens and colleagues (2007; 2011), we started with the major databases (i.e. ERIC, JSTOR, etc.) and went on to the Social Science Citation Index (SSCI), where only one relevant journal appeared.[5] In order to maximize our sample, we identified a list with over ten journals which were frequently cited in relevant studies on race/ethnicity and educational inequality in Austria. On the basis of this selection, we identified further relevant and important studies that were cited in the journal articles. As a last step, we employed detailed research on Austrian-specific bibliographic databases to classify additional studies, books, and reports relevant to our field of inquiry. Based on the publications found through this first round of sampling, we developed a detailed list with search strings to be used for re-contacting the above-named databases, which yielded a number of additional sources found within this second round of sampling.

Strikingly, we did not find any articles on race/ethnicity and educational inequality in the disciplinary journals such as the *Austrian Journal of Sociology*. Most of the contributions cited here were published in books or pedagogically oriented journals and mostly only from the 1990s onwards with a sharp increase during the 2000s. The dominant language of the publication in the sample is German rather than English. It is further important to note that there is no scientifically oriented journal of education in Austria.[6] Instead, there are some journals on education and instruction or schooling but they are not oriented towards international scientific discourse. Finally, cross-country studies are important for the context of Austria in relation to the literature on race and ethnic inequalities, which is why we included key publications in this review.

4.4 Research on race/ethnicity and educational inequality in Austria

Now we will summarize the result of our literature review. We identified five research traditions over the last 30 years.

The first research tradition, which we call (i) political arithmetic tradition (PA) due to great similarities with equivalent research traditions in countries like the United Kingdom and the Netherlands (Stevens, 2007; Stevens et al., 2011), examines studies and reports that describe rather than explain how students of different race/ethnic backgrounds perform and participate in the Austrian educational system. While this tradition started with the very first publications on migrant education in Austria at the beginning of the 1980s, it is overwhelmingly based on quantitative analyses with large-scale surveys following Austria's participation in international studies such as PISA, PIRLS and TIMSS. This tradition has also gained importance over the past ten years outside the specialist discourse due to the prominence of representative surveys on educational outcomes.

The second research tradition, (ii) family background tradition (FB), primarily investigates underachievement in education by considering the socio-economic position of the parental generation as well as related resources (cultural and social capital) to be the main explanations. This tradition has grown, side by side, with the evolution of large-scale surveys within the last decade. Thus, the great majority of studies in the FB tradition employ quantitative research designs, while qualitative and ethnographic studies are scarce.

The third research tradition investigates the impact of features and institutional arrangements of the Austrian educational system in producing educational inequalities. Therefore we call it the structures of educational systems (SOES) tradition (iii). In this category, we include research on organizational structures like age of first selection, duration of schooling and half- or whole-day schooling. This is mostly analyzed with statistical methods.

The fourth research tradition, entitled (iv) intercultural education and discrimination tradition (IED), is centered around intercultural learning as a principle of instruction and includes topics such as the (lack of) implementation, teachers' actions and attitudes, and discrimination in textbooks. It builds on concepts of cultural anthropology and employs participatory observation, interviews, questionnaires, and discourse analyses.

The fifth and final research tradition is the (v) multilinguality tradition (ML), which focuses on the development of multilinguality in Austrian schools either by concentrating on the language development of multilingual children or by depicting the implementation of the support measures for the development of multilinguality. While the first strand in this tradition builds on linguistic methodology complemented by sociolinguistics, the second strand is following a broad social science approach which uses document analyses, case analyses, and thick description.

The boundaries of these research traditions are not always clear cut. Most traditions interact with each other and in some cases it is quite hard to decide which tradition is more dominant in the particular research. Similarities, influences, and overlaps will be pointed out in the analyses and highlighted in the conclusion. An additional remark concerns the time dimension. Most of the traditions are particularly strong in a specific period closely tied to political developments and public discourse. Therefore, it is necessary to provide information on the historical context in which these traditions unfold before they are described in terms of methods, outcomes and related debates.

4.4.1   Political arithmetic tradition

In the 1980s many European countries began to examine several types of inequalities and evaluate social policy initiatives: national governments stimulated and financed large-scale surveys which allowed quantitative analysis of the educational attainment and progress of ethnic minority groups; yet, similar developments were almost non-existent in Austria. However, the few publications on the education of the children of 'guest workers' did not fail to show the detrimental situation in schools or reference the discriminatory societal structures (Matuschek, 1982; Fischer, 1986; Viehböck and Bratic, 1994). Based on accessible datasets from school administration, censuses, or micro-censuses, social science researchers from different disciplines described the situation of migrant children in Austrian schools; namely, unequal distribution across school types, over-representation in special schools, high repetition rates, large presence in low-prestige vocationally oriented schools, and large numbers leaving the educational system without any degree at all. Parallel to similar research traditions in the UK and the Netherlands, we call this research the political arithmetic tradition. It is defined by quantitative analyses with large datasets either with full coverage from school- or census-statistics or representative samples taken from national (micro-census) or international surveys (European Household Panel). This tradition also includes the first survey on the second generation in Austria by Weiss (carried out in 2005). Studies in the PA tradition increased substantially with the availability of national samples from large-scale assessment studies, such as the Programme for International Student Assessment (PISA), Progress in International Reading Literacy Study (PIRLS), and Trends in International Mathematics and Science Study (TIMSS).

These phenomena were most pronounced among the children of the labor migrants from Turkey and the former Yugoslavia. Academically oriented schools (those granting a university entrance certificate) were called 'foreigner free' until the beginning of the 1990s (DeCillia, 1994), with only 4% of pupils having a mother tongue other than German in 1992 (Perchinig, 1995, p. 133). The national averages, however, are fictitious values as there are and always were pronounced regional differences, with the federal state Vienna showing much higher proportions of immigrant children in schools. Nevertheless, large unequal distribution among different groups of origin have been observed in Vienna too: 33% of all pupils attended academically oriented schools in Vienna but only 8% of former Yugoslavians and 4% of Turkish pupils did (own calculations based on Gröpel, 1999, p. 301).

In the early 2000s, Austrian researchers from various fields (sociology, political sciences, and econometrics) started to show different aspects or changes over time. Herzog-Punzenberger (2003a) showed that at the beginning of the 2000s school success among the adult second generation was colored by the segregated school system. Among young adults aged 15 to 34 years born in Austria to Turkish parents or having immigrated before starting school, less than 0.5% held an academic degree, only 4% a university entrance certificate (AHS, BHS), and just as few a medium-level degree from a vocationally oriented school (BMS) (cf. p. 33). Finally, she was the first to look at the numbers of students with a migration background undergoing teacher education. At that point in time there were two students with Turkish citizenship heading for the teaching profession while the number of pupils with a Turkish migration background in Austrian schools had reached 30,000 (cf. p. 26). Biffl (2004) documented that on average participation rates of the Turkish and former Yugoslavian student population (aged 15–24) in the Austrian educational system increased over time (1981–2002) and that educational inequalities were reduced. She further observed a positive shift from lower basic towards vocational-oriented schools among immigrant origin students. As in many other cases (Felderer and Hofer, 2004) she based her trend analysis on a broad categorization of children of Turkish and former Yugoslavian foreigners without considering the age of the children on arrival or the effect of excluding naturalized children.

Later on, through the availability of the census data from 2001 and the question on everyday language use allowing for more than one language, more precise analyses were possible targeting the second generation born in Austria (Herzog-Punzenberger, 2007). It was shown that the share of female second generation in higher education was larger in all ethnic groups observed (Turkish, former Yugoslavian, natives) (cf. p. 94). These studies conclude that in addition to progress in either lower secondary education (Biffl, 2004) or in relation to their parents' generation (Herzog-Punzenberger, 2003a, 2003b; Kogan, 2007), ethnic minority students still obtain lower educational outcomes in upper secondary education than Austrians, especially among academic-oriented tracks. Although these studies were of great importance in continuing to highlight trends in ethnic educational inequalities, no information on competences, grades, or prior experiences were available for ethnic minority students.

4.4.1.1 *The PA tradition in the large-scale assessment period*

The number of studies that can be classified within the PA tradition in Austria sharply increased from the mid-2000s onward through the use of large-scale assessment (LSA) studies like PISA, PIRLS, and TIMSS. Those studies not only consist of standardized achievement tests but also include context questionnaires with a wide range of information on school and family. A second advantage is the possibility to statistically differentiate immigrants in school according to country of birth, parents' country of birth, and citizenship.

Starting with the first PISA survey (2000), achievement differences between immigrants and the majority of the student population aged 15–16 were reported for reading, mathematics, and (natural) science, and socio-economic and other information on migrant families was described in a new way (Blüml, 2002; Burtscher, 2004; Reiter, 2002a, 2002b). These analyses occurred for every PISA wave in short one year after the survey and in depth in more substantial reports usually three years after the survey (based on PISA, 2003; see Breit and Schreiner, 2006; Schreiner, 2006; Schreiner and Breit, 2006; based on PISA, 2006; see Breit, 2009, Herzog-Punzenberger, 2009; Schmid, Schreiner and Breit, 2009).

The findings of the PISA studies revealed that the proportion of 15–16-year-old immigrant students in Austria has grown over the last ten years. In 2000, they represented around 11% of the total student population, while, according to 2009 data, they account for 15.2% (Schwantner and Schreiner, 2010). Among them, the proportion of second generation immigrants has increased over time while numbers of first generation immigrants has decreased. From 2000 to 2009, the number of second generation immigrants aged 15–16 changed from

4% in 2000 to almost 11% in 2009. In particular, between 2006 and 2009, the numbers of second generation immigrants doubled (cf. pp. 42–43).

The majority of analytical emphasis has been on reading literacy, observable achievement differences, and co-occurrence of diverse factors. Within the four PISA waves to date, children of immigrants have been found to significantly underperform against the majority of the student population (Breit and Schreiner, 2006; Schreiner, 2006; Schreiner and Breit, 2006; Breit and Schreiner, 2007). Special attention has been drawn to children of immigrants born in Austria, the so-called second generation, who were found to perform on average among the worst in Europe (OECD, 2006). Overall, the findings on the reading abilities of second generation immigrants did not show substantial progress between the years 2000 and 2009 (compare Table 4.3) which leads to the question of whether any effective measures were taken to improve the situation following the first LSA. Moreover, literacy tests in 2006 and 2009 returned almost identical scores, and the resultant reduction in the achievement gap between migrant and native students only arose because the entire student population scored worse in 2009 than in 2006. According to the most recently available national report (Schwantner and Schreiner, 2010), children of immigrants are twice as often represented in the 'at risk' group of students in all three test subjects (30% in the group at risk compared to 15% in the overall peer group) while the group 'high achievers' is composed of 96% non-immigrant students.

Besides these findings on test results, the PISA reports shed light on many other details in education. For example, children of immigrants were found to repeat classes three times more often than their Austrian counterparts (Breit and Schreiner, 2006; Schreiner and Breit, 2006). Especially among those born outside the country, repetition rates were almost 16% compared to 4% for non-immigrant students in 2003. With the PIRLS study investigating reading competencies of pupils in their final year before leaving primary school, reporting on ethnic educational inequalities became feasible on a quantitative and representative basis also at age ten (Herzog-Punzenberger and Gapp, 2009; Unterwurzacher, 2009). However, similar to PISA, the analyses of these data suggest that children of immigrants show on average lower reading competency than their Austrian counterparts. Breaking the achievement gaps into ethnic groups, findings revealed that children of Turkish origin in particular face the greatest literacy problems at the age of ten. This trend has been replicated in the TIMSS study, a large-scale assessment survey evaluating students' competencies in mathematics and natural sciences at the end of primary school (aged nine to ten) (Breit and Wanka, 2010). More precisely, second generation students were found to perform significantly better than first generation students but still lower than their native-born peers (see Table 4.3). The relatively high levels of underachievement by second generation immigrants place Austria at

Table 4.3   Average achievements by survey, immigrant generation, type of achievement, and, year

Assessment field		Survey (students' age)					
		PISA (15/16)				PIRLS (9/10)	TIMSS (9/10)
		2000	2003	2006	2009	2006	2007
Reading	Natives	502	501	499	482	549	–
	1st Gen	**−104**	**−73**	**−48**	**−98**	**−56**	–
	2nd Gen	**−73**	**−76**	**−79***	**−55**	**−47**	–
Mathematics	Natives	–	515	515	507	–	513
	1st Gen	–	**−63**	**−65**	**−76**	–	**−51***
	2nd Gen	–	**−56**	**−80**	**−57**	–	**−36**
(Natural) Science	Natives	–	502	523	508	–	538
	1st Gen	–	**−80**	**−88**	**−103**	–	**−84***
	2nd Gen	–	**−68**	**−92**	**−74**	–	**−62**

Sources:
PISA: own calculations.
PIRLS: Suchan et al. (2007).
TIMSS: Breit and Wanka (2010).
Bold: significantly different to majority group, * significant group differences between immigrant generations.

the low end of international rankings in providing equal opportunities in education (Breit and Wanka, 2010).

Whereas naturalization did not prove significant in LSA data analyses, it did in the 2001 census data on the highest degree earned by young adults. When comparing Turkish-speaking adolescents, those with Austrian nationality had considerably higher percentages of upper secondary and tertiary degrees than those without Austrian nationality (Herzog-Punzenberger, 2007). In the first survey focusing on second generation immigrants (n=1000) in Austria in the age-group 16 to 26 years old, findings on the over-representation of immigrants in lower tracks were confirmed (Weiss, 2007) and regional differences were observed with lower disparities occurring between majority and minority youth in Vienna than in the western federal states of Salzburg, Tyrol, and Vorarlberg (Unterwurzacher, 2007).

In sum, the PA tradition in Austria during the first two decades of the reviewed time span (1980–2000) indicates the law, the labor market, the housing situation, discrimination, and the structure of the school system as reasons for the differences in access, participation, and eventual qualification of youths with or without migration backgrounds. However, the Austrian PA tradition accounting of achievements measured in standardized tests was first founded in 2000, with the first PISA testing effectively occurring in 2002 and with the first report also covering students with a migration background. Large-scale assessment studies (PISA, TIMMS, PIRLS) were used to examine achievement differences on several subjects. Overall, children of immigrants have been found to significantly underperform against the majority student population in Austria. Special attention has been drawn to children of immigrants that were born within Austria, the so-called second generation, who were also found to significantly underperform against the Austrian majority student group.

4.4.2 Family background tradition

Research on family background characteristics and ethnic inequalities in education evolved side by side with the PA tradition in Austria. First, although empirical results had been published by the end of the 1990s (e.g. Gröpel, Urbanek and Khan-Svik, 1999), the increasing availability of large-scale quantitative datasets led to considerable growth from the 2000s onwards (in particular through PISA, PIRLS or TIMSS). Researchers investigated the significance of parental socio-economic background, social and cultural capital, or material resources to explain the educational underachievement of children of immigrants in Austrian schools. Given the high correlation between the FB and PA traditions, studies in the family background tradition almost exclusively employ quantitative research designs to investigate inequalities in educational attainment, transition rates between educational tracks, and achievement at certain educational stages.

4.4.2.1 Parental socio-economic background

Due to the predominant position of first generation immigrants in the lower social strata in Austria, focusing on parental socio-economic background has been seen as promising path to pinpointing further mechanisms in explaining the educationally disadvantaged position of their children. This line of argument also traces the structural position of immigrant groups within Austrian society, considering either their time of arrival, the general skills first generation immigrants brought with them, or the fit between their skills and their ability to fill certain needs in local economies. Although not directly labeled as a 'social class versus culture' debate, the majority of studies follow this line of argumentation by employing multivariate regression analysis to show the relative impact of different factors. Socio-economic background (measured as parental occupational status and educational attainment) regularly plays a more important role in significant correlations with educational outcomes than other variables such as language spoken at home or parents born outside the survey country.

To give a few examples, various studies have observed ethnic minorities' disadvantaged socio-economic backgrounds for a considerable part account for achievement differences in reading and mathematics at the end of primary (Bacher, 2010; Breit and Wanka, 2010; Unterwurzacher, 2009) and secondary education (Bacher, 2005, 2006, 2008, 2009; Wroblewski, 2006; Breit and Wanka, 2010), at transition points from primary to lower and upper secondary education (Unterwurzacher, 2007; Bacher, 2003, 2005), in linguistic development (Khan-Svik, 2007), and on final educational attainment (Weiss, 2006, 2007a; Weiss and Unterwurzacher, 2007).

These quantitative studies do not come without methodological caveats. A great number of studies treat ethnic inequality in a dichotomous way – achievement of the Austrian students on the one side and achievement of children with a 'migration background' or 'children with a foreign mother tongue' on the other side – while detailed analyses looking closer into the heterogeneity of immigrant groups are scarce. One exception is the work conducted by Unterwurzacher (2007, 2009), using their own survey on various second generation immigrant groups in Austria. The findings suggest that enrollment differences for the academic-oriented track at the first transition point at age ten can largely be explained by parental socioeconomic status for former Yugoslavian and other immigrant descendants but that does not apply for second generation Turks (Unterwurzacher, 2007). The 'Turkish disadvantage' which persists after considering their lower socio-economic background was also observed in reading achievements using PIRLS 2007 data (Unterwurzacher, 2009) and final educational attainment (Weiss and Unterwurzacher, 2007).

4.4.2.2 Social and cultural capital

Current debates on ethnic educational inequalities in Austria are motivated by the question of how to describe the remaining variation in educational outcomes net of socio-economic differences in the family of origin. Whether specific cultural resources in the family would enhance educational success has been put to the test using Austrian LSA datasets in particular (Bacher, 2008; Breit and Wanka, 2010; Wroblewski, 2006). Studies using PISA data examined strong effects of 'cultural capital' in explaining achievement differences in reading and mathematics among Austrian and immigrant students at the age of 15 beyond socio-economic background (Bacher, 2008). The lack of cultural resources has been found to explain a large proportion of the disparities in mathematic (Breit and Wanka, 2010; Wroblewski, 2006) and reading abilities (Unterwurzacher, 2009). However, these quantitative analyses using large-scale surveys are rather limited in explaining the direct relationship between parenting behavior and educational outcomes. Instead, they use crude indicators measuring family wealth (such as place to study at home) or family 'habitus' (books at home) rather than explicit types and forms of capital and the transmission between generations.

Exceptions are recently published qualitative studies on schooling success by second generation immigrant students. Atac and Lageder (2009) interviewed children of immigrants in Viennese vocational schools. This study reveals that immigrant parents indeed lack relevant resources to support their children in schooling activities. Due to low educational levels or limited language abilities in German they are less often found to help their children with homework or attend parent-teacher conferences. But at the same time, high parental aspirations and strong emotional bonds between family members can lead to higher aspirations among the children themselves and therefore foster social mobility in the Austrian educational system – a finding that is in line with the qualitative results observed by Waechter and colleagues (Waechter, Blum and Scheibelhofer, 2007). Besides the parents, the elder siblings often act as role models and provide their younger brothers and sisters with relevant information and support for schooling activities, which makes them as effective as parents. Older siblings can act as intermediaries between younger children and their school, and their own schooling experiences can be a major source of support (Waechter, Blum and Scheibelhofer, 2007). Finally, a limited number of qualitative studies have highlighted that, in addition to family members, peers and teachers sometimes offer additional forms of support that are of great importance for immigrant children to successfully navigate the Austrian school system (Atac and Lageder, 2009; Burtscher, 2009, 2010).

In public discourse, parents' lack of fluency in the language of instruction in school (German) is one of the most prominent explanations for educational inequality although not empirically proven for data in Austria. Lack of information about the educational system on the parents' side as well as lack of communication between schools and parents was subject of analyses before the LSAs, albeit in a heuristic way (Gröpel et al., 1999; Matuschek, 1982). More recently, a study on language development in primary school children included parents and teachers in the study (Brizic 2007). With quantitative and qualitative methodology, Brizic found out that parents' attitudes towards education as perceived by the teachers had no impact on the language development of the children. At the same time, the teachers' perceptions of the parents' attitudes and the parents' factual attitudes towards education were rather different. While the teachers had a more positive appraisal of parents from the former Yugoslavia, Turkish parents were in fact more interested in educational issues. In most cases of children with language development difficulties, teachers and parents were caught in misperceptions of both each other and the educational system, which in some cases resulted in distrust. Both, however, felt helpless and thought the solution would only come about through changes made by the other (Brizic, 2007).

Overall, research on the significance of family background characteristics to explain ethnic disparities in education has grown substantially over the last decade with the increasing availability of relevant quantitative survey data. Small-scale ethnographic or qualitative studies to explore the relationship between social origin, ethnicity, and educational achievement are (at least to our knowledge) scarce in Austria. As a consequence, the majority of studies in the FB tradition are variable driven and oftentimes lack clear theoretical foundations. This applies especially for the role played by social and cultural capital in exploring the complex relationship between social class origin, ethnicity, and educational achievement. Social and cultural capital are predominantly treated as resources or indicators of family wealth rather than the classical conceptualization by Coleman (1988) or Bourdieu (1983; Bourdieu and Passeron, 1979). Additionally, parents' attitudes and behavior in relation to schooling are not understood as result of the overall setting and activities of the school, but conceptualized as a separate container where pupils should receive what they need to function well in school. This goes along with Austrian teachers' beliefs that their training in German as a second language, mutlilinguality or teaching in heterogenous classes is weakly connected to migrant student's educational disadvantage (Weiss et al., 2007, p. 45). Specific questions, such as whether certain immigrant communities possess certain forms of capital that might explain variations in achievement differences across ethnic groups, have yet to be investigated in the existing studies on race/ethnicity and educational inequality.

4.4.3   The structure of educational systems tradition

Parallel to studies in general migration research, where outcomes on an aggregate level such as naturalized immigrants' highest educational degrees or social mobility rates are often connected to the broader societal framework, researchers in the field of education also look at the macro-level and analyze the institutional arrangements of the educational system. While not all of the characteristics of educational systems have been scrutinized in the context we are discussing, the following should be mentioned:

1. Kindergarten: starting age and duration (opening hours), availability.
2. Primary education: starting age, downgrading in pre-phase (*Vorschulstufe*), duration, repetition rates, selection into special school, half-day schooling.
3. Secondary education: age at first selection, tracking, half-day schooling, short duration of compulsory schooling.

These issues came up for debate long before the school success of migrant children was considered. In the 1970s, a particularly intensive and ideological discussion raged over class-based educational inequality, with a focus on early differentiation at age ten, also called 'tracking'. This form of school organization has been anchored in the constitutional law for decades, and changes to the system would require a parliamentary majority, something still unlikely to happen in the near future despite growing evidence for the advantages of late tracking.

During the last decade (2000–2010), the question of the structural characteristics of educational systems gained importance in explaining educational outcomes more generally, not least driven by international comparative large-scale assessments such as PISA (OECD, 2005). Nevertheless, in most of the research designs, this has not been the starting point for explaining the disadvantages of students with a migration background.[7] It was rather a by-product of acknowledging the class-based character of much of the problem of research on race and ethnicity in Austria. However, the selectivity of the school system has been criticized in Austria for decades. Generally, it has an inherent logic of down-streaming, i.e. it is very unlikely that a pupil changes to a higher-status school. The main criticism was the reproductive logic of the school system in terms of family background (Bacher, 2003, 2005, 2006).

Since the 1980s, researchers have addressed institutional ramifications as driving forces for disadvantages in the educational participation and results of children with a migration background (Fischer, 1986; Khan-Svik, 1999, pp. 186–197; Gröpel, 1999; Volf and Bauböck, 2001). They criticized the individualizing perspective which either stressed the deficits of the child or the family – something quite common at that time in the German-speaking pedagogical literature. Instead, they tried to show that the selectivity of the Austrian school system was the reason for the over-representation of children of migrants in lower status school types with a lower standard curriculum, i.e. the vocational-oriented track in lower secondary school (*Hauptschule*) and special school (*Sonderschule*). Khan-Svik (1999, pp. 187–188) and Gröpel (2001, p. 220) applied the theory of '*Unterschichtung*', meaning that when a group of people enters a stratified system at the lowest rank this will enable those who formerly were at the bottom to enter the next stratum (Baker and Lenhardt, 1988, p. 40, cited in Gröpel, 2001, p. 221). For the school system, this meant that children from immigrant families, who occupied the lowest societal status at that time, would have a higher likelihood of being deferred to the lowest positions in the school system and those native children who were previously at the lowest ranks, i.e. in Sonderschule or in Hauptschule, then had a smaller chance of being down-streamed and a better chance of moving to a higher status school. They presumed an economic logic in educational organization, where pupils are channeled accordingly. For further reasons, they pointed to the fact that support measures for children with a first language other than German were not adequate, preschool in particular was described as an '*Aufbewahrungsstätte*' (place of custody) rather than a support center, which among other things explained the higher representation of students with migration backgrounds among those who had to repeat a class. Gröpel (2001, p. 219) also mentioned the limited places in institutions of early childhood education and care (*Kindergartenplätze*) as well as high fees which obviously would decrease the likelihood of the children of migrants participating.

The situation has improved since then, but the over-representation of students with migration background in special school remains a part of the discussion about race/ethnicity and educational inequality. Luciak (2008) recently pointed out that there were (still) gender, class, and ethnic disparities to be observed in schools where the only reason for such '*Zuweisung*' should be diagnosed mental or physical disability. He analyzes that while a rhetoric of diversity has been established, curriculum, didactics, school organization, and teacher education are still oriented towards homogenization and a middle-class construction of normality. Teachers basically have a hard time adjusting to the heterogeneity in classrooms, be it lingual, cultural, social, or cognitive.

While studies in this tradition have always had to use statistics to show over- and under-representation in specific school types, the first analyses to prove the effect of the different selectivity for children with migration background was based on the 2003 PISA (Bacher and Stelzer-Orthofer, 2008). In a comparison of 16 countries, of which six had early selection, between age 10 and 14, and nine had late selection, at age 15 and 16, those with early selection had significantly bigger differences in test results and school career delay (by repetition) between pupils with and without migration background, penalizing those with migration background. There was no systematic effect for age of selection on the differences between pupils with and without migration background in perceived quality of respondent-teacher interaction and interactions among pupils.[8]

To sum up, the educational structures tradition has so far concentrated on the selectivity of the school system and its down-streaming logic in Austria. It is different from the political arithmetic tradition in so far as researchers do not simply describe over- and under-representation of pupils with migration backgrounds in different school types or outcomes, but try to establish causal relationships to features of the Austrian school system. While causality is hard to establish, especially between macro-variables and micro-level outcomes, researchers in Austria have had strong hypotheses about the effects of structural features. With the availability of LSA datasets, researchers are making initial attempts to prove the effects of the first selection moment using statistical analyses in country comparisons.

4.4.4   Intercultural education and discrimination tradition

In this research tradition, we treat studies that analyze the implementation of intercultural learning (Binder, 2004; Englisch-Stölner, 2003; Luciak and Khan-Svik, 2008), focusing on teacher behavior and attitudes (Fillitz, 2003), teacher education, and textbooks (Markom and Weinhäupl, 2007). The theoretical foundation of this research lies in cultural anthropology and its critical understanding of culture as being embedded in power relations, schools as the major site of reproduction of the majority culture in modern nation-states, and ethnicity as being relational, processual, and at times instrumental and situational. If empirical, most of this research is qualitative, being sometimes supplemented with surveys of albeit small samples. Generally in this research tradition, class or socio-economic status tends to remain in the background even when some mention the unfavorable legal, economic, and housing situation of many families with migration backgrounds.

Instead of the anti-discrimination orientation found in England, the other and more positive side of intergroup relations, interculturality was to be developed as part of the curriculum and implemented in schools from 1993 onwards. Around this time several articles were published discussing the benefits and limits of intercultural education. Notably, these were also published by representatives of the school administration (Pinterits, 1990, 1991). This was not by accident nor long debated. The Ministry of Education's sudden interest in proposals of how to react to multilingual classrooms was rather a consequence, as Jaksche (1998, pp. 42–45) shows, of the influx of migrants from East and Southeast Europe, and particularly the political problematization of it. While teachers' earlier efforts to draw attention to the increase in lingual and cultural diversity were marginalized, financial and legislative measures were taken in the aftermath of the fall of the iron curtain. Astonishingly enough, since the anti-foreigner campaign (*Volksbegehren*) of the FPÖ political party was not as successful as expected, the interest of academia in questions related to multicultural and multilingual classrooms decreased again.

Jaksche (1998) was the first to critically analyze the implementation of the 'intercultural learning' principle of instruction and concluded that teachers who had previous worked in the vein of intercultural learning were, through this principle, covered by law and all other teachers and principals were not obliged to do or change anything specific.

Binder (2004) compared the implementation of intercultural learning in the Netherlands and Austria and surprisingly came to the conclusion that the difference was merely on the level of rhetoric and not so much in practice. In both countries, clear guidelines and standard procedures as well as intensive factual knowledge transfer were missing. Consequently, shape and content were dependent on the personal engagement of the teachers. Binder (2003), Binder and Daryabegi (2003), Englisch-Stölner (2003), and Frank (2003), in their case studies of lower secondary schools in Vienna and Lower Austria, also find that the implementation of 'intercultural education' is largely dependent on the personal interest of the teachers. Teachers and headmasters often simply ignored cultural and linguistic diversity and proceeded as though the pupils were a monolingual and monocultural group. Teachers complained about the lack of appropriate material, and textbooks being not adapted as well; however, as their training did not provide for a diverse classroom, many did not consider it their task to adapt to the circumstances. Parents often had very little contact with the school or the teachers and experienced language-based communication problems. This study was commissioned by the Ministry of Education and carried out with participatory observation, interviews with teachers and headmasters as well as questionnaires for pupils (n=414) and parents (n=324).

The first studies surveying teachers' attitudes and experiences in the field of intercultural education and pupils with migration background were carried out during the 2000s. Furch's study (published only in 2010) had a sample of 315 primary school teachers; a few years later a more comprehensive study, with 1400 primary and secondary school teachers (Weiss, Unterwurzacher, Strodl 2007), was initiated. Their findings were rather similar. The majority of the respondents thought that teaching should be adapted to the needs of students with migration backgrounds but implementation was weak. In Furch's study most teachers judged their knowledge on this subject to be sufficient while their actual knowledge turned out to range from insufficient to poor, even when, as 43% had done at some point in time, they had participated in intercultural training. Furch concluded that their self-image was distorted. At the time of the study, 79% had no experience with multilingual teaching material; this was interpreted as being rooted in the belief that pupils should learn German as fast as possible. These teachers mostly followed the public opinion that other languages distract children from learning German. More than half stated that migrant languages did not play a role during their classroom time and less than half were interested in learning a migrant language. 'Interculturality' was seen as a buzz-word which teachers mainly understood as differences between regional cultures. Surprisingly, even though the younger teachers had participated in intercultural training they were no more engaged in implementing intercultural learning than older teachers. The conclusion was that, despite the fact that more than half of the pupils in Viennese primary schools had a first language other than German, the primary school teachers were badly prepared for a diverse classroom with different languages, cultures, and religions at the beginning of the 2000s. In the other study (Weiss et al., 2007) the sample included teachers from all over Austria and all school types, the only pre-selection requirement being a minimum of 10% of pupils with migration backgrounds in their school. While in primary school instruction in multicultural classroom were perceived as less problematic, in secondary schools problems increased due to ethnic tensions. However, the biggest share reported knowing about specific bullying victims (39%) whereas only 22% reported hostile group dynamics in their classrooms but not necessarily bound to ethnic background. Bullying was much more frequent in general secondary schools (56%) than in academic secondary schools where pupils with migration background are less frequent. It co-occurred with a negative classroom climate. Teachers perceive religion, that is 'Islam', as the biggest problem tied to multicultural classrooms. While few teachers report experiences with conservative Muslim families that prevent girls from participating in school activities, in the same way as others they perceive Islam as an impediment to gender equality.

In Austria there is no tradition of research on school books, thus there are also no quantitative studies on the effect of textbooks on pupils' educational achievement. However, those researchers who analyze textbooks conceptualize effects as part of the secondary socialization process in which children develop their self-concept, especially concerning collective aspects.[9] This approach criticizes the values and knowledge presented in textbooks, which not only attach a higher status to Austrian middle-class culture, and more broadly to white or European expressions and manifestations, but also marginalize those of minorities or non-European provenance. This research mainly focuses on social aspects such as the ability to cooperate in diverse group settings and the ability to critically analyze diversity, hierarchy, and power relations. The link between the content of the textbooks and educational success has not been analyzed in Austria, as for example in studies on the ethnocentric curriculum in the US or the race and racial discrimination in school research tradition in England (Stevens, 2007, pp. 157–161). Children are bound to accept, if there are no convincing 'counter-offers', the content of textbooks as authoritative knowledge about groups, group relations, ethnicity, and normality, and ultimately their collective identity (Hintermann, 2007). In this way, textbooks contribute to pupils' self-concepts and possibly to the stereotype threat effect in learning (Schofield, 2005). With Austria's framework curriculum, textbooks are sometimes called 'the hidden curriculum' because teachers structure their teaching along the one book they are free to choose for each subject and year. However, the point of departure in this tradition is the implicit or even explicit view of school as being the primary site of nation-state reproduction of one homogenous culture and one language which are superior to all others. Anthropologists have analyzed diverse school-books to uncover attitudes to specific issues such as Islam or general perspectives on ethnocentrism, anti-Semitism, sexism, and heteronormativity. The most recent study (Markom and Weinhäupl, 2007) analyzes textbooks from biology, history, and geography in lower secondary school (Grades 5 to 8). They conclude that racist and anti-Semitic accounts are rare, but that clichés and downgrading stereotypes are more frequent, especially regarding 'the orient', Islam, 'the Third World', Africa, 'tribes', homosexuality, and gender roles. The superficiality in avoiding stereotyping is best exemplified by the fact that even when the text is reasonably balanced the illustrations still convey stereotypes. While the textbooks treat the reality of power imbalance, hierarchy, and exploitation, racism and discrimination are barely mentioned and receive no detailed discussion.

In sum, the intercultural education and discrimination tradition focuses not only on questions of intercultural learning in schools and the implementation of the principle of instruction in teachers' actions and attitudes, but also on textbooks. The most important results concern the variable implementation of intercultural learning in schools. Training in this area is still not compulsory in teacher education. More advanced concepts such as language awareness or cultural awareness are barely known. In many instances, interculturality is merely a buzz-word equated with cultural differences and homogenizing concepts of cultural groups; adequate material is lacking and textbooks need revision.

4.4.5 Multilinguality tradition

In this research tradition, work is mainly undertaken by linguists but also by education researchers, sociologists, and political scientists. It is research on the multilinguality of schoolchildren, the school setting regarding multilinguality, the legal ramifications as laid out by the Ministry of Education, and the implementation of the measures. Some studies focused on mother tongue teaching, either analyzing the organizational deficiencies in public schooling and its consequences (Cinar, 1998) or looking at complementary organizational provisions in the private sector (Khan-Svik 2005); others focused on the support structures for learning German as a second language (Bauer and Kainz, 2007). There were some longitudinal studies following the language development of schoolchildren over several years, either based in pedagogical (cf. Khan-Svik, 2007) or linguistic studies (Fischer, 1992, 1995; Peltzer-Karpf et al., 2006; Brizic, 2007). Otherwise this research tradition is dominated by analyses of documents and discourses.

As previously mentioned, the public discourse on pupils with migration backgrounds in Austria has centered around German language proficiency. Also the common attitude among teachers that the only problem is that immigrant parents do not speak German with their children before entering school continues to be widespread. The political approach of the Ministry of Education was more differentiated and forwardlooking.[10] In collaboration with researchers, they developed a framework for the entire complex of cultural and linguistic diversity, migration and education, as previously described: (i) the general principle of instruction called 'intercultural learning', geared towards all children; (ii) support for learning German as a second language for migrant children; and (iii) mother tongue teaching for children with a first language other than German. As the legal framework has never included 'compulsory' measures for schools, the implementation of these measures is the subject of research. However, quantitative research is scarce and evaluations on the effectiveness or outcomes of the programs are almost non-existent.

4.4.5.1 *Education of linguistic minorities as a political issue*

Since the 1980s, researchers focusing on linguistic minorities in Austria have been among the most active in contributing to scientific and public discourse on ethnicity and educational inequality while – not to give a wrong impression – the critical discourse as a whole was pretty marginalized. However, this kind of research and its institutional anchorage frequently came under threat (Fischer, 1993, p. 13), especially during the 1980s and 1990s. As a consequence of political pressure against bilingualism in the southern region of Austria and an ever present devaluation of minority languages and individuals, such as Slovene in Carinthia, researchers investigated not only bilinguality and schooling as such, but also the whole complex situation of ethnicity, ethnic identity, belonging, attachment, and discrimination (DeCillia, 1998; Boeckmann et al., 1988; Busch, 1991). One of the findings was (Fischer, 1993, pp. 13–14) that the legal ramifications of bilingual schooling laid down in the *Minderheitenschulgesetz* (Minorities School Act) of 1985 were highly disputable and predominantly seen as unfavorable for the further development of the region, the minority, its language, and the school success of the children. Instead, this law fostered segregation between monolingual and bilingual school children in a bilingual territory.

Boeckmann (1997), for example, compared bilingual speakers in the most eastern province of Burgenland who were successful in education with those in the southern province of Carinthia, contrasting the micro-social context. In this tradition, language was not seen as an isolated phenomenon but intertwined with individual and collective identity and politics. Baumgartner and Perchinig (1995) pointed out that differences between these regional contexts, albeit within the same nation-state, are deeply rooted in history. During the Austro-Hungarian monarchy, when Burgenland belonged to the Hungarian Transleithania and Carinthia to the Austrian Cisleithania, legal regulations and group relations were much more favorable in the Hungarian part compared to the German part. Even today, multilinguality is treated very differently in these two parts of Austria and is much less problematic in Burgenland than in Carinthia.

4.4.5.2 Language development of multilingual children in each of their languages

The most comprehensive in-depth study following the language development of 100 primary school children from Grade 1 to Grade 4 in Vienna was carried out by a team based in linguistic studies (Peltzer-Karpf et al., 2003). The study was commissioned by the Ministry of Education and included six classes with multilingual children from different backgrounds. To find out which factors enhance the proficiency in the language of instruction, they used a multi-methodological approach with linguistic tests (system linguistics, vocabulary, text comprehension, and text production) in the language of instruction, the first language of the children (if Bosnian/Croatian/Serbian or Turkish), and spontaneous conversation in any language combination the children wanted to use. Additionally, teachers and parents were surveyed so that the linguistic approach was accompanied by a sociolinguistic analysis. Results showed that language development in German happens differently among bilingual children than among monolingual children and that teachers have to be aware about the specificities to understand the structure of the particular mistakes etc. It does not help to support language learning in the language of instruction at the expense of the first language. As it turned out, those with the highest competence in their (non-German) first language when entering school reached the highest competence levels in (their second language) German after four years. The most important results for the development in the second language German were threefold. First, the children's self-confidence and school-related experiences of success; fear and lack of self-confidence hampers language development. Second, a good competence in and a positive approach towards the first language were more important for gains in proficiency in German than the extent of motivation to learn German. Third, the societal status of their first language also has an effect on the children. Results that proved less important than expected were the percentage of multilingual children in the class and the age of first contact with German. Moreover, while the educational background of the parents, duration of stay, and orientation to stay or return were not as important as expected, poverty was (Fleck, 2007, pp. 261–262).

4.4.5.3   *Consequences of language oppression in the country of origin*

A central question in this tradition was researched by Katharina Brizic during the 2000s and formalized in the language-capital model (2007). She tried to answer the question, why children of specific immigrant groups in different countries do have problems with language attainment while others don't. To name the most prominent ones in Europe: Turks in Germany and Austria, Moroccans in the Netherlands, and Bengali in Great Britain show large differences in educational attainment compared to natives. As lower proficiency in the language of instruction is generally seen as the reason for significantly lower success in the educational system of the country of immigration, it is an important question to ask why this happens. One of the most innovative and widely recognized findings was that the language history of many families in these groups revealed specific patterns. When parents and grandparents were members of linguistic minorities which faced oppression in their country of origin, language transmission within the family was severely hampered. Therefore not only the development of the pupils' second language, in Austria's case German, was severely delayed or restricted, but also the development of the pupils' first language or what was thought to be their first language. Often, the language the parents spoke with their children was not the parents' first language because political pressure had forced a change in their family during their own childhood. For this reason, language attainment was a rather complicated process for the pupils, despite generally being highly motivated to learn German and be successful in school.

In sum, the multilinguality tradition focuses on the development of multilinguality in Austrian schools either by concentrating on the development of the language proficiency in the pupils' first and second language or by concentrating on the implementation of measures that should support the language development of the pupils. Some of the studies follow pupils over several years and other case studies concentrate on specific groups or schools. They are mostly in-depth studies which allow insights into the micro-mechanisms of language transmission within families and are only possible within a long-term setting where trust can be built up between researchers and parents. The implementation strand simply tries to document how variable, and at times limited, support measures for language development in schools are despite the fact that the legal framework offers many possibilities. However, without funding, clear regulations for each child's support and adequate employment of teachers, especially mother tongue teachers, implementation simply does not work.

4.5 Summary and conclusion

Despite having gained considerable importance in public discourse, research on race/ethnicity and educational inequalities in Austria, contrary to other countries, remained a marginalized field within institutionalized research until recently. In the last 30 years it has developed along five research strands.

To begin with, the political arithmetic tradition consists of studies and reports that describe differences in the participation and outcomes of students from diverse ethnic backgrounds. Most researchers while coming from different disciplines agreed on discriminatory societal structures as the source for the enduring inequality in education. While researchers in the 1980s and 1990s had to rely on school statistics, census, and micro-census data, more nuanced analyses became possible with the data stemming from international comparative large-scale assessments that began with PISA 2000. Until the 1990s, due to low naturalization rates, the children's nationality was taken as the most important characteristic. Later on, during the 1990s when the share of naturalized pupils was growing, the Ministry of Education made statistics on children's first languages available. Rising numbers were observed in most school types as well as enduring over-representation in lower tracks and among drop-outs and early school-leavers, higher repetition rates, and under-representation in academic tracks. Surprisingly, under-representation in apprenticeship positions and vocational training was documented since the 1990s but did not become subject to more in-depth research. Since 2000, with Austria's participation in international tests, literacy results in reading, mathematics, and natural sciences were also compared and analyzed and showed large gaps for first- and second-generation students. At the same time, the success of mono- or bilingual schooling in the autochthonous minority languages Slovene and Burgenland-Croatian was documented, resulting in higher shares of academic success in younger-aged peers and impressive intergenerational educational mobility.

The family background tradition (FB) emerged parallel to the political arithmetic tradition in Austria. It focused primarily on the significance of family background characteristics to explain ethnic disparities in education. This tradition has grown substantially over the last decade with the increasing availability of relevant quantitative survey data. Consequently, since 2000, studies in the FB tradition are variable driven and the more detailed the data, the greater the lack of clear theoretical foundations. This especially applies to the role played by social and cultural capital in exploring the complex relationship between social class origin, ethnicity, and educational achievement. Whereas the low educational success of children with migration background was explained heuristically with reference to the socio-economic position of the families and the discriminatory societal structures in the 1980s and 1990s, with LSA data a positivistic approach is rarely accompanied with reference to institutional structures or societal frameworks.

The third research tradition, called the structure of educational systems tradition, investigates the impact of the institutional arrangement of the Austrian educational system in producing educational inequality. It focuses primarily on the early age of selection and the down-streaming logic of the Austrian school system. This has been widely discussed since the 1970s regarding social class, but not with a main focus on children with migration background. Although many other institutional variables were discussed in this literature, including issues such as the lack of kindergarten places, late age of entrance into early childhood institutions, predominance of half-day schooling, frequency of grade retention, short duration of compulsory schooling resulting in early school-leavers without certificates, and the lack of communication with parents and ethnic communities, these have not been subject of closer investigation. With the availability of LSA datasets from 2000 onwards, researchers try to show effects of the age of first selection by using statistical analyses in country comparison. Nevertheless, the empirical evidence on the influences of institutional arrangements of the Austrian education system in producing ethnic educational inequalities has only increased during recent years.

The fourth research tradition, called the intercultural education and discrimination tradition, focuses on intercultural learning as a principle of instruction, its implementation, teachers' education, training, actions, and attitudes, and discrimination in textbooks. The most important results concern the variable implementation of intercultural learning in schools, the lack of training in teacher education and the incongruent self-image of the teachers regarding their knowledge of the issue. As most studies show, interculturality often functions as a catchword and works with a clear stress on cultural differences between ethnic groups. Teaching materials in Austria still lack important aspects of intercultural education. Whereas the other research traditions mentioned so far are strongly anchored in sociology with some researchers from political science and economics, this research tradition is predominantly rooted in cultural anthropology. Therefore, qualitative methodology, participant observation, document and discourse analyses are predominant.

The multilinguality tradition, the fifth tradition, focuses on the development of multilinguality in Austrian schools, the nature and extent of support measures and the language development of bi- or multilingual schoolchildren. It does so by either concentrating on the development of proficiency in the pupils' first and second language or by concentrating on the implementation of measures that should support the language development of pupils. The former covers insights about micro-mechanisms of language transmission within families through in-depth case studies. One of the most important findings in this tradition refers to the language biography in families as a reason why specific groups appear to be particularly disadvantaged, with the language policy in the country of origin being equally important as the one in the country of residence. In contrast, the implementation-oriented strand tries to document how variable, and at times limited, support measures for language development in schools are, despite the fact that the legal framework offers many possibilities. However, without transparent rules for each child's support as well as adequate funding and employment of staff, especially mother tongue teachers, implementation simply does not work.

Overall, our review indicated that the boundaries of these research traditions are not always clear cut. Most traditions interact with each other and in some cases the research could be classified in two or more traditions. Some traditions are particularly strong in a specific period closely tied to the availability of data, political developments, and public discourse. Since the 1980s, research on migration, minorities, and educational inequalities in Austria has been dominated by a strong tradition of analysis on the macro-level considering the consequences of societal structures and intergroup relationships for the individual and its attitudes and actions. During the first decade of the 21st century education researchers entered a new phase mainly through the availability and analysis of large-scale datasets. They produced a first wave of findings on the level of the individual and its family background with a view to international comparison. As there is a lack of knowledge in the field of micro-mechanisms in teaching and learning, future research should concentrate on classroom- and school-level processes to explore how multilingual language development can be adequately supported. Research on the level of schools and classrooms waits for attention since hardly any study covers these processes.

Notes

1. The first standardized test was carried out in May 2012 in mathematics covering all students in Austrian schools attending Grade 8.

2. Own calculations on the basis of the 'Bildungsdokumentation'': http://www.statistik. at/web_de/static/schuelerinnen_und_schueler_201011_nach_geschlecht_020961.xlsx.
3. In the year 1961, the first agreement to recruit a maximum of 47,000 foreign workers was decided but many fewer came until bilateral agreements with the sending states had been signed (Wimmer, 1986).
4. Recorded in administrative data by the school principal at the moment of enrollment.
5. This journal is the *SWS Rundschau für Sozialwissenschaften.*
6. The first one was founded in 2011: '*Zeitschrift für Bildungsforschung*' (ZBF).
7. The first research project to do this was TIES (the Integration of the European Second Generation, www.tiesproject.eu), in mid-2008, which compared young adults with parents from Turkey/former Yugoslavia/Morocco to those with native parents in different education systems. For first publications, see Crul et al. (2012a, 2012b) and Schnell (2012).
8. In Austria respondents with migration background were more negative about the interactions in school than those without migration backgrounds. On this dimension Austria ranked fourth among 16 countries after Ireland, Spain and Hungary (Bacher and Stelzer-Orthofer, 2008).
9. Many researchers mention this element but only in passing and it is not properly discussed in the publications.
10. However, funds to implement the measures were lacking and research on financial flows is scarce.

References

Atac, I. and M. Lageder (2009) 'Welche Gegenwart, welche Zukunft? Keine/eine/doppelte Integration? Eine qualitative Paneluntersuchung zum Verlauf von Einstellungen und Erwartungen in Bezug auf Familie, Bildung und Beruf bei Wiener Schülerinnen und Schülern mit Migrationshintergrund'. Unpublished report. Vienna: University of Vienna.

Bacher, J. (2003) 'Soziale Ungleichheit und Bildungspartizipation im weiterführenden Schulsystem Österreichs', *Zeitschrift für Soziologie* 28 (3): 3–32.

Bacher, J. (2005) 'Bildungsungleichheit und Bildungsbenachteiligung im weiterführenden Schulsystem Österreichs – eine Sekundäranalyse der PISA 2000-Erhebung', *SWS Rundschau* 45 (1): 37–62.

Bacher, J. (2006) 'Forschungslage zu Bildungsungleichheiten in Österreich', in B. Herzog-Punzenberger (ed.), *Bildungsbe/nach/teiligung in Österreich und im internationalen Vergleich*, 7–26. Vienna.

Bacher, J. (2008) 'Bildungsgleichheiten in Österreich – Basisdaten und Erklärungsansätze', *Erziehung & Unterricht* 158 (7–8): 529–542.

Bacher, J. (2009) 'Soziale Ungleichheit, Schullaufbahn und Testleistungen', in B. Suchan, C. Wallner-Paschon and C. Schreiner (eds), *PIRLS 2006*, 79–102. Graz: Leykam.

Bacher, J. (2010) 'Bildungschancen von Kindern mit Migrationshintergrund', *Christlich-pädagogische Blätter* 123 (3): 134–136.

Bacher, J. and C. Stelzer-Orthofer (2008) 'Schulsysteme, Wohlfahrsstaatswelten und schulische Integration von Kindern mit Migrationshintergrund', in B. Leibetseder and J. Weidenholzer (eds), *Integration ist gestaltbar. Strategien erfolgreicher Integrationspolitik in Städten und Regionen*, 65–93. Vienna: Braumüller.

Bauer, F. and G. Kainz (2007) 'Die Benachteiligung von Kindern mit Migrationshintergrund beim Bildungszugang', *Wirtschafts- und sozialpolitische Zeitschrift WISO* 4/2007: 17–64.

Baumgartner, G. and B. Perchinig (1995) 'Minderheitenpolitik in Österreich – die Politik der österreichischen Minderheiten', in G. Baumgartner (ed.), *6 x Österreich. Geschichte und aktuelle Situation der Volksgruppen*, 15–25. Klagenfurt/Celovec: Drava.

Biffl, G. (2004) 'Chancen von jugendlichen Gastarbeiterkindern in Österreich', *WISO 27* (2): 37–56.

Binder, S. (2003) 'Sprache – Die Konstruktion einer Bedeutung', in T. Fillitz (ed.), *Interkulturelles Lernen*, 139–194. Innsbruck: StudienVerlag.

Binder, S. (2004) *Interkulturelles Lernen aus ethnologischer Perspektive. Konzepte, Ansichten und Praxisbeispiele aus Österreich und den Niederlanden*. Münster: Lit-Verlag.

Blüml, K. (2002) *PISA 2000*. Vol. 5. Innsbruck: Studien-Verlag.

Boeckmann, B. (1988) with K.-M. Brunner, M. Egger, G. Gombos, M. Juric and D. Larcher (Arbeitsgruppe Zweisprachigkeit und Identität): 'Identität und Assimilation' in: R. Bauböck, G. Baumgartner and K. Pintér (eds) *... und raus bist du! Ethnische Minderheiten in der Politik*, 209–223. Vienna: Verlag für Gesellschaftskritik.

Boeckmann, B. (1997) *Zweisprachigkeit und Schulerfolg: Das Beispiel Burgenland*, Frankfurt: Peter Lang Verlag.

Bourdieu, P. (1983) 'Ökonomisches Kapital, Kulturelles Kapital, Soziales Kapital', in R. Kreckel (ed.), *Soziale Ungleichheiten – Soziale Welt. Sonderband 2*. Göttingen: Schwarz & Co.

Bourdieu, P. and J.-C. Passeron (1979) *Die Illusion der Chancengleichheit*. Stuttgart.

Breit, S. (2009) 'Kompetenzen von Schülerinnen und Schülern mit Migrationshintergrund', in C. Schreiner and U. Schwantner (eds), *PISA 2006*, 46–158. Graz: Leykam.

Breit, S. and C. Schreiner (2006) 'Sozialisationsbedingungen von Schüler/innen mit Migrationshintergrund', in G. Haider and C. Schreiner (eds), *Die PISA-Studie*, 169–178. Vienna, Cologne, Weimar: Böhlau.

Breit, S. and C. Schreiner (2007) 'Familiäre sowie individuelle Kontextfaktoren und Leistung', in C. Schreiner (ed.), *PISA 2006. Internationaler Vergleich von Schülerleistungen. Erste Ergebnisse* Graz: Leykam.

Breit, S. and R. Wanka (2010) 'Schüler/innen mit Migrationshintergrund: Ein Portrait ihrer Kompetenzen im Licht ihrer familiären und schulischen Sozialisation', in B. Suchan and I.u.E.Ö.S.S. Des Bundesinstitut für Bildungsforschung (eds), *TIMSS 2007*, 96–115. Graz: Leykam.

Brizic, K. (2007) *Das geheime Leben der Sprachen*. Vol. 465. Münster [u.a.]: Waxmann.

Bundesgesetzblatt II 277/2004, legal regulation on the curriculum for academic secondary schools. http://www.ris.bka.gv.at/Dokumente/BgblAuth/BGBLA_2004_II_277/BGBLA_2004_II_277.pdf, date accessed 6 November 2012.

Bundesministerium Für Inneres (2011) *Integration. Zahlen, Daten, Fakten*. Vienna: ÖIF/Statistik Austria/BM.I.

Bundesministerium Unterricht Kunst und Kultur (BMUKK) (2011) *SchülerInnen mit anderen Erstsprachen als Deutsch. Statistische Übersicht Schuljahre 2004/05 bis 2010/11*. Vienna: Informationsblätter des Referats für Migration und Schule.

Burtscher, S. (2004) 'PISA und MigrantInnenkinder', in M. Sertl (ed.), *Integration?*, 42–55. Innsbruck, Vienna, Munich, Bozen: Studien-Verlag.

Burtscher, S. (2009) *Zuwandern-aufsteigen-dazugehören: Etablierungsprozesse von Eingewanderten*. Innsbruck/Vienna/Bozen: transblick.

Burtscher, S. (2010) 'Die Zweite Generation in Vorarlberg: Aussenseiter mit Migrationshintergrund oder Dazugehörige Einheimische? Eine Analyse anhand des Abschneidens der zweiten Generation im Bildungssystem', in M. Oberlechner and G. Hetfleisch (eds), *Integration, Rassismen und Weltwirtschaftskrise*, 205–222. Vienna: Braunmüller Verlag.

Busch, B. (1991) 'Auf den Spuren der Zweisprachigkeit', in P. Gstettner and V. Wakounig (eds) *Mut zur Vielfalt, Strategien gegen das Verschwinden ethnischer Minderheiten*, 228–241. Klagenfurt/Celovec: Drava.

Cinar, D. (1998) (ed.) *Gleichwertige Sprachen? Muttersprachlicher Unterricht für die Kinder von Einwanderern.* Innsbruck: Studienverlag.

Coleman, J. S. (1988) 'Social capital in the creation of human capital', *American Journal of Sociology* 94: 95–121.

Crul, M., P. Schnell, B. Herzog-Punzenberger, M. Wilmes, M. Slootman and R. Aparicio-Gomez (2012a) 'School careers of second-generation youth in Europe. Which education systems provide the best chances for success?', in M. Crul, J. Schneider and F. Lelie (eds), *The European Second Generation Compared: Does the Integration Context Matter?*, 101–164. Amsterdam: Amsterdam University Press.

Crul, M., M. Zhou, J. Lee, P. Schnell and E. Keskiner (2012b) 'Success against the odds', in M. Crul and J.H. Mollenkopf (eds), *The Changing Face of World Cities: Young Adult Children of Immigrants in Europe and the United States*, 25–45. New York: Russell Sage Foundation.

De Cillia, R. (1994) 'Höhere Schulen – ausländerfrei? SchülerInnen mit nichtdeutscher Muttersprache an höheren Schulen', *ahs aktuell* 88/1994: 9–13.

DeCillia, R. (1998) 'Mehrsprachigkeit und Herkunftssprachenunterricht in europäischen Schulen', in D. Çinar (ed.) *Gleichwertige Sprachen. Muttersprachlicher Unterricht für die Kinder von Einwanderern*, 229–287. InnsbruckVienna.

Englisch-Stölner, Doris (2003) 'Identität, Kultur und Differenz', in T. Fillitz (ed.), *Interkulturelles Lernen*, 195–272. Innsburck: StuidenVerlag.

Fassmann, H. and R. Münz (1994) 'Austria: A country of immigration and emigration', in H. Fassmann and R. Münz (eds), *European Migration in the Late Twentieth Century.* Boorkfield, VT: Edward Elgar Publishing.

Felderer, B. and H. Hofer (2004) Befunde zur Integration von AusländerInnen in Österreich: Endbericht; Studie im Auftrag von BM für Wirtschaft und Arbeit und BM für Finanzen. Vienna: Institut für Höhere Studien.

Fillitz, T. (2003) *Interkulturelles Lernen. Zwischen institutionellem Rahmen, schulischer Praxis und gesellschaftlichem Kommunikationsprinzip.* Innsbruck: StudienVerlag.

Fischer, G. (1986) 'Aspekte der Beschulungspolitik der Gastarbeiterkinder in Österreich', in H. Wimmer (ed.), *Ausländische Arbeitskräfte in Österreich*, 307–330. Frankfurt: campus Verlag.

Fischer, G. (1992) *Wissenschaftliche Begleitung des Schulversuches: Interkulturelles Lernen auf der Elementarstufe – Alphabetisierung türkischer Schulanfänger in ihrer Muttersprache.* Dokumentation des Schulversuchs in Wien XVII Kindermanngasse (BMUKS; Beginn September 1989). Vienna.

Fischer, G. (1993) 'Zum gegenwärtigen Stand der österreichischen Schulsprachenpolitik angesichts gesamteuropäischer Veränderungen', *Schulheft* 68/1993: 8–2.

Fischer, G. (1995) 'Alphabetisierung in der Muttersprache – Schulversuch Modell Kindermanngasse Wien', in R. Gauß, A. Harasek and G. Lau (eds) *Interkulturelle Bildung – Lernen kennt keine Grenzen*, 185–200. Vienna.

Fleck, E. (2007) '"A kuci sprecham Deutsch". Sprachstandserhebungen in multikulturellen Volksschulklassen: bilingualer Spracherwerb in der Migration', in H. Fassmann (ed.), *Zweiter österreichischer Migrations- und Integrationsbericht*, 261–262. Klagenfurt/ Celovec: Drava.

Frank, M. (2003) 'Kommunikation und soziale Beziehung', in T. Fillitz (ed.), *Interkulturelles Lernen*, 85–138. Innsbruck: StudienVerlag.

Gröpel, W. (1999) (ed.) *Migration und Schullaufbahn.* Frankfurt am Main: Lang.

Gröpel, W., M. Urbanek and G. Khan-Svik (1999) 'Darstellung und Interpretation der Untersuchungsergebnisse', in W. Gröpel (ed.), *Migration und Schullaufbahn*, 213–267. Frankfurt am Main [u.a.]: Lang.

Gröpel, W. (2001) 'Kindheit, Migration und Schullaufbahn' in W. Weidinger (ed.), *Bilingualität und Schule. Ausbildung, wissenschaftliche Perspektiven und empirische Befunde*, 162–245.Vienna: öbv & hpt.

Herzog-Punzenberger, B. (2003a) 'Die "2. Generation" an zweiter Stelle? Soziale Mobilität und ethnische Segmentation in Österreich – eine Bestandsaufnahme', http://www.interface-wien.at/system/attaches/10/original/Studie_2Generation.pdf?1246968285, date accessed 26 August 2013. Vienna: Wiener Integrationsfond.

Herzog-Punzenberger, B. (2003b) 'Ethnic Segmentation in School and Labor Market – 40 Year Legacy of Austrian Guestworker Policy', *International Migration* Review 37 (4): 1120–1144.

Herzog-Punzenberger, B. (2007) 'Gibt es einen Staatsbürgerschafts-Bonus? Unterschiede in der Bildung und am Arbeitsmarkt anhand der österreichischen Volkszählungsdaten 2001 – Ergebnisse für die zweite Generation der Anwerbegruppen', in: Fassmann, Heinz and Wiebke Sievers (eds), *Zweiter Österreichischer Migrations- und Integrationsbericht*, 242–245. Klagenfurt/Celovec: Drava Verlag.

Herzog-Punzenberger, B. and P. Gapp (2009) 'Schüler/innen mit Migrationshintergrund', in B. Suchań, C. Wallner-Paschon and C. Schreiner (eds), *PIRLS 2006. Die Lesekompetenz am Ende der Volksschule – Österreichischer Expertenbericht* Graz: Leykam.

Hintermann, C. (2007) 'Historical consciousness and identity constructions in a receiving society – an empirical analysis of migrant youth in Vienna', *SWS-Rundschau* 47 (4): 477–499.

Jaksche, E. (1998) *Pädagogische Reflexe auf die multikulturelle Gesellschaft in Österreich.* Innsbruck, Vienna: Studien-Verl.

Khan-Svik, G. (1999) 'Der sich nach oben hin zweimal verengende Flaschenhals – Die Selektion von "ausländischen" Schülerinnen und Schülern bei den Übertritten in die Mittelstufe und in die Berufsausbildung', in Gröpel, W. (ed.), *Migration und Schullaufbahn*, 186–197. Frankfurt a. M.: Peter Lang Verlag.

Khan-Svik, G. (2005) (ed.) Muttersprachliche Bildungseinrichtungen in Wien. In: Erziehung und Unterricht 155/1–2.

Khan-Svik, G. (2007) 'Anderssprachige SchülerInnen: aktuelle Studien 2000–2005', in H. Fassmann (ed.), *2. Österreichischer Migrations- und Integrationsbericht. 2001–2006.*, 257–261. Klagenfurt: Drava-Verl.- u. Druckges.

Kogan, I. (2007) 'Continuing ethnic segmentation in Austria', in A.F. Heath (ed.), *Unequal Chances*, 103–141. Oxford [u.a.]: Oxford University Press.

Landesschulrat für Kärnten, Abt. VII Minderheitenschulwesen (2011) Jahresbericht über das Schuljahr 2009/10. Abt. VII. Klagenfurt/Celovec.

Luciak, M. (2008) 'Education of ethnic minorities and migrants in Austria', in G. Wan (ed.), *The Education of Diverse Populations: A Global Perspective*, 45–64. Dordrecht, London: Springer Verlag.

Luciak, M. and G. Khan-Svik (2008) 'Intercultural education and intercultural learning in Austria – critical reflections on theory and practice', *Intercultural Education* 19 (6): 493–504.

Markom, C. and H. Weinhäupl (2007) *Die Anderen im Schulbuch. Rassismen, Exotismen, Sexismen und Antisemitismus in österreichischen Schulbüchern.* Vienna: Braumüller.

Matuschek, H. (1982) *Die Auswirkungen der 'Ausländerpolitik' auf Schul- und Berufsausbildung der jugoslawischen und türkischen Jugendlichen in Wien und Niederösterreich.* Vienna: Europ. Zentrum für Ausbildung u. Forschung auf d. Gebiet d. Sozialen Wohlfahrt.

OECD (2005) *School Factors Related to Quality and Equity. Results from PISA 2000.* Paris: OECD Publishing.

OECD (2006) *Where Immigrant Students Succeed – A Comparative Review of Performance and Engagement in PISA 2003.* Paris: OECD.

Peltzer-Karpf, A., V. Wurnig, B. Schwab, M. Griessler, R. Akkus, K. Lederwasch, D. Piwonka, T. Blazevic, and K. Brizic, K. (2003) *Bilingualer Spracherwerb in der Migration. Psycholinguistische Langzeitsutdie (1999–2003).* Unpublished project report. Vienna: BMBWK.

Peltzer-Karpf, A., V. Wurnig, B. Schwab, M. Griessler, R. Akkus, K. Lederwasch, D. Piwonka, T. Blazevic, and K. Brizic, K. (2006) *A kući sprecham Deutsch: Sprachstandserhebung in multikulturellen Volksschulklassen: bilingualer Spracherwerb in der Migration.* Unveröffentlichter Endbericht für das Unterrichtsministerium. Vienna.

Perchinig, B. (1995) 'Ausländer in Wien – Die Zweite Generation. Zahlen, Daten, Fakten', in N. Bailer and R. Horak (eds), *Jugendkultur – Annäherungen*, 113–139. Vienna: WUV.

Perchinig, B. and K. König (2003) 'Austria', in J. Niessen, Y. Schibel and R. Magoni (eds), *EU and US Approaches to the Management of Immigration*, Brussels: Migration Policy Group.

Pinterits, M. (1990) 'Gesellschaftliche Grenzen und paedagogische Moeglichkeiten Interkulturellen Lernens in Wien. Ein Interview', *Lehrerzeitung (Zentralverein der Wiener Lehrerschaft)*, 1 (1991): 7–10.

Pinterits, M. (1991) *Von der Ausländerpädagogik zum interkulturellen Lernen.* Erziehung und Unterricht, Vol. 141, Vol. 144. Vienna: Österreichischer Bundesverl.

Reiter, C. (2002a) 'Schüler/innen nichtdeutscher Muttersprache', in C. Reiter and G. Haider (eds), *PISA 2000*, 69–74. Innsbruck, Vienna: Studien-Verl.

Reiter, C. (2002b) 'Wenn die Testsprache nicht der Muttersprache entspricht', in C. Reiter and G. Haider (eds), *PISA 2000*, 61–68. Innsbruck, Vienna: Studien-Verl.

Schmid, Breit, S. and C. Schreiner (2009) 'Jugendliche mit Migrationshintergrund in berufsbildenden Schulen', in C. Schreiner and U. Schwantner (eds) *PISA 2006. Österreichischer Expertenbericht zum Naturwissenschafts-Schwerpunkt.* Graz: Leykam.

Schnell, P. (2012) *Educational Mobility of Second Generation Turks in Cross-National Perspective.* Dissertation manuscript. Amsterdam: University of Amsterdam.

Schofield, W. (2005) *Migrationshintergrund, Minderheitenzugehörigkeit und Bildungserfolg.* Forschungsergebnisse der pädagogischen, Entwicklungs- und Sozialpsychologie, http://www2000.wzb.eu/alt/aki/files/aki_forschungsbilanz_5.pdf, date accessed 30 October 2012.

Schreiner, C. (2006) 'Österreichische Jugendliche und das Lesen: Ergebnisse aus PISA 2003', *Erziehung & Unterricht* 9–10: 838–848.

Schreiner, C. and S. Breit (2006) 'Kompetenzen von Schüler/innen mit Migrationshintergrund', in G. Haider and C. Schreiner (eds), *Die PISA-Studie*, 179–192. Vienna, Cologne, Weimar: Böhlau.

Schwantner, U. and C. Schreiner (eds) (2010) *Internationaler Vergleich von Schülerleistungen. Erste Ergebnisse. Lesen, Mathematik, Naturwissenschaft.* Graz: Leykam.

Sertl, M. (2009) 'Ungehobene Schätze: Studierende mit Migrationshintergrund an der PH Wien', in *Schulheft* 135, 120–130. Innsbruck: Studienverlag.

Stanzel-Tischler, E. (2011) *Frühe sprachliche Förderung im Kindergarten.* Begleitende Evaluation. Executive Summary zu den BIFIE-Reports 1&2/2009, 5/2010 und 8/2011 (BIFIE-Report). Graz: Leykam

Statistik Austria http://www.statistik.at/web_de/static/schuelerinnen_und_schueler_2010 11_nach_geschlecht_020961.xlsx, date accessed 6 November 2012

Stevens, P. A. J. (2007) 'Researching race/ethnicity and educational inequality in English secondary schools: A critical review of the research literature between 1980 and 2005', *Review of Educational Research* 77 (2): 147–185.

Stevens, P. a. J., N. Clycq, C. Timmermann and M. Van Houtte (2011) 'Researching race/ethnicity and educational inequality in the Netherlands: A critical review of the research literature between 1980 and 2008', *British Educational Research Journal* 37 (1): 5–43.

Suchan, B., C. Wallner-Paschon, E. Stöttinger and S. Bergmüller (eds) (2007) *PIRLS 2006. Internationaler Vergleich von Schülerleistungen. Erste Ergebnisse. Lesen in der Grundschule.* Graz: Leykam.

Unterwurzacher, A. (2007) 'Ohne Schule bist Du niemand. Bildungsbiographien von Jugendlichen mit Migrationshintergrund', in H. Weiss (ed.), *Leben in Zwei Welten. Zur sozialen Integration ausländischer Jugendlicher der zweiten Generation*, 71–95. Wiesbaden: VS Verlag.

Unterwurzacher, A. (2009) 'Lesekompetenz von Schülerinnen und Schülern mit Migrationshintergrund: Einfluss des familiären Hintergrundes', in B. Suchań, C. Wallner-Paschon and C. Schreiner (eds), *PIRLS 2006. Die Lesekompetenz am Ende der Volksschule – Österreichischer Expertenbericht* Graz: Leykam.

Viehböck, E. and L. Bratić (1994) *Die zweite Generation.* Vol. 2. Innsbruck: Österreichischer Studien-Verlag.

Volf, P. and R. Bauböck (2001) *Wege zur Integration. Was man gegen Diskriminierung und Fremdenfeindlichkeit tun kann.* Klagenfurt: Drava.

Waechter, N., J. Blum and P. Scheibelhofer (2007) 'Jugendliche MigrantInnen: Die Rolle von Sozialkapital bei Bildungs- und Berufsentscheidungen', in H. Fassmann (ed.), *2. Österreichischer Migrations- und Integrationsbericht 2001–2006: Rechtliche Rahmenbedingungen, demographische Entwicklungen, sozioökonomische Strukturen*, 420–424. Klagenfurt/Celovec: Drava Verlag.

Weiss, H. (2006) 'Bildungswege der zweiten Generation in Österreich', in B. Herzog-Punzenberger (ed.), *Bildungsbe/nach/teiligung in Österreich und im internationalen Vergleich.*, 27–39. Vienna.

Weiss, H. (2007a) 'Sozialstrukturelle Integration der Zweiten Generation', in H. Weiss (ed.), *Leben in Zwei Welten. Zur sozialen Integration ausländischer Jugendlicher der zweiten Generation*, 33–69. Wiesbaden: VS Verlag für Sozialsissenschaften.

Weiss, H. and A. Unterwurzacher (2007) 'Soziale Mobilität durch Bildung? Bildungsbeteiligung von MigrantInnen', in H. Fassmann (ed.) *2. Österreichischer Migrations- und Integrationsbericht. 2001–2006*, 227–246. Klagenfurt: Drava-Verlag.

Weiss, H., Unterwurzacher, A. and R. Strodl (2007) *SchülerInnen mit Migrationshintergrund an österreichischen Schulen: Probleme aus der Sicht der Lehrkräfte. Ergebnisse einer empirischen Untersuchung.* Unveröffnetlicher Bericht für das BMBWK. [Unpublished report.]

Wimmer, H. (1986) 'Zur Ausländerbschäftigungspolitik in Österreich', in H. Wimmer (ed.), *Ausländische Arbeitskräfte in Österreich*, 5–32. Frankfurt/New York: Campus Verlag.

Wroblewski, A. (2006) 'Handicap Migrationshintergrund? Eine Analyse anhand von PISA 2000', in B. Herzog-Punzenberger (ed.), *Bildungsbe/nach/teiligung in Österreich und im internationalen Vergleich.* KMI Working Paper Series No. 10, 40–49. Vienna.

5
Belgium

Lore Van Praag, Peter A. J. Stevens, and Mieke Van Houtte

5.1 National context

This chapter presents a critical review of research on racial and ethnic inequalities in secondary education in Flanders between 1980 and 2010. Due to the educational organization of Belgium, only the Dutch linguistic community is reviewed. Belgium is a small country but has a rather complex government structure that also affects the organization of the educational system. Belgium comprises three regions (Flanders, Wallonia, and Brussels) with three linguistic communities (Dutch, French, and German) and a federal government. All have their specific governing powers. Since the federal restructuring of 1989, the Department of Education is organized by the (cultural) linguistic communities. In this chapter we focus on education in the Dutch linguistic community that covers the region of Flanders and partly Brussels. Brussels is governed by both the French- and the Dutch-speaking communities and parents have to choose between them. Because of the organization of the educational system, most research has focused on a certain linguistic community (except for Phalet et al., 2007). Before reviewing the literature, an overview is given of the educational system, immigration to Flanders, and social policy and developments in Flanders.

5.1.1 Educational system

In Flanders, education is compulsory for all children between the ages of six and eighteen. Before the age of six, children have the possibility to go to nursery education. Both primary and secondary school take six years. Primary school is similar for all children. In contrast to this, the secondary school system of Flanders is divided into three cycles of two years each. Students choose between four tracks: general or academic (ASO), artistic (KSO), technical (TSO), and vocational (BSO) secondary education. Within these tracks, a variety of specific fixed programs of subjects are offered. (Figure 5.1)

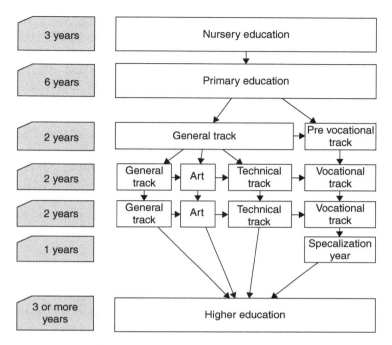

Figure 5.1 School structure in Flanders

A different status is given to the tracks, and study programs within the tracks, by parents, teachers, and pupils. Academic tracks are given more status than the 'lower', more practical tracks (Van Houtte, 2004; Stevens and Vermeersch, 2010). Changes are possible from the more general to the vocational tracks. However, the other way round seldom occurs. The educational system is characterized by the trend to start in higher academic tracks and to 'fall down' to lower tracks when not successful, often referred to as the 'cascade system'. The chosen track is important because it determines entry to higher education. Only students in academic, art, and technical tracks have the possibility to enter university. Students in vocational tracks should first follow a specialization year before they get their diploma of secondary education. Higher education is heavily subsidized and thus relatively cheap for the students. Apart from some exceptions, no entry exams are organized in higher education.

Schools have different track compositions: multilateral schools offer all the tracks while categorical schools only offer mainly ASO (academic) or TSO and BSO (technical and vocational). Most common are the categorical schools, usually distinguishing between schools for academic education and technical/vocational schools. Although different sectors (private and public) organize education, all schools are funded by the Flemish government and have the same curriculum. In Flanders, there is no centralized evaluation system and no comparable national tests are used. Teachers have considerable autonomy because they are responsible for designing, administering, and marking the examinations of the pupils they teach. In addition, at the end of each school year, teachers come together to decide whether the pupils they teach should retake their school year or pass to the next (higher) school year, and to which educational track, a decision that is based on pupils' exam results and motivational and behavioral characteristics of the pupils (Stevens, 2007b). Due to the lack of national standardized tests, different indicators of educational achievement have to be used in research. Most reports include various measures such as tracks, leaving school without a diploma, the number of students in higher education, and delay or repeating a year. Higher education is highly valued in the labor market. Getting a diploma of secondary education is an important indicator of success because without this diploma one cannot enter higher education.

This tracking system makes the Flemish education system highly stratified and this is reflected in the unequal distribution of ethnic and social groups over these tracks. Students from lower social and other racial or ethnic backgrounds are over-represented in the lower status (technical and particularly vocational) tracks and under-represented in general, more academic tracks and higher education (see also below). Schools vary according to their ethnic and social composition. Government policies want to stimulate a certain social and ethnic mix in schools but do not always succeed because parents have free school choice.

5.1.2 Immigration to Flanders (Belgium)

Since the end of World War II, Belgium has actively recruited migrants, first from Southern Europe and later from Morocco and Turkey. Migrants were imported as guest workers and were expected to return to their country of origin. After some years, it became clear that many of these migrants stayed permanently in Belgium and formed tight migrant communities. In 1973, together with other European countries, Belgium introduced a migration stop by implementing restrictive measures to restrain immigration and ceased to recruit immigrants to work in Belgium (Sierens, 2006). The rapid change into a post-industrial economy, caused an economic restructuring that especially affected immigrants who mainly worked in the industrial sector (Phalet, Deboosere, and Bastiaenssen, 2007). Nevertheless, more migrants came through procedures of family reunification and asylum. Since 1990, a new wave of immigrants from Eastern Europe entered Belgium accompanied by a wave of undocumented immigrants (Sierens, 2006; CGKR, 2010).

Statistics on recent migration flows only can be found through nationality or recent nationality change. Many persons of non-Belgian descent are naturalized and are therefore hard to trace. This is especially true for groups that have already lived in Belgium for more than one generation, such as Turkish and Moroccan populations (CGKR, 2010). Children and grandchildren from migrants are often referred to as 'allochthons', in contrast to 'autochthons' with a Belgian background. These terms are often used in a Belgian context and distinguish between persons with a migrant background (for the last two generations) and persons who lived for more than two generations in Belgium. Official statistics of the percentage of secondary school students that do not have Belgian nationality are given in Table 5.1.

As shown in Table 5.1, most students with a non-Belgian nationality come from European Union member states, especially from the Netherlands. In the total school population, 0.37% has a Moroccan nationality and 0.23% a Turkish nationality. In the general population of Flanders, most foreigners have the nationality of a member state of the EU (68%), followed by Morocco (8%), Turkey

Table 5.1 Number and percentage of students with a non-Belgian nationality in secondary school, from each continent, specified to the countries with the highest numbers of students in Belgium

Nationality	Numbers	% of foreign students in the foreign school population	% of foreign students in the total secondary school population
EU member countries	11,634	51.14	2.71
Bulgaria	*406*	*1.78*	*0.09*
Italy	*371*	*1.63*	*0.09*
The Netherlands	*8176*	*35.94*	*1.90*
Poland	*786*	*3.46*	*0.18*
Non-EU member countries	2587	11.37	0.60
Russia	*937*	*4.12*	*0.22*
Serbia	*451*	*1.98*	*0.10*
Total Europe	14,221	62.52	3.31
Africa	3109	13.67	0.72
Morocco	*1599*	*7.03*	*0.37*
America	654	2.87	0.15
Asia	4315	18.97	1.00
Afghanistan	*488*	*2.15*	*0.11*
Armenia	*523*	*2.30*	*0.12*
Turkey	*987*	*4.34*	*0.23*
Oceania	8	0.04	0.00
Other	441	1.94	0.10
Refugees from various origins	*368*	*1.62*	*0.09*
Total non-Belgian nationalities	22,748	100	5.29

Source: Flemish Ministry of Education and Training (2011b). Table adapted by the authors.

(4%), and Asian countries (6%) (FOD Economie, KMO, Middenstand en Energie, 2011). Most foreigners live in the triangle between Ghent, Antwerp, and Brussels, and in the province of Limburg (Timmerman, Vanderwaeren, and Crul, 2003).

However, official statistics only consider nationality and can be contrasted to estimations based on the language spoken at home, nationality and country of birth of the grandmother and respondent. Estimations based on research samples illustrate that nationality is not an appropriate indicator, as most students from another ethnic or racial descent are born in Belgium and have Belgian nationality. The sample of the 'Flemish Educational Assessment' (Vlaams Leerlingen Onderzoek, VLO) shows that, based on the birthplace of the maternal grandmother, approximately 14.1% of secondary school students have a non-Belgian ethnic origin (Van Houtte and Stevens, 2009). This is in accordance with other studies (Duquet et al., 2006; Timmerman, Vanderwaeren, and Crul, 2003). Moroccan and Turkish students are the most studied minority populations because of their underachievement in education and the higher proportion of students that come from these countries. Allochthonous students are often concentrated in schools with a higher percentage of students with a foreign background (Sierens et al., 2006).

5.1.3 Social policy and developments

Initially, immigrants planned a temporary stay in Belgium and this was reflected in educational policies. Except for some local and independent projects (see Verlot, 2001; Leman, 1997), few policy actions were directed at the educational achievement of immigrant children. These initial projects introduced mother language in the schools. Their aim was to relieve schools from the extra load that migrant children placed on them (Verlot, 2001). The changing political climate and the conclusion that most migrants would not return to their country, stimulated the government to invest in the education of migrant children. In 1991, the 'educational priorities policy' (*Onderwijsvoorrangsbeleid*) was introduced. Although the focus changed to children living in deprived (i.e. lower social class) families in general, it was recognized that migrants had additional challenges related to their ethnic-cultural background (Flemish Ministry of Education and Training, 2011a). The purpose of this policy was not only to resolve problems with migrants but also to focus on the positive aspects of cultural diversity (Sierens, 2006). Language education was central in this approach. Schools received more resources if they paid more attention to language and the expertise from their school teams in dealing with migrant pupils (Van den Branden and Van Avermaet, 2001). Despite the financial encouragement, very few schools implemented measures to satisfy specific minority needs. Instead, schools adopted more of an assimilation perspective and focused almost exclusively on 'Dutch language development' (De Wit, Van Petegem, and De Maeyer, 2000).

The 'educational priorities policy' was followed by the 'non-discrimination policy' in 1993. Different measures were set up to prevent discrimination actively and to stimulate a better ethnic mix in all schools. Schools voluntarily signed a declaration to fight against discrimination in their school and in return, they received extra resources. In 2002, the 'equal education opportunities policy' (*Gelijke Onderwijskansen*, GOK) proposed a more inclusive policy that would benefit the entire school instead of giving attention to the problems of (at-risk) students, including students who live outside their family, who belong to a migratory population, speak a language other than Dutch at home, live in a family with no income/a replacement income, or have a mother without a diploma. So far, three cycles of GOK policies have been implemented but it is uncertain what future policies will bring and how it can lead to more equal education opportunities (Van Avermaet, Van den Branden, and Heylen, 2010).

Before reviewing the literature, some remarks should be made about the mutual influence between social policy and educational research in Flanders (Blommaert and Verschueren, 1992; Caremans et al., 2004). In the 1980s, the lack of a coherent policy was also reflected in the lack of research on migrant children and education. Research focused on evaluating small projects (e.g. the evaluation of mother tongue projects (Boos-Nünning and et al., 1986)). In 1990, when immigrants settled permanently in Belgium, ethnicity became increasingly more a topic on the agenda of researchers (Van Damme, 2006). At the same time, more financial resources became available for research. Especially, four domains were examined: policy evaluation and support, the development of curriculum and pedagogy, the living environment of immigrants, and the development of theory to explain the educational achievement of immigrant children. Firstly, anthropological research focused on the living environment of immigrants and showed that immigrants had high expectations of educational attainment (e.g. Phalet and Claeys, 1993). As a result, the 'problem' changed from the 'immigrant child' to the 'home culture'. Secondly, many studies were funded by the Flemish government and designed to evaluate the policy initiatives and advise policy makers (e.g. Leman, 1997). Resulting from the dialogue between policy-makers and researchers, the definition and measurement of ethnic and racial minorities changed from nationality to ethnic background (Phalet et al., 2007; Verlot, 2001) and the focus of research shifted from pupils with another nationality to all groups that live in a certain (deprived) socio-cultural context (Caremans, Mahieu, and Yildirim, 2004). Thirdly, two research centers were created to study the processes and the development of didactics: the Center for Diversity and Learning, and the Center of Dutch as a Second Language. Finally, research started to focus more on the development of theory, although the data used for analyses was often gathered in order to evaluate educational policies (Verlot, 2001). In sum, the political climate and migration processes determined educational policies that, in turn, stimulated educational research in this area through funding and agenda set-ting. The entanglement between policy and research is visible throughout the literature review. Before setting out the research traditions, the scope and the methods of the sampling procedure are made explicit in the following section.

5.2 Methodology

The scope of this review is determined by five criteria. In general, only research that explicitly focuses on ethnicity and education is included. First, the sampling is limited to the time range between 1980 and 2010. Second, only research concerning secondary education is considered to be able to compare studies and to focus on specific characteristics of secondary education. Third, given the specific regional and cultural organization of the educational system in Belgium, only the Dutch linguistic community is included. Fourth, besides peer-refereed journal articles, (edited) books, and official reports, policy papers and doctoral dissertations are also considered. This is due to the fact that Flanders educational research is often intertwined with policy research. Fifth, the focus of this review is the sociological approach to race and ethnic inequali-ties in education. However, other research paradigms, such as sociolinguistics and anthropology, are included in order to understand inequality in education.

The sampling method should be seen as a snowball procedure that started from different leads. First, bibliographical databases such as Thomson Reuters (ISI) Web of Knowledge and CSA Sociological Abstracts were searched, using search-strings such as 'achievement', 'school', 'ethnic', 'racial', 'minorities', 'immigrants' 'Belgium', 'Flanders'. Because most of the research is written in Dutch, these database searches did not yield many results. Another approach was used and the publication lists of the main research centers and university departments of Flanders were searched. Finally, by examining the reference lists of this sample of literature, more relevant studies were found and included in our sample.

Different research traditions were distinguished based on the research ques-tions and research methods they used, which were sometimes in line with internationally distinguished research traditions (e.g. Stevens et al., 2011). First, the 'political arithmetic' tradition is based on large quantitative databases that describes the existing tendencies in education in Flanders and family background and educational outcomes. Second, the 'cultural and educational outcomes' tradition explains educational outcomes by referring to cultural practices. Both a qualitative anthropological and a quantitative social psy-chological approach are discussed in this tradition. Third, the 'language profi-ciency' tradition consists of mainly qualitative studies that try to understand the influence of language to develop curriculum and pedagogy. In addition, they often evaluate educational projects and policies. Fourth, the 'racism and racial discrimination' tradition focuses explicitly on racism as one group of scholars focuses on the origin of ethnocentric attitudes while a second group studies the perceptions of students' unequal treatment in schools. Fifth, the 'school effectiveness' tradition investigates school effects and processes with large quantitative datasets.

5.3 Research traditions

5.3.1 Political arithmetic tradition

The 'political arithmetic' tradition studies the differences between social categories and policy and the relationship between family background and educational success (see also Stevens, 2007a for an analysis of UK research). Several large-scale quantitative databases are set up in Flanders that allow for an analysis of ethnic inequalities in education. Findings from five databases will be discussed: the 'Longitudinal Research Secondary Education' (LOSO) project, the 'Panel Study of Belgian Households' (PSBH), Belgian Census, the 'Study of the Transition from Education to the Labor Market' (SONAR), and the 'Programme for International Student Assessment' (PISA).

From 1990 until 1997, the Flemish Ministry of Education funded the 'Longitudinal Research Secondary Education' project (LOSO)[1] (Van Damme et al., 2004; Van Damme et al., 2001; Hermans et al., 2002; Hermans, Opdenakker, and Van Damme, 2003). In this database, ethnicity is measured by the language spoken at home. Based on the data from the LOSO project, ethnic and racial minority students have more delays in their school career and will finish secondary school with a lower diploma than the majority students, after controlling for intelligence tests, achievement tests at the beginning of the secondary education, and with equal motivation and delay. An interaction effect is found between socio-economic status and ethnicity. The ethnicity of ethnic and racial minority students will only affect students with a higher socio-economic status. Students with a lower socio-economic status achieve similar to majority students. The effect of ethnicity diminishes when controlling for achievement, intelligence, and motivation to achieve at the beginning of their secondary education (Hermans, Opdenakker, and Van Damme, 2004).

Based on the 'Panel Study of Belgian Households' (PSBH),[2] Groenez, Van den Brande and Nicaise (2003) examine three indicators of social inequality: socio-economic background, ethnic and cultural background, and gender. Ethnicity is measured by the first nationality by birth and the language spoken at home. Parental socio-professional background explains a large part of the differences in school achievement and study orientation. Besides social background, ethnic and cultural barriers have an additional influence on study orientation. Children with a Maghreb (North African) background are more often referred to lower tracks in secondary education, have a higher risk leaving secondary school without a diploma, and even when they have a diploma, they are less likely to enroll in higher education.

Third, the Belgian Census in 2001 is used by Phalet and colleagues (2007) to study ethnic and racial inequalities by the highest qualifications of the birth cohort from 1973 to 1979, obtained in 2001. This study avoids the 'class' versus 'ethnicity' debate that wants to attribute minorities' educational underachievement to either class or ethnic disadvantage. Instead, the resource investment theory states that parental resources that are invested in education explain the variation in educational achievement. Parental resources, measured by social class, educational qualifications of the parents, parental housing, and the timing of parental migration and the presence of both parents, explains a large part of the variation in educational attainment. Ethnic disadvantage is perpetuated through mechanisms of class disadvantage. The analyses also highlight internal variability between ethnic minority groups' educational achievement, with Turkish students, and to a lesser extent Moroccan students experiencing an accumulation of class and ethnic disadvantage. In a following study, Fleischmann and colleagues (2011) found that structural neighborhood effects influence the school completion of Turkish, Italian, and Moroccan second generation students and these effects interact with local co-ethnic concentrations. For Moroccan Belgians, living in high-quality neighborhoods enhances educational success. However, most Moroccan Belgians live in neighborhoods with high levels of urbanization and low levels of home ownership. For Turkish Belgians, living in neighborhoods with a large number of other Turkish Belgians leads to educational success if these are stable neighborhoods. Finally, for the Italian Belgians, the presence of co-ethnic residents helps to achieve school success for residents that live in lower-quality neighborhoods, while it is rather a hindrance for those who live in more stable environments. In sum, internal variability between ethnic minority groups should be included in research in order to fully grasp the effect class disadvantage and structural neighborhood characteristics have on educational outcomes.

Fourth, the 'Study of the Transition from Education to the Labor Market' database (SONAR)[3] is a longitudinal survey of 23-, 26- and 29-year-olds designed to map the transition of education to the labor market (Duquet et al., 2006). Based on the results of the 23-year-olds, this study shows that allochthonous students lag behind other students before they enter secondary school and that this lag increases during secondary school. Interaction effects between study choice, gender, and ethnic background are observed. Boys start more often in the academic tracks but later go to technical or vocational tracks during their school career, which characterizes the Flemish educational system, also known as the 'cascade system', while girls go directly into a vocational track. Students from a North African or Turkish background have the most problematic school careers. Later generations are more oriented towards Belgian society and achieve better, suggesting an increased adaptation to the Belgian society. The first analyses show that, in line with 'the deprivation perspective', students with a disadvantageous parental background experience more problems in school while the cultural capital of the parents, measured by parental educational attainment, influences only partly the entry to secondary education.

Fifth, 'Programme for International Student Assessment' (PISA)[4] tests compare the educational outcomes of 15-year-old students over different years. According to the latest PISA assessment in 2009, Belgium combines a high average performance with large socio-economic inequalities (OECD, 2010). Results from PISA 2000 indicated ethnic and racial minorities lag behind and this gap is bigger than in other OECD countries in the survey, compared to the Belgian background students (Marks, 2005; Jacobs, Rea, and Hanquinet, 2007; Jacobs et al., 2009; Varin, 2006). Comparing the Dutch and French linguistic communities, the Dutch linguistic community scores are higher compared to the French linguistic community, but in both communities students with a non-Belgian background have lower test scores than native students. Variation also exists within the immigrant group as recently arrived immigrants have lower test scores than immigrants from the second generation. In addition, the national context can be studied through the PISA assessment. Countries with an educational system that is characterized by early tracking have more social differences (Jacobs et al., 2009). More educational inequality between students from different ethnic backgrounds in countries with early tracking is found (Dupriez, Dumay, and Vause, 2008), because in these countries, the parental environment plays a bigger role (de Heus and Dronkers, 2010). However, one should interpret the previous results with caution because only a small number of non-Belgian background students is included in the PISA sample (Jacobs et al., 2009; Agirdag, 2009b).

In sum, the 'political arithmetic' tradition in Flanders is based on large, quantitative databases that aim to offer representative descriptions of social (ethnic) inequalities in education. Most studies are policy relevant and funded by the Flemish or Belgian government. Although references are often made to sociological theories and earlier studies, the tendencies, patterns, and differences between the school career of ethnic and racial minority students are the focus of this research tradition. However, the databases are not specifically intended to study ethnic and racial inequalities in education; these studies indicate that the socio-economic background is the most important explaining factor for educational achievement. While the LOSO report indicates that ethnicity is only important for students with a higher socio-economic background, the PSBH and the Belgian Census found that, together with socio-economic background, ethnic and cultural barriers determine achievement outcomes. Furthermore, the cross-national PISA study illustrates that inequalities in Belgium are higher compared to other OECD countries. In conclusion, the 'political arithmetic' tradition excels in collecting representative data and mapping and charting out patterns in time; demonstrating the underachievement and inequality of ethnic and racial minorities in Flemish education.

5.3.2   Cultural and educational outcomes tradition

Cultural factors that influence educational outcomes are investigated (Stevens, 2007a) in the 'cultural and educational outcomes' (CEO) tradition. In Flanders, the relationship between family, national context, and education is examined. In this tradition, group identity and socialization are key concepts and comparisons are made between educational systems in the immigrant country and the country of origin. Two sub-traditions are distinguished, both focusing on culture but applying different methods and theoretical approaches. The first sub-tradition starts from an anthropological approach and uses qualitative methods. Characteristics of the immigrant culture, such as the existing nationalist ideologies and ethnic identity, the incongruence between home and school culture, and related collective problems in society are expected to be related with the educational outcomes of immigrant children. In the second sub-tradition, quantitative methods are employed and research questions arise from a social psychological framework. Cultural differences in motivation to succeed are examined and explained from the 'future time' perspective.

5.3.2.1   *An anthropological approach*

Timmerman (1994, 1999) compares Turkish girls in Belgium and Turkey and relates education to existing nationalist ideologies and ethnic identity. The author argues that, even though most Turkish youth in Belgium are born and raised in Belgium, Turkish ways of thinking are reflected in their actions and life experiences. In Turkey, education is seen as the perfect cultural apparatus to change the way of thinking of Turkish youth. But in Belgium, Turkish youth are confronted with a educational system that promotes the Belgian society. In schools with a higher number of students with Belgian backgrounds, Turkish girls are better prepared for higher education, compared to those in schools with a greater concentration of Turkish students (Timmerman, 1999). The orientation towards Turkey or Belgium is reflected in the parental school choice: children in schools with a higher percentage of students of Turkish descent more often have parents that are oriented towards Turkey, while parents with children in elite schools are more directed towards the Belgian society and invest in the education of their daughters (Timmermans, 1994). In addition, the girls' vision on education in Belgium is related to the (Turkish) nationalist orientation they have at home: while the secular-nationalist orientation or the Kemalist vision relates education to the participation of Turkish girls in Western society, the religious-nationalistic orientation sees the role of girls located in the family. Young migrant girls in higher education will follow the education supporting the Kemalist ideology and accept the Turkish nationalism that goes along with it. Turkish immigrant girls get recognition in their community because of their education and even form their own subculture. Girls gain more by participating in education than boys do. Boys already enjoy more social status in their community and education does not add so much more. The presence of other girls with a similar socio-familial perspective is a decisive factor that determines their educational career. In contrast, those who have a more religious-nationalist vision get more social status through their opposition with the Western society. In the Belgian migrant community, religious-nationalism is rising because religion offers a reference frame that many migrants lack in the Belgian society (Timmerman, 1999; 2002).

A remarkable study by Hermans (2004) applied Ogbu's (1984) theory of minority academic achievement to the situation of Moroccan immigrants in Belgium and the Netherlands based on ethnographic research. Structural positions and collective history in the immigration country lead to different motivations to study. The underachievement of Moroccan-background students in Belgium seems to contradict to Ogbu's (1984) theory. In his theory, in settler societies, a distinction can be made between voluntary (including autonomous, voluntary or immigrant, refugees, migrant or guest workers, undocumented workers), and involuntary (including binationals, involuntary or nonimmigrant minorities) immigrants, and descendants or later generations. This distinction refers to the shared collective history of different racial/ethnic groups: while voluntary minorities migrated to improve their economic and social status, this is not the case for involuntary minorities. As education is seen as a way of improving the economic and social status, educational success is of greater importance to voluntary migrants, compared to involuntary migrants. However, when this theory is applied to Belgium and the Netherlands, the voluntarily migrated Moroccans have more negative educational outcomes. Hermans (2004) argues that hindering community forces for educational achievement of immigrant in Belgium are similar to those of minorities Ogbu calls involuntary. Ogbu thinks that voluntary migrants compare themselves with the situation in the country of origin, but in Belgium, Moroccans compare themselves with Belgians. The relationship with the dominant society is seen as a conflict and this is related to issues of identity, culture, language, and ability. Moroccan students experience more often situations in which their culture is presented as inferior. Parents have often the impression that they should set aside their culture to be able to integrate into the dominant society and that school and the educational system is discriminatory. The lack of trust in teachers and the threat to their identity, culture, and religion overshadow feelings towards schooling. Furthermore, while parents have high expectations of upwards mobility through schooling, they see little evidence of this in their immediate environment. The expectations of the parents are seldom translated into effective support for schoolwork. Less weight is given to the impact of the initial voluntariness than to the situation of migrants in the migrant countries. These Moroccan 'voluntary' migrants are similar to involuntary migrants and their experiences and frames of references lead to disengagement from school. The fact that the recipient countries regarded the migration of Moroccans rather as a temporary phenomenon shaped the initial conditions of migration and integration into the society (Hermans, 2004).

5.3.2.2   *A social psychological approach*

Social psychologists are mainly interested in cultural differences in motivation to succeed in school. When activities are perceived to be instrumental to achieve valued future outcomes, such as schooling, individuals are more motivated to succeed and participate in those activities. Thus, the lack of school instrumentality for future opportunities causes a resistance to schooling (Phalet, Andriessen, and Lens, 2004). First, Phalet (1992) studies the question whether migrant groups underachieve because of lack of opportunities or lack of motivation. This stems from a long research tradition that compares cultural values from Western and non-Western cultures. In this tradition, non-Western cultures are seen as less achievement-oriented and more collectivistic or group-oriented in contrast to more individualistic and achievement-oriented Western individuals. However, a more specific typology of cultural values may correspond better to reality. In this study, motivations of Turkish migrant youth in Belgium are compared with the motivations of Belgian and Turkish students in their country of origin. Results show that Turkish migrant students want to achieve *and* be loyal to their migrant group. These rather conflicting values with respect to education, lead to a negative dilemma for Turkish migrant students: while succeeding in school will be perceived as 'Belgian' and will be perceived as a loss for the Turkish family, educational underachievement will disappoint the family as well. Resulting from this, a social promotion model is presented that proposes more connection between the Turkish migrant community and the Belgian society. In this way, their members will be more able to achieve individually. In the study of Phalet and Claeys (1993), a higher preference for achievement in Turkish migrant students, compared to Belgian students, is explained by the 'overshooting' hypothesis. This hypothesis states that Turkish migrant students' self-realization is determined by the knowledge, skills, and preferences they have from the dominant culture. In the previously discussed study from Hermans (1994), the community attached more importance to aspects related to the classic family context than to school. Succeeding in life equaled mostly being able to provide for your family and having a job.

In addition to the exploration of achievement motivations of Turkish migrant students, another study from Phalet, Andriessen and Lens (2004) starts from the 'attitude-achievement' paradox that states that attitudes towards school are ambivalent as a result of experiences with racism and discrimination.

Schooling is perceived to be less instrumental for future success by minority students. Someone's living environment determines which hypotheses gains importance. Positive instrumentality and internal regulation is necessary to accomplish intrinsic motivation and adaptive learning in multicultural classrooms and subsequently to achieve educational success. The conditions of the future time perspective were later more specified in the following study of Andriessen, Phalet and Lens (2006). Only if migrant students perceive positive instrumentality and their schoolwork is internally regulated by future goals, they will pursue educational success. Although future goals are important for both migrant and native students, migrant students attach more importance to future goals.

Concluding from the 'cultural and educational outcomes' tradition, cultural factors affect educational outcomes. Both anthropological and social psychological approaches refer to the importance ethnic and racial minority youth attach to education. Identity is seen as an important factor that guides the vision and motivation for achievement. Starting from an anthropological approach, having a nationalist ideology appears to give meaning to education and acceptance in the community. Future goals, such as participation in Belgian society, determined by the adhered orientation, matter for education. Besides the influence of the country of origin, processes in the immigrant country are not neglected. In the immigrant country, the educational system is oriented towards the Belgian society and promotes it. Therefore, immigrant children experience incongruence between home and school cultures. Following a social psychological approach, group loyalty appears to be an important motivation that complicates the motivation to succeed in school. Following the future time perspective, future goals are an important motivator but only together with a perceived positive school instrumentality and internal regulation of school tasks. The context determines the instrumentality of school and the validity of the future time perspective. Despite their achievement motivation, migrant youth does not perform well in school. Migrant students experience more limited opportunities or cultural barriers in their school careers. This leads to a more ambivalent position towards future goals. Factors such as perceived future discrimination on the labor market may be discouraging and lead to lower educational outcomes.

Future research needs to focus more on the incongruence between home and school culture. First, more research questions needs to focus on differences between the home culture of immigrant children and children from lower socio-economic families. Second, developments over time and generations are important to better understand the different relations between the immigrant country and country of origin. Third, the difference between achievement motivations and actual educational achievement needs to be examined and interpreted in their context. Fourth, the study of actual and perceived hindering community forces, as mentioned by Ogbu (1984) and Hermans (2004), and its relation with education is left unexplored. Finally, the characteristics and the dynamics of the unique immigrant culture and its relationship to education should be studied on its own.

5.3.3   Language proficiency tradition

The role of language in explaining and reducing ethnic inequalities in education has traditionally attracted considerable interest from social policy-makers and researchers in Flanders. Although language is a part of culture, this research tradition specifically focuses on language proficiency, or the ability to speak or perform in an acquired language. Subsequently, the development and evaluation of specific curricula, pedagogy, or language projects in schools are interwoven with this research tradition. Before setting out this tradition, a short history of the various language projects is given as this tradition is often related to government-funded projects and research centers. Language proficiency studies start from a sociolinguistic and anthropological approach and use mainly qualitative methods.

In 1977, the European Economic Community (EEC) supported education in mother tongue languages to avoid problems when migrant children would return to their country of origin. This led to initiatives such as 'Education in Own Language and Culture' (*Onderwijs in Eigen Taal en Cultuur*). When it became clear that migrants did not return to their country of origin, policymakers questioned the usefulness of mother tongue education. Starting from the 'linguistic interdependence hypothesis' (Cummins, 1979), it was argued that students with another mother tongue would acquire better Dutch if their linguistic skills in their mother tongue are also developed. This was reflected in research as in 1989, most studies in this research tradition in Flanders are evaluation studies of 'mother tongue' projects (e.g. the Foyer project (Leman, 1997) and the EEC pilot experiment (Jaspaert, Lemmens, and van der Zanden, 1989)). Research results from the Foyer project show the importance of additive mother tongue education and the involvement of parents with school. Only if mother tongue teachers have the same social status as their colleagues, can mother tongue education be successful. It is difficult to conclude whether mother tongue education leads to better educational outcomes because positive outcomes are also related to effective school management and adequate guidance (Leman, 1997; 1999). Later, the focus to acquire languages shifted to learning sufficient Dutch to function in Belgian society. Upward social mobility is related to knowledge of and skills in the dominant language (Blommaert, Creve, and Willaert, 2006). Hence, the use of mother tongue education was first encouraged but later became perceived as a barrier to social integration (Jaspaert, 2006; Heyerick, 1985). Finally, the language acquisition of migrant children depends on the contact possibilities with Dutch-speaking children, however, most migrant children have less opportunities as they often attend schools with large concentrations of migrant students (Heyerick, 1985).

To conclude, many studies in the 'language proficiency' tradition adopt a sociolinguistic and anthropological approach. They are initiated by concerns of educational policy-makers and practitioners and often evaluate policy measures. This is often reflected in the studies as they conclude with specific policy and curriculum recommendations. In addition, the continuing conflict in Belgium between the Dutch and French linguistic communities influences the importance that policy-makers and society more generally attach to language. The focus of this tradition is the question whether education in the mother language facilitates the learning of other languages and education (Hermans, 2002). Although mother tongue education is proposed and favored in the previous studies, no scientific conclusions can be drawn. Mother tongue education is not enough to lead to successful educational outcomes and studies did not control for other determinants of success, such as effective school management (Leman, 1997, 1999). Most research in this tradition starts from the transition from initial school to primary school and focuses on language in the primary school (e.g. Agirdag, 2010). In general, these studies indicate that most Turkish and Moroccan students have insufficient Dutch language skills to fully understand their courses. This is explained by the lack of academic knowledge of their mother tongue and incongruence between the school and the home environment (Van den Branden and Van Avermaet, 2001).

The relationship between this research tradition and educational policies is not surprising for two reasons. First, language is an interesting tool for policy-makers because policies are more easily directed towards language than to other success determinants such as socio-economic status. For example, organizing extra language courses or language support in schools is easier than eliminating socio-economic inequalities. Secondly, the learning of the language of the immigrant country is closely related to integration perspectives. Initial policy projects are directed at language, as integration was expected to follow automatically. Early reports refer to the 'language disability' of immigrants (Koninklijk Commissariaat voor het Migrantenbeleid, 1989) and indicate the lack of recognition and appreciation for the immigrants' culture. The lack of language skills and knowledge is often interpreted as an unwillingness to integrate or adapt to Belgian society. Acquiring Dutch often implies willingness to adapt to the Belgian society. In contrast, the mother tongue is not recognized as valuable capital in the educational system (Blommaert et al., 2006; Agirdag, 2009a). Some research questions remain. First, the importance of the mother tongue for education should be studied more in detail as many of the discussed studies do give more clarity about the importance of language for educational outcomes of migrant youth. Second, the interaction between language and educational developments and how these developments are related to outcomes, such as social cohesion, ethnic identity, and well-being, in and outside the school context could give more insights in the importance of language for immigrant students.

5.3.4   Racism and racial discrimination in school tradition

'Research on racism and racial discrimination in school' has already been identified as a key research tradition in previous reviews on ethnic and racial inequalities (Stevens, 2007a; Stevens et al., 2011). In Flanders, experiences and perceptions of discrimination and school effects on ethnocentrism are tested. Two groups of researchers have addressed the relationship between racism and racial discrimination and educational outcomes for migrant youth differently.

A first group of researchers use large quantitative datasets to test experiences of discrimination (Vandezande et al., 2009) and school effects on ethnocentrism (Elchardus, Kavadius, and Siongers, 1999). Based on data from the TIES project,[5] Vandezande and colleagues (2009) show that the majority of ethnic and racial minority students do not feel less comfortable at school compared to majority students. Men of Moroccan and Turkish descent more often feel discriminated over their school career compared to women. No differences in experiences of discrimination are found according to the followed track. Students experience rather incidental experiences of racism and more in relationship to the labor market than at school. Results from the study of Elchardus, Kavadius and Siongers (1999) indicate that the school should not be neglected as a socializing force. Net school effects explain a part of the variance in ethnocentrism of the pupils and the authors suggest that the school has an important socializing effect on its students, alongside other socializing agents, such as the family and cultural factors. These studies start from the prevalence of racism and discrimination in Belgian society, politics, and schools.

A second body of literature exists of ethnographic studies and explored the perception of racism and unequal treatment in secondary schools from a symbolic interactionist perspective (Stevens, 2008b; Stevens and Van Houtte, 2011). Stevens (2008a) finds that Turkish and Belgian vocational education pupils change their perception of racism according to their interactions in a particular social context. Pupils define teacher racism as a variety of different teacher attitudes and behaviors that express a less favorable opinion of ethnic-minority pupils or result in less favorable outcomes for such pupils. In addition, teachers devise particular strategies to avoid being perceived a racist. Despite being labeled as a 'racist teacher', teachers can still be perceived as 'good teachers' if they are able to fulfill their role as a teacher. In Stevens's (2008b) research, three types of pupils are considered by pupils as legitimate recipients of differential treatment from teachers: the ill, the stragglers, and deviants. Deviants can expect a less favorable treatment, whereas the ill and the stragglers are entitled to a more favorable treatment: the ill because of medical reasons and the stragglers are seen as pupils who are victims of their social situation. However, these pupils need to demonstrate a willingness to develop into 'healthy' or 'normal' pupils and failure to do so can result in them being labeled as deviants. Conflicts among pupils or between pupils and teachers can emerge over the legitimate nature of these statuses and the kind of treatment meted out to pupils in the process of status recovery. Such conflicts can in turn explain to some extent the observed variability between pupils in making claims of teacher racism or discrimination. In addition to this, Stevens (2010) finds that pupils in general have little experience with teacher racism. Teachers' attitudes and social acts are an indication of teacher racism. The perception of teacher racism is determined by six different factors: (i) intention to be a racist, (ii) the value the pupils attach to racist attitudes and social acts, (iii) the universal application of racist attitudes and social acts, (iv) being labeled as deviant, (v) unequal teacher treatment, and (vi) whether these racist attitudes obstruct teachers from being a 'good' teacher. These studies focus on teacher racism and the situations in which unequal treatment is justified by pupils.

In sum, racism and discrimination processes are often expected or assumed to have an influence on educational outcomes, but few studies have examined this in detail. No differences in experiences of racism are found in large quantitative datasets (Vandezande et al., 2008). From a symbolic interactionist perspective, the perception of racism and unequal treatment in secondary schools differs according to the interactions between students and teachers and the particular social context in which they take place (Stevens, 2008a, 2008b). Although these studies cast light on the difficulty of measuring experiences of racism, little research has been done to assess how different forms of discrimination at various levels in the society develop and affect educational and wider outcomes for ethnic minority students. In addition, there needs to be more research on students' coping strategies in response to racism and discrimination, and the impact of discrimination on different levels of the society. Finally, differences between tracks and school effects, including school policies, need to be examined (see Stevens and Görgöz, 2010).

5.3.5 School effectiveness tradition

Due to the free parental school choice, the geographic concentration of immigrant groups, and to a lesser extent the school policies, schools became ethnically segregated and in general, both immigrant and non-immigrant parents prefer 'white schools' over 'black schools' (Desmedt and Nicaise, 2006). Policymakers would like to see the school to be a reflection of the social mix in society as this is believed to stimulate social integration and cohesion. Therefore, policy-makers want to desegregate schools and create a social mix to enhance immigrant students' academic achievement and later occupational success (Mahieu, 2002). Since the 'non-discrimination policy' in 1993, the Flemish government has striven for more social mix in the schools. They did not change the free parental school choice but schools are given incentives, such as extra resources, to take more students from deprived families, such as immigrant students. In Flanders, mainly two domains are studied in this tradition: the school ethnic composition and the effective schools for ethnic and racial pupils. School effects are very interesting to policy-makers as they are easier to control and to influence (e.g. compared to family background variables). Thus, although there are also theoretical reasons to examine school effects, considerable research in this tradition is funded to evaluate policy measures and to inform educational policy-makers.

As described above, the LOSO project was initially designed to evaluate the educational system and the functioning of schools. Several studies use the LOSO data to examine school effects. Pupils who also speak languages other than Dutch at home are categorized as having an ethnic and racial background. In a study from Van Damme and colleagues (2001) language spoken at home is found to have no influence on achievement in mathematics and Dutch. Class group characteristics, such as the presence of girls or a cognitive group, are more important for these achievements. Results from the study of Opdenakker and colleagues (2002) indicate that the school ability composition is more important than the percentage of students who spoke another language at home. Based on the Flemish Trends in International Mathematics and Science study of 1999 (TIMMS)[6], Van den Broeck, Opdenakker and Van Damme (2005) find that 28% of the variation in scores of mathematics is explained at the class group level, 14% at the school level and 58% at the individual level. Class groups explain a considerable part of scores in mathematics as the intake characteristics of class groups are mainly determined by intelligence and this is strengthened by the tracked educational system of Flanders. Subsequently, a study from Jacobs and his colleagues (2009) found that students going to schools with a higher percentage of high socio-economic status students and a low number of immigrants have higher test scores than in other schools. The authors argue that school structures explain a high variation of test scores and reproduce inequality. However, Agirdag (2009b) remarks the methodological problems of this study, such as having only a small number of immigrant students in the dataset, leading to a bias in the school composition effects, and intermediate processes that explain school effects on test scores were not included.

Another large-scale quantitative survey, the 'Flemish Educational Assessment' (*Vlaams Leerlingen Onderzoek*, VLO), focuses on the relationship between the pupils and its school environment and its influences on school achievement and well-being. Based on this database, Van Houtte and Stevens (2009)[7] explore the composition of schools and native and immigrants' student interethnic friendships, social participation, and sense of belonging in school. This study is theoretically inspired by and started from Blau's structural theory (1977). According to Blau, social integration in the society is determined by the prevalence of relationships among different groups and segments of society. This structural theory is based on two assumptions: first, people prefer to associate with in-group members, and second, people choose to associate with out-group members over no association with anybody and isolation. Blau set the framework to study the relationship between ethnic school composition and the number of interethnic friendships and social integration outside school. The study of Van Houtte and Stevens (2009) confirms Blau's theory as the results show that school ethnic composition is associated with interethnic friendships and social participation for native students, but not for immigrant students, whereas socio-economic status is decisive for immigrant students' interethnic friendships. Immigrant students report more interethnic friendships than do natives. Neither immigrants' nor natives' sense of belonging in school is associated with ethnic composition. The authors suggest that mixing schools appears to have a positive influence on the social integration of Flemish youth. Although this study starts from a sociological theory, additional inspiration is found by policy aims to desegregate schools in order to avoid underachievement. In another study of Van Houtte and Stevens (2010), immigrant students' intentions to finish high school and to move on to higher education and school ethnic composition are tested. Effects of ethnic school composition are found but can be explained by the students' socio-economic status and the socio-economic context of the school. Students in 'low concentration' schools (enrolling less than 20% immigrant students) are twice as likely to plan to finish high school and to plan for higher education than those attending 'high concentration' schools (more than 50% immigrant students). Furthermore, immigrant students in high concentration schools have slightly higher aspirations to finish high school and to start higher education than those in medium concentration schools. This effect illustrates a more optimistic culture in high concentration schools. In general, the studies from Van Houtte and Stevens conclude that schools with high percentages of allochthonous students are not necessarily detrimental for students' educational aspirations. Neither do they conclude whether the government should opt for more desegregated or segregated schools. Nevertheless, the ethnic school composition has more indirect effects on educational outcomes with decisive consequences. For example, in the study of Van Maele and Van Houtte (2009), based on the same dataset, teachers' trust in parents is lower in schools with a higher proportion of immigrant students. The ethnic school composition does not have an influence on the teachers' trust in students if the socio-economic school composition is included in the model.

As already mentioned by Van Houtte and Stevens (2010), aspirations and future plans do not necessarily correspond to actual drop-out rates and enrollment in higher education. This is tested in the study of Vandezande and colleagues (2009), based on the TIES data. They find in Antwerp and Brussels that ethnically segregated schools decrease the odds of finishing schools and moving on to higher education for both immigrant and non-immigrant students. In ethnically segregated schools, there are fewer protective factors present, such as positive relationships with non-immigrant students and teachers. More immigrant students are present in lower-status tracks and these schools are more often segregated along ethnic lines. Due to this 'double cascade effect', the achievement gap between native and immigrant students increases.

School effects are also studied from a more sociolinguistic perspective. Van den Branden and Van Avermaet (2001) argue that heterogeneity in the classroom could be beneficial in terms of language learning and other skills. Students with high and low language proficiencies could help each other making tasks together. Students with a higher language proficiency benefit from learning to explain things to their peers, while students with a lower language proficiency could learn from being taught (partially) in their own language. Leman (1999) points out that language is a visible characteristic of the ethnic composition of a school and is used as a tool by the school management. By prohibiting languages from ethnic and racial minorities, more non-immigrants students can be attracted because of the more 'white' outlook of the school.

In sum, most studies that focus on school effects tested whether school ethnic composition has an influence on the non-immigrant and immigrant students in school. These studies, sometimes framed on sociological theories of in-out group relations, are inspired by public debates on and an interest of social policy-makers in the consequences of ethnic segregation in schools; schools are perceived as the ideal institution to help integrate immigrants in society. To realize this, schools are expected to reflect the social and ethnic mix in society and this vision influences parental school choice. Studies found that school characteristics influence students' outcomes. The school ethnic composition is of importance for interethnic friendships (Van Houtte and Stevens, 2009; Vandezande et al., 2009) and the development of cooperation skills (Van den Branden and Van Avermaet, 2001). In contrast, Van Damme and colleagues (2001) argue that the school ability composition is more important compared to the ethnic composition. Future research could build on this developing research tradition in various ways. First, the intermediate processes that relate school characteristics and students' outcomes could explain why and in which ways school characteristics influence their students (e.g. by different pedagogic approaches (Irizarry and Antrop-Gonzalez, 2007; Villegas, 1991)). Second, previous research by Van Houtte and Stevens (2010) found that school effects have an impact on future aspirations through the lack of accurate information about social mobility in some schools. Analogue to this research, more attention should be paid to the school culture or climate to explain variations in achievement. In the last section, an overview of the different research traditions, suggestions for future research and the limitations of this study are given.

5.4   Conclusions and discussion

In reviewing research on race and ethnic inequalities in Flanders, we could identify five main research traditions: (1) the 'political arithmetic' tradition, (2) the 'cultural and educational outcomes' tradition, (3) the 'language proficiency' tradition, (4) the 'racial and racial discrimination in school' tradition and (5) the 'school effectiveness research' tradition. The 'political arithmetic' tradition is based on large quantitative datasets and reveals the impact of socio-economic and ethnic or racial background on education. These studies indicate that most variation is explained by socio-economic background. However, ethnic and racial background is found to have an effect, but only in certain socio-economic conditions (Hermans 2004). In addition, minorities experience ethnic and cultural barriers (Groenez et al., 2003) as well as an ethnic disadvantage due to institutional discrimination (Phalet et al., 2007). Both an anthropological and social psychological approach can be found in the 'cultural and educational outcomes' tradition that focuses on cultural differences. Anthropologists paid attention to cultural orientations towards education, the country of origin, and the dominant ethnic majority values that prevail in the Flemish educational system. While social psychologists find that future goals can be motivating and lead to educational success when they are combined with a perceived positive school instrumentality and internal regulation of school tasks, lower achievement is explained by perceived discrimination in the labor market. In the 'language proficiency' tradition, qualitative methods are used to examine particular educational policies concerning language. This research tradition focuses on the question whether mother language instruction facilitates the learning of other languages and leads to better educational outcomes. This tradition is very policy-oriented and more theory-oriented research is necessary to confirm these theories and inspire future policies. Quantitative research in the 'racism and racial discrimination in school' tradition finds little evidence of experiences of racism in school (Vandezande et al., 2009). However, ethnographic research shows that perceptions of racism and unequal treatment in secondary schools vary according to the way in which concepts like 'teacher racism' and 'equal/unequal treatment' are defined through interactions between students and teachers (Stevens, 2008a, 2008b). Finally, with respect to ethnic and racial inequality in education in Flanders, the 'school effectiveness' tradition examines the impact of the school ethnic composition based on quantitative datasets. The school ethnic composition influences friendships and interactions between children from a different ethnic background during their courses.

Concluding from this review, research traditions in Flanders cannot be studied separately from social/educational policies and societal tendencies. The 'language proficiency' and the 'political arithmetic' tradition are interwoven with social and educational policy as they want to inform policy-makers. The databases from the 'political arithmetic' tradition are gathered to map out tendencies and patterns of racial and ethnic inequalities in education while the 'language proficiency' tradition evaluates educational policies and projects. Furthermore, although the 'school effectiveness' tradition is more internationally oriented and aims to identify school effects and how they are related to achievement, this research is inspired by the public concern for the integration of immigrants in the Belgian society, the phenomenon of a 'white flight' and the creation of 'concentration' schools. Nevertheless, the relationship between research and policy has changed over time. During the last decades, research practices changed from policy-oriented research, written in Dutch in order to evaluate policies and inform policy-makers, to the writing of PhD dissertations in Dutch and, more recently, to the publication of internationally peer-reviewed journal articles in English. Thus, although research remains inspired by policies, research practices in Flanders have changed and publishing in international peer-reviewed journals, and related to this: the development of social theory, gained importance.

Suggestions for future research can be made from this review. First, the inclusion of a wider variety of educational outcomes could help to understand processes that influence achievement, for example, by focusing on success determinants and including school career variables (Crul, 2000), study and school choices (Boone and Van Houtte, 2010; Sannen, Lamberts, Morissons, and Pauwels, 2009). Subsequently, influencing factors, such as immigrant community characteristics, migration policies, and the national educational context, help to contextualize the studied relationships. Intermediate processes, such as stereotype threats in school, can help to understand ethnic and racial inequality and school effects. Furthermore, by combining different socializing contexts, such as the school, family, peer groups, and leisure activities, in an ecological model, or following developments over time, a more comprehensive view can be given of the longitudinal processes and the relationship between different contexts that influence educational inequality.

Second, research that focused on cultural differences in the 'cultural and educational outcomes' and the 'language proficiency' tradition, indicated the importance of internal variability within and between ethnic and racial minority groups. More research needs to be done to grasp the different living conditions of immigrant communities (Fleischmann et al., 2011), differences between immigrant generations and the initial migration motivations (Hermans, 2004), the existence of social and ethnic capital, the ethnic composition of a city, and the structure of the immigrant communities in each city (Fleischmann et al., 2011). Subsequently, in studies from Timmerman (1995) and Hermans (1995), indications are given that the importance and significance of gender for education is culturally determined. In contrast to these cultural studies, the 'political arithmetic' tradition explains underachievement of ethnic and racial minority students mainly by the socio-economic background. However, the relation and overlap with cultural and socio-economic effects on education is not examined sufficiently, for example by comparing ethnic and racial minority students with low socio-economic background majority students.

Third, the methods used in the different research traditions lead often to different approaches and findings and are rarely combined in the same study. Even within research traditions, such as the 'racism and racial discrimination' and the 'cultural and educational outcomes' tradition, different approaches are distinguished based on the applied methods. However, they do not complement or influence each other. In contrast, the other research traditions only use quantitative or qualitative research methods and they could benefit from mixed method approach to test their theory (e.g. the 'language proficiency' tradition) or find underlying processes (e.g. 'school effectiveness' and 'political arithmetic' tradition) of their results.

Finally, some internationally distinguished research traditions are not (well) developed in Flanders such as the 'family background tradition' as in the Netherlands (Stevens et al., 2011) and the 'educational markets and educational outcomes' as in England (Stevens, 2007a) and no attention is given to the 'acting white' theory from Fordham and Ogbu (1986) which is frequently studied in the United States.

Some remarks about this review have to be made. First, only the literature of ethnic and racial inequality in secondary education in Flanders was considered, however, the comparison of the educational systems and practices between French, German and Dutch linguistic communities and the special case of Brussels may give interesting insights into the organization of education with respect to ethnic and racial minorities. No research on ethnic and racial inequality in education in the German linguistic community was found. This is a small community which is authorized for nine municipalities, and in only four of the nine municipalities, namely Eupen, Raeren, Lontzen, and Kelmis, live students with a foreign nationality (FOD Economie, KMO Middenstand en Energie, 2011). However, when comparing education in the French and Dutch linguistic community, some distinct patterns emerge. Although both communities have similar educational structures, different educational practices occur. Regional differences are found in the way these linguistic communities deal with students that do not have satisfactory results. Failing students in the Dutch linguistic community are more often oriented towards technical and vocational tracks. In contrast, students in the French linguistic community are more encouraged to repeat their year when results are not satisfactory, in order to improve achievement in the following year. Nevertheless, repeating a year did not necessarily improve students' achievement but seemed associated with psychological problems, such as having a low self-esteem. These differences can be explained by the fact that education in Flanders uses a more Anglo-Saxon approach and is oriented towards the Dutch system, while education in the French linguistic community has more in common with the French system where repeating a year is common. Although no differences in the ethnic gap were found across linguistic communities, these educational practices have resulted in distinct achievement patterns for ethnic and racial minority students. In the Dutch linguistic community, a higher proportion of ethnic and racial minority students finish secondary education with a diploma and without delays while the French linguistic community is characterized by higher drop-out rates but more ethnic and racial minority students complete secondary school in an academic track. As a consequence, a higher proportion of ethnic and racial minority students have the possibility to pursue higher education (Ouali and Réa, 1994; Varin, 2006; Jacobs et al., 2009; Phalet et al., 2007). Besides educational practices, regional governments implement different educational and social policies. For example, the French linguistic government focuses on disadvantaged students while the Dutch linguistic government differentiates and is directed at the specific situation of ethnic and racial background students (Florence and Martiniello, 2005). Finally, the organization of education in linguistic communities has resulted in the existence of a bilingual region, Brussels, where both French and Dutch linguistic communities offer education. In this region, school choice becomes more important in Brussels as parents are free to choose between these communities. Since the 1980s, Dutch-speaking schools in Brussels were seen as an insurance for the future and chosen because of the lower number of migrant children in these schools. However, schools are characterized by a larger language heterogeneity (Van den Branden and Van Avermaet, 2001; D'hondt, 1993). By studying schools in Brussels and comparing these schools with schools in Flanders, the importance of the linguistic school context and language for ethnic and racial minority students could be better understood. In sum, the comparison of different educational systems gives insight into the influence of characteristics of educational systems, approaches towards migrant populations, and the ethnic school or neighborhood school composition.

Second, although this review was limited to secondary education, by including research in initial and primary schools (e.g. Agirdag, 2009a; 2010; Agirdag, Van Houtte, and Van Avermaet, 2010; Agirdag and Demanet, 2011; Groenez, Van den Brande and Nicaise, 2003; Soenen, 2002), initial disadvantages in secondary education can be considered. In addition, the transition from secondary school to higher studies (e.g. Glorieux, Laurijssen, and Van Dorsselaer, 2008; Van Craen and Almaci, 2005; Lacante et al., 2007) and/or the labor market (Neels and Stoop, 2000; Glorieux et al., 2008; Glorieux and Laurijssen,

2009; Duquet et al., 2006; Glorieux, Laurijssen, and Van Dorsselaer, 2009; Verhoeven and Martens, 2000; Neels, 2000; Vandezande et al., 2008) are other, important areas of research that need to be considered.

In sum, five research traditions are distinguished in Flanders with specific research questions and methods. Research in Flanders has transformed from policy-oriented and small-scale projects to international publications. The combination of different research traditions and methods and a wider variety of educational outcomes, processes, and interactions are examined, will lead to more insights in explaining racial and ethnic inequality in education.

Notes

1. The LOSO project has collected data since 1990 to evaluate the system and the functioning of schools. In 1997, 6441 pupils from 90 schools were questioned at the beginning and end of every school year.
2. The PSBH is a longitudinal panel survey that started in 1992 and questioned every year until 2002. The objective of this survey was policy review and analysis, focusing on socio-economic themes and family sociology. From 1994, the PSBH was integrated in the European Community Household Panel (ECHP). In 1992, the panel started with 4438 households, including 8741 adults and 2591 children. More households were added in the seventh wave. In 2002, 2959 households, with 5362 adults and 1634 children, were retained.
3. Since 1999, the longitudinal database SONAR questioned different cohorts (1976, 1978, and 1980) at 23, 26, and 29 years. This database was funded by the Flemish Government and since 2000 part of 'Center for Careers of Pupils and Students in Education and the Transition to the Labor Market'. Results from this report were based on 9010 23-year olds from three different cohorts.
4. Belgium is one of the countries included in the PISA funded by OECD. The acquired knowledge and skills essential to participate in society from 15-year-old students was measured. Reading, mathematical, and scientific literacy were not only seen in terms of mastery of the school curriculum, but also as knowledge and skills required for adult life. Assessments have been carried out in 2000, 2003, 2006, and 2009. The Belgian results consist of the mean between the Dutch- and French-speaking communities and are sometimes separately discussed.
5. The TIES study focuses on the integration of the second generation of immigrants from Turkey, Morocco, and former Yugoslavia in eight European countries (Austria, Belgium, France, the Netherlands, Germany, Spain, Switzerland, and Sweden). In the Belgian survey, immigrants from Morocco, Turkey and a Belgian comparison group (measured by place of birth) were included. Data was collected in 2007 and 2008 (1751 respondents). For more information see Stevens et al. (2011).
6. The TIMMS questioned students in their second year of secondary education (Grade 8) in 38 countries in several years. Flanders participated in 1995 (eighth grade), 1999 (eighth grade), 2003 (fourth and eighth grade), and 2011 (fourth grade). In 1999, an extended TIMMS questionnaire was used. A two-stage design was used. First, schools were selected and, secondly, two classes were questioned in each school. A total of 133 schools, 261 classes and 4168 students are included in the sample. In addition, mathematics and sciences teachers, and principals filled in a questionnaire.

7. Data from 85 Flemish schools in the third and fifth year of these schools was gathered between 2004 and 2005 and 11,872 students and 2104 teachers were questioned.

References

Agirdag, O. (2009a). All languages welcomed here. *Educational Leadership, 66* (7), 20–25.

Agirdag, O. (2009b). Book review. Jacobs, D., Rea, A., Teney, C., Callier, L. and Lothaire, S. (2009). *De sociale lift blijft steken. De prestaties van allochtone leerlingen in de Vlaamse Gemeenschap en de Franse Gemeenschap*, Brussels: Koning Boudewijnstichting, 92 p. *Tijdschrift voor Sociologie, 3*, 318–321.

Agirdag, O. (2010). Exploring bilingualism in a monolingual school system: Insights from Turkish and native students from Belgian schools. *British Journal of Sociology of Education, 31* (3), 307–321.

Agirdag, O. and Demanet, J. (2011). Ethnic school composition and peer victimization: A focus on the interethnic school climate. *International Journal of Intercultural Relations, 35* (4), 465–473.

Agirdag, O., Van Houtte, M., and Van Avermaet, P. (2010). Ethnic school context and the national and sub-national identifications of pupils. *Ethnic and Racial Studies, 34* (2), 357–378.

Andriessen, I., Phalet, K., and Lens, W. (2006). Future goal setting, task motivation and learning of minority and non-minority students in Dutch schools. *British Journal of Educational Psychology, 76*, 827–850.

Blau, P.M. (1977). *Inequality and heterogeneity: A primitive theory of social structure* (p. 307). New York: Free Press.

Blommaert, J., Creve, L., and Willaert, E. (2006). On being declared illiterate: Language-ideological disqualification in Dutch classes for immigrants in Belgium. *Language & Communication, 26* (1), 34–54.

Blommaert, J. and Verschueren, J. (1992). *Het Belgische migrantendebat. De pragmatiek van de abnormalisering.* Antwerp: IPrA Research Center, Universitaire Instelling Antwerpen.

Boone, S. and Van Houtte, M. (2010). *Sociale ongelijkheid bij overgang van basis – naar secundair onderwijs. Eindrapport van het OBPWO-project 07.03.*

Boos-Nünning, U. et al. (1986). *Towards intercultural education. A comparative study of education of migrant children in Belgium, England, France and the Netherlands.* London: Centre for Information on Language Teaching and Research.

Caremans, P., Mahieu, P., and Yildirim, S. (2004). Over werkelijkheid, wettelijkheid en wenselijkheid in het onderwijs. In C. Timmerman, I. Lodewijckx, D. Vanheule, and J. Wets (Eds), *Wanneer wordt vreemd, vreemd? De vreemde in beeldvorming, registratie en beleid* (pp. 109–126). Leuven: Acco.

CGKR (2010). *Statistische en demografische verslag 2009.* Migranties en migrantenpopulaties in België. Brussels: Centrum voor Gelijkheid van Kansen en voor Racismebestrijding.

Crul, M. (2000). *De sleutel tot succes: Over hulp, keuzes en kansen in de schoolloopbanen van turkse en marokkaanse jongeren van de tweede generatie.* Amsterdam: Het Spinhuis.

Cummins, J. (1979). Linguistic interdependence and the educational-development of bilingual-children. *Review of Educational Research, 49* (2), 222–251.

D'hondt, A.-S. (1993). Taalproblematiek in het Brusselse onderwijs. In P. Frantzen (Ed.), *Nederlandstalige Brusselaars in een multiculturele samenleving* (pp. 151–172). Brussels: VUB Press.

de Heus, M. and Dronkers, J. (2010). De schoolprestaties van immigrantenkinderen in 16 OECD-landen. De invloed van onderwijsstelsels en overige samenlevingskenmerken van zowel herkomst- als bestemmingslanden. *Tijdschrift voor Sociologie, 31* (3–4), 260–294.

De Wit, K., Van Petegem, P., and De Maeyer, S. (2000). *Gelijke kansen in het Vlaamse onderwijs. Het beleid inzake kansengelijkheid* (p. 63). Leuven: Garant.

Desmedt, E. and Nicaise, I. (2006). Etnische segregatie in het onderwijs: horen, zien en zwijgen? In S. Sierens, M. Van Houtte, P. Loobuyck, K. Delrue, and K. Pelleriaux (Eds), *Onderwijs onderweg in de immigratiesamenleving* (pp. 91–108). Ghent: Academia Press.

Dupriez, V., Dumay, X., and Vause, A. (2008). How do school systems manage pupils' Heterogeneity?. *Comparative Education Review, 52* (2), 245–273.

Duquet, N., Glorieux, I., Laurijssen, I., and Van Dorsslaer, Y. (2006). *Wit krijt schrijft beter. Schoolloopbanen van allochtone jongeren in beeld* (p. 106). Antwerp-Apeldoorn: Garant.

Elchardus, M., Kavadius, D., and Siongers, J. (1999). Instroom of school? De invloed van scholen en andere socialisatievelden op de houdingen van leerlingen. *Mens & Maatschappij, 74* (3), 250–268.

Fleischmann, F., Phalet, K., Neels, K., and Deboosere, P. (2011). Contextualizing ethnic educational inequality: The role of stability and quality of neighborhoods and ethnic density in second-generation attainment. *International Migration Review, 45* (2), 386–425.

Flemish Ministry of Education and Training (Vlaams Ministerie van Onderwijs en Vorming). (2011a). Site van het Vlaams Ministerie van Onderwijs en Vorming. http://www.ond.vlaanderen.be.

Flemish Ministry of Education and Training. (2011b). Schoolse vorderingen en zittenblijven in het voltijds gewoon secundair onderwijs. http://www.ond.vlaanderen.be.

Florence, E. and Martiniello, M. (2005). Social science research and public policies: The case of immigration in Belgium. *International Journal on Multicultural Societies, 7* (1), 49–67.

FOD Economie, KMO Middenstand en Energie (2011). Bevolking naar nationaliteit. http://economie.fgov.be/nl/statistieken/cijfers/bevolking/.

Fordham, S. and Ogbu, J. U. (1986). Black students' school success: Coping with the burden of acting white. *Urban Review, 18* (3), 176–206.

Glorieux, I. and Laurijssen, I. (2009). *The labour market integration of ethnic minorities in Flanders. Summary of the main findings concerning the entry into the labour market of youth migrant descent* Brussels: Vrije Universiteit Brussel.

Glorieux, I., Laurijssen, I., and Van Dorsselaer, Y. (2008). *De intrede van allochtonen op de arbeidsmarkt.* (Rep. No. SSL/OD2/2008.08). Leuven: Steunpunt Studie en Schoolloopbanen.

Glorieux, I., Laurijssen, I., and Van Dorsselaer, Y. (2009). *Zwart op wit. De intrede van allochtonen op de arbeidsmarkt. [Black on white. The entry of non-natives into the labour market].* Antwerp-Apeldoorn: Garant.

Groenez, S., Van den Brande, I., and Nicaise, I. (2003). *Cijferboek sociale ongelijkheid in het Vlaamse onderwijs. Een verkennend onderzoek op de Panelstudie van Belgische huishoudens.* Leuven: Steunpunt LOA.

Hermans, D. J., Opdenakker, M.-C., and Van Damme, J. (2003). *Ongelijke kansen in het secundair onderwijs in Vlaanderen. Een longitudinale analyse van de interactie-effecten van geslacht, etniciteit en socio-economische status op de bereikte onderwijspositie: een vervolg* (Rep. No. LAO-rapport 7). Leuven: Cel voor Analyse van Onderwijsloopbanen.

Hermans, D. J., Opdenakker, M.-C., Van de gaer, E., and Van Damme, J. (2002). *Ongelijke kansen in het secundair onderwijs in Vlaanderen. Een longitudinale analyse van de interactie-effecten van geslacht, etniciteit en socio-economische status op de bereikte onderwijspositie* (Rep. No. LAO-rapport 17). Leuven: Cel voor analyse van Onderwijsloopbanen.

Hermans, P. (1994). *Opgroeien als Marokkaan in Brussel. Een antropologisch onderzoek over de educatie, de leefwereld en de 'inpassing' van Marokkaanse jongens.* Brussels: Cultuur en Migratie.

Hermans, P. (1995). Moroccan immigrants and school success. *International Journal of Educational Research, 23* (1), 33–43.

Hermans, P. (2002). Etnische minderheden en schoolsucces. Een overzicht van de diverse benaderingswijzen. In C. Timmerman, P. Hermans, and J. Hoornaert (Eds), *Allochtone jongeren in het onderwijs. een multidisciplinair perspectief* (pp. 21–42). Leuven/Apeldoorn: Garant.

Hermans, P. (2004). Applying Ogbu's theory of minority academic achievement to the situation of Moroccans in the Low countries. *Intercultural Education, 15* (4), 431–438.

Heyerick, L. (1985). Problemen van migrantenkinderen en hun leerkrachten in het Vlaams basisonderwijs. In *Buitenlandse minderheden in Vlaanderen-België* (pp. 103–122). Antwerp/Amsterdam: De Nederlandse Boekhandel.

Irizarry, J. G. and Antrop-Gonzalez, R. (2007). RicanStructing the discourse and promoting school success: Extending a theory of culturally responsive pedagogy for DiaspoRicans. *Centro Journal, 19* (2), 36–59.

Jacobs, D., Rea, A., and Hanquinet, L. (2007). *Prestaties van de leerlingen van buitenlandse herkomst in België volgens de PISA studie. Vergelijking tussen de Franse Gemeenschap en de Vlaamse Gemeenschap.* Brussels: Koning Boudewijnstichting.

Jacobs, D., Rea, A., Teney, C., Callier, L., and Lothaire, S. (2009). *De sociale lift blijft steken. De prestaties van allochtone leerlingen in de Vlaamse Gemeenschap en de Franse Gemeenschap* Brussels: Koning Boudewijnstichting.

Jaspaert, K. (2006). Taal, onderwijs en achterstandsbestrijding: enkele overwegingen. In S. Sierens, M. Van Houtte, P. Loobuyck, K. Delrue, and K. Pelleriaux (Eds), *Onderwijs onderweg in de immigratiesamenleving* (pp. 139–164). Ghent: Academia Press.

Jaspaert, K., Lemmens, G., and van der Zanden, A. (1989). *E.E.G.-Pilootexperiment Moedertaal en cultuur in het secundair onderwijs. Onderzoek naar taalvaardigheidsniveau bij Turkse en Italiaanse kinderen bij het begin van het secundair onderwijs* Hasselt: Provinciale dienst Limburg.

Koninklijk Commissariaat voor het migrantenbeleid. (1989). Integratie(beleid): een werk van lange adem. Deel II: Beleid en beleidsvisies. (p. 91). Brussels: Koninklijk Commissariaat voor het migrantenbeleid.

Lacante, M., Almaci, M., Van Esbroeck, R., Lens, W., and De Metsenaere, M. (2007). *Allochtonen in het hoger onderwijs: Onderzoek naar factoren van studiekeuze en studiesucces bij allochtone eerstejaarsstudenten in het hoger onderwijs. In opdracht van de Vlaamse Minister voor Onderwijs en Vorming, in het kader van het 'OBPWO-programma'.* Brussels/ Leuven: Vrije Universiteit Brussel/Katholieke Universiteit Leuven.

Leman, J. (1997). School as a socialising and corrective force in inter-ethnic urban relations. *Journal of Multilingual and Multicultural Development, 18* (2), 125–134.

Leman, J. (1999). School as a structuring force in interethnic hybridism. *International Journal of Educational Research, 31* (4), 341–353.

Mahieu, P. (2002). Desegregatie in functie van integratie. In C. Timmerman, P. Hermans, and J. Hoornaert (Eds), *Allochtone jongeren in het onderwijs. een multidisciplinair perspectief* (pp. 205–232). Leuven: Garant.

Marks, G. N. (2005). Accounting for immigrant non-immigrant differences in reading and mathematics in twenty countries. *Ethnic and Racial Studies, 28* (5), 925–946.

Neels, K. (2000). Education and the transition to employment: Young Turkish and Moroccan adults in Belgium. In R. Lesthaeghe (Ed.), *Communities and generations. Turkish and Moroccan populations in Belgium* (pp. 243–278). Brussels: Steunpunt demografie and VUB University Press.

Neels, K. and Stoop, R. (2000). Reassessing the ethnic gap: Employment of younger Turks and Moroccans in Belgium. In R. Lesthaeghe (Ed.), *Communities and generations. Turkish and Moroccan populations in Belgium* (pp. 279–320). Brussels: Steunpunt Demografie en VUB University Press.

OECD. (2010). PISA 2009 Results: Overcoming Social Background: Equity in Learning Opportunities and Outcomes (Vol. II). http://www.oecd.org/document/24/0,3746, en_32252351_46584327_46609752_1_1_1_1,00.html.

Ogbu, J. U. (1984). Family life and school achievement: Why poor black children succeed or fail. *The Social Service Review, 58* (4), 649–652.

Opdenakker, M.-C., Van Damme, J., De Fraine, B., Van Landeghem, G., and Onghena, P. (2002). The effects of schools and classes on mathematics achievement. *School Effectiveness and School Improvement, 13* (29), 399–427.

Ouali, N. and Réa, A. (1994). La scolarité des élèves d'origine étrangère (The schooling of pupils of foreign origin). *Cahiers de Sociologie et d'Economie Régionales, 21–22*, 7–56.

Phalet, K. (1992). Groepsgerichtheid en prestatiemotivatie bij Turkse migrantenjongeren. *Tijdschrift voor Sociologie, 13*, 157–188.

Phalet, K., Andriessen, I., and Lens, W. (2004). How future goals enhance motivation and learning in multicultural classrooms. *Educational Psychology Review, 16* (1), 59–89.

Phalet, K. and Claeys, W. (1993). A comparative-study of Turkish and Belgian youth. *Journal of Cross-Cultural Psychology, 24* (3), 319–343.

Phalet, K., Deboosere, P., and Bastiaenssen, V. (2007). Old and new inequalities in educational attainment – Ethnic minorities in the Belgian Census 1991–2001. *Ethnicities, 7* (3), 390–415.

Sannen, L., Lamberts, M., Morissons, A., and Pauwels, F. (2009). *De Vlaamse integratiekaart Deel III: Naar een Vlaamse integratiemonitor. Tussentijds verslag over de bevindingen binnen het project 2007–2011 'Ontwikkeling van de Vlaamse integratiemonitor'.* Antwerp, Hasselt: Steunpunt Gelijkekansenbeleid. Consortium Universiteit Antwerpen en Universiteit Hasselt.

Sierens, S. (2006). Immigratiesamenleving, onderwijs en overheid in Vlaanderen: een gespannen driehoeksverhouding. In S. Sierens, M. Van Houtte, P. Loobuyck, K. Delrue, and K. Pelleriaux (Eds), *Onderwijs onderweg in de immigratiesamenleving* (pp. 9–32). Ghent: Academia Press.

Sierens, S., Van Houtte, M., Loobuyck, P., Delrue, K., and Pelleriaux, K. (2006). *Onderwijs onderweg in de immigratiesamenleving.* Ghent: Academia Press.

Soenen, R. (2002). Een nieuwe sound op de jukebox: een perspectief op interculturele vorming. In C. Timmerman, P. Hermans, and J. Hoornaert (Eds), *Allochtone jongeren in het onderwijs. Een multidisciplinair perspectief* (pp. 45–68). Leuven/Apeldoorn: Garant.

Stevens, P. A. J. (2010). Racisme van leerkrachten in de klas. een exploratief onderzoek naar de betekenis en perceptie van racisme bij leerkrachten door hun autochtone en allochtone leerlingen. *Tijdschrift voor Sociologie, 31* (3–4), 330–353.

Stevens, P. A. J. (2007a).Researching race/ethnicity and educational inequality in English secondary schools: A critical review of the research literature between 1980 and 2005. *Review of Educational Research, 77* (2), 147–185.

Stevens, P. A. J. (2007b). Exploring the importance of teachers' institutional structure on the development of teachers' standards of assessment in Belgium. *Sociology of Education, 80* (October), 314–329.

Stevens, P. A. J. (2008a). Exploring pupils' perceptions of teacher racism in their context: A case study of Turkish and Belgian vocational education pupils in a Belgian school. *British Journal of Sociology of Education, 29* (2), 175–187.

Stevens, P. A. J. (2008b). Pupils' perspectives on racism and differential treatment by teachers: On stragglers, the ill and being deviant. *British Educational Research Journal, 13* (21), 1–18.

Stevens, P. A. J., Clycq, N., Timmerman, C., and Van Houtte, M. (2011). Researching race/ethnicity and educational inequality in the Netherlands: A critical review of the research literature between 1980 and 2008. *British Educational Research Journal, 37* (1), 1469–3518.

Stevens, P. A. J. and Görgöz, R. (2010). Exploring the importance of institutional contexts for the development of Ethnic stereotypes: A comparison of schools in Belgium and England. *Ethnic and Racial Studies, 33* (8), 1350–1371.

Stevens, P. A. J. and Van Houtte, M. (2011). Adapting to the system or the student? Exploring teacher adaptations to disadvantaged students in an English and Belgian secondary school. *Educational Evaluation and Policy Analysis 33* (1), 59–75.

Stevens, P. A. J. and Vermeersch, H. (2010). Streaming in Flemish secondary schools: exploring teachers' perceptions of and adaptations to students in different streams. *Oxford Review of Education, 36* (3), 267–284.

Timmermans, C. (1994). Jeunes filles de turquie – vie familiale et instruction scolaire. In N. Bensalah (Ed.), *Familles turques et maghrébines aujourd'hui. Evolution dans les espaces d'origine et d'immigration* (pp. 175–188). Louvain-la-neuve: Academia Erasme.

Timmerman, C. (1995). Cultural practices and ethnicity: Diversifications among Turkish young women. *International Journal of Educational Research, 23* (1), 23–32.

Timmerman, C. (1999). *Onderwijs maakt het verschil: socio-culturele praxis en etniciteitsbeleving bij Turkse jonge vrouwen.* Leuven: Acco.

Timmerman, C. (2002). Turkse jonge vrouwen in België, islam en nationalisme: onderwijs maakt het verschil. In C. Timmerman, P. Hermans, and J. Hoornaert (Eds), *Allochtone jongeren in het onderwijs. Een multidisciplinair perspectief* (pp. 69–94). Leuven/Apeldoorn: Garant.

Timmerman, C., Vanderwaeren, E., and Crul, M. (2003). The second generation in Belgium. *International Migration Review, 37* (4), 1065–1090.

Van Avermaet, P., Van den Branden, K., and Heylen, L. (2010). *Goed geGOKt? Reflecties op twintig jaar gelijkeonderwijskansenbleied in Vlaanderen.* Antwerp Apeldoorn: Garant.

Van Craen, M. and Almaci, M. (2005). De ondervertegenwoordiging van allochtonen in het universitair onderwijs: cijfers, oorzaken en remedies. In *Jaarboek 2005. De arbeidsmarkt in Vlaanderen* (pp. 209–228). Steunpunt WAV.

Van Damme, J. (2006). Sociale ongelijkheid in het secundair onderwijs, met aandacht voor socio-economische status, etniciteit en geslacht. een beperkte bijdrage tot de maatschappelijke discussie. In K. De Wit, L. Dom, C. Gijselinckx, J. Peeraer, and K. Stassen (Eds), *Onderwijs en samenleving. Thema's in het werk van J.C. Verhoeven* (pp. 163–186). Leuven/Voorburg: Acco.

Van Damme, J., Meyer, J., De Troy, A., and Mertens, W. (2001). *Succesvol middelbaar onderwijs? Een antwoord van het LOSO-project.* Leuven and Leusden: Acco.

Van Damme, J., Van Landeghem, G., DeFraine, B., Opdenakker, M.-C., and Onghena, P. (2004). *Maakt de school het verschil? Effectiviteit van scholen, leraren en klassen in de eerste graad van het middelbaar onderwijs.* Leuven: Acco.

Van den Branden, K. and Van Avermaet, P. (2001). Taal, onderwijs en ongelijkheid: quo vadis? *Tijdschrift voor Onderwijsrecht en Onderwijsbeleid (TORB), 2000–2001* (5–6), 393–403.

Van den Broeck, A., Opdenakker, M.-C., and Van Damme, J. (2005). The effects of student characteristics on mathematics achievement in Flemish TIMSS 1999 data. *Educational Research and Evaluation, 11* (2), 107–121.

Van Houtte, M. (2004) Tracking effects on school achievement: A quantitative explanation in terms of the academic culture of school staff. *American Journal of Education, 110* (4), 354–388.

Van Houtte, M. and Stevens, P. A. J. (2009). School Ethnic composition and students' integration outside and inside schools in Belgium. *Sociology of Education, 82* (3), 217–239.

Van Houtte, M. and Stevens, P. A. J. (2010). School ethnic composition and aspirations of immigrant students in Belgium. *British Educational Research Journal, 36* (2), 209–237.

Van Maele, D. and Van Houtte, M. (2009). Faculty trust and organizational school characteristics an exploration across secondary schools in Flanders. *Educational Administration Quarterly, 45* (4), 556–589.

Vandezande, V., Fleischmann, F., Baysu, G., Swyngedouw, M., and Phalet, K. (2008). *De Turkse en Marokkaanse tweede generatie op de arbeidsmarkt in Antwerpen en Brussel.* (Rep. No. Onderzoeksverslag CeSO/ISPO br. 8). Leuven: K.U.Leuven. Centrum voor Sociologisch Onderzoek (CeSO).

Vandezande, V., Fleischmann, F., Baysu, G., Swyngedouw, M., and Phalet, K. (2009). *Ongelijke kansen en ervaren discriminatie in de Turkse en Marokkaanse tweede generatie.* (Rep. No. Onderzoeksverslag CeSO/ISPO, 2009, nr. 11). Leuven: K.U.Leuven. Centrum voor Sociologisch Onderzoek (CeSO).

Varin, C. (2006). *Education in a federal system: A case-study of Belgium.* CUREJ – College Undergraduate Research Electronic Journal. University of Pennsylvania. http://repository.upenn.edu/curej/24.

Verhoeven, A. and Martens, A. (2000). *Arbeidsmarkt en diversiteit ... over de vreemde eend in de bijt.* Leuven: K.U.Leuven, Steunpunt Werkgelegenehid, Arbeid en Vorming (WAV-dossier).

Verlot, M. (2001). Van een beekje naar een stroom. Vijftien jaar onderzoek naar onderwijs aan migranten in Vlaanderen (1985–1999). In J. Vrancken, C. Timmerman, and K. Van der Heyden (Eds), *Komende Generaties. Wat weten we (niet) over allochtonen in Vlaanderen?* (pp. 179–212). Leuven: Acco.

Villegas, A. M. (1991). Culturally Responsive Pedagogy for the 1990s and Beyond. Trends and Issues Paper No. 6. Washington, DC: ERIC Clearinghouse on Teacher Education.

6
Brazil

*Luiz Alberto Oliveira Gonçalves, Natalino Neves da Silva,
and Nigel Brooke*

6.1 Introduction

Between 1980 and 2010, the Brazilian education system underwent dramatic change. At the beginning of the 1980s, Brazilian civil society was engaged in a widespread social movement to put an end to military dictatorship, restore democracy, and rewrite the constitution in line with democratic principles. This latter goal, achieved in 1988, set the stage for two decades of rapid educational expansion and the consolidation of a new set of democratic values throughout the system.

One of the striking characteristics of this period of transformation was the country's newfound awareness of its social inequalities. Numerous studies showed how the years of dictatorship had produced high levels of social exclusion amongst the poorest members of the population. Among the different indicators used, those related to education presented the most vivid account of what was happening in Brazilian society in terms of social and racial inequality. One of the purposes of the present review is to retrieve these earlier studies and show how they established a point of departure for all subsequent investigations into the distribution and consequences of racial discrimination in Brazilian education. But before we begin our presentation of the research on ethnic/racial inequalities in education it would be of help to the reader if we discuss the way in which the Brazilian education system is organized, the ethnic/racial composition of Brazilian society, and the main developments in terms of policy in relationship to race/ethnic inequalities in education.

6.1.1 Educational system

Figure 6.1 shows the education system to be divided into two segments. The legal denomination of the first segment is 'basic education', comprising everything from infant school to secondary school. The second segment is 'higher education'. The column on the left shows the flow of students who take the

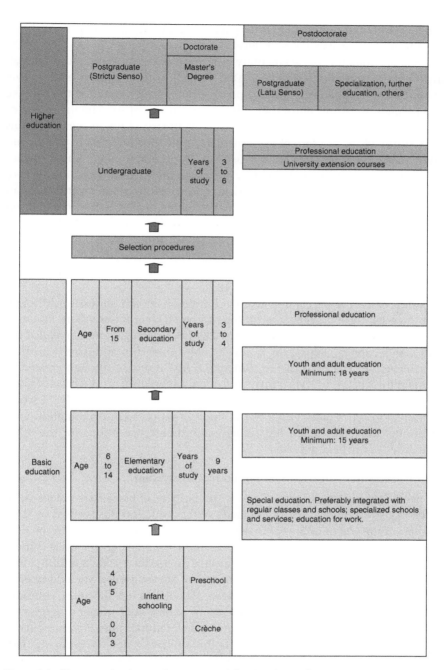

Figure 6.1   The organization and structure of the Brazilian education system
Source: Sistema Educativo Nacional de Brasil: 2002 / Ministério da Educação de Brasil (MEC/INEP) y Organización de Estados Iberoamericanos. http://www.oei.es/quipu/brasil/estructura.pdf.

regular route from preschool to university while the column on the right shows the alternatives available at each level.

The law stipulates that elementary education is compulsory and universal. In line with legislation passed in 2006 extending the duration of this level of education to nine years, the majority of states have expanded their intake and families must now enrol their children at the age of six. The first phase of elementary education now lasts five years. In theory, children remain in this phase until 11 or 12 years of age at which point they progress to the second phase where they stay until the age of 14 or 15. Secondary schooling is free for all those who finish their elementary education and is completed, again theoretically, at the age of 17 or 18. The delays provoked by grade repetition mean that many are over age on finishing the first phase of elementary school or on completing this level of education. Those who would like to finish elementary education but are over the age of 15 can make use of the youth and adult education facilities for this level. Similarly, youth and adult education offers an alternative route to the secondary education diploma for those who finish elementary education after the age of 18.

Traditionally, the public universities controlled student admissions through their own selection procedures with tests designed by university staff. Recently, as the result of a new national test created by the federal government called the National Secondary Education Exam (ENEM), university admission can now be achieved on the basis of the student's ENEM results. Although created to evaluate the quality of the country's secondary schooling on the basis of common parameters, the ministry has encouraged universities to use ENEM scores in admission procedures, either as the single criterion or in combination with traditional university-based tests. There are no entrance exams for the other modalities of further education.

6.1.2   Assessment in the Brazilian education system

Elementary schooling is organized on the basis of either yearly grades or of cycles of two to three years. In the grade system, students are assessed by their teachers at the end of each year to determine whether they progress to the next grade or are held back for a further year in the same grade. In the cycle system, on the other hand, the student is expected to recover from any difficulties through extra classes. Although the possibility of retention at the end of each cycle exists, this outcome is discouraged, which has led the most common of this method of school organization to be called 'continuous progression'. According to research, the cycle method is favored by many governments as a way to regularize the flow of students through the system by reducing high levels of student failure and grade repetition and the consequently high rates of drop-out (Jacomini, 2004; Ambrossetty, 1990). With the cycle method, students are allowed to progress without the interruptions caused by grade repetition that can be so damaging to student motivation and learning. According to the School Census carried out in 2009, 25% of all schools in Brazil use the cycle method, including the method of continuous student progression. In terms of enrollments, almost 12 million students are enrolled in schools organized in cycles, corresponding to 37.8% of all enrollments (Censo Escolar/MEC, 2009).

Elementary and secondary school students are also subjected to different types of external assessment. Apart from the National Secondary Education Exam, the Ministry of Education has also promoted the Basic Education Assessment System (SAEB) embracing two different testing procedures. The older of the two, dating from 1990, is comprised of maths and Portuguese language tests applied every two years to samples of fifth, ninth and twelfth grade public and private school students from both urban and rural areas from all the states. The second external assessment, more recent, is also comprised of maths and Portuguese language tests applied every two years, but is taken by every fifth and ninth grade student in all federal, state, and municipal urban schools with a minimum of 20 students throughout the country. The results of the latter system, called the Brazil Test, are broken down and published by region, state, municipality, and school and are used in a formula to calculate the education development index for each level. Both assessment systems also apply questionnaires to teachers, school principals, and students to gather contextual information of relevance to the study of school quality.

6.1.2.1   *How race and ethnicity became a topic of research in Brazil*

At the beginning of the 1980s, census data on the levels of schooling throughout the Brazilian population showed a high percentage of children and teenagers to be behind in their studies, along with dramatically high rates of school failure and drop-out. Studies from this period also showed profound inequalities between the rich and the poor with regards to educational and employment expectations.

Up until the 1960s, Brazilian sociology had made no connection between educational inequality and the race and ethnicity of students. The unequal distribution of education was generally believed to be the result of a lack of opportunity and the slow integration of certain social groups into class society, especially those of Afro-Brazilian and indigenous descent (Guimarães, 2004). This evolutionary view of events was based on studies that analyzed the enrollment of children and teenagers in accordance with their social background but without regard for their racial and ethnic origins. According to these studies, poverty and the different socio-economic levels of society could, by themselves, explain the educational success of some individuals and the failure and low level of schooling of others.

This viewpoint dominated sociological thinking throughout the 1970s and heavily influenced research in the area of the sociology of education.

A state-of-the-art study by Zaia Brandão (1982) with regards to school repetition and drop-out in Brazil between 1971 and 1981 pointed out that none of the studies had taken the racial or ethnic origin of the students into consideration. At that time primary schooling was still not universal and the great majority of those excluded belonged without doubt to the poorest sectors of the population. With this, the problem of access and survival of poor children and teenagers continued to dominate most of the sociological research on inequality in education for the rest of the 1980s.

The use of social class as a point of reference in educational research was heavily influenced by the sociological theories in vogue at the time. One of these theories, of Weberian inspiration, was Pierre Bourdieu and Jean-Claude Passeron's theory of reproduction (1975). Another popular theory, aligned with Marxism, was that of the ideological state apparatuses of Louis Althusser (1974). Despite their different starting points, these two theories saw the school from a purely structuralist point of view, as a mechanism for the reproduction of the dominant ideology and even as an apparatus for the repression of the working class.

With this paradigm in mind, researchers set out to find evidence of reproduction among teaching materials, in the discourse of teachers, in the curricula, and elsewhere (Nosella, 1981; Cunha, 1979, 1982). The aim was to construct a critical view of the world by denouncing the reproductive role of the school. The failure and exclusion of the great majority of students were seen as the result of the way in which school procedures placed the working classes at a disadvantage by reproducing the broader processes of social domination.

Despite their Marxist origins, the concepts of 'unitary school' and 'polytechnic school' in the work of Antonio Gramsci (1975) stand in opposition to the reproduction paradigm. In the Gramscian view, the school can become a producer of culture instead of a mere instrument of social reproduction. Given this, the research inspired by Gramsci is concerned largely with showing the mediating role played by the school and its pedagogical resources: the teacher, the textbook, school routines, etc. (Saviani, 1983; Mello, 1982; Cury, 1986). According to researchers who still follow this theoretical approach, all these resources can be used to reproduce the dominant ideology but they can also generate new, transformational knowledge, capable of liberating the working classes.

As can been seen, with these theoretical paradigms the only selection process given any importance in the Brazilian school system was that of social class. Despite this, the return to democracy in the 1980s was an important stimulus to the sociological study of the impact of racism and ethnic/racial discrimination on the educational system and the labor market, even if this innovation had to be adopted without forsaking the category of social class.

At least two factors contributed to the change. The first is associated with the increasing influence of new social movement organizations, especially those belonging to Afro-descendent and indigenous groups who had fought for historical reparations and social justice. The hiring of education researchers and specialists by the newly elected state governments was also important in this context, and lead to the article in the 1988 Constitution that eliminated all barriers to elementary schooling by declaring it universally free of all racial, social, gender, and religious discrimination. The second factor to stimulate sociological research on race and education had to do with statistics. Data containing evidence of educational inequality between different racial groups began to see the light of day.

At this point it would be appropriate to show the educational inequality data that became available in 1980, as the result of the population census carried out that year. If it were possible to compare this data with the most recent 2010 census we would also be able to show the important changes that took place over the full 30-year period of this review. However, due to the fact that the race/color categories currently in use by the Brazilian Institute of Geography and Statistics (IBGE) responsible for the country's census were established in 1991, it is the census carried out in that year instead that we have chosen for our comparisons. Up until 1991 the indigenous population was not counted as a separate race/color category but instead included as part of the mulatto population. Given our interest in maintaining the distinction between these two populations, we have therefore chosen not to present the 1980 data.

According to the 2010 census, of a total population of almost 191 million, 97 million Brazilians classified themselves as 'black' or 'mulatto', 91 million as 'white', a few more than 2 million of Asian descent, and almost 818,000 of indigenous origin (Figure 6.2).

On the basis of these population statistics it is possible to study the number of years of schooling of those of both sexes of ten years of age or more for each color/race group. Tables 6.1–6.3, containing first the data from the 1991 census and then the 2010 census, show considerable differences in the average length of schooling between each racial group and also between men and women in specific racial groups.

Based on the 1991 and 2010 censuses, the tables reveal an important overall increase in the average number of years of schooling for all racial groups. Even so, racial inequalities persist. In 2010 the white population had an average of 6.9 years of schooling while the black population had 5.0 years and the mulatto population 5.2 years. Despite having the lowest average of only 4.5 years of education in 2010, the indigenous population is the group that has advanced most, rising from an average of just 2.1 years of schooling in 1991. The highest average is found among those Brazilians of Asian descent, called 'yellow' by the organization responsible for the national census.

6.1.2.2 Public policy to reduce race inequalities in education

Besides the influence of the black movement and the circulation of data exposing the different levels of education of the various ethnic/racial segments of

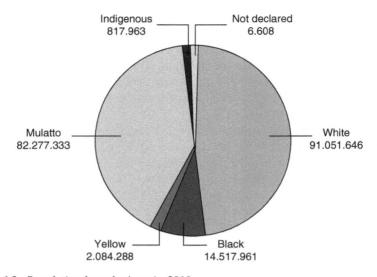

Figure 6.2 Population by color/race in 2010
Source: IBGE. Resultados Preliminares. Censo Demográfico 2010.

Table 6.1 Average years of schooling of population of ten years of age or more, by sex and color. Brazil, 1991

Sex	Average years of schooling						
				Color			
	Total	White	Black	Yellow	Mulatto	Indigenous	Not declared
Total	4.7	5.6	3.4	8.2	3.7	2.1	3.4
Men	4.6	5.6	3.4	8.5	3.5	2.2	3.5
Women	4.7	5.6	3.4	7.9	3.8	2.0	3.2

Source: IBGE, Censo Demográfico 1991.

Table 6.2 Average years of schooling of population of ten years of age or more, by sex and color. Brazil, 2010

Sex	Average years of schooling						
				Color			
	Total	White	Black	Yellow	Mulatto	Indigenous	Not declared
Total	6.2	6.9	5.0	9.0	5.2	4.5	4.1
Men	6.0	6.8	4.8	9.1	5.0	4.4	4.0
Women	6.4	7.1	5.2	8.9	5.4	4.6	4.3

Source: IBGE, Censo Demográfico 2010.

Table 6.3 Increase in average years of schooling of population of ten years or more, by sex and color. Brazil, 1991–2010

Sex	Increase in average years of schooling 1991–2010						
	Color						
	Total	White	Black	Yellow	Mulatto	Indigenous	Not declared
Total	1.5	1.0	1.6	0.8	1.5	1.4	0.7
Men	1.4	1.2	1.4	0.6	1.5	2.2	1.5
Women	1.3	1.5	1.8	1.0	1.6	2.6	1.1

Source: IBGE, Censo Demográfico 1991, 2010.

society, certain legal measures to promote new social policies may also have influenced sociological research on the theme of race/ethnicity and educational inequality. The 1988 Constitution, marking the end of dictatorship by laying down the guidelines for the consolidation of democracy, should be emphasized in this respect. For the first time in Brazilian history, the ethnic and racial plurality of the Brazilian people was given official recognition. Racism was formally acknowledged and defined as a sufficiently serious crime as to not warrant bail.

Articles of the 1988 Constitution recognized the right of different ethnic and racial groups to seek the affirmation and preservation of their cultural heritage through the medium of educational programs. Research centers were engaged to develop studies which, depending on their location within the federation, led to the introduction of elements of Afro-Brazilian culture into the school curricula, in line with the demands of the Brazilian black movement. New emphasis was also given to bilingual teaching for children and adolescents of European and Asian descent living in Brazil. Along with these changes, the idea of state and municipal agencies to foster race-related improvements through public policy began to receive support. The focus of these policies was mainly in the field of education and culture.

Although there is no proof of a direct link between changes in the country's legal framework, as established by the new constitution, and the emergence of sociological studies that recognized the ethnic/racial component of educational inequality, the expansion of research during this period and over the following decades gives credence to this belief.

The first statistical report on indigenous education in Brazil was published in 1999 by the National Institute of Educational Study and Research (INEP), a division of the Ministry of Education. The publication was the result of the first national survey of indigenous schools (Grupioni, 2006). The subsequent school census, produced by the Ministry of Education in 2005, revealed that there were 2323 indigenous schools and 8431 teachers in almost all Brazilian states, with the exception of Piauí and Rio Grande do Norte (Brasil/MEC, 2005). The National Coordination, attached to the Secretariat of Cultural Diversity (SECAD/MEC) and responsible for indigenous teacher training, estimated that 90% of the teachers in shcools for indigenous pupils were themselves of indigenous origin. According to the 2005 census, indigenous schools had 163,773 pupils studying in their ethnic language (Brasil/MEC, 2005). Of these pupils, 81.7% were enrolled in the first years of elementary school, 11.6% were in nursery schools (including crèches), 2.6% were in secondary schools, and 7.5% were taking classes in adult education courses (Brasil/MEC, 2005). In 78.2% of all indigenous schools, teaching was in the maternal language or in both the maternal language and Portuguese.

Sociological studies on the schooling of descendants of European (non-Portuguese) and Asian immigrants born in Brazil also made an appearance during the 1980–2010 period, with a focus on the following issues: family expectations, strategies to promote children's success at school, and social mobility, often accomplished through the attainment of public office and direct involvement in the management of the state.

Before concluding this overview of the contextual factors that have affected research on the topic of the relationship between educational inequality and race/ethnicity, it is worth stressing the degree of exclusion experienced by the Afro-descendant and indigenous populations. Both groups have been at considerable disadvantage at all levels of schooling, from early childhood to higher education. Current data shows the persistence of these disadvantages into the 21st century, with lower rates of educational attendance, especially among younger children, but also in secondary and higher education. Understandably, therefore, research is still concerned with strategies and policies geared towards these populations, including contentious options such as affirmative university entrance policies to improve the access of black and indigenous peoples to both graduate and postgraduate education. To illustrate the differences in school attendance, Table 6.4 summarizes the gross enrollment rates for different levels of schooling (number of students enrolled as a percentage of the total population for the appropriate age group) for each color/race population group according to the National Household Survey results for the years 1988, 1998, and 2008.

Table 6.4 shows constant improvement in the gross enrollment rates for both whites and non-whites at every level of schooling. While some of the most manifest improvements are those of non-white children at secondary and university levels, the gross enrollment rates of this group are still below average for the population as a whole and significantly lower than the white population, especially at secondary and university levels. Gross elementary school enrollments of more than 100% are explained by the effect of grade

Table 6.4 Gross enrollment rates by color/race, 1988, 1998, 2008

Level of schooling/year	Color								
	White			**Non-white**[a]			**Total**[b]		
	1988	**1998**	**2008**	**1988**	**1998**	**2008**	**1988**	**1998**	**2008**
Crèche[c]	–	9.5	20.7	–	7.7	15.5	–	8.7	18.1
Preschool or crèche[d]	–	47.0	62.9	–	44.5	56.8	–	45.8	59.6
Elementary[e]	103.3	117.3	112.5	98.2	121.8	118.4	100.8	119.5	115.7
Secondary[f]	49.4	74.0	93.3	26.7	47.1	79.5	38.6	60.7	85.5
Higher[g]	12.4	16.8	35.8	3.6	4.0	16.4	8.6	10.9	25.5

[a] Black and mulatto.
[b] Includes yellow, indigenous, and not declared.
[c] 0 to 3 years.
[d] 4 to 5 years.
[e] 7 to 14 years.
[f] 15 to 17 years.
[g] 18 to 24 years.
Source: IBGE, Microdados PNAD.

repetition and the continued enrollment of over-age students at a level of schooling that has achieved universalization. The higher gross enrollment rates for non-whites at this level indicate an even larger problem of grade repetition for this color/race group.

The leap forward in Brazilian education over the 1980–2010 period has to do with the universalization of both stages of elementary schooling (from the first to the fifth year and from the sixth to the ninth year), the consequent expansion in the proportion of the age-group continuing to secondary school, and the rapid rise in higher education enrollments. At the elementary level, where the system has been able to guarantee access to all racial and ethnic segments of society, research is shifting to the study of the internal mechanisms of discrimination and racism within schools. In order to understand the conditions that influence survival and performance and also the quality of education provided, the focus is now on the management of schools, pedagogical practice, teacher training, and relations between the different members of the school community.

In this context, it is worth mentioning Law 10.639 passed in 2003 that modified the country's basic education guidelines by introducing the history of Africa and Afro-Brazilian history into the school curricula. Attention should also be drawn to the approval of affirmative action policies to expand access to higher education for non-white students. Both measures have triggered numerous research studies on the topic of race and education.

6.2   Methods

In principle, this review required the identification of all the published research in the field of the sociology of education on the relationship between race/ ethnicity and educational inequality in Brazil between 1980 and 2010. In order to accomplish this task and then select which pieces of research to include, it was first necessary to define the universe from which the publications should be drawn. A preliminary literature search showed the majority of publications on the issue of educational inequality at all levels of education to be focused on the black (including mulatto) and white segments of Brazilian society. Very few studies presented data concerning the education of immigrant populations and their descendants or even of indigenous children and teenagers.

In a wider second search we then identified other publications between 1990 and 2010 focusing on educational expectations and school achievement of children from European and Asian immigrant families (Kreutz, 1994a, 1994b, 2000; Giron, 1998; Dalmoro, 1987; Müller, 1994; Handa, 1987; Mauch and Vasconcelos, 1994; Kaly, 2001; Pitts Jr, 2006; Demartine, 1998; Truzzi, 1992, 2008a). Other pieces of research concentrating on the education of diverse groups of indigenous children and teenagers were also located. These studies deal with the creation of indigenous schools that are now geared to their own ethnic segments, using not only curricula elaborated for each specific group, but also teaching materials appropriate to the native culture and mother tongue (Grupioni, 2003; Paes, 1999; Nascimento, 2003; Bergamaschi, 2004; Camargo and Albuquerque, 2003; Ferreira, 2006; Mélia, 1999).

The articles were then classified using an indexation criterion, which is to say that only those published in scientific journals that use forms of academic selection were considered. The point of departure for this selection was the list of articles provided by the National Association of Post-graduate Studies and Research in Social Science (ANPOCS) on their publications page. The advantage of using this source is that it lists only those papers included in the Scientific On Line Electronic Library – Brazil (SCIELO), which only includes papers that have been published in indexed journals that follow academic selection criteria. The following were included among the journals used in this review: *Revista Brasileira de Ciências Sociais* (Brazilian Journal of Social Sciences), *Revista Brasileira de Educação* (Brazilian Journal of Education), *Revista Tempo Social* (Social Times Journal), *Cadernos de Pesquisa da Fundação Carlos Chagas* (Research Records of the Carlos Chagas Foundation), *CEDES* (Education and Society) and the *Revista de Estudos Afro-Asiáticos da Fundação Cândido Mendes* (Afro-Asian Studies Journal of the Candido Mendes Foundation).

The review also considered reports of surveys or longitudinal studies carried out by research centers that contain estimates of educational inequality among different racial and ethnic groups in Brazil, at different levels of education, for the period from 1980 to 2010. As examples, this review made use of data collected by the Instituto de Pesquisa Econômica Aplicada (IPEA; Institute of Applied Economic Research), the Instituto Universitário de Pesquisa do Rio de Janeiro (IUPERJ; University Institute of Research of Rio de Janeiro), the Laboratório de Análises Históricas, Sociais e Estatísticas das Relações Raciais (LAESER; Laboratory of Economic, Historical, Social and Statistical Analysis of Race Relations) and by the Instituto Nacional de Estudos e Pesquisas Educacionais (INEP; National Institute of Educacional Study and Research). In addition to these reports, we included some classic texts on the topic of race relations in Brazil due to their theoretical and methodological importance as demonstrated by their citations in other texts and articles.

We also selected some papers published in preceding decades that reviewed the literature on educational inequality or that expressed the sociological traditions that dominated academic publications before the 1980s (Hasenbalg, 1979; Rosemberg 1980; Pinto, 1985). By comparing the authors of the 1980s with their predecessors, it was possible to identify common elements with regards their theoretical paradigms as well as the research techniques employed. It was also possible to see how education researchers have improved their methods, whether for the study of how children of European, Asian and African immigrant families were gradually integrated into Brazilian society or how indigenous education incorporated the country's different ethnic cultures after the 1988 Constitution.

Our study also gives importance to the 'color/race' category of the demographic and school censuses. It was because of these census data that a sociological research tradition centered on the analysis of the relationship between color/race and educational quality in Brazil was able to develop. The larger part of the research on race relations and educational inequality follows this tradition, with the emphasis on the relations between blacks (Afro-Brazilians) and whites. Although the concept of ethnicity had never been a reference category for the national education census, it began to be used intensively in field research from the 1990s onwards, with the creation of indigenous schools that acknowledged the ethnic characteristics of their pupils. For this reason, it was necessary to base this review on more specific definitions of ethnicity and color/race and consider these two dimensions as independent issues that have inspired different lines of research in Brazil over the last 30 years.

Sociological research, mainly to do with the sociology of education, was the first group to be selected. Once selected, the studies were subdivided into groups according to: (a) common research questions; (b) methodological approaches used in comparable situations; (c) answers provided in response to the demands of civil society organizations; and (d) the relevance for public policy regarding inclusion and/or the acknowledgement of cultural diversity.

In line with the proposed method, we identified three different traditions in the sociological research literature. These can be labelled as follows: 'charting ethnic/racial inequalities in education', 'race and school effectiveness', and 'racism and discrimination in schools'.

Although the purpose of this review is to analyze the development of these traditions since 1980, we understood it to be important to quickly describe the theory and ideology of research on the theme of race relations in Brazil prior to the 1980s so as to get an idea of the intellectual origins of current research. What this signals is our belief that current sociological studies on the theme of race and educational inequality are the direct descendants of earlier research on race relations.

6.3 Historical background

In his sociology of Brazilian sociology, Guimarães (2006) shows that the first sociological studies of Brazil's ethnic/racial composition in the first third of the 20th century were a reaction to the racist doctrines sustained by the national elite. In terms of the sociological ancestry of these and all subsequent studies, Theodoro et al. (2008) identify three 'waves of theory' that fostered the field of race relations in Brazil and continue to be relevant today.

The 'first wave' emerged at the beginning of the 20th century at a time when the theory of eugenics was popular in Brazil. The efforts of Gilberto Freyre (1998 [1933], 1939) to refute this theory were important steps towards a better understanding of the ethnic/racial basis of Brazilian society. Freyre incorporated Franz Boas's principles of cultural anthropology into his sociological formulations and thereby replaced the 'biological notion' of race with a 'cultural notion', the latter being 'a people's symbolic form of expression' (Guimarães, 2004, p. 12). This principle became the key idea behind Brazil's fame in the world as an example of 'racial democracy' and inaugurated a new strain of sociological research that came to be known as the 'cultural anthropology tradition' (Hofbauer, 2006, p. 26).

The Brazilian elite made use of the ideology of racial democracy to foment the idea that Brazil was effectively free of racism and racial discrimination, unlike other multiracial societies such as the United States. This view was to be reinforced by the studies of sociologist Donald Pierson (1971 [1945]). A follower of Robert Park and a member at the time of the Chicago School, Pierson inspired many researchers in Brazil by introducing sociological methods that relied exclusively on empirical data to describe race relations between blacks and whites and thereby played down cultural anthropology (Hofbauer, 2006; Theodoro et al., 2008). Despite this advance, Pierson did not focus on race inequalities. Instead, he studied the chances of social mobility of Afro-descendants in Brazil. The presence of the offspring of both blacks and whites among the economic and political elite and among those occupying positions of prestige was taken as a sign that the 'absence of racial discrimination' made social mobility possible.

The 'second wave' was in reaction to the ideology of racial democracy. Also starting in the 1950s and continuing with UNESCO sponsorship until the 1970s, these studies sought to challenge the myth of a 'racial paradise' by showing the prevalence of race discrimination in Brazil. However, in this early phase of reaction neither prejudice nor racial discrimination is seen as the mechanism for the reproduction of social inequalities. Instead, they are seen as deriving from the heritage of slavery and likely to disappear with the adoption of industrial capitalism in Brazil. The process of industrialization would free the Afro-descendant population from its place at the margins of class society and enable it to identify itself with a social class rather than a racial or ethnic category (Fernandes, 1964; Ianni, 1972).

The dominance of this view in sociological literature until the end of the 1970s retarded the development of studies of educational inequality based on explanations of racism. In the end it was the statistical data produced by the demographic census that would enable sociologists to construct the necessary indicators of racial inequality in Brazil.

The 'third wave' of theory in the continuing rejection of the ideology of racial democracy covers the same period as this review. Although the product of diverse sociological approaches to the question of inequality, we analyze only those studies concerned specifically with the sociology of education.

6.4 Charting ethnic/racial inequalities in education

Centered on the analysis of secondary data[1] and part of the ongoing reaction to the myth of racial democracy, the sociological research tradition we have called 'charting ethnic/racial inequalities in education' made its entrance at the end of the 1970s with the purpose of offering an objective portrait of educational inequality among the country's ethnic/racial groups. Within this tradition we find a number of transversal studies that simply portray educational inequalities by calculating differential access rates for different ethnic/racial groups and levels of schooling (Hasenbalg, 1979; Silva, 1979). By using longitudinal data, other studies attempted to identify change and continuity in inequalities over the years (Paixão, 2009; Osório and Soares, 2005). In general, the studies belonging to this tradition helped chart the difficulties of educational access of children and youths from different ethnic/racial segments. Some went further so as to isolate the ethnic/racial inequalities in the rates of survival and permanence of students within the different levels of the system.

Reinforcing a previous point, the studies designed to chart the ethnic/racial dimensions of educational inequality were made possible by two demographic data banks produced by the IBGE, the Demographic Census (Censo Demográfico) and the National Home Sample Survey (Pesquisa Nacional por Amostra de Domicilio; PNAD), both of which contained detailed educational attainment data. The data included information on age, gender, occupation of those of working age, place of residence by region, number of children, and the status of the head of the family (father, mother, oldest son or other). For the first time, these data permitted the necessary cross tabulations for a map of ethnic/racial inequality in the field of education.

As the key questions raised by the charting ethnic/racial inequalities in education tradition sought to clarify ethnic/racial inequality within the education system, it is worth describing how this inequality was actually measured. For this purpose we can use the example of the transversal studies carried out by the University Research Institute of Rio de Janeiro (IUPERJ) starting at the end of the 1970s. The purpose of these studies was to build an analytical model capable of understanding the impact of race and ethnicity variables on the production of social inequality as a whole. The authors developed their statistical model so as to describe what was then called the socio-economic achievement process. The work was derived from that of Peter M. Blau and Otis Dudley Duncan, the two sociologists most associated with the consolidation of quantitative social science methods in the United States. Blau and Duncan's studies focused on intergenerational occupational mobility or, more accurately, on the way 'parents transmit social status to their children' and showed that this transmission occurs primarily through the children's education. (Blau and Duncan, 1967, p. 32)

In an example of this tradition, Hasenbalg and Silva used the data collected in 1976 by the PNAD household survey, which, for the first time, collected data regarding color/race and social stratification. The sample was of 120,000 homes throughout the country, excluding rural areas of the northern and center-west regions. With these data, the authors applied the life-cycle model suggested by Duncan (1969). This model is usually represented by a system of structural equations, containing four exogenous variables that stand for family background (birth context, in terms of the rural/urban dichotomy, regional location, father's level of schooling and occupational status). It also contains three endogenously inferred variables (education, occupation, and income).

When applying this model, Hasenbalg and Silva took the ethnic and racial background of the respondents into consideration. The empirical data used in the structural equations demonstrated that when compared to those classified as 'whites', the groups classified as 'non-whites' were at a disadvantage with regards the three outcome variables – education, occupation and income.

With these results, the Hasenbalg and Silva model offered empirical evidence of the importance of race and ethnicity variables in the process of social stratification in Brazil. The disadvantage of non-whites was repeated at all stages of the life-cycle, including the life-cycles of individuals whose trajectories were already far removed from slavery. This helped to further refute the sociological models that still sustained this belief.

A further strain of transversal studies within the charting ethnic/racial inequalities in education tradition sought to identify inequalities within the system by calculating school survival and drop-out rates for each ethnic/racial group at given moments in time (Barcelos, 1993). In order to take these snapshots, the researchers used age and grade enrollment information to calculate the degree of school grade delay[2] for each sex and ethnic/racial group (Rosemberg, Negrão and Pinto, 1986; Rama, 1989; Levison, 1989). These studies also evaluated the physical conditions of the schools and their equipment as well as the characteristics of the teachers. These data were then correlated with the predominant ethnic/racial category for each school so as to describe the traits of educational inequality.

By using census data, other transversal studies were able to answer questions regarding inter-generational differences. Any given census could supply the average length of schooling of different age groups. For example, in a study using the 1990 census, Gonçalves pointed out the significant differences between young blacks and mulattos, from 20 to 40 years of age, and more elderly blacks and mulattos, from 60 to 80 years of age. The parameter established for this comparison was the average level of schooling of people born in the 1950s. The choice of age can be explained by the need for a study that could establish if there were educational differences between those born before and after 1950. The study revealed that the more elderly blacks and mulattos (over 60 years of age), whose childhood and youth were closer to the beginning of the 20th century, presented the highest rates of illiteracy (Gonçalves, 2000). The objective was to show the gravity of the educational situation of non-whites in Brazil, not only when compared to that of whites, but also with regards to non-whites of different generations.

The charting ethnic/racial inequalities in education tradition also produced longitudinal studies to better understand the processes of change and continuity. In this type of study the researchers customarily accompany educational cohorts comprised of individuals from different ethnic/racial backgrounds so as to detect exactly when race differences become evident (Henriques, 2001; Soares and Osório, 2005; Soares and Alves, 2003; Barcelos, 1992; Paixão, 2010). The logic underlying this model is based on the idea that when adequately specified, the statistics on years of education drawn from the population census can identify inter-generational differences in schooling (Gonçalves, 2000).

In response to the challenges of redemocratization, some studies gave further depth to the charting ethnic/racial inequalities in education tradition by analyzing not just inter-generational differences but also those within the same generation. In one such study, data was collected on the educational trajectory of all individuals born in 1980 so as to compare the schooling of whites and blacks born into the same generation (Osório and Soares, 2005). In Osório and Soares' own words, the 1980 generation was a group of 'emblematic people'. What made them different from other generations? Firstly, according to the authors, they were a generation that had gone through an educational system which, at the elementary level, had been universalized. Secondly, they were a generation that had grown up between 1980 and 2003, a period which saw racial equality embraced as a principle by government schools, racism defined as a crime by the constitution, and affirmative action discussed in a variety of contexts, especially with regards university quotas for blacks and indigenous peoples (Osório and Soares, 2005, pp. 33–34).

Observations regarding the schooling of this group started in 1987, the year in which those born in 1980 would have been seven years old and have reached what was then the recommended age for the first year of elementary school. The observations ended with the collection of the 2003 data on the supposition that in this year, if everything had gone according to normal and the students had not faced any problems along the way, they would be graduating from university (Osório and Soares, 2005). The source of data was the National Household Survey of 1987. Using computer models, Osório and Soares simulated scenarios by using a technique they called a 'statistical camera' to construct a theoretical education trajectory for all blacks and whites born in 1980. They then compared the actual path of individuals belonging to these groups with those produced by 'the camera'.

Without going into details regarding the factors responsible for the differences in the schooling of blacks and whites, Osório and Soares's longitudinal methodology helps show how the actual paths taken by each racial segment deviate from the path projected by the 'statistical camera'. However, the degree of deviation is not the same for whites and blacks. The latter group is greatly under-represented in the later stages of the educational system as the blacks are more likely to abandon their schooling along the way. Osório and Soares identify a selection effect with greater impact on the path followed by black students. Summing up, 'the statistical documentary' produced by the two authors infers that despite the universalization of access to elementary school, Afro-descendants are still at a disadvantage when their achievement or failure is compared to that of white students. Secondary education works as the principal bottle-neck for Afro-descendant students. Because it is imperative to go to secondary school in order to enter university, the reduced access of Afro-descendants to secondary education further reduces their chance of higher education. Faced by this panorama of disadvantage, researchers point to the need to compensate for the difficulties of Afro-descendants in such a way as to enable members of this group to reach the same levels of achievement as their white colleagues.

Summing up the transversal and longitudinal components of the charting ethnic/racial inequalities in education tradition, we can say that these quantitative research paradigms were a significant contribution to the deconstruction of the myth of Brazil as a racial democracy. The research carried out between 1980 and 2010 not only provided empirical evidence to confirm the importance of race in explaining school success, but also helped pinpoint the educational success or failure of each ethnic/racial segment. It also shed light on an issue that until then had had little visibility on the national scene: the level of racial discrimination inside Brazilian schools (Rosemberg, 1991). In this regard, researchers from the Institute for Applied Economic Research (IPEA) hold that it is these studies that made it clear that 'education is essential to understanding the social processes responsible for race inequalities', in Brazil (Barbosa, 2005, p. 8).

6.5 Race and school effectiveness

A number of studies have looked to see if schools can make a difference with regards the reduction of ethnic/racial inequalities. These studies focus on the Afro-Brazilian segment of the population and understand that the quality of schooling can be used to promote greater equality of educational opportunity.

As previously pointed out, at the end of the 1990s elementary schooling became universal and access to secondary and higher education became the bottle-necks. In this new environment the question of educational quality became a priority and a national assessment system for the measurement of pupil performance was established. A powerful instrument for gathering data regarding student performance and socio-demographic profiles, the System for the Assessment of Elementary Education (SAEB) also gathers information on the physical condition of schools, infra-structure, school management, and the qualifications of teachers. It was with this data that the research we identify as 'race and school effectiveness' was established. This tradition also covers research using hierarchical linear regression models (Soares and Alves, 2003), which, when applied to studies on the role of the school in combating racial inequality, supply important information regarding the mechanisms of racial discrimination within the school environment.

As a start, it is worth emphasizing how the theme of school effectiveness has been incorporated into educational research in Brazil. Brooke and Soares (2008) describe the first use of this paradigm by the Coleman study in the United States in the 1960s and the controversies provoked by its conclusions. The authors then show its adoption 30 years later in Brazil in response to political and social demands for answers to the difficult question as to why some schools produce better pupil performance than others. This question has troubled education researchers since the 1980s, especially since access to government schools was expanded to the poorest segments of the population. The research on school effectiveness started when almost 95% of children and teenagers from 7 to 14 years were enrolled in elementary schools. These studies were possible because the national SAEB assessment system had made it feasible to create a time series for measures of student performance (Brooke and Soares, 2008). These evaluations showed the recurrent educational failure of a high percentage of Brazilian students, mainly the poorest, including Afro-Brazilians. The school effectiveness paradigm questions the idea that the 'family effect' can, on its own, explain either good or bad school performance among children and teenagers. Brooke and Soares argue that, on the contrary, the paradigm holds that 'school effectiveness cannot be exclusively related to its external circumstances' and that it is necessary to identify those school factors that make a difference to the achievement of students.

However, most reviews of studies drawing on this paradigm tend to show the difficulties of determining the components of school quality that contribute to student achievement. Despite this, authors from different areas of study have made important contributions in identifying the characteristics of good quality schools (Barbosa and Veiga, 1998; Ferrâo, Barbosa and Fernandes, 2001; Falcão Filho, 1997, 2000; Mello, 1994; Franco, Alves and Ortigão, 2007; Brooke and Soares, 2008). The consensus is partial, mainly because these characteristics are dependent on specific contexts and circumstances. Even so, some characteristics do recur in different studies, indicating their importance in the assessment of school effectiveness: (a) the school principal's role and leadership, (b) the expectations of teachers and other members of staff, (c) school climate, (d) clearly delineated objectives, shared by teachers and members of staff, (e) the organization of time, (f) strategies to monitor student development, (g) strategies for in-service teacher training in every school, (h) technical assistance for every school, and (i) parental participation in school activities.

A study that exemplifies this kind of analysis was undertaken by Barbosa (2005). From a broad review of the literature, the author selected the nine items mentioned above as the definition of school quality. She then used the items to create indicators of quality for the schools included in her sample. The indicators were of a binary nature. Those items that could reinforce school quality were given a positive sign and those that could weaken it a negative one. The final score of each school was the sum of the different signs.

The study then evaluated student performance in accordance with the way the schools were classified as of high or low quality. For this, Barbosa relied on SAEB test results for student performance at the end of each cycle of schooling (fourth and eighth elementary school year) on two subjects: Portuguese language and mathematics. The results confirmed the prediction that the best averages in both subjects would be obtained by the schools considered of good quality. However, in order to gauge the effect of the school on the reduction of racial inequalities, the author restricted herself to the maths scores, as the learning of this subject depends more on the school than on the family.

Before reaching her conclusions, Barbosa (2005) added data regarding the students' social backgrounds to her model of school quality. Here she included family income, the mother's level of schooling, and the ethnic/racial origin of the student according to information supplied by the mother. In order to further study the effect of the background variables on student achievement, the author sorted the families according to two strata: level of family income, and level of mothers' schooling. With regards ethnic/racial background, the author drew on the literature on race relations in Brazil regarding the independent impact of 'color' on social inequality. For this reason the research considered the individual's color to be a distinct factor capable of exercising an effect on individual educational progress (Barbosa, op. cit., p. 107).

Summing up, the regression analysis used by Barbosa (2005) included the variable 'school quality', monthly family income, mother's schooling, and the students' 'color' as possible factors in the explanation of differences in maths performance. Of these, 'school quality' is the variable that most affects student achievement. However, when the regression formula excludes quality, the 'color' variable becomes highly significant in the determination of student achievement. The study also shows that schools of good quality make a difference to the scores of Afro-Brazilian students. When compared to white students from schools of lesser quality, these students gain almost an extra point on the SAEB scale. Moreover, the difference in the averages of white students and non-white students tends to diminish in schools of good quality, whereas in those of poor quality, the difference is maintained at higher levels.

The research carried out by Soares and Alves (2003) of the Evaluation and Educational Measurement Group (GAME) of the Federal University of Minas Gerais can be given as a second example of studies following the race and school effectiveness tradition. Concerned to improve understanding of the 'school effect' on student achievement, Soares and Alves used the 2001 SAEB data to focus on the issue of racial inequality in school test results. The authors concentrate on the low levels of maths performance of eighth year elementary education students. While the expected level of proficiency in this subject at this grade is 325 points, the average is only 245 points. The difference in the averages of white and mulatto students was 17.4 points in favor of the former. The difference of 28 points between white and black students was even greater. The authors stress that this level of racial inequality is maintained throughout the series of data collected by SAEB (Alves and Soares, 2004, p. 23). Following regression model procedures, Soares and Alves identify the 'socioeconomic gradient' that largely explains student performance results. For this reason, the researchers include two further variables in their model of analysis alongside family income and parents' level of education. These are the father's occupation and family culture. The latter variable corresponds to Bourdieu's 'cultural capital' category.

In their analysis, the authors draw attention to the importance of choosing the right type of regression model. In their opinion, the model must be appropriate for the kind of data under investigation. For the authors, therefore, the choice of model is a crucial stage in the research. In Alves and Soares's case, the procedure adopted was the 'hierarchical linear method of multiple regression', because of its ability to estimate the contribution of each of the factors described above in the explanation of maths proficiency while controlling for the contribution of the other factors in the model. For the authors, the hierarchical models are appropriate for the study of educational phenomena because these have a hierarchical structure that is empirically evident and can be described as follows: the students are grouped in classrooms, the classrooms are grouped in schools, and the schools are part of systems or located in geographical areas. These groups form a hierarchically organized chain.

In the Soares and Alves study, two hierarchical levels have been considered: (1) the student and (2) the school. At the first level, two controlling variables are introduced, the student's socio-economic background and school grade delay. At the second level, the controlling variables are: the sector to which the school belongs (government or private) and the school socio-economic profile. In summary, in order to study the effect of the variables on both student performance and on the difference between white and non-white students, the authors equalized students and schools according to their socio-economic and cognitive characteristics.

Each of the variables from the basic model was then introduced to measure the effect on student performance and test for significance. This procedure was adopted in order to show the impact of each variable on the difference between the achievement of white and mulatto students and between white and black students. When treating the results, the researchers only analyze the existence or otherwise of an effect of the selected variables on the increase or reduction in inequality in student achievement according to ethnic/racial background. There is no attempt to estimate the extent of the effect. According to the authors, the data can show the direction of the effect but are incapable of accurately estimating the size of the effect. With regards the inequalities between blacks and mulattos and between whites and blacks, the study reasserts what other studies have pointed out regarding the specificity of the student cohort in a system that is undergoing universalization but which has yet to eradicate inequality between students and between the state and private systems of education.

By synthesizing the results of this research we can also sum up the race and school effectiveness tradition. What singles this and similar studies out are the results concerning the 'school effect' on student performance. The hierarchical linear regression model has revealed that the school can have a positive effect on student achievement but does not succeed in eliminating the inequalities between different racial segments. On the contrary, in those schools with well-trained teachers and better salaries the gap in the achievement of white, mulatto, and black students is wider. Well-equipped schools with more engaged directors produce positive results, statistically speaking, but instead of reducing racial inequalities they increase the difference between white and black students. The study demonstrates, therefore, that positive school conditions promote the proficiency of white students more than that of mulatto and black students. An equally dramatic result is that inequalities are lower only in those schools in which the overall average of student achievement is low.

6.6   Racism and discrimination

This tradition is comprised of studies based on theories of social representation, ethnography, symbolic interactionism, ethnomethodology and structuralism (André and Lüdke, 1986). The research that adopts these approaches endeavors to evaluate such internal school dynamics as the relationship between teacher and pupil, classroom practice, pedagogical rituals, use of teaching materials in the classroom and others. The 'racism and discrimination' tradition has given rise to different strands of research at different moments in time, thus making it difficult to establish a chronological order of appearance. Nonetheless, it is possible to see how these strands relate to one another and the changes they have provoked regarding questions of prejudice, racism, and ethnic discrimination. It is also possible to say that in the production of knowledge on the present topic, the studies using qualitative methods preceded those using quantitative methods. The latter showed little progress until the recent consolidation of datasets that allow a broader appreciation of the Brazilian educational system. Qualitative studies, on the other hand, have opened up countless possibilities in the academic debate of prejudice, racism, racial stereotypes, and even the strategies adopted by families to protect their children from racism and xenophobia.

The racism and discrimination tradition is most clearly associated with research on the issues of (a) racial origin and socialization, (b) the symbolic manifestations of ethnic/racial prejudice, and (c) pedagogical mediation:

6.6.1   Racial origin and socialization

Researchers focusing on Afro-Brazilian topics at the beginning of the 1980s, at a time when the ideology of racial democracy was still in vogue, found great difficulty in dealing with the effects of racism and racial discrimination. The study of individual life histories gave these researchers what they needed to reconstruct the dynamics of race relations through the subjects' own interpretations

(Barbosa, 1983, 1987; Cunha Jr, 1987). These interpretations change over time. New studies undertaken over the following decades gathered information from Afro-Brazilian students in elementary school (Valente, 2002); adult and younger students (Silva, 2009); and university students (Teixeira, Praxedes and Pádua, 2006) and offer different examples of family guidance on educational success and failure and how to face up to racial discrimination.

The studies to recreate the educational trajectory of the children of European and Asian immigrant families in Brazil also rely on life histories. By and large, these studies of ethnic minorities that migrated and remained in Brazil, generated new families and entered the labor market, are sociological studies concerned with the influence of the original culture on the schooling of the Brazilian-born descendants. (Ogliari, 1999; Renk, 2001; Kreutz, 1999; Dalmoro, 1987; Rambo, 1994; Truzzi, 2008a, 2008b, 2008c).

The objective of these studies has not always been to reveal the relationship between ethnicity and educational inequality. The research has usually been more interested in analyzing how the original culture has managed to survive, especially with regards the linguistic varieties of the mother tongue, and how this has both prevented the children from suffering discrimination as well as supplying a remedy for the damage that ethnic discrimination could cause their educational trajectories. The focus of most of these studies has been on reading and writing and, more particularly, on the role of 'the mother tongue in the school achievement of the descendants of ethnic minorities' (Kreutz, 2000, p. 359)

6.6.2   Symbolic manifestations of ethnic/racial prejudice

This second theme brings together studies on the dissemination of negative stereotypes regarding blacks (Bazzili, 1999; Fazzi, 2004), indigenous peoples (Barros, 2000; Carmo, 1999; Oliveira, 2001), women (Lopes, 2002) and cultural and ethnic minorities. This tradition is made up of different strands of research that while sharing the same concern, adopt different methodological approaches when examining the symbolic manifestations of ethnic/racial prejudice. This does not mean that the different visions within this tradition are opposed to one another. Quite often the strands come together by combining elements of the different methods of analysis in accordance with the reality they intend to study.

Among the strands of the symbolic manifestations research, we find the study of prejudice and racism in textbooks and teaching materials that started in the 1980s. Based on the theory of reproduction (Bourdieu and Passeron, 1975) and on the analysis of content (Bardin, 1977), this research studies the frequency of negative stereotypes in teaching materials and then analyzes these in order to construct the image they portray of domination and subordination in Brazilian society (Silva, 1987; Negrão, 1987; Pinto, 1987a; Triumpho, 1987).

During the 1980s another strand emerges, combining the theory of communication with content analysis. The purpose of this work is no longer to analyze teaching materials but, instead, to construct a research technique to dissect children's literature in order to describe the way the producers of this written culture perceive white and non-white children (Rosemberg, 1980; Pinto, 1987). The initial concern is to characterize the sender and the intended receiver of children's literature (Rosemberg, 1980). Once these are characterized, the authors then present the social representations contained in the books. The followers of this strand of work use content analysis but introduce other elements to reduce reliance on quantitative methodology. Through these procedures, the images the senders have of their target clienteles are brought into the open (Costa, 1997; Araújo, 2001). These studies have shown that the senders (authors, picture designers, editors) do not take the ethnic/racial issue into consideration. They produce children's literature using their own imaginary frame of reference which is exclusively peopled by white children and which, thereby, creates a relationship of subordination for non-white readers (Rosemberg, Bazilli and Silva, 2003).

A further example of this general line of symbolic manifestations research can be seen as a step forward in the analysis of racism in textbooks. Carried out by the Center of Studies on Gender, Race, and Age of the Catholic University of São Paulo (Núcleo de Estudos de Gênero, Raça, e Idade; NEGRI/PUCSP), this work introduces the 'depth hermeneutics' method proposed by John B. Thompson (1995) for the study of culture and ideology. This method is subdivided into three consecutive stages: context analysis, analysis of the internal discourse of the symbolic forms themselves, and the reinterpretation of ideology (Rosemberg, Bazilli and Silva, 2003). The studies that follow this strand have shown that the forms used to express racism are symbolic and as such not only maintain the relations of domination, but also effectively generate them (Silva, 2008). Another strand that emerges almost at the same time as symbolic manifestations has as its main goal the identification of the mediators of the educational process.

6.6.3 Pedagogical mediation

The need to study racism not just in teaching materials and textbooks but also in day-to-day interactions inside the school led to the use of new methods of observational research. The challenge for researchers belonging to this new line of work was to identify those empirical elements of school relationships that needed to be observed and, even more difficult at the beginning of the 1980s, to get access to the school universe and investigate something that official school culture denied. In line with common beliefs, the great majority of Brazilian schools held that the country was free of race discrimination.

The theory of pedagogical mediation was originally based on Gramscian thinking which provided the basis for a considerable amount of research between 1980 and 2000. The point of departure for these studies was the idea that the relationship between teacher and pupil is not a direct one but one that requires mediators (Saviani, 1983; Cury, 1986; Mello, 1982). This stands in opposition to the idea that school education is derived exclusively from processes of 'knowledge transmission'.

A detailed analysis of pedagogical mediation studies shows the researchers using typically stucturalist procedures to study the school's normative instruments (school rules, course planning, curriculum, etc) and identify the different ways in which the school contributes to the dissemination of prejudice and negative stereotypes regarding Afro-descendants and indigenous peoples. The research aligned with the pedagogical mediation approach relies on pedagogical experiments in which teaching staff find ways to produce materials that deconstruct stereotyped visions and create positive images of the discriminated groups.

Now that there are policies for creating indigenous schools in accordance with the ethnic characteristics of the territory, researchers concerned with the education of indigenous groups are using the pedagogical mediation model to study the impact of new ways of representing ethnic minorities on the self-image of indigenous children and adolescents (Silva, 2002).

This line of research has acquired new strength in the current century due to the understanding that school systems should give priority to training teachers to deconstruct traditional racist discourse and the discriminatory practices that it fosters. (Cavalleiro, 2000; Gomes, 2001; Gonçalves, 2006). Pedagogical mediation stresses the use of different interview techniques borrowed from other qualitative approaches. The research explores the triangulated method of data collection that combines observation with different interview techniques so as to encompass the complexities of teacher practice.

At the same time as the research on poor teacher qualifications, another movement was going in the opposite direction. Focusing on the theme of racial inequality in schools, these studies emphasized the way some teachers manage to break the silence surrounding racial prejudice in Brazil by abandoning traditional methods of teaching. A significant number of these studies is associated with the Center for the Research of Everyday Education and Culture of the Faculty of Education of the Catholic University of Rio de Janeiro (Núcleo de Pesquisa Cotidiano, Educação e Cultura da Faculdade de Educação da Pontifícia Universidade Católica do Rio de Janeiro). These studies have introduced the theoretical-epistemological approach suggested by Walter Mignolo's theory of decolonization (Mignolo, 2005). According to these researchers, the adoption of this new approach has permitted the identification of school experiments in which the actors (teachers and specialists) are putting into practice what Mignolo has called 'colonial difference'. This is the recognition of 'other ways of construing knowledge drawn from ways of being, thinking and knowing different from European modernity but in dialogue with it' (Candau and Oliveira, 2010, pp. 34–48; Lima, 2005; Caputo, 2005).

6.7 Conclusions

The analysis of virtually all sociological research on the question of ethnic/racial inequality in education between 1980 and 2010 enabled us to identify three separate traditions of work that, while employing different methodologies and focusing on different aspects of the problem, share a similar concern to expose the nature of social inequality in Brazil. A considerable volume of previous research had studied the growth of popular social movements and the transformation of the working classes but had failed to understand the importance of race and ethnicity in the explanation of inequality. What had not been fully understood was how the indigenous peoples and those of African-Brazilian descent suffer discrimination both for their social class and their ethnic/racial ascendance.

The first research tradition, which we name 'charting ethnic/racial inequalities in education', expresses a rejection by researchers of the myth of Brazilian racial democracy. The principal studies belonging to this tradition use transversal and longitudinal data bases to show the changes but also the persistence of inequality in Brazilian society along the lines of ethnicity, race, and gender, both within and between generations.

The second tradition, concerning race and school effectiveness, seeks replies to questions regarding the role of schools in the reduction of ethnic/racial inequalities once established the evidence for differences in the levels of attainment of white and non-white students. The studies that comprise this tradition help clarify why the things that take place inside schools can have differential effects on white, black, and mulatto students. Research in this area usually relies on regression analyses in a variety of empirical settings and has shown that it is not sufficient to promote universal access to schooling. In order to reduce inequality it is also necessary to take into consideration the difference that schools can make to the educational trajectory of their students.

The 'racism and discrimation' tradition has established research on a number of fronts. On the first of these, we see the use of narrative interviews and life history research methods to focus on the reconstruction of life experiences and the efforts of families to prepare their offspring for instances of race discrimination and prejudice in school. The research has also been used to analyze the educational histories of European, Asian, and African immigrants in their process of adaptation to Brazilian society. On a second front, research has been a response to the negative stereotypes associated with blacks, people of indigenous origin, women, and ethnic minorities. The focus of these studies has been to denounce the use of stereotypes in textbooks, other teaching materials, and teaching activities. On the third front, the racism and discrimation tradition insists on the need to study how racism and ethnic/racial discrimination plays out in the interactions between teachers and students, between students themselves and between students and other members of school staff. The research methods employed are basically those of observation. These studies have contributed to the unmasking of the covert racism in Brazilian society that is manifested in the different cultural and pedagogical activities of schools.

To finalize, it is worth adding that our critical review identified a new research tendency concerned with the debate and consequences of the government's recent affirmative action policies. This debate has brought the issue of Brazilian ethnic/racial identity into the limelight. The current system of racial classification lies at the center of the debate (Brandão and Marins, 2007), attracting considerable criticism and raising a legal discussion regarding the way in which racial groups are categorized. As affirmative action is to benefit ethnic/racial minority groups, the difficulties start with the definition of who exactly is to be included. Who decides which ethnic/racial group the candidate belongs to? In order to solve this problem, several affirmative action programs have established non-traditional classification criteria: some use a self-classification system, others prefer third-person classification, and still others combine the two systems. The majority of research to study the effectiveness of these programs has stressed the importance of racial identity and the need to improve the classification methodologies.

In general, the focus of the research is the evaluation of concrete examples of affirmative action programs (Mattos, 2003; Weller, 2007; Weller and Silveira, 2008; Belchior, 2006; Cardoso, 2008). But many others of equal importance have emphasized ethnic/racial identity construction, showing that this theme is undergoing a process of renewal (Ferreira, 2009, 2010; Rosemberg, 2004). Although solid enough in themselves, the studies on this topic are still too recent and too few to be considered a new tradition in the study of educational inequality. We shall have to return to an analysis of this topic at a later date.

Notes

1. Made possible, as previously stated, by the combination of demographic census data with the more detailed educational census data.
2. A measure of the number of years a student is behind his peer group as the result of having repeated grades.

References

Althusser, L. (1974). *Ideologia e Aparelho Ideológico do Estado* (Lisboa: Presença).
Alves, M. T. G; Soares, J. F. (2004). 'Cor do Aluno e Desempenho Escolar: as evidências do Sistema de Avaliação do Ensino Básico (SAEB)'. *Encontro Anual da Anpocs*, XXVI, 25–49.

Ambrossetty, N. C. (1990). 'Ciclo Básico: uma proposta vista pelos professores'. *Cadernos de Pesquisa*, 74, 57–70.

André. M. L.; Lüdke, M. (1986). *Pesquisa em Educação: abordagens qualitativas* (São Paulo: EPU).

Araújo, L.T. (2001). *O uso do livro didático no ensino de História: depoimentos de professores da escola estaduais de ensino fundamental de São Paulo* (MA diss., Pontifical Catholic University of São Paulo).

Barbosa, I. M. F. (1983). *Socialização e Relações Raciais: um estudo de família negra em Campinas* (PhD diss., University of São Paulo).

Barbosa, I. M. F. (1987). 'Socialização e Identidade Racial'. *Cadernos de Pesquisa*, 63, 54–55.

Barbosa, M. L. O. (2005). 'As relações entre educação e raça no Brasil: um objeto em construção'. In Soares, S. [et al.] (eds), *Os mecanismos de discriminação racial nas escolas brasileiras* (Brasília: IPEA/FORD), pp. 5–20.

Barbosa, M. L.; Veiga, L. (1998). 'Eficiência e Equidade: os impasses de uma política educacional'. *Revista Brasileira de Política e Administração da Educação*, 14. 211–242.

Barcelos, L. C. (1992). 'Educação: um quadro as desigualdades raciais'. *Estudos Afro-Asiáticos*, 23, 37–69.

Barcelos, L. C. (1993). 'Educação e Desigualdades Raciais no Brasil'. *Cadernos de Pesquisa*, 86, 15–24.

Bardin, L. (1977). *Análise de Conteúdo* (Lisboa: Edições 70).

Barros, D. L. P. (2000). 'Esta é uma outra História: os índios nos livros didáticos de história do Brasil'. In Barros, D. L. P. (ed.), *Os discursos da descoberta: 55 e mais anos de discursos* (São Paulo: EDUSP/FAPESP).

Bazzili, C. (1999). *Discriminação contra personagens negros na literatura infanto-juvenil brasileira contemporânea* (MA diss., Pontifical Catholic University of São Paulo).

Belchior, E. B. (2006). *Não deixando a cor passar em branco: o processo de implementação de cotas para estudantes negros na Universidade de Brasília* (MA diss., University of Brasília).

Bergamaschi, M. A. (2004). 'Por que querem e porque não querem escolas guarani?'. *Telles*, 7, 107–120.

Bourdieu, P.; Passeron, J. C. (1975). *A Reprodução: elementos para uma teoria do sistema de ensino* (Rio de Janeiro: Francisco Alves).

Brandão, A. A.; Marins, M. T. A. (2007). 'Cotas para negros no ensino superior e formas de classificação racial'. *Educação e Pesquisa*, 33, 27–45.

Brandão, Z. (Coord.). (1982). *O Estado da arte de pesquisa de evasão e repetência no ensino de 1º grau no Brasil* (Rio de Janeiro: INEP).

Brasil. Constituição (1998). *Constituição da República Federativa do Brasil de 1988* (Brasília: Senado Federal, Centro Gráfico).

Brasil. *Lei nº 9.394, de 20 de dezembro de 1996*. Estabelece as diretrizes e bases da educação nacional. Brasília, 1996, http://www3.dataprev.gov.br/sislex/paginas/42/1996/9394. htm. Date accessed 27 May 2011.

Brasil. (1992). Instituto Brasileiro de Geografia e Estatística (IBGE). Censo demográfico 1991 (1 September 1991). Rio de Janeiro: IBGE.

Brasil. (2012). Instituto Brasileiro de Geografia e Estatística (IBGE). Censo demográfico 2010: resultados preliminares (29 October 2011). Rio de Janeiro: IBGE.

Brasil Ministério da Educação. (2005). Instituto Nacional de Estudos e Pesquisas Educacionais. *Mostre a sua raça, declare sua cor*. Brasília, Secretária de Educação Básica.

Brooke, N.; Soares, F. (2008). *Pesquisa em Eficácia Escolar: origem e trajetórias*. (Belo Horizonte: Ed. UFMG).

Cadernos de Pesquisa. (1987). Fundação Carlos Chagas. São Paulo, 63, 14–148.

Camargo, D. M. P.; Albuquerque, J. G. (2003). 'Projeto Pedagógico Xavante: tensões, rupturas na intensidade de construção curricular'. *CEDES*, 23, 338–366.

Candau, V. M. F.; Oliveira, L. F. (2010). 'Pedagogia Decolonial e Educação antirracista e intercultural no Brasil'. *Educação em Revista*, 26, 34–48.

Caputo, M. G. (2005) *Educação nos terreiros e como a escola dialoga com crianças que praticam candomblé* (PhD diss., Pontifical Catholic University of Rio de Janeiro).

Cardoso, C. B. (2008). *Efeito de Políticas de Cota na Universidade de Brasília: uma análise do rendimento e da evasão* (MA diss., University of Brasília).

Carmo, I. S. (1999). *Entre a Cruz e a Espada: o índio no discurso do livro didático de história* (MA diss., Pontifical Catholic University of São Paulo).

Cavalleiro, E. (2000). *Do silêncio lar ao silêncio do escolar. Educação e Poder: racismo, preconceito e discriminação na Educação Infantil* (São Paulo: Summus).

Costa, A. M. S. (1997). *Prática Pedagógica e Tempo Escolar: o uso do livro didático do ensino de História* (MA diss., Pontifical Catholic University of São Paulo).

Cunha, J. R. H. (1987). 'A indecisão dos pais face à percepção da discriminação racial na escola pela criança'. *Cadernos de Pesquisa*, 63, 45–68.

Cunha, L. A. (1979). 'Notas para a leitura da teoria da violência simbólica'. *Educação e Sociedade*, 5, 45–59.

Cunha, L. A. (1982). 'A Simbólica Violência da Teoria'. *Cadernos de Pesquisa*, 43, 55–57.

Cury, C. R. J. (1986). *Educação e Contradição: Elemento Metodológico para uma Teoria crítica do Fenômeno Educativo* (São Paulo: Cortes/Autores Associados).

Dalmoro, S. N. (1987). 'Escola, igreja e Estado nas colônias italianas'. *Educação e Realidade*, 12, 57–79.

Demartine, Z. B. F. (1998). 'A educação entre famílias de imigrantes japoneses: elementos para história de educação brasileira'. In Pontifícia Universidad Católica de Chile (ed.), *IV Congreso Ibero-americano de História de la Educacíon Latino-americana* (Santiago, Chile, Pontifícia Universidad Católica de Chile), pp. 23–45.

Duncan, O. D. (1969). 'Inheritance of Poverty and Inheritance of Race'. In D. P. Moynihan (ed.), *On Understanding Poverty* (New York, Basic Books), pp. 88–98.

Duncan, O. D. and Blau, P. M. (1967). *The American Occupational Structure* (New York: Wiley and Sons).

Falcão Filho, J. L. M. (1997). 'A qualidade na escola'. *Ensaio*, 5, 73–78.

Falcão Filho, J. L. M. (2000). 'Escola; ambientes, estrutura, variáveis e competência'. *Ensaio*, 8, 283–312.

Fazzi, E. C. (2004). *O drama racial das crianças brasileiras: socialização entre pares e preconceito* (Belo Horizonte: Autêntica).

Fernandes, F. (1964). *A integração do negro na sociedade de classes*. 2nd. (São Paulo: HUCITC).

Ferrão, M. E.; Barbosa, M. E.; Fernades, C. A. (2001). 'A escola brasileira faz diferença? uma investigação do efeito escola na proficiência em matemática dos alunos da 4ª série'. In Franco, C. (ed.), *Promoção, ciclos e avaliação educacional*. (Porto Alegre: Artmed).

Ferreira, A. H. (2010). *Discursos Étnico-Raciais Proferidos por Candidatos (as) a Programa de Ação Afirmativa* (PhD diss., Pontifical Catholic University of São Paulo).

Ferreira, E. C. L. (2009). *A construção da identidade e da diferença: sobre a política e cotas e poder de representação* (PhD diss., University of Brasília).

Ferreira, S. L. (2006). 'A formação para a construção de um projeto de futuro Guarani e Kaiowá no Mato Grosso do Sul'. *Telles*, 6, 95–101.

Franco, C.; Alves, F.; Ortigão, I. (2007). 'Origem Social e Risco de Repetência: interação raça e capital econômico'. *Cadernos de Pesquisa*, 37, 161–180.

Freyre, G. (1998). *Casa Grande e Senzala* (Rio de Janeiro: Editora Record).

Freyre, G. (1939). *Sobrados e Mocambos, decadência do patriarcado rural e desenvolvimento do urbano* (Rio de Janeiro: Ed Nacional).

Fundação Instituto Brasileiro de Geografia e Estatística. *Pesquisa Nacional por Amostra de Domicílio (PNAD 1976)*, http://biblioteca.ibge.gov.br/.../PNAD_1976_v1t03_PR_SC_RS.pdf. Date accessed 22 March 2011.

Giron, L. S. (1998). 'Colônia italiana e educação'. *História da Educação*, 2, 87–106.

Gomes, N. L. (2001). 'Educação cidadã, etnia e raça: o trato pedagógico da diversidade'. In Cavalleiro, E. (ed.), *Racismo e Anti-racismo na Educação: repensando nossa escola* (São Paulo: Summus).

Gonçalves, L. A. O. (2000). 'Negros e Educação no Brasil'. In Lopes, E. M. T.; Faria Filho, L. M.; Veiga, C. G. (eds), *500 anos de Educação no Brasil* (Belo Horizonte: Autêntica), pp. 325–346.

Gonçalves, L. A. O. (2006). 'Educação das relações étnico-raciais: o desafio da formação docente'. *Encontro Anual da Anped*, XXIX, 45–68.

Gramsci, A. (1975). *Os Intelectuais e a Organização da Cultura* (Rio de Janeiro: Civilização Brasileira).

Grupioni, L. D. B. (2003). 'A Educação Indígena na Academia: inventário comentando as dissertações e teses sobre educação escolar indígena no Brasil (1978–2002)'. *Revista Em Aberto*, 20, 197–238.

Grupioni, L. D. B. (ed.). (2006). *Formação de Professores Indígenas: Repensando trajetórias* (Brasília: MEC).

Guimarães, A. A. S. (2004). 'Preconceito de cor e racismo no Brasil'. *Revista de Antropologia*, 47, 9–43.

Guimarães, A. A. S. (2006). 'Depois da democracia racial'. *Tempo Social*, 18, 269–287.

Handa, T. (1987). *O imigrante japonês. Histórias de sua vida no Brasil* (São Paulo: T. A. Queiroz/ Centro de Estudos Nipo-Brasileira).

Hasenbalg, A. C. (1979). *Discriminação Racial e Desigualdades Sociais no Brasil* (Rio Janeiro: Graal).

Henriques, R. (2001). *Desigualdade Racial no Brasil: evolução das condições de vida na década de 90*. Instituto de Pesquisa Econômico Aplicada, http://www.ipea.gov.br. Date accessed 23 March 2011.

Hofbauer, A. (2006). 'Ações Afirmativas e o Debate sobre o Racismo no Brasil'. *Lua Nova*, 68, 9–56.

Ianni, O. (1972). *Raças e Classes no Brasil* (Rio de Janeiro: Civilização Brasileira).

Jacomini, M. A. (2004). 'A escola e os educadores em tempo de ciclos e progressão continuada: uma análise das experiências do Estado de São Paulo'. *Educação e Pesquisa*, 30, 401–418.

Kaly, A. P. (2001). 'Os estudantes africanos no Brasil e o preconceito racial'. In Castro, M. G. (ed.), *Migrações internacionais: contribuições para políticas brasileiras* (Brasília: CNPD), pp. 463–478.

Kreutz, L. (1994a). *Material didático e currículo na escola teuto-brasileira do Rio Grande do Sul* (São Leopoldo: Unisinos).

Kreutz, L. (1994b). 'A escola teuto-brasileira católica e a nacionalização do ensino'. In Müller, T. L. (ed.), *Nacionalização e imigração alemã* (São Leopoldo: Editora Unisinos).

Kreutz, L. (1999). 'Identidade étnica e processo escolar'. *Cadernos de Pesquisa*, 107, 79–96.

Kreutz, L. (2000). 'A Educação de Imigrantes no Brasil'. In Lopes, E. M. T.; Faria Filho, L. M.; Veiga, C. G. (eds), *500 anos de Educação no Brasil* (Belo Horizonte: Autêntica), pp. 347–371.

Levison, D. (1989). *Child Care in Metropolitan Brazil* (Word Bank).

Lima, A. C. G. (2005). *A escola e o silêncio da batucada: estudo sobre a relação de uma escola pública no bairro Oswaldo Cruz e a cultura do samba* (PhD diss. Pontifical Catholic University of Rio de Janeiro).

Lopes, L. P. M. (2002). *Identidades fragmentadas: a construção discursiva da raça, gênero e sexualidade em sala de aula* (Campinas: Mercado Aberto).

Mattos, W. R. (2003). 'Ação Afirmativa na Universidade do Estado da Bahia'. In Silva, P. B. G.; Silvério, V. R. (eds), *Entre a injustiça simbólica e a injustiça econômica* (Brasília: INEP/MEC).

Mauch, C.; Vasconcelos, N. (eds). (1994). *Os alemães no sul do Brasil: cultura, etnicidade, história* (Canoas: Editora ULBRA).

Mélia, B. (1999). 'Educação Indígena na Escola'. *CEDES*, 19, 11–17.

Mello, G. N. (1982). *Magistério do I Grau: da Competência Técnica ao Compromisso Político* (São Paulo: Cortes. Autores Associados).

Mello, G. N. (1994). 'Escolas eficazes: um tema revisado'. In Xavier, A. C. J.; Sobrinho, A; Marra, F. (eds), *Gestão escolar: desafios e tendências* (Brasília: IPEA).

Mignolo, W. A. (2005). 'Colonialidade de Cabo a Rabo: o hemisfério ocidental no horizonte da modernidade'. In Lander, E. (ed.), *A colonialidade do saber: eurocentrismo e ciências sociais, Perspectivas latino-americanas* (Buenos Aires: CLACSO).

Müller, T. L. (ed.). (1994). *Nacionalização e imigração alemã* (São Leopoldo: Editora Unisinos).

Nascimento, A. C. (2003). 'Escola Indígena Guarani/Karaowá no Mato Grosso do Sul: as conquistas e o discurso dos professores-índios'. *Telles*, 5, 11–24.

Negrão, E. (1987). 'A Discriminação Racial em Livro Didático e Infanto-Juvenis'. *Cadernos de Pesquisa*, 63, 86–87.

Nosella, M. L. C. D. (1981). *As Belas Mentiras: a ideologia subjacentes aos textos didáticos* (Vitória: Ed Moraes).

Ogliari, M. M. (1999). *As condições de resistência e vitalidade de uma língua minoritária no contexto sociolinguítico brasileiro* (PhD diss., Federal University of Santa Catarina).

Oliveira, T. S. (2001). *Olhares Poderosos: o índio no livro didático e revistas*. Dissertação (MA diss., Federal University of Rio Grande do Sul).

Osório, R. G.; Soares, S. A. (2005). 'Geração 80: Um Documentário Estatístico sobre a Produção das Diferenças Educacionais entre Negros e Brancos'. In Osório, R. G.; Soares, S. A. (eds), *Os Mecanismos da Discriminação Racial nas Escolas Brasileiras* (Brasília: IPEA/ FORD), pp. 152–174.

Paes, M. H. R. (1999). 'A questão da língua na escola indígena em aldeias'. *CEDES*, 19, 76–91.

Paixão, M. (2009). *Relatório das Desigualdades Raciais*, http://www.laeser.ie.ufrj.br. Date accessed 23 May 2011.

Paixão, M. (2010). *Relatório das Desigualdades Raciais*, http://www.laeser.ie.ufrj.br. Date accessed 27 October 2011.

Pierson, D. (1971). *Brancos e Pretos na Bahia* (Rio de Janeiro: Ed Nacional).

Pinto, R. P. (1985). 'Escola e a questão da pluralidade étnica'. *Cadernos de Pesquisa*. 55, 3–17.

Pinto, R. P. (1987a). 'Educação do Negro: uma revisão da bibliografia'. *Cadernos de Pesquisa*, 62, 3–34.

Pitts, Jr. (2006). *Forging Ethnic identity through faith: religion and Syrian-Lebanese community in São Paulo* (MA diss., Vanderlit University).

Rama, G. W. (1989). 'Estrutura Social e Educação: Presença de raças e grupos sociais na escola'. *Cadernos de Pesquisa*, n. 69, 17–31.

Rambo, A. (1994). *A escola comunitária teuto-brasileira católica* (São Leopoldo: Editora Sinos).

Renk, V. (2001). *Educação de migrantes alemães católicos em Curitiba* (Curitiba: Champagnat).

Rosemberg, F. (1980). 'Discriminações étnico-raciais na literatura infanto-juvenil brasileira'. *Tempo Brasileiro*, 63, 47–69.

Rosemberg, F. (1991). 'Raça e Educação Inicial'. *Cadernos de Pesquisa*, 77, 25–34.

Rosemberg, F. (2004). 'O branco no IBGE continua branco na ação afirmativa?'. *Estudos Avançados*, 18, 21–39.

Rosemberg, F.; Bazilli, C.; Silva, P. B. (2003). 'Racismo em livros didáticos brasileiros e seu combate: uma revisão da literatura'. *Educação e Pesquisa*, 29, 125–146.

Rosemberg, F.; Negrão, E.; Pinto, R. P. (1986). *Diagnóstico sobre a situação educacional de negros (pretos e pardos) no Estado de São Paulo* (São Paulo: Fundação Carlos Chagas).

Saviani, D. (1983). *Escola e Democracia* (São Paulo: Cortes).

Silva, A. C. (1987). 'Estereótipos e preconceitos em relação ao negro no livro de comunicação e expressão de 1° grau'. *Cadernos de Pesquisa*. 63, 96–98.

Silva, A. L. (2002). *Crianças Indígenas* (São Paulo: Editora Global).

Silva, N. V. (1979). 'O preço da cor: diferenciais raciais na distribuição da renda no Brasil'. *Pesquisa e Planejamento Econômico*, 10, 21–44.

Silva, N. N. da. (2009). *Juventude, EJA e Relações Raciais: um estudo sobre os significados e sentidos atribuídos pelos jovens negros aos processos de escolarização da EJA.* (MA diss., Federal University of Minas Gerais).

Silva, P. V. B. (2008). *Racismo em Livros Didáticos. Estudos sobre negros e brancos em livros de língua portuguesa* (Belo Horizonte: Autêntica).

Soares, J. F.; Alves, M. G. T. (2003). 'Desigualdades Raciais no Sistema Brasileiro de Educação Básica'. *Educação e Pesquisa*, 29, 35–49.

Soares, S.; Osório, R. G. (eds). (2005). *Os Mecanismos da Discriminação Racial nas Escolas Brasileiras* (Brasília: IPEA/FORD).

Teixeira, I. A. C.; Praxedes, V. L; Pádua, K. C. (2006). *Memórias e percursos de estudantes negros e negras da UFMG.* (Belo Horizonte: Autêntica).

Theodoro, M.; Jacoud, L; Osório, R. G; Soares, S. (eds). (2008). *As Políticas Públicas e a Desigualdade Racial no Brasil: 120 anos após a Abolição.* (Brasília, IPEA).

Thompson, J. B. (1995). *Ideologia e Cultura Moderna: teoria social crítica na era dos meios de comunicação de massa* (Petrópolis: Vozes).

Triumpho, V. R. (1987). 'O negro no livro didático e a prática dos agentes de pastoral negros'. *Cadernos de Pesquisa*, 63, 93–95.

Truzzi, O. M. S. (1992). *De mascates a doutores: sírios libaneses em São Paulo* (São Paulo: IDESP/Sumaré).

Truzzi, O. M. S. (2008a). 'Redes em processos migratórios'. *Tempo Social*, 20, 199–218.

Truzzi, O. M. S. (2008b). 'Sociabilidade e Valores: um olhar sobre a família árabe muçulmana em São Paulo'. *Dados*, 51, 37–71.

Truzzi, O. M. S. (2008c). 'Educar na Religião: desafios para transmissão de valores entre muçulmanos em São Paulo'. *Cadernos CERU*, 19, 157–179.

Valente, A. L. (2002). 'Os negros, a educação e as políticas de ação afirmativa'. *Revista Brasileira de Educação*, 19, 76–86.

Weller, W. (2007). 'Diferenças e desigualdades na universidade de Brasília: experiências de jovens negras e suas visões sobre o sistema de cotas'. *Política & Sociedade*, 6, 133–158.

Weller, W.; Silveira, M. (2008). 'Ações Afirmativas no sistema educacional: trajetórias de jovens negras da Universidade de Brasília'. *Revista de Estudos Feministas*, 16, 21–33.

7
Canada

Katherine Lyon, Hélène Frohard-Dourlent, Paul Fripp, and Neil Guppy

7.1 Introduction

Trajectories of research fields are influenced by the accumulation of knowledge, but also by changing methodologies, trends in grant funding, and scholars' personal interests. As a result, the course of research is neither linear nor predictable, making it particularly important for researchers to periodically reflect, in a systematic manner, upon the progression of works in their areas of expertise. In this chapter, we methodically sample and analyze changing trends in Canadian sociological research regarding education, ethnicity, and inequality from 1980 to 2011. As we examine and discuss patterns in approaches and findings, we also highlight areas and methods where future work is required.

Ethnic stratification in education is distinctive in Canada given the overlapping realities of high immigration, aboriginal rights, and colonial legacies, coupled with the lasting linguistic and cultural inequality between the British and French founding charter groups. With such complex ethnic, ancestral, and linguistic diversity, numerous areas of sociological inquiry related to education have developed in Canada.

Although previous reviews of education and ethnicity have been conducted in Canada, this project adds to the existing literature by broadening the language, timeframe, and focus of the sample. In particular, our sample includes francophone and anglophone research, whereas most existing reviews are specific to either French- or English-Canadian literature (Daley and Begley, 2008; Davies and Guppy, 1998; McAndrew, 2001). Furthermore, the majority of existing studies span only a decade. Our focus not only incorporates the most recent literature, but also includes over 30 years of previous research. Finally, our inclusion of topics in education relating to First Nation peoples, immigrant and visible minority populations, and French-Canadians makes this paper one of the broader reviews in this area. In contrast, other reviews focus on a more limited scope (e.g. Kirova's (2008) review of multicultural education).

This article has three distinct sections. We begin by contextualizing the Canadian education system historically and describing sociopolitical-legal developments regarding multiculturalism. This is followed by a methods section in which we describe in detail our inclusion criteria and search process. Finally, we identify, describe, and discuss the following five research traditions that emerged from our survey of the research literature: 'mobility/meritocracy', 'discrimination/ racism', 'identity/values', 'aboriginal education', and 'institutional processes'. These groupings are based on the research focus, scope, and in some cases, methods, employed by the authors and serve as a general guide for navigating the complex research terrain in Canada in the past 30 years.

7.2   National context

7.2.1   Canada's education system

Unlike most other nations, central control of schooling is weak in Canada. Education is the purview of the provinces and territories, not the federal government. As a result, significant components of the education system, such as the curriculum, teacher certification, and funding, vary by province. First Nations education alone remains under federal jurisdiction, highlighting the colonial legacy that still impacts Canada today (Hare, 2007). Most provinces nevertheless have relatively similar school systems, beginning with kindergarten at age five or six and progressing through to Grade 12. Typically schools are divided into elementary (k–8) and secondary (9–12), although middle schools (7–9) are increasingly popular (see Figure 7.1).Tracking or streaming within schools is minimal in comparison to most European systems. Most schooling is public, with only about 10% of students attending private schools, the majority of which are religious or heritage based (with relatively few elite private schools). Most provinces have some form of standardized examination system, mainly designed to track student performance, but increasingly few provinces have final standardized graduation exams for Grade 12. The tertiary level is characterized by two separate tracks, a community college/institute track that is mainly vocationally oriented, and a university track. The majority of high school graduates proceed to some form of post-secondary training, with about 25% of 19–23 year olds attending university (AUCC, 2007, p. 21).

As will be discussed below, the Canadian education system has been shaped by the nation's diverse ethnocultural population as well as the changing political approaches to policies of multiculturalism.

7.2.2   Migration patterns and ethnic groups

Immigration has played a significant role in the past and present ethnic composition of Canada as well as the nation's changing approach to diversity. The major source countries of immigrants have changed over time due to

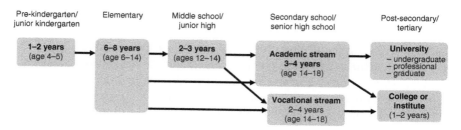

Figure 7.1   Structure of public education in Canada
Notes: 1. The structure varies by province (schooling is a provincial, not a federal, responsibility).
2. At the secondary or senior high school level the academic stream is the most prominent trajectory with less emphasis on vocational in recent decades.
3. The CEGEP university transfer program, not pictured here, is an important stream unique to the Province of Québec (between Grade 11 and university entrance).

discriminatory immigration regulations. Prior to 1960, the immigration system favored Americans, British, and Northern Europeans with white skin (Derwing and Munro, 2007, pp. 93–94). With a change in legislation as well as increased mainstream acceptance of diversity after World War II, Asia became the main source continent for immigrants. Since 2001, the top three source countries for permanent residence have been China, India, and the Philippines (Citizenship and Immigration Canada, 2009).

Currently, immigration policies prioritize three classes of immigrants: family, economic, and refugees and persons in need of protection (Citizenship and Immigration Canada, 2010). Canadian immigration has a strong history of admitting refugees based on its humanitarian ideals and temporary workers for the purpose of domestic care and seasonal labor. In 2002, policy changes resulted in younger, highly educated and bilingual workers gaining increased preference. The economic class, constituting 56% of immigrants in 2005, privileges individuals with higher education, language skills, and experience among other factors. However, skilled immigrant workers – particularly visible minorities – have a higher unemployment rate and lower income than workers born in Canada. This trend can largely be attributed to the lack of recognition of foreign educational credentials and experience by professional associations and employers (Fong and Cao, 2009; Reitz, 2001). The disconnect between immigration policies and labor market practices is particularly problematic given that most immigrants enter Canada through legal channels, in contrast to the United States where illegal immigration is a more vexing problem.

Estimating Canada's current ethnic, racial, and ancestral composition is fraught with difficulty given the diversity of ethnic heritage, the changing patterns of self-identification, and intermarriage across groups. Table 7.1 estimates ethnic composition for seven coarsely defined groupings, but is at best a rough approximation of the ethnocultural composition of modern Canada.

Table 7.1 Estimate of ethnocultural composition of Canada, 2008

	%	N
English	35	12,000,000
French	25	8,600,000
Other European	24	8,300,000
Asian	10	3,500,000
Aboriginal	3	1,040,000
African/Arab	3	1,030,000
South American	1	350,000
Total	100	34,500,000

Source: Authors' calculations from Statistics Canada, General Social Survey, 2008.

The table clearly shows the European dominance in the population, reflects a growing Asian presence over the last few decades, and emphasizes how immigration patterns in Canada have differed from the United States with respect to a much smaller black and Hispanic population. Another notable demographic characteristic of Canada is that Canadians tracing their ethnic ancestry to British stock are in a minority. Additionally, francophone populations are experiencing a relative population decline in French Canada in the face of immigration from non-francophone groups. This has heightened concerns for the preservation of their cultural heritage in the face of English-language dominance in the rest of Canada and the USA. Also significant is the fact that the visible minority population has become a larger and more vocal group in the last few decades (Fleras and Elliot, 1992). The table, based as it is on a national survey, likely underestimates the aboriginal population (other estimates would put the aboriginal population at approximately 4.4%; see Statistics Canada, 2001).

7.2.3 Relevant education and social policy developments

Strongly steeped in pro-diversity sentiments, contemporary sociological education research in Canada is inevitably shaped by the country's history of ethnic conflict and accommodation as well as by the development of formal, legally entrenched policies of multiculturalism. Although today multiculturalism is accepted as a legitimate framework within government institutions such as schools, this understanding is the result of the naturalization of the ideological frame of multiculturalism (Ng, 1995). Within Canada, multiculturalism is a process that emerged out of a history of struggle between the French and British founding charter groups, colonial oppression of First Nations peoples, and high rates of diverse and often contested in-migration.

The roots of present-day minority rights were laid as early as the 1600s when the British and French colonial powers fought to conquer land occupied by indigenous peoples.[1] After the British defeated the French in 1759, they went on to shatter aboriginal culture and institutions through assimilationist programs such as government-run residential schools, the last of which closed in the mid-1990s (Hare, 2007; see also Blackburn, 2000; Milloy, 1999). Legally mandated for First Nations children, these institutes devastated the inter-generational transmission of beliefs, language, and social structure, and were the source of child abuse, forced labor, and poor academic instruction (see below for more detail).

To maintain dominance in the face of resistance, the British developed strategic legislation to appease both the French and aboriginal groups. These accommodative yet self-serving statutes allowed for the eventual acknowledgment of diverse languages, cultures, and heritages in Canada (Joshee and Winton, 2007, p. 22). For example, the 1763 Royal Proclamation legitimated aboriginal self-government and land negotiation rights while the 1774 Québec Act ensured the survival of French language and culture. In 1876, the Indian Act granted First Nations people official status while furthering the government's control (Lawrence, 2003). These historical regulations maintain a strong contemporary presence, particularly in relation to recent court rulings granting land claims to aboriginal bands and language rights to francophone Canadians.

While these policies laid the preliminary foundations of Canadian multiculturalism, events during and after World War II led to its official entrenchment. Although the first half of the 1900s saw discriminatory immigration policies and anti-foreigner sentiments prevail, the 1947 Canadian Citizenship Act coupled with the unified war effort and increased in-migration from Europe led to more positive public associations with cultural diversity (Fleras and Elliot, 1992, p. 71; Joshee and Winton, 2007, pp. 18, 23). This new legal and cultural basis for minority rights contributed to increasing political unrest in the 1960s. Separatist nationalism grew in Québec, ethnic minorities protested the primacy of French and English language and culture, and aboriginal groups demanded recognition of their unique legal rights.

In 1971, Liberal Prime Minister Pierre Elliott Trudeau responded to pressure from the diverse ethnic communities, the French-Canadian charter group, and First Nations by introducing the policy of multiculturalism. This multicultural framework incorporated French and English as the dominant languages and strove to legitimate the cultures of all ethnic groups (Fleras and Elliot, 1992, p. 72; Ley, 2010, pp. 196–197). While this first attempt focused primarily upon cultural preservation and appreciation through festivals and programming, significant modifications occurred over the next 30 years, allowing multicultural policy to touch on systemic discrimination (Dewing and Leman, 2006, p. 5). Of note is section 27 of the Canadian Charter of Rights and Freedoms (1982) which states that the charter 'shall be interpreted in a manner consistent with the preservation and enhancement of the multicultural heritage of Canadians', thus integrating multicultural history and principles into court decisions (Government of Canada, 1982). Sections 15(1) and 15(2) demand that all people be treated equally under the law without facing discrimination based on categories including race, national or ethnic origin, color, and religion, with an exemption being made for laws and programs geared to assist marginalized groups. Additionally, the Canadian Multiculturalism Act (Government of Canada, 1988), brought in by Prime Minister Mulroney's Progressive Conservative government, clarifies the government's goals and position with regard to multiculturalism and legally binds government institutions to operate based on these ideals. Lastly, the 1984 Abella Commission, led by Judge Rosalie Abella, proposed the concept of employment equity to ensure that under-represented groups, including aboriginals and visible minorities, were not denied access to job opportunities or the ability to achieve upward mobility within a reasonably accommodating work environment. This commission led to the Employment Equity Act, which outlines that workplace practices, such as hiring, training, and advancement, must follow employment equity standards (Government of Canada, 1995). Collectively these acts create a strong anti-racist legal system within Canada (Dewing and Leman, 2006, p. 5; Ley, 2010).

Across the country, multicultural policy has not had a consistent or unified effect on educational contexts because, unlike other Western nations, education is provincially mandated in Canada (Ghosh, 2004, p. 545). Each of the ten provinces, as well as the northern territories, have the flexibility to uniquely interpret and integrate federal multiculturalism policies – policies that are particularly vague with regard to education (Guppy and Lyon, 2011). The type of multicultural education policy as well as its speed of implementation therefore varies. For example, Saskatchewan created policies as early as 1974, while Newfoundland and Labrador waited until 2008 (Dewing and Leman, 2006, p. 12; Fleras and Elliot, 1992, p. 80; Human Resources, Labour and Employment, 2008). Québec's interpretation is especially distinct as it promotes an 'intercultural' instead of 'multicultural' approach (Pagé, 1986; McAndrew, 2001, pp. 147–154). French is held as the principal culture and language of the province – a policy that is particularly influential regarding education and language of instruction (Fleras and Elliot, 1992, p. 83). Given these historical developments as well as the diversity found within schooling systems across the nation, we expected to find education research traditions focusing upon the experiences of numerous ethnic, heritage and linguistic groups, processes and issues.

7.3 Methodology

Identifying the Canadian research literature on race/ethnicity/ancestry and educational inequality required a careful process of delineating the research scope and then searching for the relevant literature. We review this process here by noting first our criteria for inclusion of research work and second our procedures for searching the research literature to identify studies for possible inclusion.

First, we followed Stevens (2007, pp. 147–148) and Stevens et al. (2011, p. 6) in defining a research tradition as 'a set of studies developed over a certain period of time, which explore the relationship between educational inequality and race/ethnicity in a similar way by focusing on similar research questions, units of analysis, or social processes'. Studies are therefore included only if they explore how race/ethnicity, and we add ancestry, interact with educational inequalities. This was not always easy to determine. On the one hand many studies have very explicit dependent variables that are clear measures of schooling outcomes (e.g. years of schooling, standardized test scores) and so long as a measure of ethnicity or race or ancestry is used as a predictor variable, then the study would be included. Many quantitative studies have this design. On the other hand numerous research works are premised on the view that different ethnic/racial/ancestral groups do more or less well in schooling because of how a particular group is either privileged or not (e.g. by the curriculum, because of discrimination). Schooling outcomes are often implicit or assumed. Many qualitative studies have this design. While we include many qualitative studies of this latter type, we also exclude many studies that, for example, probe multicultural policies and practices at a general level but are not directly linked to measured educational outcomes for specific groups.

Second, our search protocol was similar to those used in other countries:

1. We include literature written in both English and French where the research context focused upon one or more of the following: English-Canada, French-Canada, or aboriginal/First Nations. Therefore we were alert to the possible variation in research for each of these broadly defined groupings.
2. We restrict our attention to studies with a sociological approach but, as the disciplinary divisions of labor soften through an increase in transdisciplinary approaches, we are liberal in the inclusion of studies that others might reject as insufficiently sociological.
3. The focus is upon research studies examining the relationship between educational inequality and race/ethnicity/ancestry. The inclusion of ancestry is perhaps unique to Canada in that here Native Indians or aboriginal peoples are not typically included as a distinct racial or ethnic group, as these are terms used most often to discuss the migrants who came to northern North America long after indigenous communities were thriving. Ancestry is a common term that recognizes the unique historical circumstances of aboriginal peoples.
4. Only research studies published in the period from 1980 to the present are included, and we have tried to be inclusive of recent papers that we knew were in press at the time of our writing.

5. We focus mainly upon secondary (high school) education, with some studies included that capture the transition from secondary to post-secondary institutions since this is an especially important transition that has been well-studied recently. Since some provinces have middle schools, the grade level at which students enter secondary school differs slightly in research from different parts of the country. Given this discrepancy, we are liberal in our inclusion of research that includes higher elementary grades depending on the province.

6. To qualify as a research study, manuscripts had to have appeared in peer-reviewed journals, been published by a press that handles scholarly work, or been released as an official report of a governmental or non-governmental organization. Although many were available, theses and dissertations were not included in the final sample.

Our sampling procedures involved, as the first step, the extensive use of searchable electronic databases. These included Sociological Abstracts, the UBC library catalogue, ERIC, Academic Search Complete, CBCA Education, Econlit, Summon, Erudit, Cairn, and a few other databases. All searches were limited to post-1979 and included the term 'Canad*' or 'First Nations'. Other search terms which led to the most frequent hits included a version of 'educat*', 'ethnic*', 'rac*', and 'school*' (equivalent terms in French were used as well). As a second step we systematically reviewed the table of contents of the journals in which we had identified relevant literature in step one, as well as journals that we thought might have carried relevant literature but from which we had not yet found many studies. As a third step we carefully perused the list of references in the most recent literature we could find to try to identify studies which we may have missed in steps one and two (we added very few studies by this means, suggesting stages one and two were effective). Finally, as the fourth and final step we used the web to search for recent papers from authors who had previously published relevant literature, on the grounds that they may have published more recent work which we might have missed.

Based on the inclusion criteria and the sampling protocol we initially identified 193 English-language pieces and 75 French-language pieces. After reading all of these papers we reduced the final number of works included to 244. Based on the final selection of works, the following five research traditions emerged: mobility/meritocracy; individual discrimination/prejudice/racism; identity/values; aboriginal; and institutional processes. In what follows we present the key characteristics of each tradition and provide an overview of fundamental works in each area. Given the voluminous literature we amassed, we summarize trends found within each tradition while specifically mentioning only illustrative, exemplary, or noteworthy pieces.

7.4   Research traditions

7.4.1   Mobility/meritocracy

Studies in this tradition formulate their research questions around issues of equality of educational opportunity. The research is often framed by issues of meritocracy (or lack thereof), with research examining whether or not schooling is a space enabling social mobility. In Canada, John Porter's (1965) work on the vertical mosaic is pivotal. Porter portrayed ethnic groups in Canada as arrayed along a vertical mosaic of social inequality and dominance, with the British and the French, in that order, at the top, with other European groups coming next, and with non-European groups aligned along the bottom.

Often referencing the Porter tradition, the studies discussed in this section examine how racial, ethnic, or ancestral background, frequently linked to language barriers and marginalization, directly influences educational attainment or achievement, with schooling outcomes as the dependent variable. More recently, there has been a shift in focus to the rates of return to education, where educational attainment is used to predict labor market outcomes, examining how these rates of return do or do not vary across ethnic/racial/ancestral groups. This first research tradition can be broken into three subthemes focusing respectively on achievement, attainment, and financial return.

In the first subgroup, achievement is analyzed by deciding on one or several measures of academic success and comparing the outcomes of different ethnic, racial or ancestral groupings (Ledent, Murdoch, and Ait-Said, 2010). Rousseau, Drapeau, and Corin (1996), for instance, utilize the cumulative mean grades for French and math as a measure for academic achievement for refugee children. These data are analyzed against the occurrence of emotional problems, as measured by the Child Behavior Checklist, to demonstrate the association between emotional problems, learning disabilities, and the academic achievement of refugees. Similarly, in Worswick (2004), academic achievement is measured by students' scores in reading, vocabulary, and math obtained in the National Longitudinal Survey of Children and Youth. Utilizing this information, he found that students whose mother tongue is neither English nor French experience a lower performance than other students before the age of six, but that by the time they reach higher grades in school the children of immigrant parents have scores comparable to those of children of Canadian-born parents.

Research in this tradition compares minority students to majority students, but also examines differences between different minority groups (McAndrew, Ledent, and Ait-Said, 2006). In Québec, this research tradition is often supplemented by an interest in linguistic groups and in the role that language plays in maintaining or creating educational inequities (Sylvain et al., 1988). McAndrew, Ledent, and Ait-Said (2008), for example, compare the educational achievement of black students in Québec attending francophone schools with those of black students attending anglophone schools. They find subtle but significant differences between these two populations that provide different explanations for their educational underachievement, thus highlighting the importance of inter-group variations.

Research on education attainment uses ethnic, racial, or ancestral group belonging as an independent variable and analyzes the resulting differences in school attainment between these groups (Abada, Hou and Ram, 2008; Aydemir, Chen and Corak, 2008; Picot and Hou, 2011). Shamai (1992), for example, draws upon 40 years of Canadian census data to contrast the educational attainment levels of different minority groups with regard to years of schooling. Abada, Hou and Ram (2009) consider factors influencing the educational attainment of children of immigrants, particularly with regard to mobility across generations.

Lastly, research within the financial return subgroup draws upon measures of achievement and attainment and compares them against market outcomes to determine the financial payoff of education by ethnic, racial, or ancestral group (Bonikowska and Hou, 2010; Dicks and Sweetman, 1999; Geschwender and Guppy, 1995). This interest in causal links between educational attainment and social mobility has long been a focus of the literature on educational inequalities, and concern with issues of social mobility often underlies research in the other subgroups discussed in this section. Research that focuses specifically on social mobility and financial payoffs of education also seems to be undergoing a renewal of interest in recent years (Reitz, Zhang and Hawkins, 2011).

One particular policy issue that has been the focus of increasing research attention recently is the non-recognition of foreign credentials. The ability of immigrants to find good jobs, and to experience upward mobility once in the labor market, has been hampered by the resistance of Canadian employers and professional groups to recognize education qualifications earned abroad (Basran and Zong, 1998; Buzdugan and Halli, 2009; Fong and Cao, 2009; Galarneau and Morissette, 2008; Li, 2001, 2008, Reitz, 2001). Although Canada uses a selective point system to attract skilled immigrants, the inability of newcomers to transfer their education qualifications has hampered many immigrants in attaining the type of work to which they aspire.

Research in this tradition is unique given its methodological emphasis on direct causality and/or correlation between clearly defined and measurable variables. The variables employed by researchers in the subgroups of academic achievement and academic attainment vary considerably between studies. This can be seen above, in the subcategory of academic achievement, in which Worswick (2004) analyzes the impact of parents' mother tongue on academic achievement as compared to the work of Rousseau, Drapeau, and Corin (1996) which investigates the impact of the emotional problems of refugee children. Conversely, research on the financial return of education tends to focus predominantly on the linkage between the average years of education of ethnic groups and the financial return these groups command in the labor market (Dicks and Sweetman, 1999).

The quantitative approach in this category depends upon larger sample sizes, which enables these studies to contribute to understandings of broad trends frequently spanning different regions and time spans. However, this focus on broader trends in the data frequently means that the research does not target a specific age or ethnic group. Rather the research often makes comparisons between broad groups such as the absolute educational attainment of visible minority versus non-visible minority populations or the rate of return of education by coarsely designated ethnic groupings (e.g. Asians, Southern Europeans). This means that research in this tradition usually defines ethnic and racial groupings from a more essentialist perspective (treating everyone within a category as similar); this contrasts with a social constructionist approach often preferred in other research traditions that we discuss in this chapter.

Due to the need for larger sample size, research in this tradition tends to rely heavily on data collected by Statistics Canada such as the Canadian Census (Dicks and Sweetman, 1999; Geschwender and Guppy, 1995) and the National Longitudinal Survey of Children and Youth (Worswick, 2004), as well as data on provincial exam results (McAndrew, Ledent, and Ait-Said, 2006). Analyses are performed across multiple years of similar datasets (Dicks and Sweetman, 1999; Worswick, 2004) or by performing the analysis on a single dataset segmented by a common factor such as age cohorts (Geschwender and Guppy, 1995). In some instances, however, research has deviated from the use of Statistics Canada data in order to obtain more detailed information on a smaller sample group, such as the analysis of academic achievement in refugee children (Rousseau, Drapeau, and Corin, 1996), or the correlation between the degree of sorting across schools in Albertan communities and the educational inequality existing in these communities (Friesen and Krauth, 2007).

The most common tool for analysis is the use of statistical regression techniques, while controlling for extraneous factors such as age, geographic location, and language (Geschwender and Guppy, 1995; Rousseau, Drapeau, and Corin, 1996). Datasets have also been limited in a number of studies to facilitate and target the analysis of the data, for example, by age when analyzing the financial payoff of education to limit the sample being analyzed to those of working age (Geschwender and Guppy, 1995; Dicks and Sweetman, 1999). Other data exclusions have been made to remove indeterminate information such as ethnic groups who self-identify as 'Canadian' and where no evidence of their ethnic, racial, or ancestral group can be found (Dicks and Sweetman, 1999).

In sum, research framed by issues of mobility/meritocracy have focused on issues of scholastic achievement, educational attainment, and economic payoffs to schooling. Work on attainment was the earliest because of the access to large datasets provided by the federal government, with work on scholastic achievement coming next once standardized examinations began to be used more systematically for policy guidance. The more recent work on financial returns has benefitted especially from policy issues related to multicultural and employment equity issues, where the abilities of different ethnic, racial, and ancestral groups to leverage their schooling for economic returns has been of interest.

7.4.2 Discrimination and racism: The experience of prejudice as educational inequality

Discrimination exists in all facets of Canadian society, and the education system is no exception. We have included in this section works that focus primarily upon patterns of discrimination, prejudice, or racism experienced by one or more racial, ethnic, or ancestral groups through schooling. In this tradition we find an explicit emphasis on racism and prejudice as experienced and interpreted by students, both white and visible minority. As most research questions seek to examine the lived experiences of individuals, methods are consistently qualitative and almost exclusively involve small samples of interview subjects. As opposed to the often more sterile portrayals of statistical accounts of political arithmetic and path analysis from the first research tradition above, these works seek to highlight the thick descriptions (Geertz, 1973) of a life lived as a marginalized individual or group. The attempt is frequently to shed light on an 'insider's account' of how the educational system works, or fails to work, in the face of discrimination, prejudice, and racism. The implication is that such discrimination or racism is deleterious for, among other things, educational success.

The works in this category are mostly recent, suggesting a shift in researcher emphasis toward questions around explicit racism in the mid-1990s. Although the topic of racial prejudice and discrimination underlies all of the research traditions we identify, academic works in tradition two stand out as they make these issues the central focus of their analyses. This second tradition closely relates to the institutional approach presented in tradition five, but differs from it due to its student-focused, experience-based perspective (as opposed to a direct analysis of systemic processes). Codjoe (2001, p. 355), for example, integrates black students' interpretations of the curriculum and teacher expectations while not actually analyzing the curriculum or teachers' practices themselves. Due to the emphasis on individuals' experiences of prejudice, structural-level recommendations to systemically challenge racism often come out of these analyses (Codjoe, 2001). Main themes emerging in this tradition are illustrations of the ways in which discrimination takes place, individual conceptions and negotiations of racism and racialized identities, and activist attempts to challenge racism.

Due to its focus on individual experiences, works in this tradition provide evidence to show how discrimination occurs and what the negative outcomes can be for those targeted. For example, Ouestlati, Labelle, and Antonius (2006) focus on experiences of Arab immigrants (both Muslim and Christian) in Québec. Their study confirms what previous research had pointed out in other places: Arab Québecers experience racism regularly, and the situation worsened after 9/11 for Christians and Muslims alike. At school, the pervasiveness of stereotypes and prejudice regarding both religion and culture lead to insults, difficulties establishing friendships with Franco-Canadian students, and exclusionary practices (in group work, for example). Participants also reported difficulties in ensuring that school authority figures recognize and punish anti-Arab sentiment, or even accommodate diverse religious practices.

In order to comprehend how racism operates, it is necessary to understand how race and prejudice are conceptualized and interpreted by those in the education system. The concept of individual negotiation is well illustrated in Dei's (1997) examination of how black/African-Canadian youth manage their identities in the Toronto school system. He distinguishes between youth who articulate their identity as being members of a given racial group (black/African) in contrast to others who are becoming black/African, and thus more reflective of their politically aware racialized identity. Varying concepts of race and identity are uncovered and mapped by research in this area to help explain changing expressions of racism (e.g. 'new racism' – Raby, 2004, p. 368; see also 'color-blind racism' – Bonilla-Silva, 2010). Drawing on interviews with teenage girls in Toronto, Raby (2004) shows how understandings of racism are complex and contradictory. The youth in her sample primarily downplay the existence of racism, remove its systemic components by individualizing experiences, and consistently center and neutralize whiteness.

A related strain of research targets the challenges encountered by students and teachers who seek to quell racism at school. Lundrren (2006) focuses on the experiences of racially diverse student and teacher activists and highlights themes such as the denial of racism and the setbacks faced by these activists around that public denial. This research describes specific conceptions of racism and agency in relation to those conceptions. Researchers generally take a position that diversity is beneficial and that strong institutional measures need to be taken to alter power balances, and dominant narratives and histories.

In this research tradition, the three predominant strains – activist challenges, student racial negotiations, and experiences of discrimination – shed light on the multifaceted dimensions and implications of processes of racialization at the individual level. Thanks to the qualitative methods employed, scholars illuminate intricate layers of individual experiences. However, due to the highly contextualized and detailed accounts involving small numbers of research participants, this tradition's contribution has less to do with presenting generalizable findings than with uncovering concepts that may be used to understand broader patterns of discrimination.

7.4.3   Identity/values

As opposed to a focus on discrimination, prejudice, or racism, studies in this research tradition are framed by an attention to cultural differences in regard to schooling. While these differences may sometimes lead to discrimination (e.g. religious shaming), the core focus here is upon different groups seeking to adapt to or redefine education so that it might work in their particular interest. The focus of these studies is not on the conflicts of racism, but on how the cultural values and individual identities of groups or individuals have been socially constructed. A central premise here is that the education system, especially in a country with a legally-mandated multicultural agenda, must be accommodating to the cultural differences of students in the system in order for those students to be academically successful.

One particularly strong theme is concentrated upon the utility of independent or private schools as institutions to promote cultural heritage while simultaneously fostering academic achievement. Choosing ethnically defined schools (e.g. an Islamic school) is a strategy for distinct ethnic communities to protect their cultural heritage while simultaneously being sheltered, at least in the school setting, from different cultural values (e.g. more permissiveness with sex and alcohol) and outright discrimination. So, for example, Asanova (2005) examines schooling for immigrant students from the former Soviet Union, Lenoir-Achdjian (1999) looks at political, religious, and social choices that Armenian parents make when choosing which schools to send their children to, and Zine (2007) focuses upon how Islamic schools seek to resist 'cultural assimilation' and engage in 'cultural survival'.

Zine's (2007) work, examining four independent Islamic schools, focuses upon school choices for parents and students. She explores, in particular, the tension between resisting cultural assimilation to the Canadian mainstream and promoting the cultural survival of Muslim values and traditions. Independent religious schools, the most prevalent form of private schooling that exists in Canada, segregate students into relatively culturally homogeneous classrooms, thus restricting their interaction and hence socialization with a more diverse array of young people. This restricts a more universal civic engagement with the diverse, plural society characterized by multiple ethnic and religious groups.

The alternative to independent or private schooling is participation in the public school stream (where approximately 90% of Canadian students study). Studies examining how students from different ethnic groups negotiate these public settings constitute another strong research trend. Members of different ethnic groups have been more or less successful with respect to academic achievement and these studies tend to highlight possible explanations for falling above or below the average performance level of all students. Sometimes the focus is upon specific ethnic groups as in Collet's (2007) work with Somali students, Triki-Yamani and McAndrew's (2009) focus upon Muslim students,

Dei's (2008) or Smith, Schneider, and Ruck's (2005) research on black/African-Canadian youth, or Goldstein's (2003) or Li's (2004) work on immigrant Chinese high school students. Beauchesne, Limoges, and Paul (1983) compared similar processes among three groups in Québec – francophone students, and students from Spain and Asia.

The concept of negotiation, a core theme in this area, is well illustrated in Mbuya Mutombo's (2003) exploration of two minority ethnic groups from sub-Saharan Africa and the Antilles. Students who accept the social hierarchy established by the majority group tend to do better in schools while those who challenge this social organization tend to not do well in school because they see education as a tool of domination. This research has obvious parallels to that of Dei's discussed in Section 7.4.2.

In the province of Québec similar themes are explored in the context of the accommodation and integration of minority groups. Here scholars pay attention to the ways schools accommodate religious, cultural, and racial diversity in everyday processes (Benimmas, 2010; Bernatchez and Bourgeault, 1999; Gérin-Lajoie and Jacquet, 2008; Laferrière, 1983; McAndrew, 2001, 2013; McAndrew, Jacquet and Ciceri, 1997). While this research combines elements of classroom practices and education policy, the emphasis is on what is considered reasonable accommodation. Many works place special emphasis on Québec in terms of the integration of immigrants as well as francophone students (Jacquet et al., 2008). There is also a stream of this tradition focusing upon teenage disengagement with schooling with a focus upon particular ethnic groups (Dei, 2003).

Comparisons between ethnic or racial groups are, to date, relatively infrequent. One exception is Faircloth and Hamm (2005), who examine how members of four different ethnic groups experience 'belonging' or feeling comfortable within the education setting, and the impact of this sense of belonging on academic achievement. Similarly, Taylor and Krahn (2005) contrast the educational aspirations of students from different ethnic groups. Ruck and Wortley (2002) compare the perceptions of different ethnic groups to school disciplinary practices and the effect of these perceptions on educational engagement. Finally, Ryan (1997) uses more qualitative methods to explore inter-ethnic relationships in a culturally diverse school setting, trying to tease out how different groups construct their identities and the possible implications of this for school success.

In sum, most of the research in these subthemes of school choice and negotiation are characterized by thick descriptions *à la* Clifford Geertz (1973) – they provide rich ethnographic details of a particular ethnic group. This allows for a well-developed understanding of the experiences of the students from different ethnic backgrounds but it makes comparisons between groups difficult. There are a few studies providing comparisons of experiences between ethnic groups, as noted immediately above, but this is an area where more work needs to be done. Work like Annette Lareau's from the US, where the ethnographic research design incorporates theoretically rich comparisons, still needs to be undertaken in Canada.

7.4.4   Aboriginal education

This is our most easily defined category, focused as it is upon schooling among aboriginal or indigenous peoples. Research on the academic success of indigenous peoples warrants its own category given their unique status as the only population group native to Canadian soil. As such, they are neither an ethnic minority nor a founding charter group (i.e., English or French). Their distinct ancestral history, and treatment by the Canadian government, has resulted in a proliferation of research specific to aboriginal experiences. Furthermore, policy-makers, aboriginal leaders, and social commentators continue to see schooling as one viable solution for a host of problems confronting indigenous peoples and their communities (Satzewich, 1997, p. 1299). This is particularly salient because schooling outcomes of indigenous people are frequently low, have been in relative decline compared to other population groups, and have garnered substantial research interest.

Across a wide range of educational metrics, aboriginal students have poorer outcomes than their non-aboriginal peers. Whether it is with respect to years of schooling or credentials achieved (Dahm, 1995, p. 1005), aboriginal students have lower levels of attainment (Elgersma, 2001). Similarly weak relative levels of attainment hold when the focus is upon measured cognitive achievement as evidenced by school grades or standardized achievement tests (Richards, Vining, and Weimer, 2010). Even more worrying than the lower levels of attainments is the probability that the outcome gap between aboriginals and non-aboriginals may be widening, even though for both groups attainment is increasing (ibid., p. 51; Cherubini et al., 2010; Siggner and Costa, 2005).

Figure 7.2 shows, for young people aged 20–24, high school completion rates. Among the non-aboriginal population, 88% of people have completed high school while for aboriginal people the percentage is 60. What Figure 7.2 also reveals is that among aboriginal peoples there is great variation in completion rates, with Métis being more likely to graduate (75%), than either First Nations (52%) or Inuit (40%). Explanations for this internal variation have much to do with region (Inuit people living in the more remote Arctic and Métis tending to be more likely to live in urban centers) and colonial legacy (with First Nations peoples having been subject to residential schooling (see below)).

Richards, Vining, and Weimer (2010) examine the gap in standardized test scores between aboriginal and non-aboriginal young people in the province of British Columbia. They begin by asking whether it is the more economically marginalized status of aboriginal peoples that explains the gap. Their conclusion is that while aboriginal people typically are less economically privileged, this more marginal status does not account for much of the educational gap.

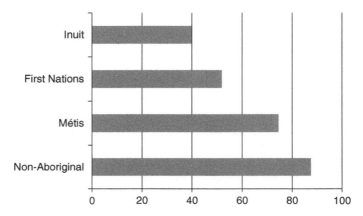

Figure 7.2   Percentage of people aged 20–24 graduating from high school, by aboriginal/ non-aboriginal status (2006 Canadian Census data)

They point instead to a 'culture of low academic expectations – among teachers, students' peers, or both' (ibid., p. 59), a culture that is promoted, they argue, by the concentration of aboriginal students in specific schools. This perspective, however, has been heavily criticized as one that, reminiscent of 'culture of poverty' explanations once popular in sociological research, puts the blame on an already marginalized population rather than interrogating the effect of colonization and persistent systemic racism.

At least three important conclusions flow from this work. First, the gap between aboriginal and non-aboriginal students persists and looks to be growing. Second, there is more research needed to sort out the strongest explanations for this growing gap. Third, there appear to be school-level effects that are amenable to some forms of policy intervention. There is some disagreement in the literature as to whether or not concentrating aboriginal students in specific schools is a good thing, although the most recent work suggests that it is not as deleterious as Richards, Vining, and Weimer implied (Friesen and Krauth, 2010). In our judgment the bulk of the research literature, based on both quantitative and qualitative research, suggests that school environments that promote culturally appropriate aboriginal-interventions (e.g. including traditional First Nations knowledge on the environment) will help indigenous students prosper in educational achievement (see Baydala et al., 2009; Carr-Stewart and Steeves, 2009; Cherubini and Hodson, 2008; Greenwood, de Leeuw, and Ngaroimata Fraser, 2007; Marker, 2009; Pirbhai-Illich, 2010).

As another example, attention has also focused upon teacher training, and in particular the training of aboriginal teachers, to help enhance the school environment for the academic success of indigenous students. Both Harper (2000) and Kitchen et al. (2010) have undertaken qualitative work pointing to the need for better, more culturally responsive preparation programs. This is an especially problematic area because of the legacy of colonial policies bearing on aboriginal schooling.

These colonial policies, which serve as another dominant explanation for the weaker academic performance of aboriginal students, are epitomized by the legacy of residential schooling (Blackburn, 2000; Haig-Brown, 1988; Milloy, 1999; Satzewich and Mahood, 1995). Residential schooling was premised on the idea that aboriginal people needed to adapt to European culture and in particular learn English and become Christian. Educating children, rather than changing the views of adults, was the operative strategy. Aboriginal children were placed in schools far from their communities, where aboriginal languages were not allowed, and where only European ideas and practices were permitted. The legacy of these schools among aboriginal students was one of humiliation and shaming, where physical and emotional abuse, and child labor exploitation were prevalent. Even though in the late 1990s most churches apologized for their roles in this program, and although the federal government set up a financial compensation package for residential school survivors, education remains a poisonous institution in the memories of many aboriginal people. The ghosts of this legacy continue to haunt aboriginal youth and their communities.

In sum, increasing research attention is turning to collaborative ways for indigenous peoples and others to work together to promote viable options for schooling successes (Canadian Council on Learning, 2007; Raham, 2009). A key trade-off is to on the one hand provide a culturally sensitive curriculum and learning milieu, while on the other hand also provide the training and skills that are necessary for success both with respect to aboriginal community heritage and long-term economic sustainability.

7.4.5   Institutional processes

The last research tradition that we examine focuses upon the numerous embedded processes in the bureaucracy of schooling, including official policy, curriculum, teacher training and pedagogy, and parental and community input in schooling and school board decisions. Due to its broad scope, tradition five covers the most scholarly terrain and constitutes 40% of all articles in the review. As with all institutions, these overlapping processes systemically normalize certain assumptions and practices while making invisible the possibility of or need for others. Due to education's role as a crucial agent of socialization in our society, researchers in the social sciences have paid particular attention to how these underlying processes of normalization have affected the outcomes and experiences of schooling for young Canadians.

Here the unit of analysis typically highlights some aspect of the educational system, whether a procedure, policy, or practice, that acts in a way to differentially impact racialized individuals and groups. While tradition three focuses on the perceptions and agency of specific minority groups, and tradition two pays attention to explicit racism, this last tradition allows insight into the structure of educational systems and the ways in which these systems provide uneven fields for learning and advancement. Although discrimination certainly plays a role here, this tradition more often captures embedded or seemingly invisible processes of stratification.

7.4.5.1   Policy

Much research has focused upon the role of multicultural policy in managing racial and ethnic diversity at school (Bertheleu, 2001; McLeod, 1987; see Daley and Begley, 2008 for an overview of the past decade; see Laferrière, 1983 for an historical perspective on this issue). This emphasis is not surprising given Canada's constitutionally entrenched commitment to multiculturalism in all government institutions. Scholars in this area provide useful overviews of the historical roots and development of multicultural education policies across the provinces (see Ghosh, 2004, pp. 545–548). Questions of diversity extend to all areas of education including language education policies (Eslingohn, 1989; Reynolds, 1991). For example, Hebertonne (1992) considers whether the linguistic and cultural needs of minority students are being met, and Tavares (2000) traces changes in language programs offered over time. Diverse approaches to multiculturalism, including more radical school-based anti-racist initiatives (Potvin and Carr, 2008; Potvin, McAndrew, and Kanouté, 2006) as well as questions about the potential for addressing race and sexual orientation together in policy (Snider, 1996) are also developing.

A small amount of material consists of action-oriented reports, often conference-based and organized by academic or community organizations, with the aim of evaluating and improving multicultural policies and their implementation in education (Barr, 1993; McLeod, 1980). Conference presentations printed in McLeod (1980), for example, cover multicultural education with regard to provincial approaches, school board administration, curriculum, and teacher education. Much of this research presumes, correctly in our judgment, that greater diversity, more attention to anti-racist practices, and enhanced multicultural mandates will improve the educational outcomes for all students, and draws on an impressive body of literature on these topics in the United States. What may be lacking are studies demonstrating that this presumption has an evidentiary basis based on calculable, positive outcomes. Consistent with government multicultural and immigration goals, assumptions about the inherent desirability of ethnic diversity are fundamentally engrained within education scholarship. While scholars often critique conceptions and implementations of multiculturalism at all levels of government, they consistently adhere to the notion that multiculturalism itself, in one form or another, is beneficial.

Challenges in the implementation of race relations policies have been monitored by scholars such as Echols and Fisher (1992) who consider the links between formal policy and practical application. Their work shows that race-related policies are often reflected in curriculum changes while other school practices continue unaltered. Further, they find that these policies are most effective in culturally diverse schools. More critical approaches to multiculturalism (Gérin-Lajoie, and Jacquet, 2008) include abstract conceptual analyses as well as concrete evaluations of specific policies' ability to address the needs of ethnically marginalized groups (Rahim, 1990).

We note that special attention is given to Québec due to its unique response to federal multiculturalism. As we have already noted, the federal government's multiculturalism model frames Québec and the francophone minority in Canada as little more than another minority group, thus undermining francophones as a founding charter group. Given the small population of francophones in North America, this history is compounded by a preoccupation for cultural and linguistic survival in Québec and amongst francophone scholars. As a result, scholars in Québec have historically resisted multiculturalism and its accompanying policies, preferring to embrace the concept of 'interculturalism', which is meant to facilitate and encourage exchanges across cultural differences while maintaining the centrality of francophone language and culture (McAndrew, 2001; see also collections on this topic, Ouellet, 1986; Ouellet and Pagé, 1991). Ghosh (2004) highlights how this is reflected in the province's education policies, particularly with regard to language of instruction. Talbani (1993) further discusses Québec's policy of intercultural education and considers the rights of minority groups in relation to the legal policy of placing their children in French-speaking schools. The intensity of debates in Québec surrounding the question of girls wearing hijabs to school (Ciceri, 1998) illustrate that tensions also underlie the concept of interculturalism.

7.4.5.2 Curriculum

Curriculum is a telling component of the schooling system as it reflects the expert knowledge deemed most appropriate at any given time period. Embedded within seemingly objective subjects are assumptions about intended audience in addition to numerous choices about what content was included, excluded, or not even considered. Over the past 30 years the need for racially inclusive curriculum and methods of working toward their creation has been well established (Cancel, 2009). Most analyses highlight problematic curricular aspects such as portrayals of specific ethnic groups along with broader conceptions of immigration, diversity, and racism (Blondin, 1990; Werner et al., 1980; see also Bromley, 2011 on the inclusion of human rights and multiculturalism in civic education in British Columbia; McAndrew, 1986 on representations of racism, immigration, and the 'multi-ethnic reality' of Canada; McAndrew,

Oueslati and Helly, 2007 on the treatment of Islam and Muslim cultures; and Mujawamariya, 2000 for diversity in the Ontario science curriculum). For example, Lebrun (1999) examines the figure of the 'foreigner' in Québec youth literature and traces the shift from 'foreigners' being portrayed as background characters and sidekicks to heroes. She notes that this change can be partly linked back to the increasing presence of recent immigrants (or those coming from families of recent immigrants) amongst youth literature authors. There is also limited discussion of the role of specific topics, such as Afrocentrism in inclusive curriculum (Dei, 1996). Content and discourse analysis is the dominant research method in this area, leaving room for different approaches to curriculum examination.

7.4.5.3   *Teacher training and practices*

Teachers are trained within institutional frameworks and go on to employ specific pedagogical standpoints in the classroom which ultimately impact the development of students' academic trajectories and racialized worldviews. As a result, teachers and training processes thoroughly influence numerous aspects of the education system. Given the potential of training programs to highlight classroom diversity and power relations, scholars have rightfully emphasized this area in a growing body of research. Training programs and the experiences of teachers in those programs are analyzed with the aim of understanding how processes and patterns in teacher training impact systemic racism in the education system (as well as how the inclusion of multicultural practices may help normalize understandings of race and ethnicity in schools).

Teacher's conceptions of whiteness in particular emerged as a strong trend beginning in the 1990s as scholars such as Peggy McIntosh (1990) and her now classic piece, 'White Privilege: Unpacking the Invisible Knapsack' began making white privilege visible. White teacher candidates' conceptions of and responses to white privilege are a central theme in teacher training research. Solomon et al. (2005, pp. 160–162), for example, note strategies used by instructor candidates including a narrative of 'liberalist notions of individualism and meritocracy' in which racialized privileges are denied based upon claims of equal opportunity and effort-based rewards. Policy recommendations suggest that more emotional and psychological support is required as issues of racism and privilege are tackled, and more applicable and concrete classroom strategies need to be provided for new instructors. Appropriate training is essential as the degree to which teachers are trained to deal with ethnic, cultural, and religious diversity is proven to shape the experiences of immigrant children and their parents (Benimmas, 2010; Ghosh, 1991; Jacquet, 2007).

In contrast, the experiences of visible minority teacher candidates are more often referenced in relation to discrimination and linguistic challenges. For example, Mujawamariya (2001) interviewed associate teachers from Franco-Ontarian classrooms and found evidence of discriminatory beliefs toward visible minority teacher candidates. This discrimination was oriented around the idea that 'outsiders' must conform to the dominant francophone culture. Dlamini and Martinovic (2007) further show that teachers-in-training for whom English is a second language harbor deep concerns about cultural acceptance, recognition of their authority, and approval of their accent by both students and host teachers.

The classroom practices of current teachers are also examined extensively in the literature. Here we see some attention to intersectionality, as is highlighted by Millington et al. (2008) case-study of physical education classes in British Columbia. They conclude that sport-related education contexts privilege dominant white masculine identities while subjugating the gender performances of Canadian-born and immigrant Chinese boys. The authors highlight the formal, if abstract, goals of anti-racism in the curriculum in contrast to the informal classroom practices of teachers who were not aware of any racial dynamics taking place. Findings show that teachers' instructions are not easily comprehended by ESL students, that vocal assertiveness and strong English speaking abilities are rewarded, and that activities such as football (familiar to the white Canadian boys) are routinely selected. As a result, the Chinese-Canadian boys lack an understanding of the exercises as well as the ability to influence the selection of class activities. Policy recommendations in this area include ensuring increased consistency between formal curriculum mandates and classroom practices.

The pedagogical practices and assumptions of teachers are additionally considered in relation to their impact upon student success and development (Morin, 1993). Here we note a large diversity in methods and concepts employed. Clifton and Bulcock's (1987) work highlights a more quantitative approach to measuring teachers' influence on student success. Drawing upon a causal model, the author's argue that teacher expectations do impact students' classroom grades, however, that teachers develop these expectations based not upon students' ethnicity (ascribed status) but rather upon their past academic performance and cognitive ability (achieved status). This quantitative approach and use of clearly defined terms and measures of achievement differs significantly from more post-structural and qualitative studies such as Rivière's (2008). In her ethnographic analysis of an Ontario drama classroom, Rivière evaluates the instructor's understanding of ethnic diversity and privilege and the resulting pedagogical approach and dramatic exercises employed in class. She determines that the students' racial conceptions (for example, the continued uncritical use of cultural stereotypes in skits) and identity development were effected as a result.

7.4.5.4   *Parent and community involvement in schooling*

Another systemic process involves the patterns of interaction between the education system and parents and community groups. Studies frame these relationships in terms of schools' integration of recent immigrant parents, the role of parents in student success, and community involvement in policy creation. Parents for whom English is a second language often face barriers to full participation in their children's education (Guo, 2006). Scholars have identified factors such as linguistic barriers and trouble adapting to the new system as key areas school boards need to address to ensure the involvement of all families (Dagenais, 2008; Kanouté, 2007). Research also considers the ways in which parents of specific ethnic minority groups are involved with their children's education (for example, assisting with homework) and the impact of their involvement on students' academic trajectories and social integration (Benimmas, 2010; Croteau, 2006; Icart, 2009; Kanouté, 2007; Kanouté et al., 2008; Liboy and Venet, 2011). Others document how parents' school choices and involvement are linked to and construct ethnic identity (Lenoir-Achdjian, 1999). Overall, research suggests that parental participation is crucial for immigrant children's success but made difficult by a number of structural factors. Finally, the role of the broader community in influencing school policy, especially regarding inclusive education, is considered with special emphasis on marginalization and mobilization. Zine (2001) explores the narratives created by community members as they challenged alterations to Toronto School Board equity policies in the early 1990s. She notes in particular that a hierarchy of marginalization was constructed as different minority groups competed for the most recognition and status within equity policy materials (in this case between religious groups and the gay community).

These four subthemes focusing on parent and community involvement, teacher training and practices, curriculum content, and policy, all highlight key structural components of the education system. While we constructed these clearly divided categories for the purpose of describing research patterns, it must be noted that in practice there is significant overlap; each component influences the operation of others. As mentioned above, scholars have reflected upon this overlap by researching the links between curriculum content and classroom practices (Millington et al., 2008) and measuring the impact that teacher training and pedagogy can have on students' experiences and success (Clifton and Bulcock, 1987; Rivière, 2008). Future research may identify connections that have yet to be thoroughly developed, such as how specific multicultural approaches (rather than teaching practices) impact student achievement, or how school administrators influence teaching pedagogy.

Methods in this tradition most often include interviews, ethnography, discourse and content analysis, and in some cases quantitative methods. It is worth noting that scholars have begun to study not just systems of oppression, but the corresponding systems of privilege as well. This strain of research, involving studies of whiteness in particular (primarily for teacher candidates and, in fewer cases, students), has the potential to add necessary layers to understandings of racialized inequality in schools. A potential approach that is missing are discussions of cases where policies and practices of multiculturalism were implemented effectively, or cases in which teacher training or classroom pedagogies appeared effective in challenging problematic racial hierarchies (although determining what constitutes 'effective' is fraught with difficulty). By studying how privilege has been recognized, or how discrimination can be identified and reduced, scholars in this tradition may present policy suggestions based not solely upon identified problems, but upon potential solutions.

7.5 Discussion and conclusion

Having reviewed the key characteristics of each research tradition, it is important to note trends observed *across* multiple traditions. These larger overlapping patterns relate, in particular, to methodologies and core concepts, external research influences, differences between English and French-language works, and changes in the volume of research published.

With regard to methods employed, we discern a general temporal shift across the literature reviewed. Closer to the 1980s, studies frequently utilized quantitative analyses with large data sets. With the rising popularity of post-structural, feminist, and qualitative methods, more recent research draws upon ethnographic and interview-based methods, demonstrates an interest in smaller, more contextualized samples, and makes an allowance for fluid, negotiated identities.

This change reflects broader sociological debates taking place regarding race and ethnicity which have been integrated in education research. For example, we note two dominant approaches to conceptions of race in our sample. Some research takes racial identity for granted (e.g. using it as a variable) while other research looks at the way that racialization is a construction facilitated by educational processes. These unique assumptions and frameworks lead to dramatically different research questions, methods, and findings, even for similar topics. This is highlighted by contrasting research analyzing the impact of teacher expectations on students. Clifton and Bulcock's (1987) piece measures the influence of ethnicity (conceptualized as an ascribed status variable) on student success, while Rivière's (2008) work examines the negotiation and development of racialized identities through teachers' classroom practices (discussed in tradition five). For these scholars, their unique conceptions of race mean they observe entirely different processes taking place at school.

Overall, we note that the majority of research on racial inequalities in education tends to assume that racialized identities are 'things' or 'facts' that exist outside of discourse. A smaller amount of work we discuss engages with the way that racial differences are created. Most research starts with the assumption that people can be categorized into racialized groups, and that these categories are then acted upon by (rather than being negotiated through) schooling processes. The work of Oyserman et al. (2003) provides an interesting hybrid between often opposing approaches to the question of racial categorization and academic disengagement. Focusing on 'racial-ethnic self-schemas (RES)' (p. 333), the authors measure individuals' conceptions of racial self-identification and inclusion in racialized groups of various scopes. Findings show that students are least likely to face academic disengagement if their RES includes both their in-group and the larger society. This quantitative model-based research allows students' subjective conceptions of racial-ethnic grouping to be measured in relation to their likelihood of disengaging from schooling. This is one way of bridging the gap between complex identities and large, generalizable samples. Specialized surveys and measurement tools are necessary for this approach, however, making it a challenge for researchers utilizing larger surveys for secondary analyses. As numerous scholars rely on data produced by Statistics Canada, this could present a significant problem. Despite its limited feasibility, the work of Oyserman et al. (2003) provides useful conceptual and methodological approaches to be considered and built upon.

In addition to diverse understandings of race, we find two polarized approaches to conceptualizing what educational inequality is and how it should be resolved. With the rationalization of the education system, a large group of scholars target measures of inequality in achievement. The emphasis here is upon understanding what factors influence academic success and how to decrease disparities in success across ethnic groups. Another equally large stream focuses on the importance of cultural diversity and the celebration of that diversity. Proponents of this approach more often evaluate curriculum content and multicultural policies with the aim of ensuring that all racial groups are equally and respectfully represented. Although related, these two frameworks ultimately target different components of inequality. The first measures inequality through academic performance (linked to social mobility and labor market success) while the second measures inequality through representations of cultural knowledge, history, and difference (with the outcomes being somewhat less linear and clearly defined). This discrepancy is not surprising given the many interpretations and stages of federal multiculturalism in Canada, ranging anywhere from celebratory to anti-racist.

The patterns of change found in this research are commensurate with broader changes in the field of sociology and the professional academy more widely. As the intellectual divisions of disciplinary boundaries become more porous, contributions from scholars in diverse fields overlap. As advances in methodology proliferate, analyses become deeper and richer (as in larger samples with cross-time designs or with comparative ethnographic sites; both developments in Canada that are only just beginning to influence this research area). With sociology itself becoming more eclectic in the methodologies of its practitioners, and with cultural explanations rising in prominence, it is not surprising to see both of these disciplinary trends surface in the educational research reviewed above.

Despite the different historical narratives of French and English Canada, works produced in either language utilized similar frameworks, methods, and research questions. Even though the concept of interculturalism is largely preferred to the concept of multiculturalism in the French literature, this distinction did little to differentiate scholars across Canada, as they shared similar concerns and approaches for thinking about racialized inequalities in education. It is important to note, however, that a stream of linguistic-focused research questions did emerge in French-language pieces. We decided not to include these in our final sample since a purely linguistic scope did not satisfy the requirements of research focusing specifically on race, ethnicity, and ancestry (and language opened a much larger scope for inclusion).

Although we found only minor differences between provinces in terms of research produced, the provincial structure of the education system has implications for research funding processes. There is a disconnect between the structure of education and the way in which funding is distributed, namely that education is provincially mandated yet the bulk of research funding is federally directed through bodies such as the Social Science and Humanities Research Council of Canada (SSHRC). As a result, provincially funded research is limited and more often contractually based. On the contrary, federally funded studies are abundant yet frequently disconnected from direct policy initiatives and more closely driven by scholars' own interests. Ultimately, the decoupled structure of provincial government authority over education and federal government authority over research funding has significantly impacted the connection between education research and policy. Complicating this further is the decision of the federal government, prior to the 2011 census completion, to have the 'long form' census filled out on a voluntary basis. Effectively this means that a great deal of data previously collected by Statistics Canada as a mandated aspect of the decanal census will now be unrepresentative of the population. Questions of race, ethnicity, and ancestry have featured prominently in the 'long form' census and thus this source of data will soon be lost.

The volume of works in each category is another topic worthy of discussion. Tradition five was the largest by far, suggesting that a substantial portion of Canadian education research focuses upon embedded institutional factors. Particularly promising about this research trend is its potential to abet meaningful, systemic changes. The documentation of problematic components of education processes such as teacher training, curriculum content, and policy creation can be useful for policy-makers seeking to implement institutional changes. However, one potential limitation notable across all five traditions (with the exception of teacher training suggestions found in tradition five) is the lack of thorough, concrete recommendations emerging from research. Scholars produce strong analyses that highlight problematic elements, but are not as effective in articulating well thought out and manageable solutions for improvement.

Over time a general expansion of research is observed across all five categories, with our sample results increasing on average by about 60% during every five year period from 1980 to 2010 (this growth is particularly visible in tradition two which emerges primarily in the mid- and late 1990s). We expect that several factors are at play here. Methodologically, the search engines and databases consulted may have improved their record-keeping for works in more recent decades. Further, an increase in online publications and other publishing avenues may be responsible for a growing number of works being published in the more recent years of our sample. Additionally, the progression of transdisciplinary research may have allowed more articles now to be classified as sociological than in previous times. Finally, education and ethnicity may simply be gaining more attention as a research field.

The recent ascendance of human rights as a focus of progress and equality also has much to do with the growing interest of scholars dedicated to research in this broad topic. Education or schooling is frequently understood as both a solution to many social ills and as an individual as well as a national asset for human betterment. Having an educational system that promotes the welfare of all citizens, regardless of ancestry, ethnicity, or race is thus a major public policy concern. Our review of this diverse research canvas, although uncovering concepts and methods that do not always correspond, paints a well-developed picture of the various layers of Canadian schooling systems and the institutions and axes of oppression and privilege that interact with it.

Notes

1. We use the words aboriginal and indigenous interchangeably although, as with the politics of identity more generally, definitions are contested. While our preference would be to capitalize these terms, as 'European' is typically capitalized in Canada, aboriginal and indigenous are rendered here in lower case to be consistent with usage in the rest of this volume. Typically aboriginal peoples in Canada are either North American Indians (or First Nations peoples as is increasingly common), Métis (descendants of intermarriages between Indians and Europeans), and Inuit (from the Arctic regions of Canada).

References

T. Abada, F. Hou and M. Ram (2008) *Group Differences in Educational Attainment Among the Children of Immigrants.* Statistics Canada Catalogue no. 11F0019M – No. 308, Ottawa Ontatio. 32p. Analytical Studies Branch Research Paper Series, date accessed 13 July 2011, http://www.statcan.gc.ca/pub/11f0019m/11f0019m2008308-eng.pdf.

T. Abada, F. Hou and M. Ram (2009) 'Ethnic differences in educational attainment among the children of Canadian immigrants', *Canadian Journal of Sociology (Online)* 34 (1): 1–28.

J. Asanova (2005) 'Educational experiences of immigrant students from the former Soviet union: a case study of an ethnic school in Toronto', *Educational Studies* 31 (2): 181–195.

Association of Universities and Colleges of Canada (AUCC) (2007) *Trends in Higher Education: Volume 1, Enrolment* (Ottawa: Association of Universities and Colleges of Canada).

A. Aydemir, W. Chen and M. Corak (2008) *Intergenerational Education Mobility among the Children of Canadian Immigrants*, Statistics Canada Catalogue no. 11F0019M – No. 316. Ottawa, ON. 38p. Analytical Studies Branch Research Paper Series, date accessed 13 July 2011, http://www.statcan.gc.ca/pub/11f0019m/11f0019m2008316-eng.pdf.

J. Barr (1993) *Multicultural, Intercultural and Anti-racism Education: A Vision for the Future: Equality, Equity, and Empowerment*, Consortium on Cultural Diversity in Education, Canadian Council for Multicultural and Intercultural Education, and British Columbia Multicultural Education Society (Vancouver: BC Multicultural Education Society).

G. Basran and L. Zong (1998) 'Devaluation of credentials as perceived by visible minority professional immigrants', *Canadian Ethnic Studies* 30 (3): 6–23.

L. Baydala, C. Rasmussen, J. Birch, J. Sherman, E. Wikman, J. Charchun and J. Bisanz (2009) 'Self-beliefs and behavioural development as related to academic achievement in Canadian aboriginal children', *Canadian Journal of School Psychology* 24 (1): 19–33.

A. Beauchesne, J. Limoges and D. Paul (1983) 'La distance sociale inter-ethnique dans le milieu scolaire', *Revue des sciences de l'éducation* 3 (9): 453–467.

A. Benimmas, Atlantic Metropolis Centre, and Centre of Excellence for Research on Immigration, Integration and Cultural Diversity (2010) *L'intégration des élèves immigrants, la relation école-familles immigrées et l'adhésion à la mission de l'école francophone acadienne selon les perceptions des parents immigrants et des futures enseignantes* 26 (Halifax: Centre Métropolis Atlantique).

S. Bernatchez and G. Bourgeault (1999) 'La prise en compte de la diversite culturelle et religieuse a l'ecole publique et l 'obligation d'accommodement' – apercu des legislations et des jurisprudences au Canada, aux Etats-Unis, en France et en Grande-Bretagne', *Canadian Ethnic Studies* 31 (1): 159–172.

H. Bertheleu (2001) 'La politique Canadienne du multiculturalisme: citoyennete, accommodements institutionnels et equite', *Sociétés Contemporaines* 43 (3): 31–51.

C. Blackburn (2000) *Harvest of Souls: The Jesuit Missions and Colonialism in North America 1632–1650* (Montreal: McGill-Queen's University Press).

D. Blondin (1990) *L'apprentissage du racisme dans les manuels scolaires* (Montreal: Editions Agenced'Arc).

A. Bonikowska and F. Hou (2010) 'Reversal of fortunes or continued success? Cohort differences in education and earnings of childhood Immigrants', *International Migration Review* 44 (2): 320–353.

E. Bonilla-Silva (2010) *Racism without Racists: Color-Blind Racism and Racist Inequality in Contemporary America*, 3rd ed. (Lanham: Rowman and Littlefield).

P. Bromley (2011) 'Multiculturalism and human rights in civic education: the case of British Columbia, Canada', *Educational Research* 53 (2): 151–164.

R. Buzdugan and S. Halli (2009) 'Labor market experiences of Canadian immigrants with focus on foreign education and experience', *International Migration Review* 43 (2): 366–386.

Canadian Council on Learning (2007) *Redefining How Success Is Measured in First Nations, Inuit and Métis Learning* (Ottawa: Canadian Council on Learning).

C. Cancel (2009) 'Minorité franco-nunavoise et majorité inuit: Tensions et coopération dans les débats sur l'éducation', *Études/Inuit/Studies* 33 (1–2): 153–171.

S. Carr-Stewart and L. Steeves (2009) 'First nations educational governance: a fractured mirror', *Canadian Journal of Educational Administration and Policy* 97: 1–16.

L. Cherubini and J. Hodson (2008) 'Ontario Ministry of Education polity and aboriginal learners' epistomologies: A fundamental disconnect', *Canadian Journal of Education Administration and Policy* 73: 1–33.

L. Cherubini, J. Hodson, M. Manley-Casimir and C. Muir (2010) "Closing the gap' at the peril of widening the void: implications of the Ontario Ministry of Education's policy for aboriginal education', *Canadian Journal of Education* 33 (2): 329–355.

C. Ciceri (1998) 'La question du foulard islamique dans les écoles publiques', *Cahiers de l'Urmis* 4: 59–71.

Citizenship and Immigration Canada (CIC) (2009) 'Canada – permanent residents by source country', date accessed 1 October 2011, http://www.cic.gc.ca/english/resources/statistics/facts2010/permanent/10.asp.

Citizenship and Immigration Canada (CIC) (2010) 'Canada – permanent residents by gender and category, 1986 to 2010', date accessed 3 October 2011, http://www.cic.gc.ca/english/resources/statistics/facts2010/permanent/01.asp.

R. A. Clifton and J. W. Bulcock (1987) 'Ethnicity, teachers' expectations, and student performances in Ontario schools', *Canadian Journal of Education / Revue Canadienne de l'éducation* 12 (2): 294–315.

H. M. Codjoe (2001) 'Fighting a "public enemy" of back academic achievement – the persistence of racism and the schooling experiences of black students in Canada', *Race, Ethnicity and Education* 4 (4): 343–375.

B. A. Collet (2007) 'Islam, national identify and public secondary education: perspectives from the Somali diaspora in Toronto, Canada', *Race, Ethnicity and Education* 2 (10): 131–153.

K. Croteau (2006) 'Les representations de l'univers educatif et la trajectoire migratoire au coeur des strategies d'accompagnement parental: L'insertion scolaire de jeunes peruviens immigrants en estrie', MA thesis (Université de Sherbrooke).

D. Dagenais (2008) 'La prise en compte du plurilinguisme d'enfants issus de familles immigrantes en contexte scolaire: une analyse de cas', *Revue des sciences de l'éducation* 2 (34): 351–375.

D. Dahm (1995) *Highlights of Aboriginal Conditions 1991, 1986: Demographic, Social and Economic Characteristics* (Ottawa: Department of Indian Affairs and Northern Development).

P. Daley and M. Begley (2008) 'Fragmentation sociale et cohesion sociale en education au Canada', *Canadian Ethnic Studies* 40 (1): 125–139.

S. Davies and N. Guppy (1998) 'Race and Canadian education' in V. Satzewich (ed.) *Racism and Social Inequality in Canada* (Toronto: Thompson Educational Publishing), pp. 131–156.

G. Dei (1996) 'The role of Afrocentricity in the inclusive curriculum in Canadian school', *Canadian Journal of Education* 21 (2): 170–186.

G. Dei (1997) 'Race and the production of identity in the schooling experiences of African–Canadian youth', *Discourse*, 18 (2): 241–257.

G. Dei (2003) 'Schooling and the dilemma of youth disengagement', *McGill Journal of Education* 38 (2): 241–256.

G. Dei (2008) 'Schooling as community: race, schooling, and the education of African youth', *Journal of Black Studies* 38 (3): 346–366.

T. M. Derwing and M. J. Monro (2007) 'Canadian policies on immigrant language education' in R. Joshee and L. Johnson (eds) *Multicultural Education Policies in Canada and the United States* (Vancouver: UBC Press), pp. 93–106.

M. Dewing and M. Leman (2006) 'Canadian multiculturalism' current issue review – parliamentary research branch, Library of Parliament Research Publications

(93–6E), date accessed 25 September 2010, http://www2.parl.gc.ca/content/lop/researchpublications/936-e.htm.

G. Dicks and A. Sweetman (1999) 'Education and ethnicity in Canada: an intergenerational perspective', *Journal of Human Resources* 34 (4): 668–696.

S. N. Dlamini and D. Martinovic (2007) 'In pursuit of being Canadian: examining the challenges of culturally relevant education in teacher education programs', *Race, Ethnicity and Education* 10 (2): 155–175.

F. Echols and D. Fisher (1992) 'School action plans and implementation of a district race relations policy', *Canadian Ethnic Studies* 24 (1): 58–79.

A. Elgersma (2001) Les femmes autochtones – un portrait d'après le recensement de 1996 Gouvernement du Canada, Ministère desAffaires indiennes et du Nord Canada.

J. H. Eslingohn, M. Ashworth, Ontario Institute for Studies in Education, Canada. Multiculturalism, and Association of B.C. Teal (1989) *Multicultural Education and Policy: ESL in the 1990s: A Tribute to Mary Ashworth* (Toronto: Ontario Institute for Studies in Education).

B. S. Faircloth and J. V. Hamm (2005) 'Sense of belonging among high school students representing 4 ethnic groups', *Journal of Youth and Adolescence* 34 (4): 293–309.

A. Fleras and J. L. Elliot (1992) *Multiculturalism in Canada* (Scarborough: Nelson Canada).

E. Fong and X. Cao (2009) 'Effects of foreign education on immigrant earnings', *Canadian Studies in Population* 35 (1–2): 87–110.

J. Friesen and B. Krauth (2007) 'Sorting and inequality in Canadian schools', *Journal of Public Economics* 91 (11–12): 2185–2212.

J. Friesen and B. Krauth (2010) 'Sorting, peers and achievement of aboriginal students in British Columbia' *Canadian Journal of Economics* 43 (4): 1273–1301.

D. Galarneau and R. Morissette (2008) 'Immigrants' education and required job skills', *Perspectives on Labour and Income* (December): 5–18.

C. Geertz (1973) 'Thick description: toward an interpretive theory of culture' in C. Geertz (ed.) *The Interpretation of Cultures: Selected Essays* (New York: Basic Books), pp. 3–30.

D. Gérin-Lajoie and M. Jacquet (2008) 'Regards croisés sur l'inclusion des minorités en contexte scolaire francophone minoritaire au Canada', *Éducation et francophonie* 36 (1): 25–43.

J. Geschwender and N. Guppy (1995) 'Ethnicity, educational attainment, and earned income among Canadian-born men and women', *Canadian Ethnic Studies* 27 (1): 67–83.

R. Ghosh (1991) 'L'éducation des maitres pour une société multiculturelle' in F. Ouellet and M. Pagé (eds) *Pluriethnicité, education et société: Construire un espace commun* (Québec: Institut québécois de la recherche sur la culture), pp. 207–229.

R. Ghosh (2004) 'Public education and multicultural policy in Canada: the special case of Québec', *International Review of Education* 50 (5–6): 543–566.

T. Goldstein (2003) 'Contemporary bilingual life at a Canadian high school: Choices, risks, tensions, and dilemmas', *Sociology of Education* 76 (3): 247–264.

Government of Canada (1982) *Canadian Charter of Rights and Freedoms* (Ottawa: Ministry of Justice), date accessed 3 October 2011, http://laws.justice.gc.ca/eng/charter/index.html.

Government of Canada (1988) Canadian Multiculturalism Act (Ottawa: Minister of Justice), date accessed October 3 2011, http://laws.justice.gc.ca/en/C-18.7/index.html.

Government of Canada (1995) *Employment Equity Act* (Ottawa: Minister of Justice), c.44, date accessed 3 October 2011, http://laws-lois.justice.gc.ca.

G. Greenwood, S. de Leeuw and T. Ngaroimata Fraser (2007) 'Aboriginal children and early childhood development and education in Canada: linking the past and the present to the future', *Canadian Journal of Native Education* 30 (1): 5.

Y. Guo (2006) 'Why didn't they show up? rethinking ESL parent involvement in K–12 education', *TESL Canada Journal* 24 (1): 80.

N. Guppy and K. Lyon (2011) 'Multicultural education in Canada' in C. Kassimeris and M. Vryonides (eds) *The Politics of Education* (New York: Routledge), pp. 114–135.

C. Haig-Brown (1988) *Resistance and Renewal: Surviving the Indian Residential School* (Vancouver: Tillacum Library).

J. Hare (2007) 'First Nations education policy in Canada: building capacity for change and control' in R. Joshee and L. Johnson (eds) *Multicultural Education Policies in Canada and the United States* (Vancouver: UBC Press), pp. 51–68.

H. Harper (2000) '"There is no way to prepare for this": teaching in First Nations schools in northern Ontario – issues and concerns', *Canadian Journal of Native Education* 24 (2): 144–157.

Y. M. Hebertonne (1992) 'Multicultural education and the minority language child', *Canadian Ethnic Studies* 24 (3): 58.

Human Resources, Labour and Employment (2008) 'Government announces provincial policy on multiculturalism', date accessed 3 June 2011, http://www.releases.gov. nl.ca/releases/2008/hrle/0603n05.htm.

J.-C. Icart (2009) 'Participation parentale et réussite scolaire: les communautés noires de Montréal et les écoles secondaires publiques francophones', *Les Cahiers de la CRIEC* 33: 95–105.

M. Jacquet (2007) 'La formation des maîtres à la pluriethnicité: pédagogie critique, silence et désespoir', *Revue des sciences de l'éducation* 33 (1): 25–45.

M. Jacquet, D. Moore and C. Sabatier (2008) L'intégration des jeunes immigrants francophones africains dans les écoles francophones en Colombie Britannique, Atlantic Metropolis Centre, Halifax, Working Paper No. 9.

R. Joshee and S. Winton (2007) 'Past crossings: US influences on the development and Canadian multicultural education policy' in R. Joshee and L. Johnson (eds) *Multicultural Education Policies in Canada and the United States* (Vancouver: UBC Press), pp. 17–27.

F. Kanouté (2007) 'Intégration sociale et scolaire des familles immigrantes au Québec', *Informations Sociales* 143 (7): 64–74.

F. Kanouté, M. VatzLaaroussi, L. Rachedi and M. Tchimou Doffouchi (2008) 'Familles et réussite scolaire d'élèves immigrants du secondaire', *Revue Des Sciences De l'Éducation* 34 (2): 289.

A. Kirova (2008) 'Critical and emerging discourses in multicultural education literature: a review', *Canadian Ethnic Studies* 40 (1): 101–124.

J. Kitchen, L. Cherubini, L. Trudeau and J. Hodson (2010) 'Weeding out or developing capacity? Challenges for aboriginal teacher education', *Alberta Journal of Educational Research* 56 (2): 107–124.

M. Laferrière (1983) 'L'éducation des enfants des groupes minoritaires au Québec', *Sociologie et sociétés* 15 (2): 117–132.

B. Lawrence (2003) 'Gender, race, and the regulation of native identity in Canada and the United States: an overview', *Hypatia* 18 (2): 3–31.

M. Lebrun (1999) 'L'étranger dans la littérature québécoise pour la jeunesse: L'affirmation d'un personnage à part entière', *Canadian Ethnic Studies* 31 (1): 92–108.

J. Ledent, J. Murdoch and R. Ait-Said (2010) 'Le cheminement et les résultats scolaires des jeunes d'origine immigrée à Montréal', *Centre Métropolis du Québec: Immigration et métropoles* 42.

A. Lenoir-Achdjian (1999) 'Le choix d'un espace scolaire pour les parents de la diaspora arménienne: un choix religieux, un choix politique, un choix social', *Canadian Ethnic Studies* 31 (2): 115–136.

D. Ley (2010) 'Multiculturalism: A Canadian defence' in S. Vertovec and S. Wessendorf (eds) *The Multiculturalism Backlash: European Discourses, Policies and Practice* (London: Routledge), pp. 190–206.

P. Li (2001) 'The market worth of immigrants' educational credentials', *Canadian Public Policy* 27 (1): 1–16.

P. Li (2004) 'Parental expectations of Chinese immigrants: a folk theory about children's school achievement', *Race, Ethnicity and Education* 7 (2): 167–183.

P. Li (2008) 'The role of foreign credentials and ethnic ties in immigrants' economic performance', *Canadian Journal of Sociology* 33 (2): 291–310.

M.-G. Liboy and M. Venet (2011) 'Participation des familles immigrantes à l'école: points de vue des parents congolais à Edmonton (Alberta)', *Journal of International Migration and Integration* 12 (2): 155–171.

D. E. Lundrren (2006) 'Rocking the racism boat: school-based activists speak out on denial and avoidance', *Race, Ethnicity and Education* 9 (2): 203–221.

M. Marker (2009) 'Indigenous resistance and racist schooling on the borders of empires: Coast Salish cultural survival', *International Journal of the History of Education* 45 (6): 757–772.

J.-P. Mbuya Mutombo (2003) 'Identité et performances scolaires. les élèves issus de groupes minoritaires au Québec, leurs points de vue', *Journal of International Migration and Integration / Revue De l'Intégration Et De La Migration Internationale* 4 (3): 361–393.

M. McAndrew (1986) 'Le traitement du racisme, de l'immigration et de la réalité multi-ethnique dans les manuels scolaires francophones au Québec', *Canadian Ethnic Studies/ Etudes Ethniques Au Canada* 18 (2): 130–143.

M. McAndrew (2001) *Immigration et diversité a l'école: Le débat Québecois dans une perspective comparative* (Montréal: Les presses de l'Universite de Montréal).

M. McAndrew (2013) *Fragile Majorities and Education: Belgium, Catalonia, Northern Ireland, and Quebec* (Montreal and Kingston: McGill-Queen's University Press).

M. McAndrew, B. Oueslati and D. Helly (2007) 'L'évolution du traitement de l'islam et des cultures musulmanes dans les manuels scolaires québécois de langue française du secondaire', *Canadian Ethnic Studies* 39 (3): 173.

M. McAndrew, M. Jacquet and C. Ciceri (1997) 'La prise en compte de la diversité culturelle et religieuse dans les normes et pratiques de gestion des établissements scolaires: Une étude exploratoire dans cinq provinces Canadiennes', *Revue Des Sciences De l'Education* 23 (1): 209–232.

M. McAndrew, J. Ledent and R. Ait-Said (2006) 'La performance des élèves des communautés noires aux examens ministériels du secondaire Québécois: Cohortes 1994, 1995, 1996', *Journal of International Migration and Integration / Revue De l'Intégration Et De La Migration Internationale* 7 (3): 301–326.

M. McAndrew, J. Ledent and R. Ait-Said (2008) 'La réussite scolaire des jeunes des communautés noires au secondaire' Rapport de recherche. Montréal, QC: Immigration et métropoles, date accessed 1 August 2011, http://site.ebrary.com/lib/ubc/docDetail. action?docID=10277095&force=1.

P. McIntosh (1990). White privilege: Unpacking the invisible knapsack. *Independent School*, Winter, 31–36.

K. A. McLeod (1980) *Intercultural Education and Community Development* (Toronto: Guidance Centre, Faculty of Education, University of Toronto).

K. A. McLeod (1987) *Multicultural Education: A Partnership* (Toronto: Canadian Council for Multicultural and Intercultural Education).

B. Millington, P. Vertinsky, E. Boyle and B. Wilson (2008) 'Making Chinese-Canadian masculinities in Vancouver's physical education curriculum', *Sports, Education and Society* 13 (2): 195–214.

J. Milloy (1999) *A National Crime: The Canadian Government and the Residential School System, 1879–1986* (Winnipeg: University of Manitoba Press).

N. Morin (1993) 'Étude des attentes des enseignants, du concept de soi scolaire et du rendement en mathématiques des élèves d'origine immigrante de sixième, septième et huitième années', MA thesis (University of Ottawa).

D. Mujawamariya (2000) 'Ils ne peuvent pas enseigner dans nos écoles: le dilemme des étudiants-maîtres des minorités visibles nés au Canada', *Revue ontaroise d'intervention sociale et communautaire* 6 (2): 138–165.

D. Mujawamariya (2001) 'Associate teachers facing integration of visible minorities into the teaching profession in francophone Ontario', *Canadian Ethnic Studies* 33 (2): 87.

R. Ng (1995) 'Multiculturalism as ideology: a textual analysis' in M. Campbell and A. Manicom (eds) *Knowledge, Experience, and Ruling Relations: Studies in the Social Organization of Knowledge* (Toronto: University of Toronto Press).

F. Ouellet (1986) *Pluralisme et école: Jalons pour une approche critique de la formation interculturelle des éducateurs* (Québec: Institut québécois de la recherche sur la culture).

F. Ouellet and M. Pagé (1991) *Pluriethnicité, éducation et société: Construire un espace commun* (Québec: Institut québécois de la recherche sur la culture).

B. Ouestlati, M. Labelle and R. Antonius (2006) 'Incorporation citoyenne des québécois d'origine arabe: conceptions, pratiques et défis', *Cahiers du CRIEC* 30.

D. Oyserman, M. Kemmelmeier, S. Fryberg, H. Brosh and T. Hart-Johnson (2003) 'Racial-ethnic self-schemas', *Social Psychology Quarterly* 66 (4): 333–347.

M. Pagé (1986) 'L'éducation interculturelle au Québec: bilan critique' in F. Ouellet (ed.) *Pluralisme et école: Jalons pour une approche critique de la formation interculturelle des éducateurs* (Québec: Institut québécois de la recherche sur la culture), pp. 271–301.

W. G. Picot and F. Hou (2011) *Preparing for Success in Canada and the United States: The Determinants of Educational Attainment among the Children of Immigrants*, 332 (Ottawa: Statistics Canada, Social Analysis Division).

F. Pirbhai-Illich (2010) 'Aboriginal students engaging and struggling with critical multi-literacies', *Journal of Adolescent & Adult Literacy* 54 (4): 257–266.

J. Porter (1965) *The Vertical Mosaic: An Analysis of Social Class and Power in Canada* (Toronto: University of Toronto Press).

M. Potvin and P. R. Carr (2008) 'La 'valeur ajoutée' de l'éducation antiraciste: conceptualisation et mise en oeuvre au Québec et en Ontario', *Éducation et francophonie* 36 (1): 197–216.

Potvin, M., McAndrew, M. and Kanouté, F. (2006) L'éducation antiraciste en milieu scolaire francophone à Montréal: Diagnostic et prospectives. *Rapport de recherche au ministère du Patrimoine Canadien, Chaire de recherche du Canada Éducation et rapports ethniques*.

R. Raby (2004) '"There's no racism at my school, it's just joking around": Ramifications for anti-racist education', *Race, Ethnicity and Education* 7 (4): 367–383.

H. Raham (2009) *Best Practices in Aboriginal Education: A Literature Review and Analysis for Policy Directions* (Office of the Federal Interlocutor, Indian and Northern Affairs Canada).

A. Rahim (1990) 'Multiculturalism or ethnic hegemony: A critique of multicultural education in Toronto', *The Journal of Ethnic Studies* 18 (3): 29–46.

J. G. Reitz (2001) 'Immigrant success in knowledge economy: Institutional change and immigrant experience in Canada, 1970–1995', *Journal of Social Issues* 57 (3): 579–613.

J. G. Reitz, H. Zhang and N. Hawkins (2011) 'Comparisons of the success of racial minority immigrant offspring in the United States, Canada and Australia', *Social Science Research* 40 (4): 1051–1066.

A. G. Reynolds (1991) *Bilingualism, Multiculturalism, and Second Language Learning: The McGill Conference in Honour of Wallace E. Lambert* (Hillside: Lawrence Erlbaum Associates).

J. G. Richards, A. R. Vining and D. L. Weimer (2010) 'Aboriginal performance on standardized tests: Evidence and analysis from provincial schools in British Columbia', *Policy Studies Journal* 38 (1): 47–67.

D. Rivière (2008) 'Whiteness in/and education', *Race, Ethnicity and Education* 11 (4): 355–368.

C. Rousseau, A. Drapeau and E. Corin (1996) 'School performance and emotional problems in refugee children', *American Journal of Orthopsychiatry* 66 (2): 239–251.

M. D. Ruck and S. Wortley (2002) 'Racial and ethnic minority high school students' perceptions of school disciplinary practices: a look at some Canadian findings', *Journal of Youth and Adolescence* 31 (3): 185–195.

J. Ryan (1997) 'Student communities in a culturally diverse school setting: identity, representation and association', *Discourse: Studies in the Cultural Politics of Education* 18 (1): 37–53.

V. Satzewich (1997) 'Indian agents and the "Indian problem" in Canada in 1946: Reconsidering the theory of coercive tutelage', *The Canadian Journal of Native Studies* 27 (2): 227–257.

V. Satzewich and L. Mahood (1995) 'Indian agents and the residential school system in western Canada', *Historical Studies in Education* 7: 41–65.

S. Shamai (1992) 'Ethnicity and educational achievement in Canada, 1941–1981', *Canadian Ethnic Studies* 24 (1): 43–57.

A. Siggner and R. Costa (2005). Aboriginal Conditions in Census Metropolitan Areas, 1981–2001. Statistics Canada Catalogue number 89-613-MIE – No. 008.

A. Smith, B. H. Schneider and M. D. Ruck (2005) '"Thinking about makin' it": Black Canadian students' beliefs regarding education and academic achievement', *Journal of Youth and Adolescence* 34 (4): 347–359.

K. Snider (1996) 'Race and sexual orientation the (im)possibility of these intersections in educational policy', *Harvard Educational Review* 66 (2): 294–303.

P. Solomon, J. Portelli, B.-J. Daniel and A. Campbell (2005) 'The discourse of denial: how white teacher candidates construct race, racism and "white privilege"', *Race Ethnicity and Education* 8 (2): 147–169.

Statistics Canada (2001) 'Aboriginal peoples of Canada', date accessed 28 June 2011, http://www12.statcan.ca/english/census01/products/analytic/companion/abor/canada.cfm.

P. A. J. Stevens (2007) 'Researching race/ethnicity and educational inequality in English secondary schools: A critical review of the research literature between 1980 and 2005', *Review of Education Research* 77 (2): 147–185.

P. A. J. Stevens, N. Clycq, C. Timmerman and M. Van Houtte (2011) 'Researching race/ethnicity and educational inequality in the Netherlands: A critical review of the research literature between 1980 and 2008', *British Educational Research Journal* 37 (1): 5–43.

L. Sylvain, L. Laforce, C. Trottier and P. Georgeault (1988) 'Les cheminements scolaires des francophones, des anglophones et des allophones du Québec au cours des années soixante-dix', *Revue des sciences de l'éducation* 14 (2): 225–244.

A. Talbani (1993) 'Intercultural education and minorities: policy initiatives in Quebec', *McGill Journal of Education* 28 (3): 407.

A. J. Tavareso (2000) 'From heritage to international languages: Globalism and western Canadian trends in heritage language education', *Canadian Ethnic Studies* 32 (1): 156–171.

A. Taylor and H. Krahn (2005) 'Aiming high: Educational aspirations of visible minority immigrant youth', *Canadian Social Trends* (79): 8–12.

A. Triki-Yamani and M. McAndrew (2009) 'Perceptions du traitement de l'islam, du monde musulman et des minorités musulmanes par de jeunes musulmans(es) du cégep au Québec', *Diversitéurbaine* 9 (1): 73–94.

W. Werner, B. Connors, T. Aoki and J. Dahlie (1980) *Whose Culture? Whose Heritage? Ethnicity within Canadian Social Studies Curricula* (Vancouver: UBC Centre for the Study of Curriculum and Instruction).

C. Worswick (2004) 'Adaptation and inequality: Children of immigrants in Canadian schools', *Canadian Journal of Economics* 37 (1): 53–77.

J. Zine (2001) '"Negotiating equity": The dynamics of minority community engagement in constructing inclusive educational policy', *Cambridge Journal of Education* 31 (2): 239–269.

J. Zine (2007) 'Safe havens or religious "ghettos"? Narratives of Islamic schooling in Canada', *Race, Ethnicity and Education* 10 (1): 71–92.

8
China

Hua-Yu Sebastian Cherng, Emily Hannum, and Chunping Lu

8.1 Introduction

Since China's market reforms and opening up in the 1980s, growing literatures in Chinese and English have addressed issues associated with educational opportunity for ethnic minorities. Overall, despite certain similarities in subject matter and, in some cases, common authorship, these literatures have emerged in different forms. Consistent with a Marxist perspective that pervades both minority education policy and much of the scholarly writing about it, much of the Chinese literature faults underlying economic underdevelopment at the regional level and poverty at the household level as key sources of minority disadvantage. Some newer pieces, a few of which draw from a multicultural education framework, offer critical perspectives on minority education policies, but this body of literature is still small. Cultural disconnects between home and school are featured in this literature, but with a few exceptions, cultural attitudes of particular groups are cited as the barrier to educational success, rather than aspects of the organization and content of educational institutions or labor market conditions that might exacerbate unfavorable attitudes. Finally, much of the empirical work is applied and focused on problems, generally associated with poverty or underdevelopment, that need to be solved to support the goals of development, patriotism, and integration of minority populations.

Like the Chinese literature, a substantial portion of the English literature could be characterized as policy discussion, with emphasis on the integrative goals and implications of minority education policy. Moreover, the English-language literature recognizes the significance of economic poverty and geographic disparity in contributing to educational disparities. However, while some of the work is descriptive and neutral in tone, much of the work has a more critical edge than found in the Chinese language literature. The operating premise of much of the literature is one of deep questioning of the goals and tactics surrounding minority education policies. Empirical work has focused on characterizing the nature and scope of educational stratification by ethnic group, and on illuminating links between schooling processes and the conveyed and constructed ethnic identities of students, cultural disconnects between home and school, and incentives and disincentives for school continuation.

This chapter provides an overview of the Chinese- and English-language scholarship related to ethnicity and inequality in education. We begin by providing an overview of China's ethnic classification and education systems. Next, we present the search strategy used to identify papers for this literature review. Finally, we describe Chinese- and English-language research. We close by discussing key differences and similarities between the two literatures, and by highlighting the need for both literatures to connect more directly to comparative sociological research on ethnicity and education.

8.2   National context

8.2.1   Ethnic minorities in China

The name used to refer to ethnic groups in China today, *minzu* (民族), is a 20th-century adaptation of the cognate Japanese term, *minzoku* (民族), and is often translated as 'ethnic nation', 'ethno-nation', or 'nationality' (Gladney, 2004). The specific categories in use today were largely set in place after the People's Republic of China was founded in 1949, as the state set out to identify and recognize as minority nationalities those who qualified among the hundreds of groups applying for national minority status. Following the Soviet model, decisions were based on the 'four commons': language, territory, economic life, and psychological make-up, meaning that ethnic minorities were identified as having common linguistic, economic, geographic, or cultural characteristics that distinguished them from the so-called Han majority population (Fei, 1981; cited in Gladney, 2004). Scholarly debates about their aptness notwithstanding, these classifications have become fairly set over time, with few new categories created in the ensuing years (Gladney, 2004; see Tsung, 2009, pp. 72–74 for examples of the complexity of the initial classifications). Today, the Chinese government officially recognizes 55 minority nationalities (少数民族, *shaoshu minzu*), along with the Han majority nationality (汉族, *hanzu*), a 'naturalized' category, and an 'unknown' category that encompasses about 350 other ethnic groups not recognized individually (Wong, 2000, p. 56).

The officially designated minority population in China grew from 5.8% of the total in the 1964 census to over 8% by the fifth population census in 2000 (West, 2004). According to the sixth national census conducted in 2010, the total minority population of mainland China was 113.79 million, accounting for 8.49% of the total population and roughly the size of the total population of Mexico. Compared with 2000, the minority population increased by 7.36 million, which is an increase of 6.92%. The growth rate for the Han population in the same period was 5.74% (National Bureau of Statistics, 2011). China's minority populations are culturally and linguistically diverse, as suggested by the fact that they span the Sino-Tibetan, Indo-European, Austro-Asiatic, and Altaic language families (Hannum and Wang, 2012, Map 1).

China has designated a system of regional autonomous areas in locations where large numbers of ethnic minorities reside (China, 2000, sec. 3). At the highest levels are the five province-level autonomous regions: the Inner Mongolia Autonomous Region, founded in 1947; the Xinjiang Uygur Autonomous Region, founded in 1955; the Guangxi Zhuang Autonomous Region, founded in 1958; the Ningxia Hui Autonomous Region, also founded in 1958; and the Tibet Autonomous Region, founded in 1965. Also, below province-level administrative divisions are autonomous prefectures and autonomous counties, which can exist outside of autonomous regions. China's regional ethnic autonomous zones are in 21 provinces and 741 county-level administrative regions (Ma, 2007).

Ethnic minorities disproportionately reside in the poor western region of China, with 71.63% of minorities living in this region. In the central region, 15.95% of the total ethnic minority population of China resides, and 12.42% reside in the eastern region. The western region accounts for 91.63% of all ethnic autonomous counties, or 741 regions, the majority of which reside in five minority autonomous regions. 5.13% of ethnic autonomous counties are located in the central region and 3.24% are in the eastern region. Among these county administrative units, almost 40% are designated as 'national poverty' counties (National Bureau of Statistics, 2011). However, there is great variability across individual groups in patterns of residence and vulnerability to poverty (Hannum and Wang, 2012).

8.2.2   China's educational system

China has a centralized education management system, and there has been much uniformity across the country in terms of curricula, textbooks, and examinations, particularly at the transition from high school to college.[1] With the exception of some special preparatory education classes, the education system for minorities and China's national educational system are very similar (Table 8.1). China's educational system includes general education, vocational education, and adult education, with the greatest resources and attention invested in general education. General education consists of nine years of compulsory education, divided into six years of elementary school and three years of junior middle school. Compulsory education plus three years of high school are considered basic education. Children six years of age are required to attend primary schools, most often located near their residence, and there is no examination requirement to transition in junior middle school. Junior middle school graduates, however, generally have to pass an entrance examination

Table 8.1   China's education system

Age	Number of years school				
25–27	3	Doctorate			Post-graduation/ work
22–24	3	Masters			
18–21	4	Undergraduate	Vocational education (tertiary education)	Tertiary level technical schools	Self-study
15–17	3	Academic high school	Secondary vocational education		Adult secondary education
12–14	3	Academic junior high school	Junior vocational school		Adult literacy programs
6–11	6	Elementary school			
3–5	3	Preschool/ kindergarten education			

Source: Ministry of Education, 2010.

to enroll in upper secondary schools (Ministry of Education, 1983; 2001).[2] An entrance examination is also typically required for entrance into the university system, and remains the primary entrance requirement for the majority of universities in China (Hannum, An, and Cherng, 2011).

More than ten years ago, China initiated a large-scale expansion of its education system. Before this time, many students from rural areas or poor households enrolled in technical schools. However, after expansion, many junior high school graduates entered academic high schools that focused more on preparation for entry into colleges and universities. In 2009, 44.8% of all junior middle school graduates entered academic high schools, 47.2% entered vocational education schools, and 8% entered the labor market (Ministry of Education, 2010). Higher education has expanded very rapidly in China, but the job market for college graduates has become much less favorable.[3]

8.2.3   Minority education policies

In 2009, 17,391,000 ethnic minority students were enrolled in basic education (Table 8.2) (Ministry of Education, 2010). In ethnic minority areas, the proportion of primary school students receiving preschool education is lower than the national average.[4] Ethnic minority students are more likely than the Han to enroll in secondary vocation school, as opposed to academic high school.

Table 8.2 Ethnic minority students in 2009

Level of school	Number of ethnic minority students	Percent of total student population
Academic high school	1,787,100	7.34
Secondary vocation school	1,072,000	17.23
Junior high school	5,012,200	9.22
Primary school	10,591,200	10.52
Special education	32,800	7.66
Preschool education	1,894,200	7.13

Source: Ministry of Education, 2010.

In recent decades, educational access for ethnic minorities has expanded rapidly due to government efforts. In 1980, the Ministry of Education and the State Ethnic Affairs Commission strengthened its commitment to the education of ethnic minorities by introducing the Law on Regional Ethnic Autonomy and also recommending that funds subsidize minority education in areas with a large number of ethnic minorities, in addition to standard education funding (Ministry of Education, 1983). In 2002, the State Council released a policy which emphasized accelerated development for minority education, and in China's tenth Five-Year Plan period (2001–2005), the central government invested 60 billion yuan for construction, of which 57% was designated to develop the western region and ethnic minority areas (Ministry of Education, 2010). In 2004, the central government also invested heavily to support the construction of boarding schools in rural areas and to further develop ethnic minority universities (Ministry of Education, 2004). From 2006 on, the government also decided that students attending school in rural areas of the western region would be exempt from all tuition and fees. China also implemented the 'Three Guarantees' – guaranteed learning, food, and housing – in rural Tibet. In 56 counties in the Xinjiang Uyghur Autonomous Region, the government provided free books and waived many schooling fees, and subsidized boarding costs (Ministry of Education, National Commission on Development and Reform, Ministry of Finance, 2007). Beyond these policies, there are numerous policy issues relevant to education in minority areas, ranging from language and curriculum policies, inland boarding school policies, to affirmative action policies. Many of the studies in both Chinese and English focus on policies and policy implementation issues; we will discuss additional policies in turn at relevant points in the review.

8.3 Methodology

We review Chinese- and English-language literatures in turn, rather than integrating the two throughout; we close with a discussion of connections and disconnects. Though there are, of course, exceptions, studies in these two language traditions often operate from disparate theoretical starting points, conform to different norms of academic writing, and speak to different audiences in different socio-political contexts. Consequently, there are domains of discourse that are prevalent in one tradition that are much less common in the other. For example, there is a body of Chinese-language literature that analyzes the Marxist philosophies that underlie China's ethnic minority education policies. While this literature and perspective is acknowledged in the English literature, there is not really a cognate body of work engaging this topic in English. A key disconnect is that much of the literature in Chinese is implicitly about solving a highly sensitive problem in national educational and economic development, whereas much of the literature in English speaks to an academic audience fundamentally concerned with inequalities and identities. We discuss disconnects and connections between the different language literatures in the conclusion.

For our Chinese-language search, we restricted our study to Chinese-language literature focused on mainland Chinese ethnic minority education. We excluded literature about Taiwan, Hong Kong, and Macao. The literature we reviewed was published from 1980 to 2010 and encompassed research drawing on sociological, pedagogical, and ethnological perspectives on minority education and inequality. We employed three specific search protocols. First, we searched China's largest periodical and journal database, the Chinese National Knowledge Infrastructure (CNKI), for titles with combinations of the following keywords: nationality, education, and equality/equity. We also searched online for books in China's National Library, which is China's largest professional book collection. Initial searches yielded close to 400 articles and 150 books, of which 80 articles and 30 books were selected for quality and relevance.

For literature in English on ethnic minority education in China, we searched Sociological Abstracts and ERIC for articles with titles containing the words 'China', 'education', and 'ethnic' or 'minority'. We then performed the same search on WORLDCAT to obtain books. Given the relatively recent emergence of literature in English on this topic, we did not put date restrictions into our search, but no work found pre-dated the 1980s. We supplemented the materials found in these systematic ways with other material we were aware of that was related to ethnic minorities and the context or outcomes of education.

8.4   Chinese-language traditions

We organize the Chinese-language research into six themes: Marxism and ethnic minority education, patriotism and national unity in education for ethnic minority students, multicultural education, determinants of ethnic differences in education, school facilities and teacher quality, and preferential/affirmative action policies. These traditions focus on the guiding ideology of ethnic minority education and its emphasis on national unity, ethnic differences in educational experiences and outcomes, and ways in which policies should address these educational differences.

8.4.1 Marxism and ethnic minority education

One line of research has described the influence of Marx, Lenin, and Stalin on China's ethnic minority education system. Jia (2000, 2007) traces how China's definition of ethnicity borrows heavily from Marx, Engels, and Stalin; that is, the notion of ethnicity, or groups that share a common history of formation, language, geography, economic life, and culture, arises when societies transition from local, tribal communities to states which encompass different ethnic groups. Ma (2007) analyzes the influence of Stalin and Lenin on the goals of ethnic minority education. The author finds that Stalin and Lenin both argue that ethnic distinction is a large source of conflict among the common people, and that assimilation of all groups will eliminate ethnic differences and contention. As a socialist state, China should therefore create policies which assimilate all ethnicities under one mainstream culture. Because Marxism is the guiding ideology of the Communist Party of China, it is difficult to find sociological studies that offer direct criticism of Marxism or educational inequality in China.

8.4.2 Patriotism and national unity in education for ethnic minority students

The Marxist ideology of assimilation and unity serves as the foundation for the second tradition found in Chinese-language research on ethnic minority education. This second research tradition focuses on the implementation of the Marxist ideals of integration, unity, and improvement in ethnic minority education. Emphasis on national unity and patriotism in ethnic minority education traces its policy origins to as early as 1983, when the Ministry of Education studied and implemented views which strengthened patriotism and propaganda in education in schools in minority areas (Ministry of Education, 1983). Scholarship in this tradition states that the integration of ethnic minorities into mainstream society through schooling is necessary for both the development of ethnic minority regions and the preservation of social stability. Most authors who do mention issues of ethnic minority identity argue that students who integrate into mainstream values do not compromise their minority identities.

One body of literature focuses on inland class and boarding schools for ethnic minority students, and argues that these programs improve education for ethnic minority students and promote national unity and the culture of minority groups. In 1985, the central government launched 'Tibetan classes' (*Xizang ban*), which are cohorts of mainly Tibetan students in classrooms and provinces in majority-Han areas of China (particularly major cities). The overall purpose of these classes was to accelerate the development of Tibet and strengthen patriotism (Ministry of Education, the General Office of Tibet Autonomous Region People's Government, 2007). The state deemed these classes an early success, and in April 1988, the State Education Commission stated that these schools were vital in order to reform and develop education in Tibet. As of 2007, Tibetan classes across China included 4840 junior high school students, 6780 junior vocational students, 13,000 high school students, and 9100 college and university students (Ministry of Education, the General Office of Tibet Autonomous Region People's Government, 2007). Similarly, 'Xinjiang classes' (*Xinjiang ban*) were established in 1987, and have expanded to 1.5 million students in recent years (Ma, 2011; Xia, 2007). One ethnographic study of middle school students enrolled in a 'Tibetan class' in an eastern city argued that students were able to accept both the state ideology of ethnic unity and integration while also claiming a sense of Tibetan culture through the students' attachment to common Tibetan symbols (Zhu, 2006).

Other work investigates language programs that educate ethnic minority students in Chinese, called '*min kao han*, 民考汉'. This body of Chinese-language literature argues that these programs are highly beneficial to ethnic minority students. Ma (2008) surveyed parents of ethnic minority students in Xinjiang, and found that parents increasingly favored that their children learn Mandarin in lieu of their native language. This same study also found that students themselves were willing to learn Chinese and preferred Chinese-language programs. Zhu (2009) argued that '*min kao han*' students not only benefited from Chinese-language education, but also from exposure to 'mainstream' cultural values. The author found that students who integrated into mainstream society did not necessarily lose their ethnic identity, and that many ethnic minority students enrolled in '*min kao han*' programs formed 'double identities' of Chinese and minority cultures.

One notable study of implementation of patriotic education in Tibet found that curricula did not sufficiently address contradictions between mainstream knowledge taught in schools and local cultural values (Zhu, 2007). In qualitative case-studies of townships in primary schools in rural areas, the author found that the nuances of each school environment were not always incorporated into teaching, and that parents mentioned tension arising from this conflict. The author recommended that formal school curriculum should present traditional Tibetan culture, including local culture, history, and geography.

8.4.3   Multicultural education

A third line of research discusses the viability of multiculturalism in the Chinese context. Multiculturalism, as defined by Chinese literature, encompasses the notions that different cultures are equal and mutually influence each other (Teng, 1997). Some scholars argue that multicultural education can teach ethnic minority students about both mainstream and minority cultures while emphasizing the value of national unity (Ma, 2007; Teng, 1997). Learning about different cultures can also help eliminate ethnic and cultural discrimination experienced by many ethnic minority students (Teng, 1997; Wan, 2006).

Other scholars have compared multicultural education in Western countries with China's Marxist ideology. In comparative studies of the teaching objectives and theories of Western multicultural education and minority education in China from a historical perspective, Wan (2006, 2008) conclude that issues addressed by Western multicultural and minority education are very distinct from China's ethnic education issues, and Western multicultural models could not simply be adopted in original form for the China context. The authors argue that in the West, the principle responsibility and demand of multicultural education is to address issues with rights and political equality. However, in China, the authors argue, the concerns with ethnic minority education focus on economic, social, and cultural development. Scholars also state that current ethnic minority education policies, such as a set of reforms in 2001 that require schools to address the cultural heritage of ethnic groups (Ministry of Education, 2001), already promote diversity and mutual interaction (Wan, 2006; Yu, 2010).

Multicultural frameworks have also been used to criticize education that is based on one mainstream culture. Yuan (2004) argues that a dominant Han culture permeates much of the education system in China, and much of this 'official knowledge' is different from ideas taught in various ethnic minority cultures. This knowledge is found in unified standards, curricula, and textbooks that often ignore the diversity of local culture, ethnic minority languages, and cultural differences. Qian (2007) found in a study of ethnic minorities in the northwest a curriculum that contradicts local customs in favor of more mainstream values. The author argues that students gradually lose their ethnic identity as they progress in their education, and that this is of growing concern since curricula that emphasize national unity are replacing ones that emphasize diversity in the schools in ethnic minority areas.

8.4.4 Determinants of ethnic differences in education

This tradition of research relies principally on quantitative analysis of education data, and focuses on 'uneven development' of the educational systems in ethnic minority regions in China.[5] Some authors argue that the educational disadvantage experienced by many ethnic minority groups is due to regional and urban–rural differences in education, while others argue that economic and cultural differences are also important.

First, a body of literature documents regional differences in educational systems. In general, the eastern region has the most developed educational system and the highest quality of education. The western region, in comparison, is significantly underdeveloped. Urban areas in most regions provide much better access to quality schools than rural areas. There are also differences in educational access and allocation of educational resources among ethnic groups (Ma, 2003; Wang, 2002). For example, in 2000, 15.14% of individuals aged 15 and over in China were illiterate (Development Planning Division of the Ministry of Education, 2000). In minority regions in the West, the percentage was 22.43%. A number of other educational gaps exist, such as compulsory education enrollment rates, drop-out rates, and retention rates, shown in Table 8.3. In addition, there are also substantial differences in school conditions and funding between western minority areas and the eastern region. For example, only 0.28% of school facilities and campuses in the eastern region were officially classified as being in a 'dilapidated state', but 2.62% of schools were dilapidated in the northwest region in 1999 (Yang, 2006). Provincial funding for education was also 4.86 times greater in five eastern provinces (Beijing, Shanghai, Zhejiang, Jiangsu, Guangdong) in 2003 than five northwestern provinces (Shaanxi, Gansu, Qinghai, Ningxia, Xinjiang) (Yang, 2006).

Other studies emphasize the importance of urban and rural educational systems in explaining ethnic differences in education. Hong (2010), using survey data from western regions, found that ethnic differences in enrollment in basic education enrollment are due to urban–rural divides and class inequality, not ethnic inequality. The author also found that while the probability that ethnic minority children are enrolled in high school is still significantly lower than for Han children, the difference can be explained mainly by urban and rural, regional, and class differences. Ma (1998) found that in 1990, the illiteracy rate in rural areas of Tibet was 77.2%, but only 37% in urban areas. There were also differences in school attendance rates between urban and rural children (Table 8.4).

Other work argues that economic poverty is an important factor in explaining educational inequality. One study found that financial difficulties were the

Table 8.3 Averages of educational indicators in different regions of China in 2000

	Enrollment rate of primary school aged children	Drop-out rate of primary school-aged children	Primary school enrollment rate	Primary school five-year retention rate	High school entrance rate
National	99.09	0.90	94.37	92.48	49.52
East	99.72	0.25	97.24	98.10	52.56
West	97.86	1.13	89.96	84.02	45.70
Western minority areas	95.78	1.50	84.37	74.84	47.43

Source: Development Planning Division of the Ministry of Education (2010).

Table 8.4   Enrollment rates for primary school-aged children (7–11 years) in Tibet

	1988	1989	1990
City	88.8	87.3	89.4
Town	69.0	86.2	54.6
Rural areas	49.4	43.3	50.7
Total	55.7	53.1	54.6
All girls	54.3	47.6	63.1

Source: Tibet Autonomous Region Bureau of Statistics: 1989:549; 1991:396.

primary reason minority children from poor families were not in school (Liu and Yang, 2007). Another study, based on survey data from the Autonomous Prefecture of Xishuangbanna, Yunnan Province, described ethnic minority education in this region before and after the implementation of compulsory education with guaranteed funding (Teng, 2004). The author found that even after reform, many families could still not afford average school fees. Some scholars have proposed that provincial and local governments establish priority development areas to improve education in impoverished ethnic minority areas (Hu and Wen, 2001; Wan, 2006).

Finally, another body of literature suggests cultural reasons for ethnic differences in education. A number of studies which focus on specific ethnic minority groups, such as the Yao, argue that there is not sufficient parental support and encouragement of children's education (Qian, 2007; Yuan, 2004). One study of two Muslim minority groups, the Salar and Bonan, found that the drop-out rate of students who reported strong religious beliefs was higher than those who were non-religious. The author argued that parents, who were instrumental in passing on cultural and religious values to their children, should also emphasize the value of education (Qian, 2007). Similarly, Bo (1986) found that Yao parents in mountainous regions did not see formal education as a wise investment, and preferred their children to help cultivate local farms. Wang (1990) found that there was still widespread resistance among Tibetan families in rural areas to sending their children to school, despite rewards for school attendance and fines for non-attendance. Related work focuses on gender differences in schooling for ethnic minorities. One study of ethnic minority schools with high female drop-out rates argued that parents resisted sending girls to school (Qian, 2007). However, research on the Miao and Dong Autonomous Prefecture in Guizhou, researchers found that families cited safety as an important factor, and argued that this concern could explain why drop-out rates for girls were generally higher than for boys (Han, 1999; Wang, 2006). Studies proposing cultural explanations have not developed or tested systematic theories about the educational, social, economic, or policy conditions under which cultural resistance to local educational systems emerges.

8.4.5   School facilities and teacher quality

Another thread of work focuses on school facilities and teacher quality. Most research in this body of literature focuses on compulsory education and regions with a large number of ethnic minorities, including Guizhou's ethnic minority regions and minority autonomous areas of Gansu, Xinjiang, Tibet, and Yunnan (Zhou, 1985; Bai, 1986; Ma, 2004; Teng and Su, 1998; Wang, 2006). These studies employ a number of methodological approaches, including ethnography, questionnaires, and interviews. Overall, these studies find that impoverished ethnic minority areas lack educational resources. Many scholars working on this topic recommend that governing bodies adopt preferential policies to increase educational investment in these areas and help teachers understand and integrate local culture and social norms into teaching.

One body of literature emphasizes problems of teacher quality in ethnic minority regions of China. In 2009, many provinces and prefectures had a higher percentage of teachers who were substitutes than national average (Table 8.5). For example, in Linxia Hui Autonomous Prefecture in Gansu Province, substitute teachers comprised 15.99% of total primary school teachers and 24.04% of fulltime teachers (Minority Education Department of Gansu Provincial Department of Education, 2010). Of these teachers, only a small number of substitute teachers had a college degree or higher and most had no professional training in pedagogy (Zhao, 2010). Other work also finds that there is a severe shortage of bilingual teachers in many ethnic minority areas and that there are no bilingual teacher training institutions (Ma, 2007; Teng, 2001; Xu, 2009).

Another line of research in this tradition focuses on the shortage of investment in education in ethnic minority regions. Studies which focus on primary and secondary education in ethnic minority areas find that schools often lack laboratory equipment, library materials, and other resources (Teng and Su, 1998; Xu, 2009). In a case-study of schools which serve Yao children, Yuan (2004) found that the far distance that students had to travel to school hindered their attendance, resulting in a large number of school drop-outs.

8.4.6   Preferential/affirmative action policies

The final research tradition of Chinese-language literature focuses on the purpose of preferential policies towards ethnic minorities. China currently implements a number of preferential policies for ethnic minorities which affect education, employment, family planning, and Communist Party membership. In October 1980, the government addressed issues of representation of

Table 8.5 Number of substitute teachers and percentage of the teaching workforce in ethnic minority autonomous regions and western multi-ethnic provinces, 2009

	Elementary school		Junior middle school	
	Number of substitute teachers	Percent workforce that are substitute teachers	Number of substitute teachers	Percent workforce that are substitute teachers
China		4.14		1.97
Xinjiang	7,761	5.46	2,858	2.51
Tibet	416	2.18	0	0
Guangxi	16,410	6.92	2,210	1.37
Inner Mongolia	3,399	2.87	2,345	2.39
Ningxia	1,697	4.83	1,291	4.59
Guizhou	8,036	3.88	1,044	0.74
Yunnan	13,586	5.49	89	0.57
Sizhuan	17,806	5.49	4,112	1.45
Qinghai	3,404	11.27	1,921	8.27
Gansu	12,872	8.42	2,238	1.88

Source: Development Planning Division of the Ministry of Education, (2010). National Educational Development Statistical Report 2009.

ethnic minorities in higher education by stating that the proportion of ethnic minorities enrolled in higher education should not be less than the proportion of ethnic minorities in the population (Ma, 2007).

The limited number of articles and books in this tradition rely more on theoretical arguments rather than empirical study. Some authors argue that affirmative action policies are necessary to address unbalanced economic development of ethnic minority regions, while others discuss the negative consequences of these policies. Some scholars argue that due to a disproportionate number of ethnic minorities residing in impoverished areas of China, policies should be created to foster educational development and 'mainstream language and values' in these areas (Hu and Wen, 2001; Wan, 2006).

However, other scholars believe that these policies may have a number of negative consequences. Zhang and Liu (2010) argue that bilingual education may hinder the integration and upward mobility of ethnic minorities. Specifically, the author argues that because only ethnic minorities can enroll in '*min kao min*, 民考民', or ethnic minority classes taught in the minority language, students' future options may be limited. Other scholars also argue that affirmative action policies for ethnic minorities should only target individuals who live in remote or impoverished areas and not ethnic minorities who live in more affluent regions (Ao, 2006). Another argument is concerned with 'reverse discrimination', in which the favoring of ethnic minorities students may disadvantage Han students (Ao, 2006; Teng and Ma, 2005).

8.5   English-language traditions

English-language literature on ethnic minority education can be categorized into three broad traditions: policy overviews, analyses of the relationships between education and ethnic identity, and studies of educational stratification. Policy overviews are in some cases exploratory cataloging projects, and in others, more serious critical investigations of the nature of relevant policies such as affirmative action, higher education, and language policies. Much of the research on education and ethnic identity focuses on the role of the state and of students themselves in constructing ethnic identities. Finally, literature on educational stratification, which is not generally highly theorized, has sought to establish empirical patterns and trends in access, attainment, and the economic context and outcomes of education.

8.5.1   Policy overviews

A number of studies have undertaken a basic descriptive task of cataloging existing minority education policy in the contemporary period. Many scholars have noted the pendulum shifts in minority education policy, with the Cultural Revolution marked by extreme assimilationist policies and the subsequent reform era dating from the late 1970s marked by a broad variety of policies aimed at promoting minority education and development (Bass, 1998, pp. 18–21; Dai and Dong, 2001; e.g. Postiglione, 2009; Tsung, 2009, Chapter 4). Iredale, Bilik, and Su (2001) and Hannum and Wang (2012) provide brief reviews of reform era minority education policies in the context of broader development policies and demographic trends, highlighting provincial 'twinning' of rich provinces with poor and minority provinces and autonomous regions for educational support; preferential treatment of minority areas in poverty alleviation targeting; and various affirmative action policies for matriculation into colleges and universities; subsidies for minority students, and establishment of inland (*neidi*, 内地) minority boarding schools in China's heartland (Hannum and Wang, 2012; Iredale, Bilik and Su, 2001). Zhou and Hill have compiled an extensive series of studies addressing multiple dimensions of affirmative action policies in China (Zhou and Hill, 2010). Clothey (2005a) has catalogued policies related to higher education, including university admission quotas that reserve spots only for minorities at universities, admissions policies under which minorities can be accepted with lower entrance scores on the Unified Examination for University Entrance (*gaokao*, 高考), and the establishment of 12 national minority institutes and one national minority university dedicated specifically to the higher education of minority students (Clothey, 2005a; see also Lang, 2010 on this topic). Candidates for nationalities institutes may sit the *gaokao* in their native language, some applicants to minority region comprehensive universities and polytechnic institutes may also take the exam in their native language, and minority students may take higher education courses in their region's main nationality language (Clothey, 2005a).[6]

A related line of work has considered language policies (for a recent review covering the course of the PRC period, see Tsung, 2009, Chapter 5). The Chinese constitution has two provisions concerning language (Ma, 2007): Article 4 states that each ethnic group has the freedom to use and develop its own language and writing system, and Article 19 states that the national government will promote a common language to be used throughout the country. The reform era dating from the late 1970s has seen increased support by policymakers for the use of minority scripts in literacy education and for increased bilingual education, with the goal that schools with a majority of minority language users can use minority languages as the primary medium of instruction (Adamson and Feng, 2009, p. 323; Lin, 1997; Ministry of Education, 1986, Article 6; Ministry of Education, 1995, Article 12; Ross, 2006, p. 25; Sautman, 1999, p. 289). In a 1980 publication, the Ministry of Education and the China State Ethnic Affairs Commission required that every ethnic group with a language and writing system use that language for educational instruction, while also learning spoken and written Mandarin (Ma, 2007). Education laws of 1986 and 1995 emphasize popularization of Mandarin, as well as use of minority languages. For example, the 1995 law states:

> The Chinese language, both oral and written, shall be the basic oral and written language for education in schools and other educational institutions. Schools or other educational institutions which mainly consist of students from minority nationalities may use in education the language of the respective nationality or the native language commonly adopted in that region. Schools and other educational institutions shall in their educational activities popularize the nationally common spoken Chinese and the standard written characters. (Article 12)

Ross's (2006, pp. 23–28) review of language policy notes a significant commitment to minority language maintenance and bilingual education in China's language laws, but also discusses significant changes over time in policy priorities and problems in implementation. Other scholars have also observed that there are gaps between policy and implementation, and that there are immense discrepancies in bilingual practice across minority regions, with regard to both state policies and local arrangements (Adamson and Feng, 2009; Feng and Sunuodula, 2009; Gao, 2010; Postiglione, 2009). Regional and local considerations – linguistic, demographic, and political – shape the ways in which bilingual and multicultural education can be and are incorporated into education across China.[7] Linguistic and demographic factors matter a lot: Ma (2007), referencing Zhou (1989, p. 31), states that when governmental educational authorities were planning and developing bilingual education, the principle they employed was consideration of the existing local language environment, along with social and economic development needs, pedagogical benefits, and preferences of residents. Scholars classify the modes of bilingual education in China as falling into transition models (transitioning to Mandarin) or maintenance models (maintaining the origin language), with the determination between the two affected by the existence of a well-established writing system and the ethnic composition of local areas (Feng, 2005, p. 534; Lin, 1997; Teng, 2002).

Political considerations are also important. Scholars have argued that the design and implementation of minority language policies relates to the histories and political statuses of the groups and regions involved (Adamson and Feng, 2009; see also Feng and Sunuodula, 2009).[8] For example, Catriona Bass notes that in the wake of the resurgence of a pro-independence movement in Tibet in the late 1980s, the primary political goal for minority education – ethnic unity – was reasserted, and concessions to Tibetan language and culturally relevant curriculum made in the 1980s were partially eroded (Bass, 1998, p. 4). This development also led to retrenchment on some preferential policies to promote secondary and higher education among Tibetans, due to fears about these policies causing tension between nationalities.

Postiglione (2009) notes that *neidi* middle schools accepting Tibetan students in the 1980s recruited mainly from elementary schools where the medium of instruction was Chinese, although students were still instructed in Tibetan for one year to ease the language transition. In later years, these schools started to accept more students from Tibetan-language elementary schools, and in 1993, students were no longer categorized by the language of instruction in elementary school. In interviews with students, the author found that *neidi* schools did not improve Tibetan language skills, and in many cases, students reported their knowledge of Tibetan language had deteriorated.

Similar to the case of Tibet, in Adamson and Feng's (2009) assessment, the difficult and contentious climate for political control in Xinjiang is reflected in the value attached to a distinct cultural identity by the people and a somewhat coercive edge to the promotion of standard Chinese as a language of instruction early on in school careers. The provision of English is mandated from the third year of primary school, but English teaching is very limited compared to other many other parts of the PRC (Adamson and Feng, 2009, p. 328; Feng and Sunuodula, 2009, p. 696; see also Tsung and Cruickshank, 2009 for a case-study in two schools in Xinjiang consistent with the notion of very limited English availability). Adamson and Feng write, 'the coercive nature of the language policies implemented in Xinjiang suggests that the rhetoric of a collaborative approach to language policies in minority areas uttered at the state level is not always translated into reality at the regional level, when national cohesion is deemed to be at stake' (2009, pp. 330–331).

At the other extreme is the case of the Zhuang, a group that Adamson and Feng characterize as highly assimilated and 'until recently, [demonstrating] little interest in cultural diversity' (2009, p. 330). Adamson and Feng argue, in this case, that the prime status accorded to standard Chinese and the lower 'vernacular' status accorded to the Zhuang language in the curriculum appeared consistent with a consensus (at least as observed in their fieldwork) about the appropriate roles for the languages, although the authors also argue that there is a lack of regional government commitment to 'genuinely collaborative' language policies (2009, p. 326). English is offered, by policy, from the third year of primary school, but the predominance of standard Chinese as the language of instruction for English classes disadvantages Zhuang students.

The challenge of balancing preservation of minority languages against instrumental pressures favoring Chinese, and sometimes English, is a common theme. In Adamson and Feng's (2009) assessment, the Yi in Liangshan Autonomous Prefecture in the Sichuan Province, in an impoverished area of western China, attach high value to maintaining a distinct cultural identity. Yet, Yi stakeholders face the systemic pressure for academic success in standard Chinese in the form of high-stakes tests. This situation inhibits the capacity and motivation of teachers to teach the Yi language, and the engagement of some Yi students. Here, English teaching is characterized as piecemeal. Gao's (2010) study found certain parallels in a bilingual school in Yanbian Korean Autonomous Prefecture, despite dramatic differences in context. Koreans in Yanbian live in the rustbelt northeast, an area in the old industrial heartland that was reasonably advantaged prior to the massive shut-downs of state-owned enterprises. Koreans are a group with a history of very high educational attainment and they are a group whose home language is increasingly an economic asset – relevant to rising cross-border trade with Korea. Yet, as in the case of the Yi, the author of this study found a strong tension among school teachers themselves between the desire to preserve Korean culture and identity, and the strong push toward promoting a curriculum that would enhance high performance in standard Chinese for test-taking, and thus economic mobility (see also Choi, 2010, p. 172; Gao, 2010).[9]

Adamson and Feng (2009, p. 331) conclude that 'additive trilingualism', in which the learning of three languages is without mutual detriment, must address "the low social status ascribed to minority languages because of their lack of associated economic and political capital; the high status accorded to standard Chinese and English; reinforced by systemic mechanisms, such as university entrance exams; geopolitical tensions ...; and a lack of resources to teach English to the level achieved in more affluent parts of the PRC" (Adamson and Feng, 2009, p. 331). As Ma (2007, p. 11) observes, the low perceived value of minority languages in general is reflected in the low number of Han people who learn minority languages, even where those languages are considered official languages. Language policy can be linked very directly to issues of equity. Standard Chinese and, increasingly, English are key to the strong test performance necessary for promotion in the Chinese educational system and for economic mobility.[10]

8.5.2   Education and ethnic identity

8.5.2.1   The 'civilizing project' of the state

As Postiglione (2009, p. 5) writes, 'the extent to which schools in China create an atmosphere that has positive institutional norms toward diverse cultural groups is limited by notions of cultural backwardness'. A significant line of research in English is grounded in this observation. Drawing on critical anthropological and sociological perspectives, much of this work focuses on the ideological objectives of the state, and their impact on students.

Citing Stevan Harrell's work, many of the English-language publications on ethnicity and education refer to education as an element of the 'civilizing projects' of the Chinese state (Harrell, 1995, p. 3). As Hansen notes,

> through the state educational system, the Chinese government transmits its ideology of the nation and of the relationships among the peoples in China who have come to be categorized into static ethnic groups. Education of minorities plays a central role in implicitly reproducing notions of cultural inequality while explicitly promoting [ethnic unity (*minzu tuanjie*, 民族团结)].
> (Hansen, 1999)

Minorities are taught the names of the groups to which they belong, and the implications of belonging to that group, versus the Han majority, as indisputable, scientific facts (Hansen, 1999). They learn that minorities were 'backward' at the time of liberation, relative to the Han majority, in economy and culture, and that the CCP helped them to develop so that they could live in a multi-ethnic socialist society, and they also learn ancient history that highlights common ties to the Chinese (Hansen, 1999). Schools take as an explicit goal to 'enhance the cultural quality', i.e. to civilize, minority populations (ibid., p. 160).

More recent work focusing on boarding schools for minority children has taken up this theme. Zhiyong Zhu's (2007, p. 256) ethnographic study of Tibetans in an inland (*neidi*) boarding school makes the argument that in these schools, the identity of 'Tibetan' comes to the foreground in organizing students' daily school life. Tibetan primary school graduates are selected and sent to boarding schools far from Tibet and not allowed to return home for years at a time.[11] The boarding schools have a clear mission of inculcating students with an integrative message: creating ties between Tibet and China's inland areas. Schools convey a notion of Tibetan identity that includes membership in the Chinese nation, along with cultural distinction that is part of the 'treasure trove of Chinese culture' (2007, p. 277). The identity conveyed by the schools – and indeed the premise for their existence – is the economic and educational 'backwardness' (*luohou*, 落后) and pre-modernity of Tibet, and the superiority of the Han. This idea is reinforced in the perceptions of Tibet and Tibetans, reinforced by official narratives, which pervade the community surrounding the school.

Yangbin Chen has conducted a parallel study of Uyghur students in an inland school (Chen, 2008). The work focuses on inland 'Xinjiang classes'. Like the Tibetan boarding schools, the existence of these 'Xinjiang classes' is also predicated on the assumption of backward, poor-quality education in Xjinjiang proper. Policy documents laying out the plan for 'Xinjiang classes' highlight the goals of patriotism, national unity, modernization, and development of the homeland. The classes aim 'to train quality senior secondary school graduates, who achieve overall developments in morals, intellect, physics, and atheism. The graduates must possess ideals, morals, culture and discipline, uphold national unity, and are dedicated to the Great Development of the Western Region' (Chen, 2008, p. 45). Minority customs are to be respected, but at the same time, any religious practice is prohibited (Chen, 2008, p. 45). Chen details the integrative aims of these schools, which are very similar to those laid out in Zhu's (2007) work.

8.5.2.2   *Construction of ethnic identity*

The other side of the 'civilizing project' is the ethnic identity constructed, partly in response, by students. Hansen (1999, p. 159) notes that, 'the classroom is an arena where processes of ethnic identification become highly relevant to students, who are confronted with the government's monopolizing interpretation of their identity'. Hansen's and Shen and Qian's fieldwork in the southwest and Yi's fieldwork in the northwest suggest that students are also confronted with a daily curriculum that suggests to them the uselessness, or at least low level of relevance, of their own language, history, religion and customs to state education (Hansen, 1999, p. 159; Shen and Qian, 2010, p. 57; Yi, 2006).

Zhu's study of Tibetans in an inland boarding school suggests a high degree of internalization of the narratives of identity offered in schools, but Zhu also discusses additional dimensions of identity asserted by students that diverge from the official narrative. Zhu highlights identities and values rooted in Buddhist religion and ethics as a key dimension of identity that diverges from state ideologies. Chen's work on inland Xinjiang classes similarly highlights Muslim religious traditions as an area of resistance to state ideologies of ethnic identity (Chen, 2008). Yi (2006) argues that minority education policy in China is shaped by a strong perception that religious-based allegiances undermine the capacity of minority people to be loyal political and cultural citizens of the Chinese state – particularly in the case of the northwest, and particularly for Tibetans and Uyghurs (p. 41).

Students in Zhu's (2007) and Chen's (2008) studies seem to reflect on their identities and their responsibilities to their homelands in ways that reflect the overt and implicit goals of the schools in which they study and the attitudes of the Han people they encounter there. The students discuss their religious identities and values, as well as the extreme personal and family sacrifice involved in being selected and attending an inland school. Chen, moreover, argues that these students' ethnic social capital is *strengthened* by the schooling experience, as these students become highly dependent on family support back home, and on co-ethnic support in the school environment, to succeed (Chen, 2008).[12]

Hansen argues that the impact of state schools on student identity has been ambiguous: Chinese state education is part of a 'hegemonic project' to modernize society and define the nation, and thus plays a role a resurgence of ethnic identities all over China. This project has had fragmenting, as well as intensifying, effects on ethnic identities, as illustrated in profoundly different responses to the expansion of formal education of the historically integrated Naxi and the more marginalized Dai (Thai) minorities in Yunnan. Consistent with this view, Zhu and Chen highlight that the context of boarding schools brings ethnic identity to the fore in Tibetan and Uyghur students' daily lives – and not always in ways that are consistent with the policy intentions. Postiglione, Zhu, and Jiao (2004) studied the ethnic identity formation of rural Tibetan children in schools in Tibet proper, and use multiple sources of data, including policy analyses, student recruitment and curriculum data, and interviews with students and teachers. The authors find signs of resistance: despite official policy rhetoric that emphasizes national unity and patriotism, there are still many symbols of Tibetan culture that reinforce Tibetan identity. The authors argue that this dual representation of state and local interests lends support for a more 'even-handed' approach to cultural policies. Clothey draws a similar conclusion based on her study of students at the Central University for Nationalities (Minzu Daxue, 民族大学, now known in English by the transliterated name Minzu University): the university's overt goal is promoting ethnic unity and a sense of Chinese patriotism, but the experiences of students there foster a sense of individual ethnic identity, not necessarily in line with official goals (Clothey, 2005b).

8.5.3   Incentives and disincentives for buy-in to the educational system

Field-based studies in China have suggested that members of ethnic groups develop unfavorable attitudes toward education if they do not observe tangible economic benefits from education among members of their own communities or if they perceive that the school system is incompatible with aspects of their own cultures (Hansen, 1999; Harrell and Mgebbu, 1999; Postiglione, 2007). Harrell and Mgebbu (1999) showed that expectations of rewards decisively influence educational participation among the Yi ethnic group in Sichuan. On the basis of fieldwork in schools in Qinghai Province, Lin Yi argues that the devaluation of Tibetan culture within the state school system in Northwest China precludes activation of the cultural capital possessed by Tibetan children, and can create atmospheres in the schools that are socially hostile. As a result, the social mobility of these children can be hindered (Yi, 2006).

In Tibet proper, Postiglione and his colleagues found that despite alleviation of school tuition and fees in efforts to address high drop-out rates in rural Tibet, many families preferred to have their children work at home due to a perceived low quality of education and inability of schools to provide graduates with competitive jobs (Postiglione, Jiao, and Gyatso, 2005). Postiglione's (2007) fieldwork illustrates a number of problems that serve to disincentivize children from engaging with education. Poor rural schools attended by Tibetans have little of the income-generating potential of urban schools, and for these schools, attracting good teachers is difficult. Further, poverty has a reinforcing effect, as parents in poor rural villages do not necessarily observe examples of education leading to economic improvements and thus are often unwilling to provide financial support for children's schooling. Yet, as important as regional and economic factors are in explaining ethnic differences in education, additional factors are also significant. Postiglione also highlights that the content of schooling may be perceived as being inconsistent, or even oppositional, to Tibetan traditions.

Similarly, Hansen (1999) argued that educational disparities between the Dai, Naxi, Hani, and Jinuo in Yunnan can be traced to ethnic differences in perceptions of the economic benefits of education and the accord or opposition between their cultural heritage and the educational system. Focusing on the two cases of the Naxi and the Dai, Hansen argues that the Naxi were thoroughly enmeshed in Confucian education during the Qing dynasty. Due to this long history of acceptance of Chinese education, the Naxi have been able to obtain a degree of social mobility and status that has made it possible to express an educated identity that is at the same time an ethnic identity – within acceptable political bounds. Educated Naxi are in a position to influence the educational system from the inside (see also Yu, 2010, on this point).

In contrast, Hansen notes that the Dai first encountered Chinese schools in the Republican period, and experienced them as a colonial-style imposition – a forced alternative to the monastic educational institutions in place previously. Chinese education is more widely available than ever, but Hansen suggests that there persists a wide range of problems in convincing Dai children to remain in school, and that the practice of Buddhism and monastic education are thriving with economic modernization and increased cross-border contact with Thailand (Hansen, 1999, p. 165). She suggests that educated Dai, unlike the Naxi, are likely to dissociate themselves from their village's cultural heritage (Hansen, 1999). Shen and Qian's (2010) fieldwork suggests that education is not necessarily widely viewed as a viable route to social mobility among the Dai.

A 'cultural rupture' between home and school may contribute to the problem (Shen and Qian, 2010). Shen and Qian's (2010) fieldwork among the Dai in Yunnan suggests that there are considerable differences between Dai students' home and school lives, in terms of the content of a curriculum that is highly exam oriented and contains little material on Dai daily lives, history, religion, or culture, and in terms of expected orientations and behaviors. Language use in school may also contribute to this disconnect, bilingual policies notwithstanding. Shen and Qian's fieldwork indicated that most students reported difficulty learning standard Chinese, and that the use of the Dai language by students is 'peremptorily reprimanded' by teachers (2010, p. 57). Similarly, Bass notes that Chinese language of instruction in upper secondary creates a barrier to enrollment and promotion to the 'fast' stream for Tibetans, *visàvis* Han students in Tibet (Bass, 1998). Yet, Bass also connects this issue, at least in part, to politics: she argues that political considerations have hindered balanced reflections on what language policies are most sensible, from a pedagogical perspective (p. 258).

8.5.4   Educational stratification

Detailed empirical attention to documenting the scope of educational inequalities by ethnic group has been limited in the English-language literature. Much of the quantitative work on access and attainment, executed by stratification researchers in sociology and development economists, has been exploratory. It addresses both access and attainment, and the economic context and outcomes of education. This work links conceptually to many of the issues raised in the field-based studies cited above, but those connections are not generally explicitly present in the work.

8.5.4.1   *Access and attainment*

Analyses of data from a 1992 survey of children demonstrated substantial ethnic differences in enrollment among rural 7–14-year-olds, with rates for ethnic Chinese boys roughly double those for girls from certain ethnic groups (Hannum, 2002). The same study showed that the ethnic gap could be attributed, in part, to compositional differences in geographic location of residence and socio-economic background (Hannum, 2002). There is no general tendency of a greater gender gap for minorities than for the ethnic Chinese, but significant differences in the gender gap emerge across individual ethnic groups. Evidence from census data showed that ethnic disparities in junior high school transitions increased between 1982 and 1990. More recent analyses of national census and survey data show generalized improvement in educational attainment for China's ethnic minority groups, but considerable gaps still persist across individual groups (Hannum and Wang, 2012; Sun and Qi, 2007). Language fluency in standard Chinese appears to matter for educational attainment, but in different ways in different regions (Hong, 2010). Work has yet to really theorize the patterns of advantage and disadvantage that exist across individual groups.

8.5.4.2   *The economic context and outcomes of education*

As theorized in the anthropological, field-based studies of ethnic differences in the experience of education, the likely outcomes of schooling are an important potential factor feeding back into the educational attainment process. Several studies have established the different context and outcomes of education by ethnic group. Minorities, on average, are poorer than the majority in China, though the trend is toward poverty reduction for all groups and a reduced ethnic poverty gap (Gustafsson and Ding, 2009; Hannum and Wang, 2012). On the other hand, an income gap favoring the Han appeared to have widened between 1988 and 1995 (Gustafsson and Shi, 2003). Analyses of data from the early 2000s show that minorities as a group are less likely to have access to waged employment and earn less than Han, though estimates of the scale of the gap differ widely by data source (Hannum and Wang, 2012). Yet, minorities also had higher returns to education, on average, compared to the ethnic majority population (Hannum and Wang, 2012; see also Sun and Xu, 2010 for evidence from Gansu Province).

A major part of the story of income, poverty and employment gaps has to do with segregation: many ethnic minority groups live in much more disadvantaged contexts, from a development perspective (Gustafsson and Ding, 2006; Hannum and Wang, 2012). This situation also raises the potential problem that social returns to schooling are less likely to be enjoyed by minority regions, to the extent that 'brain drain' is an issue in these places (Zhang and Wang, 2010, pp. 23–24).

However, studies have also indicated that the 'average' labor market situation of minorities is unlikely to apply in a uniform way. For example, studies of particular ethnic groups' labor market experiences show considerable diversity of experience. An analysis of 1982 and 1990 census data from the Xinjiang Uygur Autonomous Region revealed that the Uyghur population was more likely to be working in agriculture, and that rising ethnic disparities in occupational attainment point to a growing ethnic gap in educational credentials as the most likely source of this change (Hannum and Xie, 1998). More recent analyses of the 2005 mini-census showed a continued Han–Uyghur difference in non-agricultural employment (Wu and Song, 2010) Excluding those in agriculture, Uyghur were more likely to work in government or institutions than either Han locals or migrants, and also more likely to become self-employed. Earnings inequality was negligible in government or institutions, but it increased with the marketization of the employment sector (Wu and Song, 2010). More recently, a resumé audit study focusing on firms indicated discrimination against applicants with Uyghur names in China's urban labor market (Maurer-Fazio, 2011). In neighboring Gansu Province, a different story emerges for the urban Hui and Han populations. A study of labor market inequalities between the Han and Hui minority in urban Lanzhou shows evidence of labor market discrimination in access to state-sector employment: ethnic differences in the likelihood of state-sector employment persisted net of education and other background differences (Zang, 2008). At the same time, gaps were lessened at higher levels of education, highlighting the implications of education for broader stratification patterns.

8.6 Discussion

In some sense, there is a great deal of common ground connecting the Chinese- and English-language literatures. These literatures focus on similar case-studies, settings, and problems. It is striking that much of the work in both languages comes from scholars working outside of the field of sociology of education. Much of the existing work comes out of educational stratification, anthropology, or development economics traditions, or is conducted by educational researchers operating outside of sociological traditions and frameworks altogether.

Yet, there are certain differences across the two literatures. These literatures draw on different ideological starting points. They conform to different norms of academic composition and speak to different audiences in different socio-political contexts. In one realm, authors write carefully on topics that are both highly sensitive and highly salient to the national development agenda, and often seek to provide direct suggestions about improvement strategies. In the other realm, authors speak primarily to an academic audience. As a consequence, the focus and tone in the two literatures sometimes diverge. Certain lines of policy-related work appear primarily in Chinese. For example, there is a debate in the Chinese literature between Marxist and multicultural perspectives that is not prominent in the English literature. Many Chinese-language studies espouse and explicate a Marxist ideology of ethnic minority education. These studies focus on the ways that education can and should emphasize national unity and patriotism. Although most of the policy literature supports this ideology and policies and programs based on this framework, there are a handful of scholars writing in Chinese who are critical of this perspective. These authors argue that assimilative schooling often ignores other values, which may lead to the disappearance of distinct cultures. Many of these scholars favor what they call a multicultural approach, which places equal emphasis on all cultural groups.

In the remainder of this concluding section, we discuss a few key themes, noting where relevant when and how interpretations differ significantly in the two literatures. We discuss how the literatures on ethnic disparity address the role of poverty, the role of culture, the role of policy, and the tensions between language offerings that prioritize cultural preservation and those that prioritize social mobility in a globalized China.

8.6.1 The role of poverty

A discussion and empirical documentation of 'uneven development' of educational systems, facilities, and teachers is prominent in the Chinese literature. Much of this research suggests that ethnic differences can be explained by regional economic development differences and class disparities, as well as associated differences in access to adequate school facilities and teachers. This work parallels a line of quantitative work in English that has sought to establish empirically the disparities across ethnic groups in educational outcomes. The English literature on educational stratification by ethnicity in China attests to successes in expanding access to schools to previously excluded groups, to persisting disparities across many groups, and, like the Chinese literature, to the significance of economic and geographic context in contributing to persisting ethnic disparities in education. While it is clear in both literatures that many of the ethnic gaps in outcomes can be explained *statistically* by incorporating variables accounting for geographic location, what this fact really tells us is very unclear. In the Chinese literature, and in some of the English literature, a prominent interpretation is that the problem of minority education is one primarily of poverty and insufficient economic development. Without discounting the obvious importance of poverty as a significant contributing factor to educational disparities by ethnic group, the qualitative work in both languages certainly suggests that other issues are also at play.

8.6.2 The role of culture

Cultural issues are commonly cited in the qualitative literature as contributing factors. Some of the work in Chinese puts forth what might be termed a 'cultural deficit' model – characteristics of groups such as religion or gender norms may depress educational levels. Some of this literature does not really reflect on the school structures or practices that may contribute to unwillingness to attend schools. There is a contrasting notion of cultural disconnect in the multicultural tradition in Chinese and in much of the ethnographic literature in English. The cultural disconnect literature describes school and classroom settings where members of certain ethnic minority groups face discouraging, disincentivizing messages of linguistic and cultural inferiority; however, there is tremendous variation in experience across minority groups.

8.6.3 The role of policy: The education project, intended and unintended

A related strand in both literatures includes a substantial number of papers that catalogue existing minority policies and highlight the integrative goals of policies. The assimilative functions of minority education as promoting development and national unity are problematized in some of the multicultural literature in Chinese, and quite commonly in the English literature. Further, the English-language research and a few of the Chinese studies suggest that the assimilative mission of minority education utilizes tactics that devalue or suppress certain minority identities. Yet, a few studies in English suggest that ethnic identities and networks are in some cases strengthened by the experience.[13]

8.6.4   Trade-offs? Globalization, instrumentalism and language preservation

A theme in both language literatures is the instrumental pressure for language assimilation, even in the context of language policies that seek to preserve minority languages. Both literatures describe an educational system that has policies in place for preservation of minority languages, and both describe a system that tends to promote the dominant culture and standard Chinese language acquisition. Scholars writing in both languages acknowledge the instrumentality of this latter approach for fostering economic mobility, and highlight the rising economic incentives faced by schools, teachers, and students to privilege standard Chinese and English over minority languages. However, the English literature focuses strongly on the costs of an approach that devalues minority language and culture, whereas even the more critical Chinese language literature tends to frame the problem as an omission, and not a devaluation, of minority language and culture. In both literatures, the pressures outside the purview of the school system for students to be fluent in standard Chinese and proficient in English are challenging the preservation of minority languages.

8.7   Conclusions

This review has sought to provide an enumeration of some key themes emerging in two linked literatures: themes of the complex interrelationships of ethnicity with cultural, policy, development, and language issues. We have also highlighted certain divergences in the literatures, and suggested certain reasons why this divergence is present. While there are of course many exceptions, a key element of the divergence is that economic development and poverty alleviation are key orienting issues in the Chinese literature, while much of the English literature is oriented to a largely academic audience interested very centrally in issues of inequality and ethnic identity.

Studies in both languages pave the way for comparative sociologists of education to learn from the case of China. Close analyses of China's diverse groups and institutional arrangements hold great potential for theoretical and policy-relevant insights. Yet, certain new work is needed to move forward in this direction. Few studies in either language develop a strong comparative framework for investigating or characterizing the policies in China or the problems associated with education amongst minority communities. In addition, though some of the studies are very well theorized, most are not framed in a way that facilitates dialogue with comparative scholarship in the sociology of education, or comparative theories about ethnicity and education. This situation is understandable, given the still-nascent state of the field and the need for empirical description to aid in theory building. However, more heavily theorized work, and more comparatively framed work, will be needed to enable the Chinese experience to be informed by and inform the development of the field of sociology of education.

Notes

1. The high degree of uniformity remains true today in relative terms, despite policies that have promoted more local content and the development of some non-standard admissions procedures in higher education (Hannum, An and Cherng, 2011).
2. In 2009, a very small proportion of elementary school students, 0.17%, enrolled in vocational junior high schools (Ministry of Education, 2010).
3. The rising number of college graduates in urban areas of China, coupled with dwindling number of jobs that demand college degrees, has created a concern over whether higher education can lead to middle-class attainment (Jennings, 2010). In 2009, over 6 million new college graduates entered the labor market, many with the goal of finding white-collar employment in major cities (Ministry of Education, 2010). However, a dearth of jobs in industries that many graduates would find desirable has led many to settle for low-paying manufacturing jobs. Recent media has described college graduates, who live in cramped conditions in cities and swarm to work each rush hour, as members of the 'ant tribe' (Jennings, 2010).
4. In 2009, the primary school enrollment rate was 17.25% in Tibet, 75.24% in Xinjiang, 78.04% in Ningxia, 89.39% in Guangxi, 94.97% in Inner Mongolia. The enrollment rate for the country was 89.94% (Ministry of Education, 2010).
5. Literature in this tradition uses the Chinese phrase for unbalanced development, or 不均衡发展 (*bujunheng fazhan*).
6. See Zhang and Verhoeven (2010) for a discussion of access to higher education among ethnic minorities in Yunnan Province, based on what appears to be a purposive sample of higher education freshman students.
7. For a discussion of legislation from different regional and local governments in China, see Zhou (2005); for in-depth case-studies of bilingual education in Yunnan and Sichuan, see Xiao (1998) and Teng (2002).
8. Feng and his colleagues (Adamson and Feng, 2009; Feng and Sunuodula, 2009) present a case-study of the status in the curriculum of minority languages, namely Uyghur, Yi and Zhuang, *vis à vis* standard Chinese and English in the Xinjiang Uyghur Automous Region, the Liangshan Yi Autonomous Prefecture in Sichuan Province, and the Guangxi Zhuang Autonomous Region. Their arguments draw on field visits to each site, including interviews with stakeholders and policy document analysis.
9. Consistent with the Korean case just cited, Ojijed's (2010) study of attitudes toward Mongolian, standard Chinese, and English amongst a small purposive sample of

students at Inner Mongolia Normal University was suggestive of a high instrumental value attached to the latter two languages, relative to Mongolian.

10. While much work has catalogued minority education policies and discussed potential impacts, it is striking that few studies have sought to investigate in a direct manner the impact of specific policies around language use in schools. An exception is Tsung and Cruickshank's (2009) comparison of a minority mother tongue school and a mixed school in Xinjiang, which, the authors suggest, indicated that mixed schooling will not address disparities in educational outcomes, as learning materials in the minority language remained poorly resourced.

11. See Wang and Zhou (2003, p. 99) for a list of inland Tibetan schools and classes.

12. In another paper, Chen (2010) focuses on the continuing importance of the family element of social capital for Uyghur students, despite the impediment of distance.

13. An interesting example of the disconnect between these viewpoints is the tension between China-based and overseas scholars' interpretations of the boarding school phenomenon. Postiglione finds that North American and Australian scholars' reactions to boarding schools are highly critical, due to their very overt assimilation agenda and, likely, the extremely unfortunate histories with ethnic boarding schools elsewhere. A prominent view in China is that boarding schools provide a high quality education to students who would otherwise be unable to access it. These schools explicitly seek to strengthen ties between minority areas and China's heartland, but certain research suggests that students' ethnic identities are actually reinforced by the boarding experience (e.g. Chen, 2008).

References

Chinese references cited

敖俊梅 (Ao Junmei) (2006). 个体平等,抑或群体平等——少数民族高等教育招生政策理论探究. 清华大学教育研究, 27(6), 70–74.

柏果成 (Bai Guocheng) (1986). 瑶山民族教育调查报告.贵州民族学院学报 (社会科学版), 2, 87–94.

柏果成 (Bo Guocheng) (1986). 瑶山民族教育调查报告.贵州民族学院学报(社会科学版), (2), 87–94.

甘肃省教育厅民族教育处 (Minority Education Department of Gansu Provincial Department of Education) (2010). 甘肃省民族地区教育综合统计报表 (2009/2010). 内部资料.

国家统计局 (National Bureau of Statistics) (2011). 2010 年第六次全国人口普查主要数据公报 (第1号). http://www.stats.gov.cn/was40/gjtjj_detail.jsp?searchword=%C8%CB%BF%DA%C6%D5%B2%E9&presearchword=%C8%CB%BF%DA%C6%D5%B2%E9&channel id=6697&record=40.

韩嘉玲 (Han Jialing) (1999). 中国贫困地区的女童教育研究: 贵州省雷山县案例调查.民族教育研究, 2.

胡鞍钢、温军 (Hu Angang, Wen Jun) (2001). 社会发展优先:西部民族地区新的追赶战略.民族研究, 3, 12–23.

贾东海 (Jia Donghai) (2000). 马克思主义民族理论与政策五十年研究回顾.兰州, 甘肃人民出版社.

贾东海 (Jia Donghai) (2007). 马克思主义民族理论与民族政策研究——中国化的实践.

教育部 (Ministry of Education) (1983). 教育部关于学习贯彻《关于加强爱国主义宣传教育的意见》的通知. 中国教育年鉴 (1982–1984). 北京:中国大百科全书出版社出版.

教育部 (Ministry of Education) (2001). 基础教育课程改革纲要(试行). 中华人民共和国教育部网站. www.moe.edu.cn.

教育部 (Ministry of Education) (2004). 内地新疆高中班办学工作取得初步成效. 中华人民共和国教育部网站. http://www.moe.gov.cn/publicfiles/business/htmlfiles/moe/moe_317/200409/941.html.

教育部 (Ministry of Education) (2010). 2009 年全国各级各类学历教育学生情况. 教育部网站. http://www.moe.edu.cn/publicfiles/business/htmlfiles/moe/s4959/201012/113484.html.

教育部,国家发展改革委,财政部 (Ministry of Education, National Commission on Development and Reform, Ministry of Finance) (2007). 关于《国家西部地区"两基"攻坚计划 (2004–2007年)》完成情况的报告. http://www.moe.gov.cn/publicfiles/business/html files/moe/s3034/201001/xxgk_78196.html.

教育部发展规划司编 (Development Planning Division of the Ministry of Education) (2000).《中国教育事业发展统计简况 (1999)》.

教育部发展规划司编 (Development Planning Division of the Ministry of Education) (2010). 2009 全国教育事业发展简明统计分析.

刘精明、杨江华 (Liu Jingming, Yang Jianghua) (2007). 关注贫困儿童的教育公平问题. 华中师范大学学报, 46(2), 120–128.

马敏 (Ma Jei) (2011). 新疆内高班内初班年招生规模 2014 年将分别达到 1 万人.天山网. Date accessed 26 January 2011, http://www.xjts.cn/news/content/2011-01/26/content_5554129.htm.

马戎 (Ma Rong) (1998). 西藏地区教育事业的发展.中国藏学, 2, 3–24.

马戎 (Ma Rong) (2003). 中国各族群之间的结构性差异. 社会科学战线, 4.

马戎 (Ma Rong) (2007). 当前中国民族问题研究的选题与思路. 中央民族大学学报 (哲学社会科学版), 34(3), 12–38.

马戎 (Ma Rong) (2008). 新疆民族教育的发展与双语教育的实践.北京大学教育评论, 6(2), 2–41.

马茜 (Ma Qian) (2004). 多民族地区教育学业成就的地域性阐释:以云南省中甸县第一中学为个案. 广西民族学院学报 (哲社版), 26(3), 32–37.

钱民辉 (Qian Minhui) (2007). 断裂与重构: 少数民族地区学校教育中的潜在课程研究. 西北民族研究, 52(1), 58–68.

滕星 (Teng Xin) (2001). 文化变迁与双语教育——凉山彝族社区教育人类学的田野工作于文本撰述. 北京:教育科学出版社.

滕星 (Teng Xin) (2004). 小康社会与西部偏远贫困地区少数民族基础教育.云南民族大学学报 (哲学社会科学版), 21(4), 148–150.

滕星, 马效义 (Teng Xin, Ma Xiaoyi) (2005). 中国高等教育的少数民族优惠政策与教育平等. 民族研究, 5, 10–18.

滕星, 苏红 (Teng Xin, Su Hong) (1997). 多元文化社会与多元一体化教育.民族教育研究, 1, 18–31.

滕星, 苏红 (Teng Xin, Su Hong) (1998). 中国少数民族地区现代化过程与教育机会平等.教育科学, 1, 9–11.

万明钢 (Wan Minggang) (2006). 多元文化视野价值观与民族认同研究.北京: 民族出版社.

万明钢, 白亮 (Wan Minggang, Bai Liang) (2008). 西方多元文化教育与我国少数民族教育之比较. 民族研究, 6, 32–41.

王鉴 (Wang Jian) (2002). 西部民族地区教育均衡发展的新战略.民族研究, (6), 9–17.

王嘉毅 (Wang Jiayi) (2006). 西北少数民族基础教育发展现状与对策研究. 北京:民族出版社.

王振岭 (Wang Zhenling) (1990). 发展藏族教育必须从实际出发 讲求实效——多玛县少数民族教育调查报告, 1, 110–116.

西藏自治区统计局 (Tibet Autonomous Region Bureau of Statistics) (1989). 1989: 549; 1991: 396.

夏仕武 (Xia Shiwu) (2007). 中国少数民族教育.五洲传播出版社.

许洁英 (Xu Jieying) (2009). 加快少数民族教育发展,切实促进教育公平.西北师范大学学报, 46(1), 75–78.

杨军 (Yang Jun) (2006). 西北少数民族地区基础教育均衡发展研究. 民族出版社.

袁同凯 (Yuan Tongkai) (2004). 走进竹篱教室: 土瑶学校教育的民族志研究.天津: 天津人民出版社.

张善鑫、刘旭东 (Zhang Shanxin, Liu Xudong) (2010). 少数民族教育公平问题探析——一位校长的教育人类学口述研究.当代教育与文化.

赵明仁 (Zhao Mingren) (2010). 甘肃省中小学教师队伍建设及管理调研报告.未发表.

中央统战部办公厅、教育部办公厅、西藏自治区人民政府办公厅 (Ministry of Education, the General Office of Tibet Autonomous Region People's Government) (2007). 全国内地西藏班办学和教育援藏工作会议纪要.中华人民共和国教育部网站, http://www.moe.gov.cn/publicfiles/business/htmlfiles/moe/A09_xxgk/200705/xxgk_62393.html.

周庚鑫 (Zhou Gengxin) (1985). 必须加快少数民族地区教育改革的步伐——滇西南四县初等教育情况调查.民族研究, 3, 60–64.

朱志勇 (Zhu Zhiyong) (2006). 学校教育情境中族群认同的建构——内地西藏班的个案研究.南京师大学报 (社会科学版), 4, 82–88.

祖力亚提.司马义 (Zhuliyati, Simayi) (2009). 族群认同感建构的社会学分析:以新疆"民考汉"为例. 西北民族研究, 63(3), 65–75.

English references cited

Adamson, B., and Feng, A. (2009). A Comparison of Trilingual Education Policies for Ethnic Minorities in China. *Compare: A Journal of Comparative and International Education*, 39(3), 321–333.

Bass, C. (1998). *Education in Tibet*. New York: St. Martin's Press.

Chen, Y. (2008). *Muslim Uyghur Students in a Chinese Boarding School: Social Recapitalization as a Response to Ethnic Integration*. Maryland: Lexington Books. http://books.google.com/books?id=roiuY7bnb80C.

Chen, Y. (2010). Crossing the Frontier to Inland China. *Chinese Education & Society*, 43(1), 46–57.

China, I. O. of the S. C. of the P. R. of. (2000). *National Minorities Policy and Its Practice in China* (Vol. 2009). http://www.china.org.cn/e-white/4/4.3.htm.

Choi, S. (2010). Globalization, China's Drive for World-class Universities (211 Project) and the Challenges of Ethnic Minority Higher Education: The Case of Yanbian University. *Asia Pacific Education Review*, 11(2), 169–178.

Clothey, R. A. (2005a). China's Policies for Minority Nationalities in Higher Education: Negotiating National Values and Ethnic Identities. *Comparative Education Review*, 49(3), 389–409.

Clothey, R. A. (2005b). *Strangers in a Strange Place: The Experience of Ethnic Minority Students at the Central University for Nationalities in Beijing*. Pittsburgh, PA: University of Pittsburgh.

Dai, Q., and Dong, Y. (2001). The Historical Evolution of Bilingual Education for China's Ethnic Minorities. *Chinese Education & Society*, 34(2), 7.

Education, M. of. (1986). *People's Republic of China Law on Compulsory Education* (Vol. 2009).

Education, M. of. (1995). *People's Republic of China Education Law* (Vol. 2011).

Fei, X. (1981). *Toward a People's Anthropology*. Beijing: New World Press.

Feng, A. (2005). Bilingualism for the Minor or the Major? An Evaluative Analysis of Parallel Conceptions in China. *International Journal of Bilingual Education and Bilingualism*, 8(6), 529–551.

Feng, A., and Sunuodula, M. (2009). Analysing Language Education Policy for China's Minority Groups in Its Entirety. *International Journal of Bilingual Education and Bilingualism*, 12(6), 685–704.

Within this social context distinct research traditions have evolved which examine issues of race and ethnic inequalities in educational processes. Qualitative ethnographic studies of educational processes and schooling in particular are a fairly new research trend in Cyprus with the majority appearing as published work during the last ten years. These studies have come about mainly as a reaction to the questionnaire survey style of quantitative research which characterized much educational research until then. Carried out by anthropologically and sociologically-minded and trained researchers who sought to provide more in-depth and contextually rich accounts of school learning, these studies focused mostly on issues of identity construction especially as this takes place in key school sites such as the classroom.

A major concern of these studies is what *actually* happens in school, rather than what is simply prescribed by the curriculum or what is expected to happen. Though most of these studies privilege the classroom as the most important site of school learning, a few are also concerned with what happens outside the classroom both within the school (e.g. break time, school trips, etc.) and beyond the school (e.g. the home and the neighborhood). These studies are placed, on the one hand, within the overall context of a well-established nationalism that characterizes contemporary Cyprus as a politically and territorially divided country, a fact that is ideologically reflected in educational policy and practice, and, on the other hand, within the context of an emerging racism resulting from the arrival since the early 1990s of large numbers of economic migrants on the island.

In brief, one strand of these studies focuses on how the schooling experience results in particular constructions of 'self' and 'other' especially in the context of a nationalistic educational system, while another strand explores the outcome of racialization and ethnicization processes in schools as a result of the presence of non-majority children whether these belong to ethnic minorities on the island or immigrant groups. The focus here is on what is called 'ethnogenesis' (Singer, 1962) or 'new tribalism' (Greeley, 1971), or 'the quest for peoplehood' (Gordon, 1978). Another strand examines the way textbooks and the curriculum represents the 'others', while another looks into teachers and intercultural education.

This chapter starts with a brief overview of the national educational context of Cyprus. It then goes on to describe four traditions of educational research on race, ethnicity, and inequalities by presenting relevant publications.

9.2 National context

9.2.1 The educational system of Cyprus

In the Republic of Cyprus education is provided by both the public and private sectors. Education in public primary and secondary schools is free for all students, whereas private schools charge tuition fees. The official language of instruction in all public primary and secondary schools is Greek. In private schools the language of instruction is either English or Greek, or both. Until 2010 it was mandatory that all children at the age of five years and ten months attend the first grade of primary school. The compulsory age for attendance was lowered recently to include preschool level as well (ages of four and above). The 'compulsory educational' system requires students to attend school until the age of 15.

After the completion of primary school all students proceed to secondary school for six years (three years of lower secondary and another three years of upper secondary education). The transition from primary to secondary schools depends primarily on the school certificate obtained from the primary schools or on the entrance exam in some selective private schools. The Ministry of Education determines the compulsory curriculum that public school students must follow during the course of their studies, which, up to the first year of the upper secondary education, is uniform for all students. In the second year of students' attendance in the upper secondary school, students have the opportunity to select courses of their interest together with the few mandatory courses given. This choice to a great extent determines the kind of studies or vocational training students will follow after that.

Tertiary education in Cyprus is provided by colleges, which offer mostly vocational courses, and private and public universities. Admissions to public universities are through national entrance examinations, whereas students can enroll in private universities with their high school leaving certificate. There is high attendance at higher education, both in Cyprus and at universities abroad. Around 80% of secondary school leavers proceed to some form of tertiary education, ranking Cyprus among the countries in the Western world with the highest number of university graduates (Figure 9.1).

9.2.2   Main migration patterns and composition and size of ethnic minority groups

Demographic data derived from the Statistical Service offer us information regarding migration and ethnicity of the total population in Cyprus. The data show that migration in Cyprus has gradually increased during the last ten years. Specifically, in 1998 8801 people were immigrants whereas in 2009 the number of immigrants reached 11,675 people. The highest number of migration movements that occurred in Cyprus was in 2005 when 24,419 people immigrated to Cyprus.

Some of the recorded reasons which led people to immigrate to Cyprus were educational or employment opportunities and/or long-term permanent settlement. In the 1990s, a large number of people from Asian countries immigrated to Cyprus looking forward to achieving better life conditions. They worked

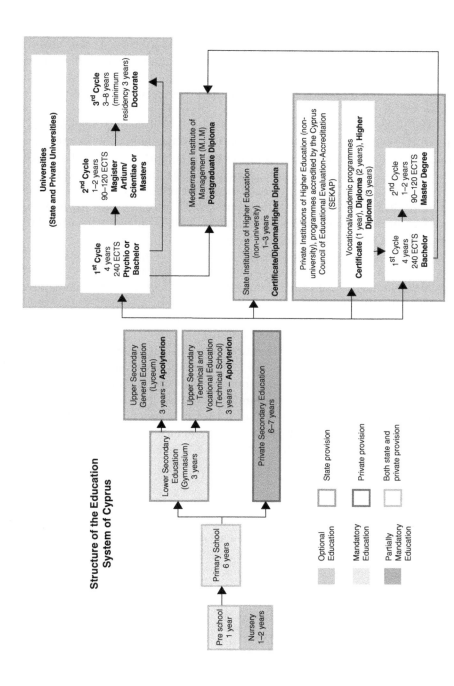

Figure 9.1 Structure of the education system of Cyprus
Source: http://www.highereducation.ac.cy/en/educational-system.html.

as child/elderly caretakers, and/or domestic workers. However, current data show that in 2009, the countries from which the highest number of immigrants came were Romania (a total of 1410 Romanian citizens) and Greece (1221 Greek citizens). Table 9.1 depicts a list of the countries of origin of most of the immigrants in Cyprus in 2008 and 2009.

Official records also demonstrate that there has been an increase in the number of illegal immigrants arriving in Cyprus. Specifically, data derived from the police annual report show that in 2007, 7770 people migrated illegally to the Republic of Cyprus. The report also shows that most people who arrived illegally to Cyprus came from the northern Turkish-occupied areas of the country ($n = 5162$). In 2009 the number of illegal immigrants increased to 8037, whereas in 2010 numerical data show that there was a decrease in the number of illegal immigration to the Republic of Cyprus; however, the number is not significantly different from 2009, that is, 8005 people illegally arrived to Cyprus (Police Department Annual Report, 2009).

Regarding school attendance, in the 1990s only certain ethnic minorities were visible in the Cypriot student population, such as Maronites, Turkish Cypriots, Armenians, and Latins. Currently, Greek Cypriot students constitute 86.05% of the student population in primary schools, whereas the four constitutionally recognized minority groups constitute just 0.54% of this population. This 0.54% includes: 0.18% Turkish Cypriots, 0.27% Maronites, and 0.09% Armenians. These percentages are very small but are very significant since members of these groups hold high political positions that influence legislative decisions regarding educational issues. Current data obtained from the Ministry of Education and Culture (2011) shows that a total number of 6744 foreign students registered nationwide for primary education (3465 boys and 3279 girls). Moreover, various data sources demonstrate that 3726 foreign students attend secondary public schools (2291 in lower secondary schools and 1435 in upper secondary schools). More foreign students are registered

Table 9.1   Immigrants in Cyprus (2008 and 2009)

	Country of origin of immigrants in 2009	N (total number) 2008	N (total number) 2009
1	Greece	1381	1221
2	Romania	1216	1410
3	Philippines	1221	799
4	Sri Lanka	540	688
5	United Kingdom	981	811
6	Russia	398	280
7	Bulgaria	816	691
8	Poland	544	181

in Nicosia ($n = 784$) than any other region of Cyprus. It is evident that a large number of students who attend lower secondary schools come from countries such as Bulgaria ($n = 241$), Georgia ($n = 440$), Greece ($n = 474$), and Romania ($n = 203$). A similar situation is present also in upper secondary schools, where the majority of attending students come from Georgia ($n = 387$), Greece ($n = 323$), and Russia ($n = 141$).

9.2.3 Developments in educational and social policies

One of the educational reforms that the Ministry of Education and Culture decided to implement in 2008 was a program of intercultural education and a program for integrating foreign students in public schools. Due to the fact that the number of students (from different ethnic backgrounds) enrolled in public schools had been increasing each academic year, educational policy-makers sought to achieve a 'smooth' integration of these children into public schools. The measures that the Ministry of Education introduced to avoid stigmatization and discrimination of migrant students included the dispersion of bilingual students into different schools in all provinces and the integration of these students in classes with native Greek-speaking students (Ministry of Education and Culture of Cyprus, 2009). Also, teachers and academic staff were specifically trained to be prepared and aware of how to deal with and assist foreign students to easily adjust to the Cypriot educational conditions.

Specific practices have been introduced for the learning of the Greek language, such as the development of intensive Greek classes that take place at a time that does not affect other academic activities in school. Schools are encouraged to adopt innovative teaching methods in order to assist migrant students to be integrated into the public school environments. It must be noted that, while the language being used refers to 'integration', in effect these policies are assimilation-related policies. In 2008, initially the program was implemented to only 352 bilingual students nationwide. Following the completion of the program's evaluation procedure by the Educational Research and Evaluation Centre in 2010, the Ministry of Education and Culture aimed to extend this program in all Cypriot public schools (Ministry of Education and Culture of Cyprus, 2009). Currently, all new bilingual students who enroll in public schools are equipped with an 'induction guide' that aims to inform them and their parents about the Cypriot educational system (Eurydice, 2010).

Within the social and educational context described above several pieces of research have been conducted either as part of doctoral theses or as part of drafting national reports on the state of the presence of migrant students in Cypriot schools or lastly as part of externally funded research projects in collaboration with research teams from European universities.

9.3   Methodology

The methodology followed in writing this chapter was to select papers that were published on the subject in journals and national reports as well as studies published in the national context. We also reviewed relevant postgraduate theses on these topics by students studying for their doctoral degrees. The criteria for selection were rather relaxed given the fact that there is a scarcity of research on this topic in Cyprus. Because the research community of Cyprus who deals with such issues is relatively small, many pieces of research were identified using personal networks and connections. The fact that there are limited references in electronic databases was confirmed by using well-known academic search engines (e.g. ERIC, EBSCO). There are, broadly speaking, four research traditions in Cyprus which deal with issues pertinent to the content of the present volume.

9.4   Research traditions

The first tradition, 'ethnographies of identity construction' focuses on the role of schooling in children's national identity constructions in the context of Cyprus' political and territorial division through the use of detailed ethnographic investigations of school life. The second tradition, 'ethnographies of racism', also through the use of ethnographic methods, explores the role of schooling in processes of racialization and ethnicization as a result of the recent increase of immigrant presence in schools. The third tradition, 'studies of curricula and textbooks', focuses on the critical analysis of curricula and textbook production in public schools with a view to deconstructing their ideological content. The last tradition, 'studies of teachers and intercultural education', focuses on the role of teachers in the production and reproduction of educational inequalities and on the recent policy turn towards intercultural education.

9.4.1   Ethnographies of identity construction

Ethnographies of identity construction (EIC) focus on the role of school in children's identity constructions as this takes shape within the existing nationalistic educational system which encourages particular constructions of 'self' and 'other' in divided Cyprus. The first in-depth ethnographic study of identity construction within a school context was carried out during 1996–1997 as part of a doctoral dissertation (see Spyrou, 1999) and subsequently published in a series of articles (e.g., Spyrou, 2000, 2001a, 2001b, 2002, 2006). The study was unique mainly because it adopted a child-centered approach which problematized earlier approaches to socialization which mostly treated children as passive objects under the direct and overpowering influence of adults, whether these were teachers or parents. The study was ethnographic in nature, and focused on the daily lives of elementary school children who attended two different schools, one urban school in Nicosia near the buffer zone which divides the island in two, and the other in a rural village community south-west of Nicosia. Participant observation and interviewing were the principal methods for data collection used, though the researcher also collected and analyzed children's drawings and essays, and administered a series of pile-sorting and ranking exercises with the children. The study's key aim was to examine children's national identity constructions both inside the school and in contexts outside the school, such as the home and the playground. Taking as its starting point the theoretical assumption that children are social actors who are able to impact their social worlds, even in contexts such as the school where their power and ability are largely limited by institutional constraints, the study explored the daily lives of children both within and outside of school thus situating identity construction within the larger social and political contexts which shape children's lives. According to Spyrou, the continuing Hellenocentric character of Greek Cypriot schools, as reflected in the curriculum, provides an overall framework for the practice of teaching that allows limited room for challenging the ideological status quo. As a result of the nationalistic character of education, most teachers, even those who are critical of nationalism in other contexts, end up essentializing and stereotyping national identities. By focusing on teacher–student and student–student exchanges as these unfold during classroom lessons, the study reveals the dynamics of identity construction as a process whereby history, nation, and identity acquire meaning and substance through social interaction. The educational preoccupation with the 'Turks' as the nation's enemy *par excellence* penetrates all aspects of school life and creates an oppositional logic which sustains a firm and problematic boundary between 'self' and 'other'. Yet, despite these structural constraints, both teachers and children from time to time challenge, resist or rework, and negotiate received knowledge to construct alternative understandings of identity to those entailed within the nationalist outlook of the educational system. Through detailed ethnographic accounts of children's everyday lives in school and beyond, this study initiated a critical discussion on educational process and practice, and what this entails for constructions of 'self' and 'other' in the context of a divided society.

The key findings from Spyrou's study have been confirmed by subsequent studies and especially Philippou's study with 10-year-old Greek Cypriot students (fifth grade, primary school) carried out during 2000–2001. Philippou's study (see especially Philippou, 2005) which explored children's national and European identities also found that children's representations of national identities were essentialist and ahistorical, and very much influenced by the highly Hellenocentric ideological context of the school and the educational system at large. Children's representations of their European identities were more instrumental in character because of the perceived benefits for Cyprus from joining the European Union but these identities were essentially imagined only in relation to Greek Cypriots rather than all Cypriots (i.e., they excluded Turkish Cypriots). Similarly, and in line with Spyrou's findings, Philippou found that a so-called 'Cypriot' identity was also very much defined by children as being exclusively 'Greek Cypriot' and monoethnic.

At the secondary school level, Christou's (2006, 2007) work with students at a Greek Cypriot school provides a fruitful and productive account of the role of schooling in the negotiation of memory and history. Christou's analysis of the slogan 'I don't forget and I struggle' which has become the single most quoted slogan on which an educational ideology of liberation and reunification of the island has been built, reveals what she terms a 'double imagination': on the one hand, the slogan becomes a call for students to imagine how peace will eventually prevail and their island will be reunited; on the other hand, it leaves them with few options of what this future might look like and how it might be achieved but through the well-known recipe of the past, the armed national struggle for liberation. As Christou writes, 'the aspiration to unify Cyprus is contradicted by the lack of understanding of what this solution means and the continuing desire to relive old glories' (2006, pp. 301–302).

A number of other studies have also explored the overall ideological climate of public education in Cyprus and its role in shaping the identities of young Greek Cypriot children (see for instance, Zembylas, 2010a; see also 2010b). Zembylas (2010a), using an intersectional approach which highlights the overlapping effects of nationalism and racism as ideologies of exclusion (see also Spyrou, 2009) provides an ethnographic case-study of the educational context for studying constructions and experiences by both Greek Cypriot majority students and Turkish-speaking minority students. The intersection between nationalism and racism in these schools brings into sharp focus the power of each to reinforce the other. As Zembylas shows, each group's understanding of these two ideologies differs given that their schooling experiences are radically different. The majority status of Greek Cypriot children and the institutional backing they have operating in a largely nationalistic educational context reinforces their sense of superiority as 'white Greeks' set in opposition to the 'dark Turks'.

To sum up, the EIC tradition produced a small but significant amount of work which supports the thesis that the Greek Cypriot educational system operates within a nationalistic framework and utilizes a Hellenocentric approach to education. These studies illustrate how this system works in practice to facilitate the construction of an 'us' versus 'them' worldview among children, but they also highlight the dynamics of this process which also gives rise to resistance and negotiation of received dominant identity narratives by both teachers and students in the flow of everyday school life. Utilizing qualitative, ethnographic approaches, these studies provide rich and detailed accounts of children's daily engagements with ideology and their identity constructions.

9.4.2   Ethnographies of racism

Ethnographies of racism (ER) focus on processes of racialization and ethnicization as these unfold in school and particularly in relation to immigrant children. These studies aim to deconstruct dominant educational discourses which sustain, on the one hand, nationalist ideologies and, on the other, racist ideologies and practices which encourage prejudice, stereotyping, and discrimination against certain ethnic groups. As is the case with the EIC tradition described above, the ER tradition is also preoccupied with school practices, and especially with the way school administrators and procedures, as well as teachers, contribute to the reproduction of structures of inequality and the exclusion of immigrant or ethnic minority students.

The findings reported by these studies confirm the general finding reported by studies carried within the EIC tradition, namely that Greek Cypriot schools operate within an ideological climate which reinforces feelings of superiority ('Greeks are better and far superior than other ethnic groups') over ethnic others, especially over those who are considered to be enemies of the nation such as the Turks or happen to be in subservient social positions to Greek Cypriots, as is the case with economic migrants who work in Cyprus.

In a study which focuses explicitly on the issue of racism through an investigation of 10–16-year-old children's attitudes and perceptions of immigrants, Zembylas and Lesta (2010) analyze the interpretive repertoires used by children to report their understanding of immigrants and of their presence in Cyprus. The study, which combines a survey with qualitative interviews, focuses on the complexity in children's stances and repertoires. Though the survey reports a whole range of responses, from negative to positive, it is clear that more than half of the children (54%) exhibit negative or mildly negative stances towards ethnic others. These children view immigrants as dirty, dangerous, and criminals, to mention a few of the attributes they report, and in general express feelings of antipathy, disgust, and fear towards them. They consider that the presence of immigrants makes Cyprus worse off, and that the rise in the rate of crime is primarily due to immigration. Interestingly, some of these children report that they are aware their stances and behaviors are racist. However, others lack this capacity and seem to be mostly unaware that their racist actions have an impact on immigrants. The relatively small number of children (about one-quarter) who have positive stances towards immigrants highlights the potential for alternative constructions of immigration and immigrants. From a theoretical standpoint, of more interest is the group of children who express more ambivalent and contradictory stances towards immigrants. On the one hand, for these children, immigrants exhibit many of the characteristics pointed out by children who had more clearly negative stances (e.g. immigrants are criminals, bad, wild, and should leave Cyprus); on the other hand, they consider that there is a lot to learn from immigrants and that it is important to get to know them better. These contradictory stances suggest, perhaps, that there is a plurality of discourses and value systems which co-exist giving rise to positive, negative, and mixed repertoires among children.

A number of other studies focus on the impact of racism and racist practices on children who are constructed as ethnic minorities or immigrants within the school system, whether these are Turkish-speaking children (mostly Turkish Cypriot and Roma children, but also other children who speak Turkish such as Kurdish asylum seekers) (e.g. Spyrou, 2004; Trimikliniotis and Demetriou, 2009; Zembylas, 2010a), Pontian children (e.g. Theodorou, 2011a, 2011b; Trimikliniotis, 2001) or children who belong to particular immigrant groups and categories such as Iraqi-Palestinian or Eastern European children (e.g. Papamichael, 2011). Most of these studies provide a critical look at the emerging educational and other problems which have appeared in recent years as a result of the rise in the populations of these 'other' children in Greek Cypriot public schools. For instance, Spyrou (2004), in his ethnographic study of schools with Turkish-speaking children, identifies a number of educational problems faced by these children. These include: a curriculum which is designed primarily for the majority (i.e. for Greek-speaking children) thus largely ignoring the differences of immigrant and ethnic minority children from the majority; serious problems with discipline, aggression, and conflicts with children both within and outside of the classroom; incidents of prejudice and racism such as name-calling and labeling; and difficulties in communication and high levels of absenteeism by Turkish-speaking children and lack of teacher–parent communication.

Papamichael's (2011) more extensive ethnographic study of an ethnically mixed primary school – with one-third of the children being of Eastern European background and rapidly increasing numbers of asylum-seeking Iraqi-Palestinian children – reveals more clearly the role of teachers in differential racialization of the two minoritized groups of children. Papamichael explores the role of diverse factors such as the children's national origin, their skin color and gender, and their time of arrival at the school, to show how the constructions which emerge – whether positive or negative – are the outcome of the strategies and practices adopted by different teachers, and the acts of resistance or negotiation adopted by different children, even when faced with the same structural constraints. Though Papamichael shows us that most teachers, most of the time, unintentionally and without fully recognizing the effect of their practices, collude with and reproduce school racist practices, her study also provides us with productive insights into the nuances of racializion processes in school settings as these unfold in a dynamic fashion within specific contexts occupied by specific actors.

Theodorou's (2011a) work explores a further dynamic of the racialization processes at work which involves children themselves as both victims and perpetrators of othering. As Theodorou explains, Pontian children who are themselves immigrants and often otherized by the majority (i.e., Greek Cypriot children and occasionally teachers), are often also involved in othering their non-European immigrant classmates by internalizing Eurocentric stereotypes and assumptions about the putative superiority of white Europeans.

An exception to the above studies which are mostly preoccupied specifically with the role of schools in racist practices, Spyrou's (2009) study of Greek Cypriot children's constructions of Filipino and Sri-Lankan domestic workers explores the more general attitudes of two groups of children, those whose families employ domestic workers and those whose families don't. Though children's constructions and feelings towards these women are not always negative, but are rather characterized by contradictions and ambiguities, the overall context which shapes these women's presence in Cyprus (i.e. the fact that they are economically subordinate but also constructed as racially inferior by prevailing discourses coupled with their status as females) gives rise to attitudes and understandings on the part of the children which, even when on the surface they appear to be positive, are in fact qualified statements which reveal a deep sense of discomfort and a sense of superiority in relation to these women.

To summarize the ER tradition, we could say that ethnographic studies of racism, especially in educational contexts, have been slowly but steadily contributing to our understanding of racialization processes at work and how these processes shape both majority and minority children. Being primarily qualitative and ethnographic in their approaches to studying children's and implicated adults engagement with racism, ethnocentrism, prejudice, and stereotyping, these studies shed light on the dynamic processes at work which give rise to these problematic social phenomena. It is important to note that conceptually it is not easy to separate the ER tradition from the EIC tradition mainly because identity construction intersects with both nationalism and racism and therefore any classification of studies within one or the other tradition is more a matter of theoretical emphasis rather than distinct categorization.

9.4.3 Curriculum/textbooks

The next group of studies examine the way the curriculum and textbooks contribute to either strengthening or soothing ethnic divisions for much of the recent history of the Cypriot state.

One of the older studies focusing on curricula development in Cyprus is that carried out by Koutselini (1997) nearly 15 years ago. Koutselini's study sought to investigate how the national problem of Cyprus, and its development during various periods of its history, affected educational policy and consequently the secondary school curricula. Following the lead of earlier studies, Koutselini suggested that curriculum choices were to a significant extent determined by the political situation in Cyprus. Furthermore, she showed that the philosophy and character of Greek Cypriot secondary education was shaped under the pressure of monolithic cultural considerations which prevented structural changes to its educational system. She identifies three periods of curriculum changes corresponding to major political events First, the period of colonial rule (1935–1960) when the opposing groups were the colonial government and the Greek Board of Education in Cyprus (which represented the interests of the Greek Orthodox church and the government of Greece). Second, the period of independence (1960–1974) when the debate over the secondary school curriculum was between pragmatic labor-related demands, which advocated increased technical and vocational education offerings and generally reduced offerings of humanistic or subjects deemed 'useless', and nationalist supporters who regarded any reduction in ancient Greek courses as a hidden plot against the national cause of *enosis*. Third, the period from 1974 to 1990 which saw a focus shift to an independent educational policy and the internationalization of education.

Within the context of the shifts in educational policy described above, Philippou's doctoral thesis (2004) and subsequent publications based on her thesis (2007a, 2007b) explored how the European dimension was conceptualized as a subtle approach to alleviate the ethnocentrism of history and geography curricula, and to shift pupils' extreme views as a result of any remnants of the previous educational policy's focus on ethnocentrism. Her study pointed to the potential of education in providing children with a wider range of 'tools' with which to construct their identities. Further, she argued that in a context where 'Europe' is a 'normativity' and the 'Other = Turk' is polarized, the European dimension might be useful to hybridize a European identity so as to include the 'Others'. In a latter paper Philippou (2009) examined how 'Europe' is constructed in Greek Cypriot civic education and its interplay with the internal citizenship debates and political divisions of the country. Although 'Europe' provides a framework from which policy documents increasingly draw to introduce curricular innovation, European citizenship is not substantially addressed in the syllabi and textbooks. Nationalistic discourses of citizenship 'appropriate' 'Europe' in ways which legitimize both ethno- and Euro-centrism and which fail to alleviate existing tensions between ethno-national and state identities in Cyprus. To address this question, among others, she focused on current official secondary school civic curricula used Greek Cypriot schools to explore how Cypriot and European citizenship are constructed within the text; analytical tools are drawn largely from nationalism theories and their implications for discussions of European integration. She argued that local and European debates seem to have influenced the curricula used in Greek Cypriot state schools in conflicting ways, which do not address the issues underlying the Cyprus problem.

Within the context of a divided island Papadakis (2008a, 2008b) conducted a comparative study of schoolbooks used to teach the history of Cyprus in primary and secondary education on the two sides of the divided island, with study material being analyzed according to guidelines outlined in UNESCO's handbook on textbook research. Despite their different political goals, the two nationalisms that emerged in Cyprus shared the same form, namely, an ethnic nationalism stressing common history, descent, language, culture, and religion with the people of the 'motherlands', Turkey and Greece. Greek Cypriots and Turkish Cypriots were only taught the history of Greece and the history of Turkey respectively, while the history of Cyprus has only relatively recently been introduced and with considerably less time allotted for its teaching. On the Greek Cypriot side, the history of Cyprus has been presented as an extension of the history of Greece, and on the Turkish Cypriot side as an extension of the history of Turkey. Papadakis's study found that Greek Cypriot schoolbooks currently in use on the island and older Turkish Cypriot schoolbooks employed until 2004 employ similar models of ethnic nationalism. According to his analysis, both present history 'from above', focusing on dynastic change and diplomatic and political history; both are male-centered, with little attention being paid to social history, internal differences, interaction, and cooperation; both sets of textbooks adopt monoethnic and ethnocentric approaches to the subject matter, rejecting any conceptualization of Cyprus as a multicultural and multi-ethnic space in past and present. Further, he argues that the view of history they contain is strongly dualistic, depicted in terms of black and white, good and evil. An interesting observation that he makes is that there was a substantial revision of history schoolbooks on the Turkish Cypriot side after the left-wing party CTP came to power in 2003, leading to the production of new textbooks during 2004. These textbooks represented a radical change in terms of content and methodology, highlighting not just conflict, internal divisions, and discontinuities, but also social and cultural interactions and cooperation between the two communities. The new model of history presented had noteworthy implications regarding the notions of memory and trauma, blame, and retribution, as well as allowing for the possibility of making one's own choices regarding political allegiance in the present.

Beyond the main ethnicity divide of Cyprus and the multiculturalism front, Angelides, Stylianou, and Leigh (2004) examined the ways schools shape students' multicultural awareness. They stated that it was necessary to implement an educational awareness in all students within the primary schools of Cyprus concerning the negative attitudes that were developed towards the foreign students. The authors point out that negative attitudes such as 'racism, xenophobia, ethnocentrism' and violent behaviors by Cypriot students toward foreign students was a reality in Cypriot schools. They describe a single episode where a foreign student felt that she could not be integrated in the school environment due to the lack of support by the educational system and not by other Cypriot students. The researchers believed that the Cypriot educational system does not motivate students to acquire knowledge about other ethnic groups and cultures. For example, in 2004 all history and religious textbooks included information that related only to the Cypriot and Greek related topics. As a result, the lack of knowledge regarding other ethnic backgrounds, histories and ethnic origins, leads to the development of stereotypical attitudes towards these students. Consequently, these negative attitudes could further result in violent behavior towards this group of students. Despite the fact that the system might not assist the foreign students to efficiently integrate into the Cypriot school environment, the group of students studied was willing to be part of Cypriot society and to enjoy all aspects of the Cypriot culture, such as religious and national celebrations, customs, and traditions (Angelides et al., 2004).

In order to recognize the vital impact of the educators on the student's identity formation, Spyrou's (2002) study, which was presented in a previous section, may be looked at again in relation to this issue. Specifically, the author examined how the educational system influenced the way students form their own and others' ethnic identities. The author observed that in order to teach history courses (e.g. Greek liberation struggles) in class, the teachers tended to provide a vivid context that might cause various negative effects. As the author explicitly stated, the teacher provided an example (for instance, the Turkish soldiers brutally murdered the Greek population to conquer a specific area) that enhanced the hatred of students towards the Turks. Consequently, as Spyrou (2002) argues, the students shaped their understanding of the Turks as the 'enemies' and attributed their negative beliefs and hostility to this group of people. In addition, Spyrou (2002) affirmed that this kind of teaching method compels students to segregate themselves from other ethnic groups. Particularly, Greek Cypriots tend to acknowledge themselves as 'us' and people of Turkish origin as 'them' (Spyrou, 2006).

This section dealt with the way textbooks and curricula treated the historical context to cultivate ethnocentric identities in a politically turbulent period. The ethnic divide has dominated much of the research agenda of many researchers until recently when the notion of multiculturalism emerged and added a newfound focus in the research repertoire of researchers to which we now turn.

9.4.4   Teachers and intercultural education

This section looks at the research which focused on teachers and intercultural education which incorporates not only the ethnicity divisions and stereotypes seen in previous sections but also the integration of migrant students in Cyprus.

A research study by the Centre for Educational Research and Evaluation (KEEA, 2010 examined whether educators in Cyprus are aware and trained on how to promote solidarity and assist the integration of foreign students. The authors focused more on the importance of the intercultural knowledge of the educators and on how they can acquire this knowledge. The research findings show that more than half of the sample of educators were trained on intercultural issues, by either attending seminars or by taking courses during their graduate and undergraduate studies. Moreover, results showed that educators were well prepared to implement practical methods to enhance the intercultural awareness of all students. However, the study showed that even though educators were aware of the institutional instructions set by the Ministry of Education and Culture regarding teaching methods applied to foreign students, few of them were familiar with the guide developed by the Ministry of Education on welcoming students into the school environment. Also, a large number of teachers were not informed about the seminars offered by the Ministry of Education regarding methods of teaching Greek as a second language. It is important to note that most of the educators wished for more training on issues of multiculturalism and on practical ways to support the integration of foreign students in the school environment.

Papamichael (2009), through a qualitative study with unstructured interviews with teachers and head teachers, investigated the teacher's role in the policy and practice of intercultural education in Greek Cypriot primary schools, amidst an environment which has gradually transformed the educational setting of Cyprus to a multicultural one.

Zembylas (2010a) showed the vital influence of educators on students by discussing the importance of the implementation of the 'integrated education' in Cypriot schools by educators. As Zembylas (2010a) discussed in his study, this type of education was derived from the conception of the 'inclusive education', which is the amalgamation of a diversity of students in one class or school. The author asserted that this type of educational measure assisted all students who come from different ethnic, social, and religious backgrounds, to integrate more easily in the mainstream Cypriot school environment and to avoid being stereotyped or discriminated. It is assumed that based on this 'integrated' educational system, all educators must be aware that their class encompasses students with different cultural, ethnic, and religious backgrounds. They also need to be informed about these differences and be academically prepared to provide all students with the necessary tools to understand and accept diversity in their class, and school in general. If educators are willing to accept and respect differing opinions and beliefs among the students, this would be an effective tool for influencing all students' reactions and attitudes towards intercultural circumstances (Zembylas, 2010a). The researcher strongly stated that the exclusive method of 'reconciliation pedagogies' is just the acknowledgement of cultural and ethnic differences, and it is not sufficient to assist students in forming their assumptions and further in understanding interculturalism.

Furthermore, Zembylas (2010b) demonstrated that when 'integrated education' was applied in a private Greek Cypriot school, this approach was effective on students' attitudes and behaviors. The particular interrelations of groups of students that were examined in the research included Greek Cypriot and Turkish Cypriot students. It was evident that there were many rivalries among these groups due to the increasing stereotypical and racist beliefs and attitudes towards each other. Teachers showed themselves to be increasingly aware of issues pertaining to several different cultures. Specifically, educators in this school tend to show understanding and acceptance of all students' beliefs and encourage children to think critically and analyze these issues based on their own views. Other teachers use various practical ways to bring Greek Cypriot and Turkish Cypriot students together, such as the establishment of a students' 'club' that would include students from all ethnicities. However, the effort that teachers put in creating school harmony is demanding since most of the students struggle to cooperate and not all of the academic staff is involved in this effort.

Another study conducted by Symeou et al. (2009) revealed how teachers reacted and felt when having Roma students in their class. More specifically, the authors showed that most Greek Cypriot teachers were not adequately equipped with the necessary knowledge and educational materials to teach classes where Roma students were enrolled. Even though there was an inadequate supply of instructional materials that would effectively train and assist teachers to help Roma students, teachers also had to cope with the unwillingness of Roma parents to cooperate with them. According to the authors, some Roma parents decided that their children might not attend school to avoid the negative effects of exclusion, segregation, and racist actions against them. Therefore, Symeou et al. (2009) argued that a methodological training program provided to the teachers could support them to overcome these difficulties. Such a program attempted to increase teachers' understanding regarding Roma historical and social background, and therefore, they would recognize more easily the learning and social needs of these students. Moreover, the program's goal was to facilitate the willingness of Roma parents to be committed to their children's academic state, and therefore to reinforce their school attendance.

As Cyprus appears to be moving more to the multicultural agenda there is a growing body of research work on intercultural education which focuses on the co-existence of multiple ethnicity groups in the educational system. This is a move away from the well-researched area on the rivalries that may be found in educational settings between the two main ethnic communities of Cyprus, and may be interpreted as a consequence of the long-lasting ethnic division of the country whereby the feeling is that little can be done to reverse a permanent partition along ethnic lines.

9.5   Summary conclusion

In this chapter we have identified and reviewed four main traditions of research for studying inequalities in educational processes in Cyprus: (1) ethnographies of identity construction, (2) ethnographies of racism, (3) studies of curricula and textbooks, and (4) studies of teachers and intercultural education. The research tradition we have identified as ethnographies of identity construction focuses primarily on school-based studies of identity construction with children being the principal research targets. These studies provide context-specific in-depth explorations of children's school lives and, especially, of the role of schooling and educational ideology on children's sense of national identity. Taken as a whole these studies shed light on the role that formal education plays in constructing oppositional identities ('us' versus 'them') in Cyprus which is divided as a result of Turkey's 1974 invasion and occupation. The second research tradition we have identified and discussed – ethnographies of racism – focuses mainly on the exploration of processes of racialization and ethnicization which take place in school as a result of the increased presence of immigrant children in recent years. These studies are also primarily ethnographic in nature and seek to problematize educational policies and practices and their role in reproducing inequalities in relation to immigrant children. In addition to the policies which guide educational practice, these studies explore the role of school administrators and of teachers in particular in order to deconstruct the assumed equality that is supposed to exist in school life. Regarding the way textbooks and curricula have been researched over recent years, one may observe that education has been a vehicle for promoting the politics of ethnocentrism to the extent that the Greek Orthodox church of Cyprus, which appears to monitor the content of textbooks, reacts forcefully when there is even a hint that they may deviate from the ethnocentric agenda of Hellenism and Greek-Orthodox Christianity. The ethnic divide that has dominated much of the research agenda of many researchers until recently appears to be losing out to the multiculturalism agenda possibly in the realization that the de facto partition of the country cannot be changed in the foreseeable future.

The still-limited number of studies on educational inequalities in Cyprus has yet to have any significant impact on social policy development, though they have given rise to public dialogue on the issue. It is clear from the existing literature that there are emerging inequalities in education which need to be addressed. However, given that the phenomenon of in-migration in Cyprus is fairly recent, coupled with the fact that Cyprus is a divided country whose educational system sustains a nationalistic outlook, a challenging task still lies ahead as far as developing social policies that will address the emerging problems effectively. At the same time, these are the same factors that entice more and more researchers in Cyprus to explore issues of diversity and inequality.

Though the four research traditions and the work carried out to date has provided significant insights into the workings of the educational system in Cyprus and its role in the production and reproduction of inequalities, much more needs to be done in mapping and assessing the empirical realities of the situation. Mixed methods approaches that map and contextualize at the same time the experiences of different migrant groups in school would help provide the currently missing larger picture of the phenomenon, while also accounting for gaps of knowledge in relation to particular migrant groups and ethnic minorities. Similarly, large-scale quantitative studies on a representative population that test the insights of the context-specific qualitative case-studies on in/out-group relations carried to date would enhance our understanding of the larger structural mapping of this phenomenon. Another fruitful direction for future research would be to explore the role of the family and the home in relation to that of the school, as well as the respective roles of the church and the military to provide for a more comprehensive analysis of the factors that play a role in understanding and explaining educational inequalities. Last but not least, a focus on wider outcomes that move beyond the in/out-group focus, which has been predominant to this day, could also provide a more comprehensive understanding of educational inequalities in Cyprus.

References

Angelides, P., Stylianou, T. and Leigh, J. (2004) 'Multicultural education in Cyprus: A pot of multicultural assimilation', *Intercultural Education*, vol. 15, no. 3, pp. 307–315.

Christou, M. (2006) 'A double imagination: Memory and education in Cyprus', *Journal of Modern Greek Studies*, vol. 24, no. 2, pp. 285–306.

Christou, M. (2007) 'The language of patriotism: Sacred history and dangerous memories', *British Journal of Sociology of Education*, vol. 28, no. 6, pp. 709–722.

Eurydice (2010) *Information on education systems and policies in Europe: National summary sheets on education systems in Europe and ongoing reforms.* http://eacea.ec.europa.eu/education/eurydice/eurybase_en.php#cyprus.

Gordon, M. M. (1978) *Human Nature, Class, and Ethnicity*, New York: Oxford University Press.

Greeley, A. M. (1971) *Why can't they be like us? Americas white ethnic groups*, New York: E. P. Dutton.

KEEA (2010) *Η Διαπλιτισμική Ετοιμότητα των Κύπριων Εκπαιδευτικών Πρωτοβάθμιας Εκπαίδευσης*. Research Report. http://www.pi.ac.cy/pi/index.php?option=com_content&view=article&id=451&Itemid=304&lang=el.

Koutselini, M. (1997) 'Curriculum as political text: The case of Cyprus', *History of Education*, vol. 26, no. 4, pp. 395–407.

Ministry of Education and Culture of Cyprus (2009) *Annual Report*, Nicosia: Konos Ltd.

Ministry of Education and Culture (2011) *Primary education in Cyprus*. http://www.moec.gov.cy/dde/index/html.

Papadakis, Y. (2008a) *History education in divided Cyprus: A comparison of Greek Cypriot and Turkish Cypriot schoolbooks on the 'history of Cyprus'*. International Peace Research Institute, Oslo: PRIO Report.

Papadakis, Y. (2008b) 'Narrative, memory and history education in divided Cyprus', *History & Memory*, vol. 20, no. 2, pp. 128–148.

Papamichael, E. (2009) 'Greek Cypriot teachers and classroom diversity: Intercultural education in Cyprus', in L. Saha and A. G. Dworkin (Eds), *International Handbook of Research on Teachers and Teaching*, vol. 21, New York: Springer, pp. 605–642.

Papamichael, E. (2011) *Exploring Intercultural Education Discourses and Everyday Practices in a Greek-Cypriot Primary School*. Ph.D. diss., University of London.

Philippou, S. (2004) *The European Dimension in Education and Pupils' Identity: A Study of the Impact of a Primary School Curricular Intervention in Cyprus*. Ph.D. diss., University of Cambridge.

Philippou, S. (2005) 'Constructing national and European identities: The case of Greek-Cypriot pupils', *Educational Studies*, vol. 31, no. 3, pp. 293–315.

Philippou, S. (2007a) 'On the borders of Europe: Citizenship education and identity in Cyprus', *Journal of Social Science Education*, vol. 6, no.1, pp. 68–79.

Philippou, S. (2007b) 'Re-inventing 'Europe': The case of the European dimension in Greek-Cypriot geography and history curricula', *The Curriculum Journal*, vol.18, no. 1, pp. 57–88.

Philippou, S. (2009) 'What makes Cyprus European? Curricular responses of Greek-Cypriot civic Europe', *Journal of Curriculum Studies*, vol. 41, no.2, pp. 199–223.

Police Department (2009) *Annual Report*. http://police.gov.cy/police/police.nsf/dml report_gr/dmlreport_gr?OpenDocument.

Singer, L. (1962) 'Ethnogenesis and Negro-Americans today', *Social Research*, 29 (Winter), pp. 419–432.

Spyrou, S. (1999) *Small Ethnic Worlds: Identity, Ambiguity, and Imagination in Greek Cypriot Children's Lives*. Ph.D. diss., Binghamton University.

Spyrou, S. (2000) 'Education, ideology, and the national self: The social practice of identity construction in the classroom', *The Cyprus Review*, vol. 12, no. 1, pp. 61–81.

Spyrou, S. (2001a) 'Those on the other side: Ethnic identity and imagination in Greek Cypriot children's lives', in H. Schwartzman (Ed.), *Children and Anthropology: Perspectives for the 21st Century*. Westport, CT/London: Bergin & Garvey, pp. 167–185.

Spyrou, S. (2001b) 'One and more than one: Greek Cypriot children and ethnic identity in the flow of everyday life', *DisClosure: A Journal of Social Theory*, vol. 10, pp. 73–94.

Spyrou, S. (2002) 'Images of "the other": "The Turk" in Greek Cypriot children's imaginations', *Race, Ethnicity and Education*, vol. 5, no. 3, pp. 255–272.

Spyrou, S. (2004) *The Educational Needs of the Turkish-Speaking Children of Limassol*. Nicosia: Report on behalf of UNOPS.

Spyrou, S. (2006) 'Children constructing ethnic identities in Cyprus', in Y. Papadakis, N. Peristianis and G. Welz (Eds), *Divided Cyprus: Modernity, History, and an Island in Conflict*. Bloomington/Indianapolis: Indiana University Press, pp. 121–139.

Spyrou, S. (2009) 'Between intimacy and intolerance: Greek Cypriot children's encounters with Asian domestic workers', *Childhood*, vol. 16, no. 2, pp. 155–173.

Symeou, L., Karagiorgi, Y., Kaloyirou, C. and Roussounidou, E. (2009) 'Reflections on teacher training for equity and social justice: The INSETRom Cypriot experience.' *Intercultural Education*, vol. 20, no. 6, pp. 511–521.

Theodorou, E. (2011a) 'I'll race you to the top: Othering from within – attitudes among Pontian children in Cyprus towards other immigrant classmates', *Childhood*, vol. 18, no. 2, pp. 242–260.

Theodorou, E. (2011b) '"Children at our school are integrated. No one sticks out": Greek-Cypriot teachers' perceptions of integration of immigrant children in Cyprus', *International Journal of Qualitative Studies in Education*, vol. 24, no. 4, pp. 501–520.

Trimikliniotis, N. (2001) 'The educational problems of the Pontians in Cyprus: Preliminary research and report'. Nicosia: Report on behalf of the Cyprus Association of Sociologists submitted to the Ministry of Education.

Trimikliniotis, N. and Demetriou, C. (2009) 'The Cypriot Roma and the failure of education: Anti-discrimination and multiculturalism as a post-accession challenge', in N. Coureas and A. Varnava (Eds), *The Minorities of Cyprus: Development Patterns and the Identity of the Internal-exclusion*. Cambridge: Cambridge Scholars Publishing.

Zembylas, M. (2010a) 'Children's construction and experience of racism and nationalism in Greek-Cypriot primary schools', *Childhood*, vol. 17, no. 3, pp. 312–328.

Zembylas, M. (2010b) 'Racialization/ethnicization of school emotional spaces: The politics of resentment', *Race Ethnicity and Education*, vol. 13, no. 2, pp. 253–270.

Zembylas, M. and Lesta, S. (2010) *Analysis and Conclusions Report: Research on the Views of Cypriot Students in Relation to Migrants*. Nicosia: CARDET.

10
England

Peter A. J. Stevens and Gill Crozier

10.1 Introduction

The aim of this literature review is to describe and critically assess how educational sociologists in England have studied racial and ethnic inequalities in primary and secondary education between 1990 and 2010. Although studies with a similar focus have been conducted in the past (Foster, Gomm, and Hammersley, 1996; Gillborn and Gipps, 1996; Gillborn and Mirza, 2000; Nehaul, 1996; Taylor, 1988; Tomlinson, 1983; Tomlinson, 1989), most of these literature reviews had different purposes in mind and also the national political and also global landscape of race, ethnicity, and education, together with developing sociological understanding, has changed quite markedly in the past decade indicating the need for an updated overview.[1]

This chapter is divided into three main parts. First, in the section 'national context', the key characteristics of the English education system; the main migration patterns; the predominant black and minority ethnic (BME) groups and important research and policy antecedents are briefly described. Second, the process of conducting this literature review is described, with particular focus on the search strategies employed and the related criteria for inclusion. Third, five research tradtions that focus on educational inequality and race and ethnicity in England are identified and analyzed in terms of their major focus, methods, findings, and debates: (1) the political arithmetic (PA) tradition; (2) racism and racial discrimination in school (RRDS) tradition; (3) school effectiveness and school inclusion (SESI) tradition; (4) culture and educational outcomes (CEO) tradition; and (5) educational markets and educational outcomes (EMEO) tradition. Finally, this particular body of literature is critically assessed and suggestions are formulated on how to advance future research on race and ethnicity and educational inequality in England.

10.2   National context

10.2.1   The education system

In England, education is compulsory for all children between the ages of 5 and 16. As a result of the Education Reform Act 1988, four Key Stages in compulsory education were established: Key Stage 1 (5–7 years old), Key Stage 2 (–11 years old), Key Stage 3 (11–14 years old), and Key Stage 4 (14–16 years old). After compulsory education, students can follow two more years of secondary education (Sixth Form) to obtain additional qualifications (such as A-levels or vocational equivalents), which are often required for entry to higher education institutions (Figure 10.1).

More than 90% of the students attend state-funded schools, which offer education free of charge between the ages of 4 and 18. All state-funded schools follow the National Curriculum, which is made up of 12 subjects. Compulsory subjects differ at different Key Stages. In Key Stage 4, for example, all students must study English literature and language, mathematics, at least one science subject or a combination, information technology, physical education, citizenship education, religious education, sex and relationships and careers education. Not all of these will necessarily be examined. All students are also required to study at least one humanities or arts subject. Students typically move up to a higher age group automatically and as a result rarely have to retake a school year or courses (UNESCO, 2003).

At the end of compulsory education, students typically take GCSE exams, which are centrally administered tests, taken in a variety of subjects, which are

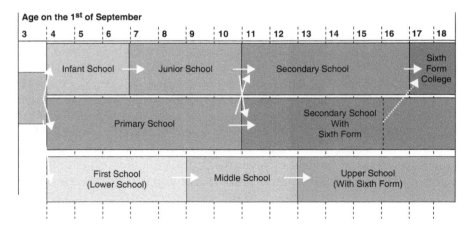

Figure 10.1   Educational system in England
Source: Knight (2007).

usually decided by the student themselves between the ages of 13 and 14 (in Year 9). Study of chosen subjects begins between the ages of 14 and 15 (Year 10), and exams are then taken between 15 and 16 (Year 11). Students are required to take the following subjects: English, mathematics, science, and physical education. At the end of the two-year GCSE course, each student receives a grade for each subject. These grades range between A* (best) to G (worst). Receiving five or more C grades is often considered the minimum requirement for taking A-levels at a sixth-form college or regular college after leaving secondary school. Students typically have to obtain at least a C or better in English and mathematics to be considered for entry at universities (UNESCO, 2003).

The Education Reform Act created an educational market in England in which schools were framed as providers which must compete against other schools for students (Gillborn and Youdell, 2000; Tomlinson, 1997; Tomlinson, 1999), and attached to each student was a financial resource. The success of the competitiveness between schools was driven by parental choice of school, and thus a set of criteria against which to measure school provision and compare the differences was introduced. The 1988 Education Reform Act was also designed, according to its originators, to improve educational 'standards' a watch word employed by successive governments for at least 20 years but never effectively translated into the experience of BME young people (Gillborn and Youdell, 2000). The original major changes introduced by the act, included the creation of a statutory 'National Curriculum', which imposed a specific curriculum framework on all state schools. 'Standards of achievement' were set at five GCSEs level A*–C and treated as a benchmark for student and school success together with a national system of testing originally at 7, 11 and 14 years. These tests are known as SATs (Standard Assessment Tests, comprising national standardized tests and teacher assessment). 'Accountability' was stressed and schools were evaluated according to the student test results; these are still published nationally under the format of league tables. The government stimulated diversity in the market and allowed schools to operate independently of the local educational authority, or 'opt out' of local control. This latter development has gone way beyond this original initiative to allow quasi public–private arrangements in the form of Academies and Free Schools making more than ever before the likelihood of the end of a state-run education system.

10.2.2 Migration patterns and main racial and ethnic minority groups in England

Since the turn of the 20th century, the UK has primarily received immigrants from Ireland and the (later former) colonies and territories of the British Empire, such as India, Bangladesh, Pakistan, the Caribbean, and Hong Kong. However, after the UN Refugee Convention in 1951, and more recently, following the enlargement of the EU, the UK has witnessed an increase in immigration from

Central and Eastern European countries and refugee populations from across the globe. Based on analysis of the 2001 Census of Population (Owen, 2003), the UK counts 4.6 million BME people (or 7.9% of the population). The largest group of BME are South Asian, accounting for 2 million people (3.5%), half of whom were Indian. Black minority people constitute another relatively large minority group, counting 1.15 million in the 2001 Census, with more than half a million Black Caribbean people. Children of mixed white and Black Caribbean heritage are the largest growing demographic group (Table 10.1).

As racial and ethnic classifications are social constructions which can refer to a multitude of means of categorization, whether self-defined or externally imposed and often change over time and context, and refer to an amalgam of characteristics, such as skin color, nationality, and culture, confusion often reigns as to what is actually measured (Sealey and Carter, 2001). However, following conventions used in the literature on race and ethnic inequalities in the UK, this chapter usually makes a distinction between 'BME students' and 'white students'. While the latter refers to students with a white skin color (sometimes subcategorized as 'White British', 'Irish', 'Traveller of Irish', or 'Any Other White' background), the former brings together different ethnic minority groups, including 'Asian' students (sometimes subcategorized as students from 'Indian', 'Pakistani', 'Bangladeshi', 'Chinese', or 'Any Other Asian' background), 'black students' (sometimes subcategorized as students from 'African', 'Caribbean' or 'Any Other African' background) and a rest-category called 'Other Ethnic Groups'.

Table 10.1   Ethnic composition of the UK based on 2001 Census of Population

Ethnic group	Number	Percent	Mean age in years	
			Males	Females
White	54,153,898	92.1	38.2	40.9
Minority ethnic groups	*4,635,296*	*7.9*	*28.2*	*28.8*
Mixed parentage	*677,117*	*1.2*	*20.1*	*21.3*
Asian and Asian British	*2,083,759*	*3.5*	*28.7*	*28.7*
Indian	1,053,411	1.8	32.0	32.4
Pakistani	747,285	1.3	25.8	25.5
Bangladeshi	283,063	0.5	24.3	23.2
Black and Black British	*1148,738*	*2.0*	*30.6*	*31.3*
Black Caribbean	565,876	1.0	35.4	35.8
Black African	485,277	0.8	26.6	27.1
Black Other	97,585	0.2	23.8	25.3
Chinese and other	*725,682*	*1.2*	*30.7*	*31.8*
Chinese	247,403	0.4	30.7	32.2
Other Asian	247,664	0.4	31.5	31.1
Other Ethnic Groups	230,615	0.4	29.7	32.1
All ethnic groups	*58,789,194*	*100.0*	*37.4*	*39.9*

Source: Adapted from Owen (2003).

10.2.3 Research and social policy antecedents

Up to the 1980s English research on educational inequality and ethnicity was strongly influenced by the deficit model of the child and family. Research conducted before 1950 relied heavily on psychological models and explained social inequalities in educational outcomes as the result of differences between social groups in terms of genetically determined cognitive abilities (IQ) (Foster, Gomm, and Hammersley, 1996).

However, from the 1950s onwards a more sociological approach, labeled the 'old sociology of education' changed the focus of attention to specific, 'deficient' cultural and structural characteristics of working-class and BME families (Foster, Gomm, and Hammersley, 1996; Nehaul, 1996; Tomlinson, 1983; Tomlinson, 1989). Questioning the idea that ability is largely inherited and emphasizing the importance of environment, these researchers sought explanations for differences in educational outcomes by looking at the importance of social background characteristics. For Asian students, underachievement was explained mainly by pointing to deficiencies considered remedial, such as language adjustment and enculturation problems, and a lower social class position. For African Caribbean students underachievement was explained by both remedial deficiencies such as cultural and familial differences, migration shock, lower social class background, and to some extent, language issues, and more intractable characteristics such as children's innate abilities and, to a lesser extent, prejudice or racism in society (ibid.).

From the 1960s onwards, some scholars started to investigate the effects of ability grouping in schools (sometimes called 'streaming', 'banding', or 'setting') on the educational attainment of white working-class children. Instead of merely looking at specific characteristics of white working-class families, the 'differentiation-polarization' theory holds that by restricting access to higher status curriculum and pedagogy to particular (mainly middle and higher social class) students, students in lower status streams become disaffected with school and develop anti-school cultures which further amplify the influence of social class background on educational inequalities (Ball, 1981; Hargreaves, 1967; Keddie, 1971; Lacey, 1970). Inspired by developments in social anthropology, these scholars combined ethnographic observations with qualitative interviewing and survey and socio-metric analysis techniques to study social relations in particular schools (Foster, Gomm, and Hammersley, 1996).

Between the 1970s and early 1980s, educational research in England changed radically as researchers focused almost exclusively on school processes, and the relationship between educational inequality and race and ethnicity and gender. Two main developments in particular help to explain this change in educational research.

The development of the 'new sociology of education' (NSE) during the 1970s constituted a first important stimulus (Foster, Gomm, and Hammersley, 1996).

NSE criticized past research, especially the 'old sociology of education', for taking the school's definition of what counted as valuable knowledge, learning ability, and motivation for granted. This approach focused on the reproduction of social class inequalities, and perceived the school as problematic because it imposed higher status on knowledge and skills characteristic of the dominant social classes (Young, 1973; Young, 1976). Although working-class students were perceived as being culturally and socially discriminated against by schools, the latter also generated resistance on their part (Willis, 1977). NSE comprised two different research traditions (Foster, Gomm, and Hammersley, 1996): a tradition influenced by symbolic interactionism and phenomenology that focused on how teachers and students played an active role in constructing the social reality of schooling (see for example Delamont, 1977; Hammersley and Woods, 1984; Hargreaves and Woods, 1984; Woods and Hammersley, 1977), and a tradition inspired by Marxist social theory (Althusser, 1971; Bowles and Gintis, 1976) that emphasized the cultural domination and social reproduction taking place in schools as generated by wider structural forces (Arnot and Whitty, 1982; Karabel and Halsey, 1977), in particular capitalism (Sharp 1981; Sharp and Green, 1975).

A second important development in the 1970s and 1980s was the increasing impact of feminism in academic work, and education in particular (e.g. Acker, 1987; Arnot, 1985; Deem, 1980; Fuller, 1984;Weiner, 1985) and the greater recognition on a political level of minority cultures and their particular needs, especially in education (Foster, Gomm, and Hammersley, 1996). These changes were encouraged by research findings that suggested persistent problems in terms of black and ethnic minorities' educational achievement and the active campaigning of BME groups, who, in the face of experiencing continuous disadvantages in society, felt increasingly excluded from the political system (Crozier, 2001;Gillborn, 2005; Nehaul, 1996; Tomlinson, 1989, 2008). While in the 1970s the English government adhered to an integration policy and tried to subsume problems experienced by black and ethnic minorities under those of the poor and disadvantaged, the committee chaired by Anthony Rampton in 1979 and Lord Swann in 1981 (DES, 1981; DES, 1985) emphasized the need for research to include the effect of racism in explaining BME underachievement, and dismissed the validity of the relationship between race and ethnicity and IQ (Nehaul, 1996; Tomlinson, 1989).

Over these past two decades immense changes in relation to race and education have taken place both intellectually and with respect to policy. Socio-political and cultural conditions influenced by global changes, the development of information technology, and immigration from different demographic groups have all contributed. More specifically, Stuart Hall's seminal paper (1992) reconceptualizing 'ethnicities' stimulated researchers to move away from essentialist and dualist notions of 'race' and ethnicity and the black–white dichotomy.

More recently (in Britain at least) the influence of critical race theory (e.g. Ladson-Billings and Tate, 1995) and critical whiteness studies (Leonardo, 2002; Garner, 2007) together with the concept of intersectionalities (Crenshaw, 1995; hooks, 1989) has further broadened the debates and posed further intellectual challenges.

In political and policy terms the racially motivated murder of a young black student, Stephen Lawrence, in London (1993) led to a recognition of institutional racism and the instigation of the Race Relations Amendment Act 2000. Moreover, the Labour government (1997–2010), aware of enduring academic underachievement of black and certain minority ethnic groups introduced a range of policies to address underachievement and school exclusions with varying success (Tomlinson, 2008). The social context of education was and continues to be influenced by the impact of globalization and the open borders of EU countries which has resulted in the changing demographics of migrants and the rise of refugees and asylum seekers due to war and famine together with the rise in terrorist activity. The latter has led to a concomitant rise in islamophobia (Stone, 2004). All of these policy developments have been detailed in Tomlinson's *Race and Education: Policy and Politics in Britain* (2008). Tensions around immigration and challenges to white identities together with perceptions of a rise in terrorism and the so-called 'war on terror' has also given rise to a reappraisal of the multicultural project in Britain (Kundnani, 2002).

In addition to these socio-political developments over the past two decades, as already indicated, we have seen the development and entrenchment of neoliberalism as applied to education. Schools and increasingly further education and higher education institutions, are constructed as businesses, and compete for students and against each other. Following the 1988 Education Act, Local Education Authorities have virtually no power or influence over schools and the implementation of any policies on race equalities is the responsibility of the school itself, although the Office for Standards in Education, Children's Services and Skills (Ofsted) inspection regime should ensure accountability. This is the back drop to our review of sociological literature on race, ethnicity, and education, and these issues will be further addressed below. The following sections will first review the research methods that underpin this review and then focus on the five research traditions identified above. These will be critically examined in terms of their research questions, methods, key findings, and debates.

10.3   Methods

In sampling literature for this review, specific but flexible protocols were employed to guide and focus the process of conducting this literature review. Some restrictions were imposed in order to allow the literature review to be conducted within the allocated space and period of time. First, it was decided to include only literature that focuses on England (rather than the UK) as the research context. Second, the literature review is restricted to contributions from the discipline of sociology that focus on the relationship between educational inequality and race and ethnicity between 1990 and 2010. Third, only research that focuses on primary and secondary education was included for analysis. As a result, studies that investigate other forms of education, such as preschool, further, higher, or adult education were not included. Finally, only peer-refereed journal articles and books (including edited collections) were considered for analysis. However, although these four criteria of inclusion strongly guided the review process, sometimes studies were considered that did not fulfill at least one of these criteria, as they were perceived as good or important examples of a specific research tradition. The imposed restrictions certainly do not suggest that other literature resources, disciplinary perspectives and/or forms of education are less important in studying race and ethnic inequality in education.

The process of sampling specific research contributions involved three specific steps. First, bibliographical databases (Sociological Abstracts, EBSCO Host and ERIC) were searched for relevant peer-refereed journal articles and books using specific search queries.[2]

Second, a manageable sample of journals from the UK was selected using the Social Science Citation Index (SSCI). These journals were systematically analyzed in terms of their content from 1990 onwards. From all the UK-based journals included in the SSCI under subject 'education and educational research', 12 were selected for review.[3] In addition, the two general British sociology journals with the highest impact factor in SSCI[4] and one specific British education journal that was not included in the SSCI,[5] but which was frequently cited in the sample of research contributions, were included in the review process.

Third, the analysis of the sample of research contributions that resulted from these two search activities identified additional important reports, journals, books, and key researchers in this area of interest, which were in turn included in the review process.

10.4   Race, ethnicity and educational inequality in England

Five major research traditions can be identified in England between 1990 and 2010. A first research tradition, called the 'political arithmetic tradition', investigates the relationship between educational inequality and race and ethnicity by offering general, more representative descriptions of how different BME students perform in education over time. This research tradition emphasizes description over explanation and prefers the use of quantitative analysis on large-scale datasets. A second research tradition, which we refer to as the 'racism and racial discrimination in school tradition' employs ethnographic, qualitative research methods to explore how school-selection processes, an ethnocentric curriculum, and white teacher racist attitudes and discriminatory behavior inform the educational experiences and outcomes of BME students. A third research tradition, called the 'school effectiveness and school inclusion tradition' uses quantitative analysis techniques on large datasets to investigate the characteristics of effective schools for students in general and for specific social (racial/ethnic) groups. A fourth research tradition which we named the 'culture and educational outcomes tradition' looks at the importance of the notion of racial/ethnic minorities' culture in influencing the educational outcomes of particular BME children. A final research tradition which we refer to as the 'educational markets and educational outcomes tradition' investigates how changes in the English educational system, realized through 1988 Education Reform Act, inform the educational experiences of various social classes and BME groups in pursuing educational opportunities.

Similarities between and differences within research traditions will be pointed out as they are analyzed in this article and brought together in the conclusion. However, two important observations can be made at this stage. Firstly, while the political arithmetic and the school effectiveness and inclusion traditions employ a positivistic epistemology and large-scale quantitative research designs, the racism and racial discrimination in schools tradition, the culture and educational outcomes tradition, and the educational markets and educational outcomes tradition seem to be informed by an interpretative epistemology and a preference for small-scale, qualitative research strategies. Secondly, the research traditions discussed in this article have strong roots prior to 1990 and developed somewhat independently from or in opposition to each other. The only exception to this is the educational markets and educational outcomes tradition. This research tradition only developed from the 1990s onwards and has been heavily influenced by the racism and racial discrimination in schools tradition: although they both prefer the use of qualitative methods and explain differences in outcomes between ethnic/racial groups as the result of discriminatory processes, the educational markets and educational outcomes tradition explores the outcomes of particular educational reforms and broadens the analysis by focusing on race and ethnicity, as well as on social class.

10.4.1 The political arithmetic tradition

Out of the old sociology of education developed a particular sociological research tradition called the "political arithmetic tradition" (PA tradition), which influenced research on race and ethnicity and educational inequality post 1980. This tradition set out from a positivist epistemology and relies mainly on quantitative research strategies in analyzing the relationship between family background and educational success (Douglas, 1964; Douglas,

Ross, and Simpson, 1968; Floud, Halsey, and Martin, 1956; Glass, 1954; Halsey, Heath, and Ridge, 1980). Writers in this tradition have been 'relatively modest in their theoretical ambition' (Heath, 2000, p. 314) and preferred 'description to explanation, and hard evidence to theoretical speculation' (ibid., p. 314).

Although researchers in the PA tradition have traditionally focused their attention on describing social class inequalities, the government's increased interest in statistical data on racial/ethnic minorities (DES, 1981; DES, 1985) stimulated the availability of such data and encouraged researchers to conduct quantitative, more representative studies on racial/ethnic minorities' school attainment (Demack, Drew, and Grimsley, 2000; DfES, 2003; DfES, 2005a; DfES, 2005b; Drew, 1995; Drew and Gray, 1990; Drew, Gray, and Sporton, 1997; Gillborn and Gipps, 1996) and, more recently, school exclusions (see Section 10.4.4).

Recent data published by the Department for Education which is based on the National Student Database (NPD) and School Census records (DfE, 2012), allows for an analysis of educational achievement by ethnicity of 97–98% of all students between 2006 and 2011 (a similar analysis can be conducted on exclusion data, which is discussed below in the EMEO tradition).

Although definitions of inequality vary and are often implicit in educational research (Foster, Gomm, and Hammersley, 1996), the focus on levels of attainment in education reflects a more general shift from 'equality of access' to more radical models of 'equality of outcome' in which the dominant 'White' group is considered the reference group (Reid, 1996). However, while researchers focus increasingly on difference in outcomes, there does not seem to be a consensus on how researchers should measure 'achievement gaps'. Some researchers employ a 'percentage point difference' model (Gillborn and Gipps, 1996; Gillborn and Mirza, 2000), which measures the differences in the proportion of minority groups achieving at least a particular defined level (usually the level of achievement of the dominant 'White' group) and whether these differences have increased or decreased over time. Other researchers prefer a 'proportional' model, which considers the rate of change in level of achievement on the part of each group, relative to its starting point. Here, the achievement gap can be defined as (for example) the difference between the achievement levels of the highest- and the lowest-achieving groups as a proportion of the achievement levels of both groups (Gorard, 1999; Gorard, 2000a; Gorard, 2000b).

Applying a 'percentage point difference' model to the data in Table 10.2 (for a similar analysis on data based on the Youth Cohort Survey (YCS)[6] between 1992 and 2004, see Stevens, 2007) shows that between 2006 and 2011 all racial/ethnic groups experienced an increase in the proportion of students obtaining at least five GCSE A*–C (including English and mathematics), the national benchmark of achievement in England at the end of compulsory schooling. Furthermore, some groups, like 'Chinese' (78.5%), 'Indian' (74.4%), 'Other Asian' (62.2%) and 'Bangladeshi' (59.7%) students now outperform the dominant 'White' (58%)

Table 10.2 Achievement of at least five GCSEs level A*–C (including mathematics and English) for pupils at the end of Key Stage 4 by ethnicity, 2006–2011

Year	2006–2007	2007–2008	2008–2009	2009–2010	2010–2011	Difference in p.p. 2006–2011	Rate of improvement 2006–2011
All	45.8 (600,659)	48.2 (598,102)	50.7 (578,840)	55.1 (578,059)	58.2 (566,932)	+12.4	0.27
White	46.1	48.4	50.7	55.1	58.0	+11.9	0.26
Black							
Caribbean	33.2	36.4	39.4	43.9	48.6	+15.4	0.46
African	40.8	43.9	48.4	53.3	57.9	+17.1	0.42
Other Black	33.5	39.6	41.2	46.2	52.6	+19.1	0.57
Asian							
Indian	62.0	65.1	67.0	71.6	74.4	+12.4	0.20
Pakistani	37.3	40.0	42.9	49.5	52.6	+15.3	0.41
Bangladeshi	41.4	45.0	48.3	54.2	59.7	+18.3	0.44
Other Asian	50.8	52.4	54.3	58.1	62.2	+11.4	0.22
Chinese	70.7	69.9	71.6	75.5	78.5	+7.8	0.11

Source: Department for Education (2012).

group. However, while 'Black African' students score on average at the same level to 'White' students, 'Pakistani' (52.6%), 'Black Other' (52.6%), and 'Black Caribbean' (48.6%) students still obtain, lower outcomes than the dominant 'White' group. In addition, Gypsy, Roma and Traveller children have the lowest SATs and GCSE scores of all ethnic groups (OFSTED, 2003; DCSF, 2007).

All BME groups, except for 'Other Asian' (+11.4 p.p.) and 'Chinese' (+7.8 p.p.) students experienced a greater increase in achievement (as measured by a difference in percentage points, p.p.) over this period than the dominant 'White' category (+11.9 p.p.); with 'Black Other' (+19.1 p.p.), 'Bangladeshi' (+18.3 p.p.) and 'Black African' (+17.1 p.p.) students experiencing the greatest increase between 2006 and 2011. Furthermore, while analysis between 1992 and 2004 shows that only 'Indian' and 'White' students enjoyed a consistent year-on-year improvement, more recent data shows that all BME groups experienced a consistent year-on-year improvement between 2006 and 2011 (except for 'Chinese' students in the period 2007–2008). Finally, the data shows that the gap in achievement between 'Black Caribbean' and 'White' has decreased between 2006 and 2011 (by 3.3 p.p. or from 12.9 to 9.6). In calculating the gap between the highest- ('Chinese') and lowest-achieving ('Black Caribbean') group, it appears that the gap has decreased even more between 2006 and 2011 (by 8 p.p. or from 37.2 to 29.2).

In employing a 'proportional model' to this data we gain additional information that throws a different light on the nature of inequality between racial/ethnic groups in terms of educational outcomes. In measuring the rate of change[7] for each racial/ethnic group between 2006 and 2011, we find that the educational outcomes of all BME students increased more quickly than those of 'White' (0.26) students, except for students of 'Chinese' (0.11), 'Indian' (0.20), and 'Other Asian' (0.22) backgrounds, groups who achieve on average higher results compared to 'White' students. However, there also appears considerable variance between 'Asian' minority groups as 'Pakistani' (0.41) and 'Bangladeshi' (0.44) students experienced a far greater acceleration in terms of educational outcomes compared to 'Indian' and 'Other Asian' students. While 'Black Caribbean' students obtain on average the lowest achievement scores, they experienced the highest acceleration in terms of achievement (0.46) between 2006 and 2011, together with 'Black Other' students (0.57). In measuring the proportional achievement gap[8] between the highest- ('Chinese') and the lowest-achieving group ('Black Caribbean') between 2006 and 2011, the results show that the achievement gap has narrowed over time (from 36% to 23%). Similarly, in comparing the proportional achievement gap between 'White' and 'Black Caribbean' students, the results suggest that the achievement gap has decreased from 16% to 8% between 2006 and 2011 (DfE, 2012).

These different methods are equally valid but offer different, often complementary kinds of information and stem from different assumptions: while the 'percentage point model' measures inequality by measuring the extent to which the present situation departs from a particular standard of equity (all minority groups should achieve at least equal outcomes to 'White' students), the proportional model looks at the starting point of the different racial/ethnic groups and defines equity in terms of the rate of improvement over time (Hammersley, 2001b).

While social class and gender differences cannot explain persistent inequalities in educational outcomes between ethnic groups (Gillborn and Mirza, 2000), analysis of the Youth Cohort Survey (YCS) suggests that social class differences in attainment are larger than ethnic differences, which are in turn larger than gender differences (Demack, Drew, and Grimsley, 2000). However, in a more recent analysis Strand (2011) shows that social class accounts for 80% of the differences between 'White' and 'Pakistani' students, and for 75% of the differences between 'Black African' and 'White' pupils, but not for the achievement gap between 'Black Caribbean' and 'White' students. A study focusing on a longer period of analysis and data from the British Household Panel Survey and the Labour Force Survey suggests that although social class differences in the UK have decreased since the beginning of the 20th century, they still remain substantial and larger than gender or ethnic differences (Heath, 2000).

More generally, data on educational achievement of ethnic minorities indicates complex interactions between race and ethnicity, gender, and social class or social deprivation. Data from 2011 (DfE 2012) shows that girls as a group outperform boys in all racial/ethnic groups, except for pupils of 'Gypsy/Roma' and 'Travellers of Irish heritage'. However, differences between girls and boys differ according to racial/ethnic background and are most pronounced amongst 'Black Caribbean', 'Black African', and 'Chinese' students and are generally higher with students from a more privileged social class background. Furthermore, the largest differences in achievement between various categories of social class or social deprivation can be observed with 'White British' and 'Irish' pupils and, to a lesser extent, with students of 'Indian' and mixed-race background (see also Kingdon and Cassen, 2010). Finally, differences between students from different social classes are the smallest with 'Chinese' pupils. The observation that race/ethnicity, social class, and gender interact in complex ways in shaping inequality is confirmed by some recent longitudinal studies. Hansen and Jones (2011) use data from the Millennium Cohort Study to investigate interactions between gender and racial/ethnic inequalities and find that gender gaps are largest for 'Black', 'Pakistani' and 'Bangladeshi' children and smallest for 'White' children (see also Kingdon and Cassen, 2010). Using data from the nationally representative Longitudinal Study of Young People in England (LSYPE), Strand shows that 'Black Caribbean' and 'White' boys do not differ significantly in their progress at age 7–11 (and at age 16), and that 'Black Caribbean' girls actually made more progress than 'White' girls. However, amongst pupils from more privileged social class background 'Black Caribbean' boys and girls both made less progress than their 'White' peers (Strand, 2010, 2012).

The PA tradition has contributed to our understanding of racial/ethnic inequalities in the English educational system by describing the differences in educational outcomes between racial/ethnic groups over time, the rate of improvement experienced by these groups, and the complex interactions between race and ethnicity, gender, and social class in developing outcomes. However, researchers have warned against simplistic interpretations of quantitative summary statistics which can stimulate the development of 'moral panics' (Connolly, 2006) or a 'discourse of despair' (Gillborn and Mirza, 2000) over the underachievement of particular groups and/or a tendency to label all students from specific BME groups as underachievers (Gillborn and Gipps, 1998; Troyna, 1984). Hence, Connolly (2006) employs and advocates the use of exploratory data analysis methods (such as box-plots and histograms) to explore and illustrate the considerable variations in achievement within racial/ethnic groups and overlap between them. Similarly, Gillborn and Mirza (2000), employing data collected from Local Educational Authorities (LEA), show that all major BME groups are the highest-achieving group in at least one LEA.

10.4.2   The racism and racial discrimination tradition

From the late 1970s and early 1980s onwards a substantial number of scholars conducted ethnographic case-studies in different educational settings to gain understanding of how micro-educational processes relate to the underachievement of Asian and (especially) African Caribbean students (Archer and Francis, 2005, 2007; Bhatti, 1999; Connolly, 1998; Crozier, 2005a; Driver, 1977; Fuller, 1984; Gillborn, 1990; Gillborn, 1995; Mac an Ghaill, 1988; Troyna, 1991a; Troyna, 1991b; Troyna and Siraj-Blatchford, 1993; Wright, 1988; Wright, 1992). These studies apply an interactionist approach, and focus mainly on the processes and effects of selection, the distribution of classroom resources and the nature of the knowledge and values taught and sanctioned in schools. The results suggest that students from BME backgrounds, especially African Caribbean students, are discriminated against in terms of set or stream allocation, and the distribution of educational resources. Furthermore, it was argued that the curriculum is biased against ethnic minority cultures, by attaching higher status to a white, middle-class culture and marginalizing expressions of ethnic minority cultures. Finally, teachers are perceived to hold negative stereotypes and low expectations of BME children, often leading to them being placed in lower sets and diverted into less academic subjects.

Implicit in research on race equalities has been the debate around where the 'blame' lies. As we indicated earlier, the focus was often on the child and family itself. Even where teachers' low expectations were cited, the argument followed that this led to processes of self-fulfilling prophecy which in turn affected the child's self-esteem, expectations, behavior, and eventual educational outcomes. Although in 2011 the discourse of low aspirations as a reason for BME as well as white working-class underachievement persists, anti-racist sociologists of education have argued forcefully against such views (Atkins, 2010; Gewirtz, 1991; Spohrer, 2011). Rather they have focused on white racist attitudes and practice, and institutional racism. Various scholars (Gillborn, 1990; Gillborn, 2002; Gillborn and Youdell, 2000) dismiss the existence of differences between social groups in terms of ability or intelligence, the alleged 'cultural deprivation' of working-class families, and the assumed superiority of the forms of knowledge promoted by schools. Influenced by Bourdieu and Bernstein, particularly in relation to social class issues, they argued that what counts as valuable capital in education in terms of knowledge, skills, and ability, is a matter of social definition, imposed by powerful groups in society.

Although a rich body of literature suggests that many classroom interactions are inherently racist or discriminate against BME students, the findings of these studies were forcibly criticized by Foster in the early 1990s. One point of criticism concerned Foster's (1990b) ethnographic case-study of an inner-city, multi-ethnic secondary comprehensive school with an explicit anti-racist and multicultural agenda. Although the author acknowledged that ethnic minority students were more likely to deviate from teachers' definition of the ideal student, he argued that there was little evidence in his and other studies to support the claim that teachers discriminate or stereotype ethnic minority students. The conflicting findings from this study and the studies cited throughout this paragraph and above, generated considerable criticism of studies that highlighted the existence and importance of experiences and structures of racism in education, particularly in relationship to the validity and generalizability of their findings, and related to this, the nature of the evidence provided (Connolly, 1992; Foster, 1990a; Foster, 1991; Foster, 1992a; Foster, 1992b; Foster, 1992c; Foster, 1993a; Foster, 1993b; Foster, Gomm, and Hammersley, 1996; Gillborn, 1995; Gomm, 1993; Gomm, 1995; Hammersley, 1992; Hammersley, 1993b; Hammersley, 2001a; Troyna, 1993; Troyna, 1995; Wright, 1990).

In part these criticisms were motivated by the concern of the so-called 'methodological purists' (Troyna, 1993) with the purpose of research. According to Foster et al., for example, educational inequality research should be 'to produce knowledge relevant to public debates, not to eradicate inequality' (Foster, Gomm, and Hammersley, 1996, p. 40). By contrast, some researchers adopted a 'partisan' (Troyna, 1995) or 'critical' approach (Gillborn, 1998b; Siraj-Blatchford and Troyna, 1993; Troyna, 1994), in which research is conceived as a tool to reveal and challenge fundamental injustices. According to the former, the partisan researchers' explicit anti-racist position makes them too readily accepting of evidence pointing to indirect discrimination and differential treatment. In order to avoid pitfalls associated with an instrumentalist, relativist, standpoint theory, or foundationalist epistemology, they argued that the research community should be guided by certain rules. These rules stipulate that the overriding concern for researchers should be the truth of claims, and not their political or practical implications. Arguments should be judged on their plausibility and credibility[9] in an open research community, in which researchers are willing to change their attitudes in the light of such evidence (Foster, 1993a; Foster, Gomm, and Hammersley, 1996; Hammersley, 1993a; Hammersley, 1995). While research should be value-relevant, which means that specific value judgments are used in choosing research topics and developing descriptions and explanations, research should also be value-neutral by restricting itself to making factual conclusions (Foster and Hammersley, 2000).

From these debates and perspectives within today's context we can see how ideas and understanding has shifted and moved on. Influenced by feminists and post-structural discourses, educational researchers working in the racism and racial discrimination (RDDS) tradition currently consider the notion of 'absolute truth' highly questionable (see for example, Harding, 1987) and it is argued that within the current socio-political and economic context the demand for 'impact' and 'useful' research, stands in marked contrast to ideals of free-floating and value-free 'knowledge'. That is not to say such debates are no longer occurring but rather that the emphasis of what is paramount has shifted. Differences in how researchers define 'racism' may in part explain why some researchers claimed to find evidence of racism while others did not. For example, while Foster (1990b) defines racism mainly in terms of specific teacher practices which are legitimized by notions of cultural or biological inferiority, Bhatti (1999), Bhopal (2011), Connolly (1998), Crozier et al. (2009), Gillborn (1990), Mac An Ghaill (1999) and others define racism in terms of white teachers' intended or unintended attitudes and behaviors. Furthermore, researchers emphasized also the importance of 'institutional racism', or specific laws, regulations, and structural workings of institutions and society as well as being interconnected with individual attitudes and behavior (Gillborn, 1990, 2002; Gillborn and Youdell, 2000; Richardson, 2005; Stone, 2004; Tomlinson, 2008).

Whilst most of the RRDS tradition has focused on schools and teachers' practice, Troyna and Hatcher (1992) researched racism in children's lives through a study of mainly white children's views and attitudes. Although with the emergence of critical whiteness studies (see below) the research agenda is changing, this is one of few studies in the field of education in England that focuses on white attitudes and children's in particular. It thus makes an important contribution challenging the myth that mere association between white and black children, related to naive interpretations of Allport's (1954) contact hypothesis (see also Connolly, 2000), will lead to harmonious inter-ethnic group relations, and suggesting the need for schools to take a pro-active anti-racist stance, especially in predominantly white schools. Moreover, they argue that a school policy to deal with racist incidents in school has to be accompanied by school policies dealing with issues of race within the curriculum. The other exception to researching white settings and white attitudes is Gaine's work (1987, 1995, 2005) which looks at all-/predominantly white schools and also teacher education. As well as analyzing a range of issues, his work is innovative in that he develops anti-racist change strategies for educators.

Some researchers within the RRDS tradition looked more at successes in relation to multiculturalism and or anti-racist teaching practice. Much of this work has focused on language and diversity in the primary school (e.g. Conteh, 2003; Gregory and Williams, 2000), evaluations of broader curriculum areas (Grudgeon and Woods, 1990), and teachers' anti-racist practices (Epstein, 1993; Klein, 1993). There have also been various publications presenting ideas and strategies for teaching in primary and secondary schools and teacher education (Cole et al., 1997; Dadzie, 2000; King and Reiss, 1993; Multiverse 2006–2010: www.multiverse.ac.uk). Others have researched some of the consequences of racism other than (although related to) underachievement. This includes for example work on school exclusions (Wright et al., 2000; Wright et al., 2005; Parsons, 2008, 2009). More recently some sociologists of education have taken the focus of successful outcomes for BME students, in part to challenge the socio-cultural pathologization of black young people (Rhamie, 2007; Rhamie and Hallam, 2002).

The emergence of discourses of identities (and post-structural feminism as part of that) within the sociology of education, has stimulated researchers in the RDDS tradition to investigate the (re)construction of young BME students' collective ethnic and gender identities and its relationship to racism and educational achievement. For example, Archer (2003) and Shain (2011) have focused on South Asian masculinity and schooling. Their work, written at a time of a rise in islamophobia, referred to earlier and moral panics around 'Islamism' and Asian gangs (Alexander, 2000) has made an important contribution to counter pervasive stereotypes arising from this context. It has also occurred however alongside a certain preoccupation with boys' (irrespective of ethnicity) education and their apparent underachievement. Work on Black Caribbean boys such as Sewell's research is such an example. Whilst this work has been important in foregrounding the issue of black students' underachievement, the focus on boys in particular masks the same or similar issues facing black girls, frequently rendering them invisible (Mirza, 2009). Further it has been argued that Sewell's (1997) work reinforces the pathologization of the black male as recalcitrant, disaffected, and a product of the feckless family. For Sewell the problem lies with the 'culture' of African Caribbean families. Critics of post-structuralist and by implication identity studies, have argued that structural analysis is eschewed and in this case structural racism and racist attitudes and practice. The focus has thus returned to, or perhaps never deviated from, the individual. Nevertheless, foregrounding identities has made a range of important contributions including the challenge to essentialist ideas of identity as homogeneous, simplistic dualist criticisms, as well as the challenge to damaging stereotypes already indicated.

Within the race and ethnicity identities discourse there has also been some limited research on Asian girls (Basit, 1995, 1997; Shain, 2003) which challenges the stereotype of the passive, conforming Asian girl. Basit's work in particular presents a more holistic picture of a range of Muslim girls' educational desires and expectations, and contextualizes a range of factors that impact on their outcomes. Studies of African Caribbean girls (Mirza, 1992, 2009; Rollock, 2007; Wright, 2010) attempt to celebrate their identities positively whilst also pointing to discriminating experiences and constraints on their life chances.

The development of 'critical race theory' (CRT), 'critical race feminism' (CRF) and 'critical whiteness studies' (CWS) aims to foreground the focus on race and racism. This work originated in the USA but over the past decade has been developed in the UK, largely by the work of Gillborn (2006, 2008) and Preston (2007). David Gillborn (1996, 2005) and some of the non-British research contributions published in the British-based journal *Race, Ethnicity and Education* (Hatchell, 2004; Leonardo, 2002; Levine-Rasky, 2000; Raby, 2004) have also helped develop critical whiteness studies (CWS) within the British educational research context. 'Whiteness' is perceived as a racial discourse that attempts to 'homogenize diverse white ethnics into a single category (much like it attempts with people of color) for purposes of racial domination' (Leonardo, 2002, p. 32). The primary aim of CWS is to 'unveil the rhetorical, political, cultural, and social mechanisms through which 'whiteness' is both invented and used to mask its power and privilege' (Giroux, 1997, p. 102). In his 2008 book Gillborn employs CWS as a conceptual tool to develop an analysis of critical race theory. Gillborn (2008) analyzes different kinds of empirical data (including official statistics, research and policy reports, and messages conveyed through radio, TV, and newspapers) to unveil and criticize the numerous, usually subtle, strategies employed by (usually white) individuals to reproduce and legitimize existing black–white racial inequalities.

Critics of CRT such as Cole (2009) question the tenuous links with structural and institutional factors and also criticize CRT for an obfuscation of social class dimensions. In response to this, theorists of intersectionalities, through a consideration of the interlinking of social and cultural identities such as class, gender, as well as race and ethnicity, (Crenshaw 1995) have attempted to address these criticisms; in the UK within education this can be mainly attributed to the emerging work of Safia Mirza (2009) and Bhopal and Preston (2011). However, research employing an intersectional approach to develop our understanding of in/equalities within an education context still remains to be undertaken.

Within the movement of anti-racism and the RRDS research tradition there have been a range of criticisms. In the 1980s and early 1990s differences between multicultural education and anti-racist education raged. More specifically, the anti-racists argued that multiculturalism obfuscated the main issues of tackling racism itself and provided a 'softer' option for practitioners (Crozier, 1989; Troyna, 1993). Whilst these differences remain, as already indicated, the research terrain has shifted. The 'multicultural project' as it has been called, has come under attack from the government and media particularly in the light of the Bradford, Oldham, and Rochdale riots (in 2001) and terrorist attacks by British-born Muslims in 2005. However, this particular criticism is more likely to unite the multiculturalists and anti-racists as it is seen to come from the assimilationist lobby (Race, 2011).

Criticisms of anti-racism have tended to come more from sociologists outside of education. Modood (2005) for example has argued that addressing 'culture' is particularly and more relevant for South Asian students. His argument has been criticized however for allegedly polarizing oppression, suggesting that Black Caribbean young people are accepted by the white majority because of the popularity of hip hop and such cultural manifestations (see also below) and have become more integrated into British society. From a broader perspective Gilroy (1992) has taken exception to anti-racism or certain manifestations of this, arguing that tackling racism is marginalized and frequently compartmentalized. As he has argued: 'race' and racism are a central part, intertwined with class and gender, of structural oppression:

> [race and racism are not] fringe questions but [are a] volatile presence at the very centre of British politics actively shaping and determining the history not simply of blacks but of this country as a whole. (Gilroy, 1992, pp. 233–244)

This marginalization frequently leads to the 'bad apple' syndrome and points to the failure to tackle racism effectively (Crozier, 2011).

Other criticisms of earlier research (within our time frame) in the RRDS tradition have been concerned that focusing on BME people constructs this group as homogeneous and powerless victims of society (Gillborn, 1997). Rather, some researchers describe how specific ethnic or racial minority groups draw on their own cultural heritage and notions of social class, gender, and sexuality to actively create a culture of resistance to school, while remaining committed to the value of education itself and the importance of obtaining educational qualifications (Connolly, 1998; Epstein, 1998; Fuller, 1984; Furlong, 1977; Mac an Ghaill, 1988, 1994; Mirza, 1992; Sewell, 1997, 1998; Youdell, 2003).

For example, in his case-study in 'Connolly College', a multi-ethnic co-educational sixth-form college providing 16-plus education, Mac an Ghaill (1988) described a group of African Caribbean girls (who he calls 'The Black

Sisters'), who valued obtaining academic qualifications and could be perceived as pro-education, but at the same time rejected a racist curriculum and were generally anti-school. The girls responded to perceived racism and discrimination through 'resistance within accommodation' or by adopting a highly instrumental view on teachers and teaching processes, in which (culturally biased) 'knowledge is not valued for its own sake, but as a means to an end, that of getting qualifications' (Mac an Ghaill, 1988, p. 35). Shain's (2003) study of Asian school girls (see also below) identifies similar themes within a more contemporary context whilst at the same time challenging the stereotype of the passive South Asian girl.

Towards the end of the period of our review in particular, researchers are seen to consider the consequences of increasing cultural and economic globalization, technological developments, communication, and international political relations on the construction of identities and multiple, decentered forms of racism in society. Such a view perceives racism as more heterogeneous, changing, and often conflicting in nature, reflecting the complex interplay of gender, sexuality, social class, and ethnicity. It supports the construction of a wider research agenda to include (in the British context) racism and discrimination towards Irish and other 'White' ethnic groups (such as Gypsy, Roma and Traveller people in England, Myers and Bhopal, 2009), Eastern Europeans (Sivanandan, 2002), as well as islamophobia and the stereotyping and treatment of new migrants, refugees, and asylum seekers (Brah, Hickman, and Mac an Ghaill, 1999; Mac an Ghaill, 1999; Mac an Ghaill, 2002; McIntosh, Duncan, and Douglas, 2004). Finally, in relation to the impact of such demographic changes and concerns about national identity, there are studies that have taken up the theme of the government's community cohesion and citizenship issues. Osler and Starkey (2005) are two proponents of such work on the development of a new vision of citizenship, and the importance for educators to understand the links between the dynamics of globalization and the everyday realities of the classroom.

The RRDS tradition is by far the most developed research tradition in the UK that focuses on the relationship between race and ethnicity and educational inequality in education. There has been a wealth of case-studies that explored how minority students experience schooling and how particular institutional processes influence the educational outcomes of these students, although since the 2000s these studies are less prevalent. While these studies provide evidence that ethnic minorities experience (institutional) racism and discrimination in schools, they are less clear on how strongly teachers' particular expectations, attitudes, and practices, and the school curriculum and structural organization impact on minority students' educational outcomes and wider benefits, related to their self-esteem, social integration, and happiness. These studies are exceptionally rich in illuminating the subtle and complex processes through which racism operates in school settings. However, there are also strong appeals to broaden the focus of research.

10.4.3 The school effectiveness and school inclusion research tradition

'School effectiveness and school inclusion' research (SESI) constitutes another main body of educational research that aims to analyze, usually by means of large quantitative samples and longitudinal, multi-level analysis techniques, the relationships between internal school processes and the production of educational outcomes in general ('overall effectiveness'), and to a lesser extent, between ethnic, social class, gender and ability groups ('differential effectiveness') (Gillborn and Gipps, 1996). This body of literature arose in large part as a reaction against findings of large-scale US studies, most notably the work of James Coleman (Coleman, 1966), which suggested that schools played little role in producing differential achievement among social groups. In addition, the availability of better (longitudinal and multi-level) data, better computing power, and new statistical techniques, in particular, multi-level modeling, allowed for more sophisticated, quantitative data analysis.

However, SESI researchers tend to put much more emphasis on the importance of family processes and characteristics compared to RRDS researchers in explaining differences in achievement, but also stress that 'schools make a difference' (Foster, Gomm, and Hammersley, 1996; Mortimore, 1997; Sammons, 1989). Hence, while researchers in the SESI tradition are interested in the effect of school processes and characteristics relative to social background and family characteristics (which are often included in statistical models as 'controls'), RRDS researchers restrict their focus mainly on school processes.

A first way through which SESI researchers investigate the relationship between race and ethnicity and educational inequality is by conducting longitudinal analysis on the absolute outcomes and progress over age made by ethnic/racial minority students in education, controlling for relevant background characteristics. The difference between SESI researchers and researchers working in the PA tradition is that SESI researchers usually follow the same group of students over time, and consider both differences in absolute outcomes and relative progress as measures of inequality (instead of preferring one over the other).

In a recent analysis of data from students' attainment at the end of primary school (KS2: age 11) and the end of secondary school (KS4: age 16), gathered through the nationally representative LSYPE dataset,[10] Strand (2007, 2008) finds that students of mixed heritage seem to have similar attainment at KS2 and make similar progress over time compared to White British students. Similarly, Indian students do not seem to differ significantly from White British at KS2, but they make more progress and have pulled substantially ahead by KS4. Although Black African, Bangladeshi and Pakistani students are well behind their White British peers at KS2, they make more progress during secondary school and while the former two groups catch up with white students by KS4, Pakistani students almost close the gap by the end of KS4. However, Black Caribbean students remain a group of concern as they start well behind White British students at KS2 and make the same progress during secondary school, and, as a result remain substantially behind White British students at KS4.

The same analysis shows that after controlling for socio-economic variables, the groups with the poorest progress are: (1) White British boys in general but particularly from low socio-economic homes, (2) White British girls from low socio-economic homes, and (3) Black Caribbean, Black African, and Bangladeshi boys from high socio-economic homes. Multivariate analysis shows that four factors in particular are strongly related to attainment and progress: (1) student's educational aspirations, (2) parents' educational aspirations for their child, (3) student's academic self-concept, and (4) frequency of completing homework. However, the low attainment and poor progress of Black Caribbean students cannot be accounted for by social class or other family, school, neighborhood, and motivational variables (Strand 2010; Strand 2011; Strand and Winston 2008). In a further analysis of the LSYPE data, Strand (2012) confirms and builds on earlier findings from ethnographic case-study research in England (Gillborn and Youdell, 2000, see below) by showing that Black Caribbean students are consistently under-represented relative to white students in entry to higher (status) mathematics and science tiers, which cannot be explained by these students' prior attainment, socio-economic status, and a broad range of motivational, family, and neighborhood characteristics. The author suggests that teachers' lower expectations of Black Caribbean students, particularly related to their behavior (see also Mortimore, 1988 and Hurrell, 1995 below), might explain why these students are less likely to be placed in higher status tiers, which in interaction with anti-school peer group cultures, can explain the lower achievement and progress made by these students in secondary education.

These findings confirm earlier longitudinal studies in England based on different datasets, such as Sammons's (1995) study based on the Junior School Project (JSP)[11] and a study based on the Student Level Annual School Census (PLASC) dataset (Wilson, Burgess, and Briggs, 2005).[12] While most BME groups underachieve compared to White British students at the start and end of primary, most of them progress on average faster than their White British peers and eventually, at the end of secondary education, obtain educational qualifications that are higher, at the same level, or not much lower compared to White British students (see also: Haque and Bell, 2001; Mortimore et al. 1988; Strand, 1999). The only exception to this are students of Black Caribbean background, who as a group seem to obtain lower educational outcomes compared to White British students.

These findings are important as they seem to suggest that racial/ethnic groups (except for students of Gypsy, Roma or Traveller background) make considerable progress in secondary education and, more generally, that racial/ethnic inequalities in education do not appear to widen in secondary education. Furthermore, and in line with the PA tradition, these studies also emphasize the importance of social class over race and ethnicity: while racial/ethnic differences (except for the achievement gap between Black Caribbean and white students) seem to reduce, disappear, or become reversed as students progress through secondary education, social class differences in educational achievement become more apparent in secondary education. Reflecting on their own analysis, Wilson et al. argue that 'the group with the most problematic path through secondary schooling is disadvantaged white boys' (Wilson, Burgess, and Briggs, 2005, p. 3). However, at the same time the authors, like Strand (Strand, 2007; Strand, 2008), stress that in terms of levels achievement, the lower-than-average achievement outcomes of certain BME groups, particularly Black Caribbean should remain a major issue for policy concern. In relationship to the latter finding, Strand's recent analysis on the LSYPE data (Strand, 2012) suggests (albeit indirectly) that teachers' expectations do play a key role in directing Black Caribbean students to lower-status tiers, which in turn affects their educational outcomes. In so doing, this quantitative study builds on a rich tradition of ethnographic case-study research in England on racism and discrimination in schools.

A second way through which SESI researchers have assessed the relationship between race and ethnicity and educational inequality, is by testing whether schools are more or less effective for particular minority groups. A growing body of SESI research tends to suggest that the effects of schools do not vary across ethnic groups. In other words, primary or secondary schools that appear most effective for one (racial/ethnic) group of students are, generally speaking, equally effective for other groups (Jesson and Gray, 1991; Mortimore, 1997; Mortimore et al., 1988; Sammons, 1999; Smith and Tomlinson, 1989; Strand, 1999; Thomas et al., 1988). While these findings do not deny that processes operating within schools keep some BME groups from achieving higher educational outcomes, they imply that such processes would need to be operating consistently across all schools (Strand, 1999). In a recent study, based on analysis of an entire national cohort of students in England (PLASC dataset) between age 7 in 2000 and age 11 in 2004, Strand (2010) finds no evidence that the gap between 'Black Caribbean' and 'White' students results from 'Black Caribbean' students attending less effective schools. There is also no evidence of differential effectiveness in relation to ethnic group, in that schools that were strong in facilitating the progress of White British students were equally strong in facilitating the progress of Black Caribbean students. The author suggests that the poor progress of Black Caribbean students 'reflects a systemic issue rather than the influence of a small number of 'low quality' schools' (Strand, 2010, p. 289).

Finally, earlier work in the SESI tradition explores the relationship between race and ethnicity and educational inequality by investigating how particular processes in school impact on the educational outcomes of BME students. However, while such research complements and strongly overlaps with the RRDS tradition, SESI researchers do not seem to consider the analysis of internal school processes related to discrimination and racism as their main area of research.

Using the JSP dataset Mortimore et al. (1988) found no relationship between teachers' ratings of students' ability and children's ethnic background, once account had been taken for other background characteristics and attainment. They conclude that teachers' expectations of students (irrespective of students' ethnic background) appear to be tied to specific knowledge of previous attainment and performance in the classroom. Furthermore, teachers were found to have more individual contact with African Caribbean students than with other students, and there was no difference between groups in the amount of teacher contact related to work discussion, supervision, or feedback. At the same time the data shows that teachers perceived African Caribbean students as more disruptive and offered such students more neutral and negative feedback on their behavior compared to other students. However, as African Caribbean students experienced greater problems in reading, and teachers offered these students more reading time, the authors conclude that 'the data supply no evidence to support the view that teachers were withholding attention from any ethnic group. In fact they appeared to go out of their way to attend to black and ethnic minority students' (Mortimore et al., 1988, p. 169). At the same time, these authors recognize the limitations of their data as 'expectations can be transmitted in subtle ways and it is possible that it was precisely through such differences in teacher attention that teachers were signalling differential expectations' (Mortimore et al., 1988, p. 169).

Smith and Tomlinson (1989) collected data from 3100 children (from the age of 11 to 16) and their parents over 20 purposively selected multi-ethnic schools. Their data suggests that minority students seem to have more enthusiasm or positive feelings about school, appear to perceive fewer difficulties than 'White' children and (in the case of 'West Indian' or 'African-Caribbean' students) attend school better than 'White' students. Furthermore, having experienced 'racial hostility at school' does not seem to influence the educational outcomes of minority students and 'just one per cent of the parents mentioned racial attacks, or that black and white children don't get on' (Smith and Tomlinson, 1989, p. 305). Only eight out of 2075 parents interviewed mentioned racial prejudice among teachers, and the level of satisfaction with the school expressed by parents does not appear to differ between ethnic groups. Somewhat in line with Mortimore et al. (1988, p. 169) this study finds that while teachers are more likely to blame 'West Indian' students for their behavior than they blame 'White' or other ethnic groups, 'West Indian' students are also more likely to receive praise from their teachers compared to other minority groups and 'White' students.

The only study in the SESI tradition that has been specifically designed to test some of the underlying processes which emerged from the RRDS tradition more directly in an English educational context concerns Hurrell's quantitative study (Hurrell, 1995). In this study, Hurrell uses survey data gathered from 974 students and their teachers in four comprehensive schools in England, and data from systematic observation, the latter being employed to measure 'observed negative reactions from teacher to student' (Hurrell, 1995). In contrast to Mortimore et al. (Mortimore et al., 1988), her findings suggest that teachers did not treat black students differently, even if they were perceived as more disruptive. The author explains this by pointing to Hargreaves's suggestion that teachers might employ a strategy of 'avoidance of provocation': 'hence while they stereotype black children as disruptive, they might decide not to respond to their behavior' (Hurrell, 1995, p. 67).

In sum, compared to the RDDS tradition, SESI research paints a somewhat more positive picture of the relationship between race and ethnicity and educational inequality, and especially the role of secondary education institutions in reproducing racial/ethnic inequalities. Such research tends to suggest that school processes are not discriminating against BME students and that most of these students, despite their experienced disadvantages, manage to progress more quickly than 'White' students and obtain educational outcomes that are, for most minority groups, equal or even better than those obtained by 'White' students.

However, these findings (and SESI in general) have been criticized on the basis of methodological problems. For example, Gillborn and Gipps (1996) argue that Sammons's (1995) findings should be treated with caution as the final sample size was less than half the original size due to non-response and attrition. Furthermore, they argue that her analysis artificially boosts the outcomes in favor of racial/ethnic minorities, as the employed sample does not include students who were not entered for GCSE exams, a group in which ethnic minority students are over-represented.[13] Another research evaluation (Gillborn and Drew, 1992) criticizes Smith and Tomlinson's (1989) study for using purposive sampling (which highlights more the range of extremes, rather than describing the relative effects of most of the schools), for lumping together different racial/ethnic categories to satisfy statistical analysis requirements (for example by combining 'Afro-Caribbean' and 'mixed-other' students) and for considering parents' perceptions of racism in school as valid measures of students' experienced racism (Gillborn and Drew, 1992).[14]

More generally, SESI research has been criticized for neglecting or providing poor measures of racism and discrimination in schools and for failing to address the effect of student recruitment processes on the educational outcomes of minority students (Figueroa, 1992a; Figueroa, 1992b; Gillborn and Gipps, 1996; Hatcher, 1998). Finally, critics downplay the importance of the SESI tradition by referring to the relatively small contribution of school-effects[15] compared to family background in explaining differences in achievement (Foster, Gomm, and Hammersley, 1996; Gillborn and Drew, 1992; Hatcher, 1998).

However, in response to such criticism, advocates of SESI argue that 'its significance is considerable in a system where even minor differences may influence significantly the life chances of students' (Mortimore, 1997, p. 479). Furthermore, researchers in this area point to the equally modest contribution (3–10%) of measures of family socio-economic status or individual student's level of social deprivation in explaining variance in students' attainment (Sammons, 2006). Finally, while it is accepted that the SESI tradition can benefit from considering the findings of more critical, qualitative studies, the RDDS tradition often fails to address differential school effectiveness and inequality directly (Thomas, 2000) and can equally benefit from considering and developing SESI research on specific school processes (see for example Hurrell, 1995).

10.4.4　The culture and educational outcomes tradition

Since the development of the new sociology of education movement, educational sociologists have focused their attention increasingly more on school processes and less on cultural characteristics of the family and BME communities in explaining the relationship between race and ethnicity and educational inequality. However, one area that attracted considerable interest from sociologists over the last 25 years focuses on the importance of religion and culture in the schooling of 'South Asian' children and to a lesser extent Muslims including those from Somalia. This 'culture and educational outcomes (CEO) tradition' is different to the old sociology of education in that cultural differences are not necessarily perceived as 'deficient' and are linked to larger social processes of immigration, settlement and reception experiences, and social class.

Some authors suggest that specific religious obligations, especially those related to Islam, act as an obstacle for girls in achieving highly in education. It is argued that Muslim parents attach higher priority to considerations of religious observance than the education of their daughters (Afshah, 1989; Bhopal, 1997; Bhopal, 1998). More recently, Abbas explores in a series of publications how ethnicity (religiosity), social class, and gender relate to 'South Asian' students' educational opportunities and experiences (Abbas, 2002a; Abbas, 2002b; Abbas, 2003; see also Anwar, 1998). Although 'South Asian' parents appear to value educational achievement, 'South Asian' Muslim ('Pakistani' and 'Bangladeshi') girls perceive specific religious and traditional values as a barrier to educational and occupational success. These specific values are believed to restrict interaction with men and non-Muslims and emphasize patriarchal values or the domestic role for women. In contrast, 'South Asian' Sikhs and Hindus, irrespective of their social class position, appear to put less importance on religion and traditional values, and are less likely to adopt specific strategies that restrict acculturation in British society (Abbas, 2002a, 2003).

However, a growing body of literature criticizes the view of Muslim women as passive victims of a situation that positions them between two conflicting cultures in which they have to adopt either the role of a 'traditional woman' or an 'educated woman' (Ahmad, 2001; Basit, 1997; Knott and Kokher, 1993; Shain, 2000; Shain, 2003; Siddiqui, 1991).

First, it is argued that such a view ignores the variability in attitudes and practices within Muslim populations. Second, research suggests that Muslim parents have generally very high educational aspirations of both their daughters and sons.[16] Third, Muslim parents' attitudes to education rarely appear to be clear cut, but are more likely to be ambivalent. On the one hand, Muslim parents often fear that continued investment in education can postpone marriage to a point where it is difficult to find an appropriate partner of the same social status for their daughter. Furthermore, Muslim parents often have negative views on 'British' or 'Western' culture, which is considered too individualistic, liberal, and characterized by a lack of respect towards family and elder people. These stereotypes make those parents fearful that their daughters' involvement in such a culture will loosen their morality or 'Anglicize' them, which can harm their daughter's and their family's status in the community. On the other hand, Muslim parents perceive education also as a valuable economic investment that offers protection and social status to their children and their family, and offers their sons and daughters an opportunity to marry people from the same (high) social status. Finally, these studies emphasize the importance of agency, in that Muslim girls employ various strategies to negotiate different expectations and construct and reconstruct complex strong identities that combine an adherence to traditional and modern values, and educational goals (Ahmad, 2001; Basit, 1997; Crozier, 2004, 2006, 2009; Knott and Kokher, 1993; Shain, 2000; Shain, 2003; Siddiqui, 1991).

Furthermore, it is important to consider other social background characteristics in assessing the relationship between religion and academic success. Haque (2000) argues that the latter relationship can be influenced by the level of education of the immigrants, their area of emigration (rural versus urban), their family size, and their timing of immigration. Untangling the effects of these interacting variables appears even more important in a British context that witnesses an increase of anti-Muslim sentiments and stereotypes (Brah, Hickman, and Mac an Ghaill, 1999; Modood, 1989; Werbner, 2000). Related to the latter, Abbas (2003) suggests the importance of different reception experiences between 'South Asian' Muslims and non-Muslims in adopting specific acculturation strategies.

The focus of the CEO tradition on the development of ethnic minority cultural practices and their impact on children's educational outcomes balances somewhat the current, dominant focus in British sociology of education on school processes. However, this research tradition is relatively small compared to the other traditions, and restricts its focus to the experiences of girls and particular ethnic groups ('Sikh', 'Hindu', and especially 'Muslim' students). As a result, research in this area could further develop by focusing on the experiences of both girls and boys, and different BME groups, without essentializing culture, family, and/or 'ethnicity' as a deterministic force (Steinberg, 1981).

An example of research that explores the broader boundaries of the CEO tradition concerns the work of Levinson (2000; 2007) and Levinson and Sparkes (2003; 2005) on the interface between Gypsy/Romani ('Traveller') culture and the educational system in South West England (see also Liegeois, 1986; Liegeois, 1987; Liegeois, 1997; Okely, 1983; Smith, 1997). Relying on ethnographic observations in schools and Gypsy sites and qualitative interviews from Gypsy students and their families and teachers over a period of more than three years, the authors show how Gypsy students' disengagement with (especially) secondary school relates to the (re)construction of a Gypsy lifestyle and related identity that often is at odds with and in opposition to the cultural capital valued in school or, more generally '*Gadjo*' (or non-Gypsy) society. For example, while the school values literacy, Gypsy culture regards *basic* literacy as functional but not essential in pursuing economic goals and potentially harmful in maintaining a Gypsy lifestyle and identity. Hence, illiteracy is more than an expression of cultural autonomy or protection against assimilation, it 'becomes an ethnic identifier, a badge of honor, and far from a deficiency it is almost an accomplishment' (Levinson, 2007, p. 33).

Furthermore, the differences between social space as prescribed by a nomadic Gypsy lifestyle (which is characterized by relative fluidity and freedom) and the failure of a (more restrictive) school system to consider this can result in conflicts and disengagement of young Gypsy students from school (Levinson and Sparkes, 2005). Similarly, and of particular importance to Gypsy boys is the construction of a Gypsy male identity that values the ability of acute bargaining skills (which in turn relates to business knowledge and charm, memory, and psychological astuteness), fighting (or being tough and protecting or retaliating against threats to family or personal status), and sexual prowess (Levinson and Sparkes, 2003). While such skills were valued within the Gypsy community and perceived as 'the Gypsy (male) way of doing things'; they were devalued and considered deviant by the school (ibid.). Building on this research, and much more in line with the RRDS tradition, other scholars stress much more the prejudiced attitudes of teachers and discriminatory school processes in explaining the lower educational outcomes of students of Gypsy, Roma and Traveller background (Bhopal, 2011, Bhopal and Meyers, 2009; Derrington and

Kendall, 2004). In so doing, these researchers warn against the dangers of essentializing 'Gypsy culture' as a deterministic force, as it leads to analytic (cultural) reductionism and fosters the prevalence of stereotypes towards Gypsies.

Another recent and innovative contribution that explores the broader boundaries of the CEO research tradition concerns the work of Archer and Francis (2005a; 2005b). Based on interviews from 48 Chinese girls, 32 Chinese boys, their parents, teachers, and peers from other racial/ethnic groups (aged 14–16), they find that Chinese students construct themselves as valuing education highly and often derive self-esteem from this in relationship to their learning and classroom conduct. Chinese students were more likely to select mathematics and science as their favorite subjects and less likely to select gender-stereotypical subjects (such as PE for boys and drama for girls). This discourse of 'Chinese value of education' seems to be employed as a tool by Chinese students and their parents to construct a British Chinese identity and production of 'Chineseness'. Furthermore, the emphasis on such values might arguably help to explain why this group achieves such high outcomes in education compared to other BME students and 'White' students (see Section 10.3.2). Furthermore, these researchers find that English educators associate Chinese students' success in education to 'pathological' values that put too much emphasis on conformity, passivity, and pressure to achieve. Hence, although the particular 'cultural currency' of Chinese students helps them to achieve (as a group) in the English educational system and develop a strong (ethnic) identity, such currency appears to be devalued by English educators. Such research is innovative in that it focuses on particular cultural values and practices of an under-studied minority group and how this impacts on the educational experiences and outcomes of boys and girls. In so doing, this research also links and brings together different research traditions (CEO, RRDS, and PA tradition).

10.4.5   Educational markets and educational outcomes tradition

A final, more recent research tradition investigates the relationship between race, ethnicity, and educational inequality by critically assessing the consequences of the neoliberal policies instigated originally by the 1988 Education Reform Act in England (see Section 10.2.1 above), on the educational experiences of ethnic minority groups. Within this system, parental choice and a thorough inspection system (Ofsted) are seen to guarantee that the provision of education reaches the expected high standards, regardless of social class, gender, and ethnicity or race; this system put under surveillance schools, teachers, and in fact the parents themselves (Crozier, 1998; David, 1993). Indeed parental choice remains a key element in ensuring the success of school competitiveness. However, as much research has shown, the nature and notion of 'choice' is neither straightforward nor based on equality of opportunity (David et al., 1994; Gewirtz et al., 1995; Reay and Ball, 1998). Parental choice has done little if anything to improve poorly performing schools and the attainment of BME students, in spite of the effort and commitment of black parents (Crozier, 1996, 2005b; Reay, 1998). In fact as these and other studies have shown (Cork, 2005; Crozier and Davies, 2007; Bhatti, 1999; Vincent, 1996), schools frequently excluded parents as well as marginalizing their children. By contrast, a recent study of white middle-class parents (Reay et al., 2011) who are committed to state education sets into relief the experiences of many BME parents. The white parents because of their privileged social, educational, and economic positions, relatively effortlessly ensure that their children succeed, in spite of attending underperforming schools. Whilst even with the considerable efforts made by black parents, their children tend to fail (Cork, 2005; Wright et al., 2000).

Rather than improve standards, the competitiveness between schools has apparently exacerbated inequalities for BME students, as shown by Gillborn and Youdell's study of two English secondary schools (Gillborn and Youdell, 2000; Youdell, 2004). They illustrate how this five 'A*–C-economy' informs the nature of the specific school organization and processes. Schools are stimulated to organize their system in order to maximize the number of students obtaining five GCSE level A*–C grades. As a result, some schools allocate valuable and scarce educational resources disproportionately to students who are most likely to benefit from such support in obtaining A*–C grades. However, students that are considered unlikely to reach this specific benchmark are left with inferior resources and in effect are discriminated against, a process referred to as 'educational triage'. Central to these selection mechanisms is the idea that students' success is largely determined by measured, innate ability, which is in turn employed as a criterion for allocating students to different educational careers (through subject 'choice', set – 'choice' and examination-tier entry). Gillborn and Youdell argue that selecting by ability disadvantages BME students, and reinforces old and scientifically incorrect notions of intelligence, race, and social class.

Disproportionate school exclusions of BME students, especially boys, is shown to be an enduring problem (see for example Wright et al., 2000; Parsons, 2008, 2009). The increase of BME school exclusions following the introduction of the 1988 Education Reform Act attracted considerable interest from educational sociologists studying racial and ethnic inequalities. In this body of literature, exclusions are usually defined as 'the means by which the headteacher of a school can prevent a child or young person from attending the school, either for a fixed period (not exceeding fifteen days in a single school term) or permanently' (Blyth and Milner, 1996, p. 3).

While the exclusion data (see Table 10.3) can be analyzed in a similar way to the achievement data as discused above in the PA tradition, explanations of why schools exclude (BME) students is framed much more from an EMEO perspective. The increased competition between schools for students and higher GCSE outcomes and their related position and public image as represented

Table 10.3   Permanent exclusions of students in primary and secondary schools in England by ethnicity, 1995–2010

	1995–1996	1996–1997	1997–1998	1998–1999	1999–2000	2000–2001	2001–2002	2002–2003	2003–2004	2004–2005	2005–2006	2006–2007	2007–2008	2008–2009	2009–2010
All	12,232	12,461	12,298	10,424	8,314	9,122	9,517	9,270	9,860	9,380	9130	8680	8110	6530	5710
(%)*	(0.19)	(0.19)	(0.19)	(0.16)	(0.13)	(0.13)	(0.14)	(0.13)	(0.14)	(0.14)	(0.14)	(0.13)	(0.12)	(0.10)	(0.09)
White	10,096	10,404	10,303	8801	6890	7574	7808	6880	7860	7470	6990	6760	6350	5000	4320
	(0.18)	(0.18)	(0.18)	(0.15)	(0.12)	(0.13)	(0.14)	(0.12)	(0.14)	(0.13)	(0.13)	(0.12)	(0.12)	(0.09)	(0.08)
Black															
Caribbean	867	756	765	589	455	385	399	360	400	380	380	360	330	270	310
	(0.92)	(0.76)	(0.77)	(0.60)	(0.46)	(0.38)	(0.42)	(0.37)	(0.41)	(0.39)	(0.41)	(0.38)	(0.36)	(0.30)	(0.34)
African	216	193	203	157	145	156	159	130	200	190	230	210	270	190	210
	(0.35)	(0.30)	(0.30)	(0.21)	(0.17)	(0.17)	(0.16)	(0.12)	(0.16)	(0.14)	(0.16)	(0.13)	(0.16)	(0.11)	(0.11)
Other	241	329	287	268	218	236	214	90	120	100	90	80	100	70	80
	(0.53)	(0.70)	(0.58)	(0.50)	(0.37)	(0.39)	(0.36)	(0.32)	(0.42)	(0.36)	(0.30)	(0.26)	(0.32)	(0.20)	(0.22)
Asian															
Indian	109	82	116	71	54	47	56	50	40	70	60	60	40	40	40
	(0.07)	(0.05)	(0.07)	(0.04)	(0.03)	(0.03)	(0.03)	(0.03)	(0.02)	(0.04)	(0.04)	(0.04)	(0.03)	(0.03)	(0.02)
Pakistani	255	274	218	165	129	113	170	130	130	160	160	180	180	160	120
	(0.16)	(0.17)	(0.13)	(0.10)	(0.07)	(0.06)	(0.10)	(0.08)	(0.07)	(0.08)	(0.08)	(0.09)	(0.08)	(0.07)	(0.05)
Bangladeshi	58	59	60	42	53	44	76	40	70	50	70	70	60	50	60
	(0.10)	(0.09)	(0.10)	(0.07)	(0.08)	(0.07)	(0.11)	(0.06)	(0.09)	(0.06)	(0.08)	(0.08)	(0.06)	(0.06)	(0.05)
Chinese	14	9	11	6	<5	<5	6	<5	<5	<5	<5	<5	<5	<5	<5
	(0.06)	(0.04)	(0.05)	(0.03)	(0.01)	(0.02)	(0.03)	(0.02)	(n/a)	(n/a)	(n/a)	(n/a)	(n/a)	(n/a)	(n/a)

in the league tables, were often cited as being responsible for this increase in school exclusions. In response to market pressures, headteachers may feel or have felt more inclined to exclude disruptive students, especially if they underachieve and keep their peers from learning. However, other potential factors were also identified relating to the educational reforms instigated in 1988. These included the pressure on teachers to implement a narrow National Curriculum, Ofsted inspections, league tables, and GCSE outcomes, many of which were said to reduce the availability of resources (time, number of teachers) to support students' individual needs (Blyth and Milner, 1996; Cooper, 2002; Gillborn, 1998a; Searle, 1996; Searle, 2001). However, under the New Labour government's initiatives (1997–2010) and following the introduction of the Race Relations Amendment Act (2000) disproportionate exclusions decreased (Parsons, 2008, 2009) but the inequalities still remain, particularly in relation to Black Caribbean students.

Neoliberal policies of competitiveness and individualism can be said to have exacerbated the entrenchment of institutional racism and the obfuscation of dealing with specific manifestations and implications of racism. However, although the neoliberal policies have had an immense impact on school processes, governance, and no doubt ethos, there is no direct evidence to suggest a direct link between these and BME exclusions and academic underachievement.

10.5   Conclusion and discussion

Research in England on the relationship between race and ethnicity and educational inequality in primary and secondary education developed into a major area of research from the 1980s onwards. Inequality has been increasingly defined in terms of differences in outcomes, and the focus of research has been predominantly on the role of school processes in developing such inequalities. Although the British government stimulates the collection and analysis of quantitative data on race and ethnicity and educational inequality, most of the studies in this field employ qualitative or ethnographic methods and an interpretative approach.

The most dominant research traditions explain the existing differences in educational outcomes by pointing to processes of racism and discrimination in schools, which are either explained by the racist practices or attitudes of teachers and/or the way in which the educational system is organized. It is argued that the educational system (in terms of its curriculum, selection mechanisms, and punish and reward systems) is organized as such that it favors, usually implicitly, the interests of white, middle-class citizens at the exclusion of BME people and the lower social classes.

These findings suggest a strong influence of the new sociology of education movement in England, and related to this a strong influence of symbolic interactionism, phenomenology, and micro-sociological classroom research. In addition, research on race and ethnicity and educational inequality in England appears to be informed by developments in social policy. During the 1980s in England, the Rampton and subsequent Swann Report put racial/ethnic minorities' disadvantages, and especially racism and discrimination, firmly on the agenda of English educational research. As a result, English educational research focused its attention increasingly more on processes of racism and discrimination in schools. How might this particular rich body of research further develop especially given the ever-changing education policy developments in England? In 2012 under a coalition government and in a context of financial austerity measures, there appears to be little political interest in addressing racial inequalities in education. Further decentralization of schools with the expansion of the Academies and the introduction of Free Schools – state funded, accountable primarily to their governing bodies as well as central government (rather than the Local Authority) – may make multicultural or anti-racist strategies more difficult to implement. This new structure of schooling may also mean that academic achievements across different ethnic groups become more difficult to monitor. In particular the accountability and governance of the schools will need to be researched in order to see the impact on diverse and disadvantaged groups and whether the children and parents have greater or lesser representation of their needs.

Research on ethnic/racial inequalities in England could benefit from adopting explicit definitions of what they take as indicative of inequality consistently through their research. While research has adopted increasingly more an 'inequality of outcomes' approach (Reid, 1996), this is not always made explicit in research and sometimes different notions of equality/equity (e.g. equality in terms of outcomes or progress) are employed simultaneously (Foster, Gomm, and Hammersley, 1996). At the same time, as inequality is often reduced to particular economic outcomes such as 'achievement' and 'exclusion' which can be expected to have an impact on children's future employment opportunities and related socio-economic position, researchers could also pay attention to the effect of educational processes on a wider set of benefits, such as students' sense of (school) community, their views on diversity, globalization, their self-esteem, and well-being.

More generally, considering the predominance of qualitative, ethnographic methods and an interpretative approach in educational sociology in England, it is somewhat surprising that little attention has been given to how notions of inequality are defined and constructed in particular (educational) settings. For instance, based on ethnographic case-study research in Flemish (Belgian) and English classrooms, Stevens (2008, 2009, 2010) investigates how young people define racist teachers, and finds that students' perceptions of teachers as racist depend on the perceived intentionality of teachers' behavior, students' appreciation of certain forms of racist behavior (like the expression of 'racist humour'), the extent to which racist behavior is expressed universally to all minority BME members or only to certain ('deviant') students, conflicts between teachers and students over the appropriateness of their roles, teachers' strategies to prevent students' accusations of teacher-racism, and the status of a teacher as a 'good' teacher.

Furthermore, researchers in England could expand their research agenda by investigating and comparing the educational experiences of a broader set of BME groups. While researchers in England have traditionally focussed on the largest BME groups ('Black Caribbean', 'Black African', 'Indian', 'Pakistani', and 'Bangladeshi' students), theories explaining educational inequalities could be enriched by including smaller, but theoretically important BME groups, and, particularly, by *comparing* these groups in terms of which processes and factors contribute to the observed differences in educational experiences. For instance, researchers could compare the educational experiences of understudied BME groups that obtain particularly low outcomes (such as students of Gypsy, Roma and Traveller backgrounds (Enneli, Modood, and Bradley, 2005; Kucukcan, 1999; Levinson, 2000) and Turkish minority students, who also appear to obtain particularly low educational outcomes) with BME groups that obtain particularly high educational outcomes (such as Chinese students, see Archer and Francis, 2005, 2006; Francis and Archer 2005a, 2005b). Similarly, instead of focussing mainly on educational factors and processes that contribute to underachievement, researchers could learn from studying and comparing educational settings that are characterized by relative success.[17]

Research in England could develop a better understanding of how educational processes influence inequality by conducting comparative research on national and regional contexts that are characterized by different educational systems. For instance, in comparing English and Flemish (Belgian) teachers' adaptations to ethnic minority students in one English and one Flemish secondary school, Stevens and colleagues (Stevens, 2011; Stevens and Görgös, 2010; Stevens and Van Houtte, 2011) found that Flemish teachers assign more responsibility (and blame/praise) to ethnic minority students for their educational achievement, think of them in more negative, stereotypical ways, and lower their standards of assessment compared to their English colleagues, something that seems to be explained by: (1) the higher degree of autonomy experienced by Flemish teachers from their national (regional) educational system, (2) the lack of emphasis on anti-racism and multiculturalism in Flemish educational policies, and (3) school characteristics related to the schools' ethnic student and staff composition and school policies on anti-racism and multiculturalism (ibid.). More generally, these studies suggest the usefulness of an 'embedded context' (McLaughlin and Talbert, 2001) or 'ecological' approach (Feinstein, Duckworth, and Sabates, 2004) in understanding the development of racism. Such an approach has its origins in developmental psychology (Bronfenbrenner 1979) and classifies environmental context measures according to the level at which they are situated, in which individuals' mental frames of reference (such as their racist beliefs, collective national and ethnic group identities), interact with various (interacting) context measures, such as: social interactions between teachers and students and parents; characteristics of social groups and organizations such as schools, peer-groups and families; and characteristics of larger social contexts, including the neighborhood and national/regional educational systems (and related policies). While comparative research between England and other countries could further expand our knowledge of how educational settings, in interaction with broader social contexts influence BME students' educational and wider outcomes, research in England could add to the development of theory in this area by considering much more how researchers in different national contexts have studied issues related to race and ethnicity and educational inequality.

Finally, all the different research traditions that developed in England between 1980 and 2010 could benefit from a stronger integration and mutual recognition of qualitative and quantitative research. This would strengthen the validity and reliability of the employed research designs and instruments, and foster the development of knowledge on the relationship between race and ethnicity and educational inequality.

Notes

1. This book chapter constitutes a revised and updated version of an article previously published in 2007 in the journal *Review of Educational Research*, which can be accessed at http://rer.sagepub.com/content/77/2/147.abstract.
2. Sociological Abstracts and ERIC were searched for publications between 1980 and 2010 using the following search input: (race OR racial OR ethnic IN DE) AND (England OR English IN AB) AND (education OR school IN AB).
3. The following journals were selected, based on their relevance and ranking: *British Educational Research Journal, British Journal of Educational Studies, British Journal of Sociology of Education, Journal of Education Policy, Oxford Educational Review, Gender and Education, Race, Ethnicity and Education, Comparative Education, Educational Review, Journal of Curriculum Studies, Educational Studies*, and *Educational Research*.
4. This concerns the journals *Sociology* and *British Journal of Sociology*.
5. This concerns the journal *Cambridge Journal of Education*.
6. Twelve cohorts of people who just reached minimum school leaving age (16 years old) have been surveyed between 1985 and 2004 through the YCS. Most of these cohorts have then been tracked over the following three years to follow their progress in the educational system and/or labor market. Each 'wave' consists of a random sample of the total population (all males and females in England and Wales who had reached the age of 16) collected through schools. Questionnaires were sent to respondents and followed up by reminders and finally an attempt to contact those who failed to respond. The initial sample size varies between 12,180 (1985 wave) and

30,000 (2004 wave) and response rates have fallen over the years (69% in 1985 to 47% in 2004). Because of the low response rates, weights have been applied to correct for any known biases (for example, high-achieving students are more likely to respond to the questionnaire). The population estimates used in the weighting are: sex, Year 11 school type, region, and Year 11 attainment (Connolly, 2006; National Statistics, 2005).

7. The rate of change in achievement for (e.g.) Chinese students is measured by: CA 2011 – CA 2006 / CA 2006, where 'CA' = 'Chinese' achievement.

8. The change in proportional achievement gap is measured by comparing the proportional gap between 2006 [(CA 2006 –BCA 2006) / (CA 2006 + BCA 2006)] with that of 2011 [(CA 2011 –BCA 2011) / (CA 2011 + BCA 2011)]; where 'CA' = 'Chinese' achievement and 'BCA' = 'Black Caribbean' achievement.

9. Plausibility refers to 'how strongly does what we currently take to be research-based knowledge imply the validity of this knowledge claim' (Hammersley, 2003, p. 23), while credibility refers to 'the likelihood that the process which produced the claim is free of serious error' (Foster, Gomm, and Hammersley, 1996, p. 38).

10. The Longitudinal Study of Young People in England (LSYPE), also known as 'Next Steps', is a major panel study of young people which brings together rich and detailed data from interviews with young people and their parents with test data from the National Student Database. So far, six waves of the study have been conducted, the sixth edition being released in August 2009. The sample of the first wave consisted of about 21,000 young people aged 13 to 14 who were in Year 9 in February 2004.

11. The author employs data collected in a major study of primary school effectiveness (the Junior School Project (JSP)), which involved a stratified random sample of 50 ethnically diverse inner-London primary schools. The study followed an age cohort of roughly 2000 students over the junior phase of schooling (ages 7–10-plus years) from entry in 1980 to secondary transfer in 1984. In 1990 additional support was obtained for a more detailed multi-level analysis of the original JSP primary school dataset and for a follow-up of the age cohort at the end of compulsory schooling when public examinations (GCSEs) are taken at age 16 (1989). Hence, this particular dataset allows Sammons to follow a random sample of students over a period of nine years: from entry to junior (Year 3 and 5), over secondary transfer (Year 6) to the end of compulsory schooling (GCSE, Year 11).

12. The PLASC dataset covers all students in primary and secondary schools in England and is developed by the Department of Education and Skills (DfES) since 2002. The data can be linked to each student's test score history and contains a number of individual and school characteristics, which are used in this study as controls in assessing the relationship between race and ethnicity and development of educational outcomes. The authors use the following controls: students' gender, within-year age, mother tongue, eligibility to free school meals (as an indicator of family poverty), special education needs status (as an indicator of learning or behavioral problems), student's postcode, and school attended.

13. In response to such criticism, Sammons (2006) argues that the sample size was not depleted due to non-response but that there were difficulties in matching data for named students from central records across nine years.

14. Burgess (personal communication) argues that the study he conducted with his colleagues (Wilson, Burgess, and Briggs, 2005) is not subject to most of this criticism since (a) they follow people over time and do not exclude low-performing students excluded from GCSEs, and (b) they focus on a very large sample (almost all students) and do not suffer that much from attrition.

15. Reviews of the literature on school effectiveness suggest that models tested in multi-level research explain 30–40% of the variance in examination results, of which around 10% can be traced directly to schools (Mortimore, 1997).

16. A recent study involving 800 students selected from inner-city schools in England shows that 'Black African', 'Asian Other' and 'Pakistani' groups all have significantly higher educational aspirations than the 'White British' group, who had the lowest aspirations (Strand and Winston, 2008). The same study shows that the high aspirations of BME students are mediated through strong academic self-concept, positive peer support, a commitment to schooling and high educational aspirations in the home.

17. A rare, recent study that aims to identify the characteristics of schools that are successful in raising the achievement of African Caribbean students is Demie's (2005) study of 13 secondary schools in London. The author conducted analysis of school and LEA data and interviews with school staff, students, and governors. The data suggests that the following factors contribute to the educational success of African Caribbean students: (1) strong leadership with emphasis on raising expectations for students and teachers; (2) the use of performance data in monitoring progress; (3) development of a creative and inclusive curriculum that takes a stand against racism and meets the needs of minority students; (4) involvement of parents and clear links with the community; and (5) well-developed support teams that make use of learning mentors. Although this study links very well with SESI research that suggests that internal school processes make a difference for African Caribbean students (Wilson, Burgess, and Briggs, 2005), the methodology is problematic in that the author does not compare 'successful' with 'unsuccessful' schools. Because of the absence of a 'control group', it is not possible to determine whether the identified school characteristics are responsible for raising the achievement of African Caribbean students. Finally, it is also possible that changes in success relate to changes in intake (in terms of, for example, social class), something which is not considered in this study. Nevertheless, this study is unique in its purpose and design and should encourage further research in this area.

References

Abbas, Tahir. 2002a. 'The Home and the School in the Educational Achievements of South Asians'. *Race, Ethnicity and Education* 5:292–316.

Abbas, Tahir. 2002b. 'A Retrospective Study of South Asian Further Education College Students and their Experiences of Secondary School'. *Cambridge Journal of Education* 32:73–90.

Abbas, Tahir. 2003. 'The Impact of Religio-Cultural Norms and Values on the Education of Young South Asian Women'. *British Journal of Sociology of Education* 24:411–428.

Acker, Sandra. 1987. 'Feminist Theory and the Study of Gender and Education'. *International Review of Education* 33,4:419–435.

Afshah, H. 1989. 'Education, Hopes and Expectations of Muslim Women'. *Gender and Education* 1:261–272.

Ahmad, Fauzia. 2001. 'Modern Traditions? British Muslim Women and Academic Achievement'. *Gender and Education* 13:137–152.

Alexander, C. 2000. *The Asian Gang*. Oxford/New York: BERG.

Allport, G. W. 1954. *The Nature of Prejudice*. Cambridge, MA: Addison-Wesley.

Althusser, Louis. 1971. 'Ideology and Ideological State Apparatus'. pp. 242–280 in *Education, Structure and Society*, edited by B. Cosin. Middlesex: Penguin.

Anwar, Muhammed. 1998. *Between Two Cultures: Continuity and Change in the Lives of Young Asians*. London: Routlegde.

Archer, Louise. 2003. *Race, Masculinity and Schooling*. Berkshire: Open University Press.

Archer, Louise and Becky Francis. 2005. '"They Never Go Off the Rails Like Other Ethnic Groups": Teachers' Constructions of British-Chinese Students' Gender Identities and Approaches to Learning'. *British Journal of Sociology of Education* 26:165–182.

Archer, Louise, & Francis, Becky. 2006. Challenging Classes? Exploring the Role of Social Class within the Identities and Achievement of British Chinese Pupils. *Sociology* 40,1:29–48.

Archer, Louise and Becky Francis. 2007. *Understanding Minority Ethnic Achievement*. London/New York: Routledge.

Arnot, Madeleine. (Ed.) 1985. *Race and Gender. Equal Opportunities Policies in Education*. Oxford/New York/Sydney/Toronto: Pergamon Press.

Arnot, Madeleine and Geoff Whitty. 1982. 'From Reproduction to Transformation: Recent Radical Perspectives on the Curriculum from the USA'. *British Journal of Sociology of Education* 3:93–103.

Atkins, Liz. 2010. Smoke and Mirrors: Opportunity and Aspiration in 14–19 Education. *Discourse, Power and Resistance Conference*, April, University of Greenwich.

Ball, Stephen J. 1981. *Beachside Comprehensive. A Case-Study of Secondary Schooling*. Cambridge: Cambridge University Press.

Basit, Tehmina. 1995. '"I Want to go to College": British Muslim Girls and the Academic Dimension of Schooling'. *Muslim Education Quarterly* 12, 3:36–54.

Basit, Tehmina. 1997. '"I Want More Freedom, but Not Too Much": British Muslim Girls and the Dynamism of Family Values'. *Gender and Education* 9:425–439.

Bhatti, Ghazala. 1999. *Asian Children at Home and at School: An Ethnographic Study*. London: Routledge.

Bhopal, Kalwant. 1997. *Gender, 'Race' and Patriarchy: A Study of South Asian Women*. Aldershot: Ashgate.

Bhopal, Kalwant. 1998. 'How Gender and Ethnicity Intersect: The Significance of Education, Employment and Marital Status'. *Sociological Research Online* 3:1–16.

Bhopal, Kalwant. 2011. '"This is a School, it's Not a Site": Teachers' Attitudes towards Gypsy and Traveller Students in Schools in England, UK'. *British Educational Research Journal* 37, 3:465–483.

Bhopal, Kalwant and John Preston. (Eds) 2011. *Intersectionality and 'race' in Education*. Routledge Research in Education. New York/London: Routledge.

Bhopal, Kalwant and M. Myers. 2009. 'Gypsy, Roma and Traveller Pupils in Schools in the UK: Inclusion and "Good practice"'. *International Journal of Inclusive Education* 13, 3:219–314.

Blyth, Eric and Judith Milner. 1996. 'Exclusions. Trends and Issues'. pp. 3–20 in *Exclusions from School. Inter-Professional Issues for Policy and Practice*, edited by E. Blyth and J. Milner. London/New York: Falmer Press.

Bowles, Samuel and Herbert Gintis. 1976. *Schooling in Capitalist America*. London: Routledge and Kegan Paul.

Brah, A., M. Hickman, and Máirtín Mac an Ghaill. 1999. *Thinking Identities: Ethnicity, Racism and Culture*. London: Macmillan.

Bronfenbrenner, Urie. 1979. *The Ecology of Human Development*. Cambridge, MA: Harvard University Press.

Cole, Mike. 2009. *Critical Race Theory and Education: A Marxist Response*. London: Palgrave Macmillan.

Cole, Mike, Dave Hill and Sharanheet Shan. 1997. *Promoting Equality in Primary Schools*. London/Washington: Cassell.

Coleman, James S. 1966. *Equality of Educational Opportunity*. Washington, DC: Government Printing Office.

Connolly, Paul. 1992. 'Playing It by the Rules: The Politics of Research in "Race" and Education'. *British Educational Research Journal* 18:133–148.

Connolly, Paul. 1998. *Racism, Gender Identities and Young Children*. London: Routledge.

Connolly, Paul. 2000. 'What Now for the Contact Hypothesis? Towards a New Research Agenda'. *Race, Ethnicity and Education* 3:169–191.

Connolly, Paul. 2006. 'Summary Statistics, Educational Achievement Gaps and the Ecological Fallacy'. *Oxford Review of Education* 32:235–252.

Conteh, Jean. 2003. *Succeeding in Diversity*. Stoke-on-Trent: Trentham Books.

Cooper, Charlie. 2002. *Understanding School Exclusion. Challenging Processes of Docility*. Nottingham: Education Now Books.

Cork, Lorna. 2005. *Supporting Black Parents. Understanding and Improving Home-School Relations*. London & New York: Routledge.

Crenshaw, Kimberlé. 1995. 'Mapping the Margins: Intersectionality, Identity Politics, and Violence against Women of Color'. In *Critical Race Theory. The Key Writings that Formed the Movement*, edited by Kimberlé Crenshaw et al. New York: The New Press.

Crozier, Gill. 1989. 'Multicultural Education: Some Unintended Consequences'. In *Politics and the Process of Schooling*, edited by L. Barton and S. Walker. Milton Keynes: Open University Press.

Crozier, Gill. 1996. 'Black Parents and School Relationships: A Case Study'. *Educational Review* 48, 3:255–269.

Crozier, Gill. 1998. 'Parents and Schools: Partnership or Surveillance?' *Journal of Educational Policy* 13, 1:185–195.

Crozier, Gill. 2001. 'Excluded Parents: The Deracialization of Parental Involvement'. *Race Ethnicity and Education* 4, 4:329–341.

Crozier, Gill. 2004. Parents, Children and Schools: Asian Families' Perspectives. ESRC End of Award report (R000239671).

Crozier, Gill. 2005a. 'There's a War against Our Children: Black Parents' Views on their Children's Education'. *British Journal of Sociology of Education* 26, 5:585–598.

Crozier, Gill. 2005b. '"Beyond the Call of Duty": The Impact of Racism on Black Parents' Involvement in their Children's Education'. In *Activating Participation: Parents and Teachers Working Towards Partnership*, edited by G. Crozier and D. Reay. Stoke-on-Trent/Virginia: Stylus Publishing and Trentham Books.

Crozier, Gill. 2006. 'Family Matters: A Discussion of the Role of the Extended Family in Supporting the Children's Education, with Specific Reference to Families of Bangladeshi and Pakistani Heritage, in the UK'. *The Sociological Review* 54, 4:677–694.

Crozier, Gill. 2009. 'The Girls Will Get Married and the Lads Will Go to the Restaurants: Teacher Expectations or Parent Aspirations? Exploding the Myths about South Asian Parents' Expectations of their Children'. *Theory into Practice* 48, 4:290–296.

Crozier, Gill. 2011. 'The Politics of Education: Challenging Racial Discrimination and Disadvantage in Education in the British Context'. In *The Politics of Education: Challenging Multiculturalism*, edited by M. Vronyides and C. Kassimeris. London/New York: Routledge.

Crozier, Gill and Jane Davies. 2007. 'Hard to Reach Parents or Hard to Reach Schools? A Discussion of Home – School Relations, with Particular Reference to Bangladeshi and Pakistani Parents'. *British Educational Research Journal* 33, 3:295–313.

Crozier, Gill, Jane Davies, and Kim Szymanski. 2009. 'Education, Identity and Roma Families: Teachers' Perspectives and Engagement with INSETRom Training'. *Intercultural Education* 20, 6:537–548.

Dadzie, Stella. 2000. *Toolkit for Tackling Racism*. Stoke-on-Trent: Trentham Books.

David, Miriam. 1993. *Parents, Gender and Education Reform*. Cambridge: Polity Press.

David, Miriam, Anne West and Jane Ribbens. 1994. *Mother's Intuition? Choosing Secondary Schools*. London: The Falmer Press.

DCSF. 2007. Level 2 and 3 Attainment by Ethnicity. London: Department of Children, Schools and Families.

Delamont, Sara. 1977. 'Readings on Interactionism in the Classroom. Contemporary Sociology of the School'. London/New York: Methuen.

Deem, Rosemary. (Ed.) 1980. *Schooling for Women's Work*. London/Boston/Henley: Routledge and Kegan Paul.

Demack, Sean, David Drew, and Mike Grimsley. 2000. 'Minding the Gap: Ethnic, Gender and Social Class Differences in Attainment at 16, 1988–95'. *Race, Ethnicity and Education* 3:117–143.

Demie, Feyisa. 2005. 'Achievement of Black Caribbean Students: Good Practice in Lambeth Schools'. *British Educational Research Journal* 31:481–508.

Derrington, C. and S. Kendall. 2004. *Gypsy Traveller Students in Secondary Schools: Culture, Identity and Achievement*. Stoke-on-Trent: Trentham Books.

DES. 1981. 'West Indian Children in our Schools, A Report of the Committee of Enquiry into the Education of Children from Ethnic Minority Groups (The Rampton Report)'. Department of Education and Science, Runcorn: Cheshire.

DES. 1985. 'Education for All (The Swann Report)'. Department of Education and Science.

DfES. 2003. 'Minority Ethnic Attainment and Participation in Education and Training: The Evidence'. Nottingham/Birmingham: Department of Education and Skills and University of Birmingham.

DfES. 2005a. 'Ethnicty and Education: The Evidence on Minority Ethnic Students'. Nottingham: Department of Education and Skills.

DfES. 2005b. 'The Youth Cohort Study: The Activities and Experiences of 16 Year Olds: England and Wales 2004'. Nottingham: Department of Education and Skills.

DfE. 2012. 'GCSE and Equivalent Attainment by Student Characteristics in England'. vol. 2012: Department for Education, Runcorn: Cheshire.

Douglas, J. W. B. 1964. *The Home and the School*. London: McGibbon and Kee.

Douglas, J. W. B., J. M. Ross, and H. R. Simpson. 1968. *All Our Future. A Longitudinal Study of Secondary Education*. London: Peter Davies Publisher.

Drew, David. 1995. *'Race', Education and Work: The Statistics of Inequality*. Aldershot: Avebury Press.

Drew, David and John Gray. 1990. 'The Fifth Year Examination Acievements of Black Young People in England and Wales'. *Educational Research* 32:107–117.

Drew, Deborah, John Gray, and D. Sporton. 1997. 'Ethnic Differences in the Educational Participation of 16–19 Year Olds'. pp. 17–28 in *Employment, Education and Housing among ethnic minorities in Britain. Volume 4: The Ethnic Question in the 1991 Census of Great Britain*, edited by V. Karn. London: OPCS.

Driver, Geoffrey. 1977. 'Cultural Competence'. *New Society* 17:353–359.

Enneli, Pinar, Modood, Tariq, and Bradley, Harriet. 2005. Young Turks and Kurds: A set of 'invisible' disadvantaged groups. York: York Publishing Services: Joseph Rowntree Foundation.

Epstein, Debbie. 1993. *Changing Classroom Cultures: Anti-racism, Politics and Schools*. Stoke-on-Trent: Trentham Books.

Epstein, Debbie. 1998. 'Real Boys Don't Work: "Underachievement", Masculinity and the Harassment of Sissies'. pp. 96–108 in *Failing Boys? Issues in Gender and Achievement*, edited by D. Epstein, J. Elwood, V. Hey, and J. Maw. Buckingham/Philadelphia: Open University Press.

Feinstein, Leon, Duckworth, Kathryn, and Sabates, Ricardo. 2004. A Model of Inter-generational Transmission of Educational Success. London: Centre for Research on the Wider Benefits of Learning.

Figueroa, Peter. 1992a. 'Assessment and Achievement of Ethnic Minority Students'. pp. 401–419 in *Cultural Diversity and the Schools. Volume 1. Education for Cultural Diversity: Convergence and Divergence*, edited by J. Lynch, C. Modgil, and S. Modgil. London: The Falmer Press.

Figueroa, Peter. 1992b. 'Figueroa Replies to Tomlinson'. pp. 421–426 in *Cultural Diversity and the Schools. Volume 1. Education for Cultural Diversity: Convergence and Divergence*, edited by J. Lynch, C. Modgil, and S. Modgil. London: The Falmer Press.

Floud, J., A. H. Halsey, and F. M. Martin. 1956. *Social Class and Educational Opportunity*. London: Heinemann.

Foster, Peter. 1990a. 'Cases not Proven. An Evaluation of two Studies of Teacher Racism'. *British Educational Research Journal* 16:335–349.

Foster, Peter. 1990b. *Policy and Practice in Multicultural and Anti-Racist Education*. London/New York: Routledge.

Foster, Peter. 1991. 'Case Still Not Proven: A Reply to Cecile Wright'. *British Educational Research Journal* 17:165–170.

Foster, Peter. 1992a. 'Equal Treatment and Cultural Difference in Multi-Ethnic Schools: A Critique of the Teacher Ethnocentrism Theory'. *International Studies in Sociology of Education* 2:89–103.

Foster, Peter. 1992b. 'Teacher Attitudes and Afro/Caribbean Educational Attainment'. *Oxford Review of Education* 18:269–281.

Foster, Peter. 1992c. 'What are Connolly's Rules? A Reply to Paul Connolly'. *British Educational Research Journal* 18:149–154.

Foster, Peter. 1993a. '"Methodological Purism" or a "Defence Against Hype"? Critical Readership in Research in "Race" and Education'. *New Community* 19:609–628.

Foster, Peter. 1993b. 'Some Problems in Establishing Equality of Treatment in Multi-Ethnic Schools'. *British Journal of Sociology* 44:519–535.

Foster, Peter, Roger Gomm, and Martyn Hammersley. 1996. *Constructing Educational Inequality: An Assessment of Research on School Processes*. London: Falmer.

Foster, Peter and Martyn Hammersley. 2000. 'Case Studies as Spurious Evaluations: The Example of Research on Educational Inequalities'. *British Journal of Educational Studies* 48:215–230.

Francis, Becky and Louise Archer. 2005a. 'British-Chinese Students' and Parents' Constructions of the Value of Education'. *British Educational Research Journal* 31:89–108.

Francis, Becky and Louise Archer. 2005b. 'British-Chinese Students' Constructions of Gender and Learning'. *Oxford Review of Education* 31:497–515.

Fuller, M. 1984. 'Black Girls in a London Comprehensive School'. pp. 77–87 in *Life in School. The Sociology of Pupil Culture*, edited by M. Hammersley and P. Woods. Milton Keynes: Open University Press.

Furlong, V. J. 1977. 'Black Resistance in the Liberal Comprehensive'. pp. 212–236 in *Readings on Interactionsim in the Classroom. Contemporary Sociology of the School*, edited by S. Delamont. London/New York: Methuen.

Gaine, Chris. 1987. *No Problem Here*. London/Sydney/Johannesburg: Hutchinson.

Gaine, Chris. 1995. *Still No Problem Here*. Stoke-on-Trent: Trentham Books.

Gaine, Chris. 2005. *We're all White THANKS*. Stoke-on-Trent: Trentham Books.

Garner, S. 2007. *Whiteness: An Introduction*. Abingdon: Routledge.

Gewirtz, Deborah. 1991. 'Analyses of Racism and Sexism in Education and Strategies for Change'. *British Journal of Sociology of Education* 12, 2:183–201.

Gewirtz, S., S. J. Ball, and R. Bowe. 1995. *Markets, Choice and Equity in Education*. Buckingham: Open University Press.

Gillborn, David. 1990. *'Race', Ethnicity and Education. Teaching and Learning in Multi-Ethnic Schools*. London: Routledge/Falmer.

Gillborn, David. 1995. *Racism and Antiracism in Real Schools*. Buckingham: Open University Press.

Gillborn, David. 1996. 'Student Roles and Perspectives in Antiracist Education: A Crisis of White Ethnicity?' *British Educational Research Journal* 22:165–180.

Gillborn, David. 1997. 'Racism and Reform: New Ethnicites/Old Inequalities'. *British Educational Research Journal* 23, 3:345–361.

Gillborn, David. 1998a. 'Exclusions from School: An Overview of the Issue'. pp. 11–18 in *Second Chances. Exclusions from School and Equality of Opportunity*, edited by N. Donovan. London: New Policy Institute.

Gillborn, David. 1998b. 'Racism and the Politics of Qualitative Research: Learning from Controversy and Critique'. pp. 35–45 in *Researching in Racism in Education*, edited by P. Connolly and B. Troyna. Buckingham: Open University Press.

Gillborn, David. 2002. *Education and Institutional Racism*. London: Institute of Education.

Gillborn, David. 2005. 'Education Policy as an Act of White Supremacy: Whiteness, Critical Race Theory and Education Reform'. *Journal of Education Policy* 20:485–505.

Gillborn, David. 2006. 'Critical Race Theory and Education: Racism and Anti-Racism in Educational Theory and Praxis'. *Discourse: Studies in the Cultural Politics of Education* 27, 1:11–32.

Gillborn, David. 2008. *Racism and Education. Coincidence or Conspiracy?* London: Routledge.

Gillborn, David and David Drew. 1992. '"Race", Class and School Effects'. *New Community* 18:551–565.

Gillborn, David and Caroline Gipps. 1996. *Recent Research on the Achievements of Ethnic Minority Students*. London: Institute of Education and Office for Standards in Education.

Gillborn, David and Caroline Gipps. 1998. 'Watching the Watchers: Research, Methods, Politics and Equity. A Response to Foster and Hammersley'. *British Educational Research Journal* 24:629–633.

Gillborn, David and Heidi Safia Mirza. 2000. *Educational Inequality. Mapping Race, Class and Gender. A Synthesis of Research Evidence*. London: Office of Standards in Education.

Gillborn, David and Deborah Youdell. 2000. *Rationing Education: Policy, Practice, Reform and Equity*. Buckingham: Open University Press.

Gilroy, P. 1992. 'The End of Antiracism'. In *'Race', Culture and Difference*, edited by J. Donald and A. Rattansi. London: Sage Publications.

Giroux, Henry A. 1997. *Channel Surfing: Racism, The Media, and the Destruction of Today's Youth*. New York: St Martin's Press.

Glass, D. V. 1954. *Social Mobility in Britain*. London: Routledge and Kegan Paul.

Gomm, Roger. 1993. 'Figuring Out Ethnic Equity'. *British Educational Research Journal* 19:149–165.

Gomm, Roger. 1995. 'Strong Claims, Weak Evidence: A Response to Troyna's 'Ethnicity and the Organisation of Learning'. *Educational Research* 37:79–86.

Gorard, Stephen. 1999. 'Keeping a Sense of Proportion: The "Politician's Error" in Analysing School Outcomes'. *British Journal of Educational Studies* 47:235–246.

Gorard, Stephen. 2000a. *Education and Social Justice; the Changing Composition of Schools and Its Implications*. Cardiff: University of Wales Press.

Gorard, Stephen. 2000b. 'One of Us Cannot Be Wrong: The Paradox of Achievement Gaps'. *British Journal of Sociology of Education* 21:391–400.

Gregory, Eve and A. Williams. 2000. *City Literacies: Learning to Read Across Generations and Cultures*. London:Routledge.

Grudgeon, E. and P. Woods. 1990. *Educating All: Multicultural perspectives in the Primary School*. London/New York: Routledge.

Hall, S. (1992) 'New ethnicities'. In: *Race, culture and difference*, Donald, J. and Rattansi, A. London: Sage.

Halsey, A. H., A. Heath, and J. Ridge. 1980. *Origins and Destinations: Family Class and Education in Modern Britain*. Oxford: Oxford Clarendon Press.

Hammersley, Martyn. 1992. 'A Response to Barry Troyna's Children, 'Race' and Racism: The Limits of Research and Policy'. *British Journal of Educational Studies* 40:174–177.

Hammersley, Martyn. 1993a. 'On Methodological Purism: A Response to Barry Troyna'. *British Educational Research Journal* 19:339–342.

Hammersley, Martyn. 1993b. 'Research and "Anti-Racism": The Case of Peter Foster and his Critics'. *British Journal of Sociology* 44:429–448.

Hammersley, Martyn. 1995. *The Politics of Social Research*. London: Sage Publications.

Hammersley, Martyn. 2001a. 'Book Review: "Race and Antiracism in Real Schools", by Gillborn, David (Buckingham, Open University Press)'. *British Journal of Sociology of Education* 21:724.

Hammersley, Martyn. 2001b. 'Interpreting Achievement Gaps: Some Comments on a Dispute'. *British Journal of Educational Studies* 49:285–298.

Hammersley, Martyn. 2003. 'Too Good to be False? The Ethics of Belief and its Implications for the Evidence-Based Character of Educational Research, Policymaking and Practice'. p. 23 in *BERA Conference*. Heriot-Watt University.

Hammersley, Martyn and Peter Woods. 1984. *Life in School. The Sociology of Student Culture*. Milton Keynes: Open University Press.

Hansen, Kristine, and Elizabeth M. Jones. 2011. 'Ethnicity and Gender Gaps in Early Childhood'. *British Educational Research Journal* 37, 6:973–991.

Haque, Zubaida. 2000. 'The Ethnic Minority "Underachieving" Group? Investigating the Claims of "Underachievement" Amongst Bangladeshi Students in British Secondary Schools'. *Race, Ethnicity and Education* 3:145–168.

Haque, Zubaida and John Bell. 2001. 'Evaluating the Performance of Minority Ethnic Students in Secondary Schools'. *Oxford Review of Education* 27:357–368.

Harding, S. 1987. *Feminism and Methodology*. Milton Keynes: Open University Press.

Hargreaves, Andy and Peter Woods. 1984. *Classrooms and Staffrooms. The Sociology of Teachers and Teaching*. Milton Keynes: Open University Press.

Hargreaves, David H. 1967. *Social Relations in a Secondary School*. London: Routledge and Kegan Paul.

Hatchell, Helen. 2004. 'Privilege of Whiteness: Adolescent Male Students' Resistance to Racism in an Australian Classroom'. *Race, Ethnicity and Education* 7.

Hatcher, Richard. 1998. 'Social Justice and the Politics of School Effectiveness and Improvement'. *Race, Ethnicity and Education* 1:267–287.

Heath, Anthony. 2000. 'The Political Arithmetic Tradition in the Sociology of Education'. *Oxford Review of Education* 26:313–330.

Hooks, Bell. 1989. *Talking Back*. Boston, MA: Southend Press.

Hurrell, Philippa. 1995. 'Do Teachers Discriminate? Reactions to Student Behaviour in Four Comprehensive Schools'. *Sociology* 29:59–72.

Jesson, D. and John Gray. 1991. 'Slants and Slopes: Using Multi-Level Models to Investigate Differential School Effectiveness and its Impact on Students' Examination Results'. *School Effectiveness and School Improvement* 2:230–271.

Karabel, J. and A. H. Halsey. 1977. *Power and Ideology in Education*. New York: Academic Press.

Keddie, Nell. 1971. 'Classroom Knowledge'. pp. 133–160 in *Knowledge and Control: New Directions for the Sociology of Education*, edited by M. F. D. Young. Collier-Macmillan.

King, Anna and Michael Reiss. 1993. *The Multicultural Dimension of the National Curriculum*. London/Bristol, PA: The Falmer Press.

Kingdon, Geeta, and Robert Cassen. 2010. 'Ethnicity and Low Achievement in English Schools'. *British Educational Research Journal* 36, 3:403–431.

Klein, Gillian. 1993. *Education Towards Race Equality*. London/New York: Cassell.

Knott, K. and S. Kokher. 1993. 'Religious and Ethnic Identity among Young Muslim Women in Bradford'. *New Society* 19:593–610.

Kucukcan, Talip. 1999. *Politics of Ethnicity, Identity and Religion. Turkish Muslims in Britain*. Aldershot: Ashgate.

Kundnani, Arun. 2002. *The Death of Multiculturalism*. www.irr.org.uk/2002/april/ak00000.1.html. Accessed 26 October 2010.

Lacey, Colin. 1970. *Hightown Grammar: The School as a Social System*. Manchester: Manchester University Press.

Ladson-Billings, G. and W. F. Tate. 1995. 'Toward a Critical Race Theory of Education'. *Teachers College Record* 97, 1:47–68.

Leonardo, Zeus. 2002. 'The Souls of White Folk: Critical Pedagogy, Whiteness Studies, and Globalisation Discourse'. *Race, Ethnicity and Education* 5:29–50.

Levine-Rasky. 2000. 'Framing Whiteness: Working Through the Tensions in Introducing Whiteness to Educators'. *Race, Ethnicity and Education* 3:271–392.

Levinson, Martin P. 2000. *Education, Culture and Identity: The Case of Gypsy Children*. PhD diss., University of Exeter.

Levinson, Martin P. 2007. 'Literacy in English Gypsy Communities: Cultural Capital Manifested as Negative Assests'. *American Educational Research Journal* 44:5–39.

Levinson, Martin P. and Andrew C. Sparkes. 2003. 'Gypsy Masculinities and the School-Home Interface: Exploring Contradictions and Tensions'. *British Journal of Sociology of Education* 24:587–603.

Levinson, Martin P. and Andrew C. Sparkes. 2005. 'Gypsy Children, Space, and the School Environment'. *International Journal of Qualitative Studies in Education* 18:751–772.

Liegeois, J. 1986. *Gypsies – an Illustrated History*. London: Al Saqi Books.

Liegeois, J. 1987. *School Provision for Gypsy and Traveller Children: A Synthesis Report*. Luxembourg: European Communities Commission: Office for Official Publications of the European Communities.

Liegeois, J. 1997. *School Provision for Gypsy and Travelling Children*. Luxembourg: European Communities Commission: Office for Official Publications of the European Communnities.

Mac an Ghaill, Máirtín. 1988. *Young, Gifted and Black. Student-Teacher Relations in the Schooling of Black Youth*. Buckingham/Philadelphia: Open University Press.

Mac an Ghaill, Máirtín. 1994. *The Making of Men. Masculinities, Sexualities and Schooling*. Buckingham/Philadelphia: Open University Press.

Mac an Ghaill, Máirtín. 1999. *Contemporary Racisms and Ethnicities*, edited by A. Warde. Buckingham/Philadelphia: Open University Press.

Mac an Ghaill, Máirtín. 2002. 'Beyond a Black-White Dualism: Racialisation and Racism in the Republic of Ireland and the Irish Diaspora Experience'. *Irish Journal of Sociology* 11:99–122.

McIntosh, Ian, Sim Duncan, and Robertson Douglas. 2004. '"It's as if you're some alien ..." Exploring Anti-English Attitudes in Scotland'. *Sociological Research Online* 9.

McLaughlin, M. W., and Talbert, Joan E. 2001. *Professional Communities and the Work of High School Teachers*. Chicago: University of Chicago Press.

Myers, Martin and Kalwant Bhopal (2009) 'Gypsy, Roma and Traveller Children in Schools: Understandings of Community and Safety'. *British Journal of Educational Studies* 57, 4:417–434.

Mirza, Heidi Safia. 1992. *Young, Female and Black*. London: Routledge.

Mirza, Heidi Safia. 2009. *Race, Gender and Educational Desires. Why Black Women Succeed and Fail*. London/New York: Routledge.

Modood, Tariq. 1989. 'Religious Anger and Minority Rights'. *Political Quarterly* 60:280–284.

Modood, Tariq. 2005. *Multicultural Politics: Racism, Ethnicity and Muslims in Britain*. USA: University of Minnesota Press and UK: Edinburgh University Press.

Mortimore, Peter. 1997. 'Can Effective Schools Compensate for Society?' pp. 476–487 in *Education. Culture, Economy, and Society*, edited by A. H. Halsey, L. Hugh, B. Philip, and A. S. Wells. Oxford: Oxford University Press.

Mortimore, Peter, Pam Sammons, Louise Stoll, David Lewis, and Russell Ecob. 1988. *School Matters: The Junior Years*. Wells: Open Books.

National Statistics. 2005. *Youth Cohort Study: The Activities and Experiences of 16 Year Olds: England and Wales 2004*. London: Department of Education and Skills.

Nehaul, Kamala. 1996. *The Schooling of Children of Caribbean Heritage*. Stroke-on-Trent: Trentham Books.

OFSTED. 2003. OFSTED Inspection of Enfield Local Educational Authority (p. 41). London: Office of Standards in Education.

Okely, J. 1983. *The Traveller-Gypsies*. Cambridge: Cambridge University Press.

Osler, Audrey. and Starkey, David. 2005. *Changing Citizenship*. Berkshire: Open University Press.

Owen, D. W. 2003. 'The Demographic Characteristics of People from Minority Ethnic Groups in Great Britain'. In *Explaining Ethnic Differences*, edited by D. Mason. Bristol: Policy Press.

Parsons, Carl. 2008. 'Race Relations Legislation, Ethnicity and Disproportionality in School Exclusions in England'. *Cambridge Journal of Education* 38, 3:401–419.

Parsons, Carl. 2009. 'Explaining Sustained Inequalities in Ethnic Minority School Exclusions in England – Passive Racism in a Neoliberal Grip'. *Oxford Review of Education* 35, 2:249–265.

Preston, John. 2007. *Whiteness and Class in Education*. London/Germany: Springer.

Raby, Rebecca. 2004. '"There's no Racism at my School, it's Just Joking Around": Ramifications for Anti-Racist Education'. *Race, Ethnicity and Education* 7:367–383.

Race, Richard. 2011. *Multiculturalism and Education*. London/New York: Continuum International Publishing Group.

Reay, Diane, Crozier, Gill, and James, David. 2011. *White Middle-Class Identities and Urban Schooling*. Basingstoke, UK, Gordonsville, USA, South Yarra, Australia.

Reay, Diane and S. J. Ball. 1998. 'Making their Minds Up: Family Dynamics and School Choice'. *British Educational Research Journal* 24, 4:431–448.

Reid, I. 1996. 'Inequality and Education in Britain in the 1990's: A Diagnosis and Prescription'. *Research in Education* 57, 12–24.

Rhamie, Jasmine. 2007. *Eagles Who Soar. How Black Learners find the Path to Success*. Stoke-on-Trent: Trentham Books.

Rhamie, Jasmine and Susan Hallam. 2002. 'An Investigation into African-Caribbean Academic Success in the UK'. *Race, Ethnicity and Education* 5:151–170.

Richardson, Brain. (Ed.) 2005. *Tell It Like It Is: How Our Schools Fail Black Children*. Stoke-on-Trent: Trentham Books.

Rollock, Nicola. 2007. 'Why Black Girls Don't Matter: Deconstructing Gendered and Racialised Discourses of Academic Success in an Inner City School'. *British Journal of Learning Support* 4:197–202.

Sammons, Pam. 1989. 'School Effectiveness and School Organisation'. pp. 219–253 in *Different Cultures, Same School: Ethnic Minority Children in Europe*, edited by L. Eldering and J. Kloprogge. Amsterdam/Lisse: Swets & Zeitlinger.

Sammons, Pam. 1995. 'Gender, Ethnic and Socio-Economic Differences in Attainment and Progress: A Longitudinal Analysis of Student Achievement'. *British Educational Research Journal* 21:1995.

Sammons, Pam. 1999. *School Effectiveness: Coming of Age in the Twenty-First Century*. Lisse: Swets & Zeitlinger.

Sammons, Pam. 2006. Personal communication.

Sealey, Alison and Bob Carter. 2001. 'Social Categories and Social Linguistics: Applying a Realist Approach'. *International Journal of the Sociology of Language* 152:1–19.

Searle, Chris. 1996. 'The Signal of Failure. School Exclusions and the Market System of Education'. pp. 37–52 in *Exclusions from School: Inter-Professional Issues for Policy and Practice*, edited by E. Blyth and J. Milner. London/New York: Falmer Press.

Searle, Chris. 2001. *An Exclusive Education: Race, Class and Exclusion in British Schools*. London: Lawrence and Wishart.

Sewell, T. 1997. *Black Masculinities and Schooling: How Black Boys Survive Modern Schooling*. Stoke-on-Trent: Trentham.

Sewell, T. 1998. 'Loose Canons: Exploding the Myth of the "Black Macho" Lad'. pp. 112–127 in *Failing Boys? Issues in Gender and Achievement*, edited by D. Epstein, J. Elwood, V. Hey, and J. Maw. Buckingham/Philadelphia: Open University Press.

Shain, Farzana. 2000 'Culture, Survival and Resistance: Theorising Young Asian Women's Experiences and Strategies in Contemporary Schooling and Society'. *Discourse: Studies in the Cultural Politics of Education* 21:155–174.

Shain, Farzana. 2003. *The Schooling and Identity of Asian Girls*. Stoke-on-Trent: Trenham Books.

Shain, Farzana. 2011. *The New Folk Devils. Muslim Boys and Education in England*. Stoke on Trent, UK & Sterling, USA: Trentham Books.

Sharp, R. 1981. 'Marxism, the Concept of Ideology, and Its Implications for Fieldwork'. In *The Study of Schooling: Field-based Methodologies in Educational research and Evaluation*, edited by T. S. Popkewitz and B. R. Tabachnick. New York: Praeger.

Sharp, R. and A. Green. 1975. *Education and Social Control*. London: Routledge and Kegan Paul.

Siddiqui, H. 1991. 'Winning Freedoms'. *Feminist Review* 37:78–83.

Siraj-Blatchford, Iram and Barry Troyna. 1993. 'Equal Opportunities, Research and Educational Reform: Some Introductory Notes'. *British Educational Research Journal* 19:223–227.

Sivanandan, A. 2002. The Contours of Global Racism. http://www.irr.org.uk (accessed May 29, 2009).

Smith, David J. and Sally Tomlinson. 1989. *The School Effect: A Study of Multi-Racial Comprehensiveness*. London: Policy Studies Institute.

Smith, T. 1997. 'Recognising Difference: The Romani "Gypsy" Child Socialisation and Education Process'. *British Journal of Sociology of Education* 18:243–256.

Spohrer, Konstanze. 2011. 'Deconstructing "Aspiration": UK Policy Debates and European Policy Trends. *European Educational Research Journal* 10, 1:53–63.

Steinberg, Stephen. 1981. *The Ethnic Myth. Race, Ethnicity and Class in America.* Boston: Beacon Press.

Stevens, Peter A. J. 2007. 'Researching Race/Ethnicity and Educational Inequality in English Secondary Schools: A Critical Review of the Research Literature Between 1980 and 2005'. *Review of Educational Research* 77:147–185.

Stevens, Peter A. J. 2008. 'Exploring Pupils' Perceptions of Teacher Racism in their Context: A Case Study of Turkish and Belgian Vocational Education Pupils in a Belgian School'. *British Journal of Sociology of Education* 29, 2:175–187.

Stevens, Peter A. J. 2009. 'Pupils' Perspectives on Racism and Differential Treatment by Teachers: on Stragglers, the Ill and Being Deviant'. *British Educational Research Journal* 35, 3:413–430.

Stevens, Peter A. J. 2010. 'Racisme van Leerkrachten in de Klas: Een Exploratief Onderzoek naar de Betekenis en Perceptie van Racisme bij Leerkrachten door hun Autochtone en Allochtone Leerlingen'. *Tijdschrift Voor Sociologie* 32, 3–4:330–353.

Stevens, Peter A. J. 2011. 'Teachers' Adaptations to Ethnic Minority Students in Belgium and England'. pp. 119–144 in *Equity and Excellence in Education. Towards Maximum Learning Opportunities for all Students,* edited by Kris Van den Branden., Piet Van Avermaet and Mieke Van Houtte. London: Routledge.

Stevens, Peter A. J. and Reyhan Görgös. 2010. 'Exploring the Importance of Institutional Contexts for the Development of Ethnic Stereotypes: A Comparison of Schools in Belgium and England'. *Ethnic and Racial Studies* 33, 8:1350–1371.

Stevens, Peter A. J. and Mieke Van Houtte. 2011. 'Adapting to the System or the Student? Exploring Teacher Adaptations to Disadvantaged Students in an English and Belgian Secondary School'. *Educational Evaluation and Policy Analysis* 33, 1:59–75.

Stone, Richard 2004. *Islamophobia, Issues, Challenges and Actions.* Stoke-on–Trent/Stirling: Trentham Books.

Strand, Steve. 1999. 'Ethnic Group, Sex and Economic Disadvantage: Associations with Students' Educational Progress from Baseline to the End of Key Stage 1'. *British Educational Research Journal* 25:179–202.

Strand, Steve. 2007. 'Minority Ethnic Students in the Longitudinal Study of Young People in England'. Nottingham: Department of Children Schools and Families.

Strand, Steve. 2008. 'Minority Ethnic Students in the Longitudinal Study of Young People in England Extension Report on Performance in Public Examinations at Age 16'. Nottingham: Department of Children School and Families.

Strand, Steve. 2010. 'Do Some Schools Narrow the Gap? Differential School Effectiveness by Ethnicity, Gender, Poverty, and Prior Achievement'. *School Effectiveness and School Improvement* 21, 3:289–314.

Strand, Steve. 2011. 'The Limits of Social Class in Explaining Ethnic Gaps in Educational Attainment'. *British Educational Research Journal* 37, 2:197–229.

Strand, Steve. 2012. *Ethnicity, Gender, Social Class and Achievement Gaps at Age 16: Intersectionality and "Getting It" for the White Working Class.* Coventry: Warwick University.

Strand, Steve, and Winston, Joe. 2008. Educational Aspirations in Inner City Schools. *Educational Studies* 34, 4:249–267.

Taylor, M. 1988. *Worlds Apart: A Review of Research on Other Ethnic Minority Students.* Slough: NFER-Nelson.

Thomas, S. 2000. 'Debate. Richard Hatcher & Sally Thomas on Equity and School Effectiveness Research'. *Race, Ethnicity and Education* 3:103–109.

Thomas, S., Pam Sammons, Peter Mortimore, and R. Smees. 1988. 'Differential School Effectiveness: Comparing the Performance of Different Student Groups'. *British Educational Research Journal* 23:451–469.

Tomlinson, Sally. 1983. *Ethnic Minorities in British Schools: A Review of the Literature 1960–1982*. London: Heineman.

Tomlinson, Sally. 1989. 'Ethnicity and Educational Achievement in Britain'. pp. 15–37 in *Different Cultures, Same School: Ethnic Minority Children in Europe*, edited by L. Eldering and J. Kloprogge. Amsterdam/Lisse: Swets & Zeitlinger.

Tomlinson, Sally. 1997. 'Diversity, Choice and Ethnicity: The Effects of Educational Markets on Ethnic Minorities'. *Oxford Review of Education* 23:63–76.

Tomlinson, Sally. 1999. 'Ethnic Minorities and Education: New Disadvantages'. pp. 17–36 in *Combating Educational Disadvantage: Meeting the Needs of the Vulnerable Children*, edited by T. Cox. London: Falmer Press.

Tomlinson, Sally. 2008. *Race and Education: Policy and Politics in Britain*. Milton Keynes: Open University Press.

Troyna, Barry. 1984. 'Fact or Artefact? The "Educational Underachievement" of Black Students'. *British Journal of Sociology of Education* 5:153–166.

Troyna, Barry. 1991a. 'Children, "Race" and Racism: The Limitations of Research and Policy'. *British Journal of Educational Studies* 39:425–436.

Troyna, Barry. 1991b. 'Underachievers or Underrated? The Experiences of Students of South Asian Origin in a Secondary School'. *British Educational Research Journal* 17:361–76.

Troyna, Barry. 1993. 'Underachiever or Misunderstood? A Reply to Roger Gomm'. *British Educational Research Journal* 19:167–74.

Troyna, Barry. 1994. 'Critical Social Research and Education Policy'. *British Journal of Educational Studies* 42:70–84.

Troyna, Barry. 1995. 'Beyond Reasonable Doubt? Researching "Race" in Educational Settings'. *Oxford Review of Education* 21:395–408.

Troyna, B. and Hatcher, R. 1992. *Racism in Children's Lives*. London: Routledge.

Troyna, Barry and Iram Siraj-Blatchford. 1993. 'Providing Support or Denying Access? The Experiences of Students Designated as "ESL" or "SN" in a Multi-Ethnic Secondary School'. *Educational Review* 45:3–11.

UNESCO. 2003. *World Data on Education – Fifth Edition*. Geneva: United Nations Educational, Scientific and Cultural Organisation.

Vincent, Carol. 1996. *Parents and Teachers. Power and Participation*. London & Washington: Falmer Press.

Weiner, Gaby. 1985 (Ed.) *Just a Bunch of Girls*. Milton Keynes: Open University Press.

Werbner, Pnina. 2000. 'Divided Loyalties, Empowered Citizenship? Muslims in Britain'. *Citizenship Studies* 4:307–324.

Willis, Paul E. 1977. *Learning to Labour: How Working Class Kids get Working Class Jobs*. Farnborough: Gower Publishing Company.

Wilson, Deborah, Simon Burgess, and Adam Briggs. 2005. *The Dynamics of School Attainment of England's Ethnic Minorities*. Bristol: University of Bristol – CMPO.

Woods, Peter and Martyn Hammersley. 1977. *School Experience. Explorations in the Sociology of Education*. New York: St Martin's Press.

Wright, Cecile. 1988. 'School Process: An Ethnographic Study'. pp. 197–214 in *Family, School and Society*, edited by M. Woodhead and A. McGrath. Buckingham/Philadelphia: Open University Press.

Wright, Cecile. 1990. 'Comments in Reply to the Article by P. Foster, Cases Not Proven: An Evaluation of Two Studies of Teacher Racism'. *British Educational Research Journal* 16:351–356.

Wright, Cecile. 1992. *Race Relations in the Primary School*. London: David Fulton.

Wright, Cecile, Standen, P., John, G., German, G. and Patel, T. 2005. *School Exclusion and Transition into Adulthood in African-Caribbean Communities*. New York: Joseph Rowntree Foundation.

Wright, Cecile, Weekes, Deborah and McGlaughlin, A. 2000. *'Race', Class and Gender in Exclusion from School*. London/New York: The Falmer Press.

Wright, Cecile. 2010. 'Othering Difference: Framing identities and representation in Black Children's Schooling in the British Context'. *Irish Education Studies Journal* 29, 3:305–320.

Wrong, Dennis. 1964. 'The Oversocialized Conception of Man in Modern Sociology'. pp. 112–122 in *Sociological Theory: A Book of Readings*, edited by L. Coser and B. Rosenberg: New York: Collier-Macmillan.

Youdell, Deborah. 2003. 'Identity Traps or How Black Students Fail: The Interactions between Biographical, Sub-Cultural and Learner Identities'. *British Journal of Sociology of Education* 24:3–20.

Youdell, Deborah. 2004. 'Engineering School Markets, Constituting Schools and Subjectivating Students: The Bureaucratic, Institutional and Classroom Dimensions of Educational Triage'. *Journal of Education Policy* 19:407–431.

Young, Michael F. D. 1973. 'Curricula and the Social Organisation of Knowledge'. pp. 339–362 in *Knowledge, Education, and Cultural Change*, edited by R. Brown. London: Tavistock.

Young, Michael F. D. 1976. 'On the Politics of Educational Knowledge'. pp. 134–157 In *Worlds Apart: Readings for a Sociology of Education*, edited by J. Beck, C. Jenks, N. Keddie, and M. F. D. Young. Collier Macmillian.

11
Finland

Päivi Harinen and M'hammed Sabour

11.1 Introduction

The aim of this chapter is to analytically describe and categorize the research conducted in Finland on educational inequalities faced by students of ethnic minority backgrounds. The focus is mainly on secondary education examinations between 1990 and 2010. Because in Finland scientific attention to ethnic inequalities has been paid on only recently, the data for this analysis remained rare, and most of our criticisms are directed towards the absence of sociological perception in understanding this phenomenon.

After presenting briefly the educational system of Finland we describe the general atmosphere towards ethnic diversity in the country, which impacts also on educational paths and possibilities for minority youth. Our analysis of the existing research on ethnic minority students' positions and possibilities in the Finnish secondary education has been divided in three parts according to the discursive approaches of the studies under review: (1) ethnic diversity as a 'problem' for educational policies and patterns, (2) minority background as a risk for educational exclusion, and (3) ethnic discrimination.

The increasing discussion around multiculturalism in Finland has also stimulated academic debate and polemical political discourse about racism. In the Finnish context the term 'racism' has been broadened beyond 'race' to describe also cases where the basis of discrimination is the person's or people's ethnic or cultural background. In this chapter we follow this pattern and call for more profound analyses in order to understand different forms and levels of the manifold and statistically proven ethnic inequalities in a learning society. Sociology of cultural racism is committed to social theories that emphasize social hierarchies and positions as discursive and given conditions: e.g. educational exclusion is not an individual process and choice but based on marginalizing patterns of societies and their communities. This chapter outlines this aspect through the rare data at hand pertaining to education in Finland.

11.2 National context

11.2.1 The educational system of Finland

Finland is a Nordic welfare society, which covers social and educational services. The state's welfare policies lean on universalistic ideals: educational services are, in principle, available for all native citizens, naturalized citizens, and denizens living in the country. At the very heart of the whole Finnish educational system there is a formal principle and law concerning equality of participation opportunities (Act of Basic Education 1998). Furthermore, the newest 'Developmental Plan for Education' launched by the Ministry of Education and Culture (2011) emphasizes practices that aim at decreasing inequalities in learning outcomes that are a reflection and consequence of students' social, ethnic, or sexual backgrounds.

Figure 11.1 presents the educational system of formal schooling in Finland. Compulsory education extends to youth under 17 years old; the voluntary secondary education is offered nationwide in high and vocational schools and it is tuition free. In Finland students can be forced to retake a year if their progress is not good enough but this is quite rare as all other ways of supporting (e.g. special education measures) are used first if their progression is not going well. Both high schools and vocational schools offer paths to tertiary education that is organized in universities and polytechnics. High school students complete their studies in a national matriculation examination, but this is not a case in the fields of vocational education.

Most schools for young people in Finland are owned, regulated, and administrated by municipalities, under the financing and guidance of the state. Teacher education is ordered in universities, and the teachers are relatively highly educated with competencies regulated by an Act. It is also possible to establish private schools with public financial support, and it seems that especially private primary schools carry a reputation as elite schools and choices for 'enlightened' families. In practice, private schools are still quite rare, leaning on some alternative pedagogy (e.g. Steiner pedagogy, Montessori pedagogy), religion (e.g. Jewish, Christianity), or language (e.g. Swedish, French, Russian, German). It is noteworthy that also private schools should get their mandate and legitimation from the Finnish Educational Board.

In spite of the equality principle of schools and schooling, in Finland there can be recognized a tendency to compare schools according to some measurements – according to the grades of the students, for example. Also students' socio-economic or ethnic backgrounds are used as indicators of the hierarchies of valuation. Local educational markets are somewhat segregated as well: some high schools, for example, are more popular than others and can thus make tight entrance selection criteria whereby they get the 'best' students. There is a difference in the general cultural valuation of high school education and vocational

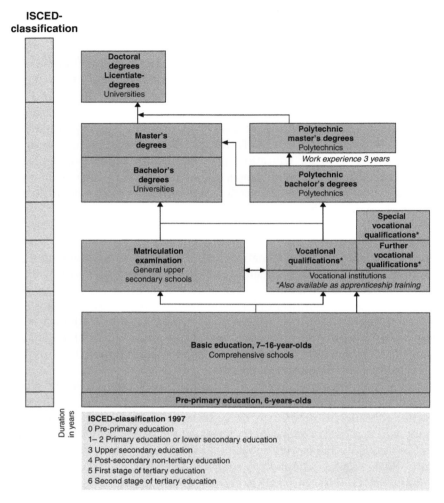

Figure 11.1   The educational system of Finland
Source: Ministry of Education and Culture, 27 February 2013 (http://www.minedu.fi/OPM/Koulutus/koulutusjaerjestelmae/?lang=en).

education as well, setting the former at an advantage over the latter. In principle, both branches of secondary education should qualify their pupils for university studies, but in practice it is more challenging for students of vocational schools to pass university entrance exams or successfully conduct university studies, as only high school curricula consist of an explicit academic qualification orientation.

In general, however, students' knowledge is relatively good. This quality has been evaluated as 'excellent' in international comparisons (e.g. in the PISA measurements). This outcome has been explained by, among other factors, the cultural and linguistic homogeneity of classrooms, and thus also by the absence of immigrant pupils and students from classrooms. For teachers, culturally homogenous classrooms seem to be pedagogically and didactically less challenging than those with multicultural compositions (Räsänen et al., 2002). Curriculum planning and teaching practices in educational institutions have often been based on the idea that all pupils have same kinds of resources and needs, in spite of their very different life conditions and cultural backgrounds. Lately, however, in national educational strategies immigrant pupils have been recognized as learners who need special attention and treatment in schools – but this has mainly been justified by pedagogical and cognitive explanations, not with immigrant students' disadvantageous positions in their social context within the landscapes of a learning society.

11.2.2 Main migration patterns and composition

As mentioned above Finland is a society where the issue of multiculturalism has been publicly noted and discussed only very recently. This rise of interest has a clear link with the relatively rapidly increasing number of immigrant people in a country that during its short independence history (from 1917) has been generally quite closed and inward-oriented. This is why the discourse – both public and scientific – around ethnic minorities or multiculturalism in Finland is very tightly connected with the concept of immigration.

The building of Finland as a nation-state has been loaded with strong emphasis on nationalism and patriotism. As the country has no colonial history, the ethnic composition of its population has been quite homogeneous. Now the situation is changing: whereas the number of the foreign-born population in Finland was 64,922 in 1990 (1.3% of the population), it was 248,135 in 2010 (4.6% of the population) (Statistics Finland, 2011; Ahponen et al., 2011). Children, youth, or young adults under 30 form almost half of the immigrant population in Finland (Statistics Finland, 2004). At their age, school is one of the most important spheres of life, both in terms of formal learning and informal peer relationships. Even though the number of immigrants is increasing continuously, also popular resistance towards the change in the ethnic composition of citizens can be recognized widely.

Finland has, of course, had small migrant and ethnic minority populations (e.g. Tatars, Roma, and the indigenous Sami) even before this new wave of migration, but their presence in (or absence from) formal education has been almost ignored in patterns and strategies of the national social and educational policies until late 1970s. This invisibility has also been connected to the independent nation-state building, where the principle of 'one nation, one language, and one culture' has been a focal device. This has led to a situation where Finnish educational institutions have been tainted by a sort of culturally ethnocentric and nationalistic sentiment that enhances national assimilation policies – aiming at the cohesion of a relatively young nation-state. This has been noticed, for example, in different analyses of curricula and textbooks.

The 1990s was the turning-point decade towards a slightly more international orientation: commitments to the European Union, as well as to other transnational coalitions, forced Finland to introduce some changes to its national policies. The waves of migration turned upside down as immigration began to be higher in numbers than emigration. The biggest groups of immigrants came from Russia, Estonia, Somalia, and the former Yugoslavia (Statistics Finland, 2011). Dual (or multiple) citizenship became legal in 2003, and 'active immigration policy' appeared as a new concept in governmental declarations. Racism and ethnic discrimination were defined as crimes in the national legislation (Pitkänen et al., 2005.) This, however, did not lead to any new and sustainable multiculturally open atmosphere: in the 1990s many neo-nationalistic movements and attitudes were recognized in Finland, as was the case also in other European countries (Sabour, 1999). Today, no mitigation in this sense can be seen. There are several neo-Nazi movements in Finland causing local conflicts between natives and immigrants, and neo-nationalistic politics got wide parliamentary support when the Finns Party[1] rose to be among the biggest parties of the National Parliament.

In the middle of the hardening attitudes towards immigration and multiculturalism we should, however, note that not all immigrants in Finland face intolerance and discrimination. There seems to be a clear 'hierarchy of differences' (Suurpää, 2002): the native population classifies those who are defined as culturally different into divergent positions in 'a continuum of acceptance and non-acceptance' (Harinen et al., 2009). It seems that for a high percentage of Finns it is much easier to cope, associate, and coexist with people of Western (American or European) origins than with other backgrounds. This preference is manifested as a form of ethnic penalty (Khattab, 2009; Reyneri and Fullin, 2011) seen in the reluctance of Finnish employers to hire immigrants and subsequently in the employment statistics that show the large proportion of immigrants with African backgrounds unemployment or educational drop-out figures (Ministry of the Interior, 2009; Ahmad, 2005; see Table 11.1). These hierarchies of differences seem also to cause tension among various groups of immigrants in the everyday life at school (Souto, 2011). However, Table 11.1 shows also a trend towards more equal conditions, as the second-generation immigrants seem to find their places in the educational system relatively more easily than before.

As we are dealing with education in this article, it is important to note that most of immigrants in the country live in large, crowded cities of western and southern Finland (Ministry of the Interior, 2013). In these educational localities competition for the most popular student positions and learning subjects are harder than average, which subsequently often puts immigrant applicants in a difficult and disadvantageous situation. In addition, today there are some

Table 11.1 Ethnic inequality in Finnish education shown by statistics

Ethnic origin	N	% in population	In general schools	In vocational schools	Out of education
Russian/Estonian 2nd gen.	525	0.4	55.5	35.7	8.9
Russian/Estonian 1st gen.	1254	0.8	44.4	45.7	10.0
Ex-Yugoslavia	271	0.2	23.6	61.6	**14.8**
West Asian/North African 2nd gen.	117	0.1	49.3	32.9	**17.9**
West Asian/North African 1st gen.	290	0.2	45.5	36.2	**18.3**
East Asian 2nd gen.	148	0.1	57.7	32.1	10.2
East Asian 1st gen.	96	0.1	45.8	34.4	**19.8**
Sub-Saharan African 2nd gen.	108	0.1	63	18.5	**18.5**
Sub-Saharan African 1st gen.	249	0.2	29.7	41.0	**29.3**
Other 2nd gen.	112	0.1	55.5	28.7	**15.9**
Other 1st gen.	138	0.1	32.7	48.3	**19.0**
Mixed origin (one Finnish parent)	588	1.5	65.1	29.0	5.9
Other-language Finn	172	0.1	57.0	28.5	**14.5**
Swedish language Finn	4779	5.1	57.6	37.8	4.7
Finnish-language Finn	14311	91.9	54.5	39.9	5.6
Total	*23158*	*100*	*54.6*	*39.7*	*5.8*

Source: Kilpi-Jakonen (2011, p. 84).

vocational schools that refuse to enroll students from immigrant background; a fact that clearly breaks the national policy concerning equality of educational participation opportunities (Helsingin Sanomat, 2012). A new trend seems to be on the rise: a large number of Finnish parents refuse to send their children to schools where immigrants form a sizeable proportion of students (Iltalehti, 2012).

11.2.3 Developments in terms of relevant educational and social policies

In Finland the formal policies have paid a considerable attention to the growing immigrant population in the country. At the strategic level the Finnish society invests significantly in immigrants' educational possibilities, especially in the fields of secondary vocational education. Courses of Finnish language are arranged systematically, and a system named 'training education' is developed for facilitating access of immigrants to secondary education. Training education aims at developing immigrants' learning capabilities within the Finnish educational system (language skills, general understanding of society and social policy etc.). Still, it seems that something important remains unnoticed as the strategies and recommendations do not reach minority youth's educational paths in a successful way, as we can deduce when analyzing figures of national statistics and comparisons such as presented in Table 11.1.

Recent educational policies have paid attention to the risk of immigrant students' educational drop-out, which is three times that of the native students (Finnish National Board of Education, 2010). The National Board of Education has financed several developmental projects in order to prevent immigrant students from dropping out, especially during secondary education. In addition, special study-counseling practices for minority pupils have been formed, and in tertiary education an intensive aim is to make both the curricula and student population much more international.

The current increase of especially youth with immigrant background in Finland has inspired researchers to turn their attention and interest towards issues of multicultural education, intercultural learning, and cultural diversity in everyday encounters in schools (e.g. Räsänen et al., 2002; Teräs et al., 2010; Souto, 2011). However, research in this area has been interested mainly in institutions and practices of primary education. Racism has, to a certain extent, been a topic in sociological research of primary education (in terms of pupil interactions, Souto, 2011), and in didactic analyses of cultural conflicts in classrooms, as well as pupils of immigrant background with 'learning difficulties' as problems for teachers' work (e.g. Räsänen et al., 2002). Overall, in Finland any scientific empirical research and evaluations concerning the field of secondary education has been carried out only recently. Even though studies concerning young people's attitudes in Finland endorse and confirm the result that native pupils of secondary vocational education have the most negative attitudes towards immigrants (e.g. the National Youth Barometer, 2005), youth researchers/ethnographers have not decided to step into vocational schools until recently. The concepts of racism or anti-racism are explicitly mentioned as research topics only casually.

In spite of many renewals, we also have to emphasize that at the turn of the third millennium the rational of economic policy began to have predominance and hegemony over other social policies (Jauhiainen et al., 2001). 'Requirements of labor markets' as a dominating, discursive reference also conditioned educational strategies and visions. Now this discourse has found its way to the latest Developmental Plan for Education (2011) and turned into recommendations to speed up individual students' learning paths and graduations. Education *an sich* is not valuable anymore, while its economic, instrumental function begins to dominate. This means that, for example, vocational studies that formerly took three years to complete are expected to last now only two. For a student, who can have incomplete Finnish language skills, this hastening trend may cause consequential and prejudicial difficulties.

11.3 Methodology

We started to seek literature for our review from the national information database of libraries by using keywords 'inequality', 'racism', 'anti-racism', 'discrimination', 'ethnicity', 'minorities', 'immigration', and 'secondary education'. The very first notion in this search was that in Finland there seems to be a systematic tendency to avoid the use of the term 'racism' when education or educational policy is under scrutiny – probably because of the negative connotation of the concept (Souto, 2011). Hence we had subsequently to loosen our searching criteria and include in our data any studies or reports that somehow deal with ethnic minority students who have completed primary education, and then check if some discussion concerning discrimination was included therein. We also had to give up the idea of seeking just sociological research because attention to secondary education has mainly occurred in the fields of pedagogical sciences. In this way, we ended up with one dissertation (concerning Finland though made in Oxford), four research articles, four descriptive and summary reports or memos of different ministries or municipalities, and one sociological statement against ethnic discrimination. Below there is a list of these texts, one of which has been published in English and the rest in Finnish.

Doctoral dissertation:

- *The Education of Children of Immigrants in Finland* (2010)

Research articles:

- *Vähemmistö, kieli ja rasismi* [Minority, language and racism] (1988)
- *Kahden opetuskulttuurin kohtaaminen: Venäjänkieliset opiskelijat toisen asteen opinnoissa* [Encounters in-between two teaching cultures: Russian-speaking students in secondary education] (2001)
- *Elämää Suomessa: Venäjänkielisten nuorten naisten kokemuksia ja tulevaisuudennäkymiä* [Life in Finland: Russian-speaking young women's experiences and future plans] (2007)
- *Maahanmuuttajien lasten siirtymät koulutukseen ja työelämään* [Immigrant children's transitions to education and working life] (2010)

National or municipal reports or memos:

- *Maahanmuuttajanuoret toisen asteen koulutuksessa* [Immigrant students in secondary education] (1999)
- *Romaniasioiden hallintotyöryhmän muistio* [A memo of an administrative working group for Roma issues] (2001)

- *Romanien pitkä matka työn markkinoille* [Roma people's long journey to the labor market] (2008)
- *Maahanmuuttajaoppilaat ja koulutus* [Immigrant students and education] (2008)

Critical statement, discussion:

- *Toisen sukupolven koulumenestyksen ymmärtäminen ja tutkiminen Suomessa* [Understanding and studying educational achievements of the second-generation immigrants in Finland] (2010)

It is noteworthy to outline that in most of the studies we found immigrant youth and young people representing ethnic minorities (e.g. Roma people, Sami people) are mainly seen as 'student at risk' *an sich* (because of their non-Finnish backgrounds), and their educational exclusion has been made visible in a statistical sense (numbers of drop-outs, educational failure). Thus the way that racism and discrimination are treated, if they are treated at all, had to be found implicitly almost between the lines. For this analysis, the main approach of the research or discussion we found are categorized in the following way: (1) studies based on an idea of cultural conflicts (that 'automatically' cause learning and teaching problems) – it has been supposed that living between two cultures and two languages causes problems for immigrant youth who are victims of unhappy circumstances *per se*; (2) studies following life-courses of 'excluded or self-excluded immigrants'; and (3) statements concentrating on everyday interaction and everyday racism in schools – this is just a new trend with only a slight impact which has risen along with the general notions of emerging racism towards immigrants.

In the following chapter we make a critical assessment into this rare research concerning ethnic plurality and discrimination in the fields of secondary education. It is noteworthy that this research has been conducted almost exclusively among vocational education students. Behind this trend there might be an assumption that minority students automatically 'must go' to vocational education, which is the culturally less-valued choice in Finland (Käyhkö, 2006). This can be seen as a serious shortcoming as many studies have shown that immigrant youth usually have a very positive attitude towards schooling in general and high schooling especially (e.g. Ministry of Education, 2008).

11.4   Ethnicity and educational inequality in Finland

11.4.1   Non-Finnish backgrounds of students as a pedagogical and didactic problem?

The main research questions behind the analyses read for this section can be condensed as following: What kinds of problems do students' of minority backgrounds cause to the Finnish educational system and its institutions – and how should the system react to solve these problems? In multicultural conditions uniform services and practices become insufficient, and cultural diversity is easily manifested as a challenge, obstacle or problem (Ålund, 1991; Heywood, 2007; Ahponen et al., 2011). This discursive tendency can clearly be seen in, for example, the ways of research funding in Finland: as immigration is something to be governed by different social policies, research money is allocated to those who are promising practical 'problem-solving'. The approach stressing 'multi-ethnicity as challenge' thus creates the mainstream research of immigration and cultural minorities in Finland, as well as the research concerning multi-ethnicity in education.

The perspective of problem solving, and ethnic minority students as challenges for teaching, is a frame for five studies analyzed for this article: (1) *Encounters in-between two teaching cultures: Russian speaking students in secondary education* (Iskanius, 2001), (2) *Immigrant students in secondary education* (Romakkaniemi, 1999), (3) *A memo of an administrative working group for Roma issues* (Ministry of Social Affairs and Health, 2001), (4) *Immigrant students and education* (Ministry of Education, 2008), and (5) *The Education of Children of Immigrants in Finland* (Kilpi, 2010). The first one is based on a questionnaire filled in by teachers (n=30), the others have used large national quantitative datasets as bases for analyses. Besides, quantitative reasoning is supplemented by qualitative interview data in these studies, except the one of Iskanius (2001). Answers have been sought by inviting some teachers from secondary education to reflect their teaching experiences, by collecting nation-wide information concerning immigrant or Roma students' educational achievements (diploma numbers), their educational choices and progress, their drop-out proportions, as well as their school experiences as students in Finland (Kilpi-Jakonen, 2011).

A lack of sufficient language skills seems to be one main theme in these studies that aim at proving the challenging nature of minority youth in secondary education. One conclusion presented is that reliable language skill tests for young non-Finns could work as a guarantee for teachers to get students, who would be capable enough to study in Finnish – and would thus not cause any extra burden on the everyday arrangements of teaching. In addition, the concept of learning culture raises questions for pedagogues concerning students' adaptation. From their point of view minority youth are located in-between two different learning cultures and thus have difficulties in adapting to the Finnish way to be at school. These difficulties are explained with cultural differences in growing up to self-discipline, punctuality, and personal autonomy; it is seen that even though education is valued in immigrant families, their youth lack the needed degree of autonomy, in order to take independent care of their studies. It is assumed then that this leads to immigrants' low educational outcomes, as described in national statistics.

The question of language is crucial also in studies focusing on Roma and Sami students at school (Ministry of Social Affairs and Health, 2001). Here, however, the arguments are the opposite: the fundamental rights of Roma and Sami students to study in their own native languages and the lack of competent teachers, as well as proper learning material, are emphasized. From this perspective, the linguistic inequalities are treated as a human right problem and defined as a strategy of structural discrimination, where ethnicity as Finns is denied or passed, in particular in relationship to the Roma. In addition, these analyses also call for recognition of ethnic equality at the school. This surely is an important notion as the educational exclusion of Roma youth in Finland has a long history (e.g. Markkanen, 2003).

The city of Helsinki is managing educational services to the biggest group of immigrant students in Finland. Helsinki is also one of the rare municipalities, who have invested in covering, local follow-up research concerning immigrant youth's educational progress and problems (Romakkaniemi, 1999). From this research we can see, for example, that even 30 percent of immigrant youth fall off from educational services and do not finish the compulsory period between 7–16 years (the same number among native Finnish youth is less than 10 percent). The biggest ethnic group among these drop-outs is formed by Somali immigrants, whose position in Finland, anyway, is precarious and who are socially rejected – the statistics show how difficult for them is to become employed and how the attitudes towards them among Finns are much more negative than towards other groups of immigrants (Sabour, 1999). However, when teachers and administrative staff of education were interviewed, they did not talk about rejection – or group-based inequality – but more about 'wrong educational choices' of immigrant youth, about a lack of proper student counseling, and about a need for more intensive individual support that should be offered to immigrant students.

The Ministry of Education (now the Ministry of Education and Culture), being an operator of the state level, has presented a system level investigation concerning immigrant students' educational achievements, their educational choices, and their possibilities in labor market after secondary education (2008). The analysis has its basis in the welfare state principle of educational equality. The scrutiny is leaning on the idea that the educational system should be improved so that it could answer to very different needs of very different students. It also pays attention to many prevailing grievances noted in the system that lead students to unequal outcomes and positions. This inequality is demonstrated clearly also by Kilpi's (2010) results that show a plain difference in native and immigrant students' diploma numbers – which, then, have a fateful significance when student places of tertiary education are contested and applied for. The national statistics show that in every school subject native students reach significantly higher grades than they immigrant fellows.

Even though these numbers show a clear structural tendency of inequality, the researchers of the Ministry end up to recommendations where individual immigrants and their counselors are put in charge and no glance are turned to the fateful, discriminative practices of educational everyday life – as was the case also in the Helsinki-report mentioned above.

To sum up: This branch of researches has a strong didactic tone with a focus on multicultural encounters between teachers and pupils. The ideas of difference and misunderstanding are guiding the definitions of problems and efforts to solve them. Answers are sought from individual guidance and support given to individual students. However, this kind of reasoning becomes relatively slight when it concentrates much attention on individual students and disregards structural, everyday discrimination which could marginalize certain and same minorities in a systematic way.

11.4.2 Educational pathways of marginalized life-courses

The main research questions behind the analyses read for this section can be condensed as following: What kinds of challenges minority students encounter during their educational careers and how could they be supported in facing these challenges? The theme of risky life-circumstances of immigrants can be recognized as a research focus behind at least three of the studies we found for this article: (1) *Immigrant students and education* (Ministry of Education, 2008, mentioned also in the previous sub-chapter), (2) *Roma people's long journey to labor market* (Ministry of Labor, 2008), and (3) *Immigrant children's transitions to education and working life* (Teräs et al., 2010). The gravid concern behind these analyses is that because it is expected that the cultural difference of minority students will create educational, pedagogic, and didactic problems that remain unsolved, this causes the minority youth's marginalized positions in the different 'markets' of society. Thus, this branch of research is based on the idea that careful tracing of the experiences of those considered as vulnerable would help in preventing educational marginalization that is quite fateful in a society that appreciates educational diplomas above all. These analyses have been conducted by using national follow-up statistics and some complementary, qualitative interviews.

When examining life-courses, the theoretical concept of transition is important. Transitions are phases where many far-reaching choices are made – and where the young ones are the most vulnerable. Transition phases between different educational stages are defined as the most important phases of choice in youth's lives (Herranen and Harinen, 2007). The studies analyzed for this article examine transitions from primary school to secondary school, and transitions from vocational education to labor market. The scrutiny leans on statistical information concerning individual life-courses, and also shows the marginalizing educational 'choices' of ethnic minorities. Here, again, Roma and Somali youth seem to be posed in the most vulnerable social positions as their educational paths become closed much more systematically than those of the others. Thus these studies, again, lead to think about systematic racist patterns of school-going – but the solutions presented in reports we analyzed are pedagogic and didactic. They, however, do not just put the blame on immigrants or other minorities (or on their culture) and do not oblige only them but also challenge the system to react and take care that there are enough supporting institutional structures and services to support the 'vulnerable ones' in their important life-course transitions (as was the case within almost all of the reports we read).

In spite of the recommended supporting arrangements, especially the transition where the compulsory (primary) education ends seems to be prone to educational drop-outs. Negative and bitter experience from school life can cumulate towards a decision not to continue school-going after the compulsory phase. This cumulative effect of bitterness can be recognized also in studies analyzed for this article. But it is, however, noteworthy that in spite of qualitative interviews where, for example, immigrant students report experiences of becoming targets of bullying at school, some of the researchers eagerly tend to seek explanations to minorities' educational (and later to their labor market) exclusion from their ethnic backgrounds, or from the supposed conflict between their cultural attitudes and the Finnish educational system (Teräs et al., 2010). These explanations seem to have weight: immigrant students' positive attitudes towards school-going reported in research data are not enough to open up the 'sociological eyes'. It seems that it would be analytically more adequate to avoid overemphasizing cultural reasoning and seek explanations also from feelings of alienation and exclusive relationships from everyday life at school (cf. Souto, 2011).

It is the most noteworthy that, again, the themes of bullying and rejecting in these life-course studies are almost only discussed (or actually slightly referred to) when the analysis focuses on Roma students. This rarity seems to reveal one Finnish national unfortunate policy in dealing with minorities: There is a historical echo from the era when the main and explicit aim of education was to hide all ethnic differences and make all children 'decent Finns'. This happened especially with Roma and Sami people (Rahikainen, 1994, pp. 41–49). The studies where Roma students are concerned contain references to bullying, discrimination and even racism exercised by teachers that other reports do not mention.

To sum up: By using statistical information this branch of researches draws images of educational pathways of minority youth. Attention is paid to transitions (e.g. from primary education to secondary education) where especially immigrant and Roma youth more systematically than the others tend to drop out schooling. This is an important notion as in the Finnish learning society failure in secondary education seems to be the strongest predictor of future problems in individual life courses.

11.4.3 Ethnic discrimination in secondary education

The main research questions behind the analyses read for this section can be condensed as following: How does discrimination impact on minority students' school going? In spite of some slight referring to discriminative treatment towards Roma students, the lack of empirical research concerning direct exclusion in secondary education in Finland is very obvious. Furthermore, nation-wide analyses that show ethnic minority youth's vulnerable positions in national educational and labor market lead to conclude and call for a necessity of new kinds of methodological approaches in research of educational equality. The term ethnic discrimination was mentioned or reflected only in four texts analyzed for this article: (1) *Minority, language and racism* (Skutnabb-Kangas et al., 1988), (2) *Life in Finland: Russian speaking young women's experiences and future plans* (Juutilainen, 2007), (3) *Roma people's long journey to labor market* (Ministry of Labor, 2008, mentioned also, and presented, in the previous sub-chapter), and (4) *Understanding and studying educational achievements of the second generation immigrants in Finland* (Markkanen, 2010).

The first examination mentioned above does not concentrate on secondary education and not just on the Finnish society but it can be noted as one of the earliest texts discussing minority children's education in Finland. This scrutiny does not contain any systematic empirical analysis (Skutnabb-Kangas et al., 1988) but was done before the 'immigration decade' of Finland (the 1990s), and that is why it is very interesting to note that racism is mentioned explicitly even in the title of the writing that concentrates on the question how to grow up as a bilingual person. Here, however, discrimination is examined loosely in the wider context; within the ethnocentrically-oriented Nordic tradition that seems to grant low credit and consideration to all what is culturally, linguistically and racially 'strange'.

The second study mentioned above (Juutilainen, 2007) is not actually focusing on education but the informants of the analysis (young Russian immigrant women), when describing their future plans a and dreams, also reported many negative school memories. In the research interviews where young immigrants' future visions were collected, the interviewees told how experiences at school where they had been victims and targets of bullying, teasing, naming, framing and violence, had affected their school-going and lowered their educational motivation which during the first school years had been intensive and high. Also these notions from Juutilainen's research data imply a need for data collection that would open up everyday relations of the educational reality.

An important question to be formulated is: Why researchers in Finland do not underline openly the possible existence racism even though their data would carry many clues towards these kinds of interpretations? This can be explained maybe by a policy level choice – to be passive is to fade out the problem? (Harinen et al., 2009) However, the last text presented in this chapter seems to be an invitation for opening up of a discussion, where reality even when is 'bold' and 'ugly' it can be pronounced aloud (Markkanen, 2010). *Understanding and studying educational achievements of the second generation immigrants in Finland* is a critical statement, where the idea that minority youth's educational outcomes are always seen as reflections of their ethnic backgrounds is strongly questioned. Markkanen makes no empirical analysis but suggests to researchers of education and educational equality to revise their culturalistic assumptions where ethnic background is posed as the most explaining variable when analyzing differences of educational experiences, choices, and outcomes. This incitation has both conceptual (approach related) and methodological implications when stating that in statistical analyses strongly preconceived variables begin to dominate the process and produce results that are in line with the hypothetic categories set beforehand – even though we may ask whether these kinds of results tell much more about the possible discriminative and selective attitudes which may exist amongst some spheres in the host society than minorities' cultures or ethnicities *an sich*.

To sum up: This branch of researches pays special attention to educational inequality as a socially produced and maintained process both in the macro and micro levels of communities. The everyday school life analyses show that minority youth are easily stigmatized with a stamp of difference and deviance. Statistical information, on its part, denotes that minority youth are facing much more educational risks (e.g. drop outs) than others. However, a slight change seems to happen in case of the so called second generation immigrants, who manage at school better than their predecessors.

11.5   Conclusion

The goal of this paper has been to describe and categorize the contemporary research concerning ethnic relations and inequality in the fields of Finnish secondary education. Minority youth has been absent from Finnish schools until the recent decades, and we are only now witnessing a wake-up of sociologists to pay scientific attention to ethnic and cultural diversity of schools and their actors. This indicates why it was hard to find data for our analysis and this notion is also the content of our main critics: the Finnish learning society obviously needs a more intensive assessment of its schools and to their ethnic diversification, from the perspective of critical sociology of education.

As the amount of data remained so thin, no special paradigms of research could be classified for this article. We have categorized the research according to three branches. The first one looks at the phenomenon pedagogically and didactically, from the point of view of encounters and confrontations of 'different ones' (Finnish teachers and minority students). It is assumed that multi-ethnicity in schools provides challenges in both parties, and the educational system needs to seek for solutions towards equal possibilities of learning. The second branch is showing us statistics of minority youth's educational risks that seem to be more numerous than those of native students. The third branch of research, finally, has a more sociological perspective while paying attention to cultural processes of everyday relations in school life. Still, it is notable that secondary education itself has been the frame of scrutiny only in a couple of analyses.

Finnish educational system emphasizes the values and ideals of educational equalities in a learning society. However, when comparing the national research results with the educational policy strategies campaigning for educational equality, it is noticeable that the noble principles do not always meet educational practices and outcomes. This notion indicates a lack of understanding that would enhance the required changes in both policies and practices of education and school-going. Especially we can recognize a lack of research concerning everyday life relationships in secondary education. In reaching this understanding, teachers' teaching experiences do not seem to be sufficient: multicultural classes are not just didactic spaces, as for young people school means much more than just a place for formal learning. School is a place where peer group memberships and friendships are created and tested, and where the feelings of social belonging or isolation are born (Ziehe, 1991; Antikainen et al., 2011, pp. 132–133). These issues have already been studied in Finnish primary education institutions, also from the perspective of multiculturalism and multi-ethnicity (e.g. Tolonen, 2001; Souto, 2011), but not yet in high and vocational schools.

Furthermore, when we are discussing educational marginalization in a learning society, attention needs to be paid not only to confrontations in everyday life at school but also to the indirect and structural discrimination that is enhanced by comparative research which tends to explain ethnic minorities' low educational outcomes with their ethnic backgrounds. As Bourdieu (1986) and Bernstein (1996) have prompted, educational institutions in Western societies are ideological institutions that favor middle class 'mainstream' population. Thus, critical sociological approach is needed where attention would be paid to ethnic minorities' manifold social inequality, which becomes culminated in their descendants' educational outcomes.

Still, in the Finnish sociology of education, an important share of academic discussion that has been taking place is mainly concerned with the question of whether educational choices are individual choices at all – or is it actually the societal system that chooses people to proper places in society, and using the educational system when doing this structural, selective work (see Antikainen et al., 2011). In this regard the classical theories of Bourdieu (1977) and Bernstein (1975) can provide an appropriate approach for illuminating this structural selection, where students' socioeconomic and cultural backgrounds become factors for hierarchical selections, which have their roots in the class structure of society. Although the critical sociology of education has a long tradition also in Finland, researches tackling ethnic inequalities are still reluctant to appropriate this kind of scrutiny where ethnic discrimination is seen as a means to maintain the unequal hierarchies of class society (Himanen and Könönen, 2010).

It goes without saying that the Finnish educational policy has not given up its aims of equality in front of quite frustrating results. Aspirations to develop the system and its institutions, as well as its practices to offer individual support for individual students in various difficulties have been continuous and purposeful. Now, however, it seems that the contemporary neo-liberal educational policy is changing the systemic vocation and course: especially the shortened graduation times in secondary education mean extra difficulties for students with foreign mother languages. They can easily become stigmatized as special cases (with 'learning difficulties'), who need special treatment, and who will face enormous obstacles in competing for studying places in tertiary education through selective entrance exam. Because. The Finnish language is crucial in this regard. Applicants from immigration background can find themselves in a disadvantaged situation in achieving success and entry to university. The evaluation of 'learning difficulties' tends to predict increasing drop-out numbers – unhappy fates in a society that classifies its members according their educational successes. Thus, an extra question could be asked: How much today's educational policies themselves are producing and maintaining, consciously or unconsciously, indirect ethnic discrimination and generate something that can be called 'ethnic punishments' (Teräs et al., 2010, p. 88)?

Beck and Beck-Gernsheim (2008) share this concern while criticizing the contemporary sociological mainstream for its commitments to nation-state frames and for the hidden nationalistic aspirations of its methodological solutions. They take a questioning stand towards this approach called methodological nationalism. This is the basic adjustment recognized also in Sanna Markkanen's statement we found for this analysis. Markkanen argues for the opening of a new path for new kinds of questions in research of educational equality (no more plain ethnic comparisons) and challenges researchers to participate in an inevitable ethnographic work in the middle of the everyday encounters of secondary education (cf. Souto, 2011). The same possibilities to participate do not mean same possibilities to success. Statistics have already shown that something has gone wrong.

The researches we have analyzed for this chapter contains many references to the fact that especially immigrants' attitudes towards schooling are very positive and they express high expectations from their education – so this is not the problem. Further, the structural nature of discrimination can be seen in statistics that report, for example, Roma and Somali people's regular educational marginalization in Finland. In the light of this it is expected that future policy will tackle how everyday patterns, on their part, produce, maintain, and support this systematic exclusion.

Note

1. 'The Finns' are politicians and their supporters, who actively resist immigration (especially immigration based on humanitarian issues) and multiculturalism. One of their slogans is: 'Return Finland to Finns!'

References

Ahmad Akhlaq (2005) *Getting a Job in Finland: The Social Networks of Immigrants from the Indian Subcontinent in the Helsinki Metropolitan Labour Market.* Helsinki: Helsinki University Printing House.

Ahponen, Pirkkoliisa, Harinen, Päivi, Honkasalo, Veronika, Kivijärvi, Antti, Pyykkönen, Miikka, Ronkainen, Jussi, Souto, Anne-Mari and Suurpää, Leena (2011) Emerging Multiculturalism in Youth Work. The Case of Finland. An article to be published in Youth & Policy.

Ålund, Aleksandra (1991) *Paradoxes of Multiculturalism. Essays on Swedish Society.* Aldershot: Avebury.

Antikainen, Ari, Dworkin, Gary A., Saha, Lawrence J., Ballantine, Jeanne, Essack, Shaheeda, Teodoro, António and Konstantinovskiy (2011) Contemporary Themes in the Sociology of Education. *International Journal of Contemporary Sociology*, Vol. 48(1), 117–147.

Beck, Ulrich and Beck-Gernsheim, Elisabeth (2008) Global Generations and the Trap of Methodological Nationalism for a Cosmopolitan Turn in the Sociology of Youth and Generation. *European Sociological Review*, Vol. 25(1), 25–36.

Bernstein, Basil (1975) *Class, Codes and Control.* London: Routledge & Kegan Paul.

Bernstein, Basil (1996) *Pedagogy, Symbolic Control and Identity: Theory, Research, Critique.* London: Taylor and Francis.

Bourdieu, Pierre (1977) *Outline of a Theory of Practice.* Cambridge: Cambridge University Press.

Bourdieu, Pierre (1986) *Distinction.* Cambridge, MA: Harvard University Press.

Developmental Plan for Education in Finland (2011) The Ministry of Education and Culture.

Finnish National Board of Education (2010) *Dropout Rates in the Finnish Educational System.* Helsinki: Ministry of Education and Culture.

Harinen, Päivi, Honkasalo, Veronika, Souto, Anne-Mari and Suurpää, Leena (eds) (2009) *Ovet auki! Monikulttuuriset nuoret, vapaa-aika ja kansalaistoimintaan osallistuminen. [Open the Doors! Multicultural Youth, Leisure and Participation in Civil Society].* Helsinki: The Finnisf Youth Research Network.

Herranen, Jatta and Harinen, Päivi (2007) Oikein valinneet jätetään rauhaan. Osallisuus, kulttuuri ja kontrolli. [Those Choosing Well are Laid off. Participation, Culture, and Control] In: A. Gretschel and T. Kiilakoski (eds) *Lasten ja nuorten kunta [Children and Youth in Municipalies].* Helsinki: The Finnish Youth Research Network.

Heywood (2007) *Political Ideologies. An Introduction*. Basingstoke: Macmillan.

Himanen, Markus and Könönen, Jukka (2010) *Maahanmuuttopoliittinen sanasto. [The Vocabulary of Immigration Policy]*. Helsinki, : Like.

Iskanius, Sanna (2001) Kahden opetuskulttuurin kohtaaminen. Venäjänkieliset opiskelijat toisen asteen koulutuksessa. [Encounters in-between two Teaching Cultures: Russian Speaking Students in Secondary Education] In: K. Perho (ed.) *Kahden kulttuurin väkeä. Suomalaiset ja venäläiset koulussa. [People of two Cultures. Finns and Russians at School]*. Joensuu: University of Joensuu, Department of Education, 73–87.

Jauhiainen, Arto, Rinne, Risto and Tähtinen, Juhani (2001) *Koulutuspolitiikka Suomessa ja ylikansalliset mallit. [Educational Policy and Supranational Models in Finland]*. Turku: The Finnish Society of Pedagogues.

Juutilainen, Päivi-Katriina (2007) Elämää Suomessa. Venäjänkielisten nuorten naisten kokemuksia ja tulevaisuudennäkymiä [Life in Finland: Russian Speaking Young Women's Experiences and Future Plans] In: P-K. Juutilainen (ed.) *Suhteita ja suunnantotoa. Näkökulmia nuorten ohjaukseen. [Relations and Orientations. Perspectives to Youth Counseling]*. Joensuu: University of Joensuu, Department of Education.

Khattab Nabil (2009) Ethno-religious Background as a Determinant of Educational and Occupational Attainment in Britain, *Sociology*, April 2009, Vol. 43(2), 304–322.

Kilpi, Elina (2010) *The Education of Children of Immigrants in Finland*. University of Oxford: St Anthony's College.

Kilpi-Jakonen, Elina (2011) Continuation to Upper Secondary Education in Finland: Children of Immigrants and the Majority Compared, *Acta Sociologica*, Vol. 54(1), 77–106.

Käyhkö, Mari (2006) *Siivoojaksi oppimassa. Etnografinen tutkimus työläistytöistä puhdistuspalvelualan koulutuksessa. [Learning to Become a Cleaner. An Ethnographic Study of Working-class Girls in Secondary Education]*. Joensuu: Joensuu University Press.

Maahanmuuttajaoppilaat ja koulutus (2008) *Immigrant Students and Education*. Helsinki: The Ministry of Education.

Markkanen, Airi (2003) *Luonnollisesti. Etnografinen tutkimus romaninaisten elämänkulusta [Naturally. An ethnographic analysis on Roma women's life courses]*. University of Joensuu: Department of Humanities.

Markkanen, Sanna (2010) Toisen sukupolven koulumenestyksen ymmärtäminen ja tutkiminen Suomessa. [Understanding and studying educational achievements of the second generation immigrants in Finland] In: T. Martikainen and L. Haikkola (eds) *Maahanmuutto ja sukupolvet. [Immigration and Generation]*. Helsinki: SKS, 133–147.

Ministry of Education (2008) *Immigrants' and Education*. Helsinki: Ministry of Education and Culture.

Ministry of Labor (2008) *Roma People's Long Journey to Labor Market*. Helsinki: Ministry of Labor.

Ministry of Interior (2009) *Immigrant Population in Finland*. Helsinki: Ministry of Interior.

Ministry of Social Affairs and Health (2001) *A Memo of an Administrative Working Group for Roma Issues*. Helsinki: Ministry of Social Affairs and Health.

National Youth Barometer (2005) *Erilaiset ja samanlaiset. [The Different and the Alike Ones]*. Helsinki: Ministry of Education and the Finnish Youth Research Network.

Pitkänen, Pirkko, Ronkainen, Jussi and Harinen, Päivi (2005) Dual Citizenship in Finland. In: Y. Schröter, C. Mengelkamp and R.S. Jäger (eds) *Doppelte Staatsbürgerschaft. Ein Gesellschaftlicher Diskurs über Mehrstaatigkeit*. Landau: Verlag Empirische Pädagogik, 256–267.

Rahikainen, Marjatta (1994) Viimeiset vaeltajat. Romanit ja saamelaiset modernisaation tiellä. [The Last Wanderers. Roma and Sami People on the Road to Modernity]. *Kosmopolis*, Vol. 24(4), 41–49.

Räsänen, Rauni, Jokikokko, Katri, Järvelä Maria-Liisa and Lamminmäki-Kärkkäinen, Tanja (eds) (2002) *Intercultural Teacher Education. From Utopia to Practice Trough Action Research*. University of Oulu: Department of Educational Sciences and Teacher Education.

Romakkaniemi, Harri (1999) *Maahanmuuttajanuoret toisen asteen koulutuksessa. [Immigrant students in secondary education]*. The City of Helsinki: Educational Office.

Romaniasioiden hallintotyöryhmän muistio (2001) *A Memo of an Administrative Working Group for Roma Issues*. Helsinki: The Ministry of Social Affairs and Health.

Romanien pitkä matka työn markkinoille (2008) *Roma People's Long Journey to Labor Market*. Helsinki: The Ministry of Labor.

Reyneri Emilio and Fullin Giovanna (2011) Labour Market Penalties of New Immigrants in New and Old Receiving West European Countries. *International Migration*, Vol. 49(1), 31–57.

Sabour M'hammed (1999) The Socio-cultural exclusion and self-exclusion of foreigners in Finland: the case of Joensuu, in Littlewood Paul et al. (ed.) *Social Exclusion in Europe: Problems and Paradigms*. London: Ashgate.

Skutnabb-Kangas, Tove, Kangas, Ilkka and Kangas, Kea (1988) *Vähemmistö, kieli ja rasismi [Minority, Language, and Racism]*. Helsinki: Gaudeamus.

Souto, Anne-Mari (2011) *Arkipäivän rasismi koulussa. Etnografinen tutkimus suomalais- ja maahanmuuttajanuorten ryhmäsuhteista. [Everyday Racism at School. An Ethnographic Study on Native and Immigrant Youth's Group Relations]*. Helsinki: The Finnish Youth Research Network.

Statistics Finland (2004) *Population in Finland*. Helsinki: Statistics Finland.

Suurpää, Leena (2002) *Erilaisuuden hierarkiat. Suomalaisia käsityksiä maahanmuuttajista ja rasismista. [Hierarchies of Difference. Finnish Perceptions of Immigrants and Racism]*. Helsinki: The Finnish Youth Research Network.

Teräs, Marianne, Lasonen, Johanna and Sannino, Annalisa (2010) Maahanmuuttajien lasten siirtymät koulutukseen ja työelämään. [Immigrant Children's Transitions to Education and Working life] In: T. Martikainen and L. Haikkola (eds) *Maahanmuutto ja sukupolvet. [Immigration and Generation]*. Helsinki: SKS, 85–109.

Tolonen, Tarja (2001) *Nuorten kulttuurit koulussa. Ääni, tila ja sukupuolten arkiset järjestykset. [Youth Cultures at School. Voice, Space and the Gendered Order]*. Helsinki: The Finnish Youth Research Network.

Ziehe, Thomas (1991) *Uusi nuoriso. Epätavanomaisen oppimisen puolustus. [The New Youth. A Defence of Unconventional Learning]*. Tampere: Vastapaino.

Internet sources

Act of Basic Education (1998) http://www.finlex.fi. 28 February 2013.

Helsingin Sanomat (2012) http://mediaseuranta.blogspot.com/2011/08/hs-maahanmuuttaja-kaannytettiin.html http://portti.iltalehti.fi/keskustelu/showthread.php?p=6649042. 28 December 2012.

Iltalehti (2012) http://portti.iltalehti.fi/keskustelu/showthread.php?p=6649042. 13 September 2012.

Ministry of Education and Culture, 27 February 2013. (http://www.minedu.fi/OPM/Koulutus/koulutusjaerjestelmae/?lang=en).

Ministry of the Interior (2013) www.intermin.fi/newslist/pbic/20081002021. 28 February 2013.

Statistic Finland (2011) www.stat.fi. 20 February 2011.

12

France

Mathieu Ichou and Agnès van Zanten

12.1 Introduction

Racial and ethnic inequalities remain an underdeveloped area of research in France. This situation can mainly be attributed to the fact that researchers have been strongly influenced, on the one hand, by a political model of integration (presented in more detail in Section 12.3.3) that has led France 'to ignore itself as a country of immigration' (Noiriel, 1988) and encouraged a color-blind approach to social reality (Lorcerie, 1994a) and, on the other hand, by Marxist political and scientific perspectives giving central importance to class in the study of society. However, since the 1980s, due to important changes in the immigrant population and in policy towards immigrants, as well as to the arrival of a new generation of researchers and the growing internationalization of French research, the number of studies in this domain has increased and diversified. There are however very few reviews of the existing scientific literature (Lorcerie, 1995, 2003; Payet, 2003; Payet and van Zanten, 1996; van Zanten, 1997b) and only one in English (van Zanten, 1997a). Therefore, the following critical survey, based on a systematic sampling of the literature and covering 30 years of research, including very recent studies, should prove useful to various, and especially anglophone, audiences.

12.2 National context

This section presents a brief overview of the French educational system, the history and current state of immigration in France, and developments in policy models that directly or indirectly affect ethnic inequalities in education.

12.2.1 The French educational system

Since 1959 education in France has been compulsory for children aged six to 16, although virtually all children begin preschool at age three (Ministère de l'Education nationale, 2011, p. 81). Primary school is common to all pupils and lasts five years, unless pupils are required to repeat one or more years as can happen in both primary and secondary schools. At age 11, on average, pupils enter a comprehensive four-year lower secondary school called *collège*. By default, pupils are assigned to the local *collège* but under certain conditions parents can choose another school (see Section 12.4.4). At the end of lower secondary school, pupils aged about 15 are assigned to different types of upper secondary school tracks based on their level of academic achievement, and their own preferences and that of their families. Higher achievers usually enter the academic or technological track of upper secondary school (*lycée*), while lower achievers usually enter a vocational *lycée* or an apprenticeship (Figure 12.1).

After three years of upper secondary school, pupils can take an exam called the *baccalauréat*, which serves both as a certificate of completion and as an entry permit to higher education. Depending on their chosen track, pupils will take the academic baccalaureate (*baccalauréat général*), the technological baccalaureate (*baccalauréat technologique*) or the vocational baccalaureate (*baccalauréat professionnel*), the latter created in 1985. Each year, around 65% of the cohort obtains a *baccalauréat* (Ministère de l'Education nationale, 2011, p. 241). Although all three types of *baccalauréat* officially grant access to higher education, they are actually strongly stratified both academically and socially (Ichou and Vallet, 2011): academic *baccalauréat* holders disproportionately come from upper- or middle-class backgrounds and usually enter university or take preparatory classes leading to the *Grandes Ecoles*; technological *baccalauréat* holders, often from lower-middle-class origins, most frequently pursue short vocational tracks in higher education, while pupils who hold a vocational *baccalauréat* generally enter the labor market directly after completion. At both primary and secondary school level, the private sector caters for a significant share of the student body. In 2010, 13.4% of primary school pupils and 21.3%

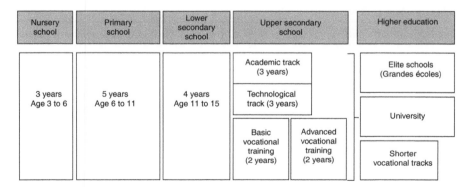

Figure 12.1 The French educational system

of secondary school pupils were schooled in the private sector (Ministère de l'Education nationale, 2011, pp. 75, 95). The public comparison of schools, through league tables, is much less developed than in other countries such as the UK, but a few magazines publish yearly upper secondary schools rankings.

12.2.2 Immigration in France

France has long been a country of immigration. The earliest waves of immigration started long before World War II and came from Eastern and Southern Europe. After the war, the dramatic need for manual workers drove a rise in labor migration. Until the mid-1970s, most immigrants to France were men from Southern Europe (Italy, Portugal, Spain) and North Africa (Algeria, Morocco, Tunisia). After the mid-1970s, family reunification and, to a lesser extent, political and labor migration have been the main reasons for immigration from Southern Europe and North Africa, as well as Turkey, sub-Saharan Africa (Senegal, Mali, Ivory Coast, etc.), Southeast Asia (Cambodia, Laos, Vietnam), and China. Immigrants from Northern Africa, most sub-Saharan African countries and Southeast Asia come from former French colonies. A recent survey shows that, among all adult residents in France, 10% are immigrants and 12% are children of one or two immigrant parents (Lhommeau and Simon, 2010, p. 13). Table 12.1 shows the proportion of first-year primary school students (*cours préparatoire*) in 1997 who were children of immigrants, by their parents' country of birth.

12.2.3 Integration models and policies

Since the 19th century, European countries have embraced ideological models of integration based on the belief of the nation-state as an organic entity, which alone can hold together the diversity of people, including different ethnic

Table 12.1 Proportion of children of immigrants in the first year of primary school in 1997, by their parents' country of birth

Pupils' parents' country of birth	% of all pupils	% of children of immigrant(s)
Native parents	75.7	
Immigrant parents	24.3	100.0
Mixed (one native parent)	14.8	60.7
Portugal	1.0	4.1
Algeria	1.2	5.1
Morocco	1.6	6.7
Tunisia	0.6	2.3
Sub-Saharan Africa	1.3	5.3
Turkey	0.9	3.8
Southeast Asia & China	0.5	2.0
Other immigrants	2.4	9.9

Source: 1997–2004 primary school panel, Ministry of Education; own calculations.

groups, sharing the same territory. Each country has nevertheless adapted these models to specific political, social, and cultural configurations. France has introduced and maintained relatively unchanged what is known as the 'Republican model of integration' (Lapeyronnie, 1993; Favell, 2001, 2003; Browne, 2009). This model is characterized by the importance given to individual rather than collective participation, by the central role attributed to rational allegiance and political membership, as opposed to blood and group membership, and by an emphasis on universalism rather than cultural differences (Schnapper, 1991). As discussed below, this model, which gives a central role to the integrative function of institutions, and particularly schools, has profoundly influenced educational policies until today (Raveaud, 2008; Lorcerie, 2010).

Authors such as van Zanten (1997a) have pointed out that this model has persisted despite its inability to take into account important changes in French society and in immigration patterns after the 1970s. The Republican model was conceived to integrate regional groups and immigrants who came mainly from Europe or from the French colonies, that is from countries where the national culture was either relatively close to French culture or still partly dominated by it. Today the immigrant population is composed of a large number of immigrants from non-EU countries. In addition, the form of assimilation promoted by the Republican model was made possible by the fact that even though immigrants occupied lower-status jobs in the industrial and construction sectors, they were integrated into an expanding economy of full employment and, a significant proportion of them, into workers' trade unions and associations as well (Dubet, 1989; Tripier, 1990; Body-Gendrot, 1995). The situation is entirely different in a period of economic recession and growing unemployment. Still another change concerns ethnic segregation. Since the late 1970s, the departure of the white middle classes and, later, the white working classes from social housing areas in urban peripheries has contributed to the increase of urban segregation.

This situation has generated more complex patterns of immigrant integration. Two studies, one based on the examination of existing statistical data and studies by Dubet (1989) and a second, based on an original research by Tribalat (1995), found a large degree of cultural assimilation among most immigrant groups with respect to cultural practices and a relatively high level of political participation among second-generation immigrants, especially among Algerian youngsters, but limited social mobility and access to the job market for most groups. Working from a perspective inspired by the work of Alejandro Portes and his colleagues (Portes and Zhou, 1993) in the United States, Safi (2006) has shown the existence of three distinctive patterns of integration in French society: (1) upward assimilation characterizes the situation of Spaniards who show great levels of cultural assimilation, socio-economic mobility and social mix; (2) downward assimilation characterizes that of Africans and, to a lesser extent, of individuals from Maghreb, who show high levels of cultural assimilation but low levels of socio-economic mobility; and (3) cultural pluralism characterizes the situation of Asian and, to a lesser extent, of Turkish immigrants. This third pattern is the most conflicting with the premises of the Republican model of integration both because socio-economic integration and upward mobility are accompanied by the preservation of group-specific cultural traits and because community networks and resources seem to play a more important role than state institutions, including schools.

12.3   Methodology

We have systematically sampled all the sociologically relevant peer-reviewed articles, books, edited books, and official reports on the subject of ethnic or racial inequalities in French secondary education from 1980 to 2010. We also adopted a flexible approach when appropriate. This flexibility proved especially important in two instances. First, while focusing on the secondary school level, we also included relevant research on primary school when we considered it particularly noteworthy or necessary to the understanding of pupils' situations in secondary school. Secondly, we sometimes included articles from non-peer-reviewed journals when they met high scientific standards and significantly contributed to the understanding of the subject matter.

In line with Stevens (2007) and Stevens et al. (2011), our sampling procedure consisted of three main stages. First, using systematic queries, we searched bibliographical databases, including two that are international (ERIC and Sociological Abstracts) and two that are French (CAIRN and Persée).[1] The second step consisted in identifying a relevant sample of French scientific journals from 1980 to 2010 and systematically examining their tables of contents for relevant articles. We considered three types of journals: high profile general sociological journals, journals focused on the sociology of education, and journals focused on the sociology of migration and ethnicity.[2] Third, we inspected the bibliographic references contained in the articles found in the two previous steps to identify even more relevant works for review.

This sampling approach resulted in identifying a large body of research, which can be categorized into five research traditions: (1) structures, curriculum, and policies for minority students (SCPM); (2) family background and ethnic inequalities in education (FBEI); (3) limited educational resources of ethnic minority families (LEREM); (4) ethnic school segregation and educational inequalities (ESSEI); and (5) ethnic relations in classrooms and schools (ERCS).

12.4   Ethnicity and educational inequality in France

12.4.1   Structures, curriculum, and policies for minority students

In this section we present research studies that have analyzed how the language, culture, religion, and educational problems of ethnic minority pupils have been integrated in the policies, curricula, and social order of schools. We analyze to what extent these policies reflect the Republican model of 'indifference to (ethnic) differences' and examine their intended and unintended consequences.

12.4.1.1 Language and culture

A prime example of the limited recognition of cultural differences by the French system is the way in which the linguistic and cultural problems of immigrant children have been addressed. The existence of linguistic 'initiation' and 'adaptation' classes was officialized in 1970. However, because the creation of these classes was seen as a breach of the Republican model and because policymakers feared that they might have negative effects on the school trajectories of immigrant children, they were treated as temporary structures both within the system and for children themselves. Until 1995, when new programs and methods on French as a second language were developed, these classes used and adapted syllabi designed for teaching French as a foreign language even though the linguistic problems of immigrant children were frequently very different in nature (Cortier, 2007). Unsurprisingly, the intercultural materials and activities that they produced and used were also quite poor and regarded with suspicion (Berque, 1985; Lorcerie, 1995). As a result, these structures have occupied a marginalized place in the system and contributed in turn to marginalize ethnic minority children (Berque, 1985; Lazaridis, 2001).

In 1973, ELCO (*Enseignement des langues et des cultures d'origine*) classes were also created that offered linguistic and cultural courses in the children's native tongue taught by teachers from their native countries and funded by foreign governments. However, the initial aim of these classes was not to promote cultural differences but to prepare for immigrants' return to their home country. After they were requalified as structures aiming to promote immigrant students' integration in French society, they have been accused of having been used by Muslim countries to transmit the religious principles of Islam and to foster anti-French sentiment among Muslim pupils. Researchers have nevertheless shown that although there are strong variations in the types of courses provided, due to differences between countries in the political role and interpretation of Islam and little administrative control over teachers and their pedagogical practices, the existence of indoctrination mechanisms has been greatly exaggerated (Barou, 1995; Lorcerie, 1994b, 2010).

As concerns the presence of elements of the culture of origin of ethnic minority children in national mainstream curricula, researchers have pointed out the limited space provided for the presentation of Arab-Islamic civilizations and for the history of immigration in history programs and textbooks, the slightly more accurate representation of migration processes in the curricula of geography, economic and social sciences (a subject only taught in one upper secondary school track), and civic education, and the strong reluctance to teach Islam as a contemporary subject (Lorcerie, 1998, 2010; Falaize, 2007).

Researchers have also shown that immigrants are generally presented in a positive but instrumental perspective, as an economic asset for France, in history, geography, and civic education textbooks, and that racism is analyzed as a phenomena belonging to colonial history or to other countries such as South Africa. They also point out that in textbook images immigrants are presented in ways that tend to degrade them, are associated with poverty, suffering, persecution and war, or are just 'invisible' (i.e. presented in the dark or represented by a symbol) (Roussier-Fusco, 2007; Lavin, 2007). Although little is known about the effects of curricula and textbooks on students' knowledge and representations of immigrants, Baccaïni and Gani (1999) found that 54% of secondary school students, including a significant (39%) proportion of ethnic minority students, of lower-class students in technological tracks and of students in private schools, think that immigrants contribute to unemployment among the native population.

12.4.1.2   Religion and the wearing of hijabs in schools

The recognition of non-Christian religions in French schools has attracted a great deal of attention. What is known as the 'hijabs' or 'headscarves' affair started in 1989 and has undergone three phases (de Galembert, 2009). The first controversy started in 1989 following the exclusion of three veiled Muslim girls from a *lycée*. It ended after the *Conseil d'Etat* rendered a judgment reminding the French public that civil servants must remain neutral in all their official responsibilities but not the clients – in this case, the students – followed by a decree from the minister of education reaffirming the secular nature of the school system but advising discussion and consultation with students and their families to find a negotiated solution (Wayland, 1997; Limage, 2000).

Local conflicts continued to occur but the second controversy only started in 1994 when a new minister of education issued a decree stating that 'ostentatious symbols' of religion should be banned from schools. This decree was followed by a limited number of exclusions, some of which were declared void by administrative judges. The third and currently last controversy started in 2003 when a law was passed allowing head teachers to exclude students wearing a headscarf if that symbol was perceived as disrupting the normal functioning of the school. Although this law has not given way to a significant number of exclusions, it has encouraged some immigrant parents to plead discrimination before the HALDE (Haute Autorité contre les discriminations et pour l'égalité), an independent administrative authority created in 2005 and disbanded in 2011.

Analyses of the positions of the different actors involved in these controversies show that the majority of intellectuals, policy-makers, and institutional actors are opposed to headscarves on the basis of three types of arguments: respecting the religious neutrality of schools, limiting the impact of a patriarchal social order on Muslim women, and fighting increasing religious fanaticism (Gaspard and Khosrokhavar, 1995; de Galembert, 2009; Limage, 2000). An additional argument is that publicly showing their Islamic beliefs may reduce girls' chances of social and professional integration (Chérifi, 2001).

However, as pointed out by Lorcerie (1996) and, in an ethnographic study, by Chazal and Normand (2007), whether wearing the hijab becomes an issue or not at the local level depends on the underlying causes and connections that school agents identify in the girls' attitudes, i.e. whether they are seen as constrained or voluntary and, if voluntary, on the factors that motivate them. The latter are frequently religious but can also be psychological and social (a reaction to stigmatization or a sign of rebellion) as well as strategic: complying with the pressures of their parents and brothers by wearing a hijab can also allow girls to gain more autonomy from their families. Kakpo (2005) also underscores the need to understand young men's attraction to Islam, which she associates with attempts to improve their self-esteem and status position when confronted with academic underachievement, unemployment, and rejection by successful Muslim women.

12.4.1.3 Positive discrimination

A limited departure from the Republican model in educational policy was also prompted by teachers' work in segregated schools and by research findings showing the failure of the model to ensure ethnic and class equality in education (see the FBEI tradition). These processes led to the creation in 1981 of Educational Priority Zones (ZEP), a compensatory program modeled after the British Educational Priority Areas, which represented the first explicit acknowledgment of the existence of socio-geographic educational inequalities (Henriot-van Zanten, 1990). In accordance with the principles of the French model of integration, the beneficiaries of this policy were not selected on the basis of personal but of territorial criteria, i.e. the degree of social and educational disadvantage in a given area. However, both because of the geographical concentration of immigrants in poor areas and because the percentage of children of immigrants at school was used as one of the main criteria of social disadvantage, the latter became a main target of this policy (Morel, 2002; Calvès, 2004; Doytcheva, 2007; Robert, 2009). In addition to that, the analysis of teachers' discourses reveals a pervasive tendency to assimilate academic underachievement and the presence of children from immigrants groups in the schools (Varro, 1997, 1999; Kherroubi and Rochex, 2002).

The ZEP, which came to be seen as the major French policy to reduce educational inequalities, proved extremely resistant to political changes throughout the 1980s and 1990s. Since the mid-1990s, they have nevertheless become the target of growing criticism because of their lack of effectiveness in improving the educational achievement of students from low socio-economic and immigrant backgrounds, even though these students' school trajectories appear slightly better than those of similar students in non-ZEP schools (Meuret, 1994; Rochex, 2008; Benabou et al., 2009).

In this context, prestigious higher education institutions such as Sciences Po and ESSEC, a renowned management school, launched new programs in 2001 and 2002, replicated later by many other *grandes écoles,* targeting disadvantaged students. These programs were a response to research studies showing a decrease in the percentage of lower-class students in elite institutions and to pressures from businessmen and politicians of immigrant backgrounds, who had started to denounce the ethnic and racial barriers to accessing these institutions. However, although they maintained the territorial dimension through the development of partnerships with disadvantaged *lycées*, these programs represent an important shift from place-based to people/place-based policies because they select a limited number of good and motivated students within each school for preferential treatment (Sabbagh, 2006; Buisson-Fenet and Landrier, 2008; van Zanten, 2009c). They target not only socially disadvantaged students but also a large proportion of ethnic minority students as well without officially acknowledging it (van Zanten, 2010).

In sum, this research tradition has revealed three important phenomena. The first is the tendency of the French educational system to create structures for ethnic minority students that are not given strong official recognition and financial support, and are therefore marginalized in the educational system and marginalize the students that they are supposed to help. The second concerns the gap between official policies and their implementation at the school level, which depends on interpretations of local situations. Finally, the last phenomenon has to do with the use of territorial and social criteria as a proxy for targeting, without officially acknowledging it, ethnic minority pupils.

12.4.2   Family background and ethnic inequalities in education

12.4.2.1   Public data, French Republican ideology, and difficulties in measuring ethnic inequalities

As in other quantitative subfields of French sociology, researchers who belong to the family background and ethnic inequalities in education (FBEI) research tradition have largely depended on data collected by public institutions, especially the Ministry of Education, the National Institute for Demographic Studies (INED) and the National Institute of Statistics and Economic Studies (INSEE).[3] Funded and administered by the state, these public institutes have also logically followed what has been called the 'color-blind Republican ideology', which lies at the heart of traditional French integration policies and official discourse, i.e. it is still legally prohibited in France to record people's self-described race or ethnicity. This ideology of color-blindness has long made it impossible to quantitatively study ethnic inequalities in education.

The FBEI research tradition has nevertheless made substantial progress since the early 1980s, both thanks to the development of data of increasing quality, especially in terms of the still indirect measure of ethnicity, and the use of more refined statistical methods. Methodological advances were fostered by the growing realization that ethnicity should not be studied in isolation, given that it is so closely intertwined with class background and family structure. In order to consider these multiple variables, older studies frequently used two- or three-way cross-tabulations, while more recent works make use of multivariate linear and logistic regression techniques.

In addition to that, researchers have in the past often been forced to use remote proxies to measure ethnicity. From the 1960s, with the seminal work of Paul Clerc (1964), until the early 1990s, ethnicity was overwhelmingly studied by taking into account pupils' nationality, very frequently reduced to a dichotomy between French citizens, supposedly representing the majority group, and foreign citizens, supposedly representing ethnic minority pupils. It soon became evident that citizenship alone was a very weak measure for ethnicity, as most ethnic minority pupils were children of immigrants and French citizens.[4] With the passage of time and the increased salience of immigration as a political, social, and sociological issue, data on pupils' parents' country of birth were collected (see footnote 3), in order to assess second-generation immigrants' educational '*intégration*'. The country of birth of pupils' parents, sometimes combined with the language spoken at home, is now *the* main proxy used by French sociologists to measure ethnicity in the context of this quantitative research tradition.

The remainder of this section critically describes the main findings within the FBEI research tradition, by successively reviewing: (1) works that compare the educational achievement of ethnic minority pupils with that of the majority group; (2) works that study the differences between academic progress made by ethnic minority pupils and their peers in primary and secondary schools; (3) recent works that use more relevant data and adopt more nuanced approaches to study educational differences between ethnic minorities, their positions within a highly differentiated secondary education system, and interactions between ethnicity and gender.

12.4.2.2 *Differences in academic achievement between children of immigrants and children of natives*

Based on the first large-scale survey focusing on education, the INED 1962–1972 panel, Clerc (1964) analyzed the academic achievement of foreign pupils and their transition rate from primary to lower secondary school. His conclusion set a precedent for future investigations of ethnic inequalities in education:

> Foreign pupils are, on average, slightly disadvantaged compared to their French peers. *However, this handicap is mainly due to the occupational structure of this population, in which 70% are the children of manual workers.* A working-class child of foreign nationality is no more [academically] disadvantaged than a French pupil from the same class background.[5] (Clerc 1964, p. 871, emphasis in the original)

In the 1980s, other studies focused on the academic achievement of foreign pupils and made clear that the main factors of their raw underachievement were to be found in their lower-class origin and, to a lesser extent, their family structure (Marangé and Lebon, 1982; Bastide, 1982; Gibert, 1989; Boulot and Boyzon-Fradet, 1984, 1988b; Boyzon-Fradet and Boulot, 1991).

However, it was not until the mid-1990s that the influence of family background on ethnic inequalities in secondary education was analyzed comprehensively by Louis-André Vallet and Jean-Paul Caille (Vallet and Caille, 1996a; see also Vallet and Caille, 1995; Vallet, 1996; Vallet and Caille, 1996b). Based on the 1989 panel study of the French Ministry of Education (see note 3), Vallet and Caille's study improves on previous literature through the use of advanced multivariate regression models and the consideration of a wide range of educational outcomes that occur along pupils' educational trajectories.[6] They show that the number of siblings, class background, and especially parental level of education explain most, if not all, of ethnic minority children's underachievement for all educational outcomes analyzed. The authors further demonstrate that, all things being equal, ethnic minority pupils are actually *more likely* than the majority group to be channeled into the academic track in the middle and end of lower secondary school. Using a later wave from the 1989 panel, Vallet and Caille (2000) showed that being a child of immigrants also has a significant and positive net effect at the end of upper secondary school on the likelihood of passing the *baccalauréat*.

12.4.2.3   Ethnic differences in academic progress

Other studies have specifically investigated the differences in academic progress made by ethnic minority children compared with pupils from the majority group and provided a convergent result: ethnic minority pupils begin primary school with a net academic disadvantage compared with children from the majority group, but progress faster in the following years (Le Guen, 1991; DEP, 1993; Mingat, 1984; Matéo, 1992; Bressoux and Desclaux, 1991; Mingat, 1987; Bressoux, 1994; Caille, 2008). In any case, a strong claim can be made that primary school does not contribute to widening ethnic inequalities in education; if anything, it would tend to reduce these inequalities, though not enough for second-generation immigrants to fully catch up with children of natives by the beginning of lower secondary school (Caille and Rosenwald, 2006).

The picture appears similar in lower secondary school. Most studies show that ethnic minority students progress more than their French peers throughout lower secondary school, when socio-economic and family background is controlled for (Mondon, 1984; Caille and O'Prey, 2002; Caille, 2008). To date, the best attempt to analyze the comparative progress in both French and mathematics of children of immigrants and children of natives from the first year of lower secondary school (age 11) to their fourth and final year (age 15) can be credited to Héctor Cebolla Boado (2008b). Based on the 1995 panel survey (see footnote 3), he shows that children of immigrants do progress faster in both subjects, but that 'their faster progress seems to stem from the fact that it is easier to improve one's marks when their initial level is low than it is when their initial level is high' (Cebolla Boado, 2008b, p. 760).

12.4.2.4   *Differences between and within ethnic groups*

The remainder of this section is devoted to reviewing mostly recent studies that aim to give a more complex and realistic picture of ethnic inequalities in education in France, mainly by analyzing educational differences between first- and second-generation immigrants, between ethnic minorities and between educational outcomes (especially between performance and tracking).

As a whole, these research studies clearly show that children of immigrants are more educated than their parents (Moguérou et al., 2010) and that, among immigrant children, the younger a child is when he or she arrived in France, the better his or her educational achievement and attainment (Tribalat, 1997; Vallet and Caille, 1996a). Even if immigrant status (i.e. being first or second generation) does matter more than ethnicity *per se* (Cebolla Boado, 2008a), one cannot deny that differences in the parents' country of birth, whether interpreted as ethnic, cultural, or economic (see Section 12.2), are associated with educational differences among ethnic minorities.

The two largest second-generation immigrant groups in France, i.e. those from North Africa (Algeria, Morocco, Tunisia) and Southern Europe (Portugal, Spain, Italy) have been the focus of many studies (Brinbaum and Kieffer, 2005, 2009; Brinbaum and Cebolla Boado, 2007; Cebolla Boado, 2006, 2008a). The general conclusion is that, all things being equal, neither group has a significantly lower performance than the majority group, although, in certain models, North African children do seem to fare worse than children of natives. Due to small sample sizes, few studies have actually managed to analyze the situation of smaller ethnic groups. However, Ichou (2013) has recently shown that the smallest and least often studied groups of children of immigrants are also those who differ the most academically from children of natives from similar social backgrounds.

The lowest performing groups are children of immigrants from Turkey and the Sahel, while children of Southeast Asian immigrants have the highest average level of academic achievement, often outperforming children of natives.

Besides academic performance, tracking has been shown to be a key influence on (ethnic minority) pupils' academic trajectories. In descriptive terms, ethnic minority pupils tend more often than the majority group to be: in special education classes[7] in primary, but especially secondary school (Lacerda and Ameline, 2001; Boulot and Boyzon-Fradet, 1992); in low-prestige short vocational tracks in upper secondary school (Lacerda and Ameline, 2001; Alba and Silberman, 2009; Palheta, 2012); and, at the *baccalauréat* level, in less 'noble' technological tracks rather than in the most prestigious scientific track (Laacher and Lenfant, 1991, 1997; Brinbaum and Kieffer, 2009). In fact, the proportion of ethnic minority pupils schooled in a specific track can be said to be inversely related to the track's social and academic prestige (Mullet, 1980).

When ethnic differences in academic performance and tracking are analyzed together, an interesting and seemingly paradoxical result emerges. In descriptive terms (i.e. without controls for socio-economic backgrounds), ethnic minority pupils perform noticeably worse than the majority group. Yet, when prior academic performance is controlled for, they tend to be *more* likely than children of natives to proceed towards the academic track of upper secondary school (Brinbaum and Cebolla Boado, 2007; Brinbaum and Kieffer, 2009; Ichou and Vallet, 2013). As is often the case in the study of ethnic inequalities in education, works that rely on descriptive bivariate analyses and those that use multivariate methods reach different and indeed opposite conclusions.

In sum, this research tradition that focuses on the quantitative descriptive study of ethnic inequalities in education has improved over the years in both the quality and accuracy of its results through the development of better data and measures of ethnicity, and the use of more advanced multivariate methods. Contrary to common wisdom, but in line with the conclusions of the international literature on the subject, the central finding in these studies is that if their class background and family structure are taken into account, ethnic minority pupils do not appear to perform less well academically than members of the majority group. However, it remains unclear how research findings are affected by the different ways 'achievement' is measured between studies, from standardized test scores to grade point averages to teachers' subjective assessments. In addition, due to limited sample sizes, both smaller ethnic minorities and differences within each ethnic group should be analyzed further by future research.

12.4.3 Limited educational resources of ethnic minority families (LEREM)

This section reviews research works focused on the description and explanation of the resources of ethnic minority families towards schooling. A wide range of educational attitudes and practices have been studied. They can broadly be structured into the following categories: educational aspirations, which is the most widely studied topic, interactions with and knowledge about school, and help from extended family and the community. To account for the specificity of the resources of ethnic minority families, some researchers point to the influence of cultural differences, while others insist on socio-economic pre-migration characteristics.

12.4.3.1 *High aspirations, social distance from school, and help from the community*

There is a large consensus among sociologists in describing the educational aspirations of ethnic minority families as higher than that of the majority group. This is the case for immigrant parents when compared with socio-economically similar native parents (Vallet and Caille, 1996a; Brinbaum and Kieffer, 2005; Caille and O'Prey, 2002; Caille, 2005, 2008; Ichou, 2010). This 'ambitious' and hopeful attitude is associated with a general trust from immigrant parents towards schools and teachers who embody knowledge (Henriot-van Zanten, 1990). These attitudes seem, by and large, to be passed on to the children's generation in the form of high aspirations and 'academic goodwill' (Caille, 2005; Cibois, 2002), especially for children of North African immigrants (Rochex, 1992; Brinbaum and Kieffer, 2005; Stuart Lambert and Peignard, 2002). The educational aspirations of second-generation immigrants compared with that of children of natives tend to be less dependent on their actual educational position and academic achievement (Caille, 2005; Brinbaum and Kieffer, 2005): even after being channeled into short vocational tracks in upper secondary school, these pupils still seem to show relatively unaltered ambitions (Caille, 2007; Palheta, 2012). The high aspirations of immigrant parents and children have been shown to be associated with higher academic achievement (Zeroulou, 1988; Zeroulou, 1985) and are therefore considered to be the most likely cause of the higher educational position of most second-generation immigrants, all things being equal (Vallet and Caille, 1996a).

These ambitious and hopeful attitudes of immigrant families cannot be understood independently of their demonstrated lack of knowledge about the school system, their difficulty in helping their children with homework, and their symbolic distance from schools and teachers. Because they were not schooled in France, immigrant parents often lack accurate knowledge about the French school system and its procedures, language, and norms (Henriot-van Zanten, 1990; Zehraoui, 1998; Dubreuil, 2001; Caille and O'Prey, 2002; Caille, 2008).

However, educational resources, often absent in the nuclear family of immigrant children, are frequently found elsewhere in the larger community. Significantly more than children of natives, ethnic minority pupils find support among elder siblings who went to school in France, or from other relatives and educated members of their ethnic or neighborhood community (Zeroulou, 1988; Laacher, 1990; Henriot-van Zanten, 1990; Lahire, 1995; Zehraoui, 1998; Santelli, 2001; Dubreuil, 2001).

12.4.3.2   *Cultural differences and pre-migration social position*

Although culturalist approaches to ethnic differences in education are not dominant in French sociology, some researchers have adopted them to explain the specific resources and difficulties of ethnic minority families towards education and schooling. In addition to or in place of traditional socio-economic interpretations, these authors maintain that each culture is associated with specific educational practices and representations (Carayon, 1992; Lagrange, 2010). For example, Vasquez (Vasquez, 1980, 1982) focused on cultural differences in time management norms to explain educational practices leading to the academic underachievement of recently immigrated children of Spanish and Portuguese families.

In a recent book entitled *Le Déni des cultures* ('The Denial of Cultures'), Hugues Lagrange (2010) uses a kinship structure-oriented culturalist framework to interpret secondary school underachievement among the children of immigrants from the Sahel region (i.e. Mali, Senegal, and Mauritania). He holds that the clash of immigrants' culture of origin and dominant French culture, in a context of urban segregation and economic inequalities, produces a subculture that impedes second-generation academic achievement. Although Lagrange's work does insist on the historical and contextual character of the group culture, culturalist approaches have been criticized on the grounds that they tend to overemphasize group homogeneity and overlook contextual and historical variation, thus presenting an essentialist view of culture (Charlot, 1990; Chauveau and Rogovas-Chauveau, 1990; Guénif-Souilamas, 1994; Payet, 1995b; Fassin, 2011).

Recognizing both the need to take into account the pre-migration experiences of immigrants and the heterogeneity of these experiences, some researchers have followed a promising path that looks at pre-migration socio-economic and educational characteristics of migrants as a determining factor of their situation in France, their attitudes towards education, and the attitudes of their children. These researchers have been influenced by a key French immigration sociologist, Abdelmalek Sayad, according to whom, 'Any study of migratory phenomena that overlooks the emigrants' conditions of origin is bound only to give a view that is at once *partial* and *ethnocentric*'. (Sayad, 2004, p. 29, emphasis in the original). Research has found that children of immigrants who succeed in school usually have parents, and even grandparents, aunts, and uncles, who were more educated, more urban, and had more economic resources than average in their country of birth (Zeroulou, 1985; Zeroulou, 1988; Laacher, 1990, 2005; Gouirir, 1998; Santelli, 2001; Ichou, 2013).

The roots of immigrant families' higher aspirations towards school can be traced back to the pre-migration status and intentions of future migrants. Upward social mobility is often a central goal of migration, but not easily attainable by first-generation migrants. Parents consequently push their children to fulfill the 'migration project' that they formulated (Charlot, 1999; Zehraoui, 1998, 1996). The academic and professional success of their children is, for the parents, an achievement by proxy, which would legitimize their migration altogether (Zehraoui, 1998; Laurens, 1995).

In sum, the research tradition focusing on the limited resources of ethnic minority families towards schooling is not a very coherent and integrated one. However, a somewhat consistent picture emerges depicting ethnic minority families, most often immigrant families, as having high educational aspirations, being less knowledgeable in school matters and participating less in schools than natives, and as resorting more to elder siblings, relatives, and the community for school help. To explain these specific educational attitudes and practices researchers in this field have alternatively focused on cultural differences and on pre-migration socio-economic characteristics. The main limitation of this strand of research is the absence of any systematic assessment of the effect, either positive or negative, of these specific resources on the academic achievement of ethnic minority students.

12.4.4 Ethnic school segregation and educational inequalities (ESSEI)

Both social and policy changes, on the one hand, and evolutions inside the field of sociology, on the other, have fostered the development of a research tradition focusing on ethnic segregation at school. As mentioned in the section on context, from the 1960s onwards the French educational system has undergone a dramatic process of both comprehensivisation and massification. The progressive disappearance of formal tracking in lower secondary school has in fact led to the development of subtler forms of differentiations in pupils' trajectories, depending on differences in languages studied, options chosen, schools attended, etc. (Henriot-van Zanten, 1990; van Zanten, 2001; Payet, 1995a; Bourdieu and Champagne, 1992). At the same time, as part of a general pattern of political devolution, the administrative autonomy of secondary schools has increased (van Zanten, 2011). This twofold process of increasing school differentiation and autonomy has contributed to make ethnic school segregation both desirable to some families and socially and sociologically more visible. However, the focus on school segregation is also due to efforts by sociologists of education from the 1980s onwards to challenge and refine the dominant 'reproduction paradigm' (Bourdieu and Passeron, 1970), by focusing on local educational processes (Duru-Bellat and van Zanten, 2012).

Researchers in the ESSEI research tradition agree that the expression 'ethnic school segregation' should only be used if three conditions are present (van

Zanten, 1996; Barthon, 1998): (1) one should be able to observe that pupils belonging to different ethnic groups are unevenly distributed between schools and within schools, over and above class-based segregation; (2) there should be specific school-related mechanisms and behaviors that shape the distribution of pupils between and within schools, over and above the spatial distribution of pupils in the neighborhood; and (3) this uneven distribution of pupils between and within schools based on their ethnicity should be shown to have negative consequences for individuals' educational achievement. This section will review how researchers have addressed these three types of issues.

12.4.4.1   *The existence of ethnic segregation at school*

Following the pioneering and oft-cited book by Léger and Tripier (1986), researchers have used ethnographic methods to study the social and ethnic composition of local schools in ethnically mixed neighborhoods and have observed a clear pattern of ethnic concentration, especially in lower secondary school (Henriot-van Zanten, 1990; Henriot-van Zanten et al., 1994; van Zanten, 2001; Payet, 1995a, 1998, 1999). Payet (1995a, 1998, 1999), amongst others, insists on one key point: ethnic segregation should not be reduced to the most visible *between*-schools disparity but should also be investigated as differences *within* school and *between* classes.

In the past 15 years, researchers have begun using statistical data to quantify ethnic school segregation and have confirmed its high level. They have shown that ethnic school segregation in lower secondary schools was both high and on the increase during the 1990s (Trancart, 1998; Barthon, 1998; Louis-Etxeto, 1998). In this field, a key innovative study was carried out by Felouzis and his colleagues (Felouzis, 2003; Felouzis et al., 2005; Felouzis and Perroton, 2009). Based on data on all 144,725 pupils from all 333 middle schools in the Bordeaux education authority, they used pupils' first names (instead of nationality unlike previous studies) to classify each of them according to their ethnicity, or as they prefer to say, their 'cultural origin'. Thanks to this creative measurement method, the authors showed that, within this education authority, 10% of the middle schools were concentrating 40% of pupils of African and Turkish cultural origins. Indeed, 'such an uneven distribution would be inconceivable according to other variables, such as pupils' class background or academic performance' (Felouzis, 2003, p. 427). The major weakness of this research lies in its geographical limitation to only one education authority around Bordeaux making it impossible to generalize its results at the national level.

12.4.4.2   *Causes of ethnic segregation at school*

Three broad factors are involved in the uneven distribution of ethnic minority pupils between and within schools: (1) urban segregation and school district zoning; (2) families' strategies of school flight; and (3) school policies and in-school practices.

Urban sociologists and geographers have shown that ethnic minorities are by no means evenly distributed between neighborhoods (Desplanques and Tabard, 1991; Rhein, 1997; Préteceille, 2009). Because pupils are normally educated in their local school at the primary and secondary level residential segregation alone can explain *part* of the uneven distribution of ethnic minorities between schools. White upper-class parents with significant economic resources frequently choose to move or already live (Préteceille, 2006; Pinçon and Pinçon-Charlot, 1994) in areas with high real estate prices next to prestigious lower and upper secondary schools (van Zanten, 2001; Oberti, 2007a). Although most costly economically, this strategy is probably the most efficient and least visible among the many strategies that families use to avoid schools with a significant concentration of pupils from immigrant backgrounds (van Zanten, 2006b; Oberti, 2007a). Aggravating the effects of residential segregation on school segregation, school district zoning often tends to group social housing areas together in a single district, thus increasing the concentration of poor ethnic minorities in specific schools (van Zanten and Obin, 2010; Barthon, 1996). Because residential segregation is higher when smaller spatial units are considered, the size of the school districts also matters: the smaller they are, the stronger the effects on segregation (Payet, 1998, 1999). Residential segregation, combined with school district zoning, has a decidedly substantial impact on ethnic school segregation. However, researchers show that school segregation is almost always higher than residential segregation (Henriot-van Zanten et al., 1994; Felouzis et al., 2005; Barthon, 1998; Léger and Tripier, 1986).

This phenomenon points to other segregation mechanisms related to family strategies of 'school flight'. Even though according to school choice regulations called *'carte scolaire'* ('school map') pupils should normally attend their district school, parents have been given increasing leeway in requesting an out-of-district public secondary school, provided they give admissible arguments (van Zanten and Obin, 2010). These arguments can range from having an elder sibling schooled in the requested out-of-district school, wishing to study a rare foreign language only offered there, being geographically closer to this school because of odd district zoning, etc. Not surprisingly, this opportunity to choose an out-of-district secondary school by using specific arguments is not used by all families equally. These 'choosers' – especially the successful ones – are overwhelmingly from the middle and upper classes (Ballion, 1986; Henriot-van Zanten et al., 1994; Payet, 1999; Broccolichi and van Zanten, 1997; van Zanten, 2009a, 2009b; Raveaud and van Zanten, 2007) and disproportionately white (Barthon, 1998).

These strategies of school flight reinforce ethnic segregation at school, first, because they are carried out mostly by white parents and, second, because a key reason for withdrawing one's child from the local public school is the perceived high proportion of ethnic minorities among its pupils. This 'ethnic proportion' is considered by many parents to be a proxy of school quality, both in terms of academic performance and overall 'climate': the more visible minorities, the lower the perceived school quality (Barrère and Martucelli, 1996; Broccolichi and van Zanten, 1997; van Zanten, 2006b, 2009b). Besides requesting an out-of-district public school, another form of school flight, which also increases ethnic segregation, consists in opting for a private secondary school. In this case, there is overwhelming evidence that white native families use private schools far more than ethnic minorities (Boulot and Boyzon-Fradet, 1988a; Boyzon-Fradet and Boulot, 1991; Héran, 1996; Brinbaum et al., 2010; Louis-Etxeto, 1998).

Yet another type of strategy pursued by middle-class families consists in keeping their children in the local public lower secondary school, while closely monitoring its functioning (Barthon and Oberti, 2000) and relying on in-school practices to produce internal segregation that would keep their children from associating with too many ethnic minority pupils. This set of behaviors characterizes 'cultural capital-rich' and 'economic capital-poor' middle-class families and corresponds to what Agnès van Zanten (2001) has termed the 'colonization' of the local school.

One should not overestimate the responsibility of parents and their strategies in creating ethnic school segregation. Indeed, in a context of local school competition, these strategies constantly interact with school policies and in-school practices aimed at enhancing the school's image in order to retain white middle-class pupils (Payet, 1995a; van Zanten, 2006a; Barthon and Monfroy, 2005, 2006). A common practice is therefore to adapt the general school policy to the perceived demands of white middle-class families, with a special focus on security and safety issues (Broccolichi and van Zanten, 1997; van Zanten, 2001, 2000). However, the main tool used by head teachers is to create academically, and therefore socially and ethnically, homogeneous classes where better-achieving white middle-class pupils are grouped together, leaving working-class ethnic minority pupils in 'bad' classes (Payet, 1995a; Barthon, 1998; Visier and Zoïa, 2010; Broccolichi and van Zanten, 1997; van Zanten, 2001, 2000).

12.4.4.3   Consequences of ethnic segregation at school

Research in this field shows that ethnic segregation generates unequal access to educational resources.[8] This concretely means that lower and upper secondary schools with high concentrations of ethnic minority pupils tend to offer less diverse and less prestigious academic options and tracks (Chauveau and Rogovas-Chauveau, 1990; Barthon, 1998; Trancart, 1998; Oberti, 2005, 2007a, 2007b). Alongside white middle-class parents' flight from schools situated in ethnically diverse neighborhoods, there is a similar trend on the part of the more experienced and senior teachers. This leaves ethnically concentrated schools with both less-experienced teachers and a high overall rate of teacher turnover (Léger and Tripier, 1986; Barthon, 1998; Trancart, 1998; Payet, 1998; Mathey-Pierre and Larguèze, 2010).

However, due to the lack of appropriate quantitative data, studies that actually analyze the effects of ethnic concentration on pupils' achievement are rather scarce. Moreover, most existing works provide only indirect evidence (see, for example, Broccolichi, 2009; Broccolichi and Trancart, 2010). Among the few more direct sociological investigations, findings do not perfectly match. Some researchers found no effect of the proportion of pupils on the average progress made by pupils during either the third year of primary school (Bressoux, 1994) or in secondary school (Cebolla Boado, 2007). In their study in the Bordeaux education authority, Felouzis and his colleagues (Felouzis, 2003; Felouzis et al., 2005) find two seemingly contradictory consequences of ethnic segregation in secondary schools: on average and all things being equal, in the most ethnically concentrated schools, standardized academic performance is lower, but access to academic upper secondary school is higher. Considering these conflicting results, no firm conclusion should be drawn on the consequences of the concentration of ethnic minorities in certain tracks or schools on average achievement.

In sum, the research tradition focusing of ethnic school segregation is one that has brought out a set of particularly consensual and robust results. The extent of ethnic school segregation has been shown to be high and is not the mere reflection of ethnic segregation at the neighborhood level. According to families' socially differentiated resources and constraints, family strategies, in interaction with school policies, partly produce this high level of ethnic segregation both between and within schools. The main weakness of this research area is the lack of robust results on the exact extent of the consequences of ethnic segregation at school on students' academic trajectories and on the overall level of educational inequalities.

12.4.5 Ethnic relations in classrooms and schools (ERCS)

In this section, we look at ethnographic studies conducted in schools and classrooms that analyze the salience of ethnicity in school professionals' views and practices. We also explore ethnic minority students' classroom behavior, feelings concerning discrimination, and social networks.

12.4.5.1 The salience of ethnicity in school professionals' views and practices

Research studies in this area have shown that although the Republican model encourages teachers to adopt color-blind attitudes, many of them resort to negative stereotypes concerning the impact of economic deprivation or of outdated and inappropriate cultural traditions to explain the attitudes and behavior of immigrants and their children (Anderson-Levitt, 1989; van Zanten,

1990). These stereotypes concern students' hygiene, beauty, dress, and politeness, as well as their intellectual potential (Zimmerman, 1980; Vasquez, 1982) and parents' inadequate socialization at home.

Ethnographic studies of primary schools have also documented the salience of ethnicity in teacher–pupil interactions. However, while a study comparing French and British teachers concludes on a clear separation in French schools between formal activities where the principle of 'indifference to differences' still applies and informal activities where ethnic minority pupils are asked to share aspects of their culture with the teacher and other children (Raveaud, 2003, 2006), another one shows that ethnicity can be salient in formal interactions, although with great variations between teachers (Roussier-Fusco, 2003). Three models seemed at work: (1) 'indifference to ethnic differences', associated with a good classroom climate but high levels of ethnic conflicts between children in the playground; (2) 'negative emphasis on children's ethnicity', associated with high levels of conflict within and outside the classroom; and (3) 'critical view of French treatment of immigrants', that generated high levels of politicization of children's discourses and relationships.

Studies on secondary school teachers have also shown considerable variation concerning the importance attributed to students' ethnicity in daily interactions (Payet, 1995; Perroton, 2000a; van Zanten, 2001). Differences between teachers are related (1) to the proportion of students from immigrant backgrounds in their classrooms, but also to (2) their age, younger teachers take ethnic differences more explicitly into account; (3) their social class, teachers from upper-class backgrounds tend to equate 'integration' with 'assimilation', while those from middle-class and working-class backgrounds appear more open to cultural differences (Légendre, 2002; Rayou and van Zanten, 2004; Sanselme, 2009); but (4) apparently not to teachers' ethnicity. According to Charles and Légendre (2006), teachers from immigrant backgrounds, who constitute a small group, are more likely to start their careers in multicultural schools but their professional *habitus* appears very similar to that of teachers from native family backgrounds.

Still other ethnographic studies point out the tendency of other school professionals, involved in enforcing discipline or in liaising with parents, to refer to their own or to students' ethnic background (Payet, 1997). These professionals have in recent years been recruited on the basis of their ethnic and local origin and implicitly encouraged to use inside knowledge of students' cultures and neighborhoods in the accomplishment of their tasks (Rinaudo, 1998; Perroton, 2000b; Charlot, Emin and de Peretti, 2002).

12.4.5.2   *Discrimination in punishment, grading, and tracking*

Evidence on teachers' discrimination of ethnic minority students is scarce. In line with John Ogbu's research in the United States (Anderson-Levitt and van Zanten, 1992), some researchers have pointed out that misunderstandings between teachers and ethnic minority students arise not only because of 'primary' cultural differences, but because of 'secondary' differences, that is attitudes that these students develop in reaction to their subordinate position in society and in anticipation of discriminatory attitudes from institutional agents. For example, Payet (1985) showed that teachers tend to perceive students from Algerian families as 'insolent', 'sly', and 'aggressive' both because of cultural differences in interactive styles and of these students' tendency to contest teachers' judgments and sanctions (Payet and Sicot, 1997; Debarbieux and Tichit, 1997).

Other studies have shown that, when making decisions about grades, assignation to different classes, and allocation to future tracks, teachers pay greater attention to the behavior of ethnic minority students, especially of boys from Maghreb and Africa, than to that of students from native backgrounds (Zirotti, 1980; Payet, 1997). These practices contribute in turn both to ethnic minority students' bad behavior and to their perception of being treated unfairly. In her ethnographic research on two 'bad classes', van Zanten (2001) showed that a significant proportion of minority students – allocated to these classes because of their behavior and not of their achievement level – felt not only rejected but bored by the low-level activities proposed by teachers, which led them to engage in disruptive behaviors and thus to be frequently sanctioned.

Tracking decisions are perceived by ethnic minority students as the most discriminatory dimension of their school experience (Akers-Porrini and Zirotti, 1992; Favre and Manigand, 2000; Brinbaum and Kieffer, 2005; Caille, 2007; Palheta, 2012), although quantitative studies (Bastide, 1982), including two using multivariate analyses (Vallet and Caille, 1996a; Caille 2008), have shown that there are no conspicuous signs of the influence of ethnicity on these decisions once other significant factors are taken into account. However, what students from ethnic backgrounds perceive is that a large proportion of them are forced, because of their grades, to take courses and tracks, especially vocational tracks, that they did not ask for (Santelli, 2001, 2007; Palheta, 2012). Brinbaum and Guégnard (2010) found that this was the case at the end of *collège* for 25% of second-generation students from Maghreb, Africa, and Turkey as opposed to 12% of second-generation students from Portugal and Asia, and 8% of pupils with French parents.

Many ethnic minority students therefore describe unsatisfactory personal experiences at school (Bouamama, 2000) as well as in higher education where many of them, especially those who come from vocational and technological tracks, fail at academic evaluations and, later, at competitive examinations for access to occupations in the public sector, including teaching (Beaud, 2002). Although these negative perceptions are not always framed in the language of discrimination a significant proportion of students mention some form of institutional racism at school (Zirotti, 1980; Akers-Porrini and Zirotti, 1992; Oberti, Sanselme and Voisin, 2009; Cortéséro, 2010).

12.4.5.3 *Peer relations, violence, and delinquency*

Qualitative studies have provided evidence on the existence of interracial and interethnic friendships in urban primary schools, but also on the ways in which they are influenced by children's gender and academic status (Xavier de Brito and Vasquez, 1994; Perroton, 2000a; van Zanten, 2000b; Fouquet-Chauprade, 2011). Roussier-Fusco (2007) has shown that the influence of these various factors leads to the formation of small groups of white girls that may include girls from ethnic minority groups if they are high achievers, and larger groups of boys from ethnic minorities that may include boys with native parents if they are underachievers.

In multicultural *collèges*, interracial and interethnic friendships are more common because of greater ethnic mix as well as higher adolescent autonomy from parents and teachers (Herpin, 1996; Xavier de Brito and Vasquez, 1996). However, the influence of academic position still remains (van Zanten, 2000b, 2005). Using data from 1300 questionnaires distributed in six *collèges* characterized by high concentrations of ethnic minority pupils and an ethnic score obtained by adding eight characteristics (students' first and last name, place of birth, school trajectory abroad, date of arrival of parents, language spoken at home, and nationality of the students and his or her parents), Fouquet-Chauprade (2011) found that a high ethnic score was associated with weak academic integration but strong social integration and a preference for friends from ethnic minority groups.

Ethnographic studies have also shown that in segregated school contexts students frequently use ethnic and racial categories to identify themselves and others but also that these categories are not necessarily used and perceived as insults (Achard et al., 1992). They are part of verbal interaction rituals whose purpose is to jibe and laugh at each other and, through that process, to cancel the stigma associated to those terms (Lepoutre, 1997). These rituals can nevertheless lead to conflicts if these categories are used to make unfavorable comparisons or establish social and moral boundaries between students with different academic statuses or from different school tracks (Payet, 1995a; Debarbieux, 1997, 1999; Debarbieux and Tichit 1997; Perroton, 2000a; van Zanten, 2001).

Other studies have established a correlation between the proportion of ethnic minority students and the perception of school climate. Debarbieux (1988) found that when children of immigrants represented only 5% or less of the school intake, only 8% of pupils thought there was violence in their school. However, in schools with 30% of children of immigrants or more, the proportion of those who thought there was a bad climate was also 30% or more (for similar results, see also Fouquet-Chapraude, 2011). Schools with large proportion of ethnic minority students do seem to be characterized by higher levels of what some authors call 'incivilities', which include insults and verbal aggressions, damages to school furniture or premises, small acts of delinquency, and bullying and fights between students (Debarbieux, 1998; Debarbieux and Tichit, 1997; Tichit, 2001). However, this does not mean that ethnic minority students are more involved than their native classmates in these acts.

Some researchers point out that school violence can be analyzed as a subtype of urban violence as schools with large proportions of children of immigrants are often located in poor areas where delinquency and violence are part of everyday life (Dubet, 1987). Others emphasize the impact of social and ethnic segregation as well as of the disorganization of these schools on the emergence of a culture of drift, deviance, and delinquency, and on the formation of gangs characterized by deviant behavior and a confrontational relationship with their immediate environment (Debarbieux, 1997; van Zanten, 2000; Moignard, 2008; Mohamed, 2011). This is not inevitable however and other studies have shown that collective and sustained efforts to enforce norms significantly reduce the number of incivilities, transgressions, and micro-violences (Débarbieux and Blaya, 2001).

In sum, research studies belonging to this last tradition show that, to varying degrees, teachers and other school agents use ethnicity as a resource to explain existing problems. Although there is little evidence of widespread ethnic discrimination, teachers do seem to focus on different dimensions when they evaluate children of immigrants and children of natives, while many ethnic minority students feel, rightly or wrongly, that they have experienced rejection and discrimination. Peer relationships in multicultural schools appear two-sided: interethnic friendships and conflicts coexist. It is difficult however to generalize the results of these, mostly ethnographic, studies because of the contextual embeddedness of the data and interpretations, and the limited number of comparisons of the processes at work within different types of schools.

12.6   Conclusion and discussion

Research on ethnicity and educational inequality in France encompasses five major research traditions. These traditions have revealed a number of consensual and robust findings.

Research in the first tradition has been conducted by political scientists and sociologists and has concentrated on policy decisions concerning educational structures, curriculum and religion. Its most important findings concern the lack of a strong political will, irrespective of the political orientation of governments, to develop ambitious educational policies for ethnic minorities, but also the existence of a growing number of policies and schemes that use area or class as a proxy for ethnicity.

Another group of studies has used statistical methods to analyze ethnic inequalities in educational achievement and attainment. Despite the scarcity of relevant data, a coherent tradition has developed from cumulative results in this field. The principal finding is that ethnic inequalities in education are, above all, class inequalities: the academic disadvantages of children of immigrants can be mostly explained by their parents' economic poverty and low levels of education.

Research in the third tradition focuses on the study of the limited resources of ethnic minorities at schools. This tradition is more fragmented and less coherent than the previous two. Researchers who have tried to identify the specific attitudes of immigrant families tend to show that these families have higher academic aspirations than those of native families but are less involved in school activities.

The fourth research tradition has focused on ethnic segregation in schools. As in the first tradition, cumulative research has resulted in particularly strong results. Ethnic segregation in schools appears to be high, even higher than ethnic residential segregation or class-based segregation in schools. The causes of this segregation can be found at the conjunction between the interests of white middle-class parents and of school agents. Its consequences are important as students educated in schools with high concentrations of ethnic minorities enjoy fewer educational resources.

Finally, the fifth research tradition is quite coherent because researchers have addressed similar questions with comparable ethnographic methods. The main findings concern the contrast between official indifference to ethnicity and its salience in the everyday activities and interactions of school agents and students in multiethnic school contexts as well as ethnic minority students' perceptions of the existence of discrimination processes in punishment, grading and, especially, tracking.

Despite this consistent body of research, several research areas remain understudied or altogether unexplored. First, more attention should be paid to differences between ethnic minority groups. Categories such as 'second-generation immigrants' should be further deconstructed and decomposed. Second, better quantitative and qualitative data on the characteristics of neighborhood and school environments are needed to refine the study of the effects of ethnic segregation in education. In particular, more detailed analyses of official and unofficial tracking processes within schools and how they affect students from immigrant and ethnic backgrounds should be conducted. Third, a promising path for future research lies in the study of the influence of pre-migration experiences and characteristics on second-generation immigrants' school behavior and academic achievement. Fourth, more research is needed to explore why and how ethnic minority students come to feel discriminated against in schools and whether this perception is related to the objective attitudes of teachers, misunderstandings between teachers and students in everyday interactions or, more generally, students' perceptions of exclusion from French society. Last, to unveil the full extent of ethnic inequality, researchers must further analyze the interaction between ethnic inequalities at school and in the labor market especially considering the fact that the latter have been shown to be high in absolute terms (Silberman and Fournier, 2006; Lefranc, 2010) and relative compared to rates in other countries, especially Germany (Tucci, 2010).

The development of these research areas and, more generally, of research on ethnic inequalities in education in the French context is nevertheless strongly dependent on changes in social policy and in intellectual thought. Despite a growing political consciousness of the problems faced by ethnic minority students at school, political and administrative discourses and choices tend to ignore ethnic and racial inequalities. This continued 'veil of ignorance' makes it difficult to obtain official statistical or documentary data to assess the extent of these inequalities and to obtain funding to conduct original quantitative and qualitative studies to further explore their different expressions, causes, and consequences. In the same way, researchers' perspectives, resulting from socialization into the French model of integration but also into research paradigms focusing on class rather than ethnicity and giving preeminence to macro-structural factors rather than to cultural and interactional dynamics has limited research on educational processes involving ethnicity. However, changes in this area are taking place more rapidly among sociologists than among educational policy-makers given the former's professional interest in objective facts and the diversification of theories and approaches brought about by their increasing integration into international research networks.

Notes

1. The queries were made using the Boolean logic allowed by the searchable databases. French and English keywords were successively used as follows: in French, (race OR racial* OR ethni* OR *migr*) AND (inégalité*) AND (éducation OR école OR collège OR lycée) AND (France OR français*); in English, (race OR racial* OR ethni* OR *migr*) AND (inequal*) AND (education OR school OR college) AND (France OR French). The asterisk (*) means 'any character.' The CAIRN and Persée databases do not allow as much flexibility and complexity in the query structure. Multiple queries using combinations of the above keywords were therefore carried out in the latter databases.
2. In total, we included 12 journals. The general sociology journals are the *Revue française de sociologie, Actes de la recherche en Sciences sociales, Sociétés contemporaines, L'Année sociologique, Sociologie, Ethnologie française, Population,* and *Revue européenne des sciences sociales.* The sociology of education journals are *Revue française de pédagogie* and *Education et sociétés.* The *Revue européenne des migrations internationales* focuses on the sociology of migration and ethnicity, while *Ville-Ecole-Intégration Diversité* (whose name has changed several times, with the first and longest lasting one being *Migrants*

Formation) is at the crossroads of migration and education studies. The latter journal is the only non-peer-reviewed journal in our literature review, included because it contains numerous relevant articles.

3. Four main surveys have been used to study the academic trajectories of children of immigrants. The first two are the 1989 and 1995 panel surveys, carried out by the French Ministry of Education, in collaboration with INSEE. These two longitudinal studies followed for at least 10 years a nationally representative sample of pupils who entered secondary school in 1989 ($n = 21,479$) and 1995 ($n = 17,830$), respectively. Both surveys contain detailed information on pupils' academic trajectories, including standardized test scores, and family background. As proxies for ethnicity, the 1989 panel survey contains information on the nationality of pupils and their parents, whether pupils were born or schooled abroad, whether parents have always lived in France and the language(s) spoken at home. In addition to this information, the 1995 panel survey includes precise data on the country of birth of pupils and their parents. The last two surveys are the 1992 Geographical Mobility and Social Insertion survey (MGIS, $n = 12,325$) and the 2008 Trajectories and Origins survey (TeO, $n = 21,761$). Both are cross-sectional surveys run by INED in collaboration with INSEE. They both focus on and oversample immigrants and children of immigrants in France. The two surveys contain information on the educational and socioeconomic characteristics of immigrants and their children, as well as data on their residential, academic, religious, marital, and linguistic practices. As proxies for ethnicity, MGIS and TeO contain detailed information on the country of birth, nationality, and migration trajectories of immigrants and children of immigrants.

4. A recent publication demonstrated that as many as 95% of children of two immigrant parents were French citizens (Borrel and Lhommeau, 2010).

5. Our translation from French. Unless otherwise stated, all quotations included in this text have been translated by us.

6. These outcomes are: the number of years repeated in primary school, whether pupils are channeled into mainstream or special education tracks at the beginning of lower secondary school, French and mathematics test scores at this time, whether they are channeled into the academic track at the end of the second year of lower secondary school, and finally whether they are channeled at the end of the fourth and final year of lower secondary school.

7. Historically conceived for children considered as mentally deficient, these classes now target underachieving children considered to have cognitive difficulties.

8. Research that specifically deals with the effects of the concentration of ethnic minority pupils in schools on ethnic relations and in-school violence is discussed as part of the ERCS research tradition.

References

Achard, Pierre, Gabrielle Varro, François Leimdorfer, and Marie-Christine Pouder. 1992. 'Quand des enfants migrants se traitent d '«arabe » dans une classe primaire'. *Revue européenne de migrations internationales* 8(2):191–209.

Akers-Porrini, Ruth, and Jean-Pierre Zirotti. 1992. 'Élèves « français » et « maghrébins ». Un rapport différent à l'orientation scolaire'. *Migrants-Formation* (89):45–57.

Alba, Richard, and Roxane Silberman. 2009. 'The Children of Immigrants and Host-Society Educational Systems: Mexicans in the United States and North Africans in France'. *Teachers College Record* 111(6):1444–1475.

Anderson-Levitt, Kathryn M. 1989. 'Degrees of Distance between Teachers and Parents in Urban France'. *Anthropology & Education Quarterly* 20(2):97–117.

Anderson-Levitt Kathryn M., and Agnès Henriot-van Zanten. 1992. 'L'anthropologie de l'éducation aux Etats-Unis: méthodes, théories et applications d'une discipline en évolution'. *Revue française de pédagogie* (101):79–104.

Baccaïni, Brigitte, and Léon Gani. 1999. 'L'immigration en France: connaissances et opinions des lycéens de terminale'. *Sociétés contemporaines* (35):131–161.

Ballion, Robert. 1986. 'Le choix du collège: le comportement « éclairé » des familles'. *Revue française de sociologie* 27(4):719–734.

Barou, Jacques. 1995. 'Enseignement des cultures d'origine: ambiguïtés et contradictions'. *Hommes & migrations* (1190):16–21.

Barrère, Anne, and Danilo Martucelli. 1996. 'L'école à l'épreuve de l'ethnicité'. *Annales de la recherche urbaine* (75):51–58.

Barthon, Catherine. 1996. 'Enfants d'immigrés dans la division sociale et scolaire: l'exemple d'Asnières-sur-Seine'. *Annales de la recherche urbaine* (75):70–78.

———. 1998. 'La ségrégation comme processus dans l'école et dans la ville'. *Revue européenne de migrations internationales* 14(1):93–103.

Barthon, Catherine, and Brigitte Monfroy. 2005. 'Illusion et realite de la concurrence entre colleges en contexte urbain: l'exemple de la ville de Lille'. *Sociétés contemporaines* (59–60):43–65.

———. 2006. 'Une analyse systémique de la ségrégation entre collèges: l'exemple de la ville de Lille'. *Revue française de pédagogie* (156):29–38.

Barthon, Catherine, and Marco Oberti. 2000. 'Ségrégation spatiale, évitement et choix des établissements'. pp. 302–310 in *L'école. L'état des savoirs*, edited by Agnès Van Zanten. La Découverte.

Bastide, Henri (ed.). 1982. *Les Enfants d'immigrés et l'enseignement du français*. Presses Universitaires de France.

Beaud, Stéphane. 2002. *80% au bac … et après? Les enfants de la démocratisation scolaire.* La Découverte.

Benabou, Roland, Kramarz, Francis, and Corinne Prost. 2009. 'The French Zones d'Education Prioritaires: Much Ado about Nothing?' *Economics of Education Review* 28(3): 345–356.

Berque, Jacques. 1985. *L'immigration à l'école de la République*. La Documentation française.

Body-Gendrot, Sophie. 1995. 'Models of Immigrant Integration in France and the United States: Signs of Convergence?' in *The Bubbling Cauldron: Race, Ethnicity, and the Urban Crisis*, edited by Michael Peter Smith, and Joe R. Feagin. University of Minnesota Press.

Borrel, Catherine, and Bertrand Lhommeau. 2010. 'Être né en France d'un parent immigré'. *INSEE Première* (1287):1–4.

Bouamama, Saïd. 2000. 'Le sentiment de "hogra". Discrimination, négation du sujet et violences'. *Hommes et migrations* (1227):38–50.

Boulot, Serge, and Danielle Boyzon-Fradet. 1984. 'L'échec scolaire des enfants de travailleurs immigrés (un problème mal posé)'. *Les temps modernes* (452–454):1902–1914.

———. 1988a. 'L'Ecole française: égalité des chances et logiques d'une institution'. *Revue européenne de migrations internationales* 4(1):49–83.

———. 1988b. *Les immigrés et l'école: une course d'obstacles. Lectures de chiffres (1973–1987)*. L'Harmattan/CIEMI.

———. 1992. 'La section d'éducation spécialisée, miroir grossissant des inégalités'. *Migrants-Formation* (89):18–31.

Bourdieu, Pierre, and Patrick Champagne. 1992. 'Les exclus de l'intérieur'. *Actes de la recherche en sciences sociales* (91–92):71–75.

Bourdieu, Pierre, and Jean-Claude Passeron. 1970. *La Reproduction: éléments d'une théorie du système d'enseignement*. Éditions de Minuit.

Boyzon-Fradet, Danielle, and Serge Boulot. 1991. 'Le système scolaire français: aide ou obstacle à l'intégration?' pp. 236–260 in *Face au racisme*, edited by Pierre-André Taguieff. La Découverte.

Bressoux, Pascal. 1994. 'Les effets de la formation initiale et de l'expérience professionnelle des instituteurs. Etude portant sur le CE2'. *Les dossiers d'Éducation et Formations* (36).

Bressoux, Pascal, and Agnès Desclaux. 1991. 'La lecture à l'école élémentaire: recherche des facteurs de progrès des élèves'. *Éducation et Formations* (27–28):61–81.

Brinbaum Yaël, and Guégnard Claude. 2010. 'Orientation, parcours de formation et insertion: quelles relations pour les jeunes issus de l'immigration?' *Relief* (30):323–338.

Brinbaum, Yaël, and Héctor Cebolla Boado. 2007. 'The School Careers of Ethnic Minority Youth in France: Success or Disillusion?' *Ethnicities* 7(3):445–474.

Brinbaum, Yaël, and Annick Kieffer. 2005. 'D'une génération à l'autre, les aspirations éducatives des familles immigrées. Ambition et persévérance'. *Éducation et Formations* (72):53–75.

———. 2009. 'Les scolarités des enfants d'immigrés de la sixième au baccalauréat: différenciation et polarisation des parcours'. *Population* 64(3):561–610.

Brinbaum, Yaël, Laure Moguérou, and Jean-Luc Primon. 2010. 'Parcours et expériences scolaires des jeunes descendants d'immigrés en France'. pp. 47–54 in *Trajectoires et Origines. Enquête sur la diversité des populations en France. Premiers résultats*, edited by Cris Beauchemin, Christelle Hamel, and Patrick Simon. INED.

Brinbaum, Yaël, and Christine Guégnard. 2011. 'Parcours de formation et d'insertion des jeunes issus de l'immigration', Net-Doc 78, CEREQ.

Broccolichi, Sylvain. 2009. 'L'espace des inégalités scolaires. Une analyse des variations socio-spatiales d'acquis scolaires dégagée des optiques évaluatives'. *Actes de la recherche en sciences sociales* (180):74–91.

Broccolichi, Sylvain, and Danièle Trancart. 2010. 'De fortes disparités de contextes et de résultats'. pp. 88–103 in *École: les pièges de la concurrence. Comprendre le déclin de l'école française*, edited by Sylvain Broccolichi, Choukri Ben Ayed, and Danièle Trancart. La Découverte.

Broccolichi, Sylvain, and Agnès van Zanten. 1997. 'Espaces de concurrence et circuits de scolarisation. L'évitement des collèges publics d'un district de la banlieue parisienne'. *Annales de la recherche urbaine* (75):5–17.

Browne, Anthony. 2009. 'Denying Race in the American and French Context'. *Wadabagei* 12(1):73–91.

Buisson-Fenet, Hélène, and Séverine Landrier. 2008. 'Être ou pas? Discrimination positive et révélation du rapport au savoir'. *Education et sociétés* (21):67–80.

Caille, Jean-Paul. 2005. 'Les projets d'avenir des enfants d'immigrés'. *Les immigrés en France*:11–22.

———. 2007. 'Perception du système éducatif et projets d'avenir des enfants d'immigrés'. *Education et Formations* (74):117–142.

———. 2008. 'Parcours et aspirations scolaires des enfants d'immigrés'. *Ville-Ecole-Intégration Diversité* (154):87–93.

Caille, Jean-Paul, and Sophie O'Prey. 2002. 'Les familles immigrées et l'école française: un rapport singulier qui persiste même après un long séjour en France'. *Données sociales*:149–159.

Caille, Jean-Paul, and Fabienne Rosenwald. 2006. 'Les inégalités de réussite à l'école élémentaire: construction et évolution'. *France, portrait social*:115–137.

Calvès, Gwénaële. 2004. 'Les politiques françaises de discrimination positive: trois spécificités'. *Pouvoirs* (111):29–40.

Carayon, Claudie. 1992. 'Jeunes enfants en situation interculturelle et difficultés en lecture: recherche d'explication'. *Revue française de pédagogie* (98):57–68.

Cebolla Boado, Héctor. 2006. 'Ethnic Disadvantage in the Transition from Lower to Upper Secondary Education in France'. *Mediterranean Journal of Educational Studies* 11(1):1–29.

———. 2007. 'Immigrant Concentration in Schools: Peer Pressures in Place?' *European Sociological Review* 23(3):341–356.

———. 2008a. 'Del preescolar a las puertas de la universidad. Un análisis de las trayectorias escolares de los estudiantes inmigrantes en Francia'. *Revista Internacional de Sociología* 66(51):79–103.

———. 2008b. 'Les enfants d'immigrés progressent-ils plus vite à l'école? Le cas français'. *Population* 63(4):747–765.

Charles Frédéric and Florence Legendre. 2006. *Les enseignants issus des immigrations: modalités d'accès au groupe professionnel, représentations du métier et de l'école. Étude comparative*. Sudel.

Charlot, Bernard. 1990. 'Penser l'échec comme événement, penser l'immigration comme histoire'. *VEI Enjeux* (81):8–24.

———. 1999. *Le Rapport au savoir en milieu populaire. Une recherche dans les lycées professionnels de banlieue*. Anthropos.

Charlot, Bernard, Laurence Émin and Olivier de Peretti. 2002. *Les aides-éducateurs: une gestion communautaire de la violence scolaire*. Anthropos.

Chauveau, Gérard, and Eliane Rogovas-Chauveau. 1990. 'La (non) réussite scolaire des « immigrés ». Où sont les différences?' *Migrants-Formation* (81):25–34.

Chazal, Dominique, and Romuald Normand. 2007. 'Le foulard dévoilé: le proche à l'épreuve du droit dans l'espace scolaire'. *Education et sociétés* (19):33–52.

Chérifi, Hanifa. 2001. 'Islam et intégration à l'école'. *Revue européenne de migrations internationales* 17(2):175–182.

Cibois, Philippe. 2002. 'La bonne volonté scolaire. Expliquer la carrière scolaire des élèves issus de l'immigration'. in *Méthodes et outils des sciences sociales. Innovation et renouvellement*, edited by Philippe Blanchard, and Thomas Ribémont. L'Harmattan.

Clerc, Paul. 1964. 'Les élèves de nationalité étrangère'. *Population* 19(5):865–872.

Condon, Stéphanie, and Corinne Régnard. 2010. 'Héritage et pratiques linguistiques des descendants d'immigrés en France'. *Hommes & migrations* (1288):44–56.

Cortéséro, Régis. 2010. Entre l'émeute et le ghetto. Quels cadres de socialisation politique pour les jeunes des banlieues populaires? *Education et sociétés* (25): 65–81.

Cortier, Claude. 2007. 'Accueil et scolarisation des élèves allophones à l'école française: contextes, dispositifs et didactiques'. *Ville-École-Intégration Diversité* (151):145–153.

Debarbieux, Eric. 1997. 'Ethnicité, effet-classe et punition: une étude de cas'. *Migrants-Formation* (109):377–401.

———. 1998. 'Violence et ethnicité dans l'école française'. *Revue européenne de migrations internationales* 14(1):77–91.

———. 1999. 'Désigner et punir. Remarques sur une construction ethnicisante au collège'. pp. 195–212 in *La justice du système éducatif*, edited by Denis Meuret. De Boeck & Larcier.

Debarbieux Eric and Catherine Blaya. 2001. *Violence à l'école et politiques publiques*. ESF.

Debarbieux, Eric, and Laurence Tichit. 1997. 'Le construit ethnique de la violence'. pp. 155–177 in *Violences à l'école. Etat des savoirs*, edited by Bernard Charlot, and Jean-Claude Emin. Armand Colin.

———. 1993. 'Évaluation CE2-6ème de septembre 1992. Résultats complémentaires et analyse'. *Les dossiers d'Éducation et Formations* (31).

Desplanques, Guy, and Nicole Tabard. 1991. 'La localisation de la population étrangère'. *Économie et statistique* (242):51–62.

Doytcheva, Milena. 2007. *Une Discrimination positive à la française? Ethnicité et territoire dans les politiques de la ville*. La Découverte.

Dubet, François. 1987. *La galère. Jeunes en survie*. Fayard.

———. 1989. *Immigrations, qu'en savons-nous? Un bilan des connaissances. Notes et Etudes Documentaires* n° 4887, La Documentation Française.

———. 1992. 'Le Racisme et l'école en France'. in *Racisme et modernité*, edited by Michel Wieviorka. La Decouverte.

Dubreuil, Bertrand. 2001. 'Immigration et stratégies familiales en milieu scolaire'. *Migrations Société* 13(75–76):73–82.

Duru-Bellat, Marie, and Alain Mingat. 1987. 'Facteurs institutionnels de la diversite des carrieres scolaires'. *Revue française de sociologie* 28(1):3–16.

Duru-Bellat, Marie, and Agnès van Zanten. 2012. *Sociologie de l'école*, 4th ed. Armand Colin.

Falaize, Benoît. 2007. 'Histoire de l'immigration et pratiques scolaires'. *Ville-École-Intégration Diversité* (149):79–84.

Fassin, Didier. 2011. 'Qu'il ne suffit pas d'être politiquement incorrect pour être scientifiquement fondé'. *Revue française de sociologie* 52(4):777–786.

Favell, Andrian. 2001. *Philosophies of Integration: Immigration and the Idea of Citizenship in France and Britain. Second edition*. Macmillan.

———. 2003. 'Integration Nations: The Nation-State and Research on Immigrants in Western Europe'. *Comparative Social Research* 22(13–42).

Favre, Joëlle, and Alain Manigand. 2000. 'Les adolescents de migrants au collège: représentations et positionnements scolaires'. *Migrations Société* 12(71):21–36.

Felouzis, Georges. 2003. 'La ségrégation ethnique au collège et ses conséquences'. *Revue française de sociologie* 44(3):413–447.

Felouzis, Georges, Françoise Liot, and Joëlle Perroton. 2005. *L'apartheid scolaire. Enquête sur la ségrégation ethnique dans les collèges*. Seuil.

Felouzis, Georges, and Joëlle Perroton. 2009. 'Grandir entre pairs à l'école. Ségrégation ethnique et reproduction sociale dans le système éducatif français'. *Actes de la recherche en sciences sociales* (180):92–101.

Fouquet-Chauprade, Barbara. 2011. *Voir le monde en couleurs. Sociologie de l'ethnicité et de la construction de soi dans les collèges ségrégués*. Doctoral Dissertation. University of Bordeaux 2.

Galembert, Claire de. 2009. 'Cause du voile et lutte pour la parole musulmane légitime'. *Sociétés contemporaines* (74):19–47.

Gaspard, Françoise, and Frédéric Khosrokhavar. 1995. *Le Foulard et la République*. La Decouverte.

Gibert, Serge. 1989. 'La scolarisation des élèves étrangers. Eléments de synthèse statistiques'. pp. 125–134 in *Les politiques d'intégration des jeunes issus de l'immigration*, edited by Bernard Lorreyte. Harmattan.

Gouirir, Malika. 1998. 'L'avenir d'une illusion: reproduction de groupes familiaux et trajectoires de filles et fils d'un « douar » immigré'. *Ville-École-Intégration* (113):136–156.

Guénif-Souilamas, Nacira. 1994. 'Représentations et pratiques éducatives des jeunes parents franco-maghrébins'. *Migrants-Formation* (98):92–104.

Henriot-van Zanten, Agnès. 1990. *L'école et l'espace local. Les enjeux des zones d'éducation prioritaire*. Presses universitaires de Lyon.

Henriot-van Zanten, Agnès, Jean-Paul Payet, and Laurence Roulleau-Berger. 1994. *L'École dans la ville. Accords et désaccords autour d'un projet politiques*. L'Harmattan.

Héran, François. 1996. 'École publique, école privée, qui peut choisir?' *Économie et statistique* (293):17–39.

Herpin, Nicolas. 1996. 'Les amis de classe: du collège au lycée'. *Économie et Statistique* (293):125–136.

Ichou, Mathieu. 2010. 'Rapprocher les familles populaires de l'école. Analyse sociologique d'un lieu commun'. *Dossiers d'études* (125):1–104.

———. 2013. 'Différences d'origine et origine des différences: les résultats scolaires des enfants d'émigrés/immigrés en France du début de l'école primaire à la fin du collège'. *Revue française de sociologie* 54(1):5–52.

Ichou, Mathieu, and Louis-André Vallet. 2011. 'Do All Roads Lead to Inequality? Trends in French Upper Secondary School Analysed with Four Longitudinal Surveys'. *Oxford Review of Education* 37(2):167–194.

———. 2013. 'Academic Achievement, Tracking Decisions and Their Relative Contribution to Educational Inequalities: Change over Four Decades in France'. in *Determined to Succeed? Performance, Choice and Education*, edited by Michelle Jackson. Stanford University Press.

Kakpo, Nathalie. 2005. 'Relégation scolaire et recherche de requalification par l'islam monographie des religiosités juvéniles dans une ville française moyenne'. *Sociétés contemporaines* (59–60):139–159.

Kherroubi, Matine and Jean-Yves Rochex. 2002. 'La recherche en éducation et les ZEP en France. 1. Politique ZEP, objets, postures et orientations de recherche'. *Revue française de pédagogie* (140): 103–131.

Laacher, Smaïn. 1990. 'L'école et ses miracles. Note sur les déterminants sociaux des trajectoires scolaires des enfants de familles immigrées'. *Politix* 3(12):25–37.

———. 2005. *L'institution scolaire et ses miracles*. La Dispute.

Laacher, Smaïn, and Alain Lenfant. 1991. 'Où vont les jeunes filles quand elles vont à l'école? Remarques statistiques provisoires sur les élèves d'origine étrangère'. *Migrants-Formation* (84):177–189.

———. 1997. 'Réussite au baccalauréat: Français et étrangers en Ile-de-France'. *Revue européenne de migrations internationales* 13(2):25–45.

Lacerda, Élise de, and Laurent Ameline. 2001. 'Les élèves de nationalité étrangère dans les premier et second degrés'. *VEI Enjeux* (125):160–186.

Lagrange, Hugues. 2010. *Le déni des cultures*. Le Seuil.

Lahire, Bernard 1995. *Tableaux de familles. Heurs et malheurs scolaires en milieux populaires*. Gallimard-Le Seuil.

Lapeyronnie, Didier. 1993. *L'individu et les minorités. La France et la Grande-Bretagne face à leurs immigrés*. Presses Universitaires de France.

Laurens, Jean-Paul. 1995. 'La migration: une chance contre l'échec scolaire?' *Hommes & migrations* (1185):19–25.

Lavin, Marie. 2007. 'L'image des immigrés dans les manuels scolaires'. *Ville-École-Intégration Diversité* (149):97–103.

Lazaridis, Marie. 2001. 'La scolarisation des enfants de migrants: entre intégration républicaine et structures spécifiques'. *VEI Enjeux* (125):198–208.

Le Guen, Martine. 1991. 'Réussite scolaire et disparités socio-démographiques'. *Education et Formations* (27–28):9–28.

Lefranc, Arnaud. 2010. 'Unequal Opportunities and Ethnic Origin: The Labor Market Outcomes of Second-Generation Immigrants in France'. *American Behavioral Scientist* 53(12):1851–1882.

Legendre, Florence. 2002 'Diversité culturelle et pratiques pédagogiques. Opinions et attitudes des professeurs des écoles de l'académie de Créteil'. *VEI Enjeux* (129):190–206.

Léger, Alain, and Maryse Tripier. 1986. *Fuir ou construire l'école populaire?* Méridiens-Klincksieck.

Lepoutre, David. 1997. *Cœur de banlieue. Codes, rites et langages*. Odile Jacob.

Lhommeau, Bertrand, and Patrick Simon. 2010. 'Les populations enquêtées'. pp. 11–18 in *Trajectoires et Origines. Enquête sur la diversité des populations en France. Premiers résultats*, edited by Cris Beauchemin, Christelle Hamel, and Patrick Simon. INED.

Limage, Leslie J. 2000. 'Education and Muslim Identity: The Case of France'. *Comparative Education* 36(1):73–94.

Lorcerie, Françoise. 1988. 'L'islam au programme'. *Annuaire de l'Afrique du Nord* 27:161–192.

———. 1994a. 'Les sciences sociales au service de l'identité nationale'. pp. 245–281 in Cartes d'identité. Comment dit-on 'nous' en politique, edited by D.C. Martin. Fondation Nationale des Sciences Politiques.

———. 1994b. 'L'Islam dans les cours de Langue et Cultures d'origine: le procès'. *Revue Européenne des Migrations Internationales* 10(2): 5–43.

———. 1995. 'Scolarisation des enfants d'immigrés. Etat des lieux et état des questions en France'. *Confluences Méditerranée* 14:27–66.

———. 1996. 'Laïcité 1996. La République à l'école de l'immigration?' *Revue française de pédagogie* (117):53–85.

———. (ed.). 2003. *L'école et le défi ethnique. Éducation et intégration*. ESF Editeur.

———. 2010. 'A French Approach to Minority Islam? A Study in Normative Confusion'. *Journal of International Migration and Integration* 11(1):59–72.

Louis-Etxeto, Daniel. 1998. 'La hiérarchisation sociale des lycées'. *Revue française de pédagogie* 124(1):55–68.

Marangé, James, and André Lebon. 1982. 'L'insertion des jeunes d'origine étrangère dans la société française'. p. 270. Ministère du Travail / Haut Comité de la population et de la famille.

Matéo, Pierre. 1992. 'Évaluation de l'impact pédagogique des bibliothèques centres documentaires au niveau du cours préparatoire'. *Revue Française de Pédagogie* (99):37–48.

Mathey-Pierre, Catherine, and Brigitte Larguèze. 2010. 'Désarroi des familles, des élèves et des professionels'. pp. 147–165 in *École: les pièges de la concurrence – Comprendre le déclin de l'école française*, edited by Choukri Ben Ayed, Sylvain Broccolichi, and Danièle Trancart. La Découverte.

Mingat, Alain. 1984. 'Les acquisitions scolaires des élèves au cours préparatoire: les origines des différences'. *Revue française de pédagogie* (69):49–62.

———. 1987. 'Sur la dynamique des acquisitions à l'école élémentaire'. *Revue Française de Pédagogie* (79):5–14.

Ministère de l'Education nationale. 2011. *Repères et références statistiques sur les enseignements, la formation et la recherche*. Direction de l'évaluation, de la prospective et de la performance.

Moguérou, Laure, Yaël Brinbaum, and Jean-Luc Primon. 2010. 'Niveaux de diplôme des immigrés et de leurs descendants'. pp. 39–46 in *Trajectoires et Origines. Enquête sur la diversité des populations en France. Premiers résultats*, edited by Cris Beauchemin, Christelle Hamel, and Patrick Simon. INED.

Mohamed, Marwan. 2011. *La formation des bandes. Entre la famille, l'école et la rue*. Presses universitaires de France.

Moignard, Benjamin. 2008. *L'école et la rue: fabriques de délinquance*. Le Monde/Presses Universitaires de France.

Mondon, Pierre. 1984. 'Quelques aspects de la scolarisation des enfants étrangers à partir des statistiques'. *Migrants-Formation* (58):6–14.

Morel, Stéphanie. 2002. *Ecole, territoires et identités: les politiques publiques françaises à l'épreuve de l'ethnicité*. L'Harmattan.

Mullet, Etienne. 1980. 'Les enfants de travailleurs migrants et l'enseignement secondaire'. *L'orientation scolaire et professionnelle* 9(3):195–252.

Noiriel, Gérard. 1988. *Le creuset français. Histoire de l'immigration, XIXe-XXe siècles*. Seuil.

Oberti, Marco. 2005. 'Différenciation sociale et scolaire du territoire: Inégalités et con-figurations locales'. *Sociétés contemporaines* (59–60):13–42.

———. 2007a. *L'école dans la ville. Ségrégation – mixité – carte scolaire*. Presses de Sciences Po.

———. 2007b. 'Social and School Differentiation of Urban Space: Inequalities and Local Configurations'. *Environment and Planning* 39(1):208–227.

Oberti, Marco, Franck Sanselme, and Agathe Voisin. 2009. 'Ce que Sciences Po fait aux lycéens et à leurs parents: entre méritocratie et perception d'inégalités. Enquête dans quatre lycées de la Seine-Saint-Denis'. *Actes de la recherche en sciences sociales* (180):102–124.

Palheta, Ugo. 2012. *La domination scolaire. Sociologie de l'enseignement professionnel et de ses publics*. Presses Universitaires de France.

Payet, Jean-Paul. 1985. 'L'insolence'. *Annales de la recherche urbaine* (27):49–55.

———. 1992. 'Civilités et ethnicité dans les collèges de banlieue: enjeux, résistances et dérives d'une action scolaire territorialisée'. *Revue française de pédagogie* 101(1):59–69.

———. 1995a. *Collèges de banlieue. Ethnographie d'un monde scolaire*. Méridiens-Klinksieck.

———. 1995b. 'Culture, ethnicité, école. Tentative de réflexion dans la tourmente'. *Migrants-Formation* (102):74–81.

———. 1997. ' 'Le sale boulot': division morale du travail dans un collège de banlieue'. *Annales de la Recherche Urbaine* (75):19–31.

———. 1999. 'Mixités et ségrégations dans l'école urbaine'. *Hommes & migrations* (1217):30–42.

———. 2003. 'Ecole et immigration. Un bilan des travaux (1996–2002), un programme de recherche (1)'. *Ville-Ecole-Intégration Enjeux* (135):103–122.

Payet, Jean-Paul, and François Sicot. 1997. 'Expérience collégienne et origine « ethnique »: la civilité et la justice scolaire du point de vue des élèves étrangers ou issus de l'immigration'. *Migrants-Formation* (109):155–167.

Payet, Jean-Paul, and Agnès van Zanten. 1996. 'L'école, les enfants de l'immigration et des minorités ethniques. Une revue de la littérature française, américaine et britan-nique'. *Revue française de pédagogie* (117):87–149.

Perroton, Joëlle. 2000a. 'Les dimensions ethniques de l'expérience scolaire'. *L'Année sociologique* 50(2):437–468.

Perroton, Joëlle. 2000b. 'Les ambiguïtés de l'ethnicisation des relations scolaires. L'exemple des relations école-familles à travers la mise en place d'un dispositif de médiation'. *VEI Enjeux* (121):130–147.

Pinçon, Michel, and Monique Pinçon-Charlot. 1994. 'Les enfants d'immigrés dans une école des beaux quartiers'. *Migrants-Formation* (96):73–81.

Préteceille, Edmond. 2006. 'La ségrégation sociale a-t-elle augmenté? La métropole parisi-enne entre polarisation et mixité. ' *Sociétés Contemporaines* (62):69–93.

———. 2009. 'La ségrégation ethno-raciale a-t-elle augmenté dans la métropole parisi-enne?' *Revue française de sociologie* 50(3):489–519.

Raveaud, Maroussia. 2003. 'Minorités, ethnicité et citoyenneté: les modèles français et anglais sur les bancs de l'école'. *Revue française de pédagogie* 144(1):19–28.

———. 2006. *De l'enfant au citoyen. La construction de la citoyenneté à l'école en France et en Angleterre*. Presses universitaires de France.

———. 2008. 'Culture-Blind? Parental Discourse on Religion, Ethnicity and Secularism in the French Educational Context'. *European Educational Research Journal* 7(1): 74–88.

Raveaud, Maroussia, and Agnès van Zanten. 2007. 'Choosing the Local School? Middle Class Parents' Values and Social and Ethnic Mix in London and Paris'. *Journal of Education Policy* 22(1):107–124.

Rayou, Patrick and Agnès van Zanten. 2004. *Les nouveaux enseignants: changeront-ils l'école?* Bayard.

Rhein, Catherine. 1997. 'De l'anamorphose en démographie. Polarisation sociale et flux scolaires dans la métropole parisienne' *Les Annales de la Recherche Urbaine* (75).

Rinaudo, Christian. 1998. 'L'imputation de caractéristiques ethniques dans l'encadrement de la vie scolaire'. *Revue européenne de migrations internationales* 14(3):27–43.

Robert, Bénédicte. 2009. *Les politiques d'éducation prioritaire. Les défis de la réforme.* Presses Universitaires de France.

Rochex, Jean-Yves. 1992. 'Ecole et immigrations. La nécessité du pluriel'. *Migrants-Formation* (89):32–44.

———. 2008 « Vingt-cinq ans de politique d'éducation prioritaire en France: une spécificité incertaine et des résultats décevants » pp. 131–177 in Marc Demeuse, Daniel Frandji, Denis Greger, Jean-Yves Rochex (eds) *Les politiques d'éducation prioritaire en Europe.* INRP.

Roussier-Fusco, Elena. 2003. 'Le modèle français d'intégration et les dynamiques interethniques dans deux écoles de la banlieue parisienne'. *Revue française de pédagogie* 144(1):29–37.

———. 2007. *L'école à l'épreuve de l'ethnicité.* Doctoral dissertation. Sciences Po.

Sabbagh, Daniel. 2006. 'Une convergence problématique: les stratégies de légitimation de la « discrimination positive » dans l'enseignement supérieur aux États-Unis et en France'. *Politix* (73):211–229.

Sanselme, Franck. 2009. 'L'ethnicisation des rapports sociaux à l'école. Ethnographie d'un lycée de banlieue'. *Sociétés contemporaines* (76):121–147.

Santelli, Emmanuelle. 2001. *La mobilité sociale dans l'immigration: itinéraires de réussite des enfants d'origine algérienne.* Presses Universitaires du Mirail.

———. 2007. *Grandir en banlieue. Parcours et devenir de jeunes français d'origine maghrébine.* CIEMI.

Sayad, Abdelmalek. 2004. *The Suffering of the Immigrant.* Polity.

Schnapper, Dominique. 1991. *La France de l'intégration. Sociologie de la nation en 1990.* Gallimard

———. 'Les enfants d'immigrés sur le marché du travail. Les mécanismes d'une discrimination sélective'. *Formation Emploi* (65):31–55.

Silberman, Roxane, and Irène Fournier. 2006. 'Les secondes générations sur le marché du travail en France: une pénalité ethnique ancrée dans le temps. Contribution à la théorie de l'assimilation segmentée'. *Revue française de sociologie* 47(2):243–292.

Stevens, Peter A. J. 2007. 'Researching Race/Ethnicity and Educational Inequality in English Secondary Schools: A Critical Review of the Research Literature between 1980 and 2005'. *Review of Educational Research Quarterly* 77(2):147–185.

Stevens, Peter A. J., Noel Clycq, Christianne Timmerman, and Mieke Van Houtte. 2011. 'Researching Race/Ethnicity and Educational Inequality in the Netherlands: A Critical Review of the Research Literature between 1980 and 2008'. *British Educational Research Journal* 37(1):5–43.

Stuart Lambert, Paul, and Emmanuel Peignard. 2002. 'Ambitions et réussites scolaires et professionnelles comparées des enfants d'immigrés'. *Revue française de pédagogie* (140):75–88.

Tichit, Laurence. 2001. 'Quartiers sud: racialisation et construits ethniques du racket à l'école'. *VEI Enjeux* (124):198–206.

Trancart, Danièle. 1998. 'L'évolution des disparités entre collèges publics'. *Revue française de pédagogie* (124):43–53.

Tribalat, Michèle. 1997. 'Chronique de l'immigration. Les populations d'origine étrangère en France métropolitaine'. *Population* 52(1):163–219.

Tripier, Maryse. 1990. *L'Immigration dans la classe ouvriere en France*. L'Harmattan.

Tucci, Ingrid. 2010. 'Les descendants de migrants maghrébins en France et turcs en Allemagne: deux types de mise à distance sociale?' *Revue française de sociologie* 51(1):3–38.

Vallet, Louis-André. 1996. 'L'assimilation scolaire des enfants issus de l'immigration et son interprétation: un examen sur données françaises'. *Revue française de pédagogie* 117(1):7–27.

Vallet, Louis-André, and Jean-Paul Caille. 1995. 'Les carrières scolaires au collège des élèves étrangers ou issus de l'immigration'. *Éducation et Formations* (40):5–14.

———. 1996a. 'Les élèves étrangers ou issus de l'immigration dans l'école et le collège français. Une étude d'ensemble'. *Les dossiers d'Éducation et Formations* 67.

———. 1996b. 'Niveau en français et en mathématiques des élèves étrangers ou issus de l'immigration'. *Economie et statistique* (293):137–153.

———. 2000. 'La scolarité des enfants d'immigrés'. in *L'école. L'état des savoirs*, edited by Agnès van Zanten.

van Zanten, Agnès. 1996. 'Fabrication et effets de la ségrégation scolaire'. pp. 281–291 in *L'exclusion. L'état des savoirs*, edited by Serge Paugam. La Découverte.

———. 1997a. 'Schooling Immigrants in France in the 1990s: Success or Failure of the Republican Model of Integration?' *Anthropology & Education Quarterly* 28(3):351–374.

———. 1997b. 'Le traitement des différences liées à l'origine immigrée à l'école française'. pp. 149–167 in *Langue, école, identités*, edited by Nadir Marouf, and Claude Carpentier. L'Harmattan.

———. 2000a. 'Le quartier ou l'école? Déviance et sociabilité adolescente dans un collège de banlieue'. *Déviance et société* 24(4):377–401.

———. 2000b. 'Massification et régulation des systèmes d'enseignement. Adaptations et ajustements en milieu urbain défavorisé'. *L'année sociologique* 50(2):409–436.

———. 2001. *L'école de la périphérie. Scolarité et ségrégation en banlieue*. Presses Universitaires de France.

———. 2005. 'Political Models and Local Practice: The Production of Ethnicity in the Schools of the Parisian Periphery'. pp. 223–234 in Robert Maier, and Wolfgang Herrlitz (eds) *Dialogues In and Around Multicultural Schools*, Max Niemeyer Verlag.

———. 2006a. 'Compétition et fonctionnement des établissements scolaires: les enseignements d'une enquête européenne'. *Revue Française de Pédagogie* (156):9–17.

———. 2006b. 'Une discrimination banalisée? L'évitement de la mixité sociale et raciale dans les établissements scolaires'. pp. 195–210 in *De la question sociale à la question raciale? Représenter la société française*, edited by Didier Fassin, and Eric Fassin. La Découverte.

———. 2009a. *Choisir son école. Stratégies familiales et médiations locales*. Presses Universitaires de France.

———. 2009b. 'Le choix des autres. Jugements, stratégies et ségrégations scolaires'. *Actes de la recherche en sciences sociales* (180):24–34.

———. 2009c. 'New Positive Discrimination Policies in Basic and Higher Education: From the Quest of Social Justice to Optimal Mobilisation of Human Resources?' pp. 478–494 in Marteen Simons, Mark Olseen and Michael Peters (eds) *Re-reading Education Policies: A Handbook Studying the Policy Agenda of the 21st Century,* Sense Publishers.

———. 2010. 'L'ouverture sociale des grandes écoles: diversification des élites ou renouveau des politiques publiques d'éducation?' *Sociétés contemporaines* (79):69–95.

———. 2011. *Les politiques de l'éducation*, 2nd ed. Presses Universitaires de France.

van Zanten, Agnès, and Jean-Pierre Obin. 2010. *La carte scolaire*, 2nd ed. Presses universitaires de France.

Varro, Gabrielle. 1997. 'Les élèves étrangers dans les discours des institutions et des instituteurs'. *Langage et société* (80):73–99.

————. 1999. 'Les futurs maitres face à l'immigration. Le piège d'un « habitus discursif »'. *Mots* (60):30–42.

Vasquez, Ana. 1980. 'Le temps social: enfants étrangers à l'école française'. *Enfance* 33(3):179–191.

————. 1982. 'Temps social, temps culturel'. *Enfance* 35(5):335–350.

Visier, Laurent, and Geneviève Zoïa. 2010. 'Le collège, la ville, et la mixité sociale: la fabrique de la distribution des élèves'. *Annales de la recherche urbaine* (106):38–47.

Wayland, Sarah V. 1997. 'Religious Expression in Public Schools: Kirpans in Canada, Hijab in France'. *Ethnic and Racial Studies* 20(3):545–556.

Xavier de Brito, Angela, and Ana Vasquez. 1994. 'La perception de l'étranger par les enfants d'une école primaire'. *Migrants-Formation* (96):57–72.

————.1996. 'L'intégration… mais qu'est-ce donc?' *Revue française de pédagogie* (117):29–37.

Zehraoui, Ahsène. 1996. 'Processus différentiels d'intégration au sein des familles algériennes en France'. *Revue française de sociologie* 37(2):237–261.

————. 1998. 'Les relations entre familles d'origine étrangère et institution scolaire: attentes et malentendus'. *Ville-École-Intégration* (114):53–73.

Zeroulou, Zaihia. 1985. 'Mobilisation familiale et réussite scolaire'. *Revue européenne de migrations internationales* 1(2):107–117.

Zeroulou, Zaïhia. 1988. 'La réussite scolaire des enfants d'immigrés. L'apport d'une approche en termes de mobilisation'. *Revue française de sociologie* 29(3):447–470.

Zimmerman, Daniel. 1978. 'Un langage non verbal de classe: les processus d'attraction-répulsion des enseignants à l'égard des élèves en fonction de l'origine familiale de ces derniers'. *Revue française de pédagogie* (44):46–70.

Zirotti, Jean-Pierre. 1980. 'Le jugement professoral: un système de classement 'qui ne fait pas de différence'. *Langage et société* (14):3–42.

13
Germany

Ingrid Gogolin and Tanja Salem

13.1 Introduction

With respect to ethnic diversity, ethnicity and educational inequality, Germany is a very specific case. Due to the division into two German republics, the country has two different histories of migration as well as treatment of ethnic and autochthonous minorities since World War II and until 1989. This also implies the existence of two different research traditions in this period. In Section 13.2, we outline these different traditions for the purpose of contextualization and illustration. Another historical shift and a new dynamic of social and educational policies can be observed since 2000. To a considerable extent, this is a reaction to the first results from the OECD-PISA studies. The proof of strong linkages between socio-economic status, cultural capital, ethnic background, and pupils' achievement motivated new political as well as research activities. To this belongs the establishment of a biannual national education report (since 2006). A 'National Educational Panel Study (NEPS)' was set up from 2009. These political activities were highly influential for the realignment of traditions in research on ethnicity and educational inequality in Germany.

The next section of our contribution describes the national context, focusing on the first four decades or so, on the Western part of Germany, and on main migration patterns, composition, and size of ethnic minority groups until 1989, and after this point in time on reunified Germany. We also present relevant developments of educational and social policies since 1989. The following section ('methodology') describes the process of sampling the literature which we included in the report. In the third section, we refer to different research traditions. From a bird's eye view, three approaches can be identified: (1) features of the education system and their relevance for inequality; (2) characteristics of migrant students and their families as causes for inequality; and (3) linguistic diversity and educational achievement. In the final section, we summarize key findings of the review and present suggestions on how research in Germany could develop.

13.2   National context: Migration, educational and social policy in Germany

As mentioned above, due to the history of Germany as a divided state until relatively recently, our chapter on 'Germany' needs to address the fact that the country has two different histories of migration and thus two different research traditions in this period from World War II to 1989, which overlaps the period of the literature review by about a decade and of course has longer-reaching consequences for the research and educational communities alike. We outline these different traditions. The main focus of this article, however, will be on migration and policy patterns and the respective research which was carried out in the former Federal Republic of Germany, i.e. the Western states of the country, until 1989, and on the actual Federal Republic since then. This is justified as follows.

Firstly, the general question of inequality as an outcome or even product of the educational or social system was vigorously discussed in the Western part, i.e. the Federal Republic of Germany (BRD), whereas in the German Democratic Republic (DDR)[1] it was no topic of public discourse. In the BRD, 'educational expansion' became a societal aim in the late 1960s. In 1970, the German Educational Council (Deutscher Bildungsrat, 1970) presented a report and recommendations for reform of the educational system, focusing on the aim to overcome the disadvantages caused by socio-economic factors, gender, cultural backgrounds, (which were at that time primarily seen as influenced by religious belief and affiliation), or by region (rural vs. urban areas) (Cortina, Baumert et al., 2005). At that time, the 'girl from a Catholic working-class family, living in a rural area' presented the quintessential educationally disadvantaged child in (Western) Germany. Whereas intense public discourse as well as research on educational inequality was initiated by the Bildungsrat report, a similar development did not take place in the German Democratic Republic. Here, by definition and political conviction, the social and educational systems were not considered to support, let alone produce inequality.

Secondly, growing ethnic and linguistic diversity as a consequence of migration can be observed in the Western German states (*Länder*). These implemented a recruitment policy for 'guest workers' since 1955. In contrast to this, the DDR austerely restricted visits or immigration from abroad. Only a limited number of foreigners were allowed to enter the country. Most of them were contract workers on a fixed-term basis or students and trainees, coming from other socialist countries. Rather than aiming to integrate them, the DDR conducted a policy of isolation of foreigners from the resident population. Thus, ethnic diversity was more or less invisible in the DDR, and the topic was irrelevant in public discourse as well as in research before the German reunification in 1989 (Krüger-Potratz, Hansen, and Jasper, 1991).

Given this background and the time frame which is set for this review, we focus on the development in the former Western part of Germany for a historical retrospection on migration patterns, composition, and size of ethnic minority groups before describing the situation after 1989 (Section 13.2.1). With respect to educational and social policy, we concentrate on the contemporary German systems which follow the traditions of the former BRD (Section 13.2.2).

Another preliminary remark has to be made here. Although there is a discourse on 'racism' and 'anti-racist education', this perspective plays a marginal role in the migration-related research sphere in Germany. This is primarily due to the historical connotation of the terminology which is inextricably linked with the extinction of the Jewish, the Romany people, disabled populations and with euthanasia in the National Socialist era. The German racism discourse was thus primarily focused on attempts to reconstruct and understand the inconceivability of this historical burden, and to contribute to a prevention of such a human disaster in future. The respective research connected especially to work which was carried out in the *Neue Frankfurter Schule* (New Frankfurt School) (for example, Adorno, Frenkel-Brunswik, Levinson, and Sanford, 1973). In the mainstream of migration-related educational and social sciences research, the race-terminology was considered as political combat term rather than a scientific terminology (Bielefeld, 1991). Considering this specific historical constellation, we focus our review on research which is related to migration, ethnic, cultural, and linguistic minorities, and the respective terminology.

13.2.1 Migration to Germany

Germany – in its different cultural and political shapes – was an area of immigration throughout its history. After World War II, however, the country faced a new dynamic of immigration. This was due to two reasons: the first was the absorption of returnees or refugees from the former Eastern European war zones until the 1960s. The second was intense recruitment of labor-force since the early 1950s, in the German *Wirtschaftswunder* (the period of economic miracle until the early 1970s).

The legal fundamentals for migration were (and still are, in adapted versions) the possibility to recruit individuals or groups of migrants for specific purposes, such as workers, artists, scientists or other specialists on one hand; the repatriation of 'ethnic Germans' at second, and at third the protection of refugees as determined by the Constitution. In 1955, the BRD signed the first recruitment agreement with Italy. From 1960, more agreements followed: with Greece and Spain (1960); Turkey (1961); Morocco (1963); Portugal (1964); Tunisia (1965); Federal People's Republic of Yugoslavia (1968), and South Korea (1970). These contracts were of limited duration. All workers from non-members of the European Economic Community (EEC) – these were initially all above-mentioned countries except Italy – were expected to re-migrate after their contracts expired.

In the first recruitment period, the workers had to come alone. With respect to human rights agreements, however, the BRD started to accept and support family unification activities from the early 1970s. In 1973, Germany stopped recruitment due to the oil crisis and decline of employment. The only legal possibility for these groups of migrants to enter the country after the recruitment stop was family unification. During the recruitment period, the proportion of foreigners in Germany grew from 1.2% in 1960 to about 4.9% in the 1970s. The number of foreigners increased from 1973 to 1988 from 4 to 4.8 million.[2]

Another legal possibility to enter the BRD is based on Paragraph 1of the Federal Law on Refugees and Displaced Persons (BVFG, 2001). This regulates the re-migration of 'ethnic Germans' (*Aussiedler*, German repatriates). The addressees of this regulation are primarily emigrants to the Russian Empire from the 17th century onwards and their offspring, who left Germany on the basis of recruitment contracts, e.g. with Peter the Great. Still today and under certain conditions, the members of this group have the right to 'remigrate'. Since 1990, the respective regulation includes particularly 'ethnic Germans' from Estonia, Latvia, Lithuania, Russia, Poland, Czech and Slovak Republic, Hungary, and Romania.

The third relevant immigrant group enters the country based on Article 116 of the Constitution (Grundgesetz, 1949), concerning the rights of refugees. The definition of refugees follows the Geneva Convention on Refugees (1951). After World War II, and in recognition of the country's historical responsibilities, these regulations were utmost liberal. However, since then due to a change of public climate and to the EU-Schengen regulations (1985), the right to enter the country as a refugee became severely restricted. In general, considerably less than 10% of a refugee cohort receives the permission to reside. Irrespective of the high dismissal rate, refugees make up the third largest group of immigrants in Germany.

In 1990, roughly 5,342,500 'foreign residents' were registered in population statistics (8.4% of the total population). In reality, the number of immigrants was significantly larger, as the criterion for entries in these statistics was 'citizenship'. Thus, all immigrants with German passports were excluded from the observation, such as the *Aussiedler*, naturalized immigrants, those with dual nationality, and children from binational marriages. Migration researchers had complained of this highly insufficient data basis since the late 1970s, as it led to a lack of information-validity for research, policy-making, and social planning. It took more than 30 years, however, to convince the statistical offices of the relevance of more detailed data on migration. Since 2005, the '*Mikrozensus*' – a regular representative household survey carried out by the National Statistical Office – includes data on 'migration background', operationalized as: place of birth (two generations in retrospect), main language at home, and citizenship.

According to *Mikrozensus* data, about 15.7 million residents with migration background lived in the BRD in 2010. As migration is a phenomenon of 'the young', and because of higher than average birth rates in migrant families, the percentage of immigrants is highest in the youngest age cohorts. In 2010, 35% of children below the age of 6 years, 32% of adolescents up to 15, and 26% of the age group 15–20 years had a migration background (Statistisches Bundesamt, 2011). More information on the relative sizes of particular immigrant groups will be presented in the next section.

Despite the continuous immigration flows since World War II, the BRD refused to accept its status as an immigration country in official politics until the turn of the 21st century. The very first official governmental statement that indicated political responsibility for the integration of migrants in the whole social and economic, cultural, and educational sphere was adopted in 2006 (Bundesregierung, 2007).

13.2.2   Educational system

Although there was no comprehensive integration policy over decades, the educational sector took action in favor of the 'foreign workers' children' (*Ausländerkinder*) since the early 1960s. At any rate, we cannot report of a concise policy. This is not least due to the fact that Germany is a federal and highly decentralized nation, especially so in the fields of educational, cultural, and social welfare policies. Education in particular is the responsibility of the individual *Länder* (federal states). The BRD until 1989 comprised of 11 *Länder*, since 1990 there have been 16.

The German *Grundgesetz* defines the range of the federal government's responsibilities within the different fields of politics and legislation. Some political fields are centrally governed (such as foreign affairs and defense), but many fields are either under joint responsibility, or they are under sole responsibility of the *Länder*. Education is specifically rigorous with respect to decentralization. The *Länder* are responsible for all decisions about general education. The federal government holds responsibility for vocational education and training. For the rest of the education system, the central government is merely able to give financial support for certain measures – if the *Länder* agree to this.

Another particularity of the German system is the fact that early years or preschool education – for children up to six years – is not considered as a part of education, but of the public social system. Thus, the responsibility here is assigned to the federal government's ministry of family and social affairs (Bundesministerium für Familie, Senioren, Frauen und Jugend, BMFSFJ). The operative basis of the preschool system is the responsibility of public agencies, partly economically driven, partly subsidized by local, regional, or supra-regional bodies, such as religious organizations or social welfare services.

In most of the *Länder*, general frameworks (*Bildungspläne*, educational plans) exist that describe the aims of the preschool system; in some *Länder*, these concern the age-group from zero to ten years. These frameworks function as recommendations only, they have no binding character. Figure 13.1 displays the basic structure of the German education system.

Most German *Länder* have established a tri-partite or more system in secondary education, which begins at around the age of ten years at so-called fifth grade. For a few years however, due to the decline of birth rates and drift to the cities, we have observed a tendency to lower the number of tiers in secondary education. Some *Länder*, such as Hamburg, Berlin, and Saxony, started establishing a two-tier system with the '*Gymnasium*' (leading to a university entry qualification) and another school type that comprises of all other forms, leading at least to a lower secondary certificate. The system is highly selective; in general, university enrollment requires a *Gymnasium* certificate (*Abitur*).

In order to guarantee the equality of education standards in the Germany as a whole, the 'Standing Conference of the Ministers of Education and Cultural Affairs of the Länder' (*Kultusministerkonferenz*, KMK) was founded in 1948. After the restoration of Germany's unity in 1990, the *Länder* which were formerly part of the DDR (Brandenburg, Mecklenburg-Western Pomerania, Saxony, Saxony-Anhalt, Thuringia, and Berlin) joined the Standing Conference. Key tasks are to safeguard the mobility between the *Länder* for pupils, university students, and teachers. In order to meet this objective, the KMK agrees on the accordance and comparability of certificates and final qualifications, and on quality standards for schools, vocational training, and higher education.

The German educational system can be described as 'loosely coupled' by agreement between the *Länder*. The system is highly decentralized and complex. The complexity is even greater with respect to the areas of preschool education and life-long learning, as these areas are determined by the principle of subsidiarity. This situation is also influential with respect to general information about the system. In established areas of reporting we find recognized data based on longstanding conventions. With respect to migration in education and social systems however, data is rather scarce. Each of the *Länder* produces its own education and social statistics, and the operationalization of migration-related data is only partly concerted.

According to official school statistics, in 2010 8.3% (about 730,000) of approximately 8.8 million students in general and vocational education had a non-German citizenship. According to *Mikrozensus* data however, there were 8.3% of 'foreign' students plus 20.3% of students with German citizenship, but migration background. About 2.6 million of the 8.8 million students in public (i.e. non-private) schools had a migration background (we refer to them as 'migrant students'). The majority of migrant students live in families from a former *Anwerbeland* (recruitment country). In 2010, 37% held Turkish

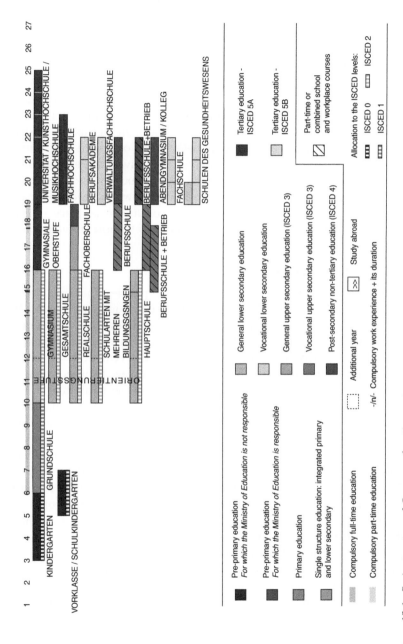

Figure 13.1 Basic structure of German education system
Source: Eurydice. http://eacea.ec.europa.eu/education/eurydice/documents/facts_and_figures/education_structures_EN.pdf.

citizenship; 11% represent former Yugoslavia. Overall, 22% were citizens of EU countries, 55% of which came from Greece, Italy, Portugal, and Spain.

The vast majority of 'migrant students' belong to the second or even third generation of residence in Germany. Nevertheless, there are strong indicators for educational disadvantage (see Section 13.4.2). There is an uneven distribution over the types of school in secondary education:[3] In 2010, 12% of German children and adolescents attended a school of the lowest track, but 33% of 'foreign students'. On the other hand, 52% of German students attended a *Gymnasium*, as opposed to 26% of 'foreign students'. The group of 'foreign students', however, is in itself very heterogeneous. The share of Russian students attending a *Gymnasium* is 46%, whereas below 20% of Italian and Turkish young people do so. About 80% of German school leavers achieve middle or highest school-leaving certificates, this applies only to about 50% of young people with foreign passports. Citizenship as indicator, however, leads to a partly inaccurate picture: If migration background is considered as place of birth (two generations) and family language, the picture gets more differentiated – although main tendencies do not change.

13.2.3   Policy developments

Considerable changes in social and educational policies can be observed in Germany after the first results of the OECD-PISA studies were published (J. Baumert et al., 2001). The political and public spheres were very alarmed because the German educational system obviously produces not only inequality to an undesired extent, but also only fairly low achievement in the average school population. Moreover, it turned out that the linkage between the socioeconomic status and pupils' achievement was closer in Germany than in most other participating countries. The ties between the coincidence of being born in a family with low economic and cultural capital and the chance of educational success were, and still are, remarkably strong. Migrant pupils are especially disadvantaged (Klieme et al., 2010). In reaction to these findings, a considerable number of new social and educational support strategies were established.

The KMK contributed to the National Integration Plan of 2006. A central element of this commitment was the establishment of model projects for the support of migrants in education (Gogolin et al., 2011). New qualification schemes for educators and teachers were established, aiming at raising their professional competence for work in culturally and linguistically diverse educational and social institutions. The impact and effects of these activities shall be observed in a biannual 'National Education Report' (Autorengruppe Bildungsberichterstattung, 2010). A 'National Educational Panel Study (NEPS)' was set up from 2009 (Blossfeld, Roßbach, and von Maurice, 2011). In order to support the integration of new immigrants, a national strategy was established.[4] A core part of this was the establishment of courses aiming at an introduction to the German language, history, and the legal system. Support of the immigrants is one side of the coin of this new strategy. The other is a raised demand for migrants to increase their own efforts to 'integrate'. Integration courses are an example of this. New immigrants now have the right to subscribe to such courses – and they are obliged to do so in order to receive certain social support. Participants have to pay for courses. They can apply for exemption from costs – provided they attend lessons regularly and pass the final test.

Such political activities were highly influential for the realignment of traditions in research on ethnicity and educational inequality in Germany, as we will demonstrate in our report.

13.3 Methods

The sampling for our study is informed by strategies introduced in earlier reviews (Stevens, 2007; Stevens et al., 2011). We started our research by probing journals which are listed in the Social Science Citation Index (SSCI), using specific search queries. Secondly, we searched for key researchers. We found seven German-based journals which included relevant articles. Both methods have specific limitations with respect to social sciences and the humanities, and publications in languages other than English, especially if they are published in journals which are not based in the USA or the UK. Respective analysis shows that the European research area is vastly under-represented in the above-mentioned instruments (Gogolin, 2012). Another limitation of the method is the publication tradition in many European countries, such as Germany. A significant share of research is published in books. This tradition is about to change, but it is relevant for the time frame of this survey.

We included peer SSCI-ranked journals such as *Kölner Zeitschrift für Soziologie und Sozialpsychologie*, *Zeitschrift für Erziehungswissenschaft*, *Zeitschrift für Soziologie*, and the *Zeitschrift für Pädagogik*. Moreover, we included relevant articles from other national or international journals on the basis of our assessment of their quality. We also included books, edited books, and book chapters which appeared in publishing houses that specialize in publications relevant for our topic. Usually, quality control systems (e.g. peer review processes) are established for the latter publications similarly to the practice in research journals.

By applying this sampling method, we identified the following research traditions: (1) features of the education system and their relevance for inequality, (2) characteristics of migrant students and their families as causes for inequality, and (3) linguistic diversity and educational achievement.

13.4 Research traditions

Research on migration, ethnicity, social disadvantage, language diversity, and educational inequality are strongly related to each other in the German context.

The three main approaches we identified all date back to first attempts in the 1970s. The debate related to the underachievement of migrant children (or in the beginning 'foreign students') started in the early 1970s, focusing at first on practical solutions to everyday problems in teaching. These pragmatic and practice-driven approaches were soon complemented by theoretical explanation and empirical clarification of educational disadvantage. Empirical studies concentrated on traditional features of the German school system, school culture, or teaching strategies and their potential negative effects in a context of increasing ethnic and cultural diversity. These studies were largely embedded in the humanities, namely anthropological and cultural theories, in combination with sociological theories of social stratification and class distinction.

The second tradition also arose from the application of social sciences approaches, with a focus on methodologies borrowed from psychology and economics. Consequently, these studies rely on quantitative or mixed-method approaches. Respective projects are also attached to socio-cultural frameworks and human capital theories, but mostly concentrate on a rational choice perspective. The third tradition includes linguistic perspectives. Here, the attempt to explain inequality is focused on the role and function of bi- or plurilingualism for educational success. In this research, historical, qualitative, and quantitative methods are often combined.

13.4.1   Features of the education system and their relevance for inequality

13.4.1.1   *Cultural mismatch*

In the 1970s, a 'foreigner pedagogy'-approach was predominant (*Ausländerpädagogik*), assuming that descent from a foreign country equated 'a foreign culture' and thus a mismatch of expectations and beliefs about school and learning between 'the foreigners' and 'the school'. Respective projects were appealed to providing short-term solutions for problems which were faced in everyday classroom practice. These initial works had neither far-reaching theoretical claims nor significant empirical foundations. The literature is dominated by reports on behavioral or learning problems of migrant children, accompanied by ethical considerations and programmatic blueprints for good ways to deal with the perceived problems. Publications aimed at providing orientation for teachers (see for example, Hohmann, 1976; Koch, 1970; Müller, 1974). From the beginning, numerous pilot projects aiming at 'best practice' solutions for schools or teacher qualification were launched by the *Länder*, partly in co-operation with the federal government. Respective evaluations were predominantly based on expert interviews about participants' satisfaction and perception of success (e.g. Esser and Steindl, 1987; Beer and Wagner, 1985; Boos-Nünning et al., 1983).

From the beginning, these approaches were accompanied by critical discussions of their theoretical foundation and, consequently, empirical validity (Heckmann, 1992). The most fundamental issue that was raised was concerned with the notions of 'culture' and 'ethnicity', often an implicit rather than explicit element of the approaches. Analysis showed that both terms had at first primarily been used in a naive manner as synonymous with 'national background' (Gogolin, 1998a). Given this connotation, the issue was raised in which respects, or if at all a legal category – citizenship – has an impact on educational processes and their results (Ruhloff, 1983). The critical debate also touched the matter of 'internal diversity' of the migrant groups. It was shown that the classification as quasi-homogenous groups of descendants from a specific state erases differences and obscures potential relationships, such as socio-economic background as causal factor for educational disadvantage (Hamburger, Seus, and Wolter, 1981; Radtke and Dittrich, 1990).

13.4.1.2 *Folgen der Arbeitsmigration für Bildung und Erziehung*

These criticisms were colligated in the application for a research priority program Folgen der Arbeitsmigration für Bildung und Erziehung (FABER; 'Consequences of labor migration for education'), funded by the German Research Foundation from 1993 to 1998. Roughly 25 fundamental research projects were subsidized. The majority of these projects aimed at sound theoretical and empirical foundations of explanations for educational disadvantage of migrant workers children by focusing on traditions and features of the German education system (Gogolin and Nauck, 2000). The following examples derive from this research in this framework and follow-up studies.

13.4.1.3 *Historical traditions*

The majority of people in Germany, in the general public as well as in the education system, perceived migration and the subsequent diversity after World War II as a 'historically new' phenomenon. In reality however, migration is a continuous feature of German history (Bade, 1992). In parts of this history, the focus was on emigration rather than immigration; in other eras, Germany was the final destination for considerable numbers of immigrants, e.g. from Eastern Europe in the 19th century. Moreover, the change of state frontiers as effects of wars repeatedly led to the emergence of minorities. Given this context, research on the apparent mismatch of public memories and historical facts, and their possible influence on features of the education system which might cause disadvantages for migrant children were obvious. The related projects applied historical theories and methodologies, namely social history approaches (Wehler, 1987–2008) and the study of archives.

To the most relevant results of this research belongs the insight that a considerable number of features which were applied to the education system from the 1960s onwards mirror the 19th- and early 20th-centuries' traditions (Hansen, 2003; Krüger-Potratz, 1999; Krüger-Potratz, Jasper, and Knabe, 1998). The authors show that the development of *national* education systems in the 19th century gave rise to the general principle that a nation is responsible for the education of only its own citizens. Thus, the inclusion of 'foreigners' and special provisions in favor of them was coupled to the existence of bi- or multilateral agreements with the state(s) of origin. This principle was again applied when first provisions for 'guest workers' children' were made. This is inherent in the fact that the right to attend 'regular' school is until today tied to the legal residence permit of a child. Children or youth with a fragile or 'illegal' status would in most cases be accepted by an individual school, but their rights to be educated can be restricted (Fuchs and Reuter, 2002). Another indicator of this principle is integral in the provisions for 'mother tongue instruction', i.e. the teaching of migrants' heritage languages. In most German *Länder*, such instruction is provided only if the state of origin takes responsibility for it (Reich, 2000).

A further traditional feature which was revitalized in reaction to migration since the 1960s was the assumption that 'integration' is a short-term process which – quasi by nature – leads to a living and learning situation with no difference to the situation of autochthonous learners; in other words: to 'normalization'. Thus, so-called reception measures for newcomers were established, lasting from six months to 24 months. After this period of support, no further provision was provided, except of extra tuition in case of severe backlog or drop-out. For children who were born and raised in Germany (which are the majority of migrant children since the 1990s), no specific support was envisaged. It took the PISA studies to convince the German public and policymakers of the fact that short-time interventions fail the objective educational equality for migrant children and youth.

13.4.1.4   Institutional discrimination

Another attempt to identify characteristics of the education system which may discriminate ethnic minorities was provided by research based on the sociology of organizations, especially Luhmann's systems theory (Luhmann, 1984). Here, the mechanisms of schools as systems were studied with the guiding question of how they 'act' in order to reproduce and protect their own existence. By regional case-studies, the authors uncovered mechanisms which were not dedicated to discriminate against ethnic minorities but functioned in this sense (Gomolla and Radtke, 2002). They traced the rhetoric which couched pedagogical decisions that were *de facto* unfavorable to children's academic careers, but appeared as if they were in favor of them. Examples are justifications for the allocation of migrant children to special needs schools. The authors showed in a regional case-study that the numbers of migrant children who were allocated to such schools rose after the numbers of autochthonous children had dropped. The statements that justified respective decisions did not refer to the children's migrant status (which would have been a violation of the respective regulations), but focused on their protection from physical or mental overload. The transfer to the special needs school was thus considered to be a good chance for the children rather than (what it actually is) the virtual exclusion of educational success.

13.4.1.5   *Perceptions of diversity*

The third approach consists of studies striving for deep analysis of educational institutions. The theoretical background here is Pierre Bourdieu's theory of practice, connected with related methodological approaches from ethnography (Bourdieu, 1977). An example is the case-study *'Großstadt-Grundschule'* ('Urban Primary School') which dealt with the question of how an exemplar urban primary school masters the challenges of ethnic diversity of the student population (cf. Gogolin and Neumann, 1997). As representative of this situation, a primary school in the city of Hamburg was observed. The student composition met the average of inner-city districts at that time: 50% held foreign passports. The aim of the study was to expose how teachers, children, and parents perceived, evaluated, and mastered the linguistically and culturally diverse educational constellation. A key finding was that the various parties were in agreement about ways to deal with diversity. They shared the view that the school is responsible for the formation of a high competence in German, as this was recognized as crucial for educational success. Despite of this 'common sense', the migrant parents and their children had clear multilingual self-concepts. Parents wanted to maintain their children's ties to the heritage language and were hoping that they acquired good competences in these languages. However, they did not demand the school take on a responsibility for heritage language support; instead this was considered as their 'private affair'. Language concepts and practices of migrant parents and their children were described with the metaphor of 'arrangement'. They undoubtedly respected the privilege of German in the public sphere, be it in school and classroom or in other communication spaces. In the private sphere however, the families and students act out their plurilingual concerns, using German as well as the heritage languages (Gogolin, 1998).

13.4.1.6   *Subject-matter teaching in multilingual classrooms*

The projects described above were mainly focused on school life and teaching in a holistic approach. In follow-up projects, more attention was paid to subject-matter teaching. First attempts concentrated on the programmatic design of 'intercultural' teaching methods (Reich, Holzbrecher, and Roth, 2000). Since the 1990s, a growing number of empirical projects concern the question if and in what ways subject-matter teaching practices in diverse classrooms are responsible for educational inequalities. Some of these studies focus on the individual students as the object of observation (Kaiser, 2003; Kaiser and Schwarz, 2003). Complementary projects investigate whether different teaching methods and pedagogical approaches have different effects on the acquisition of skills by children with and without migration backgrounds. These studies often concentrate on teachers as principal actors (see Schütte, 2009; Demidov, 1999; Kaiser, 2003; Prediger and Özdil, 2011; see also Section 13.4.3 with respect to language education).

A relevant result of these studies is the identification of systematic differences in perceptions and ways of dealing with learning tasks. Kaiser et al. (e.g. 2003) compared approaches to mathematics tasks by students with a Turkish-German, Russian-German, and monolingual German background in secondary schools. They show actual differences between the modes of access to the tasks between the three groups. The differences persist even if the learners have passed their whole education career in a German school. Furthermore the studies show that a general proficiency in German is less important for the ability to work successfully with the mathematics tasks. More important were subject-specific language skills and the command of academic language. The authors conclude that these differences in processing tasks might contribute to a systematic disadvantage of migrant students. To the indicators that sustain this assumption belongs the finding that the migrant students in the sample, even if they showed a high proficiency in everyday colloquial German, needed considerably more time than their monolingual German counterparts for decoding mathematics tasks (Gogolin, Kaiser, and Schütte, 2005; Grießhaber, 2011; Heinze, Herwartz-Emden, Braun, and Reiss, 2011).

Another relevant result is the observation that teachers tend to use different strategies of addressing students with and without a migration background. One of these strategies is the reduction of aspirations and complexity when addressing migrant students (Gogolin, 2009). This strategy may produce negative effects on students' self-conceptions as 'successful learners' as well as on their chances to acquire the subject-specific and academic language skills which are, in the end, the necessary foundation of a successful educational career.

In sum, the research tradition we presented in this section was fundamental for a considerable progress in the theoretical understanding of consequences of migration for education. Moreover, a substantial body of empirical research on characteristics of the German education system as well as teaching and learning in German schools was produced. The results show systematic patterns which are likely to contribute to the production of ethnic inequality in German schools. Moreover, they deliver good groundwork for follow-up intervention studies, aiming at the improvement of general principles as well as actual methods of teaching in ethnically and linguistically diverse classrooms.

In recent years, the attention of educational researchers to respective projects as well as the public support of respective research increased considerably. Despite of this, however, it was not accomplished by research in this tradition to convince the political sphere and the general public of the wide range and continuous relevance of the issue. It needed the research which we present in our next section to gain the attention for this.

13.4.2 Characteristics of migrant students and their families as causes for inequality

The second important research tradition we present is focused on characteristics of the migrant population rather than the educational system in order to explain ethnic inequality.

The starting point of this tradition was a discourse based on the assumption that migrant students have deficits – as compared to the autochthonous group – with respect to the competences, knowledge, and behavior which are expected by the educational system. This discourse started in the early 1970s. At first, the main impetus of related research was to find explanations for educational disadvantages in the migrants' *cultural* backgrounds. As mentioned already, this perception was based on a static, nation-related connotation of the concept of culture at first, but – not least in reaction to research results – became more and more differentiated and complex. In recent research in this tradition, the multi-modality and complexity of causes and effects are integrated in conceptual designs of projects as well as their methodological approaches.

13.4.2.1 Cultural deficit approach

Until the early 1990s, the 'cultural deficit' approach was widespread – and it still is a popular belief in general public and parts of the political sphere. Related projects mostly concentrated on reasons for educational disadvantage which were attributed to socialization in 'foreign' families and 'the culture' they represent. Consequently, most studies operating in this framework focused on a specific group of origin. The specificity was either seen in their national background (Hopf, 1987; Merkens, 1990; Bott, Merkens, and Schmidt, 1991). Most studies connected to this approach argued within a social psychology or educational psychology framework and applied related methodologies. One assumption was that specific features of familial climate and support structures had negative effects on educational success (Schönpflug and Alamandar-Niemann, 1993). Other authors assumed that migrant children's personality traits lead to 'adaptation problems' in school and thus yield or foster low achievement (Roebers and Schneider, 1995). One basic postulate of these studies was that the 'cultural differences' between migrant families and their children on the one hand, and the school and majority society on the other, lead to conflicting constellations which cause underachievement.

This research was grounded on classifications of cultures as 'modern' or 'traditional', indicated for example by more 'individualistic' and more 'collective' lifestyles (Triandis, 1988). The explanatory power of effects of cultural deficits or distance on the educational success of migrant children, however, turned out to be low or even undetectable (cf. Schönpflug and Alamandar-Niemann, 1993, pp. 144f.; see also Diefenbach, 2002; Herwartz-Emden, 2000). Consequently, this perspective fizzled out in the end of the 1980s. Some researchers, however, are still concerned with the development of differentiated approaches to cultural causes for educational disadvantage, mostly based on post-colonial studies (e.g. Ashcroft, Griffiths, and Tiffin, 1998; Hall, 1996). In this research, the international debates and research results about 'racism and discrimination in schools' are taken up and integrated into designs as well as usage of terminology (Gomolla, 2009). A change of perspective is intended: from a focus on migrants' characteristics and their 'mismatch' with the cultural demands of the reception society to the opposite notion of a deficient ability of the receiving society to deal with cultural and ethnic diversity in a non-discriminatory manner. Literature related to this perspective is usually based on qualitative, ethnographic, or biographical approaches, tracing the disadvantageous aspects of individual school careers or processes of being labeled as culturally or ethnically 'different' (Mecheril, 2003; Weber, 2003). An important finding is the reciprocity of using cultural ascriptions or stereotypes in educational settings. Weber (2003) for example, traced the 'mutual understanding' of girls with a Turkish background and their teachers in dealing with different interests in school. The teachers used the label 'Turkish culture' for their explanations of students' unwelcome behavior; the girls used the same label if they wanted to push through their own plans, for example in the context of school excursions 'Turkish' girls who did not want to take part explained to their teachers that their conservative and paternalist fathers did not allow their participation, which the teachers accepted unchallenged.

13.4.2.2   *Human capital*

A complementary approach to explain educational disadvantages by characteristics of migrants themselves developed in a research tradition which is largely based on human capital theories, mainly adopted in their sociologically expanded variants, including Coleman's concept of social capital or Bourdieu's more general concept of capital and social stratification (Bourdieu and Passeron, 1990; Bourdieu, 1986; Coleman, 1988). The observation that not all migrant students of the same 'cultural' or ethnic background succeed or fail in the same way motivated a number of projects. Furthermore, the question why different schools of the same school type or schools in different regions produce marked achievement differences, not only between migrant and autochthonous students but also within both groups was taken in to account.

The first, mainly quantitative studies in this tradition were focused on socio-economic, cultural and educational background of the migrants before their migration to Germany or on social and economic features of the country of origin. An example is Hopf (1987). The author concentrated on families from Greece, because their children belonged to the most successful groups of migrants in German schools. From analyses of socio-economic data on this group Hopf concluded that Greek migrants were a positively selected group with better school qualifications, better professional positions, and higher incomes compared to the average population in their area of origin. The author resolved that this initial situation indicates high educational aspiration and readiness to invest in the children, leading to a positive impact on the educational success of the children. This interpretation however, was challenged by other studies. Nauck (1994) for example, showed that migrants from different states of origin disposed of a similar socio-economic and educational background as the Greek migrants. Moreover, parental investment in their children and educational aspirations were similarly high. Both, however, did not lead to similar success in the education system for their children.

The discourse on such contradictory results led to a concentration on features of the receiving country as possible explanation for underachievement and inequality of migrants. At first, respective projects mainly focused on obvious socio-economic factors, such as household income and number of persons belonging to a household. The respective indicators show that the migrant population in Germany represents lower social strata than the average population, despite of the fact that recruitment policies in the 1950s–1970s intended to attract skilled workers. A number of unfavorable conditions however, such as restrictive practices in acknowledging professional or academic qualifications, and likewise constraint issuance of work permits, led to a downgrading of professional status and low income opportunities of migrant workers. Respective analysis showed for example, that in the early 2000s a 'poverty risk' was estimated for 12% of the autochthonous population, but for 28% of the migrant population. For 15-year-olds, the risk was estimated for 15% of non-migrants, but 33% of children from migrant families (see (BMAS), 2008, chapter 9). These findings paved the way to the insight that heredity of 'educational poverty' (*Bildungsarmut*) is a general characteristic of the German school system. Low educational achievement and success, according to related sociological analysis, is handed down from generation to generation in Germany due to interlocked attributes of the educational and social system (Allmendinger, 1999). The unfavorable socio-economic living conditions of migrants and related disadvantages – such as low access to better-off residential areas – led to forms of ethnic stratification in Germany (Esser, 2001). This has negative effects on educational chances not least because of the interaction of residential areas and the location of school types. As was shown by analysis for the national education reports, the hierarchically tiered school system interacts with the social structure of residential areas. Whereas low social-strata areas assemble schools which allot the lowest school leaving qualifications, the schools with academic tracks can mostly be found in 'good areas'. This leads to more or less favorable educational milieus which typically disadvantage the already disadvantaged, especially students from migrant families (see Autorengruppe Bildungsberichterstattung, 2010).

Other studies which tried to identify structural and procedural characteristics of the German school system have been conducted since the 1990s. In the context of the FABER focal project for example, Nauck and others carried out re-analysis of data from the 'Socio-economic panel study (SOEP)', a longitudinal survey on household development which has been conducted for more than 30 years (http://www.diw.de/en/soep). The panel covers data on socio-economic living conditions and on participation in education. It includes a sample of 'foreign nationals' (families with Turkish, Greek, Italian, Spanish, or [former] Yugoslavian descent). Nauck and colleagues (e.g. Nauck and Diefenbach, 1997; Nauck, Kohlmann, and Diefenbach, 1997; Nauck, Diefenbach, and Petri, 1998) identified stratified selection processes to the detriment of migrant students in schools, but even more in the transition to vocational education and the labor market. The authors point to the hierarchically tiered school system and early selection in general schooling as likely to contain causal factors for this stratification. For the transition from school to the vocational education system, mechanisms of active discrimination could be identified (Imdorf, 2010). The analysis shows that students whose families know about the general procedures and requirements – such as formal qualifications and tracks – are at an advantage for getting access to promising professions. Migrant students often lack the respective information and make choices for dead-ended qualifications or jobs (Baethge, 2010; Bommes, 1996). There is positive evidence for the fact that non-migrant families are equipped with more functional networks and information channels (Nauck, Kohlmann, and Diefenbach, 1997; Nauck, Diefenbach, and Petri, 1998). Their cultural capital – knowledge about the educational and vocational system – as well as social capital raises their children's opportunities for successful integration in vocational education and careers. Moreover, the authors reveal that education certificates of parents have a higher impact on educational success in the case of non-migrant students than for migrant students. In fact, the chance to attend an academic school track increases for children from higher-educated autochthonous families, but not in the same way for migrant students whose parents have similar educational backgrounds. In a more general conclusion, non-migrant families have better chances to transmit their different capitals over the generations than the migrant population (Nauck, 2011).

Whereas the research mentioned was concentrated on migration-related aspects of human capital, other studies showed that social status in general has a high explanatory power for education success, irrespective of the migration status of a child (see, for example, Lehmann et al., 2002; Baumert and Schümer, 2002; Baumert, Watermann, and Schümer, 2003). The gradual introduction of more sophisticated statistical methodologies and improvement of data sources allowed for multilevel analysis which could also trace hidden interrelations between different indicators. Theoretical discourse and empirical evidence showed the internal differences of 'migrants' as a group, considering that former attempts to differentiate according to 'nationality/culture' led to a dead end. The introduction of 'place of birth' as an indicator resulted in inconsistent findings. Diefenbach (2006, 2010) determined by re-analysis of panel data that Germany as the birthplace of – at least one – parent has no effect on the type of school in secondary education which children attend. In analysis of school achievement results however, correlations between place of birth and attainment were identified (e.g. DESI-Konsortium, 2006). In related discussions, the question of whether 'place of birth' is a causal factor or an indicator, pointing to other relevant living conditions is being deliberated (Clauß and Nauck, 2009; Diefenbach, 2010).

More recent attempts to explain disadvantages are concerned with the whole educational career of a child. Instead of focusing on school only, the related studies ask for effects of preschool attendance on educational success and consider the ethnic as well as social backgrounds of children (see overview in Becker, 2010). An example of related research is the study of Biedinger (2010). She asks whether the time spent in Kindergarten and the quality of environment have positive effects on three- to five-year-old children's German vocabulary, especially if these factors have a larger impact on children with a Turkish background compared to non-migrant children. The analyses are conducted with data from a project on 'Preschool Education and Educational Careers of Migrant Children'[5] which includes a two-wave panel over a one-year period. In effect, children with a Turkish background score worse on the German vocabulary test than non-migrant children at both points in time, but the migrant children's progress is steeper. By fixed effects regressions the author shows that longer preschool attendance leads to a significant improvement of German vocabulary. Both migrant and non-migrant children profit from good quality of the preschool environment. Non-migrant children profit more than migrant children from social and cultural activities inside the family, while activities outside the family have the opposite effects, especially on fostering the second language, i.e. the command of German (Biedinger, 2010).

In a further study, Biedinger et al. (2008) asked whether preschool attendance accounts for some of the educational inequality of migrant children when they enter school (usually at the age of six). In an analysis of regional school entrance data, the authors try to identify differences in school readiness between the groups as an indicator of early school success. The result was that preschool experience improves school readiness, even under control of family background. While this applies for all children, migrant children nonetheless show lower scores in the respective tests when all socio-economic factors are controlled for. Multilevel analysis indicates that the ethnic effect differs among preschools. The preschools' influences depend on their social composition: preschools with a beneficial clientele promote children's development better than those in a poorer environment. Here again, the social selectivity of housing areas shows effects.

Biedinger and Becker (2006; cf. Biedinger, 2010) found that ethnic difference decreases at the end of preschool if the duration of preschool attendance is taken into account. An open question is, if preschool attendance has short or long-term effects on educational careers. In a recent study, Becker (2010) confirms that – under control of social selectivity in access to preschools – there is strong evidence for positive effects in a long-term perspective, provided that the socio-structural position of the families is average. Although preschool attendance can contribute to the reduction of educational inequalities, the effect of social background cannot fully be compensated for.

The human capital approach unveils relevant characteristics of migrant families *and* the German school system that contribute to disadvantages of migrant children (see also Alba, Handl, and Müller, 1994; Diefenbach, 2002, 2006; Walter, 2006; Schnepf, 2007). Considerable results of this research approach are in line with findings from international comparative studies, such as Pástztor (2008).

13.4.3 Linguistic diversity and educational achievement

The third relevant research tradition we present is concerned with the role and function of linguistic diversity for educational equality. This question intrigued researchers as well as practitioners and the political sphere in Germany from the beginning of labor migration to the BRD, particularly since family reunion processes enlarged in the late 1960s. The focus and perspective of the related research, however, changed considerably over the years. First attempts were mainly concerned with the problem of introducing learners to German as quickly as possible. Their linguistic heritage, i.e. the command of their family languages, was mainly considered a deficit and barrier for the acquisition of German. This position was soon challenged by researchers who claimed that the first or heritage language is a valuable source of linguistic development and builds important stepping stones for the acquisition of German as a second language (Pommerin, 1977). Thus, a bilingualism perspective should be applied in research and practice related to language as a factor for educational achievement. The first works advocating this perspective concentrated on the specificities of the Turkish language in relation to German, considering the typological differences between these languages and on the fact that the number of children from Turkish families in German schools had vastly grown since the 1960s (Meyer-Ingwersen, Neumann, and Kummer, 1977; Neumann and Reich, 1977). Still today, Turkish is the second largest language in Germany.

Complementary to the bilingual perspective, a research tradition was stimulated by the increasing diversity of languages which are represented by groups of migrants in Germany. Here, the claim for an integration of a multilingual perspective was made. This claim was often imbedded in concepts of 'intercultural education' and research concerned with this topic (Boos-Nünning et al., 1983). An integration of the bi- and multilingual perspectives belonged to the aims of research in the FABER program.

Transdisciplinarity is a general feature of the research tradition presented here. Related projects integrate educational sciences, social sciences, and linguistics theories and methodologies. We start by presenting more recent research that delivered empirical evidence for language as a cause for educational inequality. The interpretation of the related results, however, led to a controversy about appropriate conceptualizations of language and language education in migration societies. In the second part of this section, we report on research that aims at a historical understanding of current mainstream perceptions of linguistic 'normality'. Finally, we give an outlook on new approaches which attempt to conceptualize language and education in a way that captures language diversity as a general feature of present-day societies and their schools.

13.4.3.1 *'Language' as cause for educational inequality*

There can be no doubt about the fact that access to the language of schooling is a basic requirement for potential educational success. The best ways to provide access in the case of migrants, however, to whom the language of schooling is most probably not the only, and conceivably not the most important means of communication in their everyday life, are contested. Moreover, the general perceptions of linguistic diversity in Germany are inconsistent. On the one hand, policy and other public statements claim to embrace and respect linguistic diversity. On the other, strong concerns and even rejection of linguistic diversity is expressed, especially with respect to the languages that are associated with underprivileged groups such as migrants. The latter attitude is present in some research on the causes of migrants' educational disadvantages. Especially in large-scale monitoring studies, the so-called 'languages spoken at home' are conceptualized as risk factors for educational success. This concept is applied in German follow-up research to the international comparative educational achievement studies, such as PISA (Klieme et al., 2010) or PIRLS (called *Internationale Grundschul-Lese-Untersuchung IGLU*, Bos et al., 2007) or TIMSS (Bos et al., 2008). In this influential research tradition, growing up and living with more than one language is considered to be a threat to educational attainment and, more generally, to integration. These studies deserve a lot of credit because they attracted public attention to the fact that the German education system is highly selective with respect to children's socio-economic backgrounds and the capital of their families. Moreover, they shed light on the key importance of language competence for educational careers in general. For the German general public as well as the political sphere, the insight that performance in mathematics and science is highly dependent on competence in the language of schooling was a shocking bad news – although it had repeatedly been addressed by researchers (Lehmann et al., 1995). It took the striking proof that is inherent in large-scale statistics to convince the audience of these insights.

'Language competence' in the above-mentioned studies is generally operationalized as reading ability, a receptive language proficiency. The main reason for this is the challenge in testing large samples. As yet, there are no sound support methodologies available for the analysis of great amounts of productive speech samples. Although it is plausible that reading abilities are relevant for educational attainment, a definite understanding of the interrelations between receptive and productive language competence and their contribution to educational attainment is not on-hand yet (Becker-Mrotzek and Vogt, 2009; Portmann-Tselikas and Schmölzer-Eibinger, 2002). This problem has only recently been taken up in several research projects which are supported in a research priority program promoted by the federal Ministry of Education and Research.[6]

All mentioned projects are focused on the role of German for educational success. Whereas the first studies provided a holistic view on 'the migrant students', it has become commonplace to differentiate between different groups of origin. For methodological reasons, most studies concentrate on a comparison of students with a Turkish and a Russian background; the latter category combines students from different countries of origin belonging to the former Soviet Union. The main reason for this is the lack of adequate sample sizes of other groups of origin in representative studies. A general result of the studies is that the group of Turkish origin belongs to the least successful, whereas the 'Russian' group belongs to the most successful migrants in German schools (Müller and Stanat, 2006; Stanat, 2003).

Achievement differences between these two groups are strongly influenced by their different migration histories. Whereas the Turkish group is largely composed of second-generation students with parents who themselves belong to underprivileged groups with low educational success in Germany, the 'Russian' group comprises of a considerable number of first-generation individuals who experienced parts of an educational career in the country of origin and whose parents are equipped with high-level school leaving qualifications, i.e. advantageous cultural capital (Stanat, Rauch, and Segeritz, 2010). Only exceptionally, smaller groups of origin are taken into account for theoretical considerations. An example is the Vietnamese group which, on the one hand shows considerable features of an unfavorable starting position, e.g. low socio-economic status and cultural capital of the families. Nevertheless, their children represent the most successful group of migrant students in German schools, just as it is the case in other immigrant countries. The related studies strive to trace explanations for this, but as yet did not achieve uncontested results (Walter, 2011). Neither language usage at home nor socio-economic background differentiates the Vietnamese from low-success groups of origin. In more recent studies, the role and function of social capital and learning styles are investigated.[7]

In a national representative study of educational attainment in the ninth grade of schooling (students of 15–17 years), the relevance of the language of origin for educational success was additionally explored (DESI-Konsortium, 2006). The study focused on achievement in two subjects, German and English. It indicated that bilingual migrant students showed advantages in their access to English, even when socio-economic and other background features are controlled for. This result could also be shown for students of Turkish origin (Rauch, Jurecka, and Hesse, 2010; see also Haenni Hoti, 2009). The potential advantages of bilingual living conditions seem to be taken up in the teaching of foreign languages in German-speaking countries, but not in the areas of schooling in which German is the language of instruction. The potential positive effects of transfer on language learning and learning in general (Bialystok, 2009) can thus not be exploited by the learners.

The general question, if bilingualism is a threat or an advantage for educational success, was the subject of constant debate in the German research tradition. The different points of view were exchanged and disputed in a conference entitled 'The Bilingualism Controversy' (Gogolin and Neumann, 2009). It was shown, that from a rational choicepoint of view the command of the language of origin has no specific additional effect on educational attainment or success in the labor market, as measured by income level (Esser, 2006, 2009). From a linguistic and sociology of culture perspective however, and applying different indicators of 'additional effects' than economic ones (e.g. well-being or linguistic flexibility), it could be shown that elaborate command of all languages of bi- (or multi-)lingual individuals are likely to have positive effects (Auer, 2009; see also Tracy, Weber, and Münch, 2006). The dispute led to the concurrent conclusion that the controversy is still open to debate, due to two reasons: firstly, the answers given on many questions related to this controversy are not very consistent; secondly however, it has to be admitted that the problem of linguistic diversity is deeply imbedded in historical traditions which set the frame for basic normative positions. Sometimes explicitly, more often implicitly such positions resonate not only in political or public viewpoints, but also in research. In the next section, we present attempts to expose this problem.

13.4.3.2   *Linguistic habitus*

Even though multilingualism is hardly a new phenomenon in any region of the world, migration-induced linguistic diversity was considered a 'new experience' in public as well as professional perception since World War II. This signifies that notion of 'linguistic normality' of a nation is largely embedded in a traditional European conceptualization. Languages were – and often still are – widely viewed as strongly connected with particular 'cultures' and 'their' territories. Inherent in this perspective is a monolingual norm that is bound up with the 'classical', i.e. European concept of the nation-state (Hobsbawm, 1990).

The attention of researchers for the potential role and functions of traditionalized linguistic norms as implicit rather than explicit basic principle of research, political understanding and educational practice was not least raised by the fact that evidence for active discrimination of migrant students in German schools could not be detected (Radtke and Dittrich, 1990). Moreover, the assumption that structural discrimination plays a relevant role could not indisputably be proved (Lehmann, Gänsfuß, and Peek, 1997). On the contrary, on the rhetorical level, be it expressed by teachers or captured in official political frameworks and provisions for educational practice, the equality of migrant children was perpetually claimed a self-evident aim. Especially with respect to primary education, even positive discrimination of migrant students was considered a legitimate means to support them. Teachers were advised to respect the migrant children's heritage languages and cultures. Teachers themselves asserted in interview studies that they act accordingly (Bühler-Otten, Neumann, and Reuter, 2000; Gogolin, Neumann, and Reuter, 1998).

The discrepancies between such rhetoric and factual educational inequality to the detriment of migrant students are evident. As migrants' characteristics explain educational inequality to a considerable extent, but a likewise substantial residual remains unexplained, an obvious question for further research was to what degree can the actual teaching be made responsible for generating inequality, even if the explicit aims of schooling strive to ensure equal opportunities? In the related research tradition, this question was taken up with a focus on everyday routines and habitual practices of teachers: do they function as a potential source for unintended, but effective causes of disadvantage for migrant children?

This question was tackled in historiographical analyses of the German and other European education systems which aimed to trace the foundations of the widespread linguistic self-conceptions of schools and teachers (Gogolin, 1994; Kroon, 2003; Krüger-Potratz, 2000). The analyses took up Bourdieu's concept of habitus (Bourdieu, 1983). According to this, every individual acquires in his or her socialization certain dispositions for social action that are conditioned by the own position in society. These dispositions develop in the course of the individual's engagement with the social world. They include what Bourdieu calls 'a sense of the game': an understanding of the social order and one's own position in it; a mode of classification of the world; a certain taste and tone of voice – Bourdieu calls them 'embodied social structures' (Bourdieu, 1984a, p. 65). The individual develops a certain habitus that is typical of her or his position in the social space. A habitus is a necessary prerequisite for routine activities in the sector of the social world which is relevant for an actor. Inherent are mechanisms which prompt the individual to acknowledge, legitimate, and reproduce the accustomed opinions and forms of acting of his or her social group as self-evident – a shared 'common sense' which is hidden from conscience and rules routine practice. This theoretical perspective has been transferred to groups of actors, namely to professional groups (Bourdieu, 1984b). It was also applied to the field of language, unveiling relations between language use and symbolic power in societies (Bourdieu, 1991).

By application of this perspective on historiographical analysis it could be shown, that the habitualization of a monolingual self-concept, i.e. the emergence of a 'monolingual habitus' accompanied the processes of nation building in 18th and 19th century (Gogolin, 1994). These processes, although different on the surface level of historical phenomena, can be reconstructed for European nation-states; the existence of a 'common language' is considered as the core of national identities or of 'linguistically zoned' regions within one state (Caviedes, 2003). The development of general education systems accompanied the nation-building processes, and these systems took on an important role for the creation of monolingualism in the national languages. For the case of Germany, the respective studies traced the processes of creating and securing the common opinion that German is, quasi by nature, the 'mother tongue' of every person living in the country (Krüger-Potratz, 1994). Thus, educating children in German only was considered the best and 'natural' way of schooling. Other languages which had formerly also functioned as languages of instruction (such as Greek and Latin) were then constricted to subjects of 'foreign language teaching'. As Gogolin (1994) showed, an unintended side effect of this development was the emergence of a professional habitus among teachers, that the emblematic 'normal child' is monolingual. Thus, language development – except of the acquisition of script – is expected to happen *en passant*. Consequently, schools' tasks in this field are considered as gardening what grows naturally (Hildebrand, 1920).

This concept was taken up in international comparative projects on teaching the majority language in multilingual classroom settings (Gogolin and Kroon, 2000). Applying an ethnographic approach, actual teaching in urban classrooms in England, Belgium, the Netherlands, and Germany was observed and audio-taped over a long period of schooling. In the data analyses, routines that were based on shared common beliefs which had been incorporated by the included teachers beyond all differences in the various systems were unveiled.

Language instruction was based on habitual routines which the teachers were not aware of. This included the idea that all children in their classroom possessed a common and identical instinctive feel for the language of schooling (*sprachgefühl*), which is similar to the teachers' own. This is an element of a 'monolingual habitus', because it governed teaching activities even though the teachers were aware of linguistic diversity in their classrooms.

A side effect of this routine is that the specific linguistic knowledge and skills which are inherent in the language of instruction – the register of academic language – are not systematically taught, but expected as a 'natural' basic equipment of students. This was due to the teachers' unconscious belief that children acquire these specific skills outside of school–first and foremost in the family. An effect of this belief is that those children who do not grow up in very literate environments are not systematically introduced to the particular requirements of academic language which becomes more and more important for learning over the course of a school career. Bi- or multilingual students, but also monolinguals who have less access to literacy in the language of schooling within their family environment can thus gradually be excluded from successful learning due to the linguistic presentation of contents and tasks (de Jong and Leseman, 2001).

The reported research contributed to a deeper theoretical understanding of language-related factors that may influence educational inequality. It could be shown that a monolingual 'norm – following a 200-year tradition – is part of the unconscious beliefs that rule individual practices and underlie societal structures, even where public rhetoric extols multilingualism. The dynamics of linguistic differentiation, however, that derive from global migration flows and virtually limitless media communications are not captured by such perception. A monolingual habitus reinforces the notion that multilingualism is a threat to learning and educational achievement. Individual bi- or multilingualism is particularly thought to be a risk factor for migrant children and youth, as in their case, low prestige and an underprivileged status often overshadow the capability and value of their languages and linguistic competence. First attempts to consider both the potential risk factors as well as advantages of individual bi- or multilingualism are briefly sketched in the next paragraph.

13.4.3.3 *Superdiversity*

Despite the controversial points of view presented above, the related research community has come to the shared fundamental understanding that 'the language question' will remain central for tracing causes and effects of educational inequality for quite some time. Two main reasons forced this common appreciation. The first derives from the observation of current features of migration flows, which do not concern Germany especially but Europe in general. Whereas from World War II to the late 1970s, comparatively large groups of people from a relatively small number of regions of origin migrated to Germany, the number of regions has since increased which leads to a diminishment of the single groups of origin (Krüger-Potratz and Schiffauer, 2010). According to demographic data, the migrants in Germany represent roughly 190 different nations, i.e. virtually all nations of the world according to the United Nations definition (Bundesamt für Migration und Flüchtlinge, 2010). This development has led to a 'diversification of diversity' in Europe – to 'superdiversity', as Vertovec termed it (2007). This concept includes distinctly more diversity phenomena than languages. It has been applied to the interwoven effects of diversity as caused by gender, social class, legal status, or religious affiliation, to mention just some starting points (Vertovec, 2009). Language heritages, however, belong to the most relevant elements that create super-diverse constellations in educational settings. This is not least due to the fact that the traditional pattern of heritage language attrition within three migrant generations seems to become more and more irrelevant in present-day migration. New, more fluid forms of migration, which are facilitated by increasing global interconnectedness (thanks to easily accessible and cheap modern transport systems), do invite greater loyalty towards the heritage languages. Moreover, new communication technologies support the continuous usage of these languages in the emerging mobile trans-migrant or diaspora communities (Androutsopoulos, 2006; Pries, 2007). The second reason for continuous relevance of research on languages in the context of education and inequality is related to the scope of education itself. Whereas there is relatively little room to maneuver with respect to intervention in children's social backgrounds or the living conditions of their families, the field of language education is fairly open to innovation and effective action, provided that the necessary preconditions for successful interventions are created.

13.5 Conclusion and discussion

The research dealing with ethnic and linguistic diversity and their impact on educational equality mirrors to a large extent the German socio-political and historical context, especially peculiarities of the migration regime in combination with decentralized political responsibilities. First attempts to deal with the consequences of migration for education reacted on phenomena which were attributed to the 'unfamiliar' (school) population. Especially their 'cultural' or 'ethnic difference' was a topic of interest (Heckmann, 1992). Different from discourse in other European immigration countries, these differences and their potential role for educational disadvantage were hardly discussed in terms of racial categories due to the specific historical burden that is connected to this terminology in the German context. As mentioned above, however, a considerable amount of research is focused on causes and mechanisms of discrimination. The perspectives taken here and the theoretical and methodological approaches are reminiscent in many respects of research in the framework of ethnic and racial studies in other national contexts.

A general strategy that can be observed in the first projects which were concerned with migration was their reaction to certain groups of origin. At first, migrants from Italy attracted the attention of researchers. Increasingly, other groups of origin were taken into account – always in reaction to their 'appearance' in Germany (Bade, 1994; Kalter, 2008; Krüger-Potratz, 2005). Until today, the migrants with Turkish background cause the largest amount of research, which is a reaction on the size of the group on the one hand, and on their particular 'strangeness' on the other. A considerable amount of research which is not represented in this article is related to the Islamic heritage of Turkish migrants which is often conceived as part of their ethnic identities and as causal factor for their relatively low educational success.[8]

This feature of research traditions points to the fact that there was, and still is no consistent migration regime and integration policy in Germany. The first political program that recognized immigration as a constant, irreversible element of German society appeared in 2007 (Bundesregierung, 2007). In a historical perspective, the political pattern of reaction to migration was termed 'catching-up integration policy' (*nachholende Integrationspolitik*) (Bade, 2007), indicating that recurrent attempts have to compensate for previous omissions. This pattern affected research on migration as well as practical approaches in the education system, because funding or special programs in both areas followed the principle of government that integration was a short-term task – either because of expected return of the migrants to their 'home country' or because of a belief in short-term periods of adaptation to the country of residence. These opinions led to a tradition of short-term funding in research as well as practice. Initially, research on the topic was established in a few institutes and universities, carried out by a small community of specialists.

This situation changed in the late 1980s, not least thanks to the establishment of the research priority program FABER (see Section 13.4.1). The program attracted interdisciplinary fundamental research and achieved results in theoretical as well as methodological respect which were ineluctable afterwards. FABER initiated changes of perspectives. Historical traditions of dealing with diversity and their traces in the 'common sense' of the general or political public, in research traditions and concepts and in educational practice were disclosed. Furthermore, projects shed light on the 'inner diversity' of migrants as a group and groups of migrants which share a common characteristic, such as country of origin. Moreover, the results showed the complex relationships between attributes related to migration and other markers of diversity that affect living conditions and educational opportunities, such as socio-economic state or cultural capital. Additionally, it was shown that both – the migrant population and their characteristics as well as the majority population or institutions and their characteristics – must be taken into account, if possible within a joint concise theoretical framework, in order to understand causes and effects of inequality. Last not least, the projects indicated the challenges as well as power of mixed-methods designs in the complex field of research on migration, diversity, and educational equality.

Another important impulse for enlargement of quality and scope of the respective research was the growing interest in monitoring the German educational system, as is expressed by the country's participation in international large-scale student assessment projects since the 1990s. Here, the discourse about best ways to capture diversity was taken up and operationalized in more appropriate ways, e.g. by differentiating the marker 'migrant background'. Methodological approaches allowing complex multilevel analysis were refined and new standards were established. The attempts to describe and understand a wide range of causes and effects of educational inequality can be deemed a success.

The next step however, and a pending field of research is related to the lessons which can be learned from these insights for the innovation of educational practice. We comprise of nearly saturated knowledge about individual, contextual, and structural attributes and mechanisms which affect educational attainment of migrants (and others), if they belong to underprivileged groups with low cultural capital. In the case of migrants, language diversity is a specific feature which has to be considered beyond other elements of distinctiveness. An academic void now is the question: what do we learn from these insights for the innovation of educational practice and/or structural characteristics of the education system? The next – and necessary – step in the development of the German research sphere in this respect is the design and thorough evaluation of intervention schemes which reflect ethnic, cultural, and linguistic diversity as a general and non-reversible element of the German society and education system.

Notes

1. We use the German abbreviations here, because most of the – even international – research literature refers to these rather than the English versions (BRD: Federal Republic of Germany, FRG; DDR: German Democratic Republic, GDR).
2. http://www.zuwanderung.de/ZUW/DE/Zuwanderung_hat_Geschichte/Anwerbung/ Anwerbung_node.html#doc921694bodyText3, retrieved March 2013.
3. Data reported here from Beauftragte für Migration, Flüchtlinge und Integration, 2012.
4. See http://www.bamf.de/SiteGlobals/Forms/Sprachumschaltung/DE/Sprachumsch-altung_Formular.html, retrieved March 2013, for information on the strategy as a whole.
5. 'Erwerb von sprachlichen und kulturellen Kompetenzen von Migrantenkindern in der Vorschulzeit', http://www.mzes.uni-mannheim.de/d7/de/projects/erwerb-von-sprach-lichen-und-kulturellen-kompetenzen-von-migrantenkindern-in-der-vorschulzeit-und-der-ubergang-in-die, date accessed 1 March 2013.

6. 'Research Initiative Language Diagnostics and Support'; see http://www.fiss-bmbf. uni-hamburg.de/ (accessed March 2013). Until 2010, there are no noteworthy publications from the projects available because the fieldwork had only just started.
7. See the project 'Herkunft und Bildungserfolg' which started in 2012: http://www. hebe-projekt.de/index.php.
8. We avoided the debate on religion, especially Islam, and its role and function for integration in the German society in our contribution because (a) we are no experts in this field; but (b) probably even more because the discourse is highly politicized and ideological. Only single studies tried to approach the relations between religious/ Islamic affiliation and educational achievement or, more generally, integration empirically. The results of these studies do not indicate convincing evidence for causal relations of religious, especially Islamic religious preference and educational (dis-)advantage in Germany (see, for example, the overview in Boos-Nünning and Karakaşoğlu, 2005).

References

(BMAS), B. f. A. u. S. (2008). *Lebenslagen in Deutschland. Der dritte Armuts – und Reichtumsbericht der Bundesregierung.* Berlin: BMAS. http://www.bmas.de/SharedDocs/Downloads/DE/ PDF-Publikationen-DinA4/forschungsprojekt-a333-dritter-armuts-und-reichtumsbericht.pdf;jsessionid=F3ED815E0111C9863E31DF4D2E4B2443?__blob=publicationFile.

Adorno, T. W., Frenkel-Brunswik, E., Levinson, D. J., and Sanford, R. N. (1973). *Studien zum autoritären Charakter. Posthumously Published German Version of: The Authoritarian Personality. New York 1950.* Frankfurt a.M.: Suhrkamp.

Alba, R. D., Handl, J. and Müller, W. (1994) Ethnische Ungleichheit im deutschen Bildungssystem, *Kölner Zeitschrift für Soziologie und Sozialpsychologie, 46*(2), 209–237.

Allmendinger, J. (1999). Bildungsarmut – zur Verschränkung von Bildungs – und Sozialpolitik. *Soziale Welt, 50*(1), 35–50.

Androutsopoulos, J. (2006). Multilingualism, diaspora, and the internet: Codes and identities on German-based diaspora websites. *Journal of Sociolinguistics, 10*(4), 429–450.

Ashcroft, B., Griffiths, G., and Tiffin, H. (1998). Key Concept in Post-Colonial Studies. London u.a.: Routlegde.

Auer, P. (2009). Competence in performance: Code-switching und andere Formen bilingualen Sprechens. In I. Gogolin and U. Neumann (Eds), *Streitfall Zweisprachigkeit – The Bilingualism Controversy* (pp. 90–110). Wiesbaden: VS-Verlag.

Autorengruppe Bildungsberichterstattung (Ed.). (2010). *Bildung in Deutschland 2010. Ein indikatorengestützter Bericht mit einer Analyse zu Perspektiven des Bildungswesens im demografischen Wandel. Im Auftrag der Ständigen Konferenz der Kultusminister der Länder in der Bundesrepublik Deutschland und des Bundesministeriums für Bildung und Forschung.* Bielefeld: W. Bertelsmann.

Bade, K. (1994). *Ausländer – Aussiedler – Asyl: Eine Bestandsaufnahme.* Munich: C.H. Beck.

Bade, K. J. (2007). Versäumte Integrationschancen und nachholende Integrationspolitik. In K. J. Bade and H.-G. Hiesserich (Eds), *Nachholende Integrationspolitik und Gestaltungsperspektiven der Integrationspraxis* (pp. 21–95). Göttingen: V&R Unipress.

Bade, K. J. (Ed.). (1992). *Deutsche im Ausland – Fremde in Deutschland: Migration in Geschichte und Gegenwart.* Munich: C.H. Beck.

Baethge, M. (2010). Neue soziale Segmentationsmuster in der beruflichen Bildung. In H.-H. Krüger, U. Rabe-Kleberg, R.-T. Kramer, and J. Budde (Eds), *Bildungsungleichheit revisited: Bildung und soziale Ungleichheit vom Kindergarten bis zur Hochschule* (pp. 275–298). Wiesbaden: VS-Verlag.

Baumert, J., and Schümer, G. (2002). Familiäre Lebensverhältnisse, Bildungsbeteiligung und Kompetenzerwerb im nationalen Vergleich. In Deutsches PISA-Konsortium (Ed.), *PISA 2000 – Die Länder der Bundesrepublik Deutschland im Vergleich* (pp. 159–202). Opladen: Leske+Budrich.

Baumert, J., et al. (Ed.). (2001). *PISA 2000: Basiskompetenzen von Schülerinnen und Schülern im internationalen Vergleich.* Opladen: Leske+Budrich.

Baumert, J., Watermann, R., and Schümer, G. (2003). Disparitäten der Bildungsbeteiligung und des Kompetenzerwerbs: Ein institutionelles und individuelles Mediationsmodell. *Zeitschrift für Erziehungswissenschaft, 6,* 46–71.

Becker-Mrotzek, M., and Vogt, R. (2009). *Unterrichtskommunikation. Linguistische Analysemethoden und Forschungsergebnisse. 2. überarb. und ergänzte Auflage* Tübingen: Niemeyer.

Becker, R. (2010). Bildungseffekte vorschulischer Erziehung und Elementarbildung – Bessere Bildungschancen für Arbeiter – und Migrantenkinder? In Becker, R. & Lauterbach, W. (Eds), Bildung als Privileg. Erklärungen und Befunde zu den Ursachen der Bildungsungleichheit. 4. aktualisierte Auflage (pp. 129–160). Wiesbaden: VS-Verlag.

Bialystok, E. (2009). Effects of bilingualism on cogitive and linguistic performance. In I. Gogolin and U. Neumann (Eds), *Streitfall Zweisprachigkeit – The Bilingualism Controversy* (pp. 53–67). Wiesbaden: VS-Verlag.

Biedinger, N. (2010). Ethnische und soziale Ungleichheit im Vorschulbereich. Leipzig: Engelsdorfer Verlag.

Biedinger, N., Becker, B., and Rohling, I. (2008). Early Ethnic Edcuational Inequality: The Influence of Duration of Pre-school Attendence and Social Composition. *European Sociological Review, 24*(2), 243–256.

Bielefeld, U. (Ed.). (1991). *Das Eigene und das Fremde. Neuer Rassismus in der Alten Welt?* Hamburg: Junius.

Bildungsrat, D. (1970). Empfehlungen der Bildungskommission. Strukturplan für das Bildungswesen. Stuttgart: Klett.

Blossfeld, H.-P., Roßbach, H.-G., and von Maurice, J. (Eds). (2011). *Education as a Lifelong Process. The German National Educational Panel Study (NEPS)* (Vol. 14). Wiesbaden: VS.

Bommes, M. (1996). Ausbildung in Großbetrieben: Einige Gründe, warum ausländische Jugendliche weniger Berücksichtigung finden. In D. Kiesel, R. Kersten and S. Sargut (Eds), *Ausbilden statt Ausgrenzen. Jugendliche ausländischer Herkunft in Schule, Ausbildung und Beruf* (pp. 31–44). Frankfurt am Main: Haag und Herchen.

Boos-Nünning, U., Hohmann, M., Reich, H. H., and Wittek, F. (1983). *Aufnahmeunterricht, Muttersprachlicher Unterricht, Interkultureller Unterricht.* Munich: Oldenburg.

Boos-Nünning, U., and Karakaşoğlu, Y. (2005). *Viele Welten leben. Zur Lebenssituation von Mädchen und jungen Frauen mit Migrationshintergrund.* Münster: Waxmann.

Bos, W., Hornberg, S., Arnold, K.-H., Faust, G., Fried, L., Lankes, E.-V., Schwippert, K., and Valtin, R. (Eds). (2007). IGLU 2006: Lesekompetenzen von Grundschulkindern in Deutschland im internationalen Vergleich. Münster: Waxmann.

Bos, W., Hornberg, S., Arnold, K.-H., Faust, G., Fried, L.; Lankes, E.-V., Schwippert, K., and Valtin, R. (Eds). (2008). IGLU-E 2006: Die Länder der Bundesrepublik Deutschland im nationalen und internationalen Vergleich. Münster: Waxmann.

Bott, P., Merkens, H., and Schmidt, F. (Eds). (1991). Türkische Jugendliche und Aussiedlerkinder in Familie und Schule: theoretische und empirische Beiträge der pädagogischen Forschung. Baltmannsweiler: Schneider Verlag Hohengehren.

Bourdieu, P. (1977). *Outline of a Theory of Practice.* Cambridge: Cambridge University Press.

Bourdieu, P. (1983). Der sprachliche Markt. In Bourdieu, P., Soziologische Fragen (pp. 115–131). Frankfurt a.M.: Suhrkamp.

Bourdieu, P. (1984a). *Distinction: A Social Critique of the Judgment of Taste (translated by Richard Nice)*. Boston: Harvard University Press.

Bourdieu, P. (1984b). *Homo Academicus*. Paris: Les Éditions de Minuit. English edition (1990). Cambridge: Polity Press.

Bourdieu, P. (1986). The forms of capital. In J. G. Richardson (Ed.), *Handbook for Theory and Research for the Sociology of Education* (pp. 241–258). Westport: Greenwood Press.

Bourdieu, P. (1991). *Language and Symbolic Power*. Cambridge: Polity Press.

Bourdieu, P., and Passeron, J.-C. (1990). *Reproduction in Education, Society and Culture (translation of: La Reproduction. Éléments pour une théorie du système d'enseignement, Les Éditions de Minuit, 1970)*. London: Sage.

Bühler-Otten, S., Neumann, U., and Reuter, L. (2000). Interkulturelle Bildung in den Lehrplänen. In I. Gogolin and B. Nauck (Eds), *Migration, gesellschaftliche Differenzierung und Bildung* (pp. 279–319). Opladen: Leske+Budrich.

Bundesamt für Migration und Flüchtlinge. (2010). *Migrationsbericht 2008 des Bundesamts für Migration und Flüchtlinge*. Nuremberg: Bundesamt für Migration und Flüchtlinge.

Bundesregierung. (2007). *Der Nationale Integrationsplan. Neue Wege, neue Chancen*. Berlin: http://www.bmj.bund.de/files/-/2321/181007_Nationaler%20Integrationsplan.pdf.

BVFG. (2001). Bundesvertriebenen – und Flüchtlingsgesetz. In der Fassung der Bekanntmachung vom 02. Jun 1993, BGB1. I 829, zuletzt geändert durch das Gesetz zu Klarstellung des Spätaussiedlerstatus (Spädaussiedlerstatusgesetz – SpStatG) von 06.09.2001, 26.03.2013.

Caviedes, A. (2003). The role of language in nation-building within the European Union. *Dialectical Anthropology, 27*(3–4), 249–268.

Clauß, S., and Nauck, B. (2009). The situation among children of migrant origin in Germany *Innocenti Working Paper* (Vol. 14). Florence: UNICEF Innocenti Research Centre.

Coleman, J. S. (1988). Social capital in the creation of human capital. *The American Journal of Sociology, 94, Supplement: Organizations and Institutions. Sociological and Economic Approaches to the Analysis of Social Structure*, 95–120.

Cortina, K. S., Baumert, J. et al. (2005). Das Bildungswesen in der Bundesrepublik Deutschland. Strukturen und Entwicklungen im Überblick. Ein Bericht des Max-Planck-Instituts für Bildungsforschung. Reinbek bei Hamburg: Rowohlt (= rororo, 61122).

de Jong, P. F., and Leseman, P. P. M. (2001). Lasting effects of home literacy on reading achievement in school. *Journal of School Psychology 39*, 389–414.

DESI-Konsortium. (2006). Unterricht und Kompetenzerwerb in Deutsch und Englisch. Zentrale Befunde der Studie. Deutsch-Englisch-Schülerleistungen-International (DESI).

Diefenbach, H. (2002). Bildungsbeteiligung und Berufseinmündung von Kindern und Jugendlichen aus Migrantenfamilien. Eine Fortschreibung der Daten des Sozio-Ökonomischen Panels (SOEP). In Sachverständigenkommission 11. Kinder – und Jugendbericht (Ed.), *Migration und die europäische Integration. Herausforderungen für die Kinder – und Jugendhilfe. Materialien zum Elften Kinder – und Jugendbericht* (Vol. 5, pp. 9–70). Munich: Deutsches Jugendinstitut.

Diefenbach, H. (2006). Die Bedeutung des familialen Hintergrundes wird überschätzt. Einflüsse auf schulische Leistungen von deutschen, türkischen und russlanddeutschen Grundschulkindern. In Alt, C. (Ed.), Kinderleben – Integration durch Sprache? Band 4: Bedingungen des Aufwachsens von türkischen, russlanddeutschen und deutschen Kindern (pp. 219–258). Wiesbaden: VS-Verlag.

Diefenbach, H. (2010). *Kinder und Jugendliche aus Migrantenfamilien im deutschen Bildungssystem – Erklärungen und empirische Befunde*. Wiebaden: VS-Verlag.

Esser, H. (2001). Kulturelle Pluralisierung und strukturelle Assimilation: das Problem der ethnischen Schichtung. *Swiss Political Science Review, 7*(2), 97–107.

Esser, H. (2006). *Migration, Sprache und Integration*. Berlin.

Esser, H. (2009). Der Streit um die Zweisprachigkeit: Was bringt die Bilingulität? In I. Gogolin and U. Neumann (Eds), *Streitfall Zweisprachigkeit. The Bilingualism Controversy* (pp. 53–67). Wiesbaden: VS-Verlag, Berlin: Wissenschaftszentrum Berlin, AKI-Forschungsbilanz 4.

Esser, H., and Steindl, M. (1987). *Modellversuche zur Förderung und Eingliederung ausländischer Kinder und Jugendlicher in das Bildungssystem. Bericht über eine Auswertung im Auftrag der Bund-Länder-Kommission für Bildungsplanung und Forschungsförderung*. Bonn: BLK.

Franceschini, R. (2010). Mehrsprachigkeit: Forschungsperspektiven. In C. Hülmbauer, E. Vetter and H. Böhringer (Eds), *Mehrsprachigkeit aus der Perspektive zweier europäischer Projekte: DYLAN meets LINEE* (pp. 17–39). Bern/Frankfurt a.M./New York: Peter Lang.

Fuchs, H.-W., and Reuter, L. (2002). Bildungssysteme im Ländervergleich: Rechtsgrundlagen – Strukturen – Pädagogische Innovationen, Teil I. *Hamburger Beiträge zur Erziehungs – und Sozialwissenschaft* (5), 121–144.

Göbel, K., Vieluf, S., and Hesse, H. G. (2010). Die Sprachentransferunterstützung im Deutsch- und Englischunterricht bei Schülerinnen und Schülern unterschiedlicher Sprachenlernerfahrung. *Zeitschrift für Pädagogik (ZfPäd)* (Beiheft 55), 101–122.

Gogolin, I. (1994). *Der monolinguale Habitus der multilingualen Schule*. Münster: Waxmann.

Gogolin, I. (1998a). »Arrangements« als Hindernis und Potential für die Veränderung der schulischen sprachlichen Bildung. In I. Gogolin and U. Neumann (Eds), *Großstadt-Grundschule. Eine Fallstudie über sprachliche und kulturelle Pluralität als Bedingung der Grundschularbeit* (pp. 311–344). Münster/New York: Waxmann.

Gogolin, I. (1998b). »Kultur« als Thema der Pädagogik der 1990er Jahre. Das Beispiel interkulturelle Pädagogik. In A. M. Stroß and F. Thiel (Eds), *Erziehungswissenschaft, Nachbardisziplinen und Öffentlichkeit* (pp. 125–150). Weinheim/Munich: Juventa.

Gogolin, I. (2009). Zweisprachigkeit und die Entwicklung bildungssprachlicher Fähigkeiten. In I. Gogolin and U. Neumann (Eds), *Streitfall Zweisprachigkeit. The Bilingualism Controversy* (pp. 263–280). Münster: Waxmann.

Gogolin, I. (2010). Stichwort: Mehrsprachigkeit. *Zeitschrift für Erziehungswissenschaft (ZfE), 13*(4), 529–547.

Gogolin, I. (2012). Identificación de la calidad en las Publicaciones de Investigación Educativa: Proyecto Europeo sobre los Indicadores de Calidad en la Investigación Educativa (EERQI). *Revista de Investigación Educativa (RIE), 30*(1), 13–27.

Gogolin, I., Dirim, I., Neumann, U., Reich, H. H., Roth, H.-J., Schwippert, K., ... Michel, U. (2011). *Förderung von Kindern und Jugendlichen mit Migrationshintergrund. Bilanz und Perspektiven eines Modellprogramms*. Münster/New York: Waxmann.

Gogolin, I., Kaiser, G., and Schütte, M. (2005). Mathematiklernen und sprachliche Bildung. Eine interaktionistische Perspektive auf dialogisch stukturierte Lernprozesse im Grundschul-Mathematikunterricht unter Berücksichtigung der sprachlich-kulturellen Diversität der Lernenden. In B. Schenk (Ed.), *Bausteine einer Bildungsgangtheorie* (pp. 179–195). Wiesbaden: VS-Verlag.

Gogolin, I., and Kroon, S. (Eds). (2000). *'Man schreibt, wie man spricht'. Ergebnisse einer international vergleichenden Fallstudie über Unterricht in vielsprachigen Klassen*. Münster/New York: Waxmann.

Gogolin, I., and Nauck, B. (Eds). (2000). *Migration, gesellschaftliche Differenzierung und Bildung. Resultate des Forschungsschwerpunktprogramms FABER*. Opladen: Leske+Budrich.

Gogolin, I., and Neumann, U. (Eds) (1997). Großstadt-Grundschule: Eine Fallstudie über sprachliche und kulturelle Pluralität als Bedingung der Grundschularbeit. Münster u.a.: Waxmann.

Gogolin, I., and Neumann, U. (Eds). (2009). *Streitfall Zweisprachigkeit – The Bilingualism Controversy.* Wiesbaden: VS-Verlag.

Gogolin, I., Neumann, U., and Reuter, L. (1998). Schulbildung für Minderheiten. Eine Bestandsaufnahme. *Zeitschrift für Pädagogik, 44*(5), 663–678.

Gomolla, M. (2009). Interventionen gegen Rassismus und institutionelle Diskriminierung als Aufgabe pädagogischer Organisationen In R. Leiprecht and W. Scharathow (Eds), *Rassismuskritik: Rassismus und politische Bildungsarbeit (II)* (pp. 41–60). Schwalbach/Ts.: Wochenschau-Verlag.

Gomolla, M., and Radtke, F.-O. (2002). *Institutionelle Diskriminierung. Die Herstellung ethnischer Differenz in der Schule.* Opladen: Leske+Budrich.

Grießhaber, W. (2011). Diagnose und Förderung zweitsprachlicher Kompetenzen im Mathematikunterricht. Ansätze eines systematischen Überblicks. In S. Prediger and E. Özdil (Eds), *Mathematiklernen unter Bedingungen der Mehrsprachigkeit – Stand und Perspektiven der Forschung und Entwicklung in Deutschland* (pp. 77–96). Münster/New York: Waxmann.

Grundgesetz. (1949). Grundgesetz für die Bundesrepublik Deutschland. Zuletzt geändert durch Art. 1 G v. 11.7.2012 I 1478. URL: http://www.gesetze-im-internet.de/bundesrecht/gg/gesamt.pdf (26.03.2013).

Haenni Hoti, A. (2009). Forschungsergebnisse zu Einflussfaktoren auf die Englischfertigkeiten von PrimarschülerInnen unter besonderer Berücksichtigung des Migrationshintergrunds. *Bulletin Suisse de Linguistique Appliquée* (89), 5–14.

Hall, S. (1996). „'Wann war der Postkolonialismus'? Denken an der Grenze". In Bronfen, E., Marius, B., Steffen, T. (Eds), Hybride Kulturen: Beiträge zur angloamerikanischen Multikulturalismusdebatte, Tübingen: Stauffenburg.

Hansen, G. (2003). Pluralitätsrhetorik und Homogenitätspolitik. In I. Gogolin (Ed.), *Pluralismus unausweichlich?* (pp. 59–75). Münster: Waxmann.

Heckmann, F. (1992). *Ethnische Minderheiten, Volk und Nation. Soziologie inter-ethnischer Beziehungen.* Stuttgart: Enke Verlag.

Heinze, A., Herwartz-Emden, L., Braun, C., and Reiss, K. (2011). Die Rolle von Kenntnissen der Unterrichtssprache beim Mathematiklernen. Ergebnisse einer quantitativen Längsschnittstudie in der Grundschule. In S. Prediger and E. Özdil (Eds), *Mathematiklernen unter Bedingungen der Mehrsprachigkeit – Stand und Perspektiven der Forschung und Entwicklung in Deutschland* (pp. 11–34). Münster/New York: Waxmann.

Herwartz-Emden, L. (Ed.). (2000). *Einwandererfamilien. Geschlechterverhältnisse, Erziehung und Akkulturation.* Osnabrück: Rasch-Verlag.

Hildebrand, R. (1920). *Vom deutschen Sprachunterricht in der Schule und von deutscher Erziehung un Bildung überhaupt. Mit einem Anhang über die Fremdwörter und einem über das Altdeutsche in der Schule* (15 ed.). Leipzig: Julius Klinkhardt.

Hobsbawm, E. J. (1990). *Nations and Nationalism Since 1780: Programme, Myth, Reality.* Cambridge: Cambridge University Press.

Hohmann, M. (Ed.) (1976). Unterricht mit ausländischen Kindern. Düsseldorf: Schwann.

Hopf, D. (1987). *Herkunft und Schulbesuch ausländischer Kinder.* Berlin: Max-Planck-Institut für Bildungsforschung.

Imdorf, C. (2010). Wie Ausbildungsbetriebe soziale Ungleichheit reproduzieren: der Ausschluss von Migrantenjugendlichen bei der Lehrlingsselektion. In H.-H. Krüger, U. Rabe-Kleberg, R.-T. Kramer and J. Budde (Eds), *Bildungsungleichheit revisited: Bildung und soziale Ungleichheit vom Kindergarten bis zur Hochschule* (pp. 259–274). Wiesbaden: VS-Verlag.

Kaiser, G. (2003). *Learning Mathematics within the Context of Linguistic and Cultural Diversity: An Empirical Study.* Paper presented at the European Research in Mathematics

Education III. Third Conference of the European Society for Research in Mathematics Education, Bellaria, Italy.

Kaiser, G., and Schwarz, I. (2003). Mathematische Literalität unter einer sprachlich-kulturellen Perspektive. *Zeitschrift für Erziehungswissenschaft, 6*(3), 357–377.

Kalter, F. (Ed.). (2008). *Migration und Integration. Sonderheft 48/2008 der Kölner Zeitschrift für Soziologie und Sozialpsychologie* Wiesbaden: VS-Verlag für Sozialwissenschaften.

Klieme, E., Jude, N., Baumert, J., and Prenzel, M. (2010). PISA 2000–2009: Bilanz der Veränderungen im Schulsystem. In E. Klieme, C. Artelt, J. Hartig, N. Jude, O. Köller, M. Prenzel, W. Schneider and P. Stanat (Eds), *PISA 2009. Bilanz nach einem Jahrzehnt* (pp. 277–300). Münster/New York: Waxmann.

Koch, H. (1970). Gastarbeiter in deutschen Schulen. Königswinter: Brandt-Verlag.

Kroon, S. (2003). Mother tongue and mother tongue education. In J. Bourne and E. Reid (Eds), *Language Education: World Yearbook of Education 2003* (pp. 35–47). London/Sterling: Kogan Page.

Krüger-Potratz, M. (1994). 'Dem Volke eine andere Muttersprache geben' – Zur pädagogischen Diskussion über Zwei- und Mehrsprachigkeit in der Geschichte der Volksschule. *Zeitschrift für Pädagogik* (1), 81–96.

Krüger-Potratz, M. (1999). Stichwort: Erziehungswissenschaft und kulturelle Differenz. *Zeitschrift für Erziehungswissenschaft, 2*(2), 149–165.

Krüger-Potratz, M. (2000). Schulpolitik und 'fremde Kinder'. Eine Schule, 'die die eigene Art schützt und die fremde achtet'. In I. Gogolin and B. Nauck (Eds), *Migration, gesellschaftliche Differenzierung un Bildung* (pp. 365–384). Opladen: Leske + Budrich.

Krüger-Potratz, M. (2005). *Interkulturelle Bildung. Eine Einführung.* Münster: Waxmann.

Krüger-Potratz, M., Hansen, G., and Jasper, D. (1991). *Anderssein gab es nicht: Ausländer und Minderheiten in der DDR.* Münster/New York: Waxmann.

Krüger-Potratz, M., Jasper, D., and Knabe, F. (1998). *Fremdsprachige Volksteile und deutsche Schule. Schulpolitik für die Kinder der autochthonen Minderheiten in der Weimarer Republik – ein Quellen – und Arbeitsbuch.* Münster/New York: Waxmann.

Krüger-Potratz, M., and Schiffauer, W. (Eds). (2010). *Migrationsreport 2010: Fakten – Analysen – Perspektiven.* Frankfurt am Main/New York: Campus.

Lehmann, R., Peek, R., Pieper, I., and von Stritzky, R. (1995). *Leseverständnis und Lesegewohnheiten deutscher Schüler und Schülerinnen.* Weinheim/Basel: Beltz.

Lehmann, R. H., Gänsfuß, R., and Peek, R. (1997). *Aspekte der Lernausgangslage von Schülerinnen und Schülern der fünften Klassen an Hamburger Schulen.* Hamburg: Behörde für Schule, Jugend und Berufsbildung.

Luhmann, N. (1984). *Soziale Systeme: Grundriß einer allgemeinen Theorie. English translation: Social Systems.* Stanford: Stanford University Press, 1995. Frankfurt am Main: Suhrkamp.

Mecheril, P. (2003). *Prekäre Verhältnisse. Über natio-ethno-kulturelle (Mehrfach-) Zugehörigkeit.* Münster/New York: Waxmann.

Merkens, H. (1990). Schulschwierigkeiten von Aussiedlerkindern, *Zeitschrift für Pädagogik, 25*, 265–266.

Meyer-Ingwersen, J., Neumann, R., and Kummer, M. (1977). *Zur Sprachentwicklung türkischer Schüler in der Bundesrepublik. 2 Bände.* Kronberg/Ts.: Scriptor.

Müller, A., and Stanat, P. (2006). Schulischer Erfolg von Schülerinnen und Schülern mit Migrationshintergrund: Analysen zur Situation von Zuwanderern aus der ehemaligen Sowjetunion und aus der Türkei. In J. Baumert, P. Stanat and R. Watermann (Eds), *Herkunftsbedingte Disparitäten im Bildungswesen. Vertiefte Analysen im Rahmen von PISA 2000* (pp. 221–255). Wiesbaden.

Müller, H. (Ed.). (1974). Ausländerkinder in deutschen Schulen. Stuttgart: Klett.

Nauck, B. (1994). Bildungsverhalten in Migrantenfamilien. In Büchner, P., Grundman, M., Huinink, J., Krappmann, L. (Eds), Kindliche Lebenswelten, Bildung und innerfamiliäre Beziehungen (pp. 105–141). Weinheim u.a.: Beltz.

Nauck, B., and Diefenbach, H. (1997). Bildungsbeteiligung von Kindern aus Familien ausländischer Herkunft: Eine methodenkritische Diskussion des Forschungsstandes und eine empirische Bestandsaufnahme. In Schmidt, F. (Ed.), Methodische Probleme der empirischen Erziehungswissenschaft (pp. 289–307). Baltmannsweiler: Schneider Verlag Hohengehren.

Nauck, B., Diefenbach, H., and Petri, K. (1998). Intergenerationale Transmission von kulturellem Kapital unter Migrationsbedingungen. Zum Bildungserfolg von Kindern und Jugendlichen aus Migrantenfamilien in Deutschland, *Zeitschrift für Pädagogik, 44*(5), 701–722.

Nauck, B., Kohlmann, A., and Diefenbach, H. (1997). Familiäre Netzwerke, intergenerative Transmission und Assimilationsprozesse bei türkischen Migrantenfamilien, *Kölner Zeitschrift für Soziologie und Sozialpsychologie, 49*, 477–499.

Nauck, B. (2011). Kulturelles und soziales Kapital als Determinanten des Bildungserfolgs bei Migranten? In R. Becker (Ed.), *Integration durch Bildung. Bildungserwerb von jungen Migranten in Deutschland* (pp. 71–93). Wiesbaden: VS-Verlag.

Neumann, U., and Reich, H. H. (Eds). (1977). *Türkische Kinder – deutsche Lehrer.* Düsseldorf: Schwann-Verlag.

Pásztor, A. (2008) The Children of Guest Workers: Comparative Analysis of Scholastic Achievement of Pupils of Turkish Origin Throughout Europe, *Intercultural Education, 19*(5), 407–419.

Pommerin, G. (1977). *Deutschunterricht mit ausländischen und deutschen Kindern.* Bochum: Kamp Verlag.

Portmann-Tselikas, P. R., and Schmölzer-Eibinger, S. (Eds). (2002). *Textkompetenz. Neue Perspektiven für das Lernen und Lehren* (Vol. 7). Innsbruck: Studien Verlag.

Prediger, S., and Özdil, E. (Eds). (2011). *Mathematiklernen unter Bedingungen der Mehrsprachigkeit – Stand und Perspektiven der Forschung und Entwicklung.* Münster/New York: Waxmann.

Pries, L. (2007). Transnational migration: New challenges for nation states and new opportunities for regional and global development. In A. K.-m. Sahoo and B. Maharj (Eds), *Sociology of Diaspora: A Reader* (pp. 298–320). Jaipur: Rawat Publications.

Radtke, F.-O., and Dittrich, E. (Eds). (1990). *Ethnizität – Wissenschaft und Minderheiten.* Opladen: Leske + Budrich.

Rauch, D., Jurecka, A., and Hesse, H.-G. (2010). Für den Drittspracherwerb zählt auch die Lesekompetenz in der Herkunftssprache. Untersuchung der Türkisch-, Deutsch- und Englisch-Lesekompetenz bei Deutsch-Türkisch bilingualen Schüler. *Zeitschrift für Pädagogik, 56*(55. Beiheft), 78–100.

Reich, H. H. (2000). Die Gegner des Herkunftssprachenunterrichts und ihre Argumente. *Deutsch lernen* (2), 112–126.

Reich, H. H., Holzbrecher, A., and Roth, H.-J. (Eds). (2000). *Fachdidaktik interkulturell. Ein Handbuch.* Opladen: Leske+Budrich.

Roebers, C., and Schneider, W. (1995). Zum Einfluss von Persönlichkeitsmerkmalen und Sprachkenntnissen auf die schulische Anpassung von Migrantenkindern, *Report Psychologie, 4*, 24–32.

Ruhloff, J. (1983). Bildung und national-kulturelle Orientierung. *Rassegna di pedagogica. Pädagogische Umschau, XLI*, 249–261.

Schnepf, S. V. (2007). Immigrants' Educational Disadvantage: an Examination across Ten Countries and Three Surveys, *Journal of Population Economics, 20*(3), 527–545.

Schönpflug, U. and Alamandar-Niemann, M. (1993). Erziehungsklima und Schulbiographie. Eine Untersuchung türkischer jugendlicher Migranten der zweiten Generation, *Unterrichtswissenschaft. Zeitschrift für Lernforschung, 21*(2), 126–145.

Schütte, M. (2009). *Sprache und Interaktion in Mathematikunterricht der Grundschule. Zur Problematik einer impliziten Pädagogik om Kontext sprachlich-kultureller Heterogenität.* Münster/New York: Waxmann.

Stanat, P. (2003). Schulleistungen von Jugendlichen mit Migrationshintergrund. Differenzierung deskriptiver Befunde aus PISA und PISA-E. In Deutsches PISA-Konsortium (Ed.), *PISA 2000. Ein differenzierter Blick auf die Länder der Bundesrepublik Deutschland* (pp. 243–260). Opladen: Leske+Budrich.

Stanat, P., Rauch, D., and Segeritz, M. (2010). Schülerinnen und Schüler mit Migrationshintergrund. In E. Klieme, C. Artelt, J. Hartig, N. Jude, O. Köller, M. Prenzel, W. Schneider and P. Stanat (Eds), *Pisa 2009 – Bilanz nach einem Jahrzehnt* (pp. 200–230). Münster/New York: Waxmann.

Statistisches Bundesamt. (2011). Bevölkerung und Erwerbstätigkeit. Bevölkerung mit Migrationshintergrund. Ergebnisse des Mikrozensus 2010. Fachserie 1 Reihe 2.2. https://www.destatis.de/DE/Publikationen/Thematisch/Bevoelkerung/MigrationIntegration/Migrationshintergrund2010220107004.pdf?__blob=publicationFile (01.03.2013).

Stevens, P. A. J. (2007). Researching race/ethnicity and educational inequality in English secondary schools: A critical review of the research literature between 1980 and 2005. *Review of Educational Research, 77*(2), 147–185.

Stevens, P. A. J., Clycq, N., Timmerman, C., and Van Houtte, M. (2011). Researching race/ethnicity and educational inequality in the Netherlands: A critical review of the research literature between 1980 and 2008. *British Educational Research Journal, 37*(1), 5–43.

Tracy, R., Weber, A., and Münch, A. (2006). *Frühe Mehrsprachigkeit. Mythen – Risiken – Chancen.* Stuttgart: Bande-Württemberg-Stiftung.

Triandis, H. C. (1988). Collectivism vs. individualism: A reconceptualization of a basic concept in cross-cultural social psychology. In Bagley, C. & Verma, G. K. (Eds), Personality, cognition and values: Cross-cultural perspectives on childhood and adolescence (pp. 60–95). London: Macmillan.

Vertovec, S. (2007). Super-diversity and its implications. *Ethnic and Racial Studies, 30*(6), 1024–1054.

Vertovec, S. (2009). *Conceiving and Researching Diversity.* Working Papers (09–01). Göttingen: Max-Planck-Institute for Religious and Ethnic Diversity.

Walter, O. (2006). Die Entwicklung der mathematischen und der naturwissenschaftlichen Kompetenzen von Jugendlichen mit Migrationshintergrund im Verlauf eines Schuljahres. In Prenzel, M., Baumert, J., Blum, W., Lehmann, R., Leutner, D., Neubrand, M., Pekrun, R., Rost, J. & Schiefele, U. (Eds), PISA 2003 – Untersuchungen zur Kompetenzentwicklung im Verlauf eines Schuljahres (pp. 249–275). Münster: Waxmann.

Walter, O. (2011). Der Schulerfolg vietnamesischer und philippinischer Jugendlicher in Deutschland: Eine Analyse auf der Grundlage der Erweiterungsstichprobe von PISA 2003 *Zeitschrift für Erziehungswissenschaft (ZfE), 14*(3), 397–419.

Weber, M. (2003). *Heterogenität im Schulalltag. Konstruktion ethnischer und geschlechtlicher Unterschiede.* Opladen: Leske+Budrich.

Wehler, H.-U. (1987–2008). *Deutsche Gesellschaftsgeschichte. 5 Bände.* Munich: C.H. Beck.

14
Ireland

Daniel Faas and Rachael Fionda

14.1 National context

14.1.1 The educational system of the country

Schooling in Ireland is compulsory from the age of six until 16. Most primary schools are privately owned but state-funded and provide education for children from the ages of four to 11 or 12 years. Around 95% of primary schools are denominational in their intake and management. Alternative option to parents is provided by the new Community National (CN) and Educate Together (ET) schools. CN schools were set up in response to parental demand in areas with considerable numbers of immigrants, and where children were not able to secure places in local schools. Two such schools were established in September 2008 and a further three in September 2010. These schools provide an additional option for parents, and are designed to meet the demand for different approach in providing religious and moral education. These schools provide faith formation for different religious groups during the school, distinctly different from the approach adopted by the currently 58 ET schools that teach children about different world religions with an optional faith formation component after school, organised by the parents. There has been a growing demand for alternative schools, as the proportion of the population who do not belong to the Catholic faith has increased. There are also two state-funded Islamic primary schools in Ireland, both in Dublin, and one Jewish school. All state schools follow a centralized curriculum. Pupils are not generally permitted to repeat a school year (see Department of Education, 2003). A revised primary school curriculum was launched in 1999 and outlines six areas: language; mathematics; social, environmental and scientific education (history, geography and science); arts education (music and drama); physical education; and social, personal and health education. Curriculum and assessment are centralized on a national basis, by the National Council for Curriculum and Assessment (see ncca.ie).

The second-level education sector in Ireland comprises secondary, vocational, community, and comprehensive schools. Secondary schools, which educate approximately 54% of second-level students, are privately owned and managed. The majority are conducted by religious communities and the remainder by boards of governors or by individuals. Vocational schools and community colleges educate over 33% of all second-level students; they are administered by vocational education committees which are statutory bodies set up under the Vocational Education Act of 1930. Comprehensive schools are managed by a board of management representative of the diocesan religious authority, the vocational education committee of the area and the minister for education and skills. Community schools are managed by boards of management representative of local interests. All schools are entirely funded by the state through the Department of Education and Skills (Eurydice, 2009). The second-level curriculum is divided into two cycles: a three-year junior cycle (generally catering for students 12–15 years of age) and a two-year senior cycle (generally catering for students 16–18 years of age). At both junior and senior level students can be 'streamed' according to ability; those considered to have higher academic potential study for and take exams at 'Higher Level' and those of average ability study at 'Ordinary Level'. Mathematics, English, and Irish can also be studied at 'Foundation Level' (see www.curriculumonline.ie). Stu
which levels they take, in consultation with their subje
significant implications; Higher Level exam results are
points system required for university entry (see www.cao.i
and senior cycles students may complete the Transition
is an option for students in some schools while it is com
program is not examinable and is characterized by curri
curricular initiatives, and school–community linkages.
underwent significant change during the 1990s and is c
review by the National Council for Curriculum and Asses
ing the introduction of a new subject 'Politics and So
newspaper publishes an annual league table of post-prin

Training for teachers is offered by specialist colleges f
ers, while second-level teachers complete an undergrad
one-year postgraduate course in education at an Irish u
from university to university, and this system has be
ing inadequate preparation for post-primary school tea
Whether the postgraduate education course provides p
any grounding in educating the diverse classroom an
ies from establishment to establishment. Diversity in education is either not
covered, or is covered in a deficient manner:

The narrow vision of 'Irishness' which was promoted continues to perme-
ate both the education system and society, as evidenced by the continued

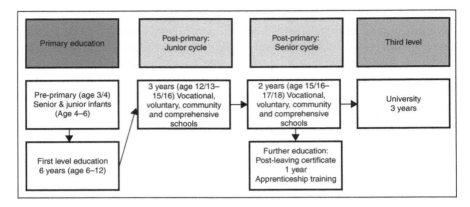

Figure 14.1   Overview of the Irish education system
Note: Adapted from Department of Education and Science, 2004.

> dominance of the Catholic Church in areas such as school ownership and teacher training, and the persistently ethnocentric curriculum.
>
> Nowlan (2008, p. 255)

In recent years the Department of Education and Skills (DES) has restructured itself and assigned certain responsibilities to external agencies such as the State Examinations Commission (Devine, 2005; Smyth et al., 2007), the intention of this move being to allow the DES to concentrate on policy issues and allow schools' management to direct the implementation of individual policy, establish their own ethos and organize the delivery of each student's education (Figure 14.1).

Much literature claims that the disempowerment faced by many students is a reflection of the habitus of the individual educators (Nowlan, 2008; Fionda, 2011), of institution-wide and national policy (Lentin and McVeigh, 2006; Kuhling and Heohane, 2007) and of the society in which the educational institution is set. DES recognizes the role disadvantage plays in preventing groups of students from accessing mainstream education: '[educational disadvantage prevents] students from deriving appropriate benefit from education in schools' (DES, 1998).

At present, the DES distributes 'circulars' to communicate to schools updates in policy, new policy initiatives, and general business. It is up to the individual school to decide on the best way to implement the policies as set out by the DES; the School Inspectorate examines whether the implementation meets the original demands of DES policy via a series of evaluations, either whole school or for each subject department. Little is known about effectiveness and best practices of implementing DES 'circulars' and other DES policies and initiatives (such as the NCCA Intercultural Guidelines, 2006, for example). Anecdotal evidence suggests such documents are not routinely used by teachers in practice (Fionda, 2011).

14.1.2   Immigration to Ireland

Although Ireland has always been a destination of in-migration including Celts, Normans, and British, it was the economic boom during the 1990s which brought unprecedented levels of prosperity and helped transform the country into one of net immigration by 1996 (Ruhs, 2005). For the first time in its history, Ireland experienced a significant inflow of migrants – both workers and asylum seekers – from outside the European Union (EU). Between 2001 and 2004, Ireland reached new peaks in non-EU immigration flows before a shift occurred toward intra-European mobility from East to West following eastern enlargement of the EU. Ireland, together with Sweden and the UK, allowed migrants from the new member states access to the labor market resulting in considerable inflows of Polish (63,090 in 2006) and Lithuanians (24,808 in 2006). Between 2007 and 2009, Ireland experienced reduced but still significant net immigration due to reduced inflows from Eastern Europe (Ruhs, 2009) (Figure 14.2). The groups which showed the largest increase between the Census 2006 and 2011 were those already well established in Ireland. The fastest growing groups were Romanians (from 8,566 to 17,995), Brazilians (from 4,720 to 9,298), Indians (from 9,342 to 17,856), Polish (from 63,090 to 115,193), Filipino (from 9,644 to 13,833), Latvians (from 13,999 to 19,989) and Lithuanians (from 24,808 to 34,847).

Now, in the context of an economic recession with unemployment around 13.5% (a threefold increase from the 4% in the mid-2000s), emigration has

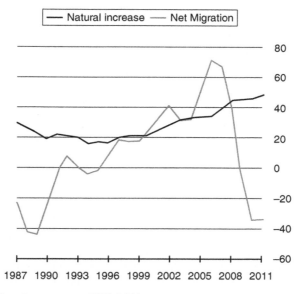

Figure 14.2   Migration patterns 1987–2011
Source: Central Statistics Office, 2011.

come to the fore again in the debates surrounding migration. For example, the Central Statistics Office noted that between April 2011 and April 2012, emigration is estimated to have reached 87,100 while the number of immigrants into Ireland fell slightly to 52,700 over the same period. Of the 87,100 people who emigrated in the year to April 2012, Irish nationals were the largest group accounting for 46,500 (CSO, 2012). Despite recent net emigration, children of immigrants and non-nationals account for 10% of the primary school level population (between four and 12 years of age) and 8% of the post-primary school level population (between 12 and 18 years of age). There is however a difference in the distribution of these students across schools at primary and post-primary levels. At post-primary level the vast majority of schools (90%) have so-called newcomer students, but many of them have a rather small proportion of between 2% and 9%. At primary level, over 40% of schools have no newcomers at all, but those that do, tend to have a greater proportion of newcomer students (ESRI, 2009; Byrne et al., 2010).

There are many studies which identify racist attitudes in Irish society in general, as well as in the education system (see for instance Lentin and McVeigh, 2006; Keogh and Whyte, 2003; Devine, 2005; Nowlan, 2008). 'Ireland lies far behind other European countries in addressing racism in terms of anti-racist legislation' (Tannam et al., 1998, p. 11). Theories of racism highlight a tendency to give with one hand while taking away with the other; this contradiction is discussed in Lentin and McVeigh (2006). Other studies claim there to be a comparatively sympathetic attitude towards migrants (Turner, 2010; such studies may be out of date considering recent economic decline.

14.1.3   Education and social policy

While many European states have adopted a number of different official policies to deal with migration-related diversity such as assimilation, integration, interculturalism, or multiculturalism (Gray, 2006; Mac Éinrí, 2007), the debate about cultural diversity, including what the appropriate educational response should be, is still very much in its infancy in Ireland (Devine, 2011a). Thus immigration has posed a number of challenges for Irish schools, which have had little prior experience of dealing with diversity. These developments in Ireland reflect wider debates about the impact of increased ethnic, cultural, and linguistic diversity on traditional conceptions of citizenship and national identity, and how educational policies and curricula should respond to these challenges (O'Connor and Faas, 2012; Faas and Ross, 2012). The main focus has been on language support for newly arrived migrant students.

Analysis of recent, context-specific literature uncovers criticism of the way official DES policy for migrants in the school system is constructed and disseminated, and of the non-uniform way in which many schools and teachers implement the policy (Devine, 2005; Nowlan, 2008; Ó Riagáin, 2013), while other studies propose solutions and recommendations (Little, 2008; Lyons and Little, 2009; Little and Lazenby-Simpson, 2009; Fionda, 2011). DES response to the changing levels of diversity in society, and therefore in the student population, began in 1999 by making funding available for English language support (Nowlan, 2008). Circular 0053/2007 (DES, 2007) is entitled 'Meeting the needs of pupils for whom English is a second language' and this three-page document was issued by DES in 2007 to address a situation which had necessitated intervention since the arrival of Ireland's new migrants at least a decade or two earlier. Earlier documents (see DES, 2003) set out availability of funding available to support migrants in the school system. Funding centers around offering language support to migrant students, which is meant to support and open access to students' mainstream learning.

Circular 0053/2007 detailed the first guidelines for official educational provision for migrant students. According to the circular, its purpose is 'to assist schools in providing an inclusive school environment to meet the needs of pupils for whom English is a second language and outline the resources that are available to assist schools in this task' (DES, 2007, p. 1). It goes on to provide limited guidelines on the subject of creating an inclusive school environment. The circular offers a brief description of the role of a language support teacher. Many such teachers describe a situation of confusion, isolation, and often blurred boundaries between a school's language support program and its special needs department (Nowlan, 2008, p. 261). Many mainstream teachers appear not to inform themselves about matters related to migrant students (Fionda, 2011), even though the circulars clearly state that mainstream teachers are responsible for migrant students in their mainstream lessons (DES, 2007, 2009a).

Circular 0015/2009, intended to replace the previous one, came in response to the recession and subsequent budget cuts across many spheres of Irish life. A review of Circular 0015/2009 indicates that ESL support was reduced to two teachers per school, except for those schools where over 90 students require ESL support. Prior to 2009, a third ESL post required just 42 students. ESL funding was cut to 100 million from 137 million. A further circular (DES, 2012) states that language support is effectively discontinued, instead it will be officially merged with learning support, and that teaching allocation will be halved.

Furthermore, the role of religious bodies as administrators in the education system has led to concern (the vast majority of Irish schools, particularly at primary level, are Catholic, Darmody et al., 2012), particularly 'the exemption that denominational schools currently enjoy from equality legislation, allowing them to discriminate in terms of student admissions and teacher appointments in order to protect their ethos' (Nowlan, 2008, p. 256), which means that a school can exclude a student from a migrant background on the grounds of their religious background – a practice which has received heavy criticism. Devine (1999) draws our attention to the long history of domination by the church in the education system. The moralization of the young, through religious instruction, continued to be perceived to be 'a fundamental part of the school course' and in line with the overall principles of the curriculum, was to be implemented in an integrated and child-centered manner (Devine, 1999, p. 21).

Emerging literature in the field has identified gaps in provision for migrant students in the Irish post-primary system and contributes to emerging literature which addresses educational policies for Ireland's migrant students and practice in schools (Devine, 2005; IILT, 2007; Little, 2008; Lyons and Little; 2009; Ó'Riagáin, 2013, Fionda, 2011). Nonetheless, Irish schools perform reasonably well according to international evaluation studies such as the Programme for International Student Assessment (PISA). PISA 2009 showed that Irish-born (native) students and non-Irish-born migrants who speak English at home had significantly higher mean reading scores than migrant students who spoke other languages at home. Unlike in most other European countries, there is no statistically significant performance gap between (first-generation) migrant students and their native peers in Ireland (OECD, 2010), though at this early stage post the significant wave of immigration it is imprudent to compare to countries with a longer history of immigration. Ireland is also characterized as an inclusive system in terms of the even distribution of migrant students across schools compared to other OECD countries (OECD, 2009), despite there being no enforcement of school choice for migrants.

14.2   Methodology

Several factors make the Irish context unique: (a) a shorter history of students from immigrant backgrounds within the education system, (b) relatively heterogeneous distribution of languages within schools, and (c) fewer context-specific studies – research is emerging but very much in its infancy. The current economic situation appears to be reversing the trend of funding; interest and research into the area, however, remain. Many studies into the Irish educational and migration context necessarily draw upon a wide range of international studies, because Irish-specific research is still emergent and limited. This is due to several interconnected causes; first and foremost that Ireland is traditionally a country of net emigration, and only during its economic boom (the so-called 'Celtic Tiger') from the mid-1990s until the crash of 2008 was immigration widespread (see also Figure 14.2).

Although, for the factors listed above, it was therefore difficult to source exclusively Irish-context literature it was decided that including only such literature was necessary to maintain the focus on the unique attributes of the Irish perspective. In presenting only studies that focused on Ireland, more effective comparisons may be made with other chapters of this book. Furthermore, and in line with Stevens (2007) and Stevens et al. (2011), and a necessary limitation given the range of Irish literature which exclusively explores the nature of educational inequality and migration, our chapter is restricted to studies conducted between 1980 and 2012. Also in line with the methodologies cited above is the decision to restrict analysis to only secondary education (referred to as second-level education in Ireland), though further rationale behind the decision is particular to the Irish context: the holistic nature of first-level education means that much practical progress has been made regarding provision for migrant students (see Little and Lazenby-Simpson, 2004). However, studies into second-level education are approached from a somewhat distinct perspective, partly due to the divided curriculum (into subject areas) and further divisions for the junior, senior and Transition Year cycles, exam type, and so forth.

In addition, the majority of the sources reviewed were peer-reviewed articles and edited books; however, this guideline was not adhered to as strictly because of the emergent nature of studies relating education and migration in Ireland much of the research carried out has not yet been published officially. Three distinct research approaches emerge from the Irish context: (1) charting ethnic inequalities and policy issues, (2) racism and education, and (3) developing newer and more critical research agendas.

14.3   Research traditions

In this section, we focus on the specific research questions, methods, results, and related debates characteristic of each of the above-named research traditions. Emphasis is placed on the Irish-specific developments in terms of social and educational policy and intellectual thought explaining each of the three identified research traditions: charting ethnic inequalities and policy issues; racism and education; and developing newer and more critical research agendas.

14.3.1   Charting ethnic inequalities and policy issues

During the aftermath of initial waves of immigration, from the mid-1990s, the Irish research agenda set out to describe the changes in society, analyze the relationship between the influx of large numbers of people from varying ethnic backgrounds and its resulting effects across political, social, and educational spheres as well as in the labor market, and to shape policy decisions. Such studies focus on pre-existing diversity and discrimination issues at national policy level and paved the way for researchers to address more domain-specific, empirical studies on racism and education (see next research tradition). Aligned with a post-structuralist perspective, the methodologies are descriptive and analytical, identifying trends over time by reviewing policy and literature.

Lentin and McVeigh (2006) provide a key reference study which identifies how inequality in Ireland is addressed via research and policy agendas, but only within an antecedent framework of discrimination, which results in a disparity between policy and practice (a trend which is picked up again in the following research traditions). According to them, racism in Irish society reflected as institutional racism in schools is revealed by, on the one hand, a tendency to 'provide for' minorities (Lentin and McVeigh, 2006, pp. 5–6), observe the current wave of 'intercultural' and 'anti-racist' education initiatives (NCCA, 2006), and on the other hand reluctance to fully implement educational programs which enable migrants to learn. There is evidence to suggest that debate in Irish society tends therefore to reinforce the unequal distribution of power (Guerin, 2002), and attitudes in the media are visibly racist (McVeigh, 2002). Policy reflects the white, Catholic hegemony in its viewpoint that racism is 'caused by the "strangeness" of incoming immigrant groups [rather than by the "host" society]' (Lentin, 2002, p. 229).

There are a profusion of large-scale guidelines and policy documents also embedded in this research tradition; some studies cross over in their purpose between providing exploratory research and suggesting policy implications. The NCCA (2005, 2006) and Irish National Teachers' Organisation (INTO) (2006) Intercultural Education Guidelines fall under this category. The more recent Intercultural Education Strategy (DES, 2010) was launched with the twofold aims of ensuring that

> all students experience an education that 'respects the diversity of values, beliefs, languages and traditions in Irish society and is conducted in a spirit of partnership' ... [and] all education providers are assisted with ensuring that inclusion and integration within an intercultural learning environment become the norm. (DES, 2010)

The strategy documents a macro-study of the context (demographic details, national legislation, and research overview) as well as setting out components of the strategy and how to implement it. It was launched by the DES in mid-September 2010 and came into practical relevance within schools with the start of the 2011/12 academic year. Anecdotal explorations show the document to be widely ignored in practice.

Similarly, the Immigration Monitor Ireland 2010 (McGinnity et al., 2011) will henceforth be an annual publication aiming to 'provide a comprehensive and concise picture of the state of Integration in Ireland and to identify where in employment, education, social inclusion and active citizenship Ireland can increase the potential for integration'. The report draws together the body of existing research on education and concludes that children from non-English-speaking backgrounds are struggling to keep up with their peers.

Early studies, and follow-up research of policy and guideline documents, argue that opening the doors to its schools but failing to provide the support necessary to access the curriculum is representative of Ireland's migration policy: a policy characterized by legislation which is 'intended to *control* rather than liberate those people who are the subjects of Irish racism' (Lentin and McVeigh, 2006, p. 2). The issue of race is 'problematized' and 'common sense' legislation (see Gramsci, 1971, p. 322, for discussion of 'common sense' notions) seeks to manage 'the problem of racial and ethnic difference' (Lentin and McVeigh, 2006, p. 2). There are a wealth of findings from the later research traditions which relate their agenda to the preceding context; namely the identification of structures which pre-date the large-scale increase of immigration and concluding that as such, recent discrimination is indicative of already present problems. Diversity in the Irish population is not new. 'Minority ethnic groups, including the indigenous Traveller community, as well as relatively small immigrant Jewish, Italian and Chinese communities, for example, have been part of Irish society for a long time' (Nowlan, 2008, p. 255). So, the recent influx of immigrants does not initiate or uncover a new problem, it reveals existing problems in the education system.

Studies from this research tradition set the tone that discrimination in schools reflects inequalities within the broader society. This largely descriptive and analytical research is limited to reviews of existing studies and policy documents. In drawing together existing research on education, legislation overviews, and large-scale demographic reports, the research highlights structures which present obstacles to migrants. The findings also uncover constructs which historically discriminate against other minority groups before the widespread immigration, such as social, cultural and religious barriers, as well as linguistic ones.

14.3.2 Racism and education

In Ireland this research agenda, which developed to describe and analyze racism in education in specific response to large numbers of migrants in the school system and affect policy (in theory), emerged from the late-1990s on and has been noticeably responsive over time to the unstable dynamics of the Irish economic circumstances. Many studies draw focus on qualitative and quantitative strategies (which paved the way for triangulation, integrating elements of qualitative approaches in the final research tradition, see next section). For example, a key study in this tradition represents the emerging interest in migration, ethnic minority, and education; Keogh and Whyte (2003), in their study on the experiences and aspirations of immigrant students in second-level schools, draw attention to the fact that within their sample schools, no Traveller students were participating in the senior cycle (Keogh and Whyte, 2003).

Studies from the wider European context also contribute to this tradition. According to such research, ESL students do not fare well; students who speak a language other than English at home still face a gap in achievement:

> The immigrant students in Ireland are a heterogeneous group. There is a gap in achievement between those students who speak English at home and those who do not. Ireland aims to provide 'inclusive, high quality education for all students'.
>
> (OECD, 2009, p. 9)

This tradition is characterized by a Bourdieuian analysis set in a framework which links academic potential to dominant cultural ideology. In schools, where the culture of the dominant group is promoted, educational differences and failure are often misrecognized as resulting from a lack of academic talent, when in reality they stem from class differences or cultural diversity (Bourdieu and Passeron, 1977, 1979). And so, while success at school is celebrated by the dominant social groups as based on merit, Bourdieuian theory questions the idea of a meritocracy and instead suggests a concern that schools merely reproduce dominant ideology by simply refusing to recognize that the established order is problematic (Bourdieu, 1993; Mills and Gale, 2007). Wacquant (1998) elaborates the theory of cultural capital thus, 'rather than education acting as an equalizer in a prejudiced society with all participants afforded equal opportunity, success in education is based on the cultural experiences, social ties and economic resources that each student has access to' (ibid., p. 216; Mills and Gale, 2007, p. 433). Irish studies initiated debate in the research which observed how migrants were subjected to 'quick fix' approaches which devalued their own 'cultural capital'. Keogh and Whyte (2003, p. 8) refer to European and human rights philosophies in their observations that provision for migrant students means not simply asking the students themselves to 'fit in', but rather a long-term and sustained effort on the part of policy-makers and schools to include and value a diverse student population:

> It means that every effort should be made to provide them with the support they need to achieve their potential and the same standard of education as their peers, without forcing them into a situation where they have to deny their ethnic and cultural heritage, traditions and beliefs.
>
> (Keogh and Whyte, 2003, p. 8)

This research tradition draws on a theoretical framework derived from Bourdieu and Gramsci, and relies upon studies from similar contexts (specifically migrant education in the UK and Canada, because these predominantly English-speaking systems have well-developed literature compared to the emerging Irish context). A significant conclusion is that practice in place for many ESL students maintains the privileges and power of dominant cultural ideology, at the cost of provision of equal chances for Ireland's new migrant students. This practice is not overtly enforced but, as Gramscian hegemony illustrates (Gramsci, 1971; Cummins, 2000; Ferguson, 2006) quietly negotiated via procedures where educational structures exclude groups who fall outside the dominant culture, by promoting an assumption where biculturalism and bilingualism are viewed as deficits (Ward, 2006), and via a state of confusion which leads to a tolerance and perpetuation of 'worst' practice. In sum, this tradition sets its research in a Bourdieuian framework and focuses on describing a rapidly emerging and new 'status quo' in relation to race and education. It seeks to illustrate, drawing on qualitative and quantitative methods, the challenges faced by education systems and students alike, and concludes that educational parity is not offered in favor of maintaining existing power structures. It is only tentative in any attempt to approach policy propositions, which leads us to the next tradition.

14.3.3 Developing newer and more critical research agendas

Key studies in this tradition set out to address what the ideal definition of 'language support' should be in Ireland and what provision for migrant students meets the specific needs of the Irish context. Researchers in this tradition suggest the disparity between policy and practice is an obstructive factor in achieving parity of educational access. This tradition continues to set its agenda within a Bourdieuian framework, and again draws on qualitative strategies.

A key study in this area is the Lyons and Little (2009) research report which widely criticizes both provision and practice. Other studies in this tradition come to similar conclusions: discrimination in schools reflects inequalities within the broader society. 'School practices are understood to be influenced by their location within the broader social and policy contexts, as well as by the individual actors in schools – students, teachers and parents' (Nowlan, 2008, p. 254; Faas, 2010), and much recent research in the field of diversity in Irish schools has concentrated on such issues (Devine, 2005). Nowlan (2008) and Devine (2005, 2011b) are also key contributors to this tradition.

Lyons and Little (2009), Nowlan (2008) and Devine (2005) conclude that Ireland's migrant students face significant obstacles in accessing education: social, cultural and religious barriers, as well as linguistic ones. Research into these issues benefits not only migrant students but also ethnic English and Irish students who, while having been born in Ireland to Irish parents, may face similar obstacles due to their social and/or economic disadvantage, and lay the foundation to prepare all students for participation in an increasingly diverse society. Devine (2011b), in a key study, concurs with Lyons and Little (2009), that as well as drawing migrant children into the curriculum via their

English language, schools have to value the cultural and personal backgrounds of the students.

Crozier et al. (2010: 209) identified the societal changes which have initiated research trends:

> Irish society shifted from being one characterised by intensive periods of emigration, to one of intense immigration. This 'unexpected immigration' during a period of rapid economic development has given rise to renewed challenges related to definitions of national identity and citizenship. Coinciding with changes in the education system arising from processes of modernisation and intense educational reform, old certainties are replaced by insecurities and challenges as to how best to work with increasing ethnic diversity in classrooms and schools.

Crozier et al. (2010) are critical of Ireland's approaches to policy development, and Kitching (2010) identifies the dangers in Ireland's apparent reluctance to learn from the mistakes of countries such as the UK in avoiding tension between migrants and local communities.

Nowlan's (2008, p. 253) findings confirm the challenges faced by a system so unprepared for the dramatic change in its student population:

> Just as society is changing, the education system needs to change in order to ensure that the schooling provided to all people prepares them for life in an increasingly pluralist society. The needs of all students must be met, including those who are not from the majority ethnic group (i.e. Irish, white and Roman Catholic).

While diversity has always existed in Irish schools (on socio-economic background and gender grounds, for example), recent immigration has uncovered insufficient provision for a diverse student body within the education system. 'Second language learners, who were seen as the "barium meal in the X-ray" showing up deficiencies in the schooling system that affected the progress of many other students' (Bourne, 2003, p. 26). Critical pedagogy is concerned with the potential role of education as a true preparation for future citizens. 'The social and political dimensions of schooling, the need to understand and transform schools and society, and the key role that educators in these processes play are core themes shared by many critical educators' (Fischman and McLaren, 2005, p. 426).

Practice which may be a result of the 'exclusive' origin of Ireland's post-primary schools, when schools were open to only a small number of wealthy families (Hyland, 1999, p. 33), is evident in Irish schools. The tendency to stream students in some schools is a legacy of this and Nowlan (2008) points out that many migrant students are placed disproportionately in lower stream groups.

Like many of the context-specific research into inequality, Nowlan's (2008) research identified with Bourdieuian traditions (see preceding research tradition). Nowlan draws on Bourdieu's ideas of cultural capital, arguing that 'society was stratified according to the possession of cultural as well as economic capital' (Nowlan, 2008, p. 254). Nowlan develops this point, reflecting that 'minority language students in particular, may be discriminated against within the education system since they lack the means to acquire the particular cultural capital which is necessary in order to do well at school' and also therefore to participate equally in society after school. According to Bourdieu, migrant students do possess rich cultural capital, that of their varied linguistic abilities and cultural experiences which are distinct from the often (more) homogeneous linguistic and cultural experiences of students born in Ireland (not ignoring the differences in social background of these students). Research shows that 'bilingual students' linguistic abilities are not valued as cultural capital ... there is a danger that stereotypes will emerge and become self perpetuating, resulting in lower expectations on the part of both students and teachers' (Nowlan, 2008, p. 262). This contrasts, for instance, with the UK where Reay et al. (2011) found that the 'socially inclusive middle-class' student and family actively embraces diversity and is open to difference, seeing themselves further enriched through the consumption of ethno-cultural – though not necessarily social – diversity.

Again, set within a Bourdieuian framework, this tradition is more progressive in its forthright approaches towards policy and ideal practice recommendations. It links small-scale case-studies, interviews, and other qualitative methods to broader theories which define some existing practices as inappropriate and puts forward model frameworks upon which to base policy.

14.3.4   Summary of research traditions

There is a tendency, widespread across all three research traditions, of approaching studies from a qualitative perspective, believed to be due to lack of data available for longitudinal quantitative studies, with the NCCA for example not generally recording ethnicity of students. Quantitative approaches are often believed to overlook the 'human story' elements of the wide range of cultural and social backgrounds of migrants, especially in second-level schools. Nowlan (2008) and Fionda (2011), for example, spent time in either one or a small number of schools and used semi-structured interviews, questionnaires, and observations to build a narrative of the students' experience of school structures. This is perhaps illustrative of the motive behind studies into the context – to put the migrant students first and uncover their perspectives. Therefore even studies with a quantitative emphasis tend to illustrate findings with qualitative components. The ESRI (2009, 2011) studies are structured in such a way as to include both qualitative and quantitative elements, and Lyons and Little (2009) emphasize that 'chalk face' narratives are imperative to obtain an accurate description of haphazard educational structures.

The research traditions all lead to the conclusion that the arrival of migrants has been useful in drawing more attention to such educational deficits, as the second research tradition (racism and discrimination at national policy level) highlights. Furthermore, studies in this area reveal a tendency to blame migration 'problems' firmly in the hands of migrants themselves. The third research tradition, which looks at education practice since the mass immigration and attempts to develop a more critical perspective, focuses on studies which observe that as society has changed the education system has struggled to keep up with it and instead maintains the cultural status quo in terms of power distribution. With Ireland's idiosyncratic context meaning there is much overlap in the traditions, in part due to the rapid pace of migration, the relative heterogeneous distribution of migrants, and then in necessary response to unstable economic conditions, the key defining features are notable. While the first research tradition, 'charting ethnic inequalities and policy issues', reviews pre-existing policy with a descriptive and analytical purpose, the second and third traditions ('racism and education' and 'developing newer and more critical research agendas') extend their methods to include qualitative analyses. The second tradition applies both quantitative and qualitative methods to describe emerging contexts, while the third tradition draws on mainly qualitative studies and offers a more critical analysis in its objective of defining an ideal policy/practice paradigm.

14.4   Conclusion and discussion

Ireland experienced large-scale immigration between 1996 and 2008, particularly following the eastern enlargement of the European Union. However, since 2008, in the context of a sharp economic downturn, emigration and especially the issue of how to integrate those already residing in Ireland has come to the fore in the debates surrounding migration. Recent government cuts led to the closure of the National Consultative Committee on Racism and Interculturalism in December 2008 and the discontinuation of Integrate Ireland Language and Training services (IILT) which means that there is no longer an Irish equivalent to the Northern Irish Inclusion and Diversity Service supporting educational institutions with linguistic and socio-cultural integration of migrant students. There is a gap between policy documents and guidelines, and the ways in which local institutions understand and respond to diversity, as noted above in the case of the NCCA Intercultural Education Guidelines. This gap between policy and practice is a key issue. Research in Ireland could therefore usefully explore how migration is managed within educational settings and what best practices have emerged including a focus on how education management understands and deals with diversity. This links to existing and new literature in the field of new managerialism in education including tracking and streaming of students (see Lynch, Devine and Grummel, 2011).

Moreover, NCCA has not revised its curricula since the 1990s despite the influx in immigration. In 2003, NCCA initiated a program of curriculum review at primary level. This review was not a specific response to diversity or migration, but is rather a general review process concerning the effectiveness of the curriculum and the extent to which it enables teachers to support children in their learning. Phase one of the review focused on English, visual arts and mathematics. Phase two focused on a further three subjects, namely Irish language, science, and social, personal and health education (SPHE). There have been no changes to the SPHE curriculum as of yet following the review with the main issues highlighted being approaches to assessment and 'curriculum overload'. History and geography have yet to be reviewed. Moreover, the Irish language requirement for primary school teachers has in effect made it very difficult to recruit teachers with a migration background. And the specificity of the Irish experience of migration includes the influence of the Catholic church in various societal sectors. Schools mediate city-level, regional, national and supranational policies in rather different ways depending on their ethos and management and future research should focus more on the micro level.

Research on migration and education in Ireland has hitherto also been of a more smaller-scale qualitative nature with the exception of the ESRI-funded study 'Adapting to Diversity: Irish Schools and Newcomer Students' (2009). Currently, several quantitative studies are ongoing including the Norface-funded project SCIP ('Causes and Consequences of Early Socio-Cultural Integration Processes among New Immigrants in Europe'). SCIP uses a panel survey to analyze how the Irish national context shapes the early stages of integration of new immigrants. It focuses especially on the integration trajectories of Polish migrants in Ireland. A related IRCHSS-funded survey 'Polonia in Dublin' aims to study working conditions, occupational mobility, networks and leisure activities of the Polish migrants in the Greater Dublin area. It found, for instance, that respondents are very highly educated, women on average have higher educational achievement than men, with almost two-thirds holding third-level qualifications; that Polish respondents in Dublin are concentrated in postcode areas 1, 7, 8 and 15; and that the vast majority rent their accommodation and only very few are owner-occupiers (Mühlau, Kaliszewska and Röder, 2010). More quantitative research that systematically maps the social, cultural, political, and economic integration of various groups of immigrants in Ireland is needed coupled with the above-mentioned qualitative or mixed-methods research into policy effectiveness and processes at the institutional level.

Until recently, Ireland has not formed part of larger-scale comparative migration and education research. To do so will enable researchers to transfer best practices within Europe and to learn from the experiences of countries with a longer migration history. Most recently, for instance, Irish researchers formed part of two European Commission-funded FP7 projects exploring the transmission of religious beliefs and values through the education system and the family (REMC); and the meanings of tolerance in a variety of contexts with a special focus on 'what needs to be done' in Europe in order to proceed to more coherent societies, while respecting ethnic, religious and cultural plurality (the ACCEPT PLURALISM project). There are a range of largely unexplored migration research themes in Ireland and Europe including, for instance, the interface between migration and sexuality. Research on bullying (see O'Moore, 2010; O'Moore, 2008) could usefully focus more on homophobic bullying and link this with earlier emigration to places like the UK (see Ryan-Flood, 2009) and possible return migration following the Irish Civil Partnership Act in 2010. For many young members of the lesbian, gay, bi- and transsexual community, sexual citizenship is replacing national identity as a master narrative (Valentine, 2001) yet very little is known about how young people from various ethno-cultural backgrounds in Ireland negotiate their belonging and what impacts their sexuality has on mobility, migration, and social well-being.

References

Bourdieu, P. (1991) *Language and Symbolic Power.* Cambridge: Polity Press.

Bourdieu, P. (1993) *The Field of Cultural Production.* Cambridge: Polity Press.

Bourdieu, P. and Passeron, J. (1977) *Reproduction in Education, Society and Culture.* London: Sage.

Bourdieu, P. and Passeron, J. (1979) *The Inheritors: French Students and Their Relation to Culture.* Chicago: University of Chicago Press.

Bourne, J. (2003) Vertical Discourse: The Role of the Teacher in the Transmission and Acquisition of Decontextualised Language. *European Educational Research Journal* 2: 496–521.

Byrne, D., McGinnity, F., Smyth, E. and Darmody, M. (2010) Immigration and School Composition in Ireland. *Irish Educational Studies* 29(3): 271–288.

Central Statistics Office (2012) *Population and Migration Estimates: April 2012*, http://www.cso.ie/en/media/csoie/releasespublications/documents/population/2012/popmig_2012.pdf

Crozier, G., Bhopal, K. and Devine, D. (2010) Editorial. *Irish Educational Studies*, 29(3): 207–212.

Cummins, J. (2000) *Language, Power and Pedagogy – Bilingual Children in the Crossfire.* Clevedon: Multilingual Matters.

Darmody, M., Smyth, E., Byrne, D. and McGinnity, F. (2012) New School, New System: The Experiences of Immigrant Students in Irish Schools. *International Handbook of Migration, Minorities and Education 2012*, 2: 283–299.

Department of Education and Science (1998) *The Education Act. Dublin:* DES, http://www.irishstatutebook.ie/1998/en/act/pub/0051/print.html.

Department of Education and Skills (2003) *Summary of All Initiatives Funded by the Department to Help Alleviate Educational Disadvantage.* Dublin: DES.

Department of Education and Skills (2004) *A Brief Description of the Irish Education System.* Dublin: DES.

Department of Education and Skills (2007) *Circular 0053/2007 – Meeting the Needs of Pupils for Whom English Is a Second Language.* Dublin: DES.

Department of Education and Skills (2009) *Circular 0015/2009 – Meeting the Needs of Pupils Learning English as an Additional Language (EAL).* Dublin: DES.

Department of Education and Skills (2012) *Circular 0009/2012 – Staffing Arrangements in Post-Primary Schools for the 2012/13 School Year.* Dublin: DES.

Devine, D. (1999) Children: Rights and Status in Education – A Socio-Historical Analysis. *Irish Educational Studies,* 18: 14–28.

Devine, D. (2005) Welcome to the Celtic Tiger? Teacher Responses to Immigration and Increasing Ethnic Diversity in Irish Schools. *International Studies in Sociology of Education,* 15: 49–70.

Devine, D. (2011a) *Immigration and Schooling in Ireland – Making a Difference?* Manchester: Manchester University Press. In Darmody, M., Tyrrell, N., and Song, S. (Eds) *The Changing Face of Ireland.* Rotterdam: Sense Publishers.

Devine, D. (2011b) 'Securing Migrant Children's Educational Well-being: Perspectives on Policy and Practice in Irish Schools', In Devine, D. (Ed.) *Ethnic Minority Children and Youth in Ireland.* Amsterdam: Springer.

Economic and Social Research Institute – ESRI (2009) *Adapting to Diversity: Irish Schools and Newcomer Students,* Research Series, Dublin: ESRI.

Economic and Social Research Institute – ESRI (2011) *Immigration Monitor Ireland* Research Series, Dublin: ESRI.

Eurydice (2009) *Organisation of the Education System in Ireland,* http://eacea.ec.europa.eu/education/eurydice/documents/eurybase/eurybase_full_reports/IE_EN.pdf.

Faas, D. (2010) *Negotiating Political Identities: Multiethnic Schools and Youth in Europe.* Farnham: Ashgate.

Faas, D. and Ross, W. (2012) Identity, Diversity and Citizenship: A Critical Analysis of Textbooks and Curricula in Irish Schools. *International Sociology,* 27(4): 574–591.

Ferguson, G. (2006) *Language Planning and Education.* Edinburgh: Edinburgh University Press.

Fionda, R. (2011) Education is a Fundamental Right: Do Immigrant Students have Equal Access to Second Level Education in Ireland? *Translocations 7.1* http://www.translocations.ie/docs/v07i01/Vol%207%20Issue%201%20-%20Peer%20Review%20-%20Education%20&%20Immigrants,%20Fionda.pdf.

Fischman, G. and Mclaren, P. (2005) Rethinking Critical Pedagogy and the Gramscian and Freirean Legacies: From Organic to Committed Intellectuals or Critical Pedagogy, Commitment, and Praxis. *Cultural Studies ↔ Critical Methodologies* 5: 425–446.

Gramsci, A. (1971) *Selections from the Prison Notebooks.* London: Lawrence and Wishart.

Gray, B. (2006) Migrant Integration Policy: A Nationalist Fantasy of Management and Control. *Translocations,* 1(1): 121–141.

Guerin, P. (2002) Racism and the Media in Ireland: Setting the Anti-Immigrant Agenda. In Lentin, R. and McVeigh, R. (Eds) *Racism and Anti-Racism in Ireland.* Belfast: Beyond the Pale.

Hyland, A. (1999) Inclusiveness in Education. In Ward, N. and Dooney, T. (Eds) *Irish Education for the 21st Century.* Dublin: Oak Tree Press.

Integrate Ireland Language and Training (2007) *A Resource Book for Language Support in Post-Primary Schools.* Dublin: IILT.

Keogh, A. and Whyte, J. (2003) *Getting On: The Experiences of Immigrant Students in Second Level Schools Linked to the Trinity Access Programmes*. Dublin: Children's Research Centre, Trinity College Dublin.

Kitching, K. (2010) An Excavation of the Racialised Politics of Viability Underpinning Education Policy in Ireland, *Irish Educational Studies*, 29(3): 213–229.

Kuhling, C. and Keohane, K. (2007) *Cosmopolitan Ireland*. London: Pluto Press.

Lentin, R. (2002) Anti-Racist Responses to the Racialisation of Irishness: Disavowed Multiculturalism and Its Discontents. In Lentin, R. and McVeigh, R. (Eds) *Racism and Anti-Racism in Ireland*. Belfast: Beyond the Pale.

Lentin, R. and McVeigh, R. (2006) *After Optimism: Ireland, Racism and Globalisation*, Dublin: Metro Éireann Publications.

Little, D. (2008) Language Learner Autonomy and the European Language Portfolio: Two English Examples. *Language Teaching*, 42: 222–233.

Little, D. and Lazenby-Simpson, B. (2004) Using the CEF to Develop an ESL Curriculum for Newcomer Pupils in Irish Primary Schools. In Morrow, K. (Ed.) *Insights from the Common European Framework*. Oxford: Oxford University Press.

Little, D. and Lazenby-Simpson, B. (2009) Immigration, Citizenship and Language. In Alderson, J. C. (Ed.) *The Politics of Language Education: Individuals and Institutions*. Cambridge: Cambridge University Press.

Lynch, K; Devine; D and Grummell, B (2011) *New Managerialism and the Care Ceiling in Education*. London: Palgrave.

Lyons, Z. and Little, D. (2009) *English Language Support in Irish Post-Primary Schools: Policy, Challenges and Deficits*. Dublin: TII, Trinity College.

Mac Éinrí, P. (2007) Integration Models and Choices. In Fanning, B. (ed.) *Immigration and Social Change in Ireland*. Manchester: Manchester University.

McGinnity, F., Quinn, E., O'Connell, P. and Donnelly, N. (2011) *Immigration Monitor Ireland 2010*. Dublin: ESRI.

McVeigh, R. (2002) Is There an Irish Anti-Racism? Building an Anti-Racist Ireland. In Lentin, R. and McVeigh, R. (Eds) *Racism and Anti-racism in Ireland*. Belfast: Beyond the Pale.

Mills, C. and Gale, T. (2007) Researching Social Inequalities in Education: Towards a Bourdieuian Methodology. *International Journal of Qualitative Studies in Education*, 20(4): 433–447.

Mühlau, P., Kaliszewska, M. and Röder, A. (2010) Polonia in Dublin: Preliminary report of survey findings (Report No.1, Demographic overview), Dublin: Trinity Immigration Initiative Trinity College Dublin.

National Council for Curriculum and Assessment (2006) *Intercultural Education in the Post-Primary School*. Dublin: DES.

Nowlan, E. (2008) Underneath the Band-Aid: Supporting Bilingual Students in Irish schools. *Irish Educational Studies* 27: 253–266.

O'Connor, L. and Faas, D. (2012) The Impact of Migration on National Identity in a Globalized Word: A Comparison of Civic Education Curricula in England, France and Ireland. *Irish Educational Studies* 31(1): 51–66.

Organization for Economic Cooperation and Development (2009) *Reviews of Migrant Education: Ireland*. Paris: OECD.

Organization for Economic Cooperation and Development (2010) *PISA 2009 Results Learning Trends: Changes in Student Performance since 2000*, Paris: OECD.

O'Moore (2008) Preventing School Bullying: The Irish Experience. In D. Pepler and W. Craig (Eds) *Understanding and Addressing Bullying*. Bloomington: Authorhouse.

O'Moore, M. (2010) *Understanding School Bullying: A Guide for Parents and Teachers*. Dublin: Veritas.

Ó Riagáin, P. (2013) The Linguistic Challenge of Multi-cultural Ireland: Managing Language Diversity in Irish Schools. In J. Ulin, H. Edwards and S O'Brien (Eds) *Race and Immigration in the New Ireland* (pp. 107–129). South Bend: University of Notre Dame Press.

Reay, D., Crozier, G. and James, D. (2011) *White Middle Class Identities and Urban Schooling*. Basingstoke: Palgrave.

Ruhs, M. (2005) *Managing the Immigration and Employment of non-EU Nationals in Ireland*, Dublin: The Policy Institute, Trinity College Dublin.

Ruhs, M. (2009) *Ireland: From Rapid Immigration to Recession*, Migration Policy Institute, http://www.migrationinformation.org/Feature/display.cfm?ID=740.

Ryan-Flood, R. (2009) *Lesbian Motherhood: Gender, Families and Sexual Citizenship*. Basingstoke: Palgrave Macmillan.

Smyth, E., McCoy, S., Darmody, M. and Dunne, A. (2007) Changing Times, Changing Schools? Quality of Life for Students. In Fahey, T., Russell, H. and Whelan, C. (Eds) *Best of Times? The Social Impact of the Celtic Tiger*. Dublin: Institute of Public Administration.

Stevens, P. (2007) Researching Race/Ethnicity and Educational Inequality in English Secondary Schools: A Critical Review of the Research Literature between 1980 and 2005. *Review of Educational Research*, 77(2): 147–185.

Stevens, P., Clycq, N., Timmerman, C. and Van Houtte, M. (2011) Researching Race/Ethnicity and Educational Inequality in the Netherlands: A Critical Review of the Research Literature between 1980 and 2008. *British Educational Research Journal*, 37(1): 5–43.

Tannam, M., Smith, S. and Flood, S. (1998) *Anti-Racism: An Irish Perspective*. Dublin: Harmony.

Turner, T. (2010) Why Are Irish Attitudes to Immigrants among the Most Liberal in Europe?, *European Societies*, 12(1): 25–44.

Valentine, G. (2001) *Social Geographies: Society and Space*. Longman: Harlow.

Wacquant, L. (1998) Pierre Bourdieu. In R. Stones (Ed.) *Key Sociological Thinkers*. New York: New York University Press.

Ward, T. (2006) *Education and Language Needs of Separated Children*. http://www.cdvec.ie/uploads/publications/LanguageNeedsChildren.pdf.

15
Japan

Kaori H. Okano

15.1 Introduction

Meritocracy in education was adopted in the middle of the 19th century by a modernizing Japan. It believed in merit-based selection of young people for what were deemed 'important' positions in order to transform a pre-modern feudal Japan into a modern nation. The government created a competitive external examination system by advocating the equality of educational opportunity. Under the post-World War II democratic system of education, it was a concern for human rights that drove merit-based selection through equal educational opportunities. The government and scholarly community have maintained a keen interest in the relationship between educational achievement and family background. This led to the institution of the large-scale Social Stratification and Mobility Survey that has been conducted every ten years since 1955.

This chapter examines how sociological studies have examined the relationship between ethnicity/race and educational equality in Japan between 1980 and 2010, and identifies three research 'traditions'. They are: (1) quantitative descriptions of minority students' educational achievements; (2) schooling processes in relation to discrimination, school interventions and identity formation; and (3) home cultures. One of the distinctive characteristics of these studies is 'localization', whereby the relationship is examined in selected localities with a focus on a single ethnic group, rather than as a national phenomenon. Even the government's repeated Social Stratification and Mobility Surveys have not included ethnicity/race as a variable. The dominant research tradition has been to study the schooling process through a large number of small-scale observational studies which explore the schooling experiences of both minority and non-minority students.

I begin with the methodology of selecting the literature for review, and then turn to a brief description of Japan's present education system, minority groups, and social policies. The ensuing section identifies three approaches in the research on the relation between race/ethnicity and educational inequality. Japan offers an interesting case as one of the few non-Western post-industrial states with a liberal democracy and a level of wealth distribution comparable to the first-world West. It is also the only non-Western country which had colonies (with the consequence of colonial subjects becoming ethnic minorities). Racial and ethnic discrimination in this context does not involve the West versus the others.

15.2   Methods

Consistent with the other chapters in the volume, I adopted the following criteria in selecting the literature to be reviewed: (1) studying the relationship between ethnicity/race and educational inequality, but not necessarily exclusively on this since the number of such studies is limited; (2) focusing squarely on Japan; (3) adopting sociological and anthropological approach; and (4) studying primary and secondary schooling. Tertiary education and non-formal and informal education are not included. Furthermore, my examination is restricted to peer-reviewed journal articles, books, book chapters, and reports by national and local governments.

The process of selecting the literature started with search of relevant databases, in both English and Japanese, starting with my existing knowledge of literature from my prior research on minorities and education in Japan (Okano, 1997, 2004, 2006, 2011; Okano and Tsuchiya, 1999; Okano and Tsuneyoshi, 2011). The English-language databases used were Sociological Abstracts, ERIC, and Bibliography of Asian Studies. Since the number of relevant studies from these databases was limited, the majority of literature came from Japanese-language sources. I searched in the Japanese-language database *Nichigai Zasshi Kiji Sakuin*, as well as focusing on the 1980–2011 issues of the three most esteemed Japanese journals in the field: *Shagaigaku Hyôron* (the journal of the Japan Sociological Association), *Kyôiku Shakaigaku Kenkyû* (the journal of the Educational Sociology Association of Japan), and *Soshioroji*. I also examined those that I found in the process of reading. The vast majority of the literature reviewed here is published only in Japanese. One of the contributions of this review is to make this research accessible to a non-Japanese-speaking readership.

15.3   Education, ethnic (and cultural) minorities, and policy developments in Japan

15.3.1   The system of education

Japan's post-war system of education was introduced under the US occupation. It was modeled on the American system of six years of primary school, three years of middle school, and three years of senior high school, with four-year undergraduate university courses. All children aged six start schooling in April, and receive nine years of compulsory education via a nationally guided curriculum. The vast majority of students attend local government schools, where ability-based tracking has been rare. Entry into senior high school requires an academic entrance examination; and over 98% of the age cohort enter senior high school. It is at this point (the end of compulsory education) that major differentiation takes place amongst students, based on academic achievement (Figure 15.1).

There are four types of senior high schools: elite academic high schools, non-elite academic high schools, vocational high schools, comprehensive high schools (which offer both non-elite academic and vocational courses), and evening high schools. Each of these types of schools has distinct school missions, and offers a curriculum to achieve that mission following the national curriculum guidelines. The majority of students are in non-elite academic high schools or in academic courses in comprehensive high schools. The vast majority of senior high school students proceed to graduation, and over half of all graduates then go to universities through entrance examinations (Okano and Tsuchiya, 1999).

Buddhist and Christian schools operate as mainstream government-sanctioned institutions, since they conform to the Ministry of Education regulations in terms of such aspects as curriculum, teaching staff, and facilities, in order to receive government funding. Some schools publicize the academic performance of their students via the internet, but this is not a government requirement. The public is able to gain a reasonable idea of where an individual school stands from the destination schools of its graduates.

Japan, like other East Asian nations, is often portrayed as a highly competitive, academic credentialist society, with university entrance examinations typifying this characterization. It needs to be remembered, however, that only a quarter (at most) participate in the highly competitive examinations to enter prestigious universities with the remainder gaining university places through their school's recommendation. Under this system students can gain a place at a participating university (not all universities offer this option) based on the school's report on his or her overall performance (e.g. academic, leadership, sports) and favorable references from teachers. With the declining birth rate and a large number of private universities, there are now more university places than there are applicants.

15.3.2   Minority students in Japan

The ethnic minorities that this chapter addresses comprise two distinct groups. One is the long-existing minorities whose origin pre-dates the end of World War II, and the other is so-called 'newcomers' who started arriving in the 1980s. The former include indigenous Ainu and Okinawans, ethnic Koreans and Chinese (descendants of former colonial subjects), and *buraku* people (descendants of

425

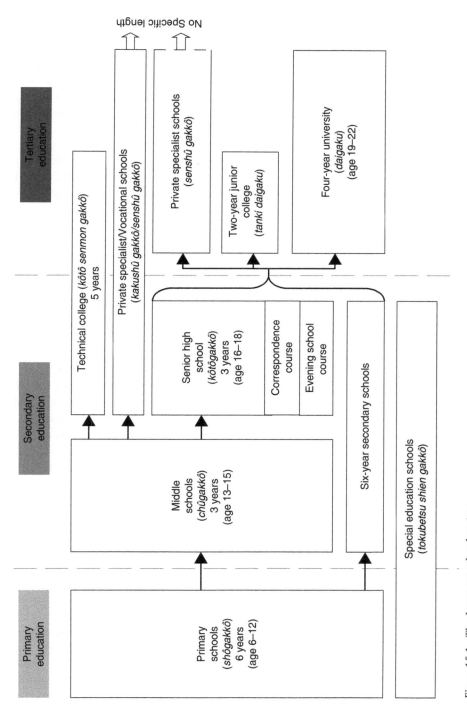

Figure 15.1 The Japanese school system

feudal outcaste population). While it is still debated whether or not *buraku* constitutes an ethnic group, I consider that they are on the grounds that *buraku* people maintain a separate 'culture' (Okano, 2011, p. 36; henceforth 'buraku'). Newcomer minority groups include Amerasians (children of American soldiers and local women in Okinawa), refugees, immigrants and guest workers, and returnees from China (women and orphans of Japanese families who left north-eastern China at the end of the war and their descendants).

It is not possible to arrive at accurate figures for the size of these groups. This is because of the national government's failure to document information on the descent of its citizens. Once a Korean takes up Japanese citizenship by naturalization or marriage, he or she becomes simply a 'Japanese citizen'. Indigenous Ainu and Okinawans are born into the category of 'Japanese'. There is no record of the number of children of mixed descent who have at least one Japanese national parent and therefore have automatically gained Japanese citizenship at birth. The estimated total minority population is between 5.78 million and 7.85 million, approximately between 5% and 6% of the total population (Okano and Tsuneyoshi, 2011, p. 6) (Table 15.1).

The indigenous peoples, Ainu and the Okinawans, were incorporated into modern Japan in the late 19th century and now reside in their respective regions of origin (the northernmost island, Hokkaidô, and southern Ryûkû Islands) and as a diaspora in metropolitan cities. Okinawa was occupied by the US after World War II until 1972, which created another minority, the children of US servicemen and local women popularly called Amerasians. The buraku people descended from the outcastes of the feudal class system. While the institutional class system was discontinued in the late 19th century, buraku people have suffered from poverty and marginalization in employment and marriage ever since.

'Oldtimer' ethnic Koreans and Chinese are descendants of former colonial subjects who came to Japan (either by force or voluntarily) during Japan's colonial occupation of those territories, and hold special permanent resident status. They are popularly called '*zainichi*' Koreans and '*zainichi*' Chinese. *Zainichi* Koreans are diverse in terms of political affiliation (Seoul or Pyongyang regimes), age, and place of residence. In Osaka and Kawasaki cities, there are large Korean communities. One-quarter of the students in many government primary schools in one Osaka ward are *zainichi* Koreans. Both Korean and Chinese communities maintain fulltime ethnic schools, which run independently of the mainstream schools. Across the country about 10% of Korean and Chinese children attend them.

Newcomers have come to Japan voluntarily since the 1980s. Returnees from China (war-displaced Japanese and their families from North East China) and Indo-Chinese refugees started arriving in the 1980s. Then Japan's economic boom attracted foreign labor from Asia and South America. The 1990 revision of immigration law, which allowed South Americans of Japanese descent to work legally as unskilled labor, accelerated the process. The South American

Table 15.1 The estimated populations of minority groups

Minority groups	Japanese citizens	Non-Japanese citizens living in Japan
Ainu (indigenous)	Exact number unknown (24,000 self-categorized in Hokkaido; 300,000 in Japan)	
Okinawan	Exact number unknown (1.37 million in Okinawa-prefecture; 300,000 in other parts of Japan)	
Amerasians in Okinawa	Exact number unknown	
People of *buraku* descent	Exact number unknown (estimated 1.5–3 million)	
Ethnic Chinese	Exact number unknown (88,123 naturalized 1972–2003; 55,708 children of Chinese-Japanese marriages 1986–2005)	606, 889 (2007)
Ethnic Koreans	Exact number unknown (320,232 naturalized 1952–2008; 263,996 Korean-Japanese marriages 1955–2007; 133,253 children of Korean-Japanese marriages 1985–2007)	593,489 (2007)
Registered foreigners, excluding Chinese and Koreans		952,593 (including 316,967 Brazilians and 202,592 Filipinos)
Naturalized Japanese citizens	Exact number unknown (133,684 in 1952–2008, excluding ethnic Chinese and Koreans)	
Children of mixed descent where one parent is a Japanese citizen	Exact number unknown	
Japanese returnees	Exact number unknown (12,000 returned in 2008)	
Totals	**Exact number unknown (3.93–5.70 million or more)**	**2,152,973**

Source: Okano and Tsuneyoshi (2011), p. 6.

nikkeijin are descended from Japanese who migrated to South America in the late 19th and early 20th centuries. While most originally planned for a short-term stay, many ended up becoming long-term residents or remained permanently. In contrast to the Japan-born long-existing minorities, newcomers do not speak Japanese and are less familiar with cultural mores.

The categories that the national government employs to indicate student diversity are: (1) citizenship/nationality, and (2) any requirement for assistance in terms of Japanese language instruction. Figures 15.2, 15.3 and 15.4 respectively show the number of registered foreigners, the number of foreign children in government schools, and the number of students who require Japanese language instruction.

15.3.3 Social policy development

The national Ministry of Education has to date not articulated a comprehensive national policy to address the cultural and ethnic diversity of the student population as a whole. Instead, it has separate policies for different groups as described below.

The government's main social policies on the education of indigenous and buraku students has been to increase their school retention rates, by improving their living conditions and employment, and by providing scholarships. The Buraku Liberation League (BLL) initiated a civil rights movement challenging discriminatory employment practices, and lobbied governments, which in 1969 resulted in a ten-year program, Special Measures for Regional Improvement. It was renewed

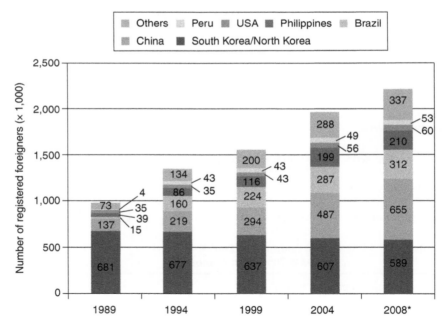

Figure 15.2 Population of registered foreigners in Japan according to the nationality
Note: The most recent data available as of September 2009.
Source: Immigration Bureau of Japan, Ministry of Justice, Japan. (2009) *Heisei 20-nenmatsu genzai ni okeru gaikokujin tourokusha toukei ni tsuite*. http://www.moj.go.jp/PRESS/090710-1/090710-1.html accessed 10 September 2009.

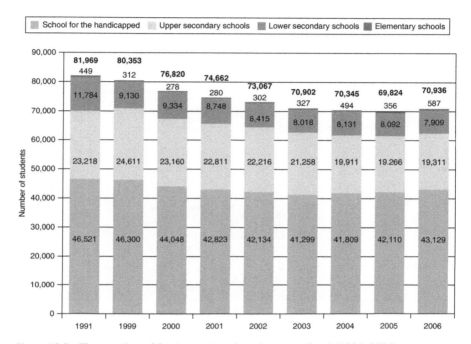

Figure 15.3 The number of foreign national students at school (1991–2006)

Note: Data were as of 1 May each year, and bold and italic numbers indicate the total numbers of students in each year.

Source: Ministry of Education, Culture, Sports, Science and Technology, Japan. (2009) *Kouritsugakkōni shūgaku suru gaikokujin jidōseito no suii*. http://www.mext.go.jp/b_menu/shingi/chousa/shotou/042/houkoku/08070301/009/002.htm accessed 10 September 2009.

in 1979 and again in 1989 continuing until 2002 when it was discontinued on the grounds that sufficient improvements had been made. The program also put '*dôwa* education' (a human rights education program taught across the curriculum to all students) on the national agenda, securing national government funding. Similarly, with respect to the Ainu, the First Hokkaido Utari Welfare Measures was implemented, at a cost of 12 billion yen, over the period 1971–1980, and then repeatedly renewed up to the present (1981–1987, 1988–1994, 1995–2001, 2002–2008, 2009–) (Hokkaidô-chô-kankyôseisaku-bu 2007, 2010). The Okinawa local government has received funding from Tokyo to improve the education of its local students. As seen later, these measures have worked to the extent that the gap in retention to Year 12 is now almost negligible.

Regarding the treatment of foreign nationals (including third- and fourth-generation Koreans), the government only issued a range of ad-hoc 'notices'. The current basic position is that all Japanese citizens are required to attend mainstream schools; and that non-citizens are expected to do the same, although this is not compulsory. The national policy has a complex history

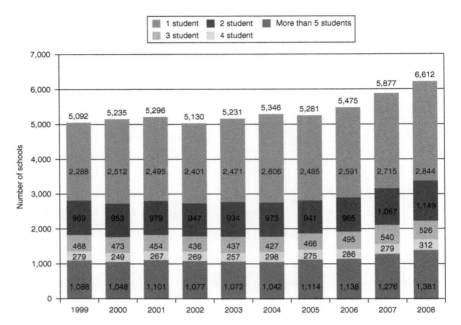

Figure 15.4   Number of children who require instruction in Japanese per school
Source: Ministry of Education, Culture, Sports, Science and Technology, Japan. (2009) *Nihongoshidō ga hitsuyō na gaikokujin jidō seito no ukeirejyoukyou tō ni kansuru chōsa.* http://www.mext.go.jp/b_menu/ houdou/21/07/__icsFiles/afieldfile/2009/07/06/1279262_2_1.pdf accessed 10 September 2009.

(Okano, 2011), but suffice to say here that the Ministry of Education's 1953 notice set the basic post-war 'principle of simple equality' (i.e., treating everyone in the same way). It stated that Korean permanent residents were to be treated in the same way as Japanese students, and all public schools were to accept them with the provision that the Korean students follow Japanese laws. However the Korean students were initially required to pay school fees, which did not apply to Japanese nationals (*Chôsenjin no gimukyôiku shôgakkô eno shûgaku ni tsuite*, 11/2/1953). Free compulsory schooling for Koreans came in 1965.

The next 25 years did not see any change in this passive policy. Then since 1991 the Ministry has gradually 'softened' the simple equality principle. For example, it retrospectively approved the operation of 'ethnic classes' (*minzoku gakkyû*) for Koreans (where students learn about their language, culture, and colonial history) at government schools under local government discretion, stating that 'ethnic classes during extra-curricular hours are exempt from the 'no special treatment' clause in the 1965 circular'. In the same year, 1991, with a sudden increase in the numbers of students from South America, the Ministry started collecting data on the demand for instruction in Japanese as a Second Language (JSL), in order to plan appropriate programs. The Ministry created a detailed JSL curriculum for primary schools in 2003, and for middle schools for 2007; and a guidebook for parents of foreign children ('Guidebook for Starting School') in several languages in 2005 (Monbukagaku-shô, 2003, 2005a, 2007). In March 2011 the Ministry issued a 68-page guidebook for schools and teachers about accepting 'foreign children' (Monbukagaku-shô, 2011), a belated addition to the large number of existing books of this kind produced by commercial publishers. The Ministry provides a homepage devoted to 'children living abroad and returnees' (*Kaigaishijo kyôiku kikoku-gaikokujin jidôseito kyôiku nado ni kansuru hômu pêji*, CLARINET); and only in March 2011 published another homepage which provides information for 'students with a special connection to foreign countries' (*gaikoku ni tsunagari no aru jidô seito no gakushû o shiensuru jôhô kensaku saito*, CASTANET).

In the current national curriculum guidelines (*gakushidô yôryô*, officially translated as 'course of study'), we see a departure from the simple equality principle. They advocate the need for special treatment for 'Japanese returnees and those in similar situations', including a clause under 'points to be considered when designing a teaching plan', that 'schools should promote their cultural adaptation to the Japanese school environment, and provide education that would effectively build on their prior overseas experience' (Monbukagaku-shô, 1998 and 2003a, 1998 and 2003b). The latest national curriculum guidelines (issued in 2008 with implementation from April 2011) for the first time acknowledged that the experiences and perceptions brought by foreign students can benefit their Japanese peers, and that schools consider providing foreign students opportunities to learn their own languages and cultures (Monbukagaku-shô, 2008a, 2008b). While these documents still adopt the category of 'foreigners'; the term is arbitrarily interpreted at the local and school levels.

It is local governments whose constituents include a large number of ethnic minorities that have more actively initiated policies to address the diverse student population, independently of the central government. In 2007 approximately 80 local governments maintained 'policies for the education of foreign nationals in Japan' (*zainichi gaikokujin kyôiku hôshin or shishin*) (Okano. 2006). Individual schools design and implement programs which support the policies, for example, bilingual Japanese as a Second Language programs in order to maintain students' home languages. Schools in localities with such policies are more readily able to run programs to assist ethnic minorities in response to emerging needs, since these programs gained more legitimacy in the eyes of local education boards and communities.

In sum, there are two main characteristics of Japan's social policies regarding ethnic minorities and education. They have been driven not by the national government, but by affected local governments and individual schools; and secondly, have targeted the education of specific ethnic/cultural minority groups, rather than all minority groups as a whole.

15.4   Three traditions in research on race/ethnicity and educational inequality

I have identified three research traditions in the studies on ethnicity and educational inequality in Japan. They are: (1) quantitative descriptions of educational outcomes; (2) case-studies of schooling processes with particular attention to discrimination, interventions, and identity formation; and (3) home culture.

15.4.1   Quantitative descriptions of ethnicity/race and educational inequality

One of the most striking features of quantitative descriptions of ethnicity/race and educational achievement in Japan is that each of them illustrates a specific ethnic group in a particular locality, and that it is almost impossible to gain a comparative picture of trends relating to these groups. Often the goals of these studies are to demonstrate the extent of the particular group's disadvantage (in terms of retention rate) and argue for continued funding from local governments.

Japan has not produced the kind of nation-wide quantitative survey that examines the relationship between 'ethnicity' and educational inequality, as described in this volume in relation to, for example, Australia and the Netherlands. This is despite the fact that sociologists in Japan have, since the 1950s, maintained a keen interest in social stratification, and the relationship between family background and educational achievement and employment success.

The nation-wide, large-scale Japan Social Stratification and Social Mobility surveys (SSM) started in 1955, following similar surveys conducted in industrialized countries at the time. It has been administered every decade since (1955, 1965, 1975, 1985, 1995, 2005). They have been funded by the government and designed by groups of sociologists, with the aim of informing the development of social policies; and have produced a large number of research papers and books. Their focus is how family social class background (as defined by occupation and education level) affects children's educational achievement and career trajectories. Up until the 1995 survey the participants were exclusively male.

To date neither race nor ethnicity has been a variable for these surveys. This is surprising when we consider that Blau and Duncan's work (1967), which illuminated the impact of race on occupational status achievement in the US, influenced Japanese sociologists in designing the subsequent Japanese survey in 1975. Kim and Inazuki (2000, p. 182) suspect that this is due to the relatively small proportion of 'foreign nationals' living in Japan compared with other industrialized countries, but foreign nationals represent only a part of ethnic diversity in Japan. To equate foreign nationals with ethnic groups is to exclude Japanese nationals of diverse ethnic descent, including indigenous peoples and those who have taken up Japanese citizenship. I would suggest that many sociologists might have uncritically assumed the homogeneous Japan thesis, or considered that the absence of reliable data on Japanese nationals of varying ethnic heritage made the task impossible. In later years, the failure to include race/ethnicity in these surveys has been considered highly problematic by some (e.g., Kawai, 1991; Shimizu, 2004; Sonoda, 2000). While studies of ethnicities appear in the urban sociology literature, ethnicity has never made it into the SSM.

In the six volumes of research papers covering the 1995 survey results, there is only one paper on ethnicity in a locality, by Kim and Inazuki (2000). It presents the findings of their own survey on *zainichi* Koreans which was based on the same questions as the 1995 SSM. Sonoda (2000) in the same volume, proposes that ethnicity be included as an important variable for future research. No papers in the third volume, on education and inequality (Kondo, 2000), mention ethnicity.

Given the absence of nation-wide quantitative descriptive studies on the relationship between race/ethnicity and educational inequality, I examine those conducted at the local level. All of these focus on a single ethnic minority group residing at a specific locality, rather than examining multiple groups.

15.4.1.1 Buraku

Amongst studies of quantitative description tradition, those on buraku children's educational achievement are by far the most numerous. They are conducted by local governments with buraku communities and a commitment to the human rights of minorities (e.g., Osakafu-kyôiku-iinkai, 1986, 1991, 1997; Fukuokaken-kyôikuiinkai-dôwakyôiku-jittai-chôsa-jikkô-iinkai, 1992; Hiroshimashi-Kyôikuiinkai-Dôwakyôikushidôka, 1996; Mieken-Kyôkuiinkai, 1996; Mino'oshi-kyôikuiinkai, 1990; Sen'nan-shi-Kyôikuiinkai, 1993). For example, Osaka prefectural education board surveys have examined educational achievement in the form of levels of literacy and numeracy, retention to post-compulsory schooling and tertiary education, school incompletion; and indicators of a suitable home environment for study (e.g. availability of study space and books, parental assistance with homework). They compared buraku children and non-buraku children in the same localities. These surveys reveal that the level of literacy and numeracy amongst buraku children have improved significantly. The gap in retention rate to post-compulsory education is almost minimal; but a significant difference remains in retention to higher education.

15.4.1.2 Ainu

The Hokkaidô prefectural government has conducted surveys on the indigenous Ainu population (Hokkaidô-chô-kankyôseisaku-bu, 2007), along with Hokkaido University's Centre for Ainu and Indigenous Studies (Sanai, 2010). They reveal that educational participation by Ainu children has increased over the years, helped by the Utari Welfare Measures that had been operative since 1971 in order to improve living conditions. The post-compulsory retention rate of Ainu children (i.e. into upper secondary school) has almost caught up to that of their non-Ainu counterparts, with a 5% gap remaining in 2006 (see Table 15.2). Of Ainu under 30 years of age, 95% completed 12 years of schooling; the figure falls with age, however (87 % of those 30–40 years old and 24 % of those over 70) (Nozaki, 2010). However, there remains a significant difference in tertiary entry rates: in 2006, less than 18% of Ainu students went on to university while nearly 40% of non-Ainu students took up tertiary study (see Table 15.3). The older generations of Ainu have achieved much lower levels of education.

Should they succeed in the competitive entrance examinations and gain a place in senior high school or university, Ainu children are still more likely to leave school before graduating. In 2009 survey (Nozaki, 2010), of those (of all age groups) who entered senior high school, 13% left before graduation in 2009; and this percentage is again higher amongst the older generations. Of those who entered university, one in five left before gaining a degree. The figure for those under 30 years old was 11%, while for those aged 60–70 it was 59% (Nozaki, 2010). It is not that Ainu people lack educational and career aspirations. Amongst those who already left school, 32% said that they had wanted to proceed to the next level of schooling, while 56% of those under 30 wanted to go to university (Nozaki, 2010, p. 63). The most frequently stated reasons for giving up a desire for further education were financial (78%), the need to obtain employment (25%), low academic achievement (14%), and mainly in the case of girls, parents' opposition (11%).

Parents' aspirations for their children's education are high: 64% want their children to attend university (i.e., post-secondary) and only 21% hope for

Table 15.2   Retention of Ainu children to upper secondary school compared with non-Ainu cohort, 1972–2006

Year	1972	1979	1986	1993	1999	2006
Ainu (%)	41.5	69.3	78.4	87.4	95.2	93.5
Non-Ainu in the same township (%)	78.2	90.6	94.0	96.3	97.0	98.3

Source: Hokkaidō-chō, Kankyōseikatsu-bu (2006). *Heisei 18-nendo Hokkaidō Ainu seikatsu jittai chōsa hōkokusho*. Sapporo: Hokkaidō-chō.

Table 15.3   Retention of Ainu children to university compared with non-Ainu cohort, 1979–2006

Year	1979	1986	1993	1999	2006
Ainu (%)	3.8	8.1	11.8	16.1	17.4
Non-Ainu in the same township (%)	31.1	27.4	27.5	34.5	38.5

Source: Hokkaidō-chō, Kankyōseikatsu-bu (2006). *Heisei 18-nendo Hokkaidō Ainu seikatsu jittai chōsa hōkokusho*. Sapporo: Hokkaidō-chō.

upper secondary school (Nozaki, 2010). Those parents who had to abandon their own desire for further education display a higher level of aspiration for their own children (Nozaki, 2010). As is the case with the national trend, Ainu in metropolitan Sapporo (Hokkaido's capital city) reach a higher level of schooling and have higher parental aspirations for their children's schooling (Nozaki, 2010). The gap between parental aspirations and their children's achievements may be due to the children's negative experiences of schooling, such as bullying and discrimination, which not only affect academic performance but also lead to alienation from school (Ueno, 2004). It may also be due to a relative lack of middle-class role-model adults who have built their careers on success at school, and also to the fact that parents are less informed regarding the workings of the school system and how to assist their children's school work.

15.4.1.3 Okinawans

Children in Okinawa have fallen behind the national benchmark in every aspect of educational participation. Okinawa prefecture has long had the worst retention rate to post-compulsory education and higher education, and the highest rate of non-graduation from high school (Nishimoto, 1999, 2001). It is also characterized by the highest unemployment and the lowest average incomes in the country. While the dominant explanation for this has been Okinawa's historical legacy, a limited employment market (due to reliance on the US military bases), and the peripheral geographical location, Nishimoto (1999) argues that the Okinawan preference for collaborative work is also an additional factor in discouraging individual competition based on merit.

15.4.1.4 Zainichi Koreans

In comparison with buraku and Ainu research, academic achievement has not been such a focus of studies of oldtimer Koreans ('*zainichi*', henceforth in roman type). The dominant approach in studying educational inequality of oldtimer Koreans have been ethnic education (*minziku kyôiku*) which enables Korean children to maintain their 'ethnic culture' and cultivate ethnic pride (Taiei Kim, 1994), institutional discrimination (which derives from the fact they are 'foreign nationals') and interpersonal discrimination in classes.

Small-scale surveys conducted by individual researchers and local governments suggest that Korean young people have performed less well compared with their Japanese counterparts, but that the gap has decreased considerably. For example, 84.9% of Korean students (in comparison with the same city average of 92.5%) went beyond compulsory schooling in 1978, but in 1990 the respective figures were 89.7% and 95.3% (Nakajima, 1994, p. 33). A 1993 survey on zainichi South Koreans (aged 18–30) revealed that the education level of those surveyed was not significantly different from the Japanese average; but that the gap between high and low achievers had increased (Fukuoka and Kim 1997: 20).

A survey of about 900 oldtimer South Korean males (using the same methods as the 1995 SSM) provided data most compatible with the SSM. It shows that there was no significant difference between ethnic Korean males surveyed and their Japanese counterparts, in terms of average years of schooling (12.35 and 12.01), and annual income (494 million yen and 531 million yen) (Kim and Inazuki, 2000, p. 189). Koreans in fact earned more. But the same survey showed that a much larger percentage of Koreans were self-employed (52% Koreans and 23% Japanese), indicating the discrimination they faced in the dominant Japanese labor market.

15.4.1.5   Newcomers

Research of this tradition on new immigrants is almost non-existent even at the local level. This is partly because new immigrants are assumed to perform poorly due to a lack of adequate Japanese language proficiency, at least in the short term. At local level researchers examined the consistently poor retention rate to post-compulsory education among new immigrants (Shimizu, 2008).

In sum, the tradition of quantitative description has asked how minority groups' achievements compared with those of non-minority students, by focusing on quantifiable survey data such as retention rate to post-compulsory schooling and academic performance. The studies found that the gap has substantially declined for all minority groups over the last several decades, but that it still exists for the entry into universities. The findings are however limited in that single-group focused studies have not enabled a comparative picture of these groups, a point that also applies to the other traditions.

15.4.2   Schooling process: Discrimination, the effects of school intervention, and identity formation

The most dominant research tradition in the literature on ethnicity/race and educational inequality has been the study of schooling processes, by means of observations and interviews. There are three aspects to this approach: (1) discrimination, (2) school intervention, and (3) identity formation of the minority students. Since most studies examine two or three of these aspects simultaneously, I will discuss them together under the broad heading of schooling processes. Chronologically, the initial emphasis was on the experience of discrimination, but studies since 1980 have added both school intervention and identity formation.

'Discrimination' ('*sabetsu*', the most frequently used term in discussions on minority education) refers to the marginalization that minority children experience in interacting with school peers and, to a lesser degree, teachers. The core of discrimination centers on the 'difference' that minority children bring to mainstream schools; but the nature of discrimination varies depending on the particular minority group. Interventions include a wide range of school-based programs to counter disadvantage, with the aim of making school a more comfortable place for minority students, assisting them to perform academically, and offering guidance for future education. The effect of these interventions is studied both in terms of advances that minority students have made in academic achievement and their educational decisions, as well as of the interactions' impact on the majority students' understanding of human rights issues. Both discrimination and school intervention affect minority students' identity formation, which in turn influences their educational achievement. This is because ethnic minority students' identity formation has a significant impact on the ways in which they appropriate what schools offer (Okano, 1995).

The focus in this tradition is on the lived experiences of students. Overt institutional discrimination exists only on the grounds of nationality (lack of Japanese citizenship) for oldtimer ethnic Koreans with special permanent resident status and new immigrants with or without such status. These studies examine interpersonal relationships, such as bullying, low expectations of academic achievement, exclusion, and marginalization, while adopting qualitative and/or ethnographic methods and examining a particular school or an ethnic community. They explore how the experiences of discrimination affect children's self-esteem, learning behaviors, expectations of themselves, educational achievement, and decisions about future academic careers and employment.

A key contribution to this research tradition is an Osaka University ethnographic study of buraku children in a rural fishing town in the 1980s (Ikeda, 1985, 1987; Nishida, 1990). It revealed home and school lives of buraku children that were not conducive to fostering educational attainment (as shall be discussed in the section on home culture), and the marginalization experienced in interacting with peers at school. This included bullying and stereotyping of buraku families. Teachers also held low expectations for buraku children's academic achievement. With large numbers of buraku children in the area, primary and middle schools suffered from 'flight' of non-buraku children. Sociologists explored factors contributing to buraku students' poor academic performance, in light of Ogbu's involuntary minority thesis (Nabeshima, 1991, 1993) and various reproduction theories including those proposed by Bowls, Bernstein, Bourdieu, and Willis (Kamihara, 2000). In contrast, buraku students in some urban schools no longer experience such overt discrimination, according to Nabeshima's interviews with buraku students and teachers, which might have contributed to many achieving well (Nabeshima, 2003). Nabeshima (2003) then explored how some schools with many buraku children manage to produce high-achieving students, in reference to the anglophone literature on effective schools. Regardless of geographical location, studies reveal that buraku children appreciate their teachers' support, who they saw as patient protection (e.g., Nishida, 1992).

I suspect that the apparent absence of overt discrimination from peers and teachers results at least partially from intervention programs that have been instituted in districts with large buraku population since the late 1960s. These interventions have included extra teachers for schools with substantial numbers of buraku children, scholarships for post-compulsory education, financial assistance (for books, school excursion, etc), and supplementary classes to assist Year 9 students to prepare for entrance examinations to senior high schools (Harada, 1999). Another notable intervention has been the initiation of '*dôwa* education' (literally 'egalitarian education') across the curriculum, whereby students learn about the history of buraku people and the unjust nature of discrimination (Hawkins, 1983; Shimahara, 1984). Schools with a substantial number of buraku children are designated as 'schools to promote *dôwa* education' (*dôwa kyôiku suishinkô*) and receive extra funding from their local education boards; they also provide professional development workshops for teachers in other schools.

A similar trend is observable in studies of zainichi Koreans. As Japan-born Koreans became less distinguishable from the majority Japanese by acquiring material resources, 'cultural mores', and Japanese language fluency over the decades, teachers, zainichi students and their parents state that overt discrimination is much less observable in classrooms than decades ago (Fukuoka and Kim, 1997; Okano, 1993). Over 90% of zainichi Korean students adopt Japanese names. Also the academic achievement of zainichi Korean students is not significantly different from their Japanese peers. Given this, research has turned to how intervention programs affect the school culture in ways that may be uncomfortable to zainichi Korean. These programs include scholarships for zainichi students, after-school ethnic education classes, extra-curricular high school clubs for the study of Korean culture (where zainichi students study their language and culture), and human rights education.

After-school ethnic education classes for Koreans (such as those in Osaka government schools) have been the major focus of studies on intervention programs. The effectiveness of these classes is influenced by the institutional status of specialist teachers (Usui, 1998) and by the relationship between ethnic class specialist teachers and regular teachers (Kishida, 1997). Zainichi students at schools which conduct human rights education across the curriculum tend to have higher levels of self-esteem and a positive outlook for their futures and therefore achieve better academically (Takenouchi, 1999). Okano's study (1993, 1997) examined how career teachers directed zainichi Korean students' decision-making about post-school destinations toward 'desirable' positions in the mainstream Japanese employment market, by discouraging them from taking up jobs in Korean business, and by providing preferential treatment in allocating jobs through the school-based job referral system on the grounds that zainichi Koreans face discrimination.

Studies on new migrants reveal more overt processes which marginalize them. This is because these students display features overtly different from the majority Japanese – they do not speak the Japanese language, are unfamiliar with the cultural mores of the school, and maintain distinctive behavioral patterns. Their parents are unable to assist them with their school work. They are initially placed in a special 'international class' (*kokusai gakkyū*) which caters for students who receive JSL (Japanese as a Second Language); as well as being members of mainstream homeroom classes. Unlike oldtimer minority students, immigrant students do not have the option of concealing their minority identity. Under these conditions, the process of marginalization for new migrants fundamentally differs from that for oldtimer minorities, in that their differences and assimilation are more emphasized (Shimizu Kokichi, 2000; Shimizu and Shimizu, 2001.

Guidance for 'cultural adaption' and JSL teaching are the two most prominent intervention programs that schools provide for new immigrant children. The main concern of the early research in the 1980s and 1990s on these programs was to 'assist' smooth integration into schooling in the 1980s and 1990s. In later years these programs have attracted critics who questioned the nature of the programs themselves. For example, based on observations, Oota (2000) argues that these programs represent Japanese schools' attempts to preserve long-existing practice for the majority Japanese, by refusing to make changes that are required to accommodate newcomers. Nakajima (2007) and Kojima (2001) question whether 'assistance' for migrant children is indeed helpful for them, noting that some teachers also raise these questions.

Later studies pay attention to a two-way process of 'cultural adaptation' and JSL teaching at school, illuminating the sense of agency that newcomer children display. Kojima's ethnography of primary schools (2006) argues that newcomer children do not simply accept what is given and suffer discrimination but selectively resist what is given and devise strategies to have more control over their lives. Yamanouchi's ethnography (1999) revealed that Brazilian middle school girls were aware of their marginalized positions in mainstream schools, and displayed their resistance by deviating from the mainstream Japanese norms (e.g. overt display of sexuality), and in so doing develop their own identity.

One of the major alienating factors for immigrant children is the uncertainty of their schooling in the future. Immigrant children's academic performance relative to the majority Japanese remains poor. Teachers initially attributed this to their lack of Japanese language skills and less than satisfactory progress in language development in the ensuing years. Studies suggest that immigrant children's language development is hindered by inadequate instruction on the part of schools, and by inadequate support at home (Miyajima and Oota, 2005; Sakuma, 2006; Kojima, 2006). Immigrant children normally acquire the fluency required for daily communication, almost indistinguishable to an untrained ear, in a few years of residence in Japan. At that point they cease to receive special JSL instruction; and the children's desire to conform to the majority accelerates this process. However linguistic studies reveal that they do not have sufficient academic language competence to achieve academically. Given the entry to post-compulsory senior high schools require competitive examinations, limited academic language competence restricts immigrant students' chances considerably.

In an effort to provide a pathway for such students some local education boards have instituted special entry examination schemes for immigrant children in respect of designated high schools (Shimizu, 2008; Okano, 2012). However, such institutional provisions alone are insufficient without immigrant-specific assistance and guidance provided by local middle schools and communities (Shimizu, 2008). Hirosaki's ethnography (2007) reveals how such assistance has influenced migrant children's decisions for post-school destinations and promoted immigrants' entry to senior high schools. An Osaka community provided a vertical network of teachers in local primary schools, middle schools, and senior high schools in order to facilitate immigrants' progression through schooling (Enokii, 2007).

The ultimate form of marginalization and exclusion of ethnic minority students is their withdrawal from school. This occurred to oldtimer minorities 50 years ago when they suffered from poverty and intolerable discrimination (resulting in now elderly oldtimers with limited literacy); but this rarely happens nowadays. Rather we now see newcomers' school non-attendance (*futôkô*, in the Ministry of Education's terminology), resulting from difficulty in keeping up with school work and feelings of isolation, in particular when study requires a more advanced level of academic language in middle school and beyond. Withdrawal can also be due to practical conditions of their parents' employment, which frequently requires moving on in search of employment, denying the family opportunities to form long-term relationships with community members. The process leading to these children's non-attendance and its consequences have been addressed in ethnographic studies by Miyajima and Oota (2005), Sakuma (2006) and Sanai (2003).

In view of this, Latin American communities established fulltime ethnic schools to provide education in their language for those who have opted out of mainstream Japanese schools. Ethnographic studies of these schools reveal that they offer a place of belonging for these young people (Sekiguchi, 2001; Haino, 2010), and that attendance in Brazilian ethnic schools is a deliberate transnational strategy which would enable the students to continue their education once returning to Brazil. But it is also true that Latin Americans without Japanese schooling (and what it entails) will find it difficult to secure permanent employment if they decide to remain in Japan in the long term (Okano, forthcoming).

Regional variations in the nature and extent of discrimination against ethnic minority groups are significant, depending on local demography and local government involvement in human rights/multiculturalism issues. In the case of new immigrants, in areas with high percentages of foreign nationals the Japanese residents tend to hold more negative feelings toward immigrants than other Japanese (Nakazawa, 2007). In the case of oldtimer buraku and ethnic

Koreans, the opposite is true, at least partly because Japanese residents have long interacted with these communities and also because these minority localities have long been involved in human rights education.

Only a limited number of the existing studies of ethnic identity discuss educational inequality. This is at least partially because improvement of material conditions was seen as a more effective means to advance educational achievement.

The studies on identity have undergone changes, as their material circumstances have significantly improved. Earlier studies emphasized that buraku children formed a negative group identity through the experience of poor material conditions and social conditions (e.g., poverty, low status, low payment occupations, poor levels of parental education and overt discrimination from the wider community), as will be seen in discussion on 'home culture'. They also internalized the majority Japanese negative perception of buraku and developed an inferior view of themselves, hiding their buraku background by 'passing' as Japanese (Wagatsuma, 1964; Hirasawa, 1983). Activists tried to develop positive buraku identity, by challenging such negative perceptions as unjust (Noguchi, 1987), or questioning the structural reasons for discrimination (a pre-modern class system) (Mori, 1990). This is precisely what *dôwa* education has pursued with some positive consequences (Shimahara, 1991). As material circumstances have improved and tangible differences became increasing invisible by the 1990s the group identity weakened (Harada, 1999; Nishida, 1992). This was in part due to the increasing awareness of human rights issues, which made overt discrimination in daily interactions less frequent. Nishida (1992) and Harada (1999) explored how buraku high school students form their identities under such circumstances and how developing a positive identity affected their academic performance and planning for their futures.

Indigenous Ainu and zainichi Koreans share a similar trajectory in shifting to a more positive identity, resulting from gradual improvement of material circumstances and less frequent discrimination. The 1997 Ainu Culture Promotion Act assisted an Ainu cultural revival to some degree. Zainichi Koreans, on the other hand, started to develop a hybrid 'zainichi Korean' identity, independent of the 'traditional' cultural features of the Korean peninsula (Taiei Kim, 1999). Studies on life stories also reveal varying types of zainichi identities amongst young people, and illuminate the plurality of zainichi identities which influence their educational decision making (Fukuoka and Kim, 1997; Kuraishi, 1996).

Studies on after-school 'Korean ethnic classes' (*minzoku gakkyû*) almost exclusively examine identity issues. These classes, held in government primary and middle schools, were started by concerned parents and teachers in the late 1940s, and later gained financial support from local governments in the Osaka region. For example, 103 Osaka metropolitan primary and middle schools ran ethnic classes in 2006, a quarter of all schools (Kouon Kim, 2009). Zainichi Korean students in schools offering ethnic classes tend to have a stronger identity as

Koreans (e.g. Taiei Kim, 1994). These classes originally focused on essentialist knowledge about Korea's culture and the zainichi history in Japan (emphasizing their unfair treatment), but were not as effective in assisting zainichi students to formulate a positive zainichi identity as was discussing their experiences with, and gaining understanding from their majority peers at school (Takenouchi, 1999). In more recent years many of the classes have become spaces for interaction amongst zainichi Koreans, empathetic majority Japanese students, buraku students, and newcomer immigrants (Kouon Kim, 2009).

Identities of new immigrants have been formed in ways that differ significantly from the experience of oldtimer ethnic minorities. These differences are overtly visible in terms of physical features, language use, mannerisms, and behavioral patterns. Newcomer minorities are diverse in their ethnic backgrounds, the largest number being ethnic Chinese and Latin Americans. The majority of the latter are of Japanese or mixed decent. Because of these tangible ethnic differences, the majority defines new immigrants in terms of what they see as essentialized and often 'traditional' cultural features (language, samba and other Latin dance styles, music and songs), and relegates these features to the periphery. Immigrant children learn that their 'culture' and language are not valued at school, are unable to perform well academically, and develop 'problematic' behavioral patterns at school (e.g., inability to focus for any length of time, early interest in the opposite sex, late homework completion, etc) (Sekiguchi, 2001; Yamanouchi, 1999).

In sum, this tradition of studying the schooling processes has explored three themes: (1) how minority students have experienced discrimination, (2) how schools' intervention programs have impacted the process, and (3) how minority students have formed ethnic identities. These studies have adopted ethnographic methods whereby a selected school is intensively researched and provides vivid descriptions of lived experiences of a single ethnic minority group. They found that the students face less overt discrimination than their parents' generation, due to improved living standards and the impact of school intervention programs.

15.4.3 Home culture approach

This tradition examines the lifestyles of ethnic minorities at home and in their communities, in order to explain their students' relatively poor academic performance. Surveys on home lives (*seikatsu jittai chôsa*) have been conducted by local governments and NGOs in order to identify aspects of ethnic minority groups' daily lives so that the findings can assist in formulation of effective social policies. This tradition has declined in recent years.

Several local governments in the Kansai and Kinki regions conducted such surveys in buraku communities and compared the results with those for non-buraku people (Osakafu-kyôiku-iinkai, 1991; Minôshi-kyôikuiinkai, 1990;

Moriguchishi-zainichi-gaikokujin-kyôikukenkyû-kyôgikai, 1994; Sen'nan-shi-Kyôikuiinkai, 1993). Aspects relating to children's education and child rearing practices include the number of books, individual study desks, attendance of cram schools, parental occupation and education levels, the parents' aspiration for their children's schooling, and whether a child has a personal television and other entertainment devices. These surveys revealed that buraku families provide fewer cultural resources, and more entertainment devices for their children, resulting in shorter time spent on studying at home.

These findings are consistent with qualitative studies, such as one of a rural buraku community by an Osaka University team (Ikeda, 1984, 1987; Nishida 1990). The ethnographic study of buraku children in a rural fishing town in the 1980s revealed aspects of the daily routine of buraku children's lives that are not conducive to children's study. For example, many of the parents received welfare payments, were engaged in dangerous or difficult physical work that were vulnerable to external factors such as weather, which resulted in a particular form of sub-culture and language use. These characteristics included a glorification of physical labor and strength, manliness, roughness and laughter, distinctive language use, a sense of close-knit community, and a lack of role models of adults who had built careers on the basis of a solid education.

Other studies also identified personal traits of buraku children that hinder their educational achievement, for example, limited capacity to focus over a period of time, to persevere, and be disciplined restricts the children's learning at school (e.g. Ikeda, 1987, p. 65). More recent changes in buraku families' child rearing practices and life-styles may have a less negative impact on their children's academic performance (Nishida, 2001; Nabeshima, 1994). Others argue that buraku children are now well-equipped with academic writing skills and understanding of abstract concepts (Osakafu-kyôiku-iinkai 1986). While attributing buraku children's failure to perform academically to culture clash between the buraku home culture and the school culture, the Osaka team also identified a limited number of buraku children who succeed against the odds.

More recent case-studies by Harada (2003) and Kamihara (2000), both on buraku communities in urban areas, reveal a somewhat different picture. In light of improved material conditions, they argue that the lack of appropriate cultural capital at home is the most significant contributor to the gap between buraku students and their non-buraku peers, although the daily experiences (*seikatsu jittai*) (as measured by, for example, low income level, instability of employment, poor quality housing), 'student sub-culture' (*seito bunka*), and self-esteem continue to influence. Buraku children are engaged in a 'recreational consumer culture' to a greater extent than non-buraku children, as seen in a greater ownership of personal televisions and computer games.

Surveys on the home lives of zainichi Koreans include questions about their participation in Korean community activities, interaction with Korean relatives and language use rather than poverty (Osaka-jinken-kenkyûkai, 1991; Tsujimoto and Kim, 1994; Taieo Kim, 1994). Studies on new migrants reveal that they tend to share a distinctive home culture. This is a result of parental absence at home (parents typically work long hours in peripheral employment market), parental inability to communicate with teachers (due to language problems), and their future plans for eventual return to their home countries (Sekiguchi, 2001; Haino, 2010).

In sum, this tradition has studied the culture of minority students' homes and communities in order to identify what contributes to the students' limited educational achievement. It adopts both quantitative surveys (e.g. the number of books in the home) and qualitative interviews (e.g. visits to homes). Studies reveal substantial diversity in the home culture, depending on parental occupations and regions.

15.5   Conclusions

I have examined how sociologists have studied the relationships between ethnicity/race and educational inequality in Japan during the period 1980 to the present, and identified three research 'traditions'. They are: (1) quantitative description, (2) schooling processes in relation to discrimination, school interventions and identity formation; and (3) home cultures. Quantitative descriptions drew on questionnaire surveys by local governments and university teams. Studies of the schooling process adopt observation and interviews with teachers, and minority students and teachers, often conducted by university-based scholars individually or in a team. Studies of home cultures uses both quantitative and qualitative methods.

One of the distinctive characteristics of these studies is 'localization'. No study has examined the relationship as a national phenomenon: and even the repeated social mobility surveys have not included ethnicity/race as a variable. Studies are based on selected localities, often with a focus on a single ethnic group. For example, Hokkaidô prefectural government has conducted surveys on indigenous Ainu (although Ainu also reside outside Hokkaidô, often in metropolitan cities), while the Okinawa prefectural government has focused on Okinawan residents. Local governments and NGOs have conducted surveys on numerous minorities in their own areas, such as Osaka authority's research on zainichi Koreans.

Given this, the dominant research tradition has been to study the schooling processes through a large number of small-scale observational studies. These studies examine three aspects in combination: discrimination, school interventions, and identity formations. Concerns include: how minority students experience discrimination from peers and teachers; how school intervention programs have assisted (or otherwise) minority students in improving academic achievement and affecting important educational decisions; how the home culture(s) of minority students have affected their school performance; and how these students develop ethnic identities in this process.

These studies reveal that in terms of retention to post-compulsory schooling the gap between ethnic minority and non-minority students had been minimized by 1990s. The gap in retention to higher education has also narrowed but still remains. The exception is the gap displayed by the new immigrants and their descendants, who started arriving in 1990s. Studies suggest that intervention programs have been effective to a degree. While minority students tended to form negative images of themselves by internalizing the majority perception of the minority groups in the schooling process, this has changed considerably due to both changing society perceptions of minorities and the success of school intervention programs on human rights.

All of these studies were intended to affect social policies regarding minority education in one way or another; but it is quantitative surveys that have provided the most immediate information for guiding social policies from early post-war years. Numerous surveys on buraku children by local governments, and repeated surveys on Ainu by Hokkaidô local governments are examples. These two groups received most attention since they are products of past institutional policies (i.e., the feudal system and internal colonization), and because they are Japanese citizens. These surveys are used to argue for the continuation of social policies for buraku and Ainu people. Quantitative surveys on zainichi Koreans (i.e., most are non-citizens) were conducted by their own organizations, who then used the results for lobbying governments.

Initiatives of qualitative studies, on the other hand, came from anthropologists and scholars of education, who were interested in the process leading to the relatively low educational achievement of minority groups that the quantitative surveys described. Teachers involved in human rights education and teachers' unions also collaborated with these scholars. This coincided with an emergence of interest in ethnography as a methodology amongst mainstream sociologists in Japan.

The dominant 'localization' trend in the Japanese research on the relationship between ethnicity/race and educational inequality is likely to continue. The potential to study the relationship as a national phenomenon (which covers all minority groups together) would be enhanced by inclusion of ethnicity/race as a variable in the regular Social Stratification and Mobility Surveys. As mentioned earlier, there are already calls for this from some sociologists in Japan. Growing interest in this research direction is also signaled by two recent publications: *Ethnicity and Education* (Shimizu ed., 2008), a collection of previously published Japanese language papers; and *Minorities and Education in Multicultural Japan* (Tsuneyoshi, Okano and Boocock, 2011), a collection of newly published English-language papers.

References

Blau, P. M., and Duncan, O. D. (1967). *The American occupational structure*. (New York: J.Wiley).

Enokii, M. (2007). 'Kodomo o tsunagu shien nettowâku zukuru' in K. Shimizu (ed.), *Kôkô o ikiru nyûkamâ* (pp. 117–139). (Tokyo: Akashi shoten).

Fukuoka, Y., and Kim, M. (1997). *Zainichi kankokujin seinen no seikatsu to ishiki*. (Tokyo: Tokyo University Press).

Fukuokaken-kyôikuiinkai-dôwakyôiku-jittai-chôsa-jikkô-iinkai. (1992). *Dôwa kyôiku jittai chôsa hôkokusho*. (Fukuoka: Fukuoka-ken Kyôikuiinkai).

Haino, S. (2010). *Burajirujin gakkô no kodomotachi*. (Tokyo: Nakanishiya).

Harada, A. (ed.). (2003). *Gakuryoku mondai e no apurôchi: Mainoriti to kaisô no shiten kara*. (Tokyo: Taba shppan).

Harada, T. (1999). 'Dôwachiku seito no aidentiti mondai: Tenkanki wo mukaeta dôwa kyôiku no kadai to tenbô'. *Osaka Daigaku Kyôikugaku Nenpô 4*, 33–43.

Hawkins, J. N. (1983). 'Educational demands and institutional response: Dowa education in Japan'. *Comparative Education Review, 27*(2), 204–226.

Hirasawa, Y. (1983). 'The burakumin: Japan's minority population'. *Integrated Education 20*(6), 3–8.

Hirosaki, J. (2007). 'Shinro tayôkô ni okeru chûgokukei nyûkamâ seito no shiro ishiki to shinro sentaku: Shien katsudô no torikumi o tsûjite no henyô katei'. *Kyôiku Shakaigaku Kenkyû, 80*, 227–245.

Hiroshimashi-Kyôikuiinkai-Dôwakyôikushidôka. (1996). *Kyôiku jittai hôkokusho*. (Hiroshima: Hiroshima-shi Kyôikuiinkai).

Hokkaidô-chô-kankyôseisaku-bu. (2007). *Heisei 18-nendo Hoddaidô Ainu seikatsu jittai chôsa hôkokusho*. Available: http://www.pref.hokkaido.lg.jp/ks/sum/somuka/ainu/jittai. htm (accessed 10 June 2008).

Hokkaidô-chô-kankyôseisaku-bu. (2010). Keizaiteki shakaiteki chii no kôjô o hakaruta-meno sôgôteki sesaku no suishin. Retrieved 29 November 2010: http://www.pref.hok-kaido.lg.jp/ks/ass/suisinhousaku.htm.

Ikeda, H. (1985). 'Hisabetsuburaku ni okeru kyôiku to bunka: Gyoson buraku ni okeru seinen no raifu sutairu ni kansuru esunogurafi'. *Osaka Daigaku Ningen Kagakubu Kiyô, 11*, 247–271.

Ikeda, H. (1987). 'Nihon shakai no mainoriti to kyôiku no fubyôdô'. *Kyôiku Shakaigaku Kenkyû, 42*, 51–69.

Kamihara, F. (2000). *Kyôiku to kazoku no fubyôdô mondai: Hisabetsu buraku no uchi to soto*. (Tokyo: Kôseisha Kôseikaku).

Kawai, T. (1991). 'Sengo nihon ni okeru kansôkôzô kenkyû no ashiato to tenki'. *Shakaigaku Hyôron, 42*, 47–56.

Kim, M. and Inazuki, T. (2000). 'Zainichi kankokujin no shakai idô' in K. Kôsaka (ed.), *Nihon no kaisô shisutemu 6: Kaisô shakai kara atarashii shimin shakai e* (pp. 181–200). (Tokyo: Tokyo Daigaku Shuppan).

Kim, T. (1994). 'Zainichi kankoku chIosenjjin no kodomotachi no ishiki no tayôsei: ijûchiiki no chigai o hikaku no jiku toshite'. *Kyôikugaku Ronshû, 20*, 34–51.

Kim, T. (1999). *Aientiti poritikusu o koete: Zainichi chIosenjin no esunishiti*. (Tokyo: Sekaishisôsha).

Kim, T. (2009). 'Taminzoku tabunka kyôiku to aratana kyôdôsei no kôchiku: Osakashiritsu shô chûgakkô no minzokugakkyû o jirei ni'. *Soshioroji, 53*(3), 91–107.

Kishida, Y. (1997). 'Tabunka kyôsei kyôiku to shiteno zainichi kankoku chôsenjin kyôiku: Minzoku kôshi to nihonjin kyôshi to no kankei o chûshin ni'. *Ibunkakan Kyôiku, 11*, 141–155.

Kojima, A. (2001). 'Nyûkamâ ukeirekô ni okeru gakkô bunka 'kyôkai waku' no henyô: Kôritsu chûgakkô nihongo kyôshi no sutorateji ni chûmokushie'. *Kyôiku Shakaigaku Kenkyû, 69,* 65–83.

Kojima, A. (2006). *Nyûkamâ no kodomo to gakkô bunka.* (Tokyo: Keisô-shobô).

Kondo, H. (ed.). (2000). *Nihon no kaisô shisutemu 3: sengo nihon no kyôiku shakai.* (Tokyo: Tokyo Daigaku shuppan).

Mieken-Kyôkuiinkai. (1996). *Mie-ken gakuryoku seikatsu jôkyô chôsa hôkoksho.* (Tsu: Mieken Kyôikuiinkai).

Mino'oshi-kyôikuiinkai. (1990). *Dôwakyôiku ni kansuru Mino'o-shi kyôiku sôgô jittai chôsa kekka hôkokusho.* (Mino'o: Mino'o-shi Kyôikuiinkai).

Miyajima, K. and Oota, H. (eds). (2005). *Gaikokujin no kodomo to nihon no kyôiku: Fushûgaku mondai to tabunka kyôsei no kadai.* (Tokyo: Tokyo University Press).

Monbukagaku-shô. (1998 and 2003a). Shôgakkô Gakushûshidô Yôryô. Retrieved 1 March 2011, http://www.mext.go.jp/a_menu/shotou/youryou/main4_a2.htm.

Monbukagaku-shô. (1998 and 2003b). Chûgakkô Gakushûshidô Yôryô. Retrieved 1 March 2011, http://www.mext.go.jp/a_menu/shotou/youryou/main4_a2.htm.

Monbukagaku-shô. (2003). Gakkôkyôiku ni okeru JSL karikyuramu shôgakkô-hen. Retrieved 15 March 2011, ttp://www.mext.go.jp/a_menushotou/clarinet/003/001/008.htm.

Monbukagaku-shô. (2005a). Gaikojin jidôseito no tame no shûgaku gaidobukku. Retrieved 15 April 2011, http://www.mext.go.jp/a_menu/shotou/clarinet/003/001.htm.

Monbukagaku-shô. (2007). Gakkôkyôiku ni okeru JSL karikyuramu chûgakkô-hen. Retrieved 15 March 2011, http://www.mext.go.jp/a_menushotou/clarinet/003/001/011.htm.

Monbukagaku-shô. (2008a). Shôgakkô Gakushûshidô Yôryô. Retrieved 1 March 2011, http://www.mext.go.jp/a_menu/shotou/new-cs/youryou/index.htm.

Monbukagaku-shô. (2008b). Chûgakkô Gakushûshidô Yôryô. Retrieved 1 March 2011, http://www.mext.go.jp/a_menu/shotou/new-cs/youryou/index.htm.

Monbukagaku-shô. (2009a). Kôtôgakkô Gakushûshidô Yôryô. Retrieved 1 March 2011, http://www.mext.go.jp/a_menu/shotou/new-cs/youryou/index.htm.

Monbukagaku-shô. (2011). Gaikokujin jidôseito ukeiru no tebiki. Retrieved 20 April 2011, http://www.mext.go.jp/a_menu/shotou/clarinet/002/1304668.htm.

Mori, M. (1990). 'Shakaiteki tachiba no jikaku to gakkô' in A. Nagao and H. Ikeda (eds), *Gakkô bunka: Shinsô eno Pâsupekuteibu.* (Tokyo: Toshindo).

Moriguchishi-zainichi-gaikokujin-kyôikukenkyû-kyôgikai. (1994). *Moriguchishi ni okeru zainichi kankoku chôsenjin o chûshin to shite jidôseito no seikatsu oyobi ishiki no jittai chôsahôkoku.* (Moriguchi: Moriguchishi-kyôiku-iinkai).

Nabeshima, S. (1991). 'Sengo gakuryoku chôsa ni miru hisabetsu buraku no kodomotachi'. *Buraku Kanhô Kenkyû, 78,* 71–101.

Nabeshima, S. (1993). 'Buraku mainorite to kyôiku tassei: JS Ogbu no jinruigakuteki aprurôchi o tegakarini'. *Kyôiku Shakaigaku Kenkyû, 52,* 208–231.

Nabeshima, S. (1994). 'Hisabetsuburaku komyuniti ni okeru katei no yôiku taido too kodomotach ni tassei iyoku ni kansuru kôsatsu'. *Buraku Kanhô Kenkyû, 98,* 69–83.

Nabeshima, S. (2003). *Kôka no aru gakkô: gakuryoku fubyôdô o norikoeru kyôiku.* (Tokyo: Kaihô shppansha).

Nakajima, T. (1994). 'Zanichi kankoku chôsenjin no esunishiti to kyôiku'. *Kyôikugaku Kenkyû, 61(3),* 29–37.

Nakajima, Y. (2007). 'Nyûkamâ no kyôiku shien no paradokkusu: Kankeino hitaishôsei ni chakumoku shita jirei kenkyû'. *Kyôiku Shakaigaku Kenkyû, 80,* 247–267.

Nakazawa, W. (2007). 'Zainichi gaikokujin no taka to gaikokujin ni taisuru henken tono kankei'. *Soshioroji, 52(2),* 75–91.

Nishida, Y. (1990). 'Chiiki bunka to gakkô: Aru gyoson buraku no fîrudonôto kara' in A. Nagao and H. Ikeda (eds), *Gakkô bunka* (pp. 123–146). (Tokyo: Yushindo).

Nishida, Y. (1992). 'Aidentiti poriteikusu no nakano aidentiti'. *Soshioroji, 37*(2), 3–20.

Nishida, Y. (2001). 'Buraku no seikatsu yôshiki: sono keishô to henka' in Burakukaihô-jinken-kenkyûsho (ed.), *Buraku no 21 kazoku: Raifuhisutori kara miru seikatsu no henka to kadai* (pp. 175–226). (Osaka: Kanhôshuppansha).

Nishimoto, H. (1999). 'Okinawa no gakuryoku mondai eno saiseisanteki apurôchi'. *Ryûkyû daigaku kyôikugakubu kiyô, 54*, 359–371.

Nishimoto, H. (2001). 'Okinawa no teigakuryoku mondai ni kansuru jisshôteki kenkyû'. *Ningen Kagaku, 9*, 1–17.

Noguchi, M. (1987). 'Kaihô undô: hokoriuru ikizama no kyôyû' in Y. Fukuoka (ed.), *Hisabetsu no bunka hansabetsu no ikizama*. (Tokyo: Akasho shoten).

Nozaki, T. (2010). 'Kyôiku hubyôdô no jittai to kyôiku ishiki' in T. Sanai (ed.), *Gendai Ainu no seikatsu to ishiki: 2008 nen Hokkaidô Ainu minzoku seikatsu jittai chôsa hôkokusho (Hokkaidô-Daigaku-Ainu-Senjûmin-Kenkyû-Sentâ)* (pp. 59–73). (Sapporo: Hokkaidô-Daigaku-Ainu-Senjûmin-Kenkyû-Sentâ).

Okano, K. (1993). *School to work transition in Japan: An ethnographic study*. (Clevedon, Avon: Multilingual Matters).

Okano, K. (1995). 'Habitus and intraclass differentiation: nonuniversity-bound students in Japan'. *International Journal of Qualitative Studies in Education, 8*(4), 357–369.

Okano, K. (1997). 'Third-generation Koreans' entry into the workforce in Japan'. *Anthropology and Education Quarterly, 28*(4), 524–549.

Okano, K. (2004). 'Minority's changing relationship with schools'. *International Review of Education, 49*(6), 1–22.

Okano, K. (2006). 'The global-local interface in multicultural education policies in Japan'. *Comparative Education, 42*(2), 473–491.

Okano, K. (2011). 'Ethnic Koreans in Japanese schools: Shifting boundaries and collaboration with other groups' in R. Tsuneyoshi, K. Okano and S. Boocock (eds), *Minorities and education in multicultural Japan: A interactive perspective* (pp. 100–125). (London: Routledge).

Okano, K. (2013). 'Ethnic schools and multiculturalism in Japan' in G. DeCoker and C. Bjork (eds), *Japanese education in the era of globalization: Enduring issues in new contexts* (pp. 85–100) (New York: Teachers College Press).

Okano, K. (2012). 'Languages and citizenship in education: Migrant languages in government schools' in N. Gottlieb (ed.), *Language and citizenship in Japan*. (New York: Routledge).

Okano, K., and Tsuchiya, M. (1999). *Education in contemporary Japan: Inequality and diversity*. (Cambridge: Cambridge University Press).

Okano, K., and Tsuneyoshi, R. (2011). 'Introduction: An interactive understanding for understanding minorities and education in Japan' in R. Tsuneyoshi, K. Okano and S. Boocock (eds), *Minorities and education in multicultural Japan: An interactive perspective* (pp. 1–26). (London: Routledge).

Oota, h. (2000). *Nyûkamâ no kodomo to nihon no gakkô*. Tokyo: Kokusai shoin.

Osaka-jinken-kenkyûkai. (1991). *Kodomo no kyôiku kankyô ni tsuite no ankêto chôsa hôkokusho: Osakashi ni oderu zainichi kankoku chôsenjin jidô seito o chûshin to shite*. (Osaka: Osakashi Gaikokujin Kyôikukenkû Kyôgikai).

Osakafu-kyôiku-iinkai. (1986). *Gakuryoku to seikatsu no kôjô o mizashite: 1985-nen hisabetsuburaku no kodomo no gakuryoku sôgô jittai chôsa hôkoku*. (Osaka: Osakafu Kyôikuiinkai).

Osakafu-kyôiku-iinkai. (1991). *Gakuryoku seikatsu kenkyûkai chôsa hôkokusho: Dôwa-chiku jidô seito no gakushû rikaido oyobi katei gakushû jôkyô nado ni tsuite*. (Osaka: Osaka-fu Kyôiku-iinkai).

Osakafu-kyôiku-iinkai. (1997). *Heisei-8-nendo gakuryoku seikatsu sôgô jittai chôsa shûkei kekka no bunseki to kôsatsu ni tsuite I II.* (Osaka: Osaka-fu Kyôikuiinkai).

Sakuma, K. (2006). *Gaikokujin no kodomo no fushûgaku: Ibunka ni hirakareta kyôiku toha.* (Tokyo: Keiso shobo).

Sanai, T. (2003). *Zainichi burazirujin no kyôiku to hoiku: Gunmaken Oota Ooizumichiku o jirei to shite.* (Tokyo: Akashi shoten).

Sanai, T. (ed.). (2010). *Gendai Ainu no seikatsu to ishiki: 2008-nen Hokkaidô Ainu minzoku seikatsu jittai chôsa hôkokusho.* (Sapporo: Hokkaidô Daigaku Ainu Senjûmin Kenkyû Sentâ).

Sekiguchi, T. (2001). 'Zainichi nikkei burajirujin seito no aidentiti no zentaizô'. *Ibunkakan Kyôiku, 15,* 162–187.

Sen'nan-shi-Kyôikuiinkai. (1993). *Sen'nan-shi gakuryoku seikatsu sôgô jittai chôsa hôkokusho.* (Sen'nan: Sen'nan-shi Kyôikuiinkai).

Shimahara, N. (1984). 'Toward the equality of a Japanese minority: The case of burakumin'. *Comparative Education, 20,* 339–353.

Shimahara, N. (1991). 'Social mobility and education: Burakumin in Japan' in M. A. Gibson and J. Obgu (eds), *Minority status and schooling* (pp. 327–353). New York: Garland Publishing.

Shimizu, K. (2000). 'Uragawa no nippon: Nikkei nanbeijin no dkasegi to gakkô kyôiku'. *Kyoôiku Shakaigaku Kenkyû, 66,* 21–39.

Shimizu, K. (ed.). (2008). *Kôkô o ikiru nyûkamâ: Osaka huritsu kôkô nimiru kyôiku shien.* (Tokyo: Akashi shoten).

Shimizu, K., and Shimizu, M. (eds). (2001). *Newcomer to kyôiku.* (Tokyo: Akashi Shoten).

Shimizu, M. (2004). 'Gakkô genba ni okeru kyôiku shakai gakusha no rinshôteki yakuwari no kanôsei o saguru: Nyûkamâ o shiensuru gakkô bunka henkaku no kokoromi o tegakari to shite'. *Kyôiku Shakaigaku Kenkyû, 74,* 111–126.

Sonoda, S. (2000). 'Tojita kaisô kenkyû kara hirakareta kaisô kenkyû e: Gurôbarujidai no kaisô mondai to nihon shakai' in K. Kôsaka (ed.), *Nihon no kaisô shisutemu 6: Kaisô shakai kara atarashii shimin shakai e* (pp. 223–240). Tokyo: Tokyo daigaku shuppan.

Takenouchi, H. (1999). 'Tabunka kyôiku to esunishitei: Zainichi kankoku chôsenjin shûjûchiku o jirei ni'. *Shakaigaku Hyôron, 49*(4), 531–543.

Tsujimoto, H., and Kim, T. (1994). *Oya to ko ga mita zainichi kankoku chôsenjin hakusho.* (Tokyo: Akashi shoten).

Tsuneyoshi, R., Okano, K. and Boocock, S. (eds). (2011). *Minorities and education in multicultural Japan: An interactive perspective.* (London: Routledge).

Ueno, M. (2004). 'Ainugo no hukkô to hukyû niokeru media riyô no torikumi nitsuie: Ainu Taimuzu to FM Nibutani hôsô no jirei o chûshin ni shite'. *Waseda Daigakuin Kyoôikugaku Kenkyûka Kiyô, 11*(2), 23–34.

Usui, T. (1998). 'Zainichi chôsenjin kyôiku no unei ni okeru shoshikitekina yôin no eikyô: Gaikokujin kyôiku shutansha kahaikyôin minzokukôshi no ichizuke no jittai bunseki o tooshite'. *Ibunkakan Kyôiku, 12,* 94–109.

Wagatsuma, H. (1964). Buraku shusshinsha no jikozô. In H. Wagatsuma (ed.), *Jiga no shakai shinri.* (Tokyo: Seishin shobô).

Yamanouchi, Y. (1999). 'Zainichi nikkei burajirujin tîn eijâ no teikô'. *Ibunkakan Kyôiku, 13,* 89–103.

16

Russia

Leokadia Drobizheva and David Konstantinovskiy

16.1 Introduction

Problems of actual Russian ethnic minorities are primarily conditioned on the multi-ethnic population of the country, which is a result of the historical development of the country. Russia comprises many regions in which numerous indigenous ethnic groups are living.

Migration streams are a new problem for Russia. These streams consist of immigrants who move to Russia for permanent residence and labor migrants who come to Russia for temporary or seasonal jobs, particularly from newly independent countries, former republics of the USSR, driven by a lower standard of living and higher levels of unemployment in their origin countries.

This chapter reviews research that was undertaken at a very important period of Russian history. In the last decades, between 1980 and 2010, large changes to political, economic, etc. conditions in Russia have taken place. Today Russian society has new features combined with several enduring ones.

For political reasons research into ethnic problems did not develop in the Soviet Union. After the changes that took place in Russia during more recent years, studies on ethnic inequality have been restarted and actualized. Researchers have paid particular attention to problems relating to equality of access to education.

This chapter includes several sections. After a description of the national context, the educational system of the country, ethnic groups and main migration patterns, and social and educational policy developments, we outline the main principles of methodology employed for this review. Then, in the section titled 'Ethnicity and educational inequality in Russia', the following research traditions are considered: languages of school education; school quality and ethnic background; socio-cultural differences and education; problems of migrants and receiving society; and students' inter-ethnic relations.

16.2 National context

16.2.1 Educational system in Russia

Preschool education is not compulsory in Russia, but it is much desired by families who wish for their children a good education, choice of profession, and successful life careers. Families can start preschool education for their children at any age. It is provided in kindergartens, as well as in various cultural and educational centers, and in the schools themselves; often it is experienced in families.

Elementary (primary) school education is compulsory. It takes three years starting at age six or seven years. From about age nine or ten, the state guarantees its citizens 'basic' education. After a total of nine years school education pupils are granted with certificates on graduation of the basic school. Students can continue their education in three ways: vocational schools, four-year colleges, and high schools.

Graduates of basic schools can apply to the vocational schools Enrolling to vocational schools is free (without exams) and after two years students can obtain employment as a blue-collar worker in industry, agriculture, etc. or as an office worker in the service sector (as an accountant, secretary, etc.). Concurrent to vocational skills, a program of general education is usually practiced.

Graduates of basic school can also enter colleges. Entrance to colleges is through competitive entry exams. After four years students can obtain the certificate of secondary special (semi-professional) education. This degree also enables graduates to work in different spheres. Vocational school graduates can also enter colleges. Adolescents who continue school learning in high schools receive high school certificates following a two-year education (Figure 16.1).

Schools can be state-owned and non-state. In 2010 private schools amounted to 1.36% of all educational institutions that provided programs of general education; there were 0.55% of all pupils enrolled in private schools (Initial data, 2010). There are also confessional schools but they are not numerous. Curriculum in non-state schools must correspond to the state standards. There are national (that is ethnical) schools (*natsional'nie shkoli*) in national (that is ethnical) regions (*natsional'nie regioni*) where education is carried out in the native language. These regions and schools are called 'national' (not 'ethnic') in Russia, in regard to the Russian tradition. In the Soviet period there was a line incorporated into the personal document identifying the 'Nationality' of the document owner, for instance 'Russian', 'Ukrainian', 'Jewish', or 'Tatar', according to the ethnicity of the person's parents or one of them. Now it is no longer mandatory, but ethnicity is still referred to as 'nationality'. Almost all schools are co-educational (girls and boys learning together), with very exceptions. Education can be free of charge or tuition fees payable. Besides that, the payment of 'non-formal' fees is widespread.

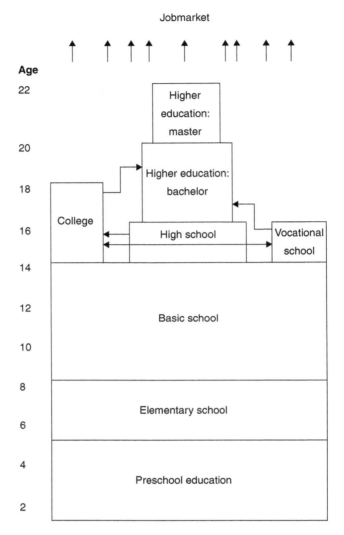

Figure 16.1   Structure of the Russian educational system

Schools vary greatly in both the quality of education processes (including teachers' qualifications, conditions of building, and so on) and education outcomes which are now measured by the Unified State Exam. Recently school ratings have appeared; but this is only a start of ranking and the public does not use it, not even in Moscow. The Unified State Examination (USE) was introduced into practice recently and includes tests on the main curriculum subjects. Its aim is the independent assessment of the student's academic achievements; entering into the universities is dependent upon the USE scores. The number of schools with high educational quality is rather limited. They are predominantly situated in the largest cities, and charge tuition fees. Thus, the learners in the good schools are principally children from wealthy families (Konstantinovskiy, 2012, pp. 17–19). The problems of access to quality schooling are one of the most pressing in today's Russia. This is reflected in the research reviewed; the accessibility of different levels of education depending on the urbanization of residence, status of parents, family economic conditions, and other factors is analyzed.

High school graduates can enter vocational schools and colleges where it is possible to obtain a professional qualification in a shorter period of time than the graduates of basic schools. There are also possibilities to enter the labor market without any professional education, on the background of a high school education. But mainly high school graduates enter universities that support daytime, evening, or distance learning. In 2010 there were 1115 higher educational institutions; 462 (41.43%) of these were private, and these enrolled 17.0% of all university students (from a total pool of 7,049,815) (Initial data, 2010). Based on their results in the USE high school graduates can be admitted to more or less prestigious universities. School contest winners have advantages. After a four-year university education students receive a bachelor degree. A bachelor can be admitted to a master's degree programs on a competitive basis and graduate in two more years.

Enrollment in a prestigious university that opens prospects of social mobility depends on the quality of school education. So the students from wealthy families have more chances to enter prestigious universities, gain access to professions and have the best variant of life career (Konstantinovskiy, 2012, pp. 14–16). In recent years both the numbers of and enrollments in universities have increased. This is particularly linked to the requirements of employers who prefer graduates. But often employers do not need an education but a qualification so many students seek a diploma, not knowledge.

Families (youngsters and their parents) make decisions about whether or not to further their children's education after basic school, or any other institution, on their own. Families also choose any educational institution independently. The principal criteria besides child's and parents' aspirations are the child's academic achievements and the family's financial resources.

College and vocational school graduates are also eligible to apply to universities. On the other hand, a university graduate can go on to obtain professional qualifications in colleges and vocational schools. To gain entrance into particular professions or obtain advanced training there are also professional courses and other forms of supplementary education. It is also possible to obtain a second higher education qualification or enroll at graduate school. In compliance with the tendencies of the labor market towards skilled workers, adult education, life-long education, and informal/non-formal education is encouraged.

16.2.2   Ethnic groups and main migration patterns

The population of Russia consists of numerous indigenous ethnic groups in regions, which are part of the Russian Federation. This is a result of the historical development of the country; modern Russia has inherited the multi-ethnic structure of the population from the Soviet Union and pre-Soviet Russia.

In the USSR Russians comprised 51.0% of the population; in Russia, 80.9% of those who mentioned their ethnicity. The most numerous after Russians are Tatars (3.7%), Ukrainians (1.7%), Bashkirs (1.15%), Chuvashs (1.05%), Chechens (1.04%), and Armenians (0.8%) (Census, 2010). The latest census recorded 182 ethnic groups living in Russia. The majority of them are indigenous peoples.

The most numerous indigenous ethnic groups have their own administrative-territorial units. After some changes had taken place in the country during the last decades the number of such administrative-territorial units increased. In Soviet Russia there were 16 autonomous republics, currently in the Russian Federation there are 21.

Some ethnic groups are referred to as national (that is ethnic) minorities (*natsional'nie men'shinstva*) – the word 'national' is used in accordance with the above-mentioned tradition. Firstly, there are the smaller indigenous groups that do not hold their own administrative-territorial units. For example, these are the people living in the east and north of Russia: Nivkhs, Ulchis, Nganasans, Yukagirs, Negidalts, Nanais, Ences, Tofalars, Oroks, and others. Aissors, Gypsies and several other peoples living in Russia are also referred to as national minorities.

Secondly, 'national minorities' includes ethnic groups that have state bodies outside Russia. They are, for example, Armenians or Georgians (even in the Soviet Union era these were among the most well-educated ethnic groups). Those diasporas have been enlarging intensively in the last decades after the collapse of the Soviet Union. The percentage of Armenians and Georgians in the Moscow population increased by three times, and that of Azerbaijanians 4.5 times, for the period from 1989 to 2002 (Zajonchkovskaja and Mkrtchan, 2009, p. 32).

Migration streams are a new problem for Russia. But these streams increased quickly. There are three main types of migration streams: compatriots or the Russian-speaking population in the newly established states, the former USSR republics, who migrate to Russia (predominantly from Middle Asia and the Baltic); immigrants who move to Russia for permanent residence; and labor migrants who come to Russia for temporary or seasonal jobs. The last two categories are also mostly citizens of new independent countries, former republics of the USSR. In majority they are the representatives of indigenous ethnic groups of these countries. The major reason for their migration is a low standard of living and high rates of unemployment in those countries.

The stream of compatriots has reduced in more recent years, subsequently the number of repatriates will continue at a rate of 50–100 thousand people per year. The number of immigrants from former Soviet republics who seek permanent residency in Russia amounted to 175 thousand people in 2006. The number of labor migrants is estimated by experts at 5 million people (Kliucharev and Mukomel, 2008, p. 310).

In the 1990s the Russian Federation already occupied the third place in the world after the United States and Germany regarding the number of immigrants received from other countries. The main proportion was shared between Moscow, St Petersburg, Yekaterinburg, and various border areas. 'Elite' migration has been replaced by the ordinary: 84% of migrants in Russia (80% in Moscow) considered themselves as the representatives of poor and extremely poor groups (Tiurukanova, 2009, p. 153).

The situation of migrants is complicated and heterogeneous. They include groups from various socio-economic statuses, and vary widely in their level of education as well. At the end of the 1990s, in Moscow 54% of Georgians, 51% of Armenians, and 27% of Ukrainians were highly qualified specialists (compared to 42% of Russians). However, 50% of migrants in Russia considered themselves as without vocational education. Researchers estimate that 9% of migrants do not have a 'good' Russian-language level and 28% are not fluent (Tiurukanova, 2009, p. 153).

16.2.3 Social and educational policy and developments

In recent decades there has been growing recognition and discussion of social and educational policies in Russian society and the academic community. Of primary importance are the problems of equality of access to education, and the quality of the education offered. Increasing equity in access to good-quality education has been declared an important part of official social policy, several steps are being taken to develop preschool education in order to smooth the inequality, and the educational system is in the process of modernization as a whole, but the results so far leave much still to be achieved (Gimpelson and Kapeliushnikov, 2011, p. 569).

These issues are essential to the total population and all ethnic groups. The social and educational policy (or at least the declared one) in the part that is related to the alignment of access to the quality education is aimed at all ethnic groups equally. However, there are some peculiarities for specific ethnic groups. To understand them, we need to delve a little further into the history of the implementation of social and educational policy in Russia.

In the first part of the Soviet period, in the 1920s, in the official public sphere the ethnic aspects of educational problems were interpreted as a concern of the Soviet rule for the education of peoples, and part of 'solving the national issue' (or '*reshenie natsional'nogo voprosa*' as it is formulated in the official documents, literally translated 'solution of the national question'). The 'solution of the national issue' was considered in the light of the 'alignment of economic and cultural development of peoples' and getting over the discrimination that existed prior to this time. This was supposed to effect involving all the ethnic groups in the social processes initiated by the Soviet authorities, including the provision of education. Almost all ethnic groups have since been involved in formal education, both general and vocational. For various reasons many groups were previously deprived of this opportunity (for some there were restrictions on their participation based on ethnic or caste status, others lacked a written language, and so on). In the 1920–1930s written languages were created for 50 ethnic groups that had previously lacked them.

Beyond the official discourse, the Soviet authorities had a practical interest in dissemination of education among minority peoples. At that time Russians made up just half of the population, and an educated personnel was needed for the desired urbanization and industrialization of various regions of the country. In addition, the Soviet ideology was propagated through the state educational system. In the last decades of the USSR it was officially considered that the 'national issue' was solved, although that was not entirely true (Bromley, 1987, p. 162). Today there still remain some anomalies in the situation for ethnic groups.

For numerically small indigenous peoples there is a special law that supports the traditional forms of economy and culture. For some of them elementary school education is organized in their mother tongue, but, generally, the language of instruction is Russian. The law offers them benefits of receiving vocational education including higher education. The benefits provided to these ethnic groups persist.

In the administrative-territorial units where more numerically large ethnic groups live the social and educational policy is formed under the influence of several factors; it is flexible and can vary according to the changing political, economic, or demographic situation. The policy problems to be solved are related to the preservation of the native language in education, the possibility of obtaining education of high level and quality by all ethnic groups, the increase of the human capital in an ethnic group, and competition between ethnic groups living in the administrative-territorial units. Policy is required to address the interests of both local (regional, ethnic) and federal levels. With some simplification it can be argued that local interests are often related to lobbying the expectations of the ethnic group, and federal interests reflect the protection of cultural integrity and preservation of at least the framework of uniformity of the educational system. This is partly reflected in the following sections of the chapter.

In the last few years the migrant population has become increasingly important in relation to social and educational policy. Within Russia, as elsewhere, popular views on the influx of migrants range from recognition and tolerance to rejection and xenophobia. But the objective situation is that with a decreasing population as a whole, and the working-age population especially (Statistical Bulletin, 2006, p. 55), Russia cannot do without the influx of migrants. So in 2005 it was decided to liberalize the policy, going forward in a new direction in order to attract migrants into the country. This makes problems of educational opportunities for all groups of population more concrete.

The problems of inequality within education identified by researchers are additionally complicated because in practice the state's social policy does not include ethnic aspects. Protection of society's most vulnerable or 'at risk' is just discernible in it. As in other states with similar situations, the invisibility of ethnicity in social policy does not eliminate the competition between ethnic groups, who claim their desire to participate in the distribution of resources – whether material, political, or symbolic.

16.3   Methodology

Since Soviet officials declared that the 'national issue' was resolved, the investigation of ethnic problems in education has not really developed in Russia. Differences in the level of education or its accessibility for ethnic groups were not discussed in scientific literature (Bromley, 1987, p. 162). But some sociological surveys and even government statistics made it possible to analyze ethnic and other forms of disparities in Soviet education (Dobson, 1988).

The study of all kinds of inequalities was excluded for a long time on ideological grounds. The myth of equal opportunities along with other myths was an important part of ideology in Soviet Russia. It was supported by official propaganda not only through repeated slogans, but also through statistical data, which had to look convincing. In particular, data on representation of industrial and farm workers, women and national minorities in the educational system were published as a proof of equal opportunities.

The Soviet society was not free from unequal opportunities including its educational system, in status transmission and other phenomena common in other societies. In spite of ideological pressure a task-oriented sociological survey on inequality in education and other youth problems was conducted in Siberia (Shubkin et al., 1968). Later this research trend was developed in other surveys (Konstantinovskiy and Shubkin, 1977). They were more intensively conducted when the political situation in the country changed, and they continue to the present time (Konstantinovskiy, 2003, pp. 232–255). It should be pointed out that the inequality of ethnic groups in education is studied most often as a part of various forms of wider inequality, for example, a status inequality. Nevertheless, there is significant literature in which inequality of ethnic groups in education is investigated.

Since research on ethnic inequalities in education in Russia has been in progress for just a few years, we can only review a small sample of studies on the topic. In practice, these studies have been conducted by Russian researchers, published in Russia, and written in Russian. This is the result of the specifics of Russian social science development more generally and traditions of research on this subject in particular. This review therefore has as an important aim to present Russian research on this topic to the broader English readership.

We used two criteria to select literature to review. The first criterion was the kind of education: we limited research to that on preschool, primary, secondary, and vocational (especially higher) education. The second criterion was on the most important problems (evident or latent) that were illuminated by the researchers: studying native languages, gaining social status by education, and so on.

Various sources were used. First, we included social science journals such as the *Journal of Comparative Research in Anthropology and Sociology*, *European Journal of Sociology* and so on; Russian journals included *Sociologicheskiy zhurnal* ('Sociological Journal'), *Sociologicheskie issledovanija* ('Sociological Researches'), and *Sociologija obrasovanija* ('Sociology of Education'). Publications made in regions and national republics along with those made in the Moscow publishing houses were also studied. We included as well official materials, for example, reports of national republics' ministries of education, and materials prepared by the state and departmental statistics. We explored also some electronic resources: Scopus, Google Scholar, Web of Sciences, Sociological Abstracts, Sociopedia and the Russian search engine Yandex, the Russian Federal Educational portal, websites of universities (for example, Moscow State University, Higher School of Economics) and institutes of the Russian Academy of Sciences (for example, Institute of Sociology, Institute of Social-Political Research), websites of the Ministry of Education and Science of Russian Federation (RF), regional Ministries of Education, and so on, for the period between 1980 and 2010.

Russian Science Citation Index and Russian Science Electronic Library (both databases that are in progress) were used as far as it was possible at the time of writing. Materials from archives of the Ethno-Sociology Department of the Institute of Sociology of Russian Academy of Sciences (RAS) and unpublished manuscripts were also useful. Finally, expert opinions and assessments expressed at seminars or conferences are also considered for this review. It was very helpful that Russian researchers of ethnic problems concentrate around the Ethno-Sociology Department of the Institute of Sociology of RAS and Russian researchers of education concentrate around Department of Sociology of Education of RAS.

16.4   Ethnicity and educational inequality in Russia

16.4.1   Languages of school education: problems and conflicts

The first research tradition explores how the growth of the national movements in ethnic regions made enlarging the role of mother language one of the main aims and conditions of the national revival. The use of ethnic minority languages in pedagogy and curriculum took on special significance since the period of crisis of the USSR. But with the lapse of time unexpected conflicts and problems were discovered.

At the end of 1980s and in the 1990s the challenging social atmosphere in national regions focused the attention of society on the issue of language used for educational tasks. In Baltic Soviet republics, Ukrainian, Armenian and Georgian national movements aspired to achieve the legal declaration of their languages as the 'official' one. The same recognition was sought in various other regions as national movements tried to achieve the recognition of their languages as the official languages of the area on an equal basis with Russian.

Those demands were realized through legislation. In the former Soviet republics, which were taking steps on the way to their independence, the languages of the titular nationalities became the only official one. The languages of minority nationalities in the constituent republics of the Russian Federation were proclaimed as official alongside Russian.

Discussion of language in education issues at national schools is based on the wording of the legislative documents. The learning of Russian language is mandatory for all Russian citizens but citizens also have the right to study in their mother tongue. This is guaranteed by the RF Constitution (Articles 68, 72, 62.2) and RF Law 'On languages of nationalities in the Russian Federation'.

In general, in primary schools humanities are taught in 16 of the minority official languages of nationalities of Russia, in two languages in basic schools, and in ten languages (Altai, Bashkir, Buryat, Mari, Tatar, Udmurt, Chuvash, Evenki, Yukagir, Yakut) predominantly in secondary schools. Obviously not all nationalities can currently possess the opportunity to study in their mother tongue; in other cases the mother tongue is taught as a curricula subject. On the whole the number of languages in which general subjects are taught rises up to 80.

In the Republic of Bashkortostan, the largest republic in Russia, 45% of all schools teach in different languages; in Tatarstan the ratio reaches 60%, and in Tyva (a republic of approximately 300,000), it is 80%. Generally in Russia 56% of the schools teach in the language of the ethnic minority or allow students to study their mother language.

In the majority of autonomous republics of RSFSR (in the USSR) from the 1970s to 1980s national languages were mostly not taught (except in the first grades of primary schools). Sociological surveys pointed out that the general population both in cities and villages apparently supported the enlargement of Russian schools (Guboglo, 1972, p. 232). But with the growth of national movements intellectuals classed the loss of mother language as one of the main abuses inflicted on the culture (Drobizheva et al., 1996, pp. 263–280), an actual expression of Russification and disruption of minority ethnic cultures.

The new status of the language of titular nationalities, as a result of changes in the country, evidently was to satisfy feelings of national pride. The network of national schools was enlarged, and in several republics (Karelia, Komi, Khakasia and others) it was re-established. As a result, many youth of different ethnic origin have gained the opportunity to choose the language of (at least part of) their education.

Unequal opportunities in the educational sphere remain not least because of the fact that university-level education in the country is still predominantly realized in Russian. It is important to note that the USE that gives admission into universities is produced in Russian only. Applications to admission to the university and colleges from those pupils who studied at schools in their mother language (at national schools) failed.

In political science a new subdiscipline of political linguistics has been formulated in which, with a regard to theories of rational choice, economic efficiency, symbolic measurements, and strategic marketing of the opportunities for social mobility, the issue of university admissions of national school graduates were studied. Some significant research using qualitative and quantitative methods has been conducted in Tatarstan (Muhariamova, 2003; Muhariamova, 2004, pp. 58–66).[1] In this republic one of the most noticeable national movements took place for the purpose of declaring the status of republic and sovereignty inside the federation, assuring the equality of languages and realization of people's rights to study in their mother language, establishing actual bilingualism. Those demands can be said to have become models, examples for other autonomies in the Russian Federation.

As a result, in 1994 63% of Russian parents in Tatarstan did consider it important for their children to learn the Tatar language (data is based on the research findings). The Tatar language was taught as a mandatory subject in Russian schools of the republic. But towards the end of the first decade of the 2000s (in 2010–2011) the situation changed, and some conflicts emerged.

Surveys among the school graduates conducted by the sociologists of Tatarstan in 2006 pointed out that the number of students preferring to study mathematics and physics in Russian is four times more than those preferring to be taught in the Tatar language; for history and social science Russian is preferred 3.0–3.5 times more than the national language. Sociologists presented excerpts from interviews with some students: 'I'd choose Russian school since Russian school graduates study all sciences easier, the university education is more available to them'; 'Tatar language is needed only for oneself'; 'One can learn Tatar language in the family' (Muhariamova and Andreeva, 2008, p. 103).

Some Russian parents were not satisfied that a lot of time was spent on Tatar language studies at the expense of Russian and that the principle of voluntarily learning of Tatar language in Russian schools was abandoned. Among the Tatar population such opinions were qualified as the absence of mutual understanding. Nowadays in Tatarstan the same distribution of lesson hours between Russian and Tatar languages still remains.

In other republics the numbers of Russians supporting the learning of languages of titular nationalities evidently started to decrease. For example, in 1994 53% of Russians in Sakha (Yakutia) wanted their children to study Yakut language, and in 1997 this number had decreased to 24% (Korostelev, 1998, p. 192).[2]

The learning of Russian at schools gives a better knowledge of the Russian language and increases the opportunities of upward social mobility for the titular nationalities students. While some Russians assess the learning of titular nationalities languages also as prospect to expand their opportunities of upward social mobility in the future; others consider it a waste of time that impedes their final preparations for Russian exams. Meanwhile, the attitude toward learning of a titular nation language reflects and contains shades of political and symbolic meaning; it is viewed as an attitude toward the culture and status of the nation itself by whose name the republic was named.

It is important that the maintenance of national (ethnic) schools is considered in political public space as a component of democracy, realization of human rights, assurance of ethnic groups' rights to study in their mother tongue with a glance to their distinctive ethno-cultural traditions. But in the late 1980s and in the 1990s education researchers did note that although the national education was considered as a part of the social system and a key factor of national revival, it was 'absolutely insufficiently studied' as to what degree those schools also covered the children's requirements in modern knowledge, whether they did assure 'the equality of starting conditions between graduates of Russian and national schools', and whether it would be considered as a discriminatory practice (Muhariamova and Andreeva, 2008, p. 9).

In defense of bilingual education Russian researchers mention that a mismatch between socialization practices at school and at home becomes an obstacle in the process of learning. This is predominantly important for children from minority families. The pupils' successes grow when teachers talk the same language as pupils do. Thereby the ideal of accommodation of ethnic minorities in school culture is proved beneficial (Avraamova, 2003, p. 108).

I.D. Frumkin sees the source of unequal opportunities not only in the content of study programs, but also in the intolerant attitude toward the culture that children carry into school from their ethnic environment (Frumkin,

2006, p. 16). Promoting the concept of poly-cultural education in modern Russia, researchers show the importance of teaching/learning respect for other cultures to increase society's capacity to live together in peace and harmony (Muhariamova and Andreeva, 2008, p. 26). In this regard, the idea of schools' diversity preference is supported (Smith and Lusthaus, 1995, pp. 378–391).

There are also other approaches to the issues of what the language of learning at school should be and in what way the prospects for social mobility of learners depend on it. In Russia, as in other countries, there are those who support the idea of maintaining national languages without studying them at school. There are also those who support the idea of firmly establishing the dominant culture in order to broaden opportunities in the modern labor market. In addition, some researchers consider language homogeneity as one of the most successful mechanisms for the creation of a single civic identity (Vorotnikov, 2007, pp. 8–10).

Summing up, we can state that the growth of national movements in ethnic regions led to the increase of studying of native languages in ethnic regions. The widespread of ethnic resurgence started during the period of crisis of the USSR almost simultaneously (but actions taken in Tatarstan became a model for the other regions). In the 1980s study in or of native languages at schools was sharply increased in national regions. Several years later (the timeframes differing in various regions but ranging from three to ten years) indigenous and Russian populations discovered that new curriculums led to insufficient knowledge of the Russian language. This situation limited social mobility by education because vocational education (especially higher education) remained exclusively the province of the Russian language. In addition, the USE (that gives admission into universities) is administered only in Russian. In the late 1980s and in the 1990s the situation became very complicated, and these problems remain unresolved. On the one hand, expressing a positive attitude towards learning a titular nation language has political significance as a component of democracy, it is interpreted as an attitude of support for the culture and status of that nation; on the other hand, differences in the level of knowledge of Russian language by graduates of Russian and national schools, from Russian and national regions, means inequalities in the starting conditions of youth persist. This is especially important for children from minority families. The Russian Federal Ministry took measures to ensuring a single educational space in the country but researchers state that today's situation is still acute.

16.4.2   School quality and ethnic background

A second research tradition explores the differences in Russian schools in terms of quality, as measured by the teaching, condition of school buildings, and technological resources that schools have. Researchers analyze the characteristics of theses disparities and their consequences for ethnic inequality.

This problem exists even in Tatarstan. In the 2000s this republic was regarded as one of the most successful and free from social problems among the 83 federal subjects of Russia. However, regarding the quality of education, teachers' qualification level the schools of the republic were ranked in the middle and sometimes in the lower half of the Russian rating system. This occurred due to predominance of rural schools with learning conducted in the Tatar language (Gohberg et al., 2007, pp. 3–30).

Researchers mention that a 'culmination' of several factors of inequality appears at national schools. Comparatively low income levels and smaller cultural capital resources of pupils' families are added to the low quality of teaching. Senior pupils at schools with national languages as the mode learning more frequently come from low-income families than pupils at other schools (they stressed in interviews 'we survive from salary to salary'). In addition, their parents are attained lower levels of education. This fact is acknowledged even in more prosperous republics such as Sakha (Yakutia), Tatarstan, and Bashkortostan. The reason is primarily that the majority of children at national schools are from rural areas or those who recently moved to cities.

The schools of the North Caucasus republics have been subject to particularly adverse, insecure conditions for a long time because of on-going terrorism and military conflicts. According to the official statistics, in 2006 one-third of Ingushetia schools occupied substandard buildings due to unameliorated deterioration, 20% required immediate reconstruction. Similarly, more than one-third of schools in Dagestan were in ramshackle houses or houses under the threat of collapse, and only 23% of pupils studied in standard-designed schools. Some republic governments' reports even noted an increase in the number of children who do not attend school (Program, 2006).

Buryatia is one of more prosperous regions regarding education. But even there rural schools where more Buryat children study differed from city schools. Those differences comprised computer equipment, internet connections, and teachers' qualifications (Report, 2004). Sakha (Yakutia) is also a republic with high indicators of education. Regarding computer equipment the schools of this republic are among the best. But in the beginning of 2010 11% of even this district's schools were in a state of disrepair (Report, 2009/2010, p. 26).

Some sociological studies have been conducted to assess the opportunities for upward social mobility of the youth of indigenous ethnic groups. The level of university admissions after school graduation were assessed and subsequent social status of children in comparison with their parents' social status was measured. For example, Ostapenko pointed out that from 1997 to 2002 in Sakha (Yakutia) more Yakut youth entered universities immediately after school graduation than ethnic Russians, and in the first stages of their labor career they overtook their parents regarding their social status. The social mobility of Tatar youth was higher than the social mobility of all youth of the republic and higher than the social mobility of youth in the regions with dominant Russian populations (for example Orenburg region). However this increase is not evenly distributed; young people living in villages, even among the Yakut and more so the Tatars, Bashkir and young people of other nationalities, appeared to have fewer opportunities for university education and upward social mobility than their urban counterparts (Ostapenko, 2002, p. 65).

Such an inequality of opportunities is acknowledged in a very negative way even in those places where the youth enjoys high quality education in general. The Deputy Minister of Economy in the Republic of Sakha (Yakutia) told the researcher during the interview, that it is more difficult for Sakha youth to obtain higher education because they are living in villages and learning in small schools, where teachers are worse. He reported that ethnic Russians in his republic have generally more educational opportunities because they are mostly living in cities where schools are better, and teaches are more qualified. Further, fewer Sakha youth than Russians continue their education in Moscow or other big cities because they do not have relatives or family networks there and Sakha parents fear have their children so far away. Moreover, parents do not wish to send their children to boarding schools: afterwards children rarely return to their parents, and on the whole parents and children no longer share a common sense of understanding, even the language of boarding school-educated children becomes different, and their parents' lifestyle in the tundra does not fit them (Archives, 1999).

To summarize, research shows that there is a great variability in educational resources between schools in Russia. Rural schools have worse education quality, teachers' qualifications, housing conditions, computer equipment, internet connections, and so on. National schools (where learning is conducted in the native language) are more frequently rural schools. Additionally, several important factors increase observable inequality. Pupils in rural schools are mainly from lower-income families than pupils at other schools, their parents have small cultural capital resources, are less educated. As a result, young people from ethnic groups living in villages have fewer opportunities after school graduation for university education and upward social mobility after school graduation than their urban counterparts. Of particular concern are those schools in regions that are characterized by adverse, insecure environments due to military conflicts. Such schools are in worse condition.

16.4.3   Socio-cultural differences and education

The third research tradition aims to chart and explain differences in educational aspirations and achievement between sub-national minority groups and the majority group of Russians. Studies point out that the prestige attached to education among various ethnic groups changed in different ways during the years of significant transformation in Russia. This dynamic would depend on a

range of factors such as the fluctuations in the regional labor market, maintenance or loss of cultural traditions, and changing conditions of the educational
infrastructure.

For example, a loss in the prestige of education among the Russian population of Tatarstan, Sakha (Yakutia), North Ossetia, Tyva, and Bashkortostan was
noticed in ethno-sociological research during the 1990s. Even poorly educated
people could become wealthy and skilled specialists would be involved in
service personals of trade networks in those years. On the other hand, education always remained prestigious among the Yakuts, Tyvinians, Ossetians
(Drobizheva, 2010, p. 131). This phenomenon cannot be explained by changes
in the labor market but rather by stable traditions, high prestige of education
and skilled work.

Using statistical data, Ostapenko pointed out that the proportion of people
with higher education among Adygeis, Altaians, Buriats, Yakuts, Kalmyks,
and Ossetians in urban areas increased approximately four times from 1960
to 1980. Among the Tatars, Mordvinians, Maris, and Chuvashs the number
of those who possessed a specialized secondary education grew more rapidly
(Ostapenko, 2002, pp. 38–39). As a result, 40–50% of urban titular nationalities
population in half of the republics in Russia held university or college diplomas
to the beginning of the 1980s when the country was undergoing considerable
transformations. Such was the situation not only for Buriats and Yakuts who
had always differed from other minority nationals with higher indicators in
education (the rate of specialists with higher education was superior to Russians
in the republics by two times), but the Adygeis, Ossetians, Altais, Kalmyks,
Kabardians, Balkars, Komis, Mordvins, Khakasses were also in an analogous
situation (Ostapenko, 2002, pp. 48, 49). Around that time people started to talk
about the overabundance of specialists, and about the fact that not all qualified specialists were employed in correspondence with their level of education.

As a result, some conflicts of interests occurred among people of various ethnicities who pretended with equal bases to be employed in intellectual work.
It is not a coincidence that more remarkable national claims and movements
for the raising of republics' status took place in Tatarstan and Sakha (Yakutia)
in the 1990s.

It is important that in the same period of time the titular nationalities moved
into a privileged position in comparison with Russians with regard to obtaining
prestigious positions in the administrative apparatus of the republics. In this
case the influence of a specific sector of labor market had an impact. This happened not only as a result of changes in the state's ethnic policy (the declared
position of Russians as a 'big brother' in the Soviet past was removed from
the public sphere). The majority of Russians living in the national republics of
Russia did not know the language of the titular nationalities. The knowledge
of two languages became preferable for obtaining leading positions in the

administrative apparatus. Russians were in failure in this respect in comparison with the representatives of the titular nationalities, who spoke fluently both languages.

In the period of transition to the market economy, the ethnic groups living in the republics with export-directed economies were in the best conditions. They could realize their educational potential more effectively. For example Bashkortostan, Tatarstan, Sakha (Yakutia), Karelia were among those republics that held companies in extractive industries.

While assessing these results, one should take into account the fact that accessibility of education among aboriginal ethnic groups (and particularly, access to education of high level and quality), as mentioned above, was influenced by the ratio of population in rural areas.

It is known that social contradictions do not always arise on the basis of real social differences including those related to the educational opportunities. Typically, contradictions are largely caused by how social hierarchies are interpreted in the everyday consciousness; herewith, social hierarchies are 'crystallized' in consequent mythologems or stereotypes.

To clarify various ideas on ethnic inequality (including those enshrined in mythologems) some special surveys were conducted from 1999 to 2002 (Drobizheva, 2002) and from 2007 to 2008 (Report, 2009).[3] The researches have proceeded from the assumption that if the social inequality in mass consciousness is linked to ethnicity (if people do believe that their ethnicity has an impact on their social status), then people will act in correspondence with those beliefs and treat representatives of other ethnic groups likewise: as a competitive equal or unequal to their groups. This is a case of self-fulfilling prophecy. The researchers have aligned themselves with the famous 'Thomas theorem', that is, if people identify situations as real, then they *are* real in regard of their consequences (Thomas and Znaniecki, 1918, p. 79). When members of contacting ethnic groups define the same intergroup reality in different ways then the grounds of social tensions and conflicts arise. This can essentially become apparent in adaptation processes of ethnic groups to the modern labor market, informational resources, and technologies.

The subjects of the study were Tatars and Russians in Tatarstan, Yakuts and Russians in Sakha (Yakutia), Russians and Tatars in Orenburg region where Tatars live in a dominant Russian populated environment, as well Russians and Tatars in Bashkortostan. Such a selection allowed the researchers to study the following issues: how ethnic groups with various traditions are drawn into transformation processes; whether and how cultural particularities influence social inequality and ideas on it; how the real inequality of ethnic groups correlates with ideas on inequality among Russians and titular nationalities in national republics; and what ethno-cultural and ethno-political factors exist among the explanatory models of movements toward the social advancement.

One of the major conclusions of the study is expressed by the fact that we often fix non-comparable social practices on the background of common processes. It is more than a decade since Yakuts in the cities of Sakha (Yakutia) overtook Russians regarding the level of education (measured by the ratio of specialists with higher education). However, the majority of Yakuts live not in the cities but in rural areas; and there the inclusion of the population in modern types of activities is not at all on a high level (especially, in terms of the dispersed population over a large sparsely populated area).

There is another situation in Tatarstan. The levels of education between Russians and Tatars are very similar. Most importantly, starting from the end of the 1980s they slightly differed from each other by the sector of employment. There are few differences on the ratio of industrial and artistic intellectuals as well. Whereas in Sakha (Yakutia) or Bashkortostan the ratio of industrial intellectuals between Russians and titular ethnic groups differs by more than four times. For the interpretations of these results the term 'glocalization' is of high importance, the term is referred to adaptations of economic practices to local conditions and linked to the description of social space reconstructions (Robertson, 1995, pp. 28, 29; Luke, 1995, pp. 91–107).

Indicators, used above, traditionally are important in Russia for perception and comprehension of the place of the group in the society by itself and to compare it with that of other groups. The ethnic groups of Russia largely differed from each other on the basis of these indicators. The variation coefficient in 1989 on the rate of highly qualified specialists among the employed city population of the republic was 33%, regarding the rate of highly qualified blue collars it was 21%, and for low and non-qualified blue collars – 18% (Ostapenko, 2002, p. 27).

Not only the ratio of prestigious employment in the ethnic community is important for its impressions of the equality or inequality; ethnic community's representation in the most prestigious groups of the whole population is also significant. For example, Yakuts had a greater percentage of high-skilled specialists (in the cities) than Russians, but among high-level administrators in the republic there were 19% of Yakuts and 61% of Russians; among the high-skilled specialists Yakuts amounted to 9%, Russians – to 68% (it is necessary to take into consideration that Yakuts comprise 31% of the population in the republic, and in the cities their percentage is even less). Yakuts interpreted their requests deeper and more versatile than many other nationalities, and that was evidently expressed in their requirements to settle control over the resources in the 1990s (Drobizheva et al., 1996, pp. 205–210).

Among Bashkirs, Tatars, Yakuts (and most other non-Russian ethnic groups) intergenerational mobility (the rate of those who improved their status in comparison with their fathers) was higher than among Russians. Half of all high-skilled Tatar and Bashkir specialists and a little less than half Yakuts in the cities (where they mostly maintain contacts with Russians) came from the families of less qualified workers.

Surveys conducted from 2007 to 2008 pointed out that in the social positions of Yakuts and Russians there were notable changes in comparison with the 1990s. In the urban population the ratios of Yakuts and Russians among specialists and technicians, businessmen and industrial leaders became closer to each other (Figure 16.2). The rate of people with higher education among the Yakuts and Russians became practically the same.

The information above shows how inadequate the assessments of the existing situation can be if we consider the equality/inequality of nationalities on any single, albeit very significant, statistical criterion. The more diverse views may exist in the everyday consciousness. At present in the Sakha (Yakutia) Republic over 30% of Yakuts and 40% of Russians believe that ethnicity does matter in regard to employment opportunities, and half of Russians believe that nationality affects the ability to take a high position in government. Yakuts consider that Russians have better opportunities to start their own business (30% of Yakuts believed that Russians had more opportunities in this field of activity, and so thought 12% of Russians). Koroteeva analyzed the economic and social opportunities of ethnic groups in the assessments of studied regions' population and arrived at the conclusion that 'people are apt to exaggerate the infringements of opportunities of their own group and minimize their privileges' (Koroteeva, 2002, p. 130).

Thus: the social processes in regions were in general the same as a whole (the same as across the country), but their variations were diverse (they were shown

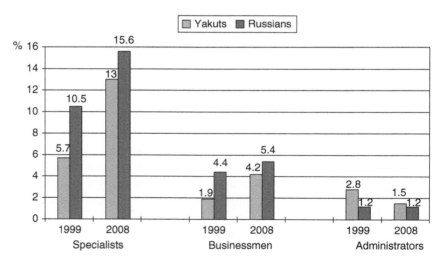

Figure 16.2 Russians and Yakuts among specialists, businessmen and administrators in Republic of Sakha (Yakutia) in 1999 and 2008

above in quantitative terms). We cannot a fit general model for all ethnic groups and all regions. Different economic and political conditions, cultural traditions, population settlement pattern, specifics of the labor market, and other factors (including very specific ethnic and regional ones) shape the local situation and its dynamic over time. Every case deserves consideration and must be investigated in the future.

16.4.4 Problems of migrants and receiving society

The next research tradition is new for Russia and therefore concerned not many publications. As was mentioned above, the issue of integration of migrants into Russian society came to the fore with increased economic-based migration. The most important role in the integration of these newcomers is assigned to education.

This applies to all three categories of migrants that were described above. Of the three, repatriates-compatriots need the least secondary socialization: they speak Russian, they know the Russian culture. However, they also need some social, cultural, and economic adaptation. The immigrants coming to Russia for permanent residence face serious problems. They need integration in all spheres. Although they come from the former Soviet republics, they do not know well the language and culture of modern Russia, orientate poorly in the socio-economic realities. This is especially true for young people who grew up in the newly independent states. Labor migrants who come for temporary jobs need further assistance, because they are often people with lower general and professional education coming from the regions where there is almost no knowledge of either the Russian language or the current Russian reality. In general, researchers (Kliucharev and Mukomel, 2008, pp. 305, 315) define the following programs of education (Table 16.1).

There is another important aspect of social and educational policy. Researchers point to xenophobic moods among the population in Russia that create difficulties for migrants (Vendina, 2009, pp. 96–97). This problem exists in Russia as in other countries. In Russia, this has become more complicated by the fact that the experience of a massive reception of immigrants in the

Table 16.1 Educational programs in the context of integration policies

Target groups	Types of educational programs		
	Linguistic	Cultural (acquaintance with traditions, customs, culture)	Professional (vocational)
Compatriots	–	+	+
Immigrants	+	+	+
Labor migrants	+	+	+

country did not exist. The majority of today's migrants are former citizens of the USSR: Ukrainians, Belarusians, Azerbaijanis, Armenians, Georgians, Uzbeks, Kyrgyzs, Kazakhs, and Tajiks. In the past they moved to Russian cities (at that time USSR) to study or work by invitation, and then stayed after the military service or university graduation. They were already adapted to Russian culture. There were almost no negative attitudes toward them. Today they are citizens of other states; moreover, they are from the states that separated from Russia. Additionally, the majority are not adapted to the Russian environment, and in their behavior they differ from the mainstream population. Sociologists from Levada Center and Department of Ethnic Sociology of Institute of Sociology (Russian Academy of Sciences) note that the cause of xenophobia is not economic competition because the migrants are involved in the niches of the labor market where the local population prefers not to work. The main reason given is the perception that the newcomers behave 'like the masters of our land' (Public Opinion, 2006, p. 162; Russian Identity, 2008, p. 125).

While taking part in international comparative studies (ESS) Russian researchers in 2006 found the most negative attitudes towards migration ('no entry permit to anybody') among 28% of the population. Of 25 European countries the number of those opponents to migration was higher than in Russia in Hungary (39%), Portugal, and Cyprus (29–30%). About 35% of respondents in Russia considered that 'not all must be allowed to arrive'; approximately the same response rate was found in Spain, Germany, Great Britain, and Norway (35–36%) (Drobizheva and Arutiunova, 2009, p. 209).

Researchers point out that it would be misleading to assume that only migrants need to know the traditions, customs, and culture of the other side:

> The integration of migrants is a two-way traffic between the cultures of recipient society and migrants [...] Recipient society also needs basic knowledge of traditions, customs, culture, peculiarities of behavior and social communication of migrants arriving from other societies. This kind of education of the recipient society should be the task of mass media and mass culture, public policy sphere. (Kliucharev and Mukomel, 2008, p. 318)

Establishment of an appropriate system for both migrants and the receiving society is an important task of politicians and managers of education. It is necessary to consider not only today's opportunities, but also long-term challenges. As is pointed out in reviewed publications, there is a need to take into account the necessity for the socialization of children of migrants, or later there is a possibility of facing the same serious social problems that Europe has already experienced (Kliucharev and Mukomel, 2008, p. 310). It is also important to cooperate with unemployed adult family members, and this is subject to additional constraints on boosting the motivation to education, especially for older people who are often not configured to integrate into the culture of the hosting country. The authors note: 'currently, Russia lacks the methods and practices of cultural education both for the unemployed adult family members of migrants, and in terms of non-formal education for migrants' youth'. It should also be borne in mind that today there are practically no professionals to work with migrants and no expert-consultants for local governments. The implementation of these significant tasks depends on federal and local authorities (Kliucharev and Mukomel, 2008, pp. 316–318, 322).

In total, we have established that researchers in this tradition concentrate on two issues today: difficulties of migrants' situations and tasks of social and educational policy. In doing so, we are observing the starting point of this research tradition in the making. While the current information and analytical base is rather poor, we can hope that social and educational policy development will be active and successful; in any case we can hope that this research tradition will be continued.

16.4.5 Students' inter-ethnic relations

How do learners of different ethnic groups feel themselves at the educational institutions? How do they treat each other? The research tradition on these issues could not be dismissed in multi-ethnic Russia, since at schools, in the universities, and other educational institutions there are children, teenagers and young people of various ethnicities. Such studies are few, but their results speak for themselves.

Some migrants moved to Russia bringing with them all their family including children who had to be taught at schools. The issues of adaptation of children, their relationships with peers, and issues mastering the Russian language they are taught in, are all the focus of researchers' attention. This research direction is very new, and advances in a lively debate among researchers.

There is an opinion that 'the migrants' children quickly adapt to the Russian schools'. At the same time the authors mentions: 'Though here we face some problems: in a range of Russian regions, including Moscow, special classes are organized for migrants' children with poor or no knowledge of Russian language' (Kliucharev and Mukomel, 2008, p. 316).

The knowledge of Russian language is considered important. Experts point out that children from urban areas of Armenia, Georgia and Azerbaijan knew Russian on arrival and were sent to ordinary/general schools. But, for example, the children of migrants that came from villages or small towns of Armenia and whose language in the home was their mother tongue were not ready to study at Russian language schools.

Big communities with wealthy sponsors established schools in their mother language. This way Armenian, Georgian, Azerbaijani and Kazakh language schools came into existence. Some schools in national languages were established for children to learn their mother language and communicate with relatives. Those were the schools in Estonian, Polish and German languages.

But there have been children from the 'problem families'. Those are mostly immigrant families from Kyrgyzstan, Tajikistan and Uzbekistan that come to earn money. Their children pass the schooling age in Russia without gaining adequate knowledge of Russian language. If they are not legal migrants (or remain unregistered for any reason) then their children cannot be enrolled in school. Then much depends on employers who are not always able or want to support them. Some evidence shows that more fortunate are the children from the families who work as yard cleaners, work taken on often by Kyrgyzs, Tajiks, or Uzbeks. If they work well their employers apply on their behalf to the nearby school for enrollment of their children. Researchers of illegal migrants convey the story of one of the respondents: 'Our boss talked to the principal of the school and now our son studies at school for free. He studies well, makes friendship with Russian children, there are no problems' (Grigoriev and Osinnikov, 2009, p. 50).

In the literature on immigration issues most frequently mentioned are the difficulties regarding employment, living conditions, medical service but not the access to education. Discriminatory practices in access to education are noted by researchers only very rarely. It is noteworthy that migrants themselves did not note the existing infringements in education when surveyed (Tiurukanova, 2009, pp. 163, 187).

How do the migrants' children feel themselves in Russian schools?

> As the experience shows, children do not like the majority of their foreign peers [...]. Not satisfactory knowledge of language, not a clear speech or accent – all these play their part here ... And children themselves communicating with their peers in Moscow often feel their 'inferiority', deprivation ... Though the majority of migrants mentions the good and neutral attitude, yet a significant part of migrants faces the ill-will. (Grigoriev, Osinnikov, 2009, pp. 50, 51)

The description quoted above corresponds with earlier surveys (Sobkin, 1984, pp. 222–225). In the years 1999–2006, in the so-called 'ordinary' schools of Moscow the percentage of ethnic intolerant teenagers increased.[4] While learners declare that ethnicity does not matter to them in the choice of friends or classmates, in fact, people of their own ethnicity prevail among friends, regarding the choice of classmates there also exists selectivity.

The research pointed out that the schoolchildren surveyed (a sample of various but not small proportions of teenagers from different ethnic groups) assumed that there was an ethnic inequality, that there were people deprived of their rights and opportunities, and also recognized the existence of the ethnic inequality in the vertical social mobility. Approximately two-fifths of Russians, Azerbaijanis and Tatars, half of Armenians and Georgians, over a third of Koreans and more than a quarter of Jews had at least one or more times read or heard malevolent or hostile remarks about their own ethnicity or the people of their ethnic group. In addition, from one-seventh to nearly one-third of Tatars, Russians, Armenians, Georgians and Azerbaijanis (listed in order of increasing rate) faced these experiences many times.

An intolerant attitude towards immigrants obviously dominates the tolerant one. One-half to two-thirds of Russian teenagers consider immigrants as people of the 'second sort' who behave improperly, contributing to the criminalization of the urban environment, competing with the old residents in the labor market, and depriving Moscow of traditional national traits. Only 10–33% of teenagers do not agree with these views (Shapiro et al., 2007, pp. 8–9, 11, 18, 26, 38–39).

Another study conducted in St Petersburg[5] has not shown any ethnic conflicts, xenophobia or lack of tolerance on the school level while discussing problems related to migrant children with the teachers and principals. At the same time the analysis of the students' communication networks prove that ethnic majority children appear to disregard ethnicity when choosing friends, whereas ethnic minority children prefer to make friends with other ethnic minorities. The researchers note that such patterns of friends' selection are also identified in European schools, and in this respect Russian students do not differ from their European counterparts.

Regarding the language difficulties it should be mentioned that children who have come to St Petersburg before or around the age of seven do not have any difficulties with linguistic adaptation. But ethnic minority teenagers who have come at the age of ten or older often need adaptation which requires special efforts from schools. In 'ordinary' schools children of migrants study better than local children, especially those who arrived in St Petersburg before school age.

There is an important observation on how migrant families of various statuses act while choosing schools for their children. The research demonstrates that the distribution of children by school depends more on social class than on ethnic background. Migrants who lack material resources and social capital prefer schools attended by children from local families with a low socioeconomic status, while children of well off and more-educated migrants are enrolled in schools with advanced curriculum. Researchers mention that 'this seems to be in accord with the theory of segmented assimilation, although with a qualification: migrants are integrated into different segments of society according to their socio-economic status without forming ethnic enclaves'.

Notwithstanding the general optimism of the publication the authors advance the following speculation in their conclusions: 'Faced by discrimination on the labor market and obstacles to social mobility after the positive experiences at school, today's students may experience in a decade deep social deprivation' (Alexandrov, Baranova and Ivaniushina, 2012).

The study conducted at the universities[6] has shown that in most cases students are inclined to tolerant attitudes toward people of other ethnic groups. About half of the interviewed students, as a rule, treat people of other ethnic groups with respect. But this does not apply to one in three students. In addition, the 40% has noted that they have faced an ill-disposed attitude because of their ethnicity this often happens with non-Russians, in particular, with Caucasians, as well as Jews. Local youth has a negative attitude toward the arrival for education purposes of young people from North Caucasus and Transcaucasia (regardless of citizenship and religion), natives from Southeast Asia and Africa. In a year, one in four students had to be engaged in conflict relations with representatives of other ethnic groups in the hometown.

The youth sees in refugees and displaced persons the reason for increased criminal activities (43.2% of students), the source of inter-ethnic conflicts (30%), and disrespect for the customs and traditions of the local population (42%). The latter association was primarily felt in relation to migrants from the Caucasian republics and Central Asia.

What are the views of students on the effectiveness of the current state policy on ethnic issues and migration? In general, researchers have received a negative opinion on the matter. Only 3.7% of those interviewed believe that much is being done by the state on the regulation of inter-ethnic relations, but that is not enough to relieve the tension. In addition, 20–30% of students are not satisfied with the measures taken by the state in the policy implementation. (Pokida, 2009, pp. 13, 15, 16).

In Peoples' Friendship University of Russia (PFUR) the issue of ethnic tolerance is adopted by the university management as a fundamental principle. A study[7] at that institution has showed that more than half of Russian students there occupy a position of openness to people of other nationalities. One-fourth of students tend more toward isolation in relation to the majority of ethnic groups, taking the following position: 'let them live and study in Russia, but I would not like to be engaged in direct contact with them'. In addition, 17% of students do not want to see people of other ethnic groups either as citizens or students in their own country, but are happy for them to visit as tourists. A small number of students (2.6%) has an openly xenophobic attitude (Demidova, 2009, p. 88).

Indeed, not always good relationships are established among students of different nationalities at the universities. This was mentioned in the interview of the Deputy Minister of Economy, Republic of Sakha (Yakutia), cited above. He described Yakut students who leave to study in the universities of big cities: 'But they differ from others by their appearance and do not always feel themselves comfortable' (Archives, 1999).

As it becomes clear, the self-feelings and relationships of young people from different ethnic groups in educational institutions are not formed easily. This relationship seems to reflect the reality that young people absorb in their families and close surroundings. Many pupils and students are open and have friendly attitudes towards other ethnic groups. However, there are high inclinations towards ethnic isolation, and negative attitudes towards the representatives of other ethnic groups. Particularly, hostile attitudes towards immigrants are recorded. At the same time, many young people are dissatisfied with the state policy on ethnic issues.

The problems of migrants' children reflect the problems faced by their parents. The conditions of migrants' children depend on the status of parents, the region of origin, and the level of urbanization of the previous residency. There are reasons to assume that it varies in different regions of Russia.

It is evident that these researches have just started. They have involved a small portion of learners. Only quantitative methods (questionnaires) are used. A more extensive and intensive study, apparently, should be undertaken in the future. More solid conclusions can be made when new research on the conditions of migrants' children within the educational system, and also a prolonged study tracing the lives of migrant children after graduation from school will be undertaken.

16.5 Conclusion

The current state of Russian studies on ethnic inequality in the educational sphere expresses the reflection and consequences of the processes taking place in Russia for decades. In the 1920s and 1930s the authority of the state was interested in the involvement of all ethnic groups of Russia in education to realize the defined objectives; ethnic aspects of educational problems were considered in scientific literature in that period of time. Afterward the investigation of such problems has not been developed by political reasons because it was proclaimed that the 'national issue' had been solved. Moreover, not all kinds of studies on inequality were possible, although some exceptions occurred. However, after the changes taken place in Russia during last decades some studies on ethnic inequality in education have been restarted.

In poly-ethnic societies any inequality in education has several dimensions, including those connected with the ethnicity. For example, the situation of selection in the labor market that is inevitable in conditions of economic competition is perceived in the public consciousness as differences in opportunities to get a plausible education and decent work. This is why the influence of ethnicity on the accessibility of education and its impact on the conditions of people in social structure of Russia draws special attention among Russian researchers.

Because research in this area has been in progress for only a few years, the literature used in this review chapter was limited in scope and number. It focuses necessarily on Russian researchers' publications and other materials written in Russian. The inequality of ethnic groups in education is more often studied as a part of various other forms of inequality, for example, a status inequality, and less as a topic on its own. Nevertheless, there is a significant literature focusing on the inequality of ethnic groups in education.

In reviewing the relevant research literature on race/ethnic inequalities in Russia between 1980 and 2010 the following research traditions can be identified: (1) Sub-national/ethnic minority languages and their educational and political implications, (2) School quality and ethnic or sub-national background, (3) Sub-national/ethnic minority background and educational aspirations and achievement, and (4) Attitude towards sub-national/ethnic minorities. In general, research has focused primarily on the experienced 'problems' of indigenous ethnic minority groups, or sub-national minority groups.

Those are the issues of national schools' status, the role of mother language and bilingualism in education for social mobility opportunities. Growth of the national movements in ethnic regions after the crisis of the USSR led to the increase of mother language's role as one of the main aims and conditions of ethnic revival. In the 1980s the studying of native languages at schools sharply increased in ethnic regions. But some time later the population discovered that new curriculums led to insufficient knowledge of Russian language. This situation limited social mobility by education because vocational education (higher especially) use Russian language almost exclusively. Learning of a titular ethnic group language has political meaning as a component of democracy, it is ascribed an attitude toward culture and status of a nation; but differing levels of knowledge of Russian language by graduates of Russian and national schools from Russian and national regions means inequality of youth's starting conditions. The problem remains unsolved and this research tradition will be continued.

Further, there is a social differentiation of ethnic groups with connection to education and role of the ethnic factor in social mobility. Different ideas on ethnic inequality have been also studied. One research tradition explores the differences between school institutional factors. Rural schools have worse education quality, teachers' qualification, housing conditions, computer equipment, and so on. But national schools are frequently rural schools. Additionally, pupils in rural schools are from low-income families more than pupils in other schools, their parents have small cultural capital resources and are less well-educated. This characteristic of the national/rural school pupil contingent increases inequality. As a result, young people from ethnic groups living in the villages have fewer opportunities after school graduation for university education and upward social mobility than their urban counterparts. It may be predicted that this research tradition will be developed while the differences between schools in Russia is so large.

The next research tradition explores differentiation in prestige attached to education, youth aspirations, realities of getting an education and notions about competition of ethnic groups in various regions. Researchers found out considerable differences between situations in various regions and analyzed their conditionality by considerable factors of reality. The social processes in regions were in general the same as a whole (the same as across the country), but their variations were various (they were shown in quantitative terms). Different economic and political conditions, cultural traditions, population settlement patterns, specifics of labor market, and other factors (including very specific ethnic and regional) have shaped the local situation and its dynamic during decades. Every case deserves consideration and must be investigated in the future.

In the last years a new problem became concrete for Russia: the problem of migration. Large streams of migrants, especially from former republics of the USSR, gushed into Russia. The most important role in the migrants' integration is assigned to education. The new research tradition concentrates on two issues: difficulties of migrants' situation and tasks of social and educational policy. This research tradition is in the making, with the result that current information and analytical base is rather poor. We can hope that this research tradition will be continued and useful for social and educational policy.

The research tradition studying how learners from different ethnic groups feel themselves at the educational institutions, and how they treat each other covers the analysis of declared statement and actual behavior of pupils and students. The researchers are focused on the study of how migrants' children feel themselves in the educational sphere: the ways they get adapted, their relations with peers from majority and minority ethnic groups, the ways they learn Russian. The materials show both encouraging and disturbing results. Here we face positive attitudes towards other ethnic groups, on one side, and intolerant attitudes, on the other side. The researchers show that the problems of migrants' children are the reflections of the problems faced by their parents. These researches have just started. The studies so far involved a small sample of students and only quantitative methods have been used. More solid conclusions can be made when further research is undertaken. There is a hope for more effective research initiatives in the future.

Within a reviving Russian sociology, the research traditions discussed above combine to mark the progress from oblivion to the modern level of social sciences in the last decades. It is necessary to use the experience and achievements of world science, and also take into account the specifics of Russian reality (which is not always easily combined). Russian researchers use all available methods, quantitative and qualitative, including questionnaires, interviews, focus groups and so on. In most cases more quantitative methods are used to develop knowledge on ethnic inequalities in education. Yet there is a need to define the theoretical approaches. While in some cases eclecticism can be noticed, positivist and structural-functional approaches are dominant.

The above research traditions, perhaps more than any others in Russia, are linked to the forming of social policy. First, they tend to focus on the analysis of the 'pain points', problem situations, and have a critical and constructive orientation. Second, they contain directly or indirectly more or less concrete proposals to resolve the problems. Finally, such researches are demanded by social policy-makers. Some case-studies (or specific directions in the study) were initiated by the Department of Interethnic Relations at the RF Ministry of Regional Development and local authorities in ethnic regions (it does not interfere with the researchers to result in an objective analysis and criticism). That is to say, there is a combination of the critical nature of the research with close collaboration of the government in order to influence and test social policy measures. The results of researches, including controversial issues are discussed at conferences and meetings in participation of researchers and policy-makers.[8]

While policy recommendations are frequently made, they are not always and not all suggestions of researchers are implemented. Sometimes the implementation is hindered by political reasons determined by the short-term specifics of the local situation. In particular, this may be linked to the particularities of public opinion in ethnic groups (myths, stereotypes are manifested here). Sometimes the implementation of measures cannot be realized due to limitations of certain resources, such as educational infrastructure (a typical case with deficiencies in rural schools). The main thing is that ethnic inequalities in education cannot be eliminated by measures that can be implemented by and within one or more social institutions, such as education or labor market. As a rule, ethnic inequality is a societal problem and requires an integrated approach.

The changes that occurred in Russia and those that are currently taking place make the examined topic increasingly actual. There is a clear demand in society for information on these issues. We should expect that the number of studies on ethnic inequality will increase. There are also reasons to expect that there will be studies on ethnic inequality specifically in education. Also, it is hoped that they will become more in-depth and will continue to increase their representativeness.

The set of opportunities opened up to citizens by their society at each period of its development is a resource used differently. Opportunities in the educational field constitute a highly important resource, especially for youth. New conditions in post-Soviet Russia must inevitably influence the education field. Such influence comes from both the global factors of contemporary Russian reality (especially, economic differentiation) and from the specific pressure on the educational system from the interested groups which have the necessary capacity to exert it. Voluntarily or not the education system gets involved into the processes of social selection. Since the significance of educational system is increasing and the prognosis is that it will keep increasing, the social processes within this system attract more attention, first of all the problem of orientation and social behavior of young people, especially their orientation towards obtaining one or another level of education and the actual opportunities for that. The contradiction between the declared equal rights for education and the real social differentiation in educational field is rightfully considered as a societal problem.

This problem would be of certain significance for any society. It turns out to be especially urgent in contemporary Russia. The questions of democracy, equal opportunities, and social mobility are extremely sharp in a transitional society. Russian sociologists have to study and evaluate (from scratch, based upon our own investigation and materials) the new social mechanisms, conflicts, and the ways to settle them.

Research shows that the inequality begins at school and is then aggravated with the transition to occupational education, especially universities. This genesis of inequality causes to consider the situation at schools particularly. However, it is improper and senseless to cast blame for ethnic equality entirely upon the system of education, to hold it responsible for everything. Here we see the reflection of what is going on in the society on the whole. The institution of education is not to be blamed for what so vividly was manifested in it. The education sphere is a mirror to our society; let us not accuse it. The purposeful activity should include not only the sphere of education. It should be large-scale, systematic, having solid organizational and financial provision.

Programs aimed to neutralize the consequences of unfavorable effects in Russia may be diverse. They should take into account the specific features of a region, an ethnic group and educational situation. Such programs require objective and multilateral evaluation which will take into consideration potential possibilities and real limitations. The development of such programs requires careful forecasting of its consequences in various aspects. It may be predicted with certainty that they will bring varied results, including new contradictions which, in their turn, will demand their solution from society. Nevertheless this cannot be an argument against scientific analysis and practical activity. It is important that society should not increase the opportunities of some groups at the expense of limiting the chances of others. The obligation of a fair society is to promote equal opportunities for people from all groups.

Notes

1. The projects are executed by the researchers of Institute of Sociology of Russian Academy of Sciences in collaboration with colleagues from the Tatarstan republic.

Research areas include: the practices of education in national languages, the state of education in the national language in the evaluation of teachers and students, the formation of ethnic identity and interethnic relations in national schools, values and career ambitions of learners, and the availability of universities for them. Methodologies include: a questionnaire survey of learners (n = 609 graduates in 2002 and n = 490 in 2006), participant observations on exams, structured interviews with learners, expert interviews with teachers, information gathering from the class registers, analysis of reports from government agencies and press. The projects are supported by the Ford Foundation and the Russian Humanitarian Foundation.

2. The projects were executed in 1997–1998 by the researchers of Institute of Sociology of Russian Academy of Sciences in collaboration with colleagues from Tatarstan, Sakha (Yakutia), Orenburg, and Magadan regions. Research areas were: the interaction between ethnic groups, the role of the mother language, social inequality of the ethnic groups in conditions of Russian reforms (access to participation in the government and to the property). The sample is multi-stage in the main types of urban and rural settlements. The aggregate sample consists of 100 observation units in each republic and region. The project is supported by the MacArthur Foundation.

3. The projects are executed by the researchers of Institute of Sociology of Russian Academy of Sciences in collaboration with colleagues from various republics and regions of the Russian Federation. The project realized during 1999–2002 was directed by L. Drobizheva. The project realized during 2007–2008 was directed by L. Drobizheva, M. Chernish, A. Bravin, and E. Yakovleva. The described aim of the research is to reveal the real state of ethnic inequality and the role of myths in its perception. The parameters of the representative sample have been developed for the main nationalities in republics and regions. In the surveys of 1999–2002 1050 respondents in Sakha (Yakutia) were interviewed,1000 in Tatarstan, 1317 in Bashkortostan, and 1160 in the Orenburg region. In the survey of 2007–2008, 1328 people were interviewed in Sakha (Yakutia). Both qualitative (survey) and quantitative (interview) methods were used.

4. The study was conducted in 2005 under the guidance of V. Shapiro. Research areas were: ethnic identity and stereotypes among pupils representing ethnic majorities and minorities; their involvement in interethnic relations and cooperation in the multi-ethnic metropolis. The sample comprised 2455 learners in Grades 8–11 from the 39 secondary schools in Moscow (including ethnic Russians, Azerbaijanis, Armenians, Georgians, Jews, Koreans, and Tatars). Subjects responded to a questionnaire titled 'You, Your Nation and Other Nations' containing 166 questions. The study was supported by the Department of Education and the Committee of Interregional Relations and National Policy of Moscow.

5. The results of the survey carried out in St Petersburg schools, spring 2010, are published. The head of research was D. Aleksandrov (National Research University, Higher School of Economics). Research areas were: the issues of ethnic and social differentiation among schools, parents' interaction with schools, teachers' attitudes to migrant minority students, and ethnic effects in communication among students. The sample comprised 104 schools from all 18 districts of St Petersburg. Researchers surveyed 419 classes (Grades 8–10 covering all students in the grade), resulting in the collection of 7380 student questionnaires. The sample is fully representative for schools with a standard curriculum. Also more than 150 interviews with migrant students, migrant parents, teachers and school administrators were performed. The total sample includes about 10% ethnic migrants. The largest migrant minority groups are Azerbaijani (26% of the entire population of ethnic minorities) and Armenians

(18%); Central Asian ethnic groups account for 14% , North Caucasians for 12%, and Georgians for 8%.

6. The 'Students in the Multi-National Megalopolises and Large Cities of Russia: Ethnic Self-Consciousness and Inter-Ethnic Relations' study was conducted by the sociological center of the Russian Academy of Public Administration in 2008. The survey was conducted among 3750 students in five Russian cities: Moscow, St Petersburg, Voronezh, Stavropol, and Orenburg. The survey involved 35 higher education institutions, including both traditional universities and regional branch institutions. The average age of respondentswas20 years. The main research areas were: ethnic consciousness for students and levels of ethnic and religious tolerance.

7. The 'Level of Ethnic Tolerance Among the Students of PFUR' study was conducted in 2007–2008 by the sociological laboratory of Peoples' Friendship University of Russia. A questionnaire survey was implemented. A multi-stage sample proportional to the faculty, the academic year, and national status of a student (citizen of Russia, CIS, or foreign countries) was prepared (*n* = 400), representing 3.5% of the sampled population.

8. For example, on 11 April 2012 the annual conference at the Institute of Sociology, Russian Academy of Sciences was held under the title 'Social Realities of Contemporary Russia'. At the first session under the theme 'Interethnic Relations and Civil Identity in the Post-reform Russia' the head of the Department of Interethnic Relations of the Russian Ministry of Regional Development, A.V. Zhuravskiy, presented his report and took part in the general discussion.

References

Alexandrov, D., Baranova, V., and Ivaniushina, V. (2012) *Migrant Children in Russia. I. Migration, Ethnicity and Segregation in St Petersburg*. http://www.hse.ru/data/2012/02/07/1262504489/Preprint%20WP1.pdf.

Archives (1999) *Archives of the Department of Ethno-Sociology, Institute of Sociology of the Russian Academy of Sciences*. (In Russian).

Avraamova, E. (2003) 'Obrazovanie kak adaptatsionnyi resurs naseleniya' ['Education as a resource of adaptation of population'], in S. Shishkin (ed.) *Problemy dostupnosti vysshego obrazovaniya [Problems of Access to Higher Education]* (Moscow: Signal). (In Russian).

Bromley, Yu. (1987) *Etnosotsial'nye protsessy: tyeoriya, istoriya, sovremennost [Ethno-Sociological Processes:Theory, History, Modernity]* (Moscow: Nauka). (In Russian).

Census (2010) *Okonchatelnie resultati Vserossiyskoy perepisi naselenia 2010 goda [The Final Results of the All-Russia Population Census in 2010]*. http://www.perepis-2010.ru/results_of_the_census/results-inform.php. (In Russian).

Demidova, I. (2009) 'Issledovanie urovnja etnicheskoy tolerantnosti studentov RUDN' ['Research of the level of ethnic tolerance of PFUR's students'], in *Studenchestvo v mnogonacionalnih megapolisah i krupnih gorodah Rossii: etnicheskoe samosoznanie i mezhetnicheskie otnoshenija. Materiali nauchno-prakticheskoy konferencii [The Students in Multi-National Megalopolises and Large Cities of Russia: Ethnic Self-Consciousness and Inter-Ethnic Relations. Materials of Theoretical and Practical Conference]*. (Moscow: Socium).

Dobson, R.B. (1988) 'Higher education in the Soviet Union: Problems of access, equity, and public policy' in G.W. Lapidus and G.E. Swanson (eds) *State and Welfare: USA/USSR. Contemporary Police and Practice* (Berkeley: Institute of International Studies, University of California).

Drobizheva, L. (2010) 'Problemy neravenstva v etnonatsionalnom prostranstve Rossii' ['Problems of inequality in ethno-national space of Russia'], *Sotsial'naya politika: ekspertiza, rekomendatsii, obzory [Social Policy: Expertise, Advice, Reviews]*, 13. (In Russian).

Drobizheva, L. (ed.) (2002) *Sotsial'noe neravenstvo etnicheskih grupp: predstavleniya i real'nost' [Social Inequality of Ethnic Groups: Representation and Reality]* (Moscow: Academia). (In Russian).

Drobizheva L., Aklaev A., Korotyeeva V. and Soldatova G. (1996) *Demokratizatsiya i obrazy natsionalizma v Rossiiskoĭ Federatsii 90-h gg. [Democratization and Images of Nationalism in the Russian Federation at 90th]* (Moscow: Mysl). (In Russian).

Drobizheva, L. and Arutiunova, E. (2009) 'Natsionalno-grazhdanskaya identichnost' i mezhetnicheskaya tolerantnost' ['National-civic identity and ethnic tolerance'] in *Rossiya v Evrope [Russia in Europe]*. (Moscow: Academia). (In Russian).

Frumkin, I. (2006) 'Osnovnie podhody k probleme ravenstva v obrazovatel'nyh vozmozhnostyah' ['The main approaches to the problem of inequality in educational opportunities'] *Voprosy obrazovaniya [Questions of Education]*, 2. (In Russian).

Gohberg, L., Zabaturina, I., Kovaleva, N., Kuznecova, V., Nechaeva, E. and Ozerova, O. (2007) 'Rezul'taty eksperimentalnyh raschetov subektov Rossiiskoi Federatsii po pokazatelyam razvitiya obrazovaniya' ['Results of experimental calculations of the Russian Federation on development indicators of education'] *Vestnik obrazovaniya [Bulletin on Education]*, 4. (In Russian).

Gimpelson, V. and Kapeliushnikov, R. (ed.) (2011) *Rossiyskiy rabotnik: obrazovanie, professija, kvalifikacija [Russian Workman: Education, Profession, Qualification]* (Moscow: Publishing house of Higher School of Economics). (In Russian).

Grigoriev, M. and Osinnikov, A. (2009) *Nelegal'nye migranty v Moskve [Illegal Migrants in Moscow]* (Moscow: Publishing house «Europe»). (In Russian).

Guboglo, M. (1972) 'Etnolingvisticheskie kontakti i dvujazichie' ['Ethnolinguistic contacts and bilingualism'], in Yu. Arutiunian (ed.) *Sotsial'noe i natsional'noe [Social and National]* (Moscow: Nauka). (In Russian).

Initial data (2010) Initial data of Ministry of Education and Science RF, 2010.

Kliucharev G. and Mukomel, V. (2008) 'Migracionnaja politika v kontekste obrazovanija' ['Migration politics in educational context'], in G. Kliucharev (ed.) *Neprerivnoe obrazovanie v politicheskom i ekonomicheskom kontekstah [Lifelong Education in Political and Economic Contexts]* (Moscow: Institute of Sociology RAS). (In Russian).

Konstantinovskiy, D. (2003) 'Education in a transition society: Growing inequality' in C. A. Torres, A. Antikainen (eds) *Handbook on the Sociology of Education. An International Assessment of New Research and Theory* (Lanham: Rowman & Littlefield).

Konstantinovskiy, D. (2008) *Neravenstvo i obrazovanie. Opyt sotsiologicheskikh issledovanii zhiznennogo starta rossiiskoi molodezhi (1960-e gody – nachalo 2000-kh) [Inequality and Education. Experience of Sociological Studies on Life Starts of Russian Youth (1960–2000)]* (Moscow: Tsentr sotsial'nogo prognozirovaniia). (In Russian).

Konstantinovskiy, D. (2012) 'Social inequality and access to higher education in Russia', *European Journal of Education*, 47, 1: 9–24.

Konstantinovskiy, D. and Shubkin, V. (1977) *Molodezh' i obrazovanie [Youth and Education]* (Moscow: Nauka). (In Russian).

Korostelev, A. (1998) 'Jazik – istochnik soglasija i protivorechiy' ['Language as source of harmony and conflicts'] in L. Drobizheva (ed.) *Sotsial'naya i kul'turnaya distantsiya. Opyt mnogonatsional'noi Rossii [Social and Cultural Distances. The Experience of Multinational Russia]* (Moscow: Izdatelstvo Instituta Sotsiologii RAN). (In Russian).

Koroteeva, V.V. (2002) 'Status etnicheskih grupp v obshchestvennom soznanii i individual'nom opyte' ['Status of ethnic groups in the public consciousness and individual experience'] in L.M. Drobizheva (ed.) *Sotsial'noe neravenstvo etnicheskih grupp: predstavleniya i real'nost' [Social Inequality of Ethnic Groups: Representation and Reality]* (Moscow: Academia) (In Russian).

Luke, T. (1995) 'New world-order and neo-world orders: Power, politics and ideology in informationalizing glocalities' in M. Featherstone, S. Lash and R. Robertson (eds) *Global Modernities* (London: Sage).

Muhariamova, L. (2003) *Yazykovye otnosheniya: politicheskiĭ analiz [Language Relations: A Political Analysis]* (Kazan: Izd-vo Kazanskogo Universiteta). (In Russian).

Muhariamova, L. (2004). 'Problema dostupnosti vysshego obrazovaniya dlya uchashchihsya natsional'nyh shkol. Etnosotsial'nye aspekty' ['The problem of access to higher education for national schools' students. Ethno-social aspects'], *Sotsiologicheskie issledovaniya [Sociological Studies]*, 3. (In Russian).

Muhariamova L. and Andreeva A. (2008) *Fenomen natsional'noi shkoly v sotsiologicheskih rakursah [The Phenomenon of the National School on Sociological Perspectives]* (Kazan: Izdatel'stvo Kazanskogo Universiteta). (In Russian).

Ostapenko, L. (2002) 'Dinamika sotsial'no-professional'nogo sostava etnicheskih grupp i problemy integratsii' ['The dynamics of socio-professional composition of ethnic groups and problems of integration'] in L. Drobizheva (ed.) *Sotsial'noe neravenstvo etnicheskih grupp: predstavleniya i real'nost' [Social Inequality of Ethnic Groups: Representation and Reality]* (Moscow: Academia, 2002). (In Russian).

Pokida, A. (2009) 'Ob osnovnih resultatah sociologicheskogo issledovanija' ['About main results of sociological research'] in *Studenchestvo v mnogonacionalnih megapolisah i krupnih gorodah Rossii: etnicheskoe samosoznanie i mezhetnicheskie otnoshenija. Materiali nauchno-prakticheskoy konferencii [The Students in Multi-National Megalopolises and Large Cities of Russia: Ethnic Self-Consciousness and Inter-Ethnic Relations. Materials of Theoretical and Practical Conference]*. (Moscow: Socium).

Program (2006) *Razvitie obrazovaniya v respublike Dagestan na 2005–2010 gg., Respublikanskaya tselevaya programma [Development of Education in the Republic of Dagestan in 2005–2010, Republican Target Program]* (Makhachkala: Ministerstvo obrasovanija Respuibliki Dagestan). (In Russian).

Public Opinion (2006) *Obshchestvennoe mnenie [Public Opinion]* (Moscow). (In Russian).

Report (2004) *Otchet Ministerstva obrazovaniya i nauki Respubliki Buryatiya za 2002–2004 gg. [Report of the Ministry of Education and Science of the Republic of Buryatia, 2002–2004]* http://www.buryatlaws.ru/index.php?ds=1005031. (In Russian).

Report (2009) *Otchet ob issledovanii 2007–2008 gg. Rukopis [Research Report 2007–2008. Manuscript]*. (In Russian).

Report (2009/2010) *Otchet Ministerstva obrazovaniya Saha (Yakutii) za 2009/2010 uchebnyi god [Report of the Ministry of Education of Sakha (Yakutia) for the 2009/2010 Academic Year]* http://www.sakha.gov.ru/minobr. (In Russian).

Review (2004) *Obzor uchebnoi literatury po natsional'noi (etnicheskoi) istorii [Review of Textbooks on National (Ethnic) History]* http:www.tataroved.ru/obrazovanie/conception/obzor. (In Russian).

Robertson, R. (1995) 'Glocalizations: Time–Space and Homogeneity–Heterogeneity' in M. Featherstone, S. Lash, R. Robertson (eds) *Global Modernities* (London: Sage).

Russian identity (2008) *Rossiiskaya identichnost' v Moskve i regionah [Russian Identity in Moscow and Regions]* (Moscow: Maks-Press). (In Russian).

Shapiro V. et al. (2007) *Podrostki i junoshestvo v mnogonatsionalnoy Moskve: formirovanie etnicheskogo samosoznanija i mezhetnicheskih otnosheniy [Teenagers and Young People in Multi-National Moscow: Formation of Ethnic Self-Consciousness and Inter-Ethnic Relations]* (Moscow: Institut sociologii RAN). (In Russian).

Shubkin, V. et al. (1968) 'Quantitative methods in sociological studies of problems of job placement and choice of occupation', *Soviet Sociology*, VII, 1: 3–24.

Smith, W., Lusthaus, Ch. (1995) 'The nexus of equality and quality in education: A framework for debate', *Canadian Journal of Education*, 20, 3.

Sobkin, V. (1984) 'The formation of national identity and value orientations among Jewish teenagers in Russia' in T. Horowitz, B. Kotik-Friedgut and S. Hoffman (eds) *From Pacesetters to Dropouts: Post-Soviet Youth in Comparative Perspective* (New York: University Press of America).

Statistical bulletin (2006) *Predpolozhitelnaja chislennost naselenia Rossiyskoy Federacii do 2025 goda: Statisticheskiy biulleten [Estimated Number of Population of the Russian Federation up to 2025: Statistical Bulletin]* (Moscow: Federal State Statistics Service, 2006.). (In Russian).

Thomas, W.L. and Znaniecki F. (1918). *The Polish Peasant in Europe and America.* (New York: Knopf).

Tiurukanova, E. (2009) 'Trudovye migranty v Moskve: "vtoroe obshchestvo"' ['Migrant workers in Moscow: "Second society"'] in Zh. Zajonchkovskaja (ed.) *Immigranty v Moskve [Immigrants in Moscow]* (Moscow: 'Tri kvadrata'). (In Russian).

Vendina, O.I. (2009) 'Kulturnoe raznoobrazie i "pobochnye effekty" etnokulturnoi politiki' ['Cultural diversity and "side effects" of ethnic-cultural policy'] in Zh. Zajonchkovskaja (ed.) *Immigranty v Moskve [Immigrants in Moscow]* (Moscow: 'Tri kvadrata'). (In Russian).

Vorotnikov, Yu. (2007) 'Russkii yazyk i problema natsionalnoi bezopasnosti Rossii' ['Russian language and Russian national security problem'] in Yu. Vorotnikov (ed.) *Yazykovaya politika v sovremennom mire [The Language Policy in the Modern World]* (St Petersburg: Zlatoust). (In Russian).

Zajonchkovskaja, Zh. and Mkrtchan, N. (2009) 'Rol migracii v dinamike chislennosti i sostava naselenija Moskvi' ['Role of migration in dynamic of Moscow population size and structure'] in Zh. Zajonchkovskaja (ed.) *Immigranty v Moskve (Immigrants in Moscow).* (Moscow: Tri kvadrata). (In Russian).

Zvezda Povolzhia (2008). Newspaper. 46 (448), 4–10 December 2008. (In Russian).

17
Republic of South Africa

Shaheeda Essack and Duncan Hindle

17.1 Introduction

The aim of the chapter is to provide a review and assess how sociologists in South Africa (SA) have studied racial and ethnic inequalities in education from 1980 to 2010. There is at present no documented review on research carried out on race, ethnicity, and educational inequality in South Africa. The socio-political nature of education in the country has generated a plethora of empirical and policy studies on race and educational inequality, although research from a sociological perspective is limited.

Research undertaken indicates that researchers proceed from dissimilar assumptions, depending on the political context. The conclusions all point to education as a tool for either maintaining racial inequality or subverting it. Research in post-apartheid SA goes to great lengths to stress the enduring legacy of educational inequality, especially among the African population.

The use of methods vary from broad descriptions as seen in policy documents to the quantitative as seen in explanatory and predictive studies. The blatant racial inequalities in education have captured the imagination of many a researcher giving rise to the use of innovative methods such us proxies, stochasticism, extrapolation, or narratives in seeking to understand the complexities. Needless to say, specific and distinct research traditions have emerged over time. All have one focus – trying to understand 'why the racial inequities in education remain' despite the implementation of progressive policies.

Of significance in the study of de-racialisation is that SA, unlike the United Kingdom (UK), the United States of America (USA) and Europe, the majority (black population) have been the victims of inferior education while the minority (white population) enjoyed legal advantage. De-racialisation is therefore in part a peripheral issue, the mainstream issue remains the quality of education for the majority who are not part of the integration project. Further, because studies cannot utilize control groups, direct comparative studies between racial groups on educational performance in a classroom setting are also not part of the research tradition.

The discussion is divided into four parts: the national context, methods, the eight research traditions, and some conclusions.

17.2   National context

This section offers an overview of the main characteristics of the SA educational system, the transition from education under apartheid to education under democracy, and key developments in policy from 1980 to 2010. In this description and analysis, it is necessary to invoke the terminology of apartheid, with four racial categories used, described here as (Black) African, Coloured, Indian and White. Where appropriate elsewhere, the (general) term black is used to include African, Coloured and Indian groups compared to white groups. This is not intended to confirm any sense of racial classification, and the terms are used only for historical or analytical reasons.

17.2.1   The educational system of the country

The following discussion is divided into the apartheid, the resistance and the post-apartheid period.

17.2.1.1   *The apartheid period*

Prior to the advent of inclusive democracy in 1994, SA had a highly fragmented education system, divided on grounds of race (primarily), language (within racial groups), and region. In all there were 19 education departments: national ones for White, Indians, and Coloureds, as well as a national department for Black Africans 'residing in South Africa'. In addition there were many Africans living in 'homelands' or self-governing territories (including Transkei, Ciskei, Bophuthatswana, KwaZulu, and Venda), which each had their own Department of Education (DoE).

On top of all this was laid a language determination, with White schools divided on the use of English or Afrikaans (official languages) as the medium of instruction, and African primary schools on the basis of language (hence ethnic identity). Sociologically, the basis for this was to avoid any notion of an 'African majority' identity; the apartheid regime hoped that by imposing enough racial, ethnic and linguistic categories in society, SA would be a nation of many minorities. These divisions were not just organizational categories: there were specific layers of material and cultural advantage and disadvantage that went with each.

17.2.1.2   *Resistance to apartheid education*

Opposition to 'Bantu Education' (where Bantu means 'Black people', particularly African) was extensive, and a core pillar of the broader anti-apartheid movement. Repression, intolerance, and inequality were driven by the education system, with children socialized into their pre-determined role either as a 'White boss' or a 'Black worker' (Kallaway, 2002). Besides the physical deprivation of poor facilities and under-trained teachers in most Black schools, the psychological trauma of being groomed for second-class citizenship was profound, and has been described by former Education Minister Naledi Pandor (1994–1999) as 'one of the most enduring legacies of apartheid', resulting in a diminished sense of self-worth. A study by Mathonsi (1988) also showed how final school results were manipulated by the apartheid state in relation to the labor absorption capacity of the country: if fewer jobs were available more students were failed so they remained in school for longer. Success at school was thereby delinked from effort and achievement and subjected to a range of external factors, which further undermined the credibility of the system.

The student protests of 1976 including their origins in relation to a directive that half of all subjects should be studied in Afrikaans are well documented (Baloyi, 2004). Besides the fact that most Black children (and their teachers) did not speak Afrikaans, its association with the apartheid system was very strong, and the directive was broadly rejected. This sparked off a national revolt, which in turn became a catalyst for much wider civil disobedience and the final changes which came about in 1994 (Landman, 1992; Muller, 1992a). In this way, students have been characterized as having led the revolution, while their parents had been 'too patient, too tolerant, for too long'.

A large part of this resistance came from the teachers themselves, who for a long time had been passive agents of the apartheid state, despite their stated dislike of what was happening (Levin, 1991; Moll, 1991; Hartshorne, 1992). By the late 1980s a growing number of teachers, some of whom had been politicized and mobilized during the student protests of the former decade, began to organize outside of the traditional teacher organizations, and adopted a more militant and aggressive stance towards the apartheid authorities. Civil society organizations were formed around the issue of education, which coalesced in the formation of the National Education Crisis Committee (NECC) as the voice of the progressive forces in regard to education. Its immediate agenda was the pursuit of a unitary and equitable education system. The broader goal was the democratization of society, captured in the slogan 'Peoples Education for Peoples Power' (Chisholm, 2006).

17.2.1.3 *The post-apartheid period*

After the first democratic elections of 1994, the Bill of Rights contained in the Constitution of the Republic of South Africa (RSA, 1996a) was promulgated. This secured an inalienable right to basic education, including adult basic education, and to further education, which the state, through reasonable measures, must progressively make available and accessible. The first year of schooling is a 'reception year', which is not compulsory. Grades 10, 11 and 12 are legally not compulsory although there is an expectation that children should complete Grade 12 and access is not denied. The Education White Paper 6, respects disabilities in learners, and provides for their needs.

Access to higher education is based on the National Senior Certificate (NSC) results at the end of Grade 12, and remains highly competitive.

Public schools are largely free of tuition fees, and are subsidized according to a re-distributive norm, geared towards redressing inequalities. This requires parents of wealthier public schools (mostly former White schools) to pay school fees to enable upkeep of the school, although poor students are exempted from these if attending such schools. Private schools do exist, and are largely funded by parents. Only 3% of children attend these. See Figure 17.1 for a description of the education system.

17.2.2   Main migration patterns and composition and size of ethnic 'minority' (majority) groups

Educational inequalities affect the majority black population. There is little documented research on the migration of foreigners into SA schools although there is evidence of movement from other African countries to SA schools. Some of this occurs across the colonial borders, where children from one country, like Lesotho, cross the border daily to attend school with their household communities.

More significant is the migration of people within SA to other parts of the country, in search of schooling. Given the poor quality of schooling in predominantly black areas, the first choice of schools is the better resourced former White school. SA has a policy of no-fee schools for over 80% of all schools, and these generally service the poorer communities, but where family resources are available, parents choose to exit such schools in favor of fee-paying public schools. While there are pro-poor policy gains, they are not sufficient to address the inequalities (Ahmed and Sayed, 2009, p. 215), and migration is the consequence.

At the local level, some children move from dysfunctional schools in the urban 'townships' to former White/Indian/Coloured schools in the 'suburbs' of the same town. Other children move from rural areas to town, often staying with relatives, sometimes on their own in order to attend better schools. Large flows of children are seen each year flowing from poorer provinces (Limpopo and the Eastern Cape (EC)) into better resourced provinces (Gauteng and the Western Cape (WC)), making planning a difficult task. As a proxy for quality, this kind of migration has to be taken seriously – these are not incidental actions.

The migration of black children out of such schools, especially in urban areas where there are possibilities of doing so, is inevitable, and has meant that the de-racialisation of SA schools has in effect meant the gradual (and selective)

General education		Further education and Training	Higher education
Primary	**Junior secondary**		
Reception to Grade 6	**Grades 7 to 9**	**Grades 10 to 12**	Universities
Reception year is not compulsory, however, the majority of children do have at least one year of preschooling.	Compulsory	Not compulsory; access not denied. High enrolments in Grade 10, but lower at Grades 11 and 12.	State run universities and private higher education institutions offer certificates, diplomas and degrees.
The curriculum from Grades 1 to 9 is a general one, including two languages, mathematics, life sciences, life orientation, economic and management sciences, arts and culture, and others.	After Grade 9, may opt to continue to Grade 10 at school or obtain the General Education and Training Certificate (GETC) and pursue employment and/or training at a Further Education and Training (FET) college.	Students sit the nationally set and moderated state examination, or an approved alternate such as the Independent Examinations Board (IEB) to obtain the National Senior Certificate at the end of Grade 12.	Certificates and diplomas (1–2 years)
			Bachelor's degree (3–6 years)
		From Grade 10, students take 7 subjects: 4 are English, a 2nd SA language, life orientation and either mathematics or mathematical literacy and 3 others from 27 options.	Honour's degree (1 year)
			Master's degree (2 years post-graduate)
			Doctorate degree

Figure 17.1 The education system of South Africa

absorption of a limited number of non-white learners into former White schools (Sujee, 2004). In many cases, the pupil population of such schools has become black, while the racial profile of the staff has not changed. While this may seem offensive, and obviously raises concerns about role-modeling, many black parents welcome the presence of white teachers for their English language ability, as well as for the generally better discipline and organization of such schools. Because of the demographics, the facts remain that the vast majority of black learners continue to learn in all-black schools, and are unlikely to encounter other races during their schooling careers. SA has thus lapsed into a system of two parts, one that is white, urban, privileged, and fee paying and the other part free, failing, and black.

By 2002, the pattern of racial integration in the different types of schools in the Gauteng province was as follows: former Coloured schools had 44% African learners and 56% Coloured learners, former Indian schools had 63% African learners and 31% Indian learners; while former White schools had 5% Coloured learners, 3% Indian, 34% African and 57% White learners (Sujee, 2004. Overall, there was a 25% shift of African learners from African schools to former White/Indian/Coloured schools, and the numbers of African learners in African schools has increased. There is no equivalent data for other provinces, which may have seen similar trends, but the extent would be greater in the more urban and compact province, making 'internal migration' more likely.

17.2.3   Developments in terms of relevant educational and social policies

Discussion on policy developments within the education system is similarly considered in terms of the apartheid, resistance to apartheid, and post-apartheid periods, each with their distinctive sociologically informed approaches and transitional assumptions.

17.2.3.1   The apartheid period

Key research in this period was policy driven, large scale and state funded aimed at justifying structural inequalities. These include the De Lange Report, the Buthelezi Commission report, the 1983 White Paper on Education, and the Education Renewal Strategy (ERS). These papers were mainly descriptive aimed at explaining the nature of educational inequality with a view to justifying it. These reports reveal how the state 'manipulated' its position of authority to legitimate educational inequality based on perverse and crude notions of racial inferiority. These reports are discussed in greater detail in Section 17.4.1 'From oligarchy to democracy'.

17.2.3.2   Resistance to apartheid period

The transformation of education was not simple. In crude terms, the question was whether 'education for liberation', was a correct strategy, or political liberation needed to precede any kind of real transformation, in which case schools should be boycotted or even burnt down until the edifice of apartheid collapsed (Alexander, 1990). This tension was never fully resolved; while significant efforts were put into trying to provide alternative curricula and materials to teachers, the mood in many schools was one in which education was willingly sacrificed in pursuit of broader 'ungovernability' and the end of the apartheid state. This ungovernability included the complete non-recognition of education authorities, which has left many schools till today without the requisite authority and discipline to be effective (Baloyi, 2004).

The major policy development by pro-democracy forces was in 1992 when the National Education Policy Investigation (NEPI) produced a comprehensive, multi-volume report that provided a well-researched argument for a systemic overhaul of the education system towards a unified, democratic, and non-racial system. In 1994, on the eve of assuming power, the African National Congress (ANC) *Policy Framework for Education and Training* was published, strongly influenced by the Congress of South African Trade Unions (COSATU) and the National Training Board (NTB). They advocated the integration of education and training within a single qualifications framework which would bring about greater equity and redress (de Clercq, 1997, p. 151). Soon thereafter, the minister of education released the First White Paper on Education and Training.

17.2.3.3 The post-apartheid period

Post-1994, SA had a unique opportunity to define and build a new education system from scratch. At the same time there was an increasing recognition that social institutions do not work this way – they change slowly, and they have to take account of what already exists. This challenge was highlighted during the long process of negotiations which led to the 1994 transition, in which education featured prominently (Hartshorne, 1992; Baloyi, 2004).

The year 1996 ushered in the first of far-reaching policy and legislative changes. These included the promulgation of the National Education Policy Act (NEPA) which defined the powers and duties of the national and provincial education ministries (Carrim, 2001, p. 101). The outgoing apartheid regime had insisted on a maximum devolution of powers in the Constitutional framework with regard to education as a way of exerting control on some areas of governance. The function was therefore designated by NEPA as a 'concurrent' responsibility of both national and provincial governments, with both having legislative and executive powers, but with provinces having the budgets and administrative responsibility for the management of schools.

Also in 1996, the South African Schools Act (Act No. 84 of 1996) ('the SASA Act') was enacted, which dealt with the funding, organization, and governance of schools (Carrim, 2001, p. 102). The SASA Act extended significant powers and functions to elected school governing bodies. Powers of admission, language policy, and other crucial elements like selecting and recommending teachers for appointment were given to schools to determine. But most significantly, schools were given the power to set and collect compulsory school fees, with complicated exemption policies intended to protect poorer learners from being excluded. This liberalization, which gave public schools more powers than their counterparts anywhere else in the world, has allowed privileged schools to remain so, with a careful selection of fee-paying parents, teachers who reflect the historical traditions of the school, and the use of school fees to employ additional teachers and procure other teaching and learning resources. Consequently, such schools perform substantially better than the majority, although whether they should be regarded as 'public' schools is debatable, since they have effectively been privatized. Ironically, many believe that free education will destroy the public school system (Paton, 2008, p. 1).

The much awaited curriculum reform came in 1997 in the form of *Curriculum 2005*, an indigenous form of 'outcomes-based education' (OBE) which departed fundamentally from the apartheid-based 'Christian national education'. The new curriculum was underpinned by the values of democracy, equity, and human rights as enshrined in the Constitution, and fundamentally altered the nature of education in SA. In 2002, the National Curriculum Statement was revised.

SA has maintained a largely functional education system around the 1994 transition, with near universal enrollment, especially among girls. However, the country has not as yet achieved the equality goals required by the Constitution, and despite progressive policies has become a conserving force in society, confirming in most cases the racial and economic inequalities in society.

17.3   Methods

The literature review faced some restrictions. First, it was decided to include only studies that focused on SA as a research context. Second, the literature review was restricted to contributions between 1980 and 2010 from the discipline of sociology that focused on the relationship between educational inequality and race or ethnicity. For SA, the focus was mainly on race. Third, only research that focused on secondary education was included for analysis. As a result, studies that investigated other forms of education, such as preschool, family, primary, higher, or adult education were not included. Finally, only peer-reviewed journal articles, commissioned reports, and (edited) books were considered for analysis. Although these four criteria for inclusion strongly guided the review process, some studies considered did not fulfill at least one of these criteria, because they were perceived relevant examples of specific research traditions such as the critical policy documents consulted. The restrictions are not meant to marginalize other literature sources, disciplinary perspectives, and/or forms of education.

The process of sampling specific research contributions involved a search of the relevant databases using specific research queries in seven selected databases for the period 1980–2010: (1). the library catalogue at the University of South Africa (UNISA) for books on http://millennium.ac.za/ and http://millennium.unisa.ac.za/airpac; (2) the SAePublications for South African Journal articles; (3) Google Scholar (http://scholar.google.com); (4) the Human Sciences Research Council (HSRC) database; (5) the journal *Perspectives in Education*; (6) the South African Institute of Race Relations (SAIRR); and (7) the *Journal of Education*. Thereafter, a manageable sample of articles were selected and systematically analyzed. Additional information identified in reports, journals, books, and by key researchers were included in the review process.

17.4   Research traditions

A literature review for the period 1980–2010 identifies eight broad research traditions: (1) from oligarchy to democracy; (2) policy development – state versus resistance movements;, (3) the impact of the removal of race-based policies; (4) racial (de)segregation: causes and consequences; (5) (de)segregation and school resources; (6) curriculum studies; (7) teacher training and pedagogy; (8) charting inequalities in student outcomes. The following section provides a descriptive analysis for each research tradition.

17.4.1   From oligarchy to democracy

The dominant research tradition prior to and even after 1994 was a structural one (Wolpe, 1988; Nkomo, 1990). Perhaps, it was also because the flaws in SA society were inherently structural in nature, based on race and gender and enforced by legislation. Human agency was a small part of the anti-apartheid equation, and much less researched.

SA remains divided in terms of race and class. Class structures remain strongly aligned to race, although there has been some re-alignment post-1994. Until 1994, the country constituted an oligarchy, in which the minority ruled the majority (Brubacher, 1969, p. 53), and democracy and political rights for the majority of SA only came into law in 1994.

17.4.1.1   *Apartheid SA/Large-scale state-funded research*

Perhaps as a result of the emphasis on 'group' identities (rather than individual agency), most of the more significant studies under apartheid were large-scale, (SA and foreign) government-funded ones, with a view to either justifying the structural inequalities or finding against them.

Structural-functionalist views of schooling assume an ordered and predictable function of schools and related socialization processes, and in some respects these were realized. Fundamental pedagogics, drawing heavily on European scientific paradigms, found many adherents in the Afrikaner universities and the state system, and sought to justify an authoritarian, differentiated education system. An article by Enslin (1988) described some of the horrific assumptions of fundamental pedagogics around the innate evilness of the child, the need for corporal punishment, and the pre-ordained nature of their development. Sadly, this research informed various efforts by the state to modernize the education system, e.g., the ERS of the mid-1990s, and even to allow for limited de-racialization of White schools.

Not surprisingly, none of these pseudo-science research efforts provided a sufficient basis to prevent the comprehensive rejection of apartheid education. Black researchers and commentators identified structural patterns and determinants, which were translated into political critiques. It is true that many Black school principals and supervisors served as agents of the state in their efforts to maintain social control. But in most respects the consequences were unintended and unpredictable; black resistance to apartheid flourished in educational settings, and education became a primary site of contestation since the initial uprisings in 1976. This was often intense and accompanied by violence (Bot and Schlemmer, 1986, p. 1), and sowed the first seeds of a notion of human agency in the deliberations about 'people's education' and its relationship to liberation.

At the same time there were emerging critical studies being undertaken, a record can be found in the Kenton Conference papers, published annually and now to be found in the *Journal of Education*. These included theoretical, Marxist analyses, as well as small-scale studies, including case-studies, and interactionist-type research. Tlhapi's (2006) study on the experience of secondary school pupils on citizenship in a democratic SA showed that learners believed that democratic citizenship emanates from a democratic political system.

In sum, research on education under apartheid was large scale, descriptive, and government funded with a view to justifying the structural inequalities. At the same time there was an emergence of critical studies with a Marxist orientation which were small scale and qualitative.

17.4.2   Policy development – State versus resistance movements

The date 16 June 1976 was 'the culmination of decades of relatively peaceful protest by Black students against the inequities of segregation and apartheid in the educational institutions of SA' (Alexander, 1990 p. 25). Black learners wanted equality of the conditions and content of learning with those enjoyed by White learners.

The greatest conflict manifested in the terrain of policy and legislation. The old system was retreating and the new system was being built in the context of political conflict between old and new social forces, and all the resultant policies and legislation were negotiated and compromised (Chisholm, 2006,

p. 144). The major protagonists were the ruling National Party (NP), the ANC, and its aligned NECC, comprising student, parent and teacher organizations.

The unannounced transition had effectively begun post-1976 with the recognition of the serious failures inherent in apartheid education policy and the ongoing social unrest which this was producing. The apartheid state initiated various research studies to understand the problem and identify possible solutions, within the paradigm of separate group identities. At the same time democratic forces, less well-organized and funded, started to tackle with a new seriousness the policy options available in resisting and then replacing apartheid education.

17.4.2.1 *The De Lange Report*

In 1981, the Human Sciences Research Council (HSRC) produced a report entitled, 'Report of the Main Committee of the HSRC Investigation into Educational Provision in South Africa'. This had been conducted under the chairmanship of Professor J.P. de Lange, at the request of the government, as a basis for educational policy change. In-depth research into the education of all race groups was conducted with a view to making recommendations on a more equitable educational policy. The proposals included the establishment of a single Ministry of Education, free and compulsory education for all race groups, and equality in all regards (albeit still racially separate) (de Lange, 1981).

In addition, a smaller sample of 300 African adults in KwaZulu was asked: 'Why do you think African children so often fail in the exams?' In response 75% blamed African teachers in various ways, 40% blamed the system of education, and 20% ascribed the problem to Black poverty. Bot and Schlemmer (1986, p. 3) note that: 'This mode of response involves the perception of what is in fact a consequence of inequality as a basis of inequality, and as such is an adaptive response, if not a 'depoliticising' viewpoint'.

17.4.2.2 *The 1983 White Paper on education*

The apartheid government published a White Paper on education in 1983, setting out its intentions for reforms in education. Regrettably it excluded the recommendations made in the De Lange report, since these were antithetical to apartheid ideology (Baloyi, 2004, p. 116). Some provisions were made for Indians and Coloureds, under the pretext of 'own affairs' governance by these racial groups, but the official policy remained 'separate but equal', with schools segregated on racial lines (Baloyi, 2004, p. 21). Not surprisingly, the White Paper was roundly rejected by democratic forces.

17.4.2.3 *The education renewal strategy*

In May 1990, with the system collapsing around them, the government announced the development of a 'strategy for education renewal', under the auspices of the Committee of Heads. The motives for renewal included the racial basis of the system, a mismatch between programs and developmental needs, and inertia and inflexibility in the system. Twenty issues were identified and submissions invited on these. In June 1991, a first discussion document was released. The educational renewal strategy (ERS) contained 68 recommendations, including the need for a centralized ministry – a major shift in government thinking. The underlying thread was the 'need to accommodate diversity', which it saw as being achieved by various forms of differentiation within a common system. The continuities with apartheid, under a different guise, were painfully obvious, and again the ERS was rejected.

17.4.2.4   *The national education policy initiative*

At around the same time, democratic forces were sharpening up their policy proposals, as part of the 'preparing to govern' phase. Under the auspices of the NECC, and drawing on extensive international funding, the 'national education policy initiative' (NEPI) was undertaken. In a post-modern fashion, over 300 research papers were commissioned on a range of key issues. These interrogated policy options, within a democratic value framework, and each set of papers culminated in a summary report, 13 of which comprise the output of the investigation.

As the moment of liberation grew nearer, these were taken further into the Implementation Plans for Education and Training (IPET) – 13 detailed plans that would inform the policy directions of the future government. Within the ANC, a political response was being formulated, drawing on the work of NEPI and the various IPETs. These were contained in the *ANC Policy Framework for Education and Training* (the 'Yellow Book'), a pre-liberation policy document on education, which became the guide to much of the legislation and policy post-1994.

17.4.2.5   *Resistance to schooling*

The turbulence of the 1980s and 1990s in the form of violent protests, teacher strikes, and class boycotts inspired research on how Black learners, overtly and covertly, rejected apartheid education in townships. Subtle forms of resistance included disrespect for authority, absenteeism by teachers and pupils, and parental non-participation in school committees (Mbonambi, 1998, p. 2). The apartheid state was challenged and civil society and education activists were alarmed at the deterioration of learning among Black learners (Reeves, 1994; Hartshorne, 1992; Samuel, 1990).

Through the use of the following methods: phenomenology, a problem-historical approach, a chronological approach, and the metabletic approach Mahumi (2004, p. 108) arrives at the conclusion that a lack of a culture of learning among black pupils cannot be attributed to a single factor but to a range of factors including the deteriorating conditions and an absence of effective teaching. Similarly, Maluleka (2001, pp. 163–164) examined the socio-educative implications of children's rights in black secondary schools. He concluded that children's lack of understanding of the concept of 'rights' led to misconceptions and resulted in instability. Most black senior secondary learners had a negative attitude on the exercise of rights leading to disrespect for authority, lawlessness, and chaos in schools.

Baloyi (2004, p. 12) adopted a problem-historical approach to establish the role of the state in establishing a culture of teaching and learning. He claimed that (a) African education degenerated from a highly disciplined and motivated culture of teaching and learning during the period 1910–1947, and (b) the culture of learning gradually collapsed during the apartheid era (1948–1994). He concluded that the crisis in Black schooling since 1976 can largely be attributed to the repressive role of the state and its unjust policies based on racial discrimination. Overt conflict only arose when the state used education to further their racist oppressive ideology. In the earlier period, despite its discriminatory colonial character, popular politics, and acceptance of state policies led to the establishment of a culture of teaching and learning. He identifies the re-establishment of the culture of teaching and learning as a pre-requisite for a successful democracy, which can only be sustained if people are well educated and disciplined. He recommends amendments to the Labour Relations Act (Act 66 of 1995) to curtail teacher strikes and promote a developmental and professional role for teachers and trade unions.

In sum, the period from around 1976 was characterized by a process of negotiation and compromise of the old forces with the new in informing the research agenda and thus shaping educational policy. The process of resistance by black teachers and learners was both overt and covert. Despite efforts by the apartheid state to arrive at an agreeable solution, all of its policies failed. Finally, the 'Yellow Book' became the guide to educational reforms and equity.

17.4.3   The impact of the removal of race-based policies on education

Sociologically based education research in the post-apartheid era has not been dominated by government. The Research Centre in the DoE was dis-established, and only the HSRC retained any real capacity for large-scale research. Studies done by them, on commission from the DoE, related to the de-racialization of schools, and the promotion of values in education. University-based research has had little impact on public policy, and the primary research driver has been independent research institutes, non-governmental organizations (NGOs) and the faculties of education at universities.

Large-scale quantitative studies conducted in 2002 by Fiske and Ladd (2004, pp. 15–16) confirm that the removal of race-based policies in education and the introduction of compulsory and equal education allowed a number of black students to enroll in former White schools. Their analysis included data from the poorest province, the EC, which was compared to data from the well-resourced WC. This provided a comprehensive analysis of integration patterns between the impoverished, predominantly rural and black EC and the relatively wealthy, urban, WC.

Ironically, they conclude that the power of school governing bodies over admissions limits the intake of black students, since this is done without attention to race equivalence, and based on the erroneous belief that social integration would lead to equal access to schools. The results imply that (a) the main determinant of educational opportunity is the quality of schools serving African students, and not the degree of integration in a few urban schools; (b) while significant progress has been made toward equity in funding, the state needs to direct more resources to schools serving low-income and historically disadvantaged families, mainly from the African community; and (c) poorly resourced schools, mainly in African areas, did not have the infrastructure, equipment, or cultural capital to effectively implement the complex OBE curriculum, while well-resourced schools thrived under the non-prescriptive paradigm (Fiske and Ladd, 2004, pp. 127–129, 170). The OBE aims were thus undermined.

The new democratic policies therefore failed to become efficient mechanisms for the redistribution of educational resources for the attainment of greater equity in education, especially for black learners (Motala and Pampallis, 2001, p. 176). Lemon (2004, pp. 269–290) suggests focusing on the urban and rural poor instead of dumping the consequences of inappropriate policies onto communities that lack the resources to implement them effectively.

In sum, the quantitative, provincial, and comparative studies of the removal of race-based policies reveals the inability of the new state to equalize educational opportunities for African learners. Qualitative and innovative methods best lend themselves to study of this phenomenon.

17.4.4   Racial desegregation

This research tradition examines the experience and consequence of migration of African/Indian/Coloured pupils to former White schools. Many of the educational changes enacted since 1994 indicate that the desegregation of schools is largely understood by many as providing black learners with greater access to better resourced former White schools. Methods draw from sociological models of analysis.

As early as 1986, White fears of the desegregation of schools were evident. An attitudinal study conducted by Bot and Schlemmer (1986) on White teachers belonging to the more liberal Natal Teachers' Society towards desegregated/multicultural schooling showed a strong polarization of views on race, although there was a high degree of consensus on issues such as White students learning the language, history, and culture of Africans, creating a single education department and multi-racial sport. In contrast, 73% believed that racial integration would lead to a lowering of standards for White children, and this fear carries through much of the predominantly white discourse to this day. Bot and Schlemmer (1986, p. 45) argued in the 1980s that segregated education is the single biggest factor in SA politics that will generate controversy and urged the White community to give urgent consideration to the challenges posed by unrest among Africans in township schools.

Whilst the quest for de-segregated schools continued, by 1997 racial integration in SA schools was still low. The assumption of a mono-directional flow was correct, and there is little movement of children in any other direction, so the majority of black children are not affected and remain in racially and ethnically homogenous contexts. Van der Berg's (2001) national study of racial integration in schools indicated that only 3.2% of Africans were in racially mixed schools. Within African schools, 99.6% of learners were African, which reflects the spatial geography determined by apartheid (Fiske and Ladd, 2004, p. 87). Former White schools remained 90% white, although 22% of whites were in racially mixed schools.

Fiske and Ladd (2004, pp. 81–100) compared the pattern of student enrollment across the four race groups in the WC and the EC. The results indicate that the former township schools still serve only African students, the former Coloured/Indian/White schools serve mostly their own communities, although 35% of learners in White schools were black. While former White schools are the most desegregated and diversified, most schools serve and will continue to serve a primarily African and rural population. While integration of schools is important, it does little to enhance the educational opportunities for the majority of black learners.

However, a study on desegregation and redistribution on 15 schools in Grahamstown in the EC ranging from private, township, informal settlements, and rural areas which looked at documents from the provincial DoE, the examinations center, and interviews concludes that class rather than race is the main determinant of educational opportunity.

17.4.4.1 *Identity, culture, and social cohesion*

While advances have been made with regard to desegregation, insufficient attention has been paid to social integration among teachers and learners from diverse backgrounds. Whilst the first level of integration, racial desegregation of pupils, is easy to achieve in schools and universities, schools struggle to integrate at the level of staffing, curriculum, and institutional culture (Jansen, 2004, pp. 118–128).

Through the conceptual lens of Bernstein's theory of code, classification, boundary, and power, Naidoo (2010) questions how far integration has progressed in an historically disadvantaged Gauteng school. She concludes that racial desegregation is achieved at student level and among lower-level staff, but not at management level. There was no evidence of an integrated institutional culture. Social boundaries maintained previous race-based power relations, while 'weaker boundaries between instrumental and non-instrumental forms of knowledge legitimised students' experiences and interests but did not facilitate access to non-instrumental forms of knowledge and thinking' (Naidoo, 2010, p. 19). At the same time the dominant discourse was racist – white teachers view black students in ways which undermine integration and reproduce racial stereotypes.

While public schools in the suburbs and cities are becoming increasingly desegregated, Bekisizwe (2004) similarly found that classroom discourse has remained unchanged, which militates against the integration of class and cultural differences and rewards students from white, middle-class backgrounds. Black children from township schools are 'soft-locked' into geographical school zones and 'soft-locked' out of former White schools because of culture, fees, and transport costs. White pupils start avoiding those schools which become all-black. Perceptions do play a powerful role in shaping parents' and students' racial attitudes (Fiske and Ladd, 2004, pp. 81–82). White parents are reported to fear the lowering of standards as teachers spend more time with disadvantaged black children.

Ntshoe (2009, pp. 85–104) believes that the school zoning policy, based on preference rather than prescription, indicates covert racism and is actually a poor instrument to redress race and class inequalities, since it recreates the apartheid-demarcated racial geographical boundaries.

Carter et al. (2009, pp. 351–364) study how students' and school officials' actions are informed by deeply embedded racialized meanings and how they reinforce the strength and rigidity of racial boundaries. They conclude that while desegregation enables learners to traverse a particular spatial plane, racial and cultural differentiation in schools continue to engender strong boundaries along these lines. Further, a study on white privilege post-1994 by Soudien (2010, pp. 35–352) through the lens of (a) global whiteness, (b) the new SA whiteness, and the (c) the new privileged black, found that the former Afrikaans schools are the least integrated of the former White schools, since Afrikaans is still used as an exclusionary medium of instruction. Contact with black people in spaces of privilege but not outside of these has been the dominant pattern. The former White schools have become places of cultural assimilation marginalizing black cultural practices.

On the positive side (Weber et al., 2009) sees an emergence of a new pattern of consciousness and behavior among some pupils, manifesting in high levels of tolerance towards other races, classes, and genders useful for building a national identity. The view is confirmed by Holtman (2005). He used the regression model to measure the relationship between the amount and quality of intergroup contact and racial prejudice as a predictor of racial attitudes.

The results show that contact was the most important predictor of race attitudes. It accounted for the strongest variation in most of the dependent measures thereby confirming that reducing prejudice for all groups runs through inter-racial contact. This is a positive development for desegregation in schools.

In sum, the educational experiment of desegregation and integration in SA schools has been ambitious and intractable. There is a disjuncture between the intentions of policy and its outcome at the grassroots level. The research correctly indicates that much needs to be done in addressing institutional and cultural integration. Whilst large-scale quantitative studies serve to provide information on demographics and geography, the micro qualitative studies highlight the intricacies of the contradictions inherent in mixed-race settings. On the positive side, research suggests that integration, if well supported and understood, has the potential to contribute to the project of nation building.

17.4.5 (De)segregation and school resources

Research post-1994 focused on the means to achieve an equitable redistribution of human and financial resources, and to provide funding to schools on a pro-poor basis. The challenge was balancing the demand for free education against limited resources (Ahmed and Sayed, 2009, p. 215). The key sources of information are census data (both school and population), datasets from the DoE, as well as the South African Living Standards Survey (SALSS), referred to as SALDRU1, that was carried out jointly by the South African Labour and Development Research Unit (SALDRU) and the World Bank.

17.4.5.1 *The pre-1994 resourcing of schools*

Pre-1994, racial divisions were not just organizational categories: there were specific layers of material and cultural advantage and disadvantage that went with each. Table 17.1 shows that pupils in the White education system were funded at levels up to 18 times greater than those in African schools; Indians and Coloureds got less than White, but more than Africans – a reflection of the

Table 17.1 Per capita expenditure on education by race: 1972–1984

	Expenditure 1983/1984	Ratio 1983/1984	Ratio 1980/1981	Ratio 1971/1972
White	R1511	9.1	6.5	18.4
Indian	R905	5.4	3.7	4.9
Coloured	R501	3.0	1.8	3.7
African	R167	1.0	1.0	1.0

Sources: White, Hansard No. 2, 4/7 February 1985, question and replies, Col 36; Coloured and Indian, personal communication from SA Institute of Race Relations; African, Hansard No. 3, 11/14 February 1985, questions and replies, Col 103.

racial hierarchy in broader society (Christie, 1991, p. 98; Lodge, 1987; Beckett, 1990; Deacon and Parker, 1998; Mncwabe, 1993; Van Zyl, 1991; Wolpe and Unterhalter, 1991).

This was a reflection of the stated goal of H.F. Verwoerd, the founder of apartheid, who saw the role of Blacks as being 'hewers of wood and drawers of water' (Kallaway, 2002). As such, the quality of outputs was also hierarchical, with very few Black children completing schooling, and even less with decent results in key areas like mathematics and science (Kahn, 1993; FRD, 1993), which became the focus of research in the post-apartheid period. Bible studies, agriculture, and 'housekeeping' were seen as more appropriate subjects and strongly encouraged; the classic pattern of colonial subjugation.

Having said this, there were many exceptions to the dominant pattern of racial inequality. First, there were many poor African schools which, despite their appalling circumstances, rose above all expectations and produced leaders like Oliver Tambo and Nelson Mandela. Many of these were 'church schools', established by missionaries in the early 20th century (Claassen, 1995; Webber, 1992). These exceptions helped to demonstrate a fundamental flaw in the apartheid paradigm, which was that 'racial categories' could not be universally applied. Secondly, from the late 1980s, private schools, including a number of church schools, began to admit pupils on a non-racial basis, which shifted the issue to one of class rather than race. In the final stages of apartheid, the state conceded defeat and provided for certain categories of White schools to admit Black learners, in an attempt to manage the deteriorating situation and prepare a new middle class (Mncwabe, 1993).

17.4.5.2   *The post-1994 resourcing of schools*

The post-1994 interprovincial variation in spending fell by more than 40%, since demographic factors determining the provincial shares of state spending include population (with rural populations given additional weight), and school-age population. Fiske and Ladd (2004) and Gustafsson and Patel (2006, p. 67) conclude that remarkable progress has been made to equalize spending across schools though it marginally favored the rich (mainly white). The concentration index measured spending equity by province and economic category. Table 17.2 shows the changes in spending that have taken place since 1994.

17.4.5.3   *The redistribution of educational resources and educational outcomes*

The focus of research post-1994 has been on the relationship between the equitable distribution of public resources across formerly White/Black/Indian/ Coloured schools, and their impact on quality and educational outcomes. Indicators for the latter are: the Grade 12 pass rate, international evaluations such as Trends in International Mathematics and Science Study (TIMMS), the Monitoring Learning Achievement (MLA) study and the report of the Southern

Table 17.2 Per learner budget allocations, by province, 1994–1995 and 2000–2001

Province	Spending per learner (rand)		Percent of national average		
	1994–1995	2000–2001	1991–1995	2000–2001	Change in percent
WC	4.074	4.230	183	130	−53
Gauteng	3.843	4.628	157	142	−15
Northern Cape	3.413	4.399	154	135	−19
Free State	2.317	3.604	104	111	+7
Kwa-Zulu Natal	2.969	2.643	93	81	−12
Mpumalanga	1.917	2.982	86	92	+6
North West	1.812	3.524	82	108	+26
Limpopo	1.669	2.780	75	85	+10
EC	1.635	2.968	74	91	+17
All provinces	**2.222**	**3.253**	**100**	**100**	**0**
Coefficient of variation	0.39	0.22			

Sources: Department of Education and the Department of Finance, reported in Perry (2000), Table 17.2. Sorted by 1994–1995 spending per learner.

Africa Consortium on Monitoring Education Quality, 2001 (SACMEQ II). The results indicate that the educational performance of SA children is extremely weak, and differences in performance between schools serving different parts of the population remain exceedingly large (Chisholm, 2004, p. 12).

The 'learner-to-educator ratio' (LER) is commonly used as one measure of educational input. In 2006, the national LER at schools was 32:1, ranging from 29:1 in Gauteng to 33:1 in Limpopo (DoE, 2006e, p. 6). The difference in LER between former Black, White, and Indian schools was still statistically significant, with a large number of former Black schools having LERs above the targets set by government (Yamauchi, 2003). Case and Deaton (1999) used LER and school facilities to study the relationship between school inputs and outcomes, including both attendance and attainment. The results show a marked correlation, with a strong and significant effect of LERS and facilities on enrollment and educational achievement.

Based on a regression analysis of matriculation pass rates, Van der Berg (2007) found that: (a) despite the massive resource shifts to Black schools, overall matriculation results did not improve, (b) attainment differentials between former White and Black schools remain large, (c) the racial composition of schools remains a major explanatory factor in outcome differentials, and (d) differentials in performance in Black schools which cannot be explained in terms of socio-economic background, LERS, or teaching resources are attributed to the quality of school management, leading to what Van der Berg (2007) terms as 'the problem of x-inefficiency rather than allocative efficiency'.

Van der Berg (2006) measured the targeting of public spending on school education from 1995 to 2000 and similarly concluded that despite the equality of educational spending, equity of educational outcome remained elusive. He identified internal efficiencies, or the lack thereof, as the reason for this. A study of continuing inequality in educational outcomes and the quality of outcomes from an economic perspective found that giving more resources may not be as urgent as improving the use of existing resources (Van der Berg, 2004).

In 2001, Van der Berg (2001, p. 405) analyzed more than 16,000 out of a total of around 25,000 schools. He concluded that the massive shift in fiscal resources to blacks coincided with a fall in fiscal resources going to whites and Indians. At the geographical level, it is likely that both rural and smaller urban areas gained massively. But differentiated teacher salaries, with better-qualified teachers disproportionately concentrated in more affluent schools, meant that fiscal inequalities remained. In addition, private resources (through fee collections) considerably supplemented resources in more affluent schools.

By looking at school effectiveness, socio-economic status, and resources in determining educational performance, Van der Berg (2008, p. 53) concludes that in 2000 socio-economic differentials still played a major role in educational outcomes, and the school system was not yet able to overcome inherited socio-economic disadvantage at the primary level and in poor African schools. Crouch and Vinjevold (2006) warn that the relationship between resources and educational outcomes is neither simplistic nor easy to analyze. Factors such as school management and teacher quality must also be accounted for.

Improving quality remains a focus, and various interventions have provided fertile ground for research. Results from a pre- and post-intervention test of the Quality Learning Project (QLP), undertaken as part of a five-year study, indicate a positive impact of selected interventions on educational outcomes (Paterson et al., 2001). A comparison of QLP schools to a control group indicates a 16% average increase in QLP schools, and a 24% increase in mathematics passes. Kanjee and Prinsloo (2005) conducted a summative evaluation on the program. They concluded that QLP schools outperformed control schools in regard to teacher proficiency, lesson pedagogy, assessment, and amount of classwork and homework. An ethnographic study by Motha (2010), concluded that children living in impoverished communities with exposure to severe disadvantages in their home environment are at greatest risk of an inferior education.

In sum, the research tradition on the distribution of educational resources and output ranges from large-scale empirical studies to micro-level studies on quality. The research points to three key conclusions: that the post-1994 government has made significant strides in equalizing the playing field; that despite the equitable redistribution of funding, inequalities of outcome remain elusive; and that poor schools in African communities have not been able to effectively deploy their resources. Quantitative data are useful in so far as they measure the impact of resources. The policy concern is converting these into outcomes. Future research might look into triangulating the economic perspective with the sociological so as to provide a complete explanation on the 'what is', 'why it is' and ideas about how the shortcomings can be addressed.

17.4.6 Curriculum studies

Post-1994, Jansen (1998), Hindle (2003), and Chisholm (2005) as cited in Bantwini (2010), agree that curriculum change has proceeded in three main waves. The first involved a cleansing of the syllabus of its apartheid terminology and legacies. This was undertaken under the auspices of the National Education and Training Forum, a transitional mechanism set up to manage the interregnum.

The second was the launch of *Curriculum 2005* in 1997, based on the principles of transformational OBE, in which content was to be shaped in a non-authoritarian and participatory manner (Fiske and Ladd, 2004). The third wave was the 2000 review of this curriculum undertaken by Chisholm. This review recommended that the curriculum be strengthened by streamlining its design, simplifying the language, and making it more accessible for teachers (Bantwini 2010, p. 85). This led to the Revised National Curriculum Statement (RNCS) in 2002.

Studies on the curriculum generate significant controversy on its perceived successes and failures. Most adopt qualitative methods, for example focus group interviews, classroom observation, ethnographic, and historiographic methods, guided by concerns on the nature of the curriculum, teacher preparedness, and the systems of supervision and assessment. Through focus groups and interviews, Vithal and Gopal (2005, p. 57) study how learners engage with the principles and practice of the new curriculum reforms such as learner-centeredness, group work, knowledge integration, and new assessment paradigms. They conclude that learners notice, experience, and articulate the changes intended and attained through curriculum reforms. The manner in which teachers articulate the agenda and purpose of the reforms is shaped by teachers as mediators.

In a study on what meanings teachers ascribe to the curriculum, Bantwini (2010, pp. 88–89) found that none of the teachers in one of the poorest districts of the EC, a province characterized by low educational standards, indicated positive responses. Two broad categories could be identified: negative, unconstructive views about the reforms, and more neutral views. Negative views were linked to perceptions of overload, too much paperwork, a shortage of teachers, and an inability to use new methods of teaching. Teachers cited a lack of understanding of the curriculum reforms and a lack of classroom support and in-service professional development for teachers for the ongoing cycle of disadvantage among their learners. Bantwini (2010) concludes that in failing to address this issue, 'the curriculum reforms did not bring justice to the disadvantaged (mainly Black learners) as was intended'.

In 2006, a small-scale empirical study by the HSRC (2006) and others focused on the socio-economic and administrative conditions in schools. Through ethnographic observation and questionnaires, answers were sought to questions about teachers and the curriculum. The results indicate that: (a) the vast majority of primary school teachers are African, female, below 41 years of age, (b) teachers are mainly Diploma holders, (c) the pool of qualified mathematics teachers is small, (d) many unqualified teachers are teaching mathematics, yet many qualified teachers are not teaching mathematics, (e) most teachers in the system were trained during the apartheid era in teacher education colleges, which did not equip them to teach the new curriculum, and (f) language ability of teachers and pupils in the medium of instruction remains a major determinant of success.

The above findings find resonance in a study of learners from three language backgrounds in inner-city Cape Town which is linguistically and culturally complex: 64% are Xhosa speaking, 21% English, 7% Afrikaans, 3% Zulu, 3.3% Sotho and 2% bilingual (English-Afrikaans). Despite a school-level commitment to accommodate linguistic diversity, there is no administrative support; the consequences of which 'perpetuate the racial and economic inequalities prevalent pre-1994' (Heugh, 2010, p. 118).

In sum, studies on curriculum transformation, supported by process-driven methods such as observations and focus group interviews focus on issues of equity with respect to learner engagement, teacher preparedness, teacher support, teacher understanding of curriculum reform, and the continued marginalization of the African teacher with a strong focus on mathematics, science, and language.

17.4.7   Teacher training and pedagogy

With the implementation of the new OBE and RNCS, research focused on pedagogy and teacher training, specifically the ability and expertise of teachers to teach, in the context of poor school performance with emphasis on black teachers, mathematics, science, and languages. Innovative qualitative methods speak directly to pedagogy as process.

17.4.7.1   Pedagogy and teacher experiences

An innovative study by Olivier et al. (2009) using participatory visual methodology, a useful tool for teacher development, within a classroom context notes that the voices of teachers who work in disadvantaged contexts, who have first-hand knowledge of factors that impede teaching and learning, are often ignored by researchers and policy-makers. The results indicate that teachers were able to learn more about themselves and their context, and re-position themselves as more effective 'teachers who care'. Wieder (2002, pp. 29–36) advocates the use of apartheid stories/narratives as a model for teachers who fought apartheid and are currently addressing class/race disparity and other social problems.

17.4.7.2 *Professional development of teachers*

The research focus has been on teacher competence, teacher upgrading, and its impact on the performance of pupils. The altered role of the teaching profession post-1994 is understood in the context of the Norms and Standards in Education (NSE), the official policy document and stated curriculum for teachers. While the NSE has formally superseded the pre-1994 apartheid legacy of inferior teaching for black learners, the identities and interests of individual academics continue to determine curriculum design and development decisions (Kruss, 2009b, p. 166).

In his study of shifts in the official curricula of initial training programs, including the Bachelor of Education (BEd) and the Postgraduate Certificate in Education (PGCE), Kruss (2009a, p. 4) focused on the content from changes since 2000. The research design involved a comparative multi-site case-study over a period of time, at five universities with different trajectories of institutional re-structuring, using interviews and document analysis.

Kruss (2009a, p. 15) concludes that the case-studies reveal a 'dominant trend towards bureaucratic compliance'. She emphasizes that there are other ways to mediate curriculum change such as recognizing potential for creating new knowledge driven by academic logic and coherence, and integrating the approaches of college and university lecturers. She argues for a stronger interchange around curriculum development, between the expertise and experience of university-based teacher educators, the Higher Education Quality Committee (HEQC), and the national and provincial departments, through the use of 'policy images'.

The image of the teacher promoted by the NSE, Jansen (2001) argues, despite its good intentions, is such that it 'denies the reality of, and fails to engage with, teachers' existing professional, emotional and political identities'. Maistry (2010, pp. 46–54) supports this claim and maintains that Continuous Professional Development (CPD) planners seldom take into account teacher biographies and the socio-economic contexts within which teachers work. He draws on the work of Wenger (1998), Bourdieu (1992), and Yosso (2005) and conducts an interpretative case-study, drawing on tenets of symbolic interactionist ethnography (Wood, 1996). The results show that cultural capital has a significant influence on a teacher's ability to negotiate participation in a community of practice.

Related research found that the greatest challenge in post-apartheid SA schools is classroom diversity in terms of race and language (Amin and Ramrathan, 2009). A case-study incorporating interviews, description, analyses, and critique, explored how first-year student teachers dealt with student diversity through four intervention phases: (1) understanding contextual diversity, (2) visiting diverse contexts, (3) making context-appropriate resources, and (4) micro teaching practice. The results indicate that (a) students were willing to teach in schools that differed from their own experience, (b) site visits were useful since they generated a positive experience to poorly resourced schools, and (c) lessons prepared by students were geared towards accommodating contextual challenges. Amin concludes that the four conceptual categories require further ongoing development and assessment.

Some of the findings on a public hearing conducted by the South African Human Rights Commission (SAHRC) reports a serious lack in teacher morale, teacher accountability, unqualified and under-qualified teachers and insufficient training in implementing the new curriculum for black teachers and learners (2006, p. 42).

17.4.7.3   Curriculum and pedagogy

Pre-service teacher educators from four provinces participated in a study investigating best practice with respect to teaching mathematics in multilingual contexts. The study linked teachers' perception of best practice and what happens in the classroom.

Using a qualitative analysis, their results indicated that five best practices emerge: (1) code switching, (2) creating an environment of trust, (3) the use of one (rather than two) medium of instruction, namely English, (4) the use of linguistic metaphors, and (5) an awareness of the multilingual context. The study warns against the danger of adopting imported practices for SA (Heugh, 2010).

A key research question on matriculation results is: 'What factors contribute to good matriculation results?' Kanjee (2006) solicits views and experiences of mathematics and science teachers from high-performing and poorly-performing schools on factors that contribute to good results. The study looked at how schools that fail to get more than 20% matriculation passes should be assisted. Inhibiting factors included poor teaching in lower grades, poverty, a lack of discipline in township schools, and inadequate subject knowledge by teachers, especially in mathematics and science. A significant finding is that students who are disadvantaged academically in terms of family resources are most likely to be instructed by teachers with less capacity to impart mathematical knowledge to students in the classroom; reinforcing the disadvantages. The poor performance of African pupils is seen as primarily a function of the poor quality of teaching.

In sum, the key findings of this tradition indicate a need for greater contextual understanding in teacher training and pedagogy. Qualitative research methods reinforce the notion that pedagogy is a human process and one that must be analyzed as such. The narrative, interpretative case-study, and symbolic interactionist ethnography become logical choices in supporting teacher development and addressing class and race disparity. The focus on NSE and teacher education qualifications reveals the presence of an imposing bureaucracy and struggles around creating an identity. Conducting public hearings is a unique method of collecting data.

17.4.8 Charting inequalities in student outcomes

Without the ability to collect fees from their often unemployed parents, poor schools have little capacity to attract qualified teachers. Many have seen very little change since 1994. Their performance is mostly dismal, as reflected in various international studies such as the TIMSS and the SACMEQ II, where SA's performance is worse than many poorer countries. Other performance measures include the matriculation results, international studies, proxy methods, extrapolation, results in mathematics and science, case-studies, and stochastic analysis.

Despite the existence of a number of poorly resourced African schools providing quality education 'the country's top schools are privileged institutions, formerly reserved for White and, to a lesser extent, 'Coloured' or Asian children' (Taylor as cited in Pendlebury and Enslin, 2004, pp. 31–50). The remaining top-performing schools fall into two groups: English-speaking schools which enroll African learners in numbers which vary from 25–75%, and Afrikaans-speaking schools containing minimal numbers of African pupils (http://www.jet.org.za).

From 1995 to 2003, school attendance was seen as a measure of participation and performance (DoE, 2006e, p. 33). The figures reveal a large drop in attendance rates for 16–18-year-olds in comparison with 7–15-year-olds. The Coloured and Asian attendance rates for 16–18-year-old is well below the national average of 72% and they are more likely to drop-out than Africans and White suggesting that drop-out is not only caused by poverty but by perceptions of the value of education (DoE, 2006e, p. 33). The low figure for Asians is attributed to its extremely small sample.

17.4.8.1 *Mathematics and science*

In 1999, a parliamentary question was asked: 'How many African students were attaining the coveted passes in the university gateway subjects?' (Kahn, 2005, pp. 140–152). In the absence of racial data on African students, the only option available was extrapolation. Kahn (2005) used the language proxy method (LPM), which was first tested in 1999 and then from 2000 onwards. The results from the 1999–2001 research confirmed three things. First, there was an increase in the number of African candidates passing higher grade (HG) mathematics but the number of passes was unacceptably low. Second, while African girl students were under-enrolled, they performed better on pass rates relative to boys in each of the four subjects, biology, mathematics, physical science and an African language in all of the four provinces. Third, against these figures it seems as if the white community generates skills at something close to saturation level (Kahn, 2005, p. 142). African students who did not take an African language scored higher.

Using Gauteng as a case-study, Reddy (2005a) examines the trends in mathematics and science performance during the period 1998–2003. She identified schools that consistently produce good results. The results indicate that although there were increased participation rates, there has been a drastic reduction in performance. In African schools the performance in HG mathematics dropped from 65% to 8%, from 60% to 36% in former White schools, from 74% to 30% in former Indian schools and from 38% to 3% in former Coloured schools. The worst performance is in African schools, which constitute the majority of SA schools (Reddy, 2005b, p. 135).

The above results are corroborated by Reddy (2005b). She tracked the progress of White and African schools in mathematics and science. Using four themes: policies, programs, participation and performance, drawing on data from TIMSS and matriculation results, she showed that former African schools scored the lowest whereas the former White schools scored the highest. Only 23% of African learners passed on the higher grade. Reddy suggests the school, rather than race should be the unit of analysis. Where there is poverty, schools must be supported to provide quality experiences to learners.

In the absence of other reliable national instruments, TIMMS, where language is used for assessment, is able to provide data for analysis of performance in mathematics and science at the primary level. Dempster and Reddy (2007) investigated the relationship between the readability of 73 text-only multiple-choice questions from TIMSS 2003 and the performance of two groups of pupils: those with limited English-language proficiency (learners attending African schools), and those with better English-language proficiency (learners attending non-African schools). They noted that high sentence complexity resulted in random guessing in non-African schools and favoring an incorrect answer in African schools. However, poor readability of some TIMSS items does not fully account for SA learners' poor performance in TIMSS.

17.4.8.2   *Participation in higher forms of education*

This research tradition is not well developed. Available research focuses on participation and drop-out rates. In the 1984 senior certificate examinations, only 10 in every 100 African learners who started schooling in 1973 wrote the exam, one gained university entrance and five failed (Hartshorne, 1986, p. 1980). In contrast, 63 out of every 100 White children who entered school at the same time wrote the exam that year.

The stochastic model of grade advancement developed by Lam et al. (2008, p. 2) focuses on the combination of high enrollment rates and high rates of grades repetition following Grade 9 by monitoring the three subsequent years of secondary schooling. The results indicate that although there is a strong impact of baseline test scores and household incomes on progress through Grades 8–11, the effect is much weaker for African students than for Coloured and White students. Therefore, the African school environment does a poor job in translating ability and resources into measured performance. Yet, African students are less likely to drop out of school because of failing a grade.

Noting that the impact of baseline test scores and income are equally large for Coloured and African students in predicting pass rates in the Grade 12 examination, they suggest that the weaker impact of baseline test scores and income for African students on retention in Grades 8–11 is due to a poor system of evaluation in those grades. Overall 84% of White students who were in Grade 9 in 2002 had advanced three grades by 2005, compared to 44% of Coloured students and 32% of Africans. Yet, 74% of the latter were still enrolled at school (Lam et al., 2008, p. 1). They conclude that a large stochastic component to grade advancement impacts greatly on who attends school, how much they invest in school, and how individual and household characteristics affect the probability of grade advancement.

Large household surveys reveal that although racial gaps in SA schools have decreased, there has been a steady decline in performance among Black learners (Lam et al., 2010). Racial gaps can be attributed to a high rate of grade repetition for Africans, with a small difference in enrollment rates across the race groups. The data also indicates a large effect of schooling on earnings, with a higher rate of return to schooling for Africans than for Whites (Lam et al., 2010, pp. 11–12).

Lam et al. (2010) analyzed the racial proportions of high school graduates who enroll in post-secondary education, and the impact of household income and scholastic ability. The results indicate that reducing financial constraints would only have a modest impact on reducing racial differences in post-secondary enrollment. Baseline income and performance in numeracy and literacy are stronger predictors of post-secondary enrollment, accounting for almost all of the difference in enrollment.

In sum, the results of the above studies indicate that the African school environment does a poor job in translating ability and resources into measured performance. Instruments used for measuring and predicting performance range from international tests such as TIMMS and SACMEQ to a study of trends, case-studies, stochastic analysis, baseline income and performance in numeracy and literacy and household surveys. Of value would be longitudinal studies examining intergenerational components of schooling including information about pupils with non-resident parents (Lam et al., 2010, p. 12).

17.5 Conclusion and discussion

From 1980 to 2010, research on the relationship between education and race has in all instances focused on one of two things: education as a tool for keeping black people subjugated to whites, or education as a tool for the advancement of all race groups. For SA, the inequalities are manifest among the majority black population. From policy to implementation, the research agenda was always meant to promote the ideas of the ruling class, the NP or the ANC forming the basis for the reciprocal relationship between education policy and research giving rise to distinct research traditions. In the main, the research methods deployed in the early 1980s were mainly commissioned reports, large-scale quantitative and descriptive studies with a spattering of qualitative studies all of which were initiated by the government aimed to influence educational policy based on the notion of racial separateness. Despite the recommendations made in these studies, the government chose to ignore them and so did the majority of black people when they rejected the government's attempts at implementing the ERS in 1990.

This rejection marked a critical phase in education as it spurred political formations (ANC) and civil society movements (NECC) to fully immerse in overhauling the education system based on principles of democracy and equality. Their activities generated numerous research articles, reports, and policy documents. Whilst grassroots research is not captured in this chapter, acknowledgement is given to the momentum and purpose it gave to both research and policy. The dominant research traditions central to the debates can be summarized as follows:

(a) Pre-1994, government-funded research in the form of reports and policy documents such as the De Lange Report and the ERS were largely descriptive with components of empirical study all aimed to justify race-based educational inequality. Reports produced by NEPI and the ANC's policy framework for education and training led to the establishment of far-reaching policy and legislative changes in education. The struggles of the 1980s gave impetus to the formalization of educational research at research institutes and universities where the key debates have been around the equalization of educational opportunities for black students and its impact on the equity of outcomes.

(b) The culture of learning among Black schools collapsed in the apartheid period, from 1948 to 1994. Research in the 1980s and 1990s focused on Black learners' resistance to schooling, namely, overt and covert violence and the deterioration/lack of a culture of learning. Unlike the pre-1994 era, qualitative methods such as phenomenology, problem-historical approach, chronological approach, interviews, focus group interviews, observation, and the metabletic approach began to dominate educational research yielding substantive results.

(c) The impacts of the removal of race-based policies on equity of outcome were studied through various sociological concepts, comparing student enrollment patterns across race groups, official records, and classroom discourse. The results indicate that social cohesion is difficult to achieve in a mixed-race classroom; often they become places of black assimilation of white culture, raising the question as to whether integration can enhance the educational opportunities for the majority.

(d) Studies on the impact of the re-distribution of economic resources on equity of outcome have been large-scale, quantitative, often relying on statistical methods such as the LER, stochastic model, regression analysis with respect to assessing matriculation results, household surveys, MLA, SACMEQ II, TIMMS, SALSS, SALDRU1, concentration index, World Bank reports, and the QLP. These studies arrive at the unwelcome conclusion that despite best efforts at the re-distribution of resources, the equity of outcome remains elusive for black learners.

(e) Key to the success of the equalizing educational opportunities was the implementation of the new curriculum: OBE, the RNCS and *Curriculum 2005*. Research focused on how students engage with the principles and practice of the new curriculum.

(f) Research on pedagogy focused on the professional development of teachers. Innovative methods such as 'participatory visual methodology' and the narrative, among others, reveal that the official policy of the NSE has not mitigated the apartheid legacy of inferior teaching for black learners. Teacher qualifications such as the CPD, BEd and PGCE are seen as possible solutions to this predicament.

(g) Performance and predictive measures centered around the matriculation results, LPM, longitudinal studies, international studies, proxy methods, extrapolation, results in mathematics and science, case-studies, household income, baseline test scores and performance in numeracy and literacy and stochastic analysis. The inequality of outcomes in mathematics and science in African schools led the government to establish the Dinaledi project. Limited studies in participation in higher forms of education highlighted the persistent inequalities and wastages in the system.

The research undertaken consistently points towards the enduring inequalities in education between black and white learners across the spectrum. The challenge around education, race and equity is an all-pervasive systemic issue affecting almost 90% of the population. The national research agenda therefore occupies a central place in the development and implementation of educational policy which must now focus on how continuing racial inequalities can be reduced. Among the many challenges that remain are:

(a) Identifying research paradigms and research questions that go beyond stating the obvious inequalities, which yield suggestions on improvement thereby giving substance and direction to the embedded nature of learner experience within a school context.

(b) The question of 'how' inequalities can be addressed is not developed in great depth. It is absent in two places: the former African schools and the mixed-race schools.

(c) Reducing the breakdown in the culture of teaching and learning in township schools.

(d) Treating the school as a unit of analysis with respect to total quality improvement.

(e) In cases of widespread poverty and struggles around adaption to newer forms of learning, inter-generational studies have the potential to provide useful insights on how previously marginalized people overcome inequality.

(f) International and national studies such as TIMMS and SACMEQ II, while valuable, but must be treated cautiously.

References

Ahmed, R. and Sayed, R. 2009. Promoting Access and Enhancing Education Opportunities? The Case of 'no-fees schools' in South Africa. *Compare* 39(2): 203–218.

Alexander, N. 1990. *Education and the Struggle for National Liberation in South Africa.* Braamfontein: Skotaville Publishers.

Amin, N. and Ramrathan, P. 2009. Preparing Students to Teach in and for Diverse Contexts: A Learning to Teach Approach. *Perspectives in Education.* 27(1): 69–77.

Baloyi, R. 2004. *The Role of the State in the Establishment of a Culture of Learning and Teaching in South Africa (1910–2004).* UNISA: DEd Dissertation.

Bantwini, B.D. 2010. How Teachers Perceive the New Curriculum Reform: Lessons from a School District in the Eastern Cape Province, South Africa. *International Journal of Educational Development.* 30(2010): 83–90.

Beckett, D. 1990. No Black and White Solutions. *Optima.* 37(3): 112–133.

Bekisizwe, N. 2004. (Re) Anglicising the Kids: Contradictions of Classroom Discourse in Post-Apartheid South Africa: Research Article. *Perspectives in Education.* Special Issue 4. 22(4): 47–57.

Bot, M. and Schlemmer, L. 1986. *The Classroom Crisis: Black Demands & White Reforms.* Indicator Project South Africa. Durban: Centre for Applied Social Sciences, University of Natal.

Brubacher, J.S. 1969. *Modern Philosophies of Education.* New York: McGraw Hill.

Carrim, N. 2001. Democratic Participation, Decentralisation and Educational reform. In *Implementing Education Policies: The South African Experience,* editors Y. Sayed and J. Jansen, Cape Town: University of Cape Town Press, 98–109.

Carter P., Caruthers, J. and Foster, J. 2009. Knowing Their Lines: How Social Boundaries Undermine Equity-Based Integration Policies in United States and South African Schools. *Perspectives in Education.* 27(4): 351–364.

Case, A. and Deaton, A. 1999. School Inputs and Educational Outcomes in South Africa. *The Quarterly Journal of Economics.* X(x): 1047–1084.

Chisholm, L. 2004. *The Quality of Primary Education in South Africa.* Background Paper Prepared for the Education for All Global Monitoring Report 2005, The Quality Imperative. Retrieved 27 May 2007 http://unesdoc.unesco.org/images/0014/001466/146636e.pdf.

Chisholm, L. 2005. The Making of the South African National Curriculum Statement. *Journal of Curriculum Studies*. 37(2): 193–208.

Chisholm, L. 2006. South Africa's New Education System: Great Intentions – Harsh Realities. In *At the End of the Rainbow?: Social Identity and Welfare State in the New South Africa*, editors G. Gunnarsen, P. Mac Manus, M. Nielsen, and H.E. Stolten, [n.p.] 143–152.

Christie, P. 1991. *The Right to Learn: The Struggle for Education in South Africa*. New expanded edition: Braamfontein: Ravan Press.

Claassen, J.C. 1995. The Education System of South Africa. In *Modern Education Systems*, editors Elise Dekker and O.J. Van Schalkwyk. Durban: Butterworths, 447–496.

Crouch, L. and Vinjevold, P. 2006. South Africa: Access before Quality, and What to Do Now? Unpublished Paper, RTI, North Carolina.

Deacon, R. and Parker, B. 1998. Education, Development and Democracy in South Africa, in *South Africa in Transition: New Theoretical Perspectives*, editors D.R. Howarth and Aletta J. Norval. Hampshire: Macmillan Press Ltd.

de Clercq, F. 1997. Effective Policies and the Reform Process: An Evaluation of South Africa's New Development and Education Macro Policies. In Kallaway, P. Kruss, G, Fataar, A. and Donn, G. *Education after Apartheid*. Cape Town: University of Cape Town Press, 145–155.

de Lange, J.P. 1981. *Report of the Main Committee of the HSRC Investigation into Educational Provision in South Africa*. Pretoria: Human Sciences Research Council.

Dempster, E.R. and Reddy, V. 2007. Item Readability and Science Achievement in TIMSS 2003 in South Africa. *Science Education*. 91: 906–925.

DoE. 2006e. *Monitoring and Evaluation Report on the Impact and Outcomes of the Education System on South Africa's Population: Evidence from Household Surveys*. Pretoria: DoE.

Enslin, P. 1988. The State of Pedagogics. *Perspectives in Education*, 10(1): 67–74.

Fiske, E.B. and Ladd, H.F. 2004. *Elusive Equity: Education Reform in Post-Apartheid South Africa*. Washington DC: Brookings Institution Press.

Francis, D. 2010. Editorial. *Perspectives in Education*. 28(3): i–ii.

FRD (Foundation for Research Development). 1993. *SA Science and Technology Indicators*. Pretoria: FRD.

Gustafsson, M. and Patel, F. 2006. Undoing the Apartheid Legacy: Pro-poor Spending Shifts in the South African Public School System. *Perspectives in Education*. 24(2): 65–77.

Hartshorne, K. 1986. The Boycott Classes of 1980 to 1984. *Indicator SA*, 3(3). Centre for Applied Social Sciences. University of Natal.

Harsthorne, K. 1992. *Crisis and Challenge: Black Education 1910–1990*. Oxford: Oxford University.

Heugh, K. 2010. When a School Principal does not Believe in the Impossible: From Multilingual Explorations to System-Wide Assessment. *Multilingualism from Below*. Pretoria: Van Schaik Publishers, 117–133.

Holtman, Z., Louw, J., Tredoux, C. and Carney, T. 2005. Prejudice and Social Contact in South Africa: A Study of Integrated Schools Ten Years after Apartheid. *South African Journal of Psychology*. 35(3): 473–93.

Jansen, J. 1998. Curriculum Reform in South Africa: a Critical Analysis of Outcomes-Based Education. *Cambridge Journal of Education*. 28(3): 321–331.

Jansen, J. 2001. "Image-ining Teachers: Education Policy & Teacher Identity in South Africa". *South African Journal of Education*. 21(4): 242–246.

Jansen, J. 2004. Race and Education After Ten Years: Conversations. *Perspectives in Education*. Special Issue 4. 22(4): 117–128.

Kahn, M. 1993. *Building the Base: Report on a Sector Study of Science and Mathematics Education.* Pretoria: Commission of the European Communities.

Kahn, M. 2005. A Class Act – Mathematics as Filter of Equity in South Africa's Schools. *Perspectives in Education.* 23(3): 139–152.

Kallaway, P. 2002. *The History of Education under Apartheid.* New York: Peter Lang Publishing Inc.

Kanjee, A. and Prinsloo, C. 2005. *Quality Learning Project: Summative Evaluation.* Paper presented at the Business Trust Offices at Woodlands Business Park, Woodlands on 14 June to the Business Trust and Project Steering Committee.

Kruss, G. 2009a. Introduction. In *Opportunities and Challenges for Teacher Education Curriculum in South Africa.* Teacher Education in South Africa Series, editor G. Kruss. Cape Town: HSRC Press.

Kruss, G. 2009b. From Bureaucratic Compliance to Creating New Knowledge: Comparative Patterns of Curriculum Change. In Opportunities & Challenges for Teacher Education Curriculum in South Africa, editor G. Kruss, Cape Town: HSRC Press, 157–174.

Lam, D., Ardington, C. and Leibbrandt, M. 2008. *Schooling as a Lottery: Racial Differences in School Advancement in Urban South Africa.* A Southern Africa Labour and Development Research Unit Working Paper Number 18. Cape Town: SALDRU, University of Cape Town.

Lam, D., Ardington, C., Branson, N., Goostrey, K., Leibbrandt, M. 2010. *Credit Constraints and the Racial Gap in Post-Secondary Education in South Africa.* Prepared for the 2010 Meeting of the Population Association of America, Dallas, TX.

Landman, R. 1992. Facts and Figures. In *South Africa – The Education Equation: Problems, Perceptions and Prospects*, editors C. Heese and D. Badenhorst. Pretoria: JL van Schaik, 36–42.

Lemon, A. 2004. Redressing School Inequalities in the Eastern Cape. *Journal of Southern African Studies.* 30(2): 269–290.

Levin, R. 1991. People's Education and the Politics of Negotiations in South Africa. *Perspectives in Education.* 12(2): 1–8.

Lodge, T. 1987. *Black Politics in South Africa since 1945.* Johannesburg: Ravan Press.

Maistry, S. 2010. Using Cultural Capital as a Resource for Negotiating Participation in a Teacher Community of Practice: A Case Study. *Perspectives in Education.* 28(3): 46–54.

Maluleka, J.S. 2001. *Socio-Educative Implications of Children's Rights.* UNISA: MEd Dissertation.

Mathonsi, P. 1988. *Black Matriculation Results: A Mechanism of Social Control.* Braamfontein, South Africa: Skotaville.

Mbonambi, P. 1998. *Sunday Times.* August 30, p. 2.

Mncwabe, M.P. 1993. *Post-apartheid Education: Towards Non-racial and Democratic Socialization in the New South Africa.* Lanham: University Press of America.

Moll, I. 1991. The South African Democratic Teachers Union and the Politics of Teacher Unity in South Africa, 1985–1990. In *Apartheid Education and Popular Struggles*, editors S. Badat, T. Botha, T. Dlamini, B. Khotseng, E. Unterhalter and H. Wolpe, Johannesburg: Raven Press, 185–202.

Motala, E and Pampallis, J. 2001. *Education and Equity: The Impact of State Policies on South African Education.* Johannesburg: Heinemann.

Motha, C. 2010. *Improving the Quality of Education in South African Schools: The Case of Orphaned Learners.* Paper Presented at the Research Indaba, Faculty of Education, University of Pretoria, 17 September 2010. PhD thesis, University of Pretoria, Pretoria, http://upetd.up.ac.za/thesis/available/etd-09252010-141318.

Muller, J. 1992a. The Three R's: Reform, Renewal or Construction. In *South Africa – The Education Equation: Problems, Perceptions and Prospects*, editors C. Heese and D. Badenhorst, Pretoria: JL van Schaik, 9–14.

Naidoo, D. 2010. A Discursive Formation that Undermined Integration at a Historically Advantaged School in South Africa. *Perspectives in Education*. 28(2): 19–29.

Nkomo M. 1990. *Pedagogy of Domination*. Johannesburg: Africa World Press.

Ntshoe, I.M. 2009. Hidden and Subtle Effects of Racism in Law and School Policy in Post-apartheid South Africa. *Southern Africa Review of Education*. 15(2): 85–104.

OECD Report. 2008. *Reviews of National Policies for Education*. Paris: OECD Publications.

Olivier, T., De Lange, N. and Wood, L. 2009. Using Participatory Video to Explore Teachers' Lived Experience. *Perspectives in Education*. 28(4): 43–51.

Paterson, A.N.M., Kanjee, A., Moore, A., Prinsloo, C.H. and Kivilu, J.M. 2001. *Quality Learning Project: Results of the Baseline Study*. Paper presented at the Quality Learning Project Indaba 3, 27 June 2001. Misty Hills Country Hotel, Muldersdrift.

Paton, C. 2008. Why Free Education Is Bad for the Country. *Financial Mail*. 10 October 2008.

Pendlebury, S. and Enslin, P. 2004. Social Justice and Inclusion in Education and Politics: The South African Case. *Journal of Education*, 34: 31–50.

Reddy, V. 2005a. *Math Schools are Not Equal: State of Math and Science Education. Tracking Development Progress*. Keynote Plenary Presented at the HSRC Winter Conference.

Reddy, V. 2005b. State of Mathematics and Science Education: Schools are Not Equal. *Perspectives in Education*. 23(3): 125–138.

Reeves, C. 1994. *The Struggle to Teach*. Cape Town: Maskew Miller.

Republic of South Africa (RSA) 1996a. Constitution of the Republic of South Africa. Pretoria: Government Printing Works.

SAHRC. 2006. A Report of the Public Hearing on the Right to Basic Education. Johannesburg; South African Human Rights Commission

Samuel, J.C. 1990. *Education: From Poverty to Liberty*. Cape Town: David Phillip.

Soudien, C. 2010. The Reconstitution of Privilege: Integration in Former White Schools in South Africa. *Journal of Social Issues*. 66(2): 352–366.

South Africa Government Online. 2013. Education. http://www.info.gov.za/aboutsa/education.htm.

SouthAfrica.info. 2013. The Languages of South Africa. http://www.southafrica.info/about/people/language.htm#ixzz1UdCsMRLf.

South African Schools Act (SASA), Act No. 84 of 1996.

Sujee, M. 2004. Deracialisation of Gauteng Schools – A Quantitative Analysis. In *Reflections on School Integration: Colloquium Proceedings*, editors M. Nkomo, C. Mckinney and L. Chisholm, Cape Town: HSRC Press, 46–51.

Tlhapi, T.J. 2006. *Secondary School Learner's Experience of Citizenship in a Democratic South Africa*. UNISA: MEd Dissertation.

Van der Berg, S. 2001. Resource Shifts in South African Schools after the Political Transition. *Development Southern Africa*. (18): 405–421.

Van der Berg, S. 2004. Enduring Inequality. An Economic Perspective on Public School Education in South Africa, with Special Focus on the Western Cape. *Africa Insight*. 34(2/3): 73–81.

Van der Berg, S. 2006. The Targeting of Public Spending on School Education, 1995 and 2000: Research Article. *Perspectives in Education*. 24(2): 49–63.

Van der Berg, S. 2007. Apartheid's Enduring Legacy: Inequalities in Education. *Journal of African Economies*. 16(5):849–880.

Van Der Berg, S. 2008. How Effective are Poor Schools? Poverty and Educational Outcomes in South Africa. *Studies in Educational Evaluation*. 34: 145–154.

Van Zyl, C. 1991. *The De Lange Report: Ten Years On: An Investigation into the Extent of the Implementation of Recommendations of the 1981 HSRC Investigation into Education.* Pretoria: HSRC Publishers.

Vithal, R. and Gopal, N. 2005. What Mathematical Learners Say About the New South African Curriculum. *Perspectives in Education.* 3(23): 45–59.

Weber, E., Nkomo, M. and Amsterdam, C. 2009. Diversity, Unity and National Developments: Findings from Desgregated Gauteng Schools. *Perspectives in Education.* 27(4): 341–350.

Webber, M. 1992. The English Liberal Education Tradition, in South Africa. In *The Education Equation: Problems, Perceptions and Prospects*, editors C. Heese and D. Badenhorst, Pretoria: JL van Schaik, 20–23.

Wieder, A. 2002. South African Teacher Stories. The Past Speaks to the Present and Future: Research Article. *Perspectives in Education*: Identity and Difference in Education: Special Issue 4 22(1): 29–36.

Wolpe, H. 1988. *Race, Class and the Apartheid State.* London: James Currey.

Wolpe, H. And Unterhalter, E. 1991. Introduction: Reproduction, Reform and Transformation: Approaches to the Analysis of Education in South Africa, In *Apartheid Education and Popular Struggles*, editors S. Badat, T. Botha, T. Dlamini, B. Khotseng, E. Unterhalter and H. Wolpe, Johannesburg: Raven Press, 1–18.

Yamauchi, F. 2003. Race, Equity, and Public Schools in Post-Apartheid South Africa: Is Opportunity Equal for All Kids? Discussion Paper BRIEFS. International Food Policy Research Institute (IFPRI).

18
The Netherlands

Peter A. J. Stevens, Maurice J. Crul, Marieke W. Slootman,
Noel Clycq, Christiane Timmerman, and Mieke Van Houtte

18.1 Introduction

This review builds on a recently published review of research on race/ethnicity in the Netherlands (Stevens et al., 2011) by including important, additional studies that were previously omitted for the period 1980–2008 and by including more recent research published during the years 2009–2010. In addition, whilst the 1980–2008 review compares the various research traditions that emerged in the Netherlands with those that developed in England, this review focuses exclusively on the Dutch context.

The chapter is divided into four main parts. First, this chapter describes the main characteristics of the Dutch educational system and immigration history and the main developments in terms of social policy between 1980 and 2010. Secondly, the process of conducting this literature review is described, with particular focus on the employed search strategies and related criteria for inclusion. Thirdly, research conducted in the Netherlands on the relationship between race/ethnicity and educational inequality is analyzed in terms of the major focus, methods, findings, and debates characteristic of specific research traditions that developed between 1980 and 2010. Finally, the conclusion and discussion section summarizes and critically analyzes the main findings of this study.

18.2 Education, migration and social policy developments in the Netherlands

This section offers a brief overview of the main characteristics of the Dutch educational system, the multicultural nature of the Netherlands, and the key developments in terms of social policy between 1980 and 2010.

18.2.1 Educational system

In the Netherlands full-time education is compulsory from the age of five until the age of 16 (Driessen, 2000b; Rijkschroeff et al., 2005; UNESCO, 2006).

Primary education is the same for all pupils and takes eight years. Dutch children enter secondary education at the age of 12. Depending on the advice[1] of the elementary school and the score of the Cito test,[2] pupils are assigned to either VMBO (pre-vocational or junior general secondary education), HAVO (senior general education) or VWO (pre-university education). It is possible for pupils who have attained the VMBO diploma to attend two years of HAVO-level education and sit the HAVO exam, and for pupils with a HAVO diploma to attend two years of VWO-level education and then sit the VWO exam (see Figure 18.1). However, in practice there is a divide between pre-vocational secondary education on the one hand and general secondary education on the other. In each of these tracks students are taught a core curriculum during the first three years, after which they prepare for their exam (which takes one year for VMBO, two years for HAVO and three years for VWO). Stratification occurs not only through enrollment in particular tracks but also through the difficulty level of the curriculum taught (Level 1–4). Each track and level has consequences for admission to vocational and higher education and the Dutch government considers obtaining a VWO, HAVO or MBO (at least Level 2) as the 'minimum level of education required to stand a serious chance of obtaining long-term, schooled employed in the Netherlands' (UNESCO, 2006).[3] Students who do not manage to obtain such a 'start-diploma' (*startkwalificatie*) are officially considered as 'early school leavers' (*vroegtijdige schoolverlaters*) (Driessen, 2000b; Rijkschroeff et al., 2005; UNESCO, 2006). In sum, the school system in the Netherlands is more stratified than for instance in the UK or Sweden and characterized by a more rigid curriculum and early selection system. Furthermore, the transition from primary to secondary education appears to be

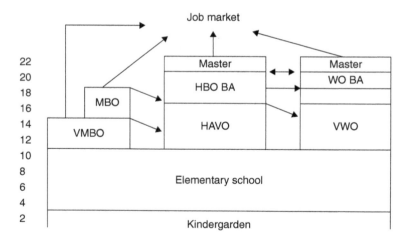

Figure 18.1   The Dutch educational system

a defining moment in a young person's educational career. Finally, obtaining a VWO, HAVO or MBO (Level 2 or higher) diploma is considered a key benchmark of success in the Dutch educational system.

18.2.2 Immigration to the Netherlands

Like many Western European countries the Netherlands became increasingly more multicultural after World War II. Particularly during the 1960s and 1970s the Netherlands attracted immigrants, mainly from Mediterranean countries like Italy, Spain, Portugal, Greece, Turkey, and Morocco, and (former) Dutch colonies, such as Surinam, the East Indies, the Moluccas and the Dutch Antilles. Most of these immigrants shared a lower educational background and immigrated mainly for economic and or (in particular East Indies and Moluccas immigrants) political motivations. Immigrants from the former Dutch colonies were usually more familiar with the Dutch system and language and as a group showed a greater variability in terms of social class. During the last two decades the Netherlands attracted refugees from Eastern Europe, Africa and the Middle East, in particular refugees from former Yugoslavia, Iraq, Iran, Afghanistan, and Somalia (Driessen, 2000b; Guirodon et al., 2004; Rijkschroeff et al., 2005). Recent statistics show that in 2007 the Netherlands counted 1.7 million non-Western immigrants or 10.6% of the total population, of which the Turkish, Moroccan, Surinamese, and Antillean immigrants constitute the largest groups of non-Western immigrants. Most research in the Netherlands focuses on the second and 'in-between' generation. In 2007 the second generation made up almost half of the total population of non-Western immigrants (Garssen and Wageveld, 2007) (Table 18.1).

Table 18.1 Composition of population in the Netherlands in 2007 by country of origin

	Number of people (× 1000)	Proportion of the population (%)	Proportion 2nd generation (%)
Turks	368.6	2.3	47.1
Moroccans	329.5	2.0	49.0
Surinamese	333.5	2.0	44.2
Antilleans	130.0	0.8	39.3
Iraqis	43.9	0.3	20.9
Afghans	37.2	0.2	15.8
Iranians	29.0	0.2	18.8
Somali	18.9	0.1	31.5
Total non-Western ethnic minorities	1,738.5	10.6	41.6
Native Dutch	13,187.6	80.6	
Total population	16,358.0		

Source: CBS Population Statistics (Garssen and Wageveld, 2007).

These migration processes impact on the social composition of schools, and statistics suggest that in 2007 15% of the students in primary and secondary school in the Netherlands are from a non-Western background (Gijsberts and Herweijer, 2007). However, due to processes of school choice (which is free in the Netherlands), residential segregation, and 'white flight' (see Section 18.4.4) ethnic minorities[4] are not distributed equally between Dutch schools but are more likely to enroll in urban schools with a high percentage of ethnic minority students; data from 2005/2006 show that almost 10% of all primary and secondary schools in the Netherlands are described as 'black schools', or schools with 70% or more ethnic minority students. This concentration is much more pronounced in the four largest cities of the Netherlands (Amsterdam, Rotterdam, Den Haag, and Utrecht), in which almost half of the schools can be described as 'black schools' (Gijsberts and Herweijer, 2007).

18.2.3   Social policy developments

In reviewing how policy on ethnic minorities developed in the Netherlands between 1970 and 2005, Rijkschroeff and colleagues (2005) identify two key goals: (1) realizing equal positions for ethnic minority and native Dutch students in education, and (2) emphasizing the value of cultural diversity and related collective identities. The authors conclude that over the last 30 years Dutch social policy has always emphasized the importance of educational equality. While socio-cultural goals were initially considered equally important, Dutch social policy reduced the importance of the socio-cultural goals over time and eventually considered such goals as problematic in realizing educational equality.

During the 1970s it was assumed that ethnic minorities (particularly those arriving from Mediterranean countries as 'guest workers') would return to their country of origins and policies focused on maintaining ethnic minorities' group identities (through mother tongue instruction or MTI) and realize a certain level of integration in Dutch society (through Dutch language instruction or DLI) (Driessen, 2000b; Eldering, 1989; OC&W, 1974; Rijkschroeff et al., 2005).

From the 1980s onwards, when it became clear that ethnic minority groups would settle permanently in the Netherlands, social policy focused on reducing socio-economic inequalities. Schools with ethnic minority and working class children were given more resources and given the opportunity to organize DLI, intensify contacts between schools and families and organize MTI and intercultural teaching (IT) (OC&W, 1981). Although all initiatives were perceived to have a positive impact on ethnic minorities' socio-economic position, MTI and IT were also organized to help develop a positive (ethnic) identity, reduce racism, and promote multiculturalism (Driessen, 2000b; Eldering, 1989). The importance attached to fighting ethnic discrimination and promoting multiculturalism is illustrated by the government's Minority Note (*Minderhedennota*) developed in 1983, which considered these two goals as equally important to improving minorities' social and economic situation. These (and future) policy developments in the Netherlands were inspired and often based on recommendations or criticism by sociologists who were actively involved in drafting and evaluating policy measures related to ethnicity and education (Guirodon et al., 2004). This close relationship between social research and policy is characteristic of the Netherlands and will be further illustrated in reviewing research traditions.

However, while initially educational policies promoted the expression and maintenance of cultural diversity and related group identities as a valuable goal in itself and a means to realize socio-economic equality and social cohesion, from 1985 onwards social policy-makers started to reverse this relationship by arguing that socio-economic integration might help to realize socio-cultural integration and social cohesion (Rijkschroeff et al., 2005). The Educational Priority Policy (EPP) developed in 1985 (OC&W, 1985) integrated earlier initiatives directed to working-class or ethnic minorities into a single framework and emphasized the importance of ethnic minority children's lower socio-economic background over their cultural differences in explaining their lower position in education (Driessen, 2000b; Eldering, 1989; Phalet, 1998).

Ten years later, and reinforced by recent events (such as the murder of politician Pim Fortuyn and film director Theo Van Gogh, see BBC, 2004) Dutch social policy considers the promotion and celebration of cultural diversity and group identities as having a negative impact on socio-economic integration and social cohesion and instead emphasizes the importance of socio-cultural integration of ethnic minority groups in Dutch society (OC&W, 1997; Rijkschroeff et al., 2005). For instance from the early 1990s onwards, the government considered MTI and IT increasingly more as a tool to facilitate Dutch language learning and learning of other subjects in school rather than a strategy to promote multiculturalism (Driessen, 2000b) and ultimately decided to cease funding of MTI related initiatives from 2005 onwards (Bronnenman-Helmers and Turkenburg, 2003).[5]

Four main conclusions can be drawn from reviewing how social policy in relationship to ethnic minorities and education developed in the Netherlands. First, there has been a consistent and strong emphasis on realizing socio-economic and particularly educational equality between different ethnic groups over time. Second, a compensatory 'capital' or 'resource' model is employed to explain educational inequalities and policies aim to develop various forms of (social, cultural, financial) capital or resources in those social groups (or schools with such groups) to increase their educational position. Third, while the Netherlands has a strong tradition of anti-discrimination and racism and the promotion of cultural diversity and related group identities, such goals are considered subordinate to the goal of realizing socio-economic

equality and evaluated according to the perceived role they can play in realizing this. Finally, research and social policy on ethnicity and educational
inequality are strongly related to each other in the Netherlands, with social
policy-makers funding large research projects aimed at evaluating, monitoring
and preparing policy initiatives and concerns and researchers in turn focusing
on and influencing social policy initiatives and agendas through their research
activities.

18.3   Methods

A particular protocol with specific selection criteria was used to draw up the
sample on which this review is based. First, it was decided to include only
literature that focuses on the Netherlands as a research context. Secondly,
the literature review is restricted to contributions that employ a sociological
approach in researching the relationship between educational inequality and
race/ethnicity between 1980 and 2010. Thirdly, this review focuses on both
primary and secondary education as considerable research has been carried
out in the Netherlands on the transition from primary to secondary schooling.
However, as a result studies that investigate other forms of education, such
as family, higher, or adult education were not included. Finally, only peer-
reviewed journal articles (edited) books, and official reports were considered
for analysis. While these four criteria of inclusion strongly guided the review
process, sometimes studies were considered that did not fulfill at least one
of these criteria, as they were perceived as good or important examples of a
specific research tradition.

The process of sampling specific research contributions involved three specific steps. First, bibliographical databases (Sociological Abstracts and ERIC)
were searched for relevant peer-reviewed journal articles and books using
specific search queries. Secondly, a manageable sample of journals from the
Netherlands was selected and systematically analyzed in terms of their content
from 1980 onwards.[6] Thirdly, the analysis of the sample of research contributions that resulted from these two search activities identified additional important studies, journals, books and key researchers in this area of interest, which
were in turn included in the review process.

In applying this sampling frame we can distinguish the following six research
traditions: those of (1) political arithmetic, (2) racism and ethnic discrimination, (3) school characteristics, (4) school choice, (5) family background, and
(6) an institutional approach. Before exploring these particular research traditions in terms of their research questions, methods, key findings, and debates,
it is necessary to describe the key characteristics and developments in terms
of the Dutch educational system, immigration processes, and social policy in
which these research traditions developed.

18.4 Ethnicity and educational inequality in the Netherlands

The following sections describe and critically analyze the different research traditions between 1980 and 2010 that focus on the relationship between race/ethnicity and educational inequality in the Netherlands. Six major research traditions are identified: those of (1) political arithmetic, (2) racism and ethnic discrimination, (3) school characteristics, (4) school choice, (5) family background and (6) an institutional approach.

18.4.1 Political arithmetic tradition

During the 1960s UK sociologists developed the political arithmetic (PA) tradition which set out from a positivistic epistemology and relies mainly on quantitative research strategies in analyzing the relationship between family background and educational success (Heath, 2000; Stevens, 2007b).

The Dutch government also started funding large-scale cohort studies in the Netherlands during the early 1990s (such as the PRIMA and VOCL studies)[7] and these datasets are used to inform and evaluate social policy initiatives by offering descriptive analyses of the achievement and progress of ethnic minority students in education over time, controlling for relevant background and school characteristics where possible (e.g. Dagevos and Gijsberts, 2007; Dagevos et al., 2003). In line with the PA tradition these reports are 'relatively modest in their theoretical ambition' (Heath, 2000, p. 314) and prefer 'description to explanation, and hard evidence to theoretical speculation' (ibid., p. 314).

The bi-annual reports produced by the SCP and CBS (Dagevos and Gijsberts, 2007; Dagevos et al., 2003; Schnabel et al., 2005; Tesser and Iedema, 2001; Tesser et al., 1999; Tesser et al., 1998) contain a wealth of statistical analyses, charting the achievements and progress of ethnic minority groups from kindergarten, over primary and secondary education to higher education and employment. In addition, these reports offer analyses on related topics in education such as Dutch language use and proficiency amongst ethnic minority families and the occurrence and importance of ethnic segregation in schools. Finally, using a broad range of population survey instruments, these reports focus on issues such as: ethnic minority people's experiences with discrimination in the labor market, attitudes of native Dutch citizens to ethnic minorities, involvement of ethnic minorities in crime, development of social policy in the Netherlands and ethnic minorities' housing and settlement patterns. This section will focus on the analyses in the last three SCP/CBS reports that investigate the achievement and progress of ethnic minority students in the Dutch educational system (Gijsberts, 2003; Gijsberts and Hartgers, 2005; Gijsberts and Herweijer, 2007; Herweijer, 2003; Turkenburg and Gijsberts, 2007).

Based on quantitative analyses of representative samples of pupils and schools in the Netherlands these reports conclude that (non-Western) ethnic minority pupils start and finish primary education with considerable arrears in mathematics and (Dutch) language compared to the native Dutch population. However, in comparing seven different cohorts, the data suggests that the arrears in language and mathematics experienced by ethnic minority pupils have reduced over time: between 1988 and 2004 pupils of Moroccan descent reduced 45% of their language and 50% of their mathematic arrears. While pupils of Turkish descent also reduced their arrears in mathematics by 50%, they only made up 33% of their arrears in language. Children from Surinamese and especially Antillean background show less progress in language and mathematics: while both groups of children reduce their arrears in language by 25%, children of Surinamese descent have only made up 38% and those of Antillean descent only 10% of their arrears in mathematics over the last six years. At the end of primary education, Antillean pupils show the lowest level of mathematics and Turkish Dutch pupils the lowest levels of Dutch language compared to all other ethnic minority groups and pupils of Dutch descent. These differences in (progress of) skills and knowledge of Dutch language and mathematics between ethnic minority groups and pupils of Dutch descent are reflected in the Cito test (see above), which is administered at the end of primary schools and used in advising pupils to particular tracks in secondary schools (Table 18.2).

At the end of primary education, the largest four non-Western ethnic minority groups obtain on average lower Cito test-scores compared to pupils of Dutch descent. While Moroccan Dutch and Turkish Dutch pupils obtained the lowest levels of Cito test scores in 1994, ten years later they show the highest increase in test-scores over time and now achieve at the same level as pupils of Suriname descent and at a higher level than pupils of Antillean descent.

Despite the remarkable progress made by Moroccan and Turkish Dutch pupils over time in primary education, ethnic minority students, particularly those from Moroccan and Turkish descent, obtain lower educational outcomes

Table 18.2   Average total scores on the Cito test at the end of primary education according to ethnicity for cohorts 1994/5–2004/5

	Turkey	Morocco	Suriname	Antillean	Dutch low SES[a]	Dutch high SES[b]
1994/5	524.1	525.1	527.1	526.8	531.9	538.0
1996/7	525.2	526.4	527.4	525.6	531.2	537.4
1998/9	526.9	526.9	529.2	525.6	530.6	536.9
2000/1	527.3	527.4	529.8	524.8	530.5	537.3
2002/3	527.3	528.3	528.3	524.7	530.6	537.3
2004/5	527.0	527.7	527.9	524.5	528.9	536.2

[a] Both parents have a diploma not higher than LBO.
[b] At least one of the parents obtained a MAVO diploma or higher.
Source: Gijsberts and Herweijer (2007).

in secondary education compared to students of Dutch descent. In 2007, at the end of the third year in secondary education in the Netherlands, almost 50% of the students of Dutch descent were enrolled in the high-status educational tracks (HAVO/VWO), whereas only 20% of the Turkish and Moroccan Dutch, 27% of the Antillean Dutch, and 30% of the Surinamese Dutch students were enrolled in such tracks. Furthermore, when students have to sit their final exams in secondary education, ethnic minority students, in particular students of Turkish descent have lower chances of passing their exams and are more likely to repeat their school year or drop out of education.

While these analyses suggest that the four largest non-Western ethnic minority groups in the Netherlands experience considerable problems and challenges throughout primary and secondary education, the data show that once ethnic minorities manage to obtain a HAVO or VWO diploma they, particularly Moroccan and Turkish Dutch students, are more likely than students of Dutch descent to continue in higher education (HBO and WO) (Table 18.3).

Over a period of ten years, ethnic minorities doubled their participation in Dutch higher education from 6% to 12–13%. However, despite the progress experienced in higher education by ethnic minorities, majority students are much more likely to enroll in higher education and are less likely to drop out or having to retake academic years. The most important determinants for students' participation in higher education seem to be the length of participation in the Dutch educational system (and related to this, whether they are first or second-generation immigrants), the socio-economic status of their parents, and the language spoken at home. In particular the latter characteristic is emphasized in explaining why Moroccan and especially Turkish students are least likely to enroll in higher education or obtain higher education qualifications

Table 18.3   Percentage of ethnic minority students in further education in three cohorts

Cohorts Ethnic group	HBO			WO		
	1995–1996	2000–2001	2005–2006	1995–1996	2000–2001	2005–2006
Turks	0.9	1.5	1.9	0.7	1.0	1.3
Moroccans	0.9	1.6	2.1	0.7	1.1	1.1
Surinamese	1.6	2.0	2.5	1.7	2.0	1.9
Antilleans	1.1	1.7	1.4	0.9	1.3	1.2
Other non-Western	1.7	3.4	4.9	2.3	3.7	6.2
Total non-Western	6.2	10.2	12.9	6.3	9.0	11.6

Source: CBS Population Statistics (Gijsberts and Herweijer, 2007).

(Crul and Wolff, 2002; Gijsberts and Herweijer, 2007; Hofman and Van Den Berg, 2002; Wolff and Crul, 2003).

The PA tradition in the Netherlands developed from the mid-1980s onwards, when the government decided to fund the development of cohort studies that allow for a descriptive analysis of the achievements and progress of ethnic minorities over time. These large-scale, quantitative studies are important in that they offer highly accurate pictures of how ethnic minorities achieve and progress through education in the Netherlands over time. In addition, basic analysis suggests the importance of ethnic minorities' social background and knowledge of Dutch language in explaining these differences in achievement. However, these studies are limited in explaining the perceived patterns of achievement and progress in education, and the extent to which particular processes and characteristics situated at the level of the school, family, peer-group, and neighborhood interact and influence educational experiences and outcomes of ethnic minority groups remains unclear.

18.4.2   Racism and ethnic discrimination tradition

In the Netherlands research on 'racism' or 'discrimination' (which is the preferred term in the Netherlands) constitutes an important and well-developed area of research. Researchers working in this area usually make use of large datasets and quantitative analysis techniques to test particular hypotheses regarding the 'meritocratic' nature of schools (Luyten, 2004; Luyten and Bosker, 2004; Meijnen, 2004) and, to a lesser extent, teachers' expectations of different social groups and students' experiences of racism (Jungbluth, 1993; Verkuyten et al., 1997). The following sections review the main findings and debates within this research tradition.

18.4.2.1   *The meritocratic nature of the Dutch educational system*

A key concern in Dutch research on racism and ethnic discrimination is the question whether the educational system selects students on the basis of merit or achieved social statuses (often measured as their performance on standardized tests and/or their measured motivation and interest) or instead on ascribed social statuses such as ethnicity (and social class and gender). To address this question researchers in the Netherlands focus their attention on key selection moments in young people's educational trajectories (*loopbaanmoment*), such as the school advice given to pupils at the end of primary education, their chance to drop out of secondary education or enrollment in high status tracks (Dekkers and Bosker, 2004; Meijnen, 2004). The following sections will focus mainly on those studies that focus on pupils' 'school advice' administered at the end of primary education, as this constitutes a crucial point of selection in the educational career of pupils and strongly influences their future educational opportunities and outcomes (Driessen and Bosker, 2007; Luyten and

Bosker, 2004; Mulder et al., 2005; Roeleveld, 2005). Furthermore, this is by far the most developed area of research on racism and discrimination in the Netherlands and also illustrates some key findings, characteristics, strengths, and weaknesses of this research tradition.

While research in the Netherlands during the 1970s and 1980s suggested that pupils' school advice at the end of primary education was mainly influenced by their test results, these studies also showed that at least 50% of the variability in school advice could not be accounted for by pupils' test results. This stimulated researchers to investigate whether pupils' gender and their social and ethnic background influences their school advice independent of their test results (Luyten and Bosker, 2004). Subsequent research, some of which used data from the first PRIMA datasets, showed that ethnic minority pupils (particularly low-achieving pupils) experienced 'positive discrimination' as they were given a more favorable advice at the end of primary education compared to native Dutch pupils than what could be expected on the basis of their test results (Bosma and Cremers, 1996; De Jong, 1987; De Jong and Van Batenburg, 1984; Driessen, 1991; Dronkers et al., 1998; Jungbluth et al., 1990; Kerkhoff, 1988; Koeslag and Dronkers, 1994; Mulder, 1993).

Some authors argue that the higher advice administered to ethnic minority students can in part explain the lower educational outcomes and higher drop-out rate of these students in secondary education, as they are placed in educational programs or tracks above their measured ability (Tesser and Iedema, 2001). However, other authors argue that for some students a higher advice can constitute an additional challenge and incentive to work hard and rise above their expected level of achievement (Hustinx, 2002; Koeslag and Dronkers, 1994). This illustrates the ambiguity and complexity surrounding the concept of 'discrimination', as a particular phenomenon can be interpreted as discriminating in both a positive and negative sense.

Some researchers argue that the higher school advice given to ethnic minority students can be explained by teachers' positive discrimination of ethnic minority students because of their lower socio-economic position (De Jong, 1987; Kerkhoff, 1988) or because of teachers' fear of being accused of racism (Jungbluth, 1985; Stevens, 2008). Other researchers claim that ethnic minority students are evaluated more favorably because they are often compared to peers in the same class who perform below the average (Brandsma and Doolaard, 1999; Driessen, 2002; Mulder, 1993; Tesser and Mulder, 1990) or because they benefit from attending schools in large cities where minority groups can exercise much more influence (De Boer et al., 2006; Dronkers et al., 1998).

However, research on more recent waves of the PRIMA datasets shows no evidence that ethnic minority students are given a higher advice after controlling for children's test scores, their cognitive ability, and motivation (Driessen, 2006; Luyten and Bosker, 2004). Furthermore, there seems no evidence to support the view that children's classroom composition and urban context have an effect on their school advice, independent of children's test results (Driessen, 2006). Finally, analyses suggest that the relationship between children's test results and their school advice in the Netherlands becomes stronger over time (Claassen and Mulder, 2003; Mulder, 1993): based on the PRIMA 1988/1999 wave Mulder (1993) finds that 70% of the variability in school advice is explained by children's test scores, which increases to 74% in the 1996/1997 wave (Dronkers et al., 1998) and to 79% in the 2000/2002 wave (Luyten and Bosker, 2004).

However, two recent studies commissioned by Amsterdam's Department of Development in Society (Dienst Maatschappelijke Ontwikkeling) found that high-scoring Turkish and Moroccan pupils were slightly more likely to receive a lower advice compared to their Dutch peers in Amsterdam (Babeliowsky and den Boer, 2007; DMOGA, 2007). Despite the main conclusion of these reports that there is no evidence for overall differences in school advice between ethnic minority and Dutch pupils and that high-achieving pupils from Surinamese and Moroccan background appear to receive on average a higher school advice than their Dutch peers with similar scores, the media focused primarily on the reported 'under-advising' of Turkish and Moroccan pupils. Following the media coverage of this report Dutch opposition parties requested the Dutch secretary of education to further investigate these findings and report back to the parliament.

The subsequent report commissioned by the government to study the alleged occurrence of 'under-advising' is based on an analysis of the most recent PRIMA wave (2004–2005) and includes more than 10,000 pupils and 500 primary schools (Driessen and Bosker, 2007; Driessen et al., 2008). The results confirm the findings of recent studies: although the main ethnic minority groups receive on average lower levels of school advice than their Dutch peers, these differences can be explained by the Cito test scores of individual students. The report also shows that while pupils in large cities receive on average lower levels of advice, these differences can in turn be explained by pupils' individual test scores. Summarizing their findings, the authors conclude that 'there is no evidence to support the claim that ethnic minority students receive systematically and substantially lower advice [than their Dutch peers]' (Driessen and Bosker, 2007, p. 11).

However, in a subsequent study, Stroucken and colleagues (2008) concluded that ethnic minority pupils of non-Western descent received lower school advice based on equal Cito test scores than pupils of Dutch descent. Finally the national inspection for education (2011) concluded that while advice for ethnic minority pupils were not systematically lower, high-performing children of Moroccan and Turkish descent received on average lower levels of advice. Another recent study by Van der Wouden (2011) based on CBS data, shows that when one looks at up-streaming and down-streaming in second-ary school in Amsterdam there is much more up- and down-streaming among second-generation Turkish and Moroccan Dutch pupils than there is for pupils of native Dutch students. This again seems to suggest that teachers are less able to determine the capacities of pupils of Moroccan and Turkish descent at the end of primary school compared to pupils of Dutch descent.

Different explanations are formulated to explain why school administra-tors in the Netherlands seem to base their school advice increasingly more on pupils' test scores and less on ascribed statuses like ethnicity (Dagevos and Gijsberts, 2007; Dagevos et al., 2003; Driessen, 2006; Tesser and Iedema, 2001). Perhaps teachers have developed a more accurate view of ethnic minority pupils' skills and capacities over time and/or they consider more the suggested negative effects of 'over-advising'. In addition, as secondary schools are increas-ingly more evaluated in public they might encourage primary schools to be more selective in terms of allocating advice or streamline processes of selection across schools. Finally, as noted above, Dutch society and social policy has changed considerable over the last few years, particularly regarding the way in which multiculturalism is approached, which might reduce white, Dutch teachers' fear to discriminate ethnic minority pupils.

The importance of 'measured ability' as a primary determinant of ethnic minority success in education is also stressed in a recent study conducted by Terwel and colleagues (Terwel et al., 2011). In this longitudinal 'embedded case study', five ethnic minority students are followed from the ages of 10 to 21 by investigating both their performances on various standardized tests and their educational trajectories as their personal experiences of their educational careers and achievements. However, this study also suggests that students' intrinsic motivation to do well and the social and educational support they obtain from teachers and parents in responding to emerging and often unan-ticipated challenges and opportunities can compensate for lower scores on standardized tests. The great variability in these experienced opportunities and challenges and their seemingly unique embeddedness in personal biographies (e.g. the sudden availability of a place in a high-status track, illness, etc) makes the authors conclude that more qualitative research is required to gain more insight in the complex processes underlying educational success.

In sum, the research findings suggest that Dutch schools became more meri-tocratic over time in that pupils' performances on tests and not their ethnic background determine their educational trajectories. However, at the same time research suggests that some sub-categories of ethnic minority groups (like high and low-achieving students) experience either more or less favorable selection outcomes. Furthermore, while these findings are consistent in relationship to students' transition from primary to secondary education and their progress in secondary education after four years (Luyten, 2004), research on drop-out in secondary schools (Beekhoven, 2004) and subject-choices (Rekers-Mombarg and Van Langen, 2004; Van Langen et al., 2004) also emphasize the importance of 'social and cultural capital', teacher support, and family background and socialization processes more generally (Terwel et al., 2011).

18.4.2.2   *Teacher expectations*

Some researchers in the racism and discrimination tradition focus their attention on teacher-expectancy effects or the 'pygmalion hypothesis' (Rosenthal and Jacobson, 1968) by investigating the relationship between social class, ethnicity, teacher expectations, and educational outcomes. One study found that part of the relationship between social class and achievement could be explained by differential teacher expectations and aspirations, which were in turn informed by social class and ability (Van der Hoeven-van Doorum et al., 1990). A study conducted several years later from a slightly larger sample of pupils included ethnic background to this model and although it confirmed the findings of the earlier study, ethnicity did not seem to be related to teacher expectations or aspirations (Jungbluth, 1993). In a more recent study which relies in part on the PRIMA (2001) database Jungbluth (2003) finds that teachers not only have lower expectations (in terms of perceived cognitive skills) of students from lower socio-economic positions but they also lower their curriculum expectations accordingly, which in turn explains differences in educational achievement, independent of students' social background characteristics, measured ability, and the schools' social composition. While these findings suggest the importance of teachers' expectations of pupils in explaining differences in achievement between pupils of different socio-economic backgrounds 'there is no indication of an ethnic bias in addition to social background' (Jungbluth, 2003, p. 129).

While these studies are unique within the context of the Netherlands, they have been criticized on methodological grounds (Terwel, 2004) and could benefit from additional case-study research that explores the importance of teachers' interactions with others and characteristics of the larger institutional contexts in which they operate in developing curriculum, pedagogy, and expectations of students (e.g. Coburn, 2004; Gillborn and Youdell, 2000; Stevens, 2007a).

18.4.2.3   *Experiences of racism and discrimination*

While most studies mentioned above focus on teachers' expectations and/or unequal treatment of ethnic minority groups, the social psychologist Verkuyten and his colleagues offer a different approach to the study of racism and discrimination in Dutch schools. Based on a series of integrated qualitative and quantitative research projects that cover populations between 90 to 800 10–12 year old pupils (Verkuyten and Thijs, 2000), these researchers offer rich descriptions of how Dutch native students perceive ethnic minority students (Verkuyten, 2001), how they and ethnic minority students perceive discrimination (Verkuyten et al., 1997), and how school characteristics influence ethnic minority's experiences with racism (Verkuyten and Thijs, 2000, 2002). The data suggest that incidents of bullying and insulting are reduced when teachers challenge such behavior. However, attention given to intercultural education increases the reported incidents of such behavior, which can either be explained by an increased level of awareness or because teachers tend to spend more time on intercultural education when there are higher levels of bullying and insulting.

Research in the Netherlands on racism and discrimination is particularly strong in that it offers a representative picture of how ethnic minorities are selected and evaluated by schools over time throughout primary and secondary education. Furthermore, by assessing the respective influence of 'ascribed' and 'achieved' statuses researchers manage to address key questions regarding the 'meritocratic nature' of the Dutch school system. The literature discussed above also illustrates the close relationship between research and social policy in the Netherlands; as research findings influence policy debates which can in turn influence further research initiatives. However, while researchers often hypothesize why schools are either more or less meritocratic, educational institutions remain largely 'black boxes' and little is known in the Netherlands about the factors and processes that influence teachers in selecting, evaluating, and teaching students throughout their educational career. Furthermore, apart from a few pioneering studies, little is known about ethnic minorities' experiences with racism and discrimination in education and the wider society and how this impacts on their motivations, aspirations, expectations, and educational outcomes.

18.4.3   Ethnic school composition

A developing body of literature in the Netherlands focuses on the importance of ethnic school composition on ethnic minority and majority pupils' educational and wider outcomes (Driessen, 2002, 2007b). Related to this, some studies investigate the consequences of attending Islamic or faith schools for ethnic minority children. While some studies in this research tradition employ ethnographic (Teunissen, 1990) or mixed-methods designs (Verkuyten and Thijs, 2000), most studies are based on sophisticated statistical analyses of large, representative datasets (Ledoux et al., 2003). The following sections critically review the main findings of Dutch research in this area.

The findings of research in the Netherlands on the effects of ethnic concentration in schools are often conflicting. While research suggests that an increase in the proportion of ethnic minority pupils in schools positively affects pupils' well-being, as measured by their relationships with their social environment, their status in school, their motivation towards learning, and their ethnic identity (Everts, 1989; Teunissen, 1990; Verkuyten and Thijs, 2000), a more recent study concludes that the ethnic composition of the pupil population has no effect on pupils' social-emotional functioning (Ledoux et al., 2003). On the other hand, ethnic minority concentration appears to lower educational outcomes. While some studies conducted in the 1980s concluded that such negative effects only affect ethnic minority pupils and only appear strong in schools with a concentration higher than 50% (Tesser and Mulder, 1990), more recent research on larger datasets, employing more sophisticated analysis techniques finds that all pupils obtain lower educational outcomes in such schools (Tesser and Iedema, 2001; Tesser and Mulder, 1990; Westerbeek, 1999).

However, research also suggests that effects of ethnic minority concentration, even cumulative effects, are relatively small (Driessen, 2007b)[8] and decrease when studies focus on younger cohorts and/or schools that have had the time to adapt to such a situation (Tesser and Iedema, 2001; Westerbeek, 1999). Furthermore, the strong variation in average achievement between schools with a high proportion of ethnic minority pupils suggests that school leadership and management styles can effectively improve educational outcomes in such schools. After conducting ethnographic research in 'white' and 'black' schools, Teunissen (1990) suggests that the following school characteristics are effective in managing 'black schools': powerful school leadership, emphasis on basic skills, evaluation of school progress, teacher expectations, and a peaceful, orderly school climate. Recent research shows that schools with a substantial proportion of disadvantaged pupils are better equipped to deal with the particular challenges imposed by such a context and take account of the diversity of pupils and their specific needs (Ledoux et al., 2003).

However, researchers do not only disagree on whether ethnic school composition has an effect on educational outcomes, they also disagree on the impact of particular characteristics of schools with a high proportion of ethnic minorities on educational outcomes for children attending such schools. For example, Hofman (1994) concludes that particular tools aimed at improving the achievement of minority subgroups seem to generate the highest increase in achievement. In contrast, a study conducted by Weide (1995) suggests that ethnic minorities benefit more from general education rather than from special activities implemented by schools to improve their achievement.

While most researchers seem to agree that the ethnic composition of a school has a relatively small effect on pupils' performances, studies also suggest that such effects may vary according to the kind of educational outcomes assessed. More specifically, the effect of schools' social composition appears higher on mathematics achievement than on achievement in languages (Hofman, 1994). Furthermore, the cognitive functioning of pupils in particular seems to be affected negatively by being taught in classes with many disadvantaged, lower-achieving or non-Dutch-speaking pupils (Ledoux et al., 2003). Such effects are often explained by arguing that teachers and pupils in schools with a high proportion of ethnic minority pupils suffer from lower levels of available, valued educational resources, especially those related to the development of Dutch language skills (Crul, 2000; Pels, 1991; Verkuyten and Thijs, 2000; Westerbeek, 1999). A recent study (Karssen et al., 2011) confirms the above results but also included a new element in the discussion by focusing on citizenship attitudes. For this outcome they found positive results for both majority and minority students in mixed schools compared to pupils in more segregated 'white' or 'black' schools.

In sum, there is a developing body of research on the effects of ethnic school composition in the Netherlands. The findings of research in this area show that such effects are small and not conclusive and as a result do not offer support for particular school (de)segregation policies (Driessen, 2007b). While qualitative and mixed-methods studies suggest that particular school policies and characteristics can help to improve minority (ethnic) students' educational achievement, and that mixed schools improve minority and majority students' citizenship attitudes, research in this area can further develop by assessing the strength and significance of these particular relationships and further exploring how the ethnic composition and ethnic differentiation of a school impacts on the pedagogy and curriculum, educational outcomes, and social cohesion in schools. The following section critically evaluates research on Islamic (faith) schools in the Netherlands, which is an area of research that is closely related to the study of ethnic school composition effects.

18.4.3.1 Islamic schools

The Dutch constitution and school system allows for the establishment of state-funded Islamic schools, similar to the Catholic, Protestant, Jewish and Hindu schools. In recent decades 'faith schools', and particularly Islamic schools, have turned into a highly controversial matter (Driessen and Merry, 2006; Merry and Driessen, 2005). Although it is commonly assumed that this form of 'ethno-religious segregation' has a negative effect on the integration of Islamic communities into mainstream Dutch society and, as a consequence on social cohesion in general (BVD, 2002), few studies focus on Islamic schools and their curriculum.

Driessen (1997) and Driessen and Bezemer (1999a, 1999b) used the PRIMA datasets to conduct unique research on the relationship between Islamic and non-Islamic schools and pupils' educational outcomes and behavior characteristics (including measures of pupils' well-being, attitudes towards school work, self-confidence, social behavior, and parental support). The authors compared these pupil outcomes in Islamic schools with pupils in schools with a similar socio-economic population and with those from a nationally representative reference group of schools (or the 'average' primary school). The findings suggest that behavioral and attitudinal characteristic differences between both pupil populations are very small or non-existent (Driessen, 1997; Driessen and Bezemer, 1999b). Furthermore, pupils in Islamic schools do not perform worse in language and slightly better in arithmetic and Cito examinations compared to pupils in schools with a similar socio-economic disadvantage. However, at the same time the data show that pupils in Islamic schools obtain far lower test results compared to pupils in the 'average' Dutch primary school. As a result, pupils in Islamic schools do not manage to perform better than pupils in average Dutch schools, even though this is stipulated as one of the advantages of Islamic schools (Driessen, 1997; Driessen and Bezemer, 1999b). In a more recent study Driessen (2007a) replicates these findings using more recent waves of the PRIMA datasets (2002 and 2004).

The general suspicion in Dutch society that Islamic schools may have a negative influence on the integration of Turkish and Moroccan immigrants stimulated the Dutch government to fund an inspection report on 'Islamic Schools and Social Cohesion' (BVD, 2002). The findings of this study are based on analyses of school reports, school plans, and other documents, interviews of school administrators, and observations in Islamic schools. This report concludes that nearly all Islamic schools have an open attitude towards Dutch society and play a positive role in the development of social cohesion (BVD, 2002). This report elicited a lot of criticism to a level that the Dutch government ordered a new study on this topic: 'Islamic schools further investigated' (*Islamitische scholen nader onderzocht*) (Dijkstra and Janssens, 2003), which also concluded that the educational approach in Islamic schools does not pose a threat for the social cohesion and the basic values of an open and democratic Dutch society.

Recent years have seen an increased pre-occupation in Western societies with the position and role of Islam and related to this the ability of European countries to integrate Muslim minorities. As a result, public debates and social policy in the Netherlands have raised concerns over the role of faith schools and particularly Islamic schools in developing social cohesion. Little research has been conducted in this area and as a result, the few studies that focus on the effects of Islamic schools in the Netherlands are highly innovative and should be a source of inspiration to educational sociologists in other European countries. The findings of Dutch research in this area suggest that such schools do not pose a threat to social cohesion in the Dutch society. However, while pupils enrolled in Islamic schools perform slightly higher on standardized tests than their peers in other, similarly disadvantaged schools, such schools cannot compensate for the experienced disadvantage as pupils enrolled in Islamic schools perform considerably lower in standardized exams than their peers enrolled in an average Dutch primary school.

18.4.4 School choice

Directly related to research on the importance of ethnic school composition and Islamic schools on educational and wider outcomes are studies that focus on the causes of school's ethnic composition. In the Netherlands, free parental school choice and the right to organize education to one's own beliefs and religious convictions are granted in the Dutch Constitution since 1917. In recent decades these rights have been linked to processes of socio-economic and ethnic segregation in the educational system, especially in primary education (Jungbluth, 2005a, 2005b; Karsten, 1994).

Researchers explain the appearance of ethnic segregation between schools mainly by pointing to free parental school choice and the establishment of faith (Islamic and Hindu) schools, in particular for secondary education (Denessen et al., 2005; Gramberg, 1998; Karsten, 1994; Karsten et al., 2006; Smit et al., 2005). However, research in the Netherlands also suggests the importance of residential segregation in explaining ethnic segregation, particularly for primary schools (Gramberg, 1998).

Karsten and colleagues (2003) studied the relation between school choice and ethnic segregation using data from 52 primary elementary schools (see also Karsten et al., 2002a, 2002b) and interviews with parents and head teachers. The findings of this study suggest that residential segregation and the location of the school are the most important factors for the explanation of school segregation in primary education. Furthermore, the interviews with the school principals showed the ethnic composition of a school was also influenced by school-specific factors like: (i) the marketing of certain school profiles, (ii) the development and practicing of different kinds of gate-keeping methods, and (iii) the encouragement of school competition with as a possible consequence 'white' and 'non-white' flight (similar results were found in: Karsten, 1994).

The relationship between school choice and ethnic school composition is reciprocal in that the ethnic composition of the school is not only influenced by school choice processes but can also influence the process of school choice (Denessen et al., 2005). However, Dutch research suggests that the impact of the ethnic composition of the school population on parental school choice processes remains small, is not conclusive and complex, in particular because different social and ethnic groups have different motivations in choosing particular schools (Karsten et al., 2003). Although parents mainly choose a school in the local area (see also Smit et al., 2005), Dutch and higher educated parents are more likely to opt for an alternative school. Furthermore, while Dutch parents prefer a school with a pupil composition that 'matches' their family background, immigrant parents find the degree of differentiation and academic reputation of the school as more important (Karsten et al., 2003). A more recent study (Coenders et al., 2004), which uses data from a random sample of Dutch adults ($n = 1008$) finds that Dutch parents are more resistant to schools with a higher percentage of immigrant students, in particular when such immigrants are defined as 'non-assimilated'. Furthermore, while Dutch respondents with a lower SES are on average more resistant to ethnic diversity in schools compared to Dutch respondents with a higher SES background, the latter group appeared more resistant to schools with a very high percentage of ethnic minorities. According to the authors these findings indicate that higher SES groups' resistance to multicultural schools is context dependent, and increases when they perceive such multiculturalism as a threat to the educational opportunities of their own children (Coenders et al., 2004).

A more recent study uses data from second grade (six-year-olds) pupils in 700 primary schools through a written questionnaire for pupils' parents and their school administrators (based on the PRIMA 1988–1999 database) to investigate the importance of group-specific reasons for school choice (Denessen et al., 2005). The analyses reveal that religious groups predominantly choose a school with the same religious affiliation as their family, and ethnic minority groups prefer schools who are considerate of their religious background. In contradiction with the research findings of the studies cited above, this study did not find any differences in school choice between parents from different social classes (Denessen et al., 2005).

A recent policy study in Amsterdam (Adviesraad Diversiteit en Integratie, 2010) illustrates how 'white flight', which is possible because of 'free choice' actually limits the notion of 'free choice' for parents. The study finds that in many neighborhoods in Amsterdam different choices made by majority and minority parents leads to the development of separate 'white' and 'black' schools. When asked, both majority and minority parents preferred mixed schools. However, because of the 'free school choice' these schools were absent in their neighborhood with the result that parents actually had less choice rather than more choice because of their 'free choice'.

In sum, as schools in the Netherlands become increasingly more segregated, researchers do not only focus on the consequences but also on the causes of ethnic segregation. A developing body of quantitative research in the Netherlands suggests that various factors like parental school choice, residential segregation, socio-economic background, school practices and ethnic composition play a role in explaining ethnic segregation in Dutch schools. However, the general, complex and sometimes contradicting findings that emerge from the sophisticated statistical analyses of large-scale databases suggests the usefulness of further in-depth case-study research in the Netherlands that explores the motivations and underlying structures that underpin the process of school choice.

18.4.5   Family background tradition

Research in the Netherlands on family background characteristics and race/ethnic inequalities in education developed over time: while researchers first investigated the relative importance of social class and ethnicity in explaining educational underachievement, more recent research focuses on particular forms of (cultural and social) capital in explaining differences in achievement between ethnic groups. The following sections further explore this particularly rich body of research.

18.4.5.1 Social class or ethnic status?

In line with social policy developments in the late 1980s and early 1990s (see Section 18.2) educational researchers in the Netherlands focused on the importance of social class in explaining the relationship between ethnicity and educational inequality. Some researchers held on to an 'immigration perspective', which considers ethnic or national descent as a decisive factor in explaining the educational position of immigrant pupils (Wolbers and Driessen, 1996). By moving to another country, immigrants have to bridge essential cultural differences in terms of mores, values, written and unwritten rules, language, and the social structure of society. On the other hand, the 'deprivation perspective' explains the underachievement of immigrant pupils by their social class background, which is supposed to reflect some crucial social, pedagogical, and material conditions, which in turn inform the educational position of the child (Wolbers and Driessen, 1996).

In this 'culture versus class debate' (Phalet, 1998, p. 101) the majority of studies employ quantitative research designs and tend to emphasize the role of social class over ethnic descent in explaining the underachievement of specific immigrant groups (Cuyvers et al., 1993; Dronkers and Kerkhoff, 1990; Kerkhoff, 1988; Van 't Hof and Dronkers, 1993; Van Langen and Jungbluth, 1990), especially for second-generation immigrants (Van Ours and Veenman, 2001; Veenman, 1996b). In a more comprehensive review covering 75 different, usually large-scale, quantitative studies Driessen (1995) finds that 68% put more emphasis on social milieu and only a minority of studies (24%) concludes that ethnic background is more important or that there is no difference between the two variables in explaining underachievement (8%). In a subsequent study, Driessen and Dekkers (1997) analyze the relationship between students' social background characteristics and educational achievement using data from the VOCL cohorts. The analyses show that test results are largely determined by social class, with gender and ethnic status having a very limited impact. However, a recent large-scale quantitative cohort study (Tolsma et al., 2007a, 2007b) suggests that ethnic minorities are more likely to enroll in lower-status tracks and less likely to enroll in university education compared to native Dutch students, a difference that persists after controlling for parental SES. Hence, the authors conclude that ethnic differences in educational attainment cannot be reduced to ethnic minorities' disadvantaged socio-economic background.

These quantitative studies have been criticized on the basis of the statistical techniques employed in data analysis, the underlying assumptions that guide the process of constructing specific statistical models, and the ambiguous and superficial nature of the proposed causal relationships. First, although most of these quantitative studies employ multiple regression, the usefulness of such a technique can be questioned because of the strong correlation or overlap between social class and ethnicity (Driessen, 1995; Latuheru and Hessels, 1996; Ledoux, 1996). Even after employing a model-comparison procedure, which is robust to the problem of multicollinearity, Latuheru and Hessels (1994) conclude that 'due to the fact that ethnic and social-economic descent are mutually contaminating, it cannot be determined whether pupils' ethnic descent contributes to an explanation of the differences in school records' (Latuheru and Hessels, 1994, p. 227). Secondly, the discussion between 'class and ethnicity' creates an artificial distinction between these variables and obscures their strong and complex inter-relations. As a result, ethnic and social class categories are perceived as separate, static, and homogeneous groups, instead of describing them as more heterogeneous, changing and interacting groups (Ledoux, 1996; Pels and Veenman, 1996; Phalet, 1998). Finally, the relationship between crude characteristics such as social class or ethnicity and educational outcomes merely begs the question how such relationships can be explained, which requires further investigation focusing on specific processes that link such crude social characteristics to specific forms of educational inequality (Driessen, 1995; Ledoux, 1996; Pels and Veenman, 1996; Teunissen and Matthijssen, 1996). While some studies try to explain the effect of ethnicity on educational outcomes by incorporating variables such as 'ethnical configuration of the family', 'time of residence in the Netherlands' and 'language spoken at home' (Kerkhoff, 1988; Wolbers and Driessen, 1996), such statistical models cannot penetrate the complexity of how ethnic background relates to various forms of educational inequality (Teunissen and Matthijssen, 1996).

18.4.5.2   *Cultural and social capital*

Some researchers conducted small-scale ethnographic or qualitative studies to explore the complex relationship between social class, ethnicity, and educational achievement. Although most of these studies, like their quantitative counterparts, focus their attention mainly on family background characteristics of the child, they tend to criticize the view that the effect of ethnicity can be reduced to social class differences. These studies explore how various forms of social and cultural capital (Bourdieu, 1992 (1979), 1999 (1983); Bourdieu and Passeron, 1977) that are valued in or available to specific ethnic communities inform the educational outcomes of ethnic minority pupils.

Pels (1991) conducted ethnographic research on mothers and teachers of Dutch and Moroccan children and concluded that Moroccan families have different 'educational styles' (*opvoedingsstijlen*) than Dutch families and schools. Moroccan families emphasize obedience and discipline and children are not supposed to ask questions or develop own initiative. In contrast, Dutch parents and primary schools stimulate individuality, independence, and children's ability to explore. Similarly, while Moroccan families tend to develop a specific cognitive style in which learning by heart or memorizing is emphasized, Dutch parents and schools seem to develop a cognitive style that emphasizes the importance of critical questioning and understanding. Therefore, it appears that the cultural capital valued by native Dutch families is closer to field-specific expectations of Dutch primary education than the capital valued in Moroccan families (Pels, 1991). Similarly, Kromhout and Vedder (1996) conducted research with African Caribbean children in elementary schools and concluded that certain forms of behavior which are labeled as aggressive by Dutch children are labeled as socially competent by African Caribbean boys in the Netherlands.

Lindo (1995, 1996) conducted qualitative interviews of Iberian (Spanish and Portuguese) and Turkish adolescents and their parents. Although these two groups are similar in terms of their economic motivations for migration, timing of migration and initial job opportunities and experiences of discrimination, Iberian immigrants tend to obtain higher educational qualifications than their Turkish peers. Lindo explains such differences by pointing to the specific structural conditions under which these immigrant groups left their country of origin and related developments of region-specific networks in the country of destination and attitudes towards integration in the host society. Iberian immigration should be perceived as a more individual enterprise, in which expectations about economic returns are confined to a small group of relatives. In contrast, Turkish immigration often involves high economic investment and expectations of the whole household in both the country of origin and country of destination. Because of the stronger social capital between Turkish immigrants in the Netherlands and their extended families in Turkey, the latter exercise more social control and often function as a barrier against cultural integration and structural mobility. This is reinforced by the development of strong region-specific networks in the country of origin through chain migration (Lindo, 1995, 1996). A more recent qualitative study explores narratives of Moroccan parents on the educational situation of their children in Belgium or the Netherlands and concludes that minority parents can also develop an oppositional culture in response to perceived injustice in the Netherlands towards ethnic minorities (Hermans, 2004).

However, while Lindo (1995, 1996) points to specific forms of social capital that appear to constrain social mobility of Turkish immigrant youth, Crul (1996, 1999, 2000) identifies various forms of social capital that can foster social mobility amongst Moroccan and Turkish youth. Crul relied mainly on interview data from Moroccan and Turkish youth and found that while support from parents did not appear to have a strong influence on educational outcomes, support from family members, peers, or teachers seemed to yield higher outcomes, as the latter are more aware of the specific demands and nature of the Dutch educational system. While parents can offer support through guidance and stimulation, family members, peers, and teachers can often offer additional forms of support such as advice and practical help. High-achieving pupils also appeared to be raised in a field (either family or school) where Dutch constituted the dominant language of communication, which in turn increases access to social and cultural capital considered valuable in the field of education (Crul, 1996, 1999, 2000), which in turn relates to the socio-economic position of the parents (Van der Veen, 2003).

Similarly, other ethnographic or qualitative studies conducted in the Netherlands conclude that although Turkish and Moroccan parents find education important, such attitudes are often not realized because of their limited ability to provide support and because of the maintenance of an oppositional culture that inhibits cultural and structural integration in Dutch society, which is in turn explained by their lack of knowledge of the Dutch language and education system (Klatter-Falmer, 1996; Ledoux, 1996; Veenman, 1996a). At the same time, the availability of specific forms of social capital that offer access to various forms of support in the process of learning is often mentioned by immigrant pupils enrolled in higher education as an important reason for their success in education (Dagevos and Veenman, 1992; Van Veen, 2001).

From 1995 onwards, and in line with the approach employed by some qualitative or ethnographic studies, quantitative researchers in the Netherlands started to investigate the relationship between social class and/or ethnic differences in educational achievement and differential access to or activation of various forms of 'social' and 'cultural' capital (De Graaf et al., 2000; Driessen, 2000a; Driessen and Smit, 2007; Driessen et al., 2005; Kalmijn and Kraaykamp, 1996; Kraaykamp, 2000; Van Veen et al., 1998). This line of research seems to be inspired by Coleman's legacy on social capital (Coleman, 1966, 1987, 1999 (1988)), and an increasing interest in US educational research on Bourdieu's theory of cultural reproduction and concept of cultural capital (DiMaggio, 1979, 1982, Lamont and Lareau, 1988; Lareau, 1999 (1987)). In addition, some recent studies (Van der Veen and Meijnen, 2000; Van der Veen and Meijnen, 2001) emphasize the importance of ethnic minority students' orientation to Dutch society (which can be defined as a form of 'identity' capital, see Cote, 1996) as a source of educational success.

In general, these studies do not lend strong support for the usefulness of Coleman's or Bourdieu's conceptualization of social or cultural capital. For example, while participation in 'high brow' culture (e.g. museum attendance) does not relate to higher educational outcomes, access to specific forms of cultural capital (such as 'parental reading behavior') that are considered crucial for achievement in a Dutch educational system relate positively with students educational outcomes (De Graaf and De Graaf, 2002; De Graaf et al., 2000; Kraaykamp, 2000; Van Veen et al., 1998). Furthermore, access to and the impact of various forms of cultural capital seems to vary according to the ethnic background of pupils (Driessen, 2000a; Verhoeven, 2006). In relationship to social capital, a recent quantitative study (Wissink et al., 2006) finds that negative relationships between parents and adolescents associate positively with developmental outcomes in all ethnic groups. However, the relationship between parenting behavior and delinquent behavior differs according to ethnicity, as restrictive control related to a higher level of delinquent behavior only for Turkish and Moroccan immigrants.

Research on the importance of family background characteristics is by far the most developed research tradition in the Netherlands that focuses on the relationship between race/ethnic inequalities in education. While initially research focused on the question whether social class or ethnicity is the most important factor in explaining underachievement, more recent qualitative and quantitative studies investigate the importance of particular forms of social and cultural capital in explaining the relationship between race/ethnicity and educational inequality.

18.4.6 An institutional approach

A relatively new tradition of research in the Netherlands looks at the importance of the institutional structure of the educational system in explaining differences in educational outcomes between different groups (Andersen and Van de Werfhorst, 2010; Crul and Vermeulen, 2003; Crul and Schneider, 2010; Dronkers et al., 2011; Heus and Dronkers, 2011; Van d Werfhorst and Mijs, 2007, 2010). Aspects of the institutional structure include: the starting age of school, the number of school contact hours, the age at which students are selected, the differentiation of the school system, and the permeability of the school system (whether or not it is easy to stream up or down from a vocational to an academic track or the other way round).

Crul (2000) was the first to do a systematic study, based on analysis of the SPVA surveys and qualitative in-depth interviews, into the importance of institutional arrangements in school for children of immigrants in the Netherlands. In his study he emphasizes the importance of the early tracking system at age 12, the intermediary classes and the permeability of the Dutch school system in explaining differences in educational achievement. Many second-generation youths in his study took what is referred to as the long route through lower and middle vocational education into higher education. This route takes them three years longer, but in the end gets them into higher education. Among other things it showed that the selection at age 12 for most second – generation

Turkish and Moroccan children in the Netherlands comes too early to be sufficiently indicative of their educational capabilities.

More recently, Crul and his team (Crul et al., 2008, 2009) looked at the importance of these and other institutional arrangements in education in a European comparative study 'The Integration of the European Second Generation' (TIES), which investigates the school and labor-market careers of second-generation youth in eight European countries using similar survey instruments.[9] The two above-mentioned Dutch research publications focused on identifying the typical Dutch institutional arrangements that help or hinder the Turkish and Moroccan second generation in school. These studies conclude that, compared to other countries (for instance France or Sweden), second-generation youth in the Netherlands enters formal education relatively late (around age four). In France almost all pupils attend preschool early, which enables the second generation to learn French as a second language in an educational environment from an early age. Secondly the selection age in the Netherlands is relatively early at age 12. The combination of late start and early selection results in a relatively large group of ethnic minority students going into the lowest tracks of VMBO (lower vocational education). The Dutch school system however does offer somewhat of a repair to the early selection. Again taking the European comparative perspective, the Netherlands is the country with the highest level of permeability between school tracks. Many second-generation youth profit from this possibility. Because of the high ambitions in the family, they are keen to get into higher education, even if it takes three years more. Crul and others (2009) also point to the enormous complexity of the Dutch school system. Nowhere in Europe is the number of possible school tracks (six) as high as in the Netherlands. This asks a lot of knowledge of the school system, something immigrant parents usually do not possess.

Van de Werfhorst and Mijs (2010) looked at school system effects, making use of studies based on different international datasets, such as PISA, TIMSS, and PIRLS. They show that inequalities are magnified by national-level tracking institutions (between-school tracking) and that standardization decreases inequalities. A high level of differentiation between school tracks (as is the case in the Netherlands) leads to more educational inequality (Van de Werfhorst and Mijs, 2007). Such a school system makes the influence of parental background characteristics more important.

Compared to research approaches discussed in the earlier sections, the emphasis in the institutional approach is on the school system itself rather than on characteristics of pupils and their parents. Or put differently: at different points in the school career, the educational system makes different demands on family or individual resources of students (Crul and Schneider, 2010). In primary school, support with Dutch as a second language is important, while in secondary school support with homework and knowledge of the schools system is vital. Further on in the school career, individual ambitions and drive are important when opting for the long route. The researchers in the political arithmetic approach and the family background approach mostly take the school system for granted or as a given.

The institutional approach especially benefits from international comparative research which brings out the specifics of national educational systems. Heus and Dronkers (2010) for example, analyzed the 'Programme for International Student Assessment' (PISA) survey to explore the educational systems and educational resources in school help, in order to explain differences in immigrant children's educational attainment. They found that in systems with teacher shortages, children of immigrants underperform. They also found that in more differentiated school systems (like the Netherlands) children of immigrants have lower test scores. Perhaps somewhat surprisingly, they found that especially children of immigrants with parents who have more resources do better in comprehensive systems. However, in a recent paper, Dronkers and colleagues (2011) again looked at school system characteristics, but now also included tracking into the equation. The most important finding of this study is that educational systems are not uniformly 'good' or 'bad', but they have different consequences for different groups: while some groups are better off in comprehensive systems, other groups are better off in moderately or highly stratified systems.

18.5 Conclusion and discussion

Educational research on the relationship between race/ethnicity and educational inequality in the Netherlands developed into a major area of research from the 1980s onwards. Educational sociologists working in this area are ultimately concerned with explaining differences in educational achievement between racial/ethnic groups. In so doing, researchers focus their attention mainly on the largest, most 'underachieving' racial/ethnic minority groups such as students from Turkish, Moroccan, and Surinamese backgrounds.

The most dominant research tradition in the Netherlands has focused its attention primarily on family background characteristics. However, more recently researchers working in the 'institutional approach' highlight the importance of characteristics of educational systems from a nationally comparative research approach in explaining the educational trajectories of ethnic minority students in different school and national contexts. While the latter 'blame' teachers, school processes and/or educational policies as the main cause of educational underachievement of racial/ethnic minority pupils, the former merely describe differences in educational outcomes or progress and/or explain such differences primarily by referring to a lack of availability or activation of valuable resources amongst ethnic minority families.

In terms of epistemology, Dutch educational researchers rely more heavily on positivism and prefer large-scale, quantitative research strategies. Three major developments can help to explain these apparent differences. First, it appears that the influence of the new sociology of education, and related influence of social constructivism, phenomenology and micro-sociological classroom research has been less influential in the Netherlands. Or, as Wesselingh (1996) puts it in evaluating the origins and development of the Dutch sociology of education:

> The strong bond with the educational reform movements of the 1970s also became looser. [...]. The research tradition stemming from [Basil Bernstein and Raymond Williams], namely the sociology of the curriculum, and the research within the school classrooms has virtually come to a standstill and thus fostered the disappearance of (micro-)sociology from the area.
>
> (Wesselingh, 1996, p. 222)

As a result, Dutch sociology of education is characterized by a small group of specialists, whose major strength lies in 'the solid empirical basis and use of advanced research techniques and analysis in their work', but for whom 'theory and reflection are not [their] strongest qualities' (Wesselingh, 1996, p. 213).

A second major influence which is particular to the Netherlands concerns the lack of interest by Dutch social policy-makers in the particular needs and interests of racial/ethnic minority groups. In Dutch social policy, the problematic social position of ethnic minority children is often reduced to their lower social class position (Driessen, 2000b; Phalet, 1998; Rijkschroeff et al., 2005). As a result, Dutch educational research did not receive a strong incentive from social policy-makers to investigate experiences of racism or racial discrimination in schools, and in the absence of a strong, critical research tradition that focuses on micro-educational processes in schools, the 'class versus ethnicity' debate remained firmly lodged into a macro-sociological, family-school perspective.

Also characteristic of research on race/ethnicity and educational inequality in the Netherlands is the close relationship between social policy-makers and the research community, with the latter often actively involved in the process of developing (or advising on) social policy and testing 'success' of policy measures through government-funded research. Furthermore, most research in the Netherlands in this area is based on analyses of large-scale quantitative datasets which are funded (albeit indirectly) by the Dutch government to assist the process of policy development and evaluation. While the close and dependent relationship of Dutch educational researchers with their government does not necessarily undermine 'good research practice', it poses questions about the extent to which such a relationship has influenced the research practice in terms of employed research questions, methods, and findings. From the above, several lessons can be drawn to improve research on the relationship between race/ethnicity and educational inequality in the Netherlands.

First, research in the Netherlands on ethnic/racial inequalities in education could develop a deeper understanding of how educational systems influence race/ethnic inequalities by conducting more in-depth case-studies or ethnographic research on the nature of specific school and classroom processes. Such efforts could help to open 'the black box' of the Dutch educational system and develop a more critical approach to specific selection processes adopted in schools, and related to this, the nature of the curriculum taught, interactions between staff and students, and processes of tracking or streaming. The more recently developed 'institutional approach' tradition seems to work towards this and particularly their international comparative approach makes findings in this area of research relevant not just for the Netherlands but for a broad range of educational and national contexts.

Secondly, while some qualitative, ethnographic work has been conducted in the Netherlands on processes and characteristics of (ethnic minority) families and educational outcomes, such research still appears to be underdeveloped and less likely to find its way into academic peer-reviewed journals compared to more positivistic, quantitative studies. Further in-depth, qualitative or ethnographic case-study research in this area can function as a continuous source of inspiration for the methodologically very strong, but theoretically exhausted quantitative family-school tradition in the Netherlands.

Thirdly, research in the Netherlands on (Islamic) and other faith schools is unique and important in a European context which is increasingly more preoccupied with the integration of Muslim minorities in 'Western' societies. The few qualitative and mixed-methods studies carried out by SESI researchers in the Netherlands suggest that future quantitative work in this area can benefit from the rich findings of small-scale qualitative studies in developing a better understanding of the complex processes, opportunities and challenges in schools with different ethnic compositions.

More generally, research on racial/ethnic inequalities in education in the Netherlands can benefit from a stronger integration and mutual recognition of qualitative and quantitative research. Such efforts are likely to be a source of inspiration to both qualitative and quantitative researchers in developing research questions and measurement instruments and help the development of knowledge in this area.

While researchers in the Netherlands focus their attention primarily on 'underachieving' ethnic or racial minority groups, their findings do not allow policy-makers and practitioners straightforward answers as to if and how achievement gaps should or could be narrowed. First, the findings suggest that the variability in achievement and more general notions such as 'inequality' and 'discrimination' can be defined and measured in different ways, leading to different interpretations of the data and conclusions. Second, research suggests that inequality is a complex and changing phenomenon. As a result research aimed at understanding inequality and policy aimed at reducing inequality is likely to be more successful if it considers the importance of the various embedded context in which inequalities develop, including school, family, peer-group, neighborhood, and regional, national, and international processes and characteristics.

Finally, following Feinstein and colleagues' 'ecological approach' (Feinstein et al., 2004) and McLaughlin and Talbert's 'embedded context approach' (McLaughlin and Talbert, 2001) future research on race and ethnic inequalities in education could benefit from considering a broad range of inter-related educational and wider outcomes, related to students' identities and well-being and by exploring how such outcomes interact and develop within the various (family, peer group, educational, economic, national, and international political) contexts in which they are embedded. This approach has its origins in developmental psychology (Bronfenbrenner, 1979) and classifies environmental context measures according to the level at which they are situated, including 'proximal' face-to-face interactions (e.g. teacher–student relationships), characteristics of institutions (school and family characteristics), and more distal factors (e.g. neighborhood characteristics, rural versus urban areas, educational policy (inter-)national political processes). Such research would offer a more comprehensive approach to the study of racial/ethnic inequalities in education and illustrate the usefulness of both quantitative and qualitative research in studying the complex, uneven, and context-dependent nature of integration processes in society.

Notes

1. At the end of primary education in the Netherlands, children are given advice regarding the educational programs or tracks they are allowed to follow in secondary education. This advice is administered by the head teacher of the child's primary school and based on their Cito (*Centraal Instituut voor Toetsontwikkeling*) test scores and an evaluation of their motivation, effort, and capacities by the pupil's teacher. On the basis of their school advice, children are oriented to either vocational or general education tracks leading to higher education within the Dutch school system. Research suggests that very few ethnic minority pupils criticize and successfully challenge their specific school-advice (Veenman, 1996a).
2. Cito is the National Institute for Educational Testing which develops and validates the official exam, known as the Cito test, in the (final) eighth year of primary school. The test uses multiple-choice questions to assess the ability of a child in the areas of language, calculation, mathematics, history, geography, biology, learning skills and world orientation (UNESCO, 2006).
3. All quotes from literature sources written in Dutch are translated in English. Readers who want to access the original quotes are encouraged to consult the cited references.

4. In the Netherlands 'ethnic minority' is used to refer to immigrant groups for whose presence the government feels a special responsibility (because of the colonial past or because they have been required by the Dutch authorities to work in the Netherlands) and who find themselves in a lower socio-economic position compared to Dutch majority population (Driessen, 2000b; Eldering, 1989; Gibson, 1997; Guirodon et al., 2004). This illustrates the problematic notion of the concept 'ethnic minority' (Sealey and Carter, 2001) and how its meaning and usage are locally constructed and reflect differences in national systems and the ideals embedded within them (Gibson, 1997).

5. The increased emphasis in Dutch social policy on the cultural integration of ethnic minorities is also illustrated by the implementation of the recent Citizenship Law (*Wet Inburgering*) which came into effect in 2006. According to this law, ethnic minorities in the Netherlands who do not have the Dutch nationality are obliged to follow and pass a citizenship course (*inburgeringsexamen*) within five years. Furthermore, ethnic minorities who want to immigrate to the Netherlands have to pass a test measuring their basic knowledge of the Dutch language and society prior to moving to the Netherlands. If successful, these immigrants are required to follow and pass the prescribed citizenship course in the Netherlands (Klaver and Ode, 2007).

6. We initially used the Social Science Citation Index (SSCI) to identify high profile journals from the Netherlands. However, as only three journals included in the SSCI appeared relevant to the topic of investigation (this concerns the journals *School Effectiveness and School Improvement*, the *Netherlands' Journal of Social Sciences* and *Pedagogische Studiën*) we selected additional journals which were frequently cited in the Dutch literature sampled through the first selection phase (this concerns the journals: *Mens en Maatschappij*, *Sociologische Gids*, *Tijdschrift voor Onderwijsresearch* and *Migrantenstudies*). As Dutch is the language of publication in most of these journals, reviewing this particular sample of studies helps in making this body of research more accessible to a non-Dutch speaking audience.

7. Since 1994 PRIMA (*Cohortonderzoek Primair Onderwijs*) is a panel study set up every other year to evaluate national educational priority policies for pupils from socially disadvantaged and/or ethnic minority families. Each wave involves about 57,000 primary school pupils selected from a sample of 600–650 schools (Gijsberts, 2003; Guirodon et al., 2004). The VOCL (*Voortgezet Onderwijs Cohort Leerlingen*) is also a panel study, set up in 1989 to follow students' progress through secondary education and involves around 20,000 students in each wave selected from a representative sample of secondary schools in the Netherlands (Guirodon et al., 2004; Herweijer, 2003).

8. Between 5–15% of the differences in average mathematics or language scores between schools could be explained by this concentration effect (Tesser and Iedema, 2001; Westerbeek, 1999).

9. The main objective of TIES is to create the first systematic and rigorous European dataset on the economic, social, and occupational integration and integration in terms of identity of second-generation immigrants in 15 cities from eight European countries: Paris and Strasburg (France), Berlin and Frankfurt (Germany), Madrid and Barcelona (Spain), Vienna and Linz (Austria), Amsterdam and Rotterdam (the Netherlands), Brussels and Antwerp (Belgium), Zurich and Basel (Switzerland), and Stockholm (Sweden). At the heart of the study is a survey involving more than 10,000 respondents (age 18–35) in the participating countries, focusing on Turkish, Moroccan, Eastern European immigrants and native citizens as a control group. The findings of this study are only recently being released and discussed (see http://www.tiesproject.eu/).

References

Adviesraad Diversiteit en Integratie (2010) *Is er dan geen smid in het land die de sleutel maken kan* (Amsterdam, Adviesraad Diversiteit en Integratie).

Andersen, R. and Van de Werfhorst, H. (2010) Educational and Occupational Status in 14 Countries: The Role of Educational Institutional and Labour Market Coordination, *British Journal of Sociology*, 61(2), 336–355.

Babeliowsky, M. and Den Boer, R. (2007) *Voortgezet onderwijs in beeld. De leerlingen en hun resultaten in het Amsterdamse VO. Schooljaar 2005/2006* (Almere, Babeliowsky Onderwijsonderzoek).

Badger, D., Nursten, J. and Woodward, M. (2000) Should All Literature Reviews Be Systematic?, *Evaluation and Research in Education*, 14(3–4), 220–230.

BBC (2004) *Gunman Kills Dutch Film Director*. http://news.bbc.co.uk/1/hi/world/europe/3974179.stm (accessed 2008).

Beekhoven, S. (2004) De Rol van Participatie en Identificatie bij het Voortijdig Schoolverlaten van Jongens, *Pedagogische Studieen*, 81, 104–124.

Bosma, H. and Cremers, P. (1996) Schooladviezen van Allochtone Leerlingen, *Tijdschrift voor Onderwijsresearch*, 21(3), 262.

Bourdieu, P. (1992 (1979)) *Distinction. A Social Critique of the Judgement of Taste* (London/ New York, Routledge).

Bourdieu, P. (1999 (1983)) The Forms of Capital, in: A. H. Halsey, L. Hugh, B. Philip and A. S. Wells (Eds) *Education. Culture, Economy, Society* (Oxford, Oxford University Press), 46–58.

Bourdieu, P. and Passeron, J.-C. (1977) *Reproduction in Education, Society and Culture* (London, Sage Publications).

Brandsma, H. and Doolaard, S. (1999) Differences in Effectiveness between Primary Schools and Their Impact on Secondary School Recommendations, *School Effectiveness and School Improvement*, 10, 430–450.

Bronfenbrenner, U. (1979) *The Ecology of Human Development* (Cambridge, MA, Harvard University Press).

Bronnenman-Helmers, R. and Turkenburg, M. (2003) Het Onderwijsbeleid ten aanzien van Minderheden, in: J. Dagevos, M. Gijsberts and C. Van Praag (Eds) *Rapportage Minderheden 2003* (Den Haag, SCP), 143–200.

BVD (2002) *Islamitische Scholen en Sociale Cohesie* (Utrecht, Binnenlandse Veiligheidsdienst).

Claassen, A. and Mulder, L. (2003) Leerlingen na de Overstap. Een Vergelijking van vier Cohorten Leerlingen na de Overgang van Basisonderwijs naar Voortgezet Onderwijs met Nadruk op de Positie van Doelgroepleerlingen van het Onderwijsachterstandenbeleid (Nijmegen, ITS).

Coburn, C. E. (2004) Beyond Decoupling: Rethinking the Relationship between the Institutional Environment and the Classroom, *Sociology of Education*, 77(July), 211–244.

Coenders, M., Lubbers, M. and Scheepers, P. (2004) Weerstand tegen Scholen met Allochtone Kinderen. De Etnische Tolerantie van Hoger Opgeleiden op de Proef Gesteld, *Mens en Maatschappij*, 79(2), 124–147.

Coleman, J. S. (1966) *Equality of Educational Opportunity* (Washington, DC, Government Printing Office).

Coleman, J. S. (1987) Families and Schools, *Educational Researcher*, 16(6), 32–38.

Coleman, J. S. (1999 (1988)) Social Capital in the Creation of Human Capital, in: A. H. Halsey, L. Hugh, B. Philip and A. S. Wells (Eds) *Education. Culture, Economy, Society* (Oxford, Oxford University Press), 80–95.

Cote, J. E. (1996) Sociological Perspectives on Identity Formation: The Culture-Identity Link and Identity Capital, *Journal of Adolescence*, 19, 417–428.

Crul, M. (1996) Succesfactoren in de Schoolloopbaan van Turkse en Marokkaanse Jongeren van de Tweede Generatie, *Tijdschrift Voor Sociologie*, 17(3), 402–420.

Crul, M. (1999) Turkish and Moroccan Sibling Support and School Achievement Levels: An Optimistic View, *Netherlands' Journal of Social Sciences*, 35(2), 110–127.

Crul, M. (2000) *De Sleutel tot Succes. Over Hulp, Keuzes en Kansen in de Schoolloopbanen van Turkse en Marokkaanse Jongeren van de Tweede Generatie* (Amsterdam, Het Spinhuis).

Crul, M., Pasztor, A. and Lelie, F. (2008) *De tweede generatie. Uitdagingen en Kansen voor de stad* (Den Haag, NICIS).

Crul, M., Pasztor, A., Lelie, F., Mijs J. and Schnell, P. (2009) *Valkuilen en springplanken in het onderwijs* (Den Haag, NICIS).

Crul, M. and Schneider, J. (2010) Comparative Context Integration Theory. Participation and Belong in Europe's Large Cities, *Journal Ethnic and Racial Studies*, 34(4), 1249–1268.

Crul, M. and Wolff, R. (2002) *Talent gewonnen. Talent verspild?* (Utrecht, ECHO).

Crul, M. and Vermeulen, H. (2003) The Future of the Second Generation: The Integration of Migrant Youth in Six European Countries, *International Migration Review*, 37(4), special issue.

Cuyvers, P., Von Meijenfeldt, F., Van Houten, H. and Meijers, F. (1993) Allochtone en Autochtone Jongeren: Hoe Groot is het Verschil?, *Sociologische Gids*, XL(2), 140–159.

Dagevos, J. and Gijsberts, M. (Eds) (2007) *Jaarrapport Integratie 2007* (Den Haag, Sociaal en Cultureel Planbureau).

Dagevos, J., Gijsberts, M. and Van Praag, C. (Eds) (2003) *Rapportage Minderheden 2003. Onderwijs, Arbeid en Sociaal-Culturele Integratie* (Den Haag, Sociaal en Cultureel Planbureau).

Dagevos, J. and Veenman, J. (1992) *Succesvolle Allochtonen. Over de Maatschappelijker Carriere van Turken, Marokkanen, Surinamers en Molukkers in Hoge Functies* (Amsterdam, Boom Meppel).

De Boer, H., Van der Werf, M. P. C., Bosker, R. J. and Jansen, G. G. H. (2006) Onderadvisering in de provincie Friesland, *Pedagogische Studieen*, 83, 452–468.

De Graaf, N. D. and De Graaf, P. (2002) Formal and Popular Dimensions of Cultural Capital: Effects on Children's Educational Attainment, *Netherlands' Journal of Social Sciences*, 38(2), 34–63.

De Graaf, N. D., De Graaf, P. and Kraaykamp, G. (2000) Parental Cultural Capital and Educational Attainment in the Netherlands: A Refinement of the Cultural Capital Perspective, *Sociology of Education*, 73(April), 92–111.

De Jong, M.-J. (1987) *Herkomst, Kennis en Kansen. Allochtone en Autochtone Leerlingen bij de Overgang van Basis- naar Voortgezet Onderwijs* (Amsterdam/Lisse, Swets and Zeitlinger).

De Jong, M.-J. and Van Batenburg, T. (1984) Etnische Herkomst, Intelligentie en Schoolkeuzenadvies, *Pedagogische Studieen*, 61, 362–371.

Dekkers, H. P. J. M. and Bosker, R. J. (2004) Het Meritocratisch Gehalte van het Voortgezet Onderwijs: Inleiding op het Themanummer, *Pedagogische Studieen*, 81(7), 75–78.

Delamont, S. (1992) *Fieldwork in Educational Settings: Methods, Pitfalls and Perspectives* (London/New York, Routledge and Falmer).

Denessen, E., Driessen, G. and Sleegers, P. (2005) Segregation by Choice? A Study of Group-Specific Reasons for School Choice, *Journal of Education Policy*, 20(3), 347–368.

Dijkstra, A. B. and Janssens, F. J. (2003) *Islamitische Scholen nader Onderzocht* (Den Haag, Sociaal en Cultureel Planbureau).

DiMaggio, P. J. (1979) Review Essay: On Pierre Bourdieu, *American Journal of Sociology*, 86(6), 1460–1474.

DiMaggio, P. J. (1982) Cultural Capital and the Schooling Success: The Impact of Status Culture Participation on the Grades of U.S. High School Students, *American Sociological Review*, 47, 189–201.

DMOGA (2007) *Basisschooladviezen en Etniciteit* (Amsterdam, Dienst Maatschappelijke Ontwikkeling Gemeente Amsterdam).

Driessen, G. (1991) Discrepanties tussen Toetsresultaten en Doorstroomniveau. Positieve Discriminatie bij de Overgang Basisonderwijs – Voortgezet Onderwijs?, *Pedagogische Studieen*, 68, 27–35.

Driessen, G. (1995) Het Relatieve Belang van Sociaal Milieu en Etnische Herkomst voor de Verklaring van Onderwijsachterstanden, *Tijdschrift voor Onderwijsresearch*, 20(4), 341–362.

Driessen, G. (1997) Islamic Primary Schools in the Netherlands: The Pupil's Achievement Levels, Behaviour and Attitudes and their Parent's Cultural Backgrounds, *Netherlands' Journal of Social Sciences*, 33(1), 42–66.

Driessen, G. (2000a) Cultureel Kapitaal en Onderwijsprestaties: Differentieren naar Etnische Groep?, *Tijdschrift voor Onderwijsresearch*, 24(3/4), 215–236.

Driessen, G. (2000b) The Limits of Educational Policy and Practice? The Case of Ethnic Minorities in the Netherlands, *Comparative Education*, 36(1), 55–72.

Driessen, G. (2002) School Composition and Achievement in Primary Education: A Large-Scale Multilevel Approach, *Studies in Educational Evaluation*, 28, 347–368.

Driessen, G. (2006) Het Advies Voortgezet Onderwijs: Is de Overadvisering Over?, *Mens en Maatschappij*, 81(1), 5–23.

Driessen, G. (2007a) Opbrengsten van Islamitische Basisscholen (ITS, Radboud Universiteit Nijmegen).

Driessen, G. (2007b) *Peer Group' Effecten op Onderwijsprestaties. Een internationaal Review van Effecten, Verklaringen en Theoretische en Methodologische Aspecten* (Nijmegen, ITS – Radboud Universiteit Nijmegen).

Driessen, G. and Bezemer, J. (1999a) Achtergronden, Kenmerken en Opbrengsten van Islamitisch Basisonderwijs, *Pedagogische Studieen*, 76(5), 332–349.

Driessen, G. and Bezemer, J. (1999b) Background and Achievement Levels of Islamic Schools in the Netherlands: Are the Reservations Justified?, *Race, Ethnicity and Education*, 2(2), 235–256.

Driessen, G. and Bosker, R. J. (2007) *Onderadvisering in Beeld* (Den Haag, Inspectie van het Onderwijs).

Driessen, G. and Dekkers, H. (1997) Educational Opportunities in the Netherlands: Policy, Students' Performance and Issues, *International Review of Education*, 43(4), 299–315.

Driessen, G. and Merry, M. (2006) Islamic Schools in the Netherlands: Expansion or Marginalization?, *Interchange*, 37(3), 201–223.

Driessen, G., Sleegers, P. and Smit, F. (2008) The Transition from Primary to Secondary Education: Meritocracy and Ethnicity, *European Sociological Review*, 24(4), 527–542.

Driessen, G. and Smit, F. (2007) Effects of Immigrant Parents' Participation in Society on Their Children's School Performance, *Acta Sociologica*, 50(1), 39–56.

Driessen, G., Smit, F. and Sleegers, P. (2005) Parental Involvement and Educational Achievement, *British Educational Research Journal*, 31(4), 509–532.

Dronkers, J., van der Velden, R. and Dunne, A. (2011) *The Effects of Educational Systems, School-Composition, Track-Level, Parental Background and Immigrants' Origins on the Achievement of 15-years Old Native and Immigrant Students. A Reanalysis of PISA 2006* (Maastricht, Research Centre for Education and the Labour Market, ROA).

Dronkers, J. and Kerkhoff, A. (1990) Sociaal Milieu, Taalvaardigheid en Schoolsucces bij Allochtonen, Dialect- en Standaardtaalsprekers, *Sociologische Gids*, XXXVII(5), 304–319.

Dronkers, J., van Erp, M., Robijns, M. and Roeleveld, J. (1998) Krijgen Leerlingen in de Grote Steden en met name Amsterdam te Hoge Adviezen?, *Tijdschrift voor Onderwijsresearch*, 21, 262–271.

Eldering, L. (1989) Ethnic Minority Children in Dutch Schools. Underachievement and its Explanations, in: L. Eldering and J. Kloprogge (Eds) *Different Cultures, Same School. Ethnic Minority Children in Europe* (Amsterdam/Lisse, Swetz & Zeitlinger), 107–136.

Everts, H. (1989) 'Witte' en 'Zwarte' Scholen: Bepaalt het Aandeel Allochtonen de Kwaliteit van het Onderwijs?, *Tijdschrift voor Onderwijswetenschappen*, 174–190.

Feinstein, L., Duckworth, K. and Sabates, R. (2004) *A Model of Inter-generational Transmission of Educational Success* (London, Centre for Research on the Wider Benefits of Learning).

Foster, P. and Hammersley, M. (1998) A Review of Reviews: Structure and Function in Reviews of Educational Research, *British Educational Research Journal*, 24(5), 609–628.

Garssen, J. and Wageveld, M. (2007) Demografie, in: J. Dagevos and M. Gijsberts (Eds) *Jaarrapport Integratie 2007* (Den Haag, Sociaal en Cultureel Planbureau), 29–46.

Gibson, M. A. (1997) Exploring and Explaining the Variability: Cross-National Perspectives on the School Performance of Minority Students, *Anthropology of Education Quarterly*, 28(3), 318–329.

Gijsberts, M. (2003) Minderheden in het basisonderwijs, in: J. Dagevos, M. Gijsberts and C. Van Praag (Eds) *Rapportage minderheden 2003* (Den Haag, Sociaal en Cultureel Planbureau), 63–142.

Gijsberts, M. and Hartgers, M. (2005) Minderheden in het Onderwijs, in: P. Schnabel, F. Leeuw and I. Van Veen (Eds) *Jaarrapport Integratie 2005* (Den Haag, Sociaal en Cultureel Planbureau), 57–79.

Gijsberts, M. and Herweijer, L. (2007) Allochtone Leerlingen in het Onderwijs, in: J. Dagevos and M. Gijsberts (Eds) *Jaarrapport Integratie 2007* (Den Haag, Sociaal en Cultureel Planbureau), 102–130.

Gillborn, D. and Youdell, D. (2000) *Rationing Education: Policy, Practice, Reform and Equity* (Buckingham, Open University Press).

Gramberg, P. (1998) School Segregation: The Case of Amsterdam, *Urban Studies*, 35(3), 547–564.

Guirodon, V., Phalet, K. and Ter Wal, J. (2004) Comparative Study on the Collection of Data to Measure the Extent and Impact of Discrimination in a Selection of Countries. Medis Project (Measurement of Discriminations). Final Report on the Netherlands (Lyon, European Comission).

Heath, A. (2000) The Political Arithmetic Tradition in the Sociology of Education, *Oxford Review of Education*, 26(3–4), 313–330.

Hermans, P. (2004) Contranarratieven van Marokkaanse Ouders: Een Weerwoord op Discriminatie, Paternalisme en Stigmatisering, *Migrantenstudies*, 20(1), 36–53.

Herweijer, L. (2003) Voortgezet Onderwijs, Beroepsonderwijs en Hoger Onderwijs, in: J. Dagevos, M. Gijsberts and C. Van Praag (Eds) *Rapportage Minderheden 2003* (Den Haag, Sociaal en Cultureel Planbureau), 111–143.

Heus de M. and J. Dronkers (2010) De schoolprestaties van immigrantenkinderen in 16 OECD-landen. De invloed van onderwijsstelsels en overige samenlevingskenmerken van zowel herkomst- als bestemmingslanden, *Tijdschrift voor Sociologie*, 3–4, 260–294.

Hofman, A. and Van den Berg, M. (2002) Ethnic-Specific Achievements in Dutch Higher Education, *Higher Education in Europe*, 28(3), 371–389.

Hofman, W. H. (1994) School Effects on Performances of Minority Pupils, *School Effectiveness and School Improvement*, 5(1), 26–44.

Hurrell, P. (1995) Do Teachers Discriminate? Reactions to Pupil Behaviour in Four Comprehensive Schools, *Sociology*, 29(1), 59–72.

Hustinx, P. (2002) School Careers of Pupils of Ethnic Minority Background after the Transition to Secondary Education: Is the Ethnic Factor Always Negative?, *Educational Research and Evaluation*, 8, 169–195.

Jungbluth, P. (1985) *Verborgen Discriminatie. Leerlingbeeld en Onderwijsaanbod op de Basisschool* (Nijmegen, ITS).

Jungbluth, P. (1993) Pygmalion and Effectiveness of 'Black' Schools; Teachers' Stereotypes and Hidden Goal Differentiation Towards Ethnic Minorities, *Tijdschrift voor Onderwijsresearch*, 18(2), 99–110.

Jungbluth, P. (2003) De Ongelijke Basisschool. Etniciteit, Sociaal Milieu, Sexe, Verborgen Differentiatie, Segregatie, Onderwijskansen en Schooleffectiviteit (Nijmegen, ITS).

Jungbluth, P. (2005a) Onderwijssegregatie en de (Re)productie van Ongelijkheid, in: P. Brassé and H. Krijnen (Eds) *Gescheiden of Gemengd. Een Verkenning van Etnische Concentratie op School en in de Wijk* (Utrecht, Forum), 33–57.

Jungbluth, P. (2005b) Trends in Segregatie in het Nederlandse Basisonderwijs naar Sociale Klasse zowel als Kleur 1994–2002, in: M. Valcke, K. De Cock, D. Gombeir and R. Vanderlinde (Eds) *Meten en Onderwijskundig Onderzoek – Proceedings van de 32e Onderwijs Research Dagen 2005* (Gent, Universiteit Gent: Vakgroep Onderwijskunde).

Jungbluth, P., Verhaak, C. and Driessen, G. (1990) Vervolgadviezen in Relatie tot Etniciteit; hoe Verhouden Prestaties, Gezinsachtergrond en Leerkrachtenoordelen zich tot Elkaar?, *Pedagogische Studieen*, 67, 231–237.

Kalmijn, M. and Kraaykamp, G. (1996) Race, Cultural Capital, and Schooling: An Analysis of Trends in the United States, *Sociology of Education*, 69(January), 22–34.

Karssen, M., van der Veen, I., Roeleveld, J. (2011) *Effecten van schoolsamenstelling op schoolprestaties in het Nederlands basisonderwijs* (Amsterdam, SCO Kohnstam Instituut).

Karsten, S. (1994) Policy on Ethnic Segregation in a System of Choice: The Case of the Netherlands, *Journal of Education Policy*, 9(3), 211–225.

Karsten, S., Felix, C., Ledoux, G., Meijnen, W. G., Roeleveld, J. and Van Schooten, E. (2006) Choosing Segregation or Integration? The Extent and Effects of Ethnic Segregation in Dutch Cities, *Education and Urban Society*, 38(2), 228–247.

Karsten, S., Ledoux, G., Roeleveld, J. and Elshof, D. (2003) School Choice and Ethnic Segregation, *Educational Policy*, 17(4), 452–477.

Karsten, S., Roeleveld, J., Ledoux, G., Felix, C. and Elshof, D. (2002a) Schoolkeuze en Etnische Segregatie in het Basisonderwijs, *Pedagogische Studien*, 79, 359–375.

Karsten, S., Roeleveld, J., Ledoux, G., Felix, C. and Elshof, D. (2002b) *Schoolkeuze in een Multi-etnische Samenleving* (Amsterdam, SCO-Kohnstamm Instituut).

Kerkhoff, A. (1988) *Taalvaardigheid en Schoolsucces. De Relatie Tussen Taalvaardigheid Nederlands en Schoolsucces van Allochtone en Autochtone Leerlingen aan het Einde van de Basisschool* (Amsterdam/Lisse, Swets and Zeitlinger).

Klatter-Falmer, J. (1996) *Turkse Kinderen en hun Schoolsucces. Een Dieptestudie naar de Rol van Sociaal Culturele Oriëntatie, Taalvaardigheid en Onderwijskenmerken* (Tilburg, Dissertation Catholic University Brabant).

Klaver, J. and Ode, A. (2007) Inburgeren in Nederland, in: J. Dagevos and M. Gijsberts (Eds) *Jaarrapport Integratie 2007* (Den Haag, SCP), 47–71.

Koeslag, M. and Dronkers, J. (1994) Overadvisering en de Schoolloopbanen van Migrantenleerlingen en Autochtone Leerlingen in het Voortgezet Onderwijs, *Tijdschrift voor Onderwijsresearch*, 19(3), 240–258.

Kraaykamp, G. (2000). Ouderlijk gezin en schoolsucces. Een verklaring met demografische, culturele en sociale aspecten. *TOR: Tijdschrift voor Onderwijsresearch*, 77(2), 179–194.

Kromhout, M. and Vedder, P. (1996) Cultural Inversion in Afro-Caribbean Children in the Netherlands, *Anthropology and Education Quarterly*, 27(4), 568–586.

Lamont, M. and Lareau, A. (1988) Cultural Capital: Allusions, Gaps, and Glissandos in Recent Theoretical Developments, *Sociological Theory*, 6, 153–168.

Lareau, A. (1999 (1987)) Social-Class Differences in Family-School Relationships: The Importance of Cultural Capital, in: A. H. Halsey, L. Hugh, B. Philip and A. S. Wells (Eds) *Education. Culture, Economy and Society* (Oxford, Oxford University Press), 703–717.

Latuheru, E. and Hessels, M. (1994) Schoolprestaties van Allochtone Leerlingen: De Invloed van Etnische Herkomst, *Tijdschrift voor Onderwijsresearch*, 19(3), 227–239.

Latuheru, E. and Hessels, M. (1996) Schoolprestaties en de Invloed van Etnische en Sociaal-Economische Herkomst, *Sociologische Gids*, XLIII(2), 100–113.

Ledoux, G. (1996) De Invloed van 'Sociaal Milieu' bij Turkse, Marokkaanse en Nederlandse Sociale Stijgers, *Sociologische Gids*, XLIII(2), 114–130.

Ledoux, G., Van der Veen, I., Driessen, G., Doesborgh, J. and Vergeer, M. (2003) *Sociale Integratie in het Primair Onderwijs* (Nijmegen/Amsterdam, ITS Nijmegen and SCO Kohnstamm Instituut Amsterdam).

Levels, M. and Dronkers, J. (2008). Educational Performance of Native and Immigrant Children from Various Countries of Origin. *Ethnic and Racial Studies*, 31(8): 1404–1425.

Lindo, F. (1995) Ethnic Myth or Ethnic Might? On the Divergence in Educational Attainment between Portuguese and Turkish Youth in the Netherlands, in: G. Bauman and T. Sunier (Eds) *Post-Migration and Ethnicity. Cohesion, Commitments, Comparison* (Amsterdam, Het Spinhuis), 144–164.

Lindo, F. (1996) *Maakt Cultuur Verschil? De Invloed van Groepspecifieke Gedragspatronen op de Onderwijsloopbaan van Turkse en Iberische Migrantenjongeren* (Amsterdam, Het Spinhuis).

Luyten, H. (2004) Succes in het voortgezet onderwijs: Capaciteiten, inzet of achtergrond?, *Pedagogische Studieen*, 81, 151–166.

Luyten, H. and Bosker, R. J. (2004) Hoe Meritocratisch zijn Schooladviezen?, *Pedagogische Studieen*, 81(8), 89–103.

McLaughlin, M. W. and Talbert, J. E. (2001) *Professional Communities and the Work of High School Teachers* (Chicago, University of Chicago Press).

Meijnen, W. G. (2004) Het Concept Meritocratie en het Voortgezet Onderwijs, *Pedagogische Studien*, 81(7), 79–87.

Merry, M. S. and Driessen, G. (2005) Islamic Schools in Three Western Countries: Policy and Procedure, *Comparative Education*, 41(4), 411–432.

Mulder, L. (1993) Secondary School Recommendations in Relation to Student and School Characteristics, *Tijdschrift voor Onderwijsresearch*, 18(2), 111–119.

Mulder, L., Roeleveld, J., Van der Veen, I. and Vierke, H. (2005) *Onderwijsachterstanden tussen 1988 en 2002: Ontwikkelingen in Basis- en Voortgezet Onderwijs* (Nijmegen/Amsterdam., ITS and SCO-Kohnstamm Instituut).

OC&W (1974) *Beleidsplan voor het Onderwijs aan Groepen in Achterstandssituaties* (Zoetemeer, Ministerie van Onderwijs, Cultuur en Wetenschappen).

OC&W (1981) *Beleidsplan Culturele Minderheden in het Onderwijs* (Zoetemeer, Ministerie van Onderwijs, Cultuur en Wetenschappen).

OC&W (1985) *Onderwijsvoorrangsplan 1985–1989* (Zoetemeer, Ministerie van Onderwijs, Cultuur en Wetenschappen).

OC&W (1997) *Landelijk Beleidskader Gemeentelijk Onderwijsachterstandenbeleid 1998–2002* (Zoetemeer, Ministerie van Onderwijs, Cultuur en Wetenschappen).

Pels, T. (1991) *Marokkaanse Kleuters en hun Culturele Kapitaal: Opvoeden en Leren in het Gezin en op School* (Amsterdam/Lisse, Swets & Zeitlinger).

Pels, T. and Veenman, J. (1996) Onderwijsachterstanden bij Allochtone Kinderen. Het Ontbrekende Onderzoek, *Sociologische Gids*, XLIII(2), 130–145.

Phalet, K. (1998) Minderheden en Schoolsucces, in: C. H. M. Geuijen (Ed.) *Werken aan Ontwikkelingsvraagstukken. Multiculturalisme* (Utrecht, Uitgeverij Lemma B.V.), 97–114.

Rekers-Mombarg, L. and Van Langen, A. (2004) Causale Modellering van het Vakkenkeuzeproces: Verschillen Tussen Jongens en Meisjes, *Pedagogische Studieen*, 81, 134–145.

Rijkschroeff, R., Ten Dam, G., Duyvendak, J. W., De Gruijter, M. and Pels, T. (2005) Educational Policies on Migrants and Minorities in the Netherlands: Success or Failure?, *Journal of Education Policy*, 20(4), 417–435.

Roeleveld, J. (2005) Effecten van Advies en Bezochte Basisschool op de Positie in het Vierde jaar Voortgezet Onderwijs, in: G. Driessen (Ed.) *Van Basis- naar Voortgezet Onderwijs. Voorbereiding, Advisering en Effecten* (Nijmegen/Amsterdam, ITS/ SCO-Kohnstamm Instituut.).

Rosenthal, R. and Jacobson, L. (1968) *Pygmalion in the Classroom* (New York, Holt, Rinehart and Winston).

Schnabel, P., Leeuw, F. and Van der Veen, G. (Eds) (2005) *Jaarrapport Integratie 2005* (Den Haag and Voorburg, Sociaal en Cultureel Planbureau, Wetenschappelijk Onderzoek en Documentatiecentrum en Centraal Bureau voor de Statistiek).

Sealey, A. and Carter, B. (2001) Social Categories and Social Linguistics: Applying a Realist Approach, *International Journal of the Sociology of Language*, 152, 1–19.

Smit, F., Driessen, G. and Doesborgh, J. (2005) Opvattingen van Allochtone Ouders over Onderwijs: Tussen Wens en Realiteit. Een Inventarisatie van de Verwachtingen en Wensen van Ouders ten Aanzien van de Basisschool en Educatieve Activiteiten in Rotterdam (Nijmegen, ITS).

Stevens, P. A. J. (2007a) Exploring the Importance of Teachers' Institutional Structure on the Development of Teachers' Standards of Assessment in Belgium, *Sociology of Education*, 80(October), 314–329.

Stevens, P. A. J. (2007b) Researching Race/Ethnicity and Educational Inequality in English Secondary Schools: A Critical Review of the Research Literature Between 1980 and 2005, *Review of Educational Research*, 77(2), 147–185.

Stevens, P. A. J. (2008) Exploring Pupils' Perceptions of Teacher Racism in their Context: A Case Study of Turkish and Belgian Vocational Education Pupils in a Belgian School, *British Journal of Sociology of Education*, 29(2), 175–187.

Stevens, Peter A. J., Clycq, Noel, Timmerman, Christiane and Van Houtte, Mieke. (2011) Researching Race/Ethnicity and Educational Inequality in the Netherlands: A Critical Review of the Research Literature between 1980 and 2008. *British Educational Research Journal*, 37(1), 5–43.

Stroucken., L., Takkenberg, D. and Beguin, A. (2008) *Citotoets en de overgang van basis naar voortgezet onderwijs*. CBS: Sociaaleconomische trends, 2e kwartaal 2008.

Terwel, J. (2004) Pygmalion in de Klas: Over de Verwachting van Leraren en de Invloed van Medeleerlingen, *Pedagogische Studieen*, 81, 58–68.

Terwel, J., Rodrigues, R. and Van de Koot-Dees, D. (2011) *Tussen afkomst en toekomst. Case Studies naar de Schoolloopbanen van Leerlingen van 10–21 jaar.* Antwerpen/Apeldoorn: Garant.

Tesser, P. and Iedema, J. (Eds) (2001) *Rapportage Minderheden. Deel 1. Vorderingen op School* (Den Haag, Sociaal en Cultureel Planbureau).

Tesser, P., Merens, J. G. F. and Van Praag, C. (Eds) (1999) *Rapportage Minderheden 1999. Positie in het Onderwijs en op de Arbeidsmarkt* (Den Haag, Sociaal en Cultureel Planbureau).

Tesser, P. and Mulder, L. (1990) Concentratie en Prestatie van Allochtone Leerlingen in het Basisonderwijs, *Migrantenstudies*, 2, 31–44.

Tesser, P., Van Dugteren, F. A. and Merens, J. G. F. (Eds) (1998) *Rapportage Minderheden 1998. De Eerste Generatie in de Derde Levensfase* (Den Haag, Sociaal en Cultureel Planbureau).

Teunissen, J. (1990) *Binnenstadsscholen: 'Witte' en 'Zwarte' Scholen in de Grote Steden* (Alphen aan de Rijn: Samsom).

Teunissen, J. and Matthijssen, M. (1996) Stagnatie in Onderwijsonderzoek naar de Etnische Factor bij Allochtone Leerlingen. Een Pleidooi voor Theoretische en Methodologische Vernieuwing, *Sociologische Gids*, XLIII(2), 87–99.

Thompson, M. and Crul, M. (2007) The Second Generation in Europe and the United States: How is the Transatlantic Debate Relevant for Further Research on the European Second Generation?, *Journal of Ethnic and Migration Studies*, 33(7), 1025–1041.

Tolsma, J., Coenders, M. and Lubbers, M. (2007a) De Onderwijskansen van Allochtone en Autochtone Nederlanders Vergeleken: Een Cohort-design, *Mens en Maatschappij*, 82(2), 133–154.

Tolsma, J., Coenders, M. and Lubbers, M. (2007b) Trends in Ethnic Educational Inequalities in the Netherlands: A Cohort Design, *European Sociological Review*, 23(3), 325–339.

Turkenburg, M. and Gijsberts, M. (2007) Opleidingsniveau en Beheersing van de Nederlandse Taal, in: J. Dagevos and M. Gijsberts (Eds) *Jaarrapport Integratie 2007* (Den Haag, Sociaal en Cultureel Planbureau), 72–101.

UNESCO (2006) *World Data on Education – 6th Edition* (Geneva, United Nations. Educational, Scientific and Cultural Organization).

Van't Hof, L. and Dronkers, J. (1993) Onderwijsachterstanden van Allochtonen: Klasse, Gezin of Etnische Cultuur, *Migrantenstudies*, 9(1), 2–26.

Van der Hoeven-van Doorum, A. A., Voeten, M. J. M. and Jungbluth, P. (1990) Het Effect van Leerkrachtenverwachtifvcvvngen en Streefniveaus op Schoolloopbanen in het Basisonderwijs, *Tijdschrift voor Onderwijsresearch*, 15(1), 23–41.

Van der Veen, I. (2001) Succesvolle Turkse, Marokkaanse en Autochtone Leerlingen in het Voortgezet Onderwijs, in: W. G. Meijnen, J. C. C. Rupp and T. Veld (Eds) *Succesvolle Allochtone Leerlingen* (Leuven/Apeldoorn, Garant).

Van der Veen, I. (2003) Parents' Education and Their Encouragement of Successful Secondary School Students from Ethnic Minorities in the Netherlands, *Social Psychology of Education*, 6, 233–250.

Van der Veen, I. and Meijnen, W. (2000) School Careers of Students from Ethnic Minorities in the Netherlands, *American Educational Research Association Conference Paper*.

Van der Veen, I. and Meijnen, W. G. (2001) The Individual Characteristics, Ethnic Identity and Cultural Orientation of Successful Secondary School Students of Turkish and Moroccan Background in the Netherlands, *Journal of Youth and Adolescence*, 30(5), 539–560.

Van der Wouden, M. (2011) Afkomst telt. Een kwantitatieve onderzoke naar typen doorstroom gedurende het voortgezet onderwijs in Amsterdam. Amsterdam: O+S.

Van Langen, A. and Jungbluth, P. (1990) *Onderwijskansen van Migranten: De Rol van Sociaal Economische en Culturele Factoren* (Amsterdam/Lisse, Swets & Zeitlinger).

Van Langen, A., Rekers-Mombarg, L. and Dekkers, H. P. J. M. (2004) Groepsgebonden Verschillen in de Keuze van Exacte Vakken, *Pedagogische Studieen*, 81, 117–129.

Van Ours, J. and Veenman, J. (2001) The Educational Attainment of Second Generation Immigrants in the Netherlands (Tilburg/Utrecht, Institute for Labour Studies, University of Tilburg and University of Utrecht), 25.

Van Veen, K., Denessen, E., Van der Kley, P. and Gerris, J. (1998) Gezin en Schoolloopbaan: een Onderzoek naar de Invloed van Cultureel en Sociaal Kapitaal in het Gezin op de Schoolloopbaan van Kinderen, *Tijdschrift voor Onderwijsresearch*, 23(1), 3–16.

Veenman, J. (1996a) *Heb je Niets, dan Ben je Niets. Tweede-Generatie Allochtone Jongeren in Amsterdam* (Assen, Van Gorcum).

Veenman, J. (1996b) *Keren de Kansen? Tweede Generatie Allochtonen in Nederland* (Assen, Van Gorcum).

Verhoeven, L. (2006) Sociocultural Variation in Literacy Achievement, *British Journal of Educational Studies*, 54(2), 189–211.

Verkuyten, M. (2001) 'Abnormalization' of Ethnic Minorities in Conversation, *British Journal of Social Psychology*, 40, 257–278.

Verkuyten, M., Kinket, B. and Van der Wielen, C. (1997) Preadolescents' Understanding of Ethnic Discrimination, *The Journal of Genetic Psychology*, 158(1), 97–112.

Verkuyten, M. and Thijs, J. (2000) *Leren (en) Waarderen. Discriminatie, Zelfbeeld, Relaties en Leerprestaties in 'Witte' en 'Zwarte' Basisscholen* (Amsterdam, THELA Thesis).

Verkuyten, M. and Thijs, J. (2002) Racist Victimisation among Children in the Netherlands: The Effect of Ethnic Group and School, *Ethnic and Racial Studies*, 25(2), 310–331.

Weide, M. G. (1995) *Effectief Basisonderwijs voor Allochtone Leerlingen* (Groningen, Rijksuniversiteit Groningen).

Wesselingh, A. (1996) The Dutch Sociology of Education: Its Origins, Significance and Future, *British Journal of Sociology of Education*, 17(2), 213–226.

Werfhorst, H. and Mijs, J. (2007) *Onderwijsdifferentiatie en ongelijkheid. Nederland in vergelijkend perspectief* (Amsterdam, Rapport in opdracht van het Ministerie van OCW).

Werfhorst, H. and Mijs, J. (2010) Achievement Inequality and the Institutional Structure of the Educational Systems: A Comparative Perspective, *The Annual Review of Sociology*, 36, 407–428.

Van de Werfhorst, Herman G. (2011) Selectie en differentiatie in het Nederlandse onderwijsbestel. Gelijkheid, burgerschap en onderwijsexpansie in vergelijkend perspectief, *Pedagogische Studiën*, 88, 283–297.

Westerbeek, K. (1999) *The Colours of My Classroom. A Study into the Effects of the Ethnic Composition of Classrooms on the Achievement of Pupils from Different Ethnic Backgrounds* (Rotterdam, CED).

Wissink, I. B., Dekovic, M. and Meijer, A. M. (2006) Parenting Behavior, Quality of the Parent-Adolescent Relationship, and Adolescent Functioning in Four Ethnic Groups, *Journal of Early Adolescence*, 26(2), 133–159.

Wolbers, M. and Driessen, G. (1996) 'Milieu of Migratie?' Determinanten van Schoolloopbaanverschillen tussen Allochtone Leerlingen in het Voortgezet Onderwijs', *Sociologische Gids*, XLIII(5), 349–366.

Wolff, R. and Crul, M. (2003) *Blijvers en Uitvallers in het hoger onderwijs* (Utrecht, ECHO).

19
United States of America

A. Gary Dworkin and Ruth N. López Turley

19.1 National context: US educational system

Prior to the 1980s, children's education in the United States was the near-exclusive domain of the individual states and not of the federal government. The Constitution of the United States made no mention or provision for the public or private education of the country's children. The consequence of this exclusion is that for most of US history there had been considerable variability in the content of educational instruction from state to state. The issue of 'states' rights,' which entails an on-going conflict between the states and the national government and which was not resolved following the American Civil War (1861–1865), has led to nuanced applications of federal programs for schools and lawsuits against the federal government by coalitions of states. Only since the 1980s has the federal government intervened in the content of instruction in the public schools. Prior to that time the role of the federal government was to protect the civil rights of citizens under the aegis of the 'Due Process clause' of the XIV Amendment to the Constitution, and there in terms of the abolition of racial segregation in the school (*Brown* v. *Board of Education of Topeka*, 1954). In the absence of a Constitutional guarantee of public education and the saliency of states' rights, the operation, curricula, and even the structure of public education in the USA continues to display considerable variability.

19.1.1 The structure of schooling in the United States

The US Department of Education's organizational chart of the public schools describes the general structure of education in US schools, although there are some individual school district and state variations (Figure 19.1). The variations in the structure remain a legacy of the absence of true national educational planning and the lack of a national curricula. In most states and school districts within states, beginning at age three, children enter nursery schools on a voluntary and often parent-paid basis. Four-year-olds enter pre-Kindergarten

(Pre-K), where reading readiness and social skills may be taught. Pre-K is not compulsory and in many school districts it may be targeted only to children from low-income families. Sometimes, other children may enroll in Pre-K at a financial cost to their parents, or be enrolled in private, for-profit Pre-K

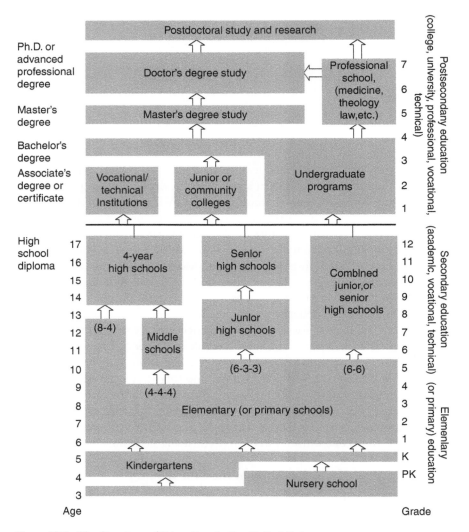

Figure 19.1   The Structure of Education in the United States

Note: Adult education programs, while not separately delineated above, may provide instruction at the elementary, secondary, or postsecondary education level. Chart reflects typical patterns of progression rather than all possible variations.

Source: U.S Department of Education. National Centre for Education Statistics. Annual Reports Program.

programs. Generally, five-year-olds enter Kindergarten, which is often not compulsory and in difficult economic times may be restricted, abridged, or even not offered in some local school districts. Elementary or primary schools operate from Grade 1 (age six) through Grade 4, 5, 6, or 8, depending upon the local system. There are also variations in the grade levels included in middle or junior high school and the grade levels included in senior high school.

Upon completion of high school students who continue their formal education will attend a vocational or technical school, which offers a certificate, a junior or community college, which offers an associate degree, or a baccalaureate program at a four-year college or university, which offers a bachelor's degree. The selection of which institution a student attends is in part a function of their career or vocational interests, partly related to their academic performance in high school and their standardized test score results, and partly due to their motivation and personal finances. Nevertheless, there are also open-admission colleges that accept all students with high school diplomas, regardless of their high school grades or standardized test scores. A similar set of processes affect whether students obtain formal education beyond the baccalaureate degree. Master's degree and later doctoral degree studies are available to selected students with a bachelor's degree, but again are based on grades in college and standardized test scores. Those college graduates interested in professional degrees such as in medicine, theology, law, business administration, etc. will attend professional schools after completing college. Such schools are selective and are limited to students with high grade averages and good test scores, as well as evidence of substantial motivation to complete the course work and pass a certification examination. Finally, a small proportion of those receiving doctoral degrees or professional degrees may proceed to postdoctoral study and research. There are individual variations to these themes, as well as nuanced content across different parts of the country.

The percentage of the school age population that participate at each progressive level of schooling diminishes somewhat, as students drop-out or do not enter more advanced levels of educational attainment Furthermore, the differential in participation at each level varies by race, ethnicity, socio-economic status, and gender. Drop-out rates are proportionally higher for Hispanic, Native American (American Indians), and African American students compared with white and Asian American students. Males and students living in poverty also have higher drop-out rates than do females and middle-class students. Balfantz and Legters (2004) observed that many of the nation's urban schools are drop-out factories where fewer than 50%of a cohort will make normal progress from grade to grade. Dworkin (2008a) described the problems of drop-outs in the public grade K–12 schools as a 'New American Dilemma'.

The makeup of the public and private school student populations differ markedly by race and ethnicity. According to the National Center for

Education Statistics of the United States, K–12 private schools have student bodies that are 73% white, while public schools have student bodies that are 55% white. African Americans represent 17% of the public school population and 9% of the private school population. Hispanics or Latinos account for 21%of the public school population and 9% of the private school population. Asian and Pacific Islanders make up 6%of the private school student bodies and 5%of the public school student bodies. Finally, Native Americans account for 1%of the public school population and much less than 1% of the private school population.

According to the Institute for Education Sciences of the National Center for Education Statistics (NCES, US Department of Education), nearly 50 million students were enrolled in K–12 public schools in 2009, with 69.9% enrolled in Grade Pre-K through Grade 8 and, of course, 30.1% enrolled in Grades 9–12. In addition to public school enrollment, the report notes that 5.5 million students are enrolled in private schools (this figure has declined from 6.3 million in 2001, plausibly from the heightened level of public school accountability implemented under the 'No Child Left Behind Act of 2001' (NCLB). In addition, approximately 5% of all public schools are 'charter' schools. As NCES notes,

> A public charter school is a publically funded school that is typically governed by a group or organization under a legislative contract or charter from the state; the charter exempts the school from selected state or local rules and regulations. In return for funding and autonomy, the charter school must meet the accountability standards articulated in its charter. (NCES, 2011, p. 24)

Research on charter schools suggest that the benefits of such schools tends to be inconclusive, with most charters performing less well academically than the public schools in the same communities (Carnoy et al., 2005; Bracey, 2005; Ballou et al., 2008). Generally, speaking, the charter school movement has been endorsed by more conservative school reformers, while other conservatives, especially from the Milton Friedman Foundation, have called for a school voucher system, whereby parents can apply public school tax monies to private school tuition for their children (see the critique of the foundation's surveys regarding the demand for private school vouchers in Lorence and Dworkin, 2007).

19.1.2   Immigration to the United States

Throughout the middle of the 19th and all of the 20th centuries the USA has been defined as 'a nation of immigrants'. The trend has not slowed down and, according to recent census data, by 2050, two-thirds of all Americans will either be immigrants or children of immigrants. However, the national origins of the immigrants have undergone radical changes since the beginning of the 20th century (Gibson and Lennon, 1999). Table 19.1 portrays the changes in

Table 19.1 National origins of immigrants 1901–2010

	1901–1910	1911–1920	1921–1930	1931–1940	1941–1950	1951–1960	1961–1970	1971–1980	1981–1990	1991–2000	2001–2010
Europe	92.5	76.3	60.3	65.9	60.1	59.3	33.8	17.8	9.6	15.8	13.0
Asia	2.8	3.4	2.4	2.9	3.1	6.2	12.9	36.4	38.4	26.4	27.0
Canada	2.0	12.9	22.5	20.5	16.6	11.0	12.4	2.6	1.6	2.7	2.0
Latin America	2.1	7.0	14.4	9.7	17.7	22.5	39.2	40.4	47.2	51.7	54.0
Africa	0.1	0.1	0.2	0.3	0.7	0.7	0.8	2.0	2.6	3.4	4.0
Other	0.4	0.3	0.1	0.6	1.7	0.3	1.0	0.8	0.5	>0.1	>0.1

Sources: US Bureau of the Census, Census of Population 1960–2000 and 2010; Table adapted from Dworkin and Dworkin (1999).

the national origins of immigrants reported in the decennial censuses between 1900 and 2010. At the beginning of the 20th century the majority of immigrants came from Eastern and Southern Europe. Restrictive quotas imposed in 1924 altered the mixture. Quotas were modified in 1965 and in 1986, limited legal status (in terms of a 'green card', or work permit) was granted to many of the undocumented adults, most of whom came from Latin America. It remains a US policy to deport undocumented individuals, especially if they are accused of a crime. Some states have passed laws requiring the law enforcement officers to verify the legal status of individuals they suspect to be undocumented.

Today, approximately 81% of the immigrant population, and also the immigrant children in the schools, come from Latin America and Asia (Camarota, 2012). The majority of the parents rely on their children to translate information sent by schools from English into their home language. Many are in poverty when they arrive and are likely to have to send their children to low-income schools. Thus, the parents may not be able to provide their children with the requisite cultural and social capital to allow them to compete effectively in the schools. Further, children of immigrants represent about a quarter of all US children, four-fifths of which were born in the US and are therefore citizens, though many of them do not receive the benefits to which they are entitled because their unauthorized parents are reluctant to access services for fear of deportation (Urban Institute, 2006). Regardless of their citizenship status, all children of immigrants are of critical importance to the nation's future because they are the fastest-growing segment of the US population (Haskins and Tienda, 2011).

Immigrant families represent a particularly disadvantaged group because they not only tend to have larger families and practice a parenting style associated with poor and working-class parents, but they also experience significant language and cultural barriers that inhibit parent involvement in their children's schooling. Furthermore, recent immigrant families also possess significantly less social capital (Coleman, 1988) that can lead contingent upon the messages from the ethnic reference groups to a devaluation of schooling by the family and limited information about the workings of schools. One exception, however has been the reliance upon the Vietnamese immigrant ethnic social capital and social capital articulates well with values of cooperation, hard work, respect for authority that are preferred by school personnel (Bankston, 2004; Kao, 2004). Although some children of immigrants outperform their school peers (also known as the 'immigrant paradox', the children of Latin American immigrants, especially Mexican immigrants, often have lower academic performance levels and are more likely to drop out of high school (Crosnoe and Turley, 2011). Cohort drop-out rates among Hispanic immigrant students, especially those who remain classified as 'limited English proficient' (LEP) are often has high as 75% (Dworkin, 2008b). 'One of the nation's top domestic problems is the poor educational achievement of immigrant youth, both those brought by their immigrant parents to the United States and those born in the United States', declared a recent Princeton/Brookings policy brief (Haskins and Tienda, 2011). Reports from George Washington University's National Clearinghouse for English Language Acquisition and Language Instruction Educational Programs (NCELA) indicate that immigrant children whose home language is not English at ages 9, 13, and 17 score significantly lower on the language and mathematics sections of the NAEP (National Assessment of Educational Progress), than do non-immigrant English speakers. They also have significantly lower NAEP scores than do students who were former English-language learners (who are fully fluent in English). This suggests that immigrant children have a test-score deficiency that is likely partially to be made up once they become fluent English speakers. However, even those immigrant students who eventually become fluent in English perform less well than native speakers (Fry, 2007, 2008; Wilde, 2010).

Early research on immigrants (see especially Glazer and Moynihan, 1963 and Gordon, 1964) suggested that once the immigrant families and their children had assimilated into the core culture and adopted English as their home language, upward mobility and improved academic outcomes would quickly follow. However, later work by Ogbu (1978), as well as Lee (1998) on Vietnamese immigrants and Valenzuela (1999) on Latino immigrants suggested that assimilation was neither easy, nor a cure-all for upward mobility and academic success for immigrant children. Work on the immigrant paradox by Rumbaut (1997) challenged the benefits of assimilation, as the children and grandchildren of Hispanic immigrants became detached from a supportive culture and the ability to speak Spanish, and were less likely than their parents to work hard in school. The nature of the immigrant experience, issues of the home country, and finally, the level of social capital attained by the immigrant families (Kao, 2004; Bankston, 2004; and Noguera, 2004) all tended to serve as screens through which immigrant student outcomes would be filtered.

Work by Portes and Zhou (1993) introduced 'segmented assimilation theory', whereby the previously advanced Gordon (1964) model of 'straight-line', inter-generational assimilation and mobility could vary in three distinctive ways due to structural barriers that affect the children of immigrant groups, including restrictions on educational opportunities due to the quality of the local public schools and limitations imposed by the local labor market. In one outcome in the segmented model the children of immigrants may progress toward cultural and structural assimilation into the dominant (white, middle-class) society. In another outcome, the children of immigrants be experience downward mobility *viz* their parents and drift into delinquency and opposition to the core culture and dominant society. Finally, some outcomes for more advantaged children of immigrants might involve a degree of pluralism, or what Portes and Zhou called 'selective acculturation', whereby the traditions and culture of the home country are selectively retained, while the practices, language, and traditions of the host society are also selectively embraced (Brown and Bean, 2006). Some researchers have suggested that the more negative outcomes for the children of immigrants today may be a result of 'racialization', or the application of negative stereotypes and discriminatory practices to them because of they resemble phenotypically the society's racial minorities. Like the older assimilation theories discussed by Gordon (1964), segmented assimilation theory has been subjected to criticism because of difficulties in measurement and the absence of critical tests of its applicability in school experiences (Zhou, 1997; Brown and Bean, 2006; Kroneberg, 2008).

19.1.3   Social policy: The standards-based school accountability movement as the national context of educational research

Current US social policies that have dictated US education practices, and in turn, US educational research emerged from the Reagan administration's report *A Nation at Risk* (1983) written by the National Commission on Excellence in Education. The central premise of the report was that because school children in America were deficient in science, mathematics, and other academic skills, the country was at risk of falling behind other nations in producing a globally competitive labor force. Dworkin and Tobe (2012) chronicled the waves of school reforms that followed the 1983 commission report, including *America 2000* in the first Bush administration, *Goals 2000* in the Clinton administration, *No Child Left Behind* (*NCLB*) in the younger Bush administration, and *Race to the Top* in the current Obama administration. Successive waves of legislated reforms called for more rigorous accountability imposed upon schools and teachers, leading to competency testing of teachers in some states (following *A Nation at Risk*), decentralized decision-making and a call for world-class academic standards (following *America 2000*), the use of high-stakes standardized testing to assess student achievement (*Goals 2000*), and the use of the results of high-stakes testing to assess schools and teachers (*No Child Left Behind* and a *Race to the Top*). The later reforms (especially *No Child Left Behind*) incorporated progressively increasing standardized passing criteria for sub-groups of students (based on ethnicity, poverty status, home-language status) to judge school and teacher performances. Low performances resulted in the right of students to change schools and determined whether schools should be closed and re-opened as charters with new personnel. Extensive research evaluating the effect of the No Child Left Behind Law has appeared in sociological publications over the past decade, including summary articles in the journal *Sociology of Education* in 2005 (Karen, 2005; Dworkin, 2005; Ingersoll, 2005; Epstein 2005) and a volume supported by the American Institute for Research (Sadovnik et al., 2007).

The call for school reform was championed by conservatives, business leaders, and middle-class parents who objected to a perceived over-emphasis on cultural issues associated with student diversity and multiculturalism that followed court decisions regarding school desegregation prompted by the Civil Rights movement. Previously excluded groups were making claims that seemed to threaten the hegemony of groups with more power, prestige, and property. Berliner and Biddle (1995) labeled *A Nation at Risk* (1983) a product of a 'manufactured crisis' intended to result in the weakening of the public schools and the passage of legislation that would permit the middle class to redirect their public school tax dollars toward private school tuition. Berliner and Biddle's work stems from the conflict perspective in sociology. Pressure to create more charter schools and to provide private school vouchers has remained an emphasis of groups whose sense that their hegemony over educational opportunities is being threatened by previously underserved groups. The Standards-based School Accountability movement rests on an array of assumptions about public schools and human motivation. The core premise of the movement has been that the public schools are broken and that only through *external* intervention can they be fixed. Further, the imposition of free market forces and competition, which advocates of the reforms suggest have worked so well for American industry, will turn the schools into more efficient and effective systems for the delivery of educational services. Recently, Mehta (2013) has documented how the accountability paradigm emerged and ultimately changed the politics of American education, including new assumptions about schools and school actors.

School accountability systems assume that schools and school personnel cannot adequately evaluate how well they are preparing the nation's children for college and careers, instead, assessments must be based on externally-imposed standards and tests. Externally-imposed accountability systems, by their very nature, assume that some outside agent needs to hold accountable individuals whom if left to their own efforts would fail to teach adequately or would not make adequate academic progress. *NCLB* and *Race to the Top* contend that through threats, the prospect of school closures and the termination of school employees, the school districts will work harder and help students raise their achievement test scores by legitimate means. Consequently, schools and school personnel are often forced to focus on the *appearance* of desired learning outcomes and not necessarily the actual attainment of the substance of those learning outcomes. There have been numerous analyses of how state education agencies, school districts, schools, and school personnel 'game the system'. A few of these analyses include those by Booher-Jennings (2005), Booher-Jennings and Beveridge (2007), Weitz-White and Rosenbaum (2007), and Dworkin (2008a). Nichols and Berliner (2007) noted that states also 'game the system', particularly by altering data on drop-outs and graduates by counting only twelfth graders who graduated, thereby ignoring the students who had dropped out earlier. Additionally, work by Dworkin and his associates (1997, 2003, 2009, and 2012) has traced how each of the waves of school reform affected the morale of teachers and the likelihood that teachers will burn out. As more draconian policies were proposed by state legislature when schools failed to meet test-passing standards, both the level of teacher burnout and the extensiveness of the levels of teacher experience that were affected by burnout expanded. Burnout was no longer the malady of neophyte teachers, but a condition that afflicted most if not all of a teaching population.

Considerable attention has been paid to the issue of standardized testing mandated by *NCLB* and *Race to the Top*. Many political and business leaders content that high-stakes testing insures that students graduate with the requisite skills to enter and succeed in the labor market or in tertiary programs such as college or technical school. Those opposed to high-stakes testing, including many educational researchers, warn that such practices cause the curricula to be narrowed and 'dumbed-down' and results in schools focusing more on test-taking skills than on academic content (McNeil, 2000). Additionally, it has been claimed that high-stakes testing diminishes the value of a high school diploma by reducing learning to what is tested. Heubert and Hauser (1999) in their report published by the National Research Council observed that high-stakes tests are often unreliable, not necessarily valid indicators of student knowledge, and particularly unfair to children from low-income families, poor schools, and children of color. Numerous investigators, including Sheldon and Biddle (1998), Heubert and Hauser (1999), Kornhaber and Orfield (2001), and Dworkin (2005) have challenged the validity of the use of a single indicator (a test score) to make a policy decision on a student or a teacher. Kane and Staiger (2002) demonstrated that the tests are particularly unstable when multi-year testing is done on low-income children. The test is often unfair to children who do not do well on standardized multiple-choice tests. Several researchers assert that high-stakes testing is associated with increased rates of student drop-out behavior (Haney, 2000; Abrams and Haney, 2004, McNeil, 2005; Heubert and Hauser, 1999; McNeil et al., 2008). Others, including Madaus and Clarke (2001) and Toenjes and Dworkin. (2002), have questioned the direct linkage between high-stakes testing and the drop-out rate.

Following a discussion of the methods that have been used to survey the sociological and educational research literature in the US and to categorize the research traditions that have been prevalent over the past 30 years, the chapter will focus upon a central theme of much research in the United States: the magnitude and causes of the test-score gap among students from different racial, ethnic, and socio-economic statuses. A comprehension of the achievement test-score gaps is predicated on an understanding of the nature of educational inequality in American schools. After that discussion the chapter will proceed to an examination of plausible causes of the achievement test-score gaps and how those gaps affect and are affected by a range of other school-related variables, from school desegregation to teacher attitudes and behaviors, as well as teacher competencies. Concerns about test-score gaps among student groups has propelled considerable social and educational policy in the United States and affected the behaviors of myriad educational stakeholders. It will be explored from three research traditions: those that emphasize the student, the family, and the school, respectively. It must be understood, however, that each of the research traditions can most usefully be seen as components of a holistic assessment of the test-score gaps, rather than as mutually exclusive and competing interpretations.

19.2   Methodology

The volume of literature on racial and ethnic inequality in US education is too massive and the array of topics that characterize the research literature is too extensive to be accommodated by a single chapter, even if journal searches are restricted to the past 30 years. This is especially the case because it is in the past three decades that an enormous quantity of research had been stimulated by large-scale, national datasets funded in part by the US Department of Education, thereby facilitating data collection and making possible a plethora of competently-done studies. Furthermore, it has been in the past 30 years that the Standards-based School Accountability movement raised a plethora of questions about school performances of various groups and the competitiveness of the American educational system. Consequently, our survey is limited to key research traditions in the analysis of racial and ethnic educational inequality. However, we utilized Stevens (2007, pp. 147–148) as a model to guide the methods of our literature review.

The extensiveness of the database necessitated a set of rules for inclusion of publications. We limited our selection of publications to refereed journal articles and to books that have been widely cited in the sociology of education or educational research literature. Nearly all were published between 1980 and 2012. The only exception to the timeframe was the inclusion of monographs or articles that were prominent in the definition of the research themes that fit within the 1980–2012 period. Thus, in discussing the role of student achievement and the racial test-score gap, or issues of school desegregation as it affects achievement, pivotal works from the 1960s and 1970s that still define the current research parameters are included, in part to establish an historical context for the current research.

Issues of inequality in American education are manifold. In focusing on racial and ethnic inequality, as well as inequalities associated with social class, we concentrate on the persistent, and frequently expanding, test-score gap between minority and majority group students. There are three research traditions that have addressed the gap over the time period from which we draw our research literature: explanations for test-score gaps among racial and ethnic, and social class differences among students, differences among families, and differences among schools. These three research traditions have flourished in the past 30-plus years under the aegis of an expanding school accountability movement in US society. Often identified as the 'Standards-based School Accountability movement', the drive toward greater accountability has focused the US education agenda around standardized test scores which are usually high-stakes, with often draconian consequences for students, teachers, and schools. Located within the three research traditions are studies that explore the education and social capital among students and their families, including differences between native-born and immigrant families; differences between public and private schools; teacher competency and teacher expectations and labeling behaviors; academic tracking, student drop-out behavior, and remedial practices for low student performances, including retention in grade; and research focusing on the effects of school segregation and desegregation on student learning outcomes. Much of the research has paid attention to differences in academic achievement between students in the nation's inner cities, where poverty and racial/ethnic minorities are concentrated and students from the more affluent suburbs, often where more robust educational resources are concentrated.

19.3   Findings and the research traditions

19.3.1   Dimensions of racial and ethnic inequality in US schools

Poverty in the public schools is often measured by whether students are eligible for subsidized lunch funded by the US Department of Agriculture (students are categorized as being eligible for free lunch, eligible for reduced-price lunch, or not eligible for free/reduced price lunch). According to the National Center for Education Statistics, in 2009 the percentages of African American and Hispanic students in poverty in public elementary schools was 44% and 45%, respectively (2011, p. 87). The percentage of white students eligible for subsidized lunch in elementary school was 6%. Asian and Pacific Islanders and American Indians/Alaskan Natives had percentages of 17% and 31%, respectively. By high school, the percentages on free or reduced lunch drop precipitously. A total of 18% of African American and Hispanic public high school students were subsidized, while only 2%of whites, and 6%of Asian and Pacific Islanders were subsidized. Finally, 16%of American Indians and Alaskan Natives receive subsidized lunches in public high schools. The differential between elementary and high school poverty rates as measured by subsidized lunch status was not due to improved economic conditions for high school students. Rather, high school students are often reticent to be labeled as on free or reduced lunch because of peer pressure. They resist letting their parents register them for subsidized lunch and are unlikely to eat such lunches if they were offered to them. Parents are also less likely to register their older children and less concerned about whether the children have had lunch. Additionally, some of the decline in lunch participation reflects differentials in the drop-out rates among children in poverty. High school age students in poverty are more likely to have dropped out of school than those not in poverty, thereby changing the relative percentages of children on subsidized lunch status.

Despite proclamations of the declining significance of race in American society and American education (Wilson, 1980; Gamoran, 2001), racial divisions and gaps remain a salient marker of differentials in life chances. Added to race are issues of ethnicity, social class, and often gender in differentiating educational opportunity, attainment, and occupational outcomes. In fact, Gordon (1964, 1978) once held that the contours of American society are shaped by the pervasiveness of 'ethclass', the conjoined effects of the cross-classification of race/ethnicity and social class. Ethclass speaks to the extent to which life chances are not solely a function of race or ethnicity on the one hand or social class on the other. Rather, the intersection of the two aspects of stratification effect outcomes for individuals and well as groups.

Table 19.2 displays racial and ethnic differences in selected education participation and outcome measures. The table summarizes the outcomes for the five major groupings by race and ethnicity reports by the US Department of Education: 'African Americans', 'Hispanics', 'Non-Hispanic Whites', 'Asian and Pacific Islanders', and 'American Indians/Alaskan Natives'. Rounding errors explain why percentages do not always total 100%. The first column reports

Table 19.2 Racial and ethnic differentials in the United States

	School type			K-8 % Retained in grade	Status Drop-out rate	High school graduation rate	Post- secondary enrolled rate*	Post- secondary graduation rate
	% of Pop.	% Public	% Private	Poverty Rate					
African American	12.3	17	9	24.4	16	10	82	14	39
Hispanic	16.1	21	9	25.3	11	10**	81	12	50
White	64.6	55	73	9.4	8	5	91	63	62
Asian & Pacific Islanders	4.5	5	6	12.5	–	2	93	7	69
American Indian & Alaskan Native	0.8	1	<1	36.0***	–	15	75	1	39

* Excludes international students.
** 32% drop-out rate for foreign-born Hispanics.
*** Varies by age group.
Sources: US Department of Education, National Center for Education Statistics, *Condition of Education: 2004, 2008, 2010, 2012* (cited as Aud et al., 2010, 2011, 2012 and Planty et al., 2008); *Digest of Education Statistics: 2005, 2010* (cited as Snyder et al., 2006 and Snyder and Dillow, 2011).

the percentages of each group represented in both the public and private K–12 student population. Columns two and three are the relative percentages of the groups composing the public school and the private school populations. It is clear from these two columns that white students make up the vast majority of both public and private school population, but that they more completely dominate the private school population. With the exception of Asian and Pacific Islanders, minority students are more concentrated in the public schools than in the private schools.

Data for the fourth column is taken from the *Current Population Survey 2010*, and represents the percentage of children 18 years of age and younger who live in families either with a female head or a male head. Those children living with a female head have even higher poverty rates. Thus, nearly one-quarter of all African American children and one-quarter of all Hispanic children live in families defined as having incomes at or below the federal poverty line.

One-eighth of all Asian and Pacific Island children also live in families at or below the poverty line and fewer than 10% of white children are likewise in poverty. One-third of all Native American (American Indian) and Alaskan Native children live in families that are defined as in poverty, although the rate varies by the age of the child, with younger children associated with an even higher rate of poverty than older children.

'Retention in grade' is a measure of academic failure, especially in elementary and middle school. African American students have the highest grade-retention rate, followed by Hispanic students, while white students have a rate that is one-half that of African Americans.

Data were not available on Asian and Pacific Islanders and American Indians and Alaskan Natives. The literature on the effectiveness of retention in grade is mixed, although many researchers suggest that it has the consequence of harming self-esteem, while not producing achievement gains (Hauser, 2001; Shepard and Smith, 1989; Jimerson, 1999; Jimerson et al., 2002; Orfield, 2009). Other research suggests that early retention is more likely to improve subsequent achievement, while later retention heightens the likelihood that the student will drop out of school (Lorence, 2006; Lorence et al., 2002; Alexander et al., 1994, 2005).

19.3.2   US achievement gaps

The National Assessment of Educational Progress (NAEP) is the largest nationally representative and continuing assessment of what US students know and can do in various subject areas (NAEP website). It tests students only at ages 9, 13, and 17, and although it does not provide scores for individual students or schools, it is very good at assessing national trends, particularly long-term trends dating back to the 1970s (NAEP website). In general, the NAEP test-score gaps between white students and black and Hispanic students have decreased somewhat over time, but they remain quite large and significant. In particular, the Hispanic–white reading test-score gap among 9-year-olds has narrowed since 1975 but remains large and significant; among 13-year-olds, the reading gap has not changed much in over three decades; and among 17-year-olds, the reading gap has narrowed since 1975 but again remains large and significant (Rampey et al., 2009). The same pattern applies to the black–white test-score gap: the gaps have narrowed since 1975 but remain large and significant (Rampey et al., 2009). To illustrate, in reading, black and Hispanic 17-year-olds score about the same as white 13-year-olds. This is better than in 1975, when white 13-year-olds scored *better* than black and Hispanic 17-year-olds. The same patterns are found in math test scores, where once again, black and Hispanic 17-year-olds score about the same as white 13-year-olds, and this pattern hasn't changed since 1973. During some years Hispanic mean scores have been slightly higher than African American mean scores, but the differences are slight and the advantages reverse from year to year. For 17-year-olds, the slight advantages of Hispanic students over African American student could also reflect the relatively higher drop-out rate among Hispanic youth, in which more lower-performing Hispanic students leave school (Figures 19.2–19.9).

19.3.3   Major research traditions for explaining these gaps

Because of the comparatively vast quantity of research within sociology of education dedicated to understanding racial and ethnic inequalities in educational access and outcomes, it is not surprising that the research traditions incorporate several theoretical orientations and methodological approaches. Over the past 30 years researchers from conflict theory, consensus theory, rational choice

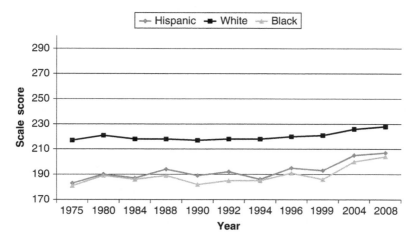

Figure 19.2   NAEP reading scores for 9-year-olds

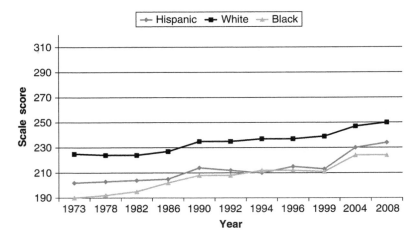

Figure 19.3   NAEP math scores for 9-year-olds

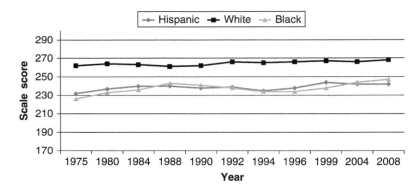

Figure 19.4   NAEP reading scores for 13-year-olds

and exchange theory, as well as social interactionist theory have attempted to explain educational access and equity and the effect of policies and practices on the achievement and attainment of minority and majority students. Some perspectives have viewed schooling as a tournament, with winners and losers varying in terms of their possession of different levels of human, cultural, and social capital; others see education from a Marxist and critical perspective in which schools function to reproduce the class structure. Some perspectives examine even larger structures shaped by neoliberalism and globalization in which assumptions about the competitiveness of nations are measured by the results of international tests, including PISA, TIMSS, or PIRLS. Considerable US research, especially that which focuses on test-score gaps, relies on data from

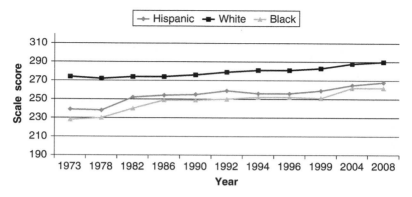

Figure 19.5 NAEP math scores for 13-year-olds

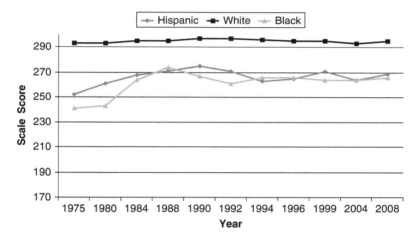

Figure 19.6 NAEP reading scores for 17-year-olds

the NAEP (National Assessment of Educational Progress), which tests mathematics, reading, science, writing, the arts, civics, economics, geography, US history, and in the future will test technology and engineering literacy. The NAEP is administered by the National Center for Education Statistics of the U. S. Department of Education.

Research on racial and ethnic inequality utilizes both quantitative and qualitative methodologies and incorporate consensus, conflict, rational choice and interactionist theories, as well as explanations that consider cultural and social capital, globalization and schools as global institutions, and critical approaches to attack neoliberalism. However, research directly addressing the magnitude of the test-score gap tends to rely on quantitative methods because the

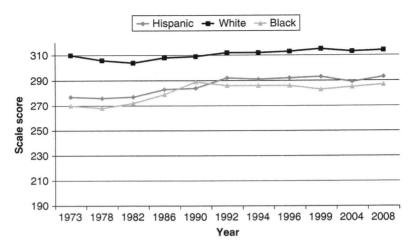

Figure 19.7   NAEP math scores for 17-year-olds

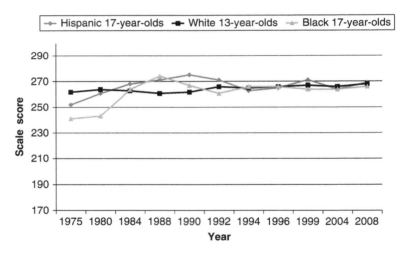

Figure 19.8   NAEP reading scores for 17 and 13-year-olds

assessment of the magnitude of the gaps are quantitative in nature and often call for regression (or hierarchical linear models) using covariates to explain variances in test scores. By contrast, many studies of the effects of home environments and school policies and practices that affect the test-score gap have relied on qualitative data. The impetus for much of the quantitative research based on large national samples comes from the report entitled *The Equality of Educational Opportunity* (Coleman et al, 1966), which was mandated by the Civil Rights (1964) Act. In the years following the 'Coleman Report', sociologists

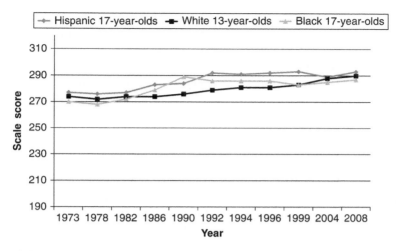

Figure 19.9 NAEP math scores for 17 and 13-year-olds

and educational researchers worked with extensive, large-scale longitudinal surveys, many supported by the US Department of Education. The Institute for Education Sciences of the National Center for Education Statistics (US Department of Education) lists no fewer than 22 national datasets accessible for research (see http://nces.ed.gov/surveys?SurveyGroups.asp?group=1). Most of these attitudinal surveys and statistical databases have led to significant publications by educational and sociological researchers in the USA. A small sampling of the surveys would include 'High School and Beyond', the 'National Educational Longitudinal Survey', the 'Educational Longitudinal Study', the 'Crime and Safety Survey', the 'National Longitudinal Survey of the High School Class of 1972', and the 'Early Childhood Longitudinal Study'. Longitudinal statistical data on schools and school districts would include the 'Common Core of Data', the 'High School Transcript Studies', the 'Schools and Staffing Surveys', and the 'School Survey on Crime and Safety'.

In the US, the study of racial and ethnic inequalities in education has undergone several key shifts resulting in research traditions that emphasize different explanations for the persistent gaps in achievement and attainment. These research traditions started with an emphasis on the role of students, then families, followed by schools. To be clear, these research traditions are not mutually exclusive, as many researchers within each tradition include measures important to the other traditions, and they overlap in terms of the time periods in which they gained prominence. However, each research tradition clearly lifts up one sphere (student, family, school) over the others, and each tradition has informed education reform efforts, some of which have resulted in reductions in racial and ethnic inequalities, but significant gaps remain. There is considerable complexity associated with the three categories of explanations for differentials in student achievements. Thus, while the rubrics 'student', 'family', and 'school' depict the foci of the explanations, singly they do not speak to the complexity of the issue or to the numerous variations of explanations that are subsumed under each category. The three traditions, while they are interlinked describe each of these research traditions approximately in the order in which they gained prominence, although all three research traditions continue to shape education research in the US.

19.3.3.1   Emphasis on students

In the 1940s and 1950s, educational attainment research documented the gaps between black and white students and predominantly emphasized student-level factors such as various measures of intelligence and cognitive ability, personality characteristics, and aspirations (e.g., Witty and Theman, 1943). External factors were certainly considered, but student-level characteristics dominated because of the advent of psychometric testing, which took off in the 1930s, attempting to measure individual traits such as knowledge, abilities, attitudes, personality, and intelligence (Michell, 1999). Prior to the publication of the Coleman Report black–white comparisons in cognitive performance were based on convenient samples that were fraught with considerable methodological errors (Hedges and Nowell, 1998).

Two decades after the work of Coleman and his colleagues, Jencks and Phillips edited a collection of analyses racial differences in test-score performance under the title *The Black–White Test Score Gap* (1998). Chapters in the volume relied on an array of nationally representative probability samples of public school and private school students, including re-analyses of the data from Coleman's *Equality of Educational Opportunity*, the National Longitudinal Study of the High School Class of 1972, High School and Beyond surveys of 1980 and 1982, National Longitudinal Survey of Youth, 1980, the National Education Longitudinal Study of 1992, as well as the National Assessment of Academic Progress (NAEP, also known as 'the nation's report card'). Jencks and Phillips and their contributors examined biases in testing, test labeling (or construct invalidity of a test), and test content (class-based knowledge); heredity versus environment issues; family background and home advantages; and peer group effects, including peer pressures found in high-poverty, minority schools against students doing well academically (the finding by Fordham and Ogbu [1986] that in inner-city schools black youth may be told that doing well is 'acting white'). Jencks and Phillips' contributors examined the effects of negative labels and lowered expectation by teachers on the academic achievement of black students. Much of the work that focuses on labeling by teachers or 'definitions of the situation' by the students clearly draw theoretical insights from a blending of conflict and interactionist theories in sociology.

An emphasis on individual traits continues to have central importance in the fields of psychology and social psychology. Perhaps the most promising student-level interventions to show significant gains in reducing the racial achievement gap are those that address stereotype threat, which occurs when students underperform due to fear of confirming negative stereotypes, such as the stereotype that blacks are less intelligent than whites (Steele and Aaronson, 1995). Recent randomized field experiments show that a social-psychological intervention – an in-class writing assignment designed to reaffirm students' sense of personal adequacy – significantly improved the grades of African Americans and reduced the achievement gap by 40% (Cohen et al., 2006).

Grissmer, Flanagan, and Williamson (1998) observed that the greatest narrowing of the black–white test-score gap occurred in the 1970s, when government invested in minority schools and the US Supreme Court supported desegregation plans that would reduce African American racial isolation (and hence exposure to disadvantaged schools). As government backed away from these supports, especially in the 1980s and 1990s, as schools in the inner city deteriorated, and support systems for poor children declined (Wilson, 1987, 1996) gains made earlier diminished or partially reversed. However, to challenge the contention that race rather than socio-economic status accounts for the test-score gap, Jencks and Phillips note the following findings:

(a) When black or mixed-race children are raised in white rather than black homes, their preadolescent test scores rise dramatically;
(b) Even non-verbal scores are sensitive to environmental change (generally described as the 'Flynn effect' [1984];
(c) Black–white differences in academic achievement have narrowed throughout the twentieth century. (Jencks and Phillips, 1998: p. 3)

19.3.3.2   Emphasis on families

In the 1960s, a shift of emphasis occurred in which the characteristics of families and significant others were highlighted. This shift was fueled by a famous Coleman Report. which largely attributed unequal educational outcomes to family background and socio-economic status and reported that these factors were more important than differences in school resources The emphasis on families and significant others was developed further by sociologists at the University of Wisconsin using a sample of Wisconsin farm-raised males and accordingly became known as the Wisconsin model of status attainment (Sewell, Haller, and Portes, 1969). The model stems from consensus theory in general and structural functionalism in particular, as it conceptualizes the mechanisms of occupational stratification as functional for society in that through self-selection the best and the brightest are recruited to do the most important work (judged by their higher occupational status). This educational and occupational attainment model included student-level characteristics such as aspirations, mental ability, and academic performance, but it emphasized a strong influence of significant others, measured as parental encouragement for going to college, teachers' encouragement for going to college, and having close friends who planned to go to college (Sewell et al., 1969). Jencks et al. (1983) raise issues of measurement error in the Sewell et al. data and offer a revised model that has more explanatory power, as it used achievement test scores rather than aptitude test results as a measure of ability, examines more closely educational plans beyond high school, and relies less on expected future earning than did the original study. Kerckhoff (1976) maintained that the Wisconsin status attainment model could better be described as a status allocation model, in which school effects assigned students to long-term outcomes, thereby reproducing the stratification system.

The role of families continues to have prominence in the study of educational outcomes, especially in sociology, where the study of families can be divided into two main categories: family structure and parenting style. Aspects of family structure, such as the presence of two parents or step-parents, the number of siblings, and birth order are all associated with educational outcomes (Downey, 1995; Wojtkiewicz and Holtzman, 2011). For example, as the number of siblings increases, parents of eighth graders tend to talk less frequently with their children about school-related matters, they have lower educational expectations, they know fewer of their children's friends by name, they know fewer of their children's friends' parents by name, they are less likely to have educational objects in the home, and are not able to save as much money for college as parents with fewer children (Downey, 1995). These trends are relevant for racial and ethnic disparities in education, not only because all of these factors are important for determining educational outcomes, but also because they are linked to family size, and racial and ethnic minorities tend to have larger families than whites. Roscigno (1999), using National Educational Longitudinal Survey and US Census data for 1990, reported that family background, especially race, and the level of poverty in a neighborhood interact such that in equally impoverished neighborhoods, African American students experience more educational disadvantage than do white students.

One measure of the effect of families is the size of achievement gaps prior to the start of schooling, and studies show that even before schooling begins, socio-economic achievement gaps are significant. Downey et al. (2004) reported that on the first day of Kindergarten, Asian American children are about 0.42 months ahead of white children, while black children are about 0.52 months behind white children, and Hispanic and Native American children are about 1.21 months behind white children.

Parenting styles also matter for educational outcomes because schools have standardized views of the proper role of parents' participation in schooling, placing a higher value on middle-class parenting styles (Lareau, 1987). Stemming from interactionist theories in sociology, Lareau's (2002) research suggests that there are two main styles of parenting, which she refers to as concerted cultivation and accomplishment of natural growth. Concerted cultivation refers to parents who actively cultivate their children's development through a series of adult-organized activities carefully selected to enrich their educational experiences, whereas natural growth refers to parents who allow their children to have more control over their leisure time, enabling their children to spend more time in unstructured activities alone or with friends and relatives (Lareau, 2002). Lareau reported a very clear pattern wherein middle-class parents were much more likely to practice concerted cultivation, while poor and working-class parents were much more likely to practice natural growth. Although she reported that race had much less of an impact on parenting than social class, the fact is that racial and ethnic minorities are much more likely to be members of lower social classes, making them more likely to practice natural growth parenting, and whites are much more likely to be members of higher social classes, making them more likely to practice concerted cultivation parenting.

19.3.3.3 Emphasis on schools

19.3.3.3.1 School desegregation and its effects on learning. The role of schools in explaining racial and ethnic inequalities was prominent during era of the Civil Rights movement, which led to the passage of the Civil Rights Act of 1964, legislation that outlawed major forms of discrimination, including racial segregation in schools (Pub. L. 88–352). After legal segregation ended, continued racial disparities were largely attributed to family background, as described above. However, the role of schools again rose to prominence in the 1980s when President Ronald Reagan's National Commission on Excellence in Education released a report entitled *A Nation at Risk: The Imperative for Educational Reform*, which called into question previously-held attitudes regarding American dominance in math, science, and technology (Goldberg and Harvey, 1983). All of the commission's recommendations for addressing student failure focused on the role of schools, including the content of the curriculum, school passage and graduation standards, the length of the school day and school year, teacher salaries and evaluations, and meeting the needs of students who have special needs, are minorities, or socio-economically disadvantaged.

Schools continue to be scrutinized regarding their role in explaining racial and ethnic disparities. Using eight national datasets, Phillips et al. (1998) found that although black first graders were about half a standard deviation below white first graders in math, reading, and vocabulary test scores, by the end of high school, black students were a full standard deviation behind white students, suggesting that schools may exacerbate racial inequality. However,

Phillips et al. (1998) recognized that children spend a significant amount of time outside of school in environments that may vary even more than schools, making it unclear whether the school context matters more than the non-school context.

Although schools seem to exacerbate racial disparities, they also seem to improve economic disparities. For example, Heyns (1978, 1987) found that the test-score gap between advantaged and disadvantaged students grew during the summer months, when children are not in school and non-school influences dominate. Similarly, Entwisle and Alexander (1992) found that socio-economic gaps in reading grew at a faster rate during the summer than during the academic year. Furthermore, a meta-analysis of 39 studies reported that middle-class students experienced summer gains while lower-class students experienced summer loss (Cooper et al., 1996), and later analyses by Alexander et al. (2007) concluded that schools actually play an important compensatory role which can only be observed by comparing student gains both at the beginning and at the end of the school year. Similarly, Downey et al. (2004) found that nearly every gap they studied grew faster during the summer months than during the academic school year. However, Downey et al. reported that the black–white gap was a conspicuous exception, suggesting that although schools can serve as equalizers of some aspects of social inequality, it is likely that racial and ethnic inequality persists even in the school setting.

Focusing on the schools also means focusing on the teachers with a concern about how much value teachers and teacher-quality adds to educational outcomes of the nation's children. The question can be distilled as follows. Is it better for a student to be assigned to a high-performing teacher in a generally low-performing school, or to be assigned to a lower-performing teacher in a high-performing school? If teacher effects are more important than school effects then the assignment to high-performing teachers regardless of school context is preferable. If school effects predominate then it is more important to assign children to high-performing campuses, regardless of the level of competence of the teacher. A second question is one of relative equity. If there are a finite number of excellent teachers – those who routinely raise student achievement above some set level – then should those teachers be assigned to the high-achieving students or the low-achieving students? If teacher effects are significant, then a theory of justice is operative in such assignments. Assigning high-achieving students to the best teachers may make the work setting more pleasant for the teachers and can raise the ceiling on the level of performance of the students. Assigning low-achieving students to the best teachers may ensure that a floor is placed below those students below which they may not likely descend.

Tobe (2009) examined teacher value-added effects on student learning in mathematics in a large urban school district in Texas. She was able to link individual student standardized test results across time with prior year class-room test performances of their teachers. She separated teachers into those whose prior year's classes scored in the top quartile, middle two quartiles, and bottom quartiles on the state-mandated achievement test. She likewise sorted students into three groups based their prior year's test performances: those who previously had performed in the top quartile on the state test, those in the middle two quartiles, and those in the bottom quartile. She then asked whether high, medium, or low-performing students did better the next year on the state test if they were assigned to a teacher whose prior classes were high, medium, or low performers. That is, she asked whether the students changed their state-wide percentile rank (across some 400,000 students per grade level) depending on the type of teachers they were assigned to the subsequent year. The findings were consistent across teachers and students. Previously high, medium, and low-performing students gained between 0.5 and 0.8 of a standard deviation in the subsequent year if they were taught by a high-performing teacher. Previously, high, medium, and low-performing students lost between 0.5 and 0.7 of a standard deviation if they were assigned to a low-performing teacher. The same outcomes were found for average-performing students who were assigned to high or low-performing teachers. Finally, average-performing teachers neither increased nor decreased their children's achievements.

At least since the Coleman Report estimates of school effects on student learning outcomes have been a substantial focus of educational research. In their 1966 report, Coleman and his colleagues found that schools contributed much less of the variance in student achievement than did other factors, especially home effects. Critiques of the report led to revised methods that could better tease out the effects of schools (see Mosteller and Moynihan, 1972; Hanushek and Kain, 1972; Jencks, 1972, and most recently Borman and Dowling, 2010).

Public confidence in the public schools has fluctuated between the 1960s and the present, with low estimations of how well schools were doing occurring in the 1980s following the release of *A Nation at Risk* (1983), and then rising slightly over the next 30 years. However, the high level of confidence in the public schools that existed in the 1950s and 1960s has never returned. Beginning with the Standards-based School Accountability movement that emerged in the 1980s, increasing attention has been place on how well teachers prepare students to achieve. The school reforms of the 1990s and beyond have considered teacher effects and more recently a focus on 'teacher value-added' effects. Hanushek and Rivkin (2010) noted that studies of teacher value-added effects have made two observations: that teacher value-added estimates of teacher effects on student performance and future performance vary considerably across studies and that the commonly used and legislatively mandated measures of teacher competence, including experience, post-graduate training and advanced degrees, and scores on certification exams, provide little predictive power in accounting for teacher effectiveness. This may be especially true in high poverty and minority schools (where concerns about teacher effects are most often focused) because student achievement is often quite variable from year to year for the same students (Kane and Staiger, 2002) and because the ability of teacher to pass competency tests or to have earned advanced degrees may not measure how well she/he relates to and communicates with students.

19.3.3.3.2 Teacher Competency.   This is an important point because school accountability mandates, include *No Child Left Behind* (2001) and *Race to the Top* (2009) specify that schools are expected to have highly qualified teachers, which is defined as being certified in the area in which they teach and/or having had an academic major in college in that area. Marrett (1990) noted that in high-poverty and minority schools the likelihood of teachers being certified in the teaching area, especially in science and mathematics, was less than in middle-class and majority schools. Data reported by the US Department of Education indicated that in predominantly minority high schools 1015% of the teachers in the subject areas of math, science, and language arts had neither a certification nor an academic major in the subject matter they taught; this compares with only 4–5%of the teachers in predominantly majority high schools (US Department of Education, National Center for Education Statistics, 2004, pp. 152–154). Ingersoll (1999, 2005) has shown that teacher shortages were not the cause of the differences in deployment, but rather that allocation schemes tend to place better-trained teachers in majority schools because majority and middle-class parents would object more strenuously if the allocations were otherwise. Nevertheless, the uniform presence of highly qualified teachers as defined by NCLB was seen as too difficult to attain quickly. Thus, the US Congress modified the definition of highly qualified under a provision known as HOUSSE, or High, Objective, Uniform State Standard of Evaluation as an alternative method for judging the competence of teachers. Under the HOUSSE provision, a teacher was considered to be highly qualified if she/he had previously taught the subject. Nevertheless, Kane et al. (2008) has warned that merely because a teacher is certified in the subject field in which she/he teaches or has had an academic major in that field does not mean that she/he is effective in producing improved student achievement. Thus, mandates for certification in the subject field in which one teaches or possession of an academic major in college in that field does not guarantee competency in teaching.

Despite HOUSSE provisions, there remain schools that are difficult to staff, often associated with higher levels of crime, low levels of student achievement, and high drop-out rates – schools that Balfantz and Legters (2004) have characterized as 'drop-out factories'. Relying on data from the National Educational Longitudinal Study of 1988 (NELS 88/00) and the Common Core of Data (CCD), both from the National Center for Education Statistics of the US Department of Education, Reininger (2013) demonstrated that new teachers often prefer to teach in the neighborhoods in which they grew up. Hard-to-staff schools with high student drop-out rates may have access to a more diminished pool of potential new teachers from which to draw, as individuals who drop out are not likely to become school teachers, thereby further making the replacement of teachers who quit more difficult.

19.3.3.3.3 Public versus private schooling.   Private schools may be church affiliated, as in the case of parochial schools (Catholic) or other religious groups (Christian, Jewish, Muslim, Hindu, Buddhist, and many others) or secular and not affiliated with any religion. Coleman, Hoffer, and Kilgore (1982) and Coleman and Hoffer (1987) explored the extent to which basis for parochial and some non-Catholic private school produced student learning outcome advantages over public schools. Coleman and Hoffer held that the Catholic school advantage was due to the assignment of more and more difficult homework, the ability to expel disruptive students, and what they called 'functional communities', or the extent to which the parents, students, and teachers were in agreement about school expectations, norms, and commitment to achievement. Bryk et al. (1993) cited what they termed the 'communal school organization' (shared values and activities among the various school participants, as well as greater faculty collegiality) in order to demonstrate the Catholic school advantage over public schools. More recent research by Duncan and Sandy (2007) analyzing the National Longitudinal Survey of Youth, reported that private schools hold a 12-point difference in academic achievement over public schools, but that all but a non-significant amount of the difference can be accounted for by demographic differences between the students attending the two categories of schools. Summarizing recent research, including longitudinal surveys, Bracey (2008) reports that student demography and parental involvement play a much greater role in student achievement differences than do school effects. Further, the longitudinal analysis conducted by Wenglinsky for the Center on Education Policy (2007) indicates that by the time the students were young adults having attended a private school or a public school did not account for outcomes such as civic-mindedness, nor job satisfaction among respondents. It is interesting that much of the current research on the public–private debate has shifted in a direction opposite to that generally found in educational research in the US. The shift has been from a focus on schools and differences in school performances to a focus on how demographic and family factors differentiate student learning outcomes.

How do we adjudicate between the propositions that schools may exacerbate racial disparities while simultaneously slowing the growth of economic gaps? This is precisely the question addressed by Condron (2009), who argues that while the school context is more important for explaining racial gaps, the non-school context is more important for explaining the economic gaps. Condron (2009) attributes the racial gaps to school segregation, in which minority (especially African American) students attend overwhelmingly one-race schools, often with more limited school resources, a smaller percentage of teachers certified in the areas they teach (Marrett, 1990), and frequently where students chide classmates who do well academically or where student believe that education does not lead to upward mobility for them (Ogbu, 1978 and Mickelson, 1990). Condron notes that there is an extensive literature on the effect of school segregation of black and white learning outcomes, citing significant works by Bankston et al. (1997); Berends et al. (2008); Borman et al. (2004, 2005); Mickelson (2001, 2003); Roscigno (1998) and Myerson et al. (1998). The majority of low-income people in the US are white, often from rural areas. The result is that the effects of poverty *per se*, on achievement incorporates white experiences as well as those of many minorities. Home disadvantages may account for lower achievement among the poor (Lareau, 1987, 2002), especially among white students.

Reardon and Bischoff (2011) have examined patterns of residential segregation by social class and reveal that between 1970 and 2000 neighborhood segregation by income has increased dramatically. There are now fewer mixed-income neighborhoods, and hence mixed-income schools, regardless of race than a generation ago. African American neighborhoods have become even more segregated by income than white neighborhoods. The result is that children from poor families are unlikely to attend school with more advantaged classmates, whose parents have the economic and social capital to make sure that schools provide valued educational resources. This finding further accounts for test-score differentials that have been reported, especially among minority students from low-income families. Recently, Lewis et al. (2010) authored a report to The Council of the Great City Schools, emphasizing that among children living in poverty, African American males in urban areas face the greatest crises with respect to education and a vast array of life chances.

In another study Reardon (2011, 2013) analyzed 12 national datasets on student achievement and reported that over the past 50 years (since 1960), the test-score gaps between students in the 90th percentile on family income and those in the 10th percentile grew substantially, even while test-score gaps between African American and white students narrowed. Significant gaps in achievement grew in comparisons of children from upper-income family with children from middle-income families, as well as between children from middle-income families and children in lower-income families. The implication is that increasingly social class will be the central factor differentiating student advantage and disadvantage and that income inequality will result in significant gaps within racial and ethnic groups.

Research on the role of schools in determining racial and ethnic gaps high-lights three main explanations: school segregation, academic tracking within schools, and the potential bias of teachers. A particularly important aspect of schools for which there is much evidence is the school's racial and ethnic com-position and level of segregation. Although school racial segregation was ruled unconstitutional in *Brown* v. *Board of Education of Topeka* (1954), efforts to deseg-regate schools were met with great resistance, including violent confrontations when white students, administrators, and political leaders attempted to physi-cally prevent the first African American students from entering all-white schools. With significant intervention by the federal government, racial integration in schools increased from the 1960s until the 1980s, but it reverted to a pattern of increasing segregation during the late 1980s through the present (Orfield, 2002). By 2006–2007, the percentage of students attending predominantly minority schools (with a minority population of 90–100%) was 40% for Latinos, 39% for blacks, 20% for American Indians, 16% for Asian Americans, and only 1% for whites; in contrast, the percentage of students attending predominantly white schools (with a white population of 90–100%) was 77% for whites, 44% for Asian Americans, 29% for blacks, and 27% for Latinos (Orfield, 2009).

Among Latinos, the children of Mexican immigrants tend to hyper-segregate, clustering in schools with especially high percentages of minority students (Crosnoe and Turley, 2011). Furthermore, the children of Mexican immigrants are over-represented in 'problem schools' plagued by a lack of academic focus, an unsafe climate, larger school size, resource deprivation, and lack of organization, even after controlling for socio-economic status (Crosnoe, 2005). All of these patterns suggest that, despite earlier legal efforts to eradicate school segregation, white and minority students continue to attend separate and highly unequal schools.

The *Brown* v. *Board of Education of Topeka* (1954 and the 1955 implementa-tion order) decisions overturned the long-standing Supreme Court decision, *Plessy* v. *Ferguson* (1896), which held that accommodations, including school-ing, could be separate for racial groups provided that they were approximately equal. However, equality was defined in terms of nominal categories. Thus, for example, regardless of the quality of facilities, if African American schools had a library of ten books and white schools had a library of thousands of books, they would be considered equal, as both groups had libraries. The plaintiffs for the African American students successfully held in the *Brown* decision that sep-arate could never be equal and that segregation of the schools violated the 'Due Process' clause of the XIV Amendment to the US Constitution. The US Justice Department and the federal courts enforced desegregation of white and African American schools (and later Latino schools in 1974). Because of residential segregation, black, white, and Latino students lived in different neighborhoods that were designated to attend different schools. Busing became an appropriate and legal solution (supported by Supreme Court decisions from 1968 onwards), whereby students in minority-group schools were sent to majority-group schools and vice versa. In reality, most busing within school districts involved only sending minority students to schools that had been all white, as orders to send white students to minority schools resulted in white parents moving to all-white suburbs or placing their children in private schools. A second wave of desegregation strategies after 1974 involved metropolitan desegregation plans. Such plans consolidated school districts by merging urban, predominantly minority districts with predominantly majority districts in the suburbs. The intent of all such plans was to produce a greater level of the equality of educational opportunity, especially for minority students.

Differentials in the birth-rate of minority and majority group children meant that the nation could no longer depend upon well-educated majority group students to populate the highly skilled labor force of the country. Thus, the school reform and accountability from the 1980s and beyond raised concerns about test-score gaps among racial and ethnic groups of students. A significant aspect of US educational research has thus focused first on the extent to which desegregation has occurred, the extent to which there remain differentials in student learning outcomes by race and ethnicity, and the extent to which desegregation efforts (as well as resistance to such efforts) have affected differentials in student learning by racial and ethnic groups. A continuing concern has been whether the test-score gaps among racial and ethnic groups has changed and whether desegregated schools could account for a narrowing of the gap.

19.3.3.3.4 Academic Tracking.   In addition to school-level segregation, rigid tracking systems are used to segregate students within schools, and although they are designed to facilitate teaching students at various skill levels, researchers have noted the systematic influence of non-meritocratic factors such as socio-economic status, gender, race, and ethnicity (Oakes, 1985). More recently, Mulkey et al. (2009) summarized the literature on tracking and detracking (removing student from tracks) on student achievement. Cohen and Lotan (1997) observed that instruction approaches that avoid tracking can be successful and Gamoran (1992) concluded that tracking is a complex and complicated process which requires an understanding of micro-processes in the classroom and a level of flexibility to enable track mobility. Inflexible track assignments produce diminished learning and numerous other negative impacts on students. Among the findings supported by work since 1980, Mulkey et al. (2009, p. 1088) summarized five sets of outcomes associated with tracking: (1) higher tracks enjoy a faster pace of instruction; (2) students in the higher tracks often have more effective teachers; (3) students in lower tracks are often in classrooms where there are more student-initiated disruptions that interfere with instruction; (4) teachers in low-achieving groups are less likely to provide encourage their students to achieve more; and (5) placement in high tracks often heightens student self-esteem and more favorable teacher estimates of the students, both of which lead to greater future academic achievement. Lucas (1999) and Lucas and Gamoran (2002) have observed that racial and ethnic differentials in the assignment of students to college or non-college tracks. As Lucas and Gamoran noted, 'race matters for tracking, and tracking matters for racial differences in measured achievement' (2002, p. 188).

19.3.3.3.5 The effect of teacher biases and labeling. Not only can teacher certification and teacher quality affect student achievement, but teacher perceptions about the abilities of different groups of students has also been linked to the academic performance of such students. Studies of teacher labeling and teacher expectations, informed by interactionist theories in sociology, have queried the extent to which such expectations create self-fulfilling prophecies. Generally, the initial studies relied upon small samples. The research tradition began with the work of Rosenthal and Jacobson (1968), as well as studies by Dusek (1975, 1985), Braun (1976), Cooper (1979), Rist (1970), Bowles and Gintis (1976, 2002), and Clifton et al. (1986). Rist's (1970) study best describes the research tradition. He held that teachers have tastes for particular kinds of students and tend to evaluate more positively students who most resemble their preferred kind of student. Since most teachers come from middle-class origins or from families in which the head of household held professional, managerial, and technical occupations (Dworkin, 1980), there is a bias toward students who are well-behaved, neat, and quiet. Middle-class and majority-group students more closely resemble the teacher's preference. Such students also command a broader vocabulary, as noted by Bernstein (1971). Teachers will pay more positive and rewarding attention to such students than to those who do not fit the teacher's preferences. Students who receive less rewarding attention may withdraw from school, learn less and perform less well on tests. Like the original Rosenthal and Jacobson (1968) study, teachers in Rist's (1970) study were informed that some of their students were gifted, while other teachers were provided with no such prior labeling of students. Teachers who assumed that their children were gifted made more eye contact with the students, asked the students fewer rhetorical questions, allowed the students more time to answer questions, and generally praised the students more than teachers who were not provided information that their children were gifted. Despite the fact that the students were randomly assigned to the gifted label, those who were so designated performed better during the school year and had higher standardized test scores. Luce and Hoge (1978), on the other hand, found that when there were independent assessments of actual student abilities were made, the true relationship between initial labels and student learning outcomes was spurious, in part because teachers were able, over the academic year, to determine whether the labels provided at the beginning of the year were credible.

Further, there is a clear association between the tracking of students and the labels that teachers attach to those students. The relationship is often reciprocal. Teacher labels and expectations about students often influence the track into which students are placed and once placed in a track, teachers rely on the track label to govern expectations about the students' future performances. The teacher labels further affect the performances of the students, thereby producing a self-fulfilling prophecy. Using a national dataset (NELS, 1992), Kelly and Carbonaro (2012) found marked differentials in college-going expectations among teachers of high school students with discrepant track placements (in different tracks for different classes). When the students were in their high track classes their teachers held significantly higher college-going expectations for them than when the same students were in their lower track classes.

19.3.3.3.6 Teacher morale and student learning in an era of accountability.   The study of teacher burnout and turnover has received considerable attention since the concept was first coined in the 1970s (Freudenberger, 1974; Maslach and Jackson, 1981; Maslach, 1978, 1993). In the years following the expansion of the Standards-based School Accountability movement, some research has examined how school accountability, school reform, and teacher competency testing has affected teacher morale, burnout, and intentions to quit teaching (Tedesco, 1997; Leithwood, et al., 1996; Day et al., 2005; Friedman, 2003; Dworkin, 1987, 1997, 2001, 2009; Dworkin, Saha, and Hill, 2003; Dworkin and Tobe, 2012).

A defining characteristic of resilient, committed teachers is their willingness to make extra efforts on behalf of their students especially those students are struggling academically. Burnout saps enthusiasm and energy leading teachers to hold negative attitudes toward their students (Dworkin, 1987, Dworkin, Saha, and Hill, 2003; Tobe, 2009). Some research on teacher morale has focused on the extent to which disruptive students increase job stress among teachers and, in turn, their level of burnout. Friedman (1991, 1995) reported that typical student behavior patterns (disrespect, inattentiveness, and sociability) contributed to predicting teacher burnout. Studies by Brouwers and Tomic (2000), Burke, Greenglass and Schwarzer (1996) reveal that student disruptions divert teacher attention away from instruction and thereby diminish the teachers' sense of accomplishment (a component of burnout). Further, disruptions can lead to confrontations that are stressful. Student disruptions tend to more adversely affect novice and/or poorly-trained teachers (Friedman, 1995), whose own hold on classroom management and professional self-confidence may be weak. The significance of teacher burnout for the test score gap is that (1) teacher burnout is highest in schools with low student achievement, especially in an era of high-stakes accountability systems, and (2) teacher burnout results in diminished teacher energy and enthusiasm, which often results in diminished willingness to assist struggling students, thereby exacerbated low student achievement. That inner-city, high-poverty schools with low student achievement experience higher burnout rates than low-poverty schools, especially since the implementation of school accountability systems that evaluate teachers on the learning gains of their students (Dworkin, 2009; Dworkin and Tobe, 2012), minority–majority test-score gaps within school districts can be seen as indicators of teacher burnout and its consequences.

It must be understood that while each of the three research traditions offers plausible explanations for the differentials in student achievement among the racial and ethnic groups, a comprehensive explanation must draw from all three (student effects, family effects, and school effects). Furthermore, conjoined family and school effects incorporate variables that may be correctly located in neighborhoods and communities. School effects incorporate not only school educational resources, campus demographic variables, including campus and class sizes, and school policies, but also social psychological factors that affect teacher morale, burnout, and willingness to make extra efforts for students who bring to school few home resources. Current research recognizes the interplay among the three research traditions. There is often a bundling of student, family, and school effects such that certain kinds of students from certain kinds of families and neighborhoods find themselves in certain kinds of schools, with given educational policies and practices, resources, and teacher competencies, certifications, and attitudes about the abilities of their students. Nevertheless, much current research is drawn from the school effects tradition, as policy concerns examine how schools can exacerbate and perpetuate inequalities, and in turn, test-score gaps among student groups. A focus on school effects also provides an economy of scale in the implementation of social policies aimed as ameliorating low test scores.

19.4 Discussion and conclusion

A chain of historical factors in the United States have been influential in defining much of the research in sociology and education that addresses racial and ethnic inequalities. The Civil Rights movement, especially during the 1950s and 1960s challenged by means of social action the prevalent racial segregation, especially in the American South. Nearly concurrent with the movement were an array of US Supreme Court decisions that struck down racial segregation in the public schools and established mandates and procedures to implement such desegregation. The Civil Rights Act of 1964 and additional federal legislation strengthened the process to secure equality of educational opportunity. One essential argument in the original *Brown* v. *Board of Education* decision of 1954 was that segregated schooling resulted in an inferior education for African American children. The 1964 Civil Rights Act called for a national study to assess the extent to which there had been compliance with the *Brown* decision and to determine the extent to which desegregation had promoted greater educational equality. The Coleman Report followed in 1966 and constituted the largest study of attitudes, outcomes, and educational achievement that had been conducted up to that time. The report, *Equality of Educational Opportunity* (1966), established a precedent for large-scale, quantitative assessments of student learning outcomes and resulted in the recognition of a test-score gap among minority and majority students.

Research which followed the Coleman Report addressed the extent to which student and home effects or school effects could explain the test-score gap, ultimately leading to sophisticated analyses that teased out the extent to which poverty accounts for low performances (including such factors as diminished home resources and less parental involvement in the education of their children) or whether the quality of schools that minority children attend differ in meaningful ways from those attended by majority-group children could account for test-score differentials. School-based issues included studies of the effects of per child expenditures, teacher quality, beliefs by children of color as to whether education leads to upward mobility represent as factors that could account for test scores. Likewise, comparisons of public, private, and charter schools arose out of a concern for the effect size of school variables.

Resistance to school desegregation was immediate and has resulted in 'white flight' to the suburbs, where minority proportions were considerably smaller, and to private schools that also had under-representation of minority students. In response to demands by minority groups school desegregation and the focus on the rights of minority groups led to changes in curricula designed to increase awareness of minority contributions to the country's history and sensitivity to cultural differences within the society. Pressure for increased cultural awareness associated with the perception that the claims for equality of educational opportunity for minorities were legitimate led to both push back from middle-class whites whose hegemony over educational opportunities was being challenged, and from big business that feared that US competitiveness in the globalizing world was being eroded. By the mid-1980s, state legislatures enacted mandates for higher academic standards which followed the release of *A Nation at Risk* (1983) by the President's Commission on Excellence in Education. The federal report predicted a decline in American productivity and competitiveness due to the deterioration of academic standards in the nation's schools. Each of the reauthorizations of the federal Elementary and Secondary Education Act of 1965 reflected responses to the 1983 report by incorporating greater federal involvement in the curricular side of public education in the USA. Thus began the Standards-based School Accountability movement that resulted in changes in schooling specified in *A Nation at Risk* (1983), *American 2000* (1991), *Goals 2000* (1994), *No Child Left Behind* (2001), and *Race to the Top* (2009).

Research that focuses on the magnitude of test-score gaps by their nature tend to be quantitative, relying on the large national datasets funded by the US Department of Education and the Institute for Education Sciences within that department. Other studies have relied on state-wide datasets collected by some of the state education agencies and again, have necessitated quantitative analyses. Some of the studies that seek to ascertain linkages between educational practices at schools or neighborhood and home environments may rely on more qualitative data, while still others may be quantitative in nature. There are also studies that run in parallel, assessing an issue using quantitative analysis, while another component or even an off-shoot from the original study uses qualitative analysis. Thus, the original Coleman Report, which used statistical modeling to assess the test-score gap was accompanied by a qualitative study of the process of desegregation and re-segregation in selected American cities (Mack, *Our Children's Burden* [1968]). The assessment of home versus school effects on learning have recently be re-analyzed by Borman and Dowling (2010) using quantitative analysis, while one of the most cited studies of home effects was a qualitative study by Lareau (1987, 2002).

A significant portion of research associated with educational inequality is either policy research or policy-relevant research. Sometimes the federal government, state education agencies, or even local school districts fund projects to assess the effectiveness of educational practices, including changes in class sizes, mainstreaming special education students, programs to mitigate summer setback among children from low-income families, the effectiveness of single-sex classrooms, teacher value-added effects, grade retention, high school exit exams, peer effects of academic majors, educational and occupational aspirations, and the transition from school to work. Recently, Ballantine and Dworkin (2012) surveyed research topics in American sociology of education through a review of 177 articles published over the past decade (2001–2011) in the American Sociological Association journal *Sociology of Education*. They were able to categorize 140 of the articles into three groups of topics. The remainder of the articles addressed methodological issues or were only tangential to the three general topics. In order of frequency of articles, they were 'stratification and inequality in access to quality education and careers' (50.7%), 'accountability, school reform, and high-stakes testing' (35.7%), and 'globalization and its effects' (13.6%). The first category addressed much of the research on the test-score gap, especially that between African American and white students.

The theoretical orientations associated with inequality in American education and the test-score gap have incorporated all of the major theory groups in sociology, including structural-functional or consensus theory, conflict theory, and symbolic interaction.

Over the last 30 or more years research addressing racial and ethnic inequality in American education in general and the test-score gap among minority groups and the majority population has emphasized three areas of causal inference. The first focused on individual students, with attention placed on what student-level factors might account for low achievement among minorities and the poor. Due to the statistical methodology employed in the Coleman Report much of the variance in test-score differences between racial groups of students was attributed to student and home effects. Likewise, Fordham and Ogbu (1986) and later Mickelson (1990) saw student beliefs and peer group attitudes as contributing to lower minority-student achievement. Current research has not abandoned student-level effects, particularly when multilevel modeling or hierarchical linear modeling (HLM) is used in quantitative studies often based on large samples. However, it is much less likely that issues of race and intelligence or analyses that 'blame' students for their academic failures carry as much currency in the social sciences and education as they might have a generation or two ago. In fact, there was considerable condemnation of the controversial book *The Bell Curve* (1994) written by Herrnstein and Murray because of its attempt to attribute racial (and social class) differences among groups to issues of heritable intelligence, a theme recited for a century by champions of racism. The book was followed by well-reasoned attacks by numerous professional associations within the social sciences (see especially, the reviews written by Hauser, Taylor, and Duster for the journal of sociological reviews, *Contemporary Sociology* 1995).

Nevertheless, a focus on the student as the explanation of the test-score gap has been part of public policy in education emanating from the Standards-based School Accountability movement begun in the 1980s, although the movement applies blame equally to student, parents, teachers, and schools. Thus, policies that retain failing students in grade or deny graduation to students who fail high school exit exams, as well as responses to disruptive students and actions to reduce bullying behavior remain focused on the student as the responsible party. However, parents and teachers may also be incorporated in the attribution of blame for these negative events.

The second category of explanations for academic failure has focused on dysfunctional families, or families in which there have been intergenerational experiences of low academic performances and drop-out behaviors. Considerable research has noted that drop-out behavior tends to be concentrated in families that have had intergenerational academic failures and where older sibling of the 'at-risk' students had dropped out of school (LeCompte and Dworkin, 1991; Hammond et al., 2007). Academic advantages that arise out of home resources have been well documented by the work of Lareau (1987, 2000, 2002). A considerable amount of attention has been placed on immigrant families, in part because the United States has often been characterized as a 'nation of immigrants' and because undocumented immigrants are a salient political issue in the country. The US Supreme Court decision in *Plyler* v. *Doe* (457 U.S. 202, 1982) held that undocumented school-aged children are protected under the 'Equal Protection Clause' of the XIV Amendment to the US Constitution and are thus entitled to a free public education. Frequently, immigrant children are among the most disadvantaged students in schools. When parents are undocumented their families fear discovery and deportation and thus do not demand that the schools provide their children with the education to which they are entitled. However, even assimilation is not a cure for the children and grandchildren on some immigrants. Rumbaut (1997) documented the numerous disadvantages of assimilation and the resultant immigrant paradox, whereby Hispanic students detached from a supportive culture and sometimes concentrated in low-performing schools do less well academically, economically, and in terms of health than their parents or even grandparents.

The third group of explanations focuses on schools and teachers and represents the largest portion of current research on student learning outcomes. Academic failure and test-score gaps are seen in this research as a result of school resources, including funding level, the quality of the faculty, and failures among campus and school district administrators to redress campus problems. Balfantz and Legters (2004) reported on 'drop-out factories' where there is 'poor promoting power' in the schools. That is, these are schools in which fewer than 50% or 60%of the freshman class will become seniors in four years. Accountability systems prescribed by the federal re-authorization of the Elementary and Secondary Education Act in 2001 (*No Child Left Behind*) and 2009 (*Race to the Top*) imposed sanctions for schools that repeatedly failed to raise student achievement.

An array of variables is addressed in research drawn from the tradition that examines school effects in accounting for test-score gaps. This chapter emphasized several of these contributing factors, ranging from the public responses to school desegregation to the emergence of a Standards-based School Accountability movement. A backlash against the focus on awareness of the cultural contributions of the nation's ethnically and racially diverse populations, resulted in a call for a return to basics. Further, the white middle class sought to restore its hegemony over education and careers, while the private corporate sector sought to ensure that the future labor force would be competitive in a globalizing world. The results were a greater focus on externally-imposed standards (external to the schools and educators), measured by standardized tests the results of which were used to evaluate schools, teachers, and school administrators. If students did not meet performance levels usually established either by state legislatures or state education agencies with the approval of the US Department of Education, a series of draconian steps were prescribed. Most were punishing to schools and school personnel and were based on a theory of motivation that holds that people can best be motivated to work hard if they are threatened with dire consequences (Dworkin, 2008a). The implementation of the school and teacher accountability systems have demoralized teachers and heightened teacher burnout (Dworkin, 2009). In turn, decreased teacher morale had resulted in more teachers blaming their students for the low achievement that threatens their jobs. Such student-blaming behaviors, accompanied by the already-present negative labeling of students by their teachers, has accelerated negative student attitudes about schooling and increased the drop-out rate of the most at-risk students.

The substantial array of issues that characterizes education, both public and private, in the United States has led to a research agenda in sociology and education that is multifaceted, often contradictory, and frequently policy relevant. Considerable federal, state and local research funding has addressed the manifold social issues in education, thereby increasing the proportion of the policy-relevant research discussed in the current chapter. In fact, the sheer volume of research into educational inequality in the United States has led us to need to view only a small portion of the salient studies of educational issues that impact racial and ethnic minorities in the country. However, we elected to comment on a strategic issue in sociology and education: the nature and causes of the test-score gap between minorities and the majority population. Although, Gamoran (2001) predicted that the 21st century would no longer be concerned with racial and ethnic inequalities in education, supplanting it with social class inequalities, the reality in the second decade of the new century is that race and ethnicity still matters. In part because educational disadvantages due to race and class remain intertwined for many children, schools and the larger society cannot move beyond the conjoined nature of these inequalities. Affluence and poverty do cut across racial and ethnic lines, but the United States is remains a society where race still matters. Even the election of Barack Obama as the first African American President of the United States in 2008 and his re-election in 2012 has not meant that prejudice, stereotyping, discrimination, and substantial differentials in educational opportunity have disappeared. It is also the case that such vestiges of racism continue to characterize the experiences of a larger percentage of African American, Latino, Native American, and immigrant children. Because of the nature of much research in the sociology of education it also means that the agendas of sociologists and other educational researchers will continue to focus on gaps in access and achievements of minority children for many decades to come. While the present chapter addresses research over the past 30 years, it must be acknowledged that it is not simply backward looking. The disadvantages experienced by minority and immigrant children today will not disappear even in the next 30 years. In fact, in a globalizing world where the magnitude and quality of educational attainment differentiates peoples, many of the issues associated with academic gaps are likely to be even more salient in the future.

In fact, future research on racial, ethnic, and social class inequality in American education and the sociology of education is likely to emphasize two current trends. Studies that seek to explain the factors that affect student academic achievement (as well as test-score gaps among groups) will be addressed using increasingly more sophisticated statistical modeling, as evidenced by the study by Borman and Dowling (2010) in their use of the Coleman Report data. It is entirely appropriate that methodological advances will be reflected in research in education and the sociology of education. An assessment by Saha and Keeves (2003) chronicled the many advances in analytical techniques that came out of educational research and especially in the sociology of education. Additionally, future research will likely explore more thoroughly the extent to which the experiences of different racial and ethnic minorities and students in poverty are differentially affected by the variables associated with lower achievement levels. The work of Condron (2009) has pointed the way for some of this research, suggesting that lower academic achievement among racial and ethnic minorities may be driven by school effects, while lower achievement among poor white students may be driven non-school effects. Reardon's (2011) work on the growing divide in test scores by social class will stimulate much research, as it suggests that social class, rather than race will become the central independent variable in the study of educational inequality in the United States. Future research, including analyses of test-score gaps among student groups is likely to isolate better school policies and practices and individual attitudes and behaviors that mediate the effects of various school, family, and student outcomes among racial, ethnic, and social class groupings. Finally, much educational research is based on large samples and therefore requires levels of funding that the national and state governments generally provide. It is expected that governmental agencies will continue to play a significant role in defining some of the research questions and relevant methodologies. However, increasingly scarce federal and state funds may place limits on the creation of new datasets and require researchers to be especially creative in testing new hypotheses with existing datasets. Policy relevance will be a hallmark of future research on gaps in student achievement as school practitioners and governmental officials continue to seek out 'what works' in addressing educational inequalities.

Note

The authors would like to thank Adara Robbins, an undergraduate at Rice University, for her assistance in locating references for this chapter.

References

Abrams, L., and Haney, W. (2004). Accountability and the grade 9 to 10 transition: The impact on attrition and retention rates. pp. 181–206 in G. Orfield (Ed.), *Dropouts in America: Confronting the Graduation Rate Crisis.* Cambridge, MA: Harvard University Press.

Alexander, K. L., Entwistle, D., and Dauber, S. L. (2005). *On the Success of Failure, 2nd Edition.* Cambridge, England: Cambridge University Press.

Alexander, K. L., Entwistle, D., and Olson, L. S. (2007). Lasting consequences of the summer learning gap. *American Sociological Review* 72: 167–80.

Aud, S., Hussar, W., Johnson, F., Kena, G., Roth, E., Manning, E., Wang, X., and Zhang, J. (2012). *The Condition of Education 2012* (NCES 20120–045). US Department of Education, National Center for Education, US Department of Education. Washington, DC.

Aud, S., Hussar, W., Kena, G., Bianco, K., Frohlich, L., Kemp, J., and Tahan, K. (2011). *The Condition of Education 2011* (NCES 2011–033). National Center for Education Statistics, US Department of Education. Washington, DC.

Aud, S., Hussar, W., Planty, M., Snyder, T., Bianco, K., Fox, M., Frohlich, L., Kemp, J., and Drake, L. (2010). *The Condition of Education 2010* (NCES 2010–028). National Center for Education Statistics. Institute of Education Sciences, US Department of Education. Washington, DC.

Balfantz, R., and Legters, N. (2004). Locating the dropout crisis: Which high schools produce the nation's dropouts? pp. 57–84 in G. Orfield (Ed.), *Dropouts in America: Confronting the Graduation Rate Crisis.* Cambridge, MA: Harvard Education Press.

Ballantine, J. H., and Dworkin, A. G. (2012). Sociology of education in the United States. pp. 189–213 in J. Toschenko and A. Osipov (Eds), *Sociology of Education around the World*, Russia: State University of Novgorod Press. (In Russian.)

Ballou, Teasley, B., and Zeidner, T. (2008). Charter school effects on achievement: Where we are and where we are going. In M. Berends, M. G. Springer, H. J. Walberg and A Primus (Eds), *Charter School Outcomes.* New York: Lawrence Erlbaum Associates.

Bankston III, C. L. (2004). Social capital and its relevance to minority and immigrant populations. *Sociology of Education* 77 (2): 176–179.

Bankston III, C. L., Calda, S. J., and Zhou, M. (1997). The academic achievement of Vietnamese students: Ethnicity as social capital. *Sociological Focus* 30: 1–16.

Berliner, D. C., and Biddle, B. J. (1995). *The Manufactured Crisis: Myth, Fraud, and the Attack on America's Public Schools.* MA: Addison Wesley.

Bernstein, B. (1971). *Class, Codes, and Control*, Vol. 1, Part III. London: Routledge & Kegan Paul.

Booher-Jennings, J. (2005). Below the bubble: Educational triage and the Texas accountability system. *American Educational Research Journal* 42 (2): 231–268.

Booher-Jennings, J., and Beveridge, A. (2007). Gains, strains, gaming, and results: The Prevalence and impact of elective and de facto test exemption in the Houston independent school district. In A. R. Sadovnik, J. A. O'Day, G. W. Bohrnstedt., and K. M. Borman (Eds), *No Child Left Behind and the Reduction of the Achievement Gap: Sociological Perspectives on Federal Education Policy.* New York: Routledge.

Borman, K. M. (2005). *Meaningful Urban Education Reform: Confronting the Learning Crisis in Mathematics and Science.* Albany, NY: SUNY Press.

Borman, K. M., Eitle, T. M., Michael, D., Eitle, D. J., Lee, R., Johnson, L., Cobb-Roberts, D., Dorn, S., Shircliffe, B. (2004). Accountability in a post-desegregation era: The continuing significance of racial segregation in Florida's schools. *American Educational Research Journal* 41: 605–631.

Borman, G., and Dowling, N. M. (2010). Schools and inequality: A multilevel analysis of Coleman's Equality of Educational Opportunity data. *Teachers College Records* 112 (5): 1201–1246.

Bowles, S., and Gintis, H. (1976). *Schooling in Capitalist America: Educational Reform and the Contradictions of Economic Life*. NY: Basic Books.

Bowles, S., and Gintis, H. (2002). Schooling in capitalist America revisited. *Sociology of Education* 75 (1): 1–18.

Bracey, G.W. (2005). Charter schools' performance and accountability: A disconnect. Education Policy Research Unit (EPRU), Education Policy Studies Laboratory (EPSL-0505–113–EPRU, Arizona State University. http://edpolicylab.org.

Bracey, G. W. (2008). Schools-are-awful bloc still busy in 2008: The 18th Bracey report on the condition of public education. *Phi Delta Kappan* 90 (2): 103–114.

Braun, C. (1976). Teacher expectation: Sociopsychological dynamics. *Review of Educational Research* 46: 185–212.

Brouwers, A., and Tomic, W. (2000). The longitudinal study of teacher burnout and perceived self-efficacy in classroom management. *Teaching and Teacher Education* 16: 239–253.

Brown v. *Board of Education of Topeka* (1954), 347 U.S. 483.

Brown, S. K., and Bean, F. D. (2006). Assimilation models, old and new: Explaining a long-term process. *Migration Information Source,* Migration Policy Institute. http://www.migrationinformation.org/USfocus/print.cfm?ID=442.

Bryk, A. S., Lee, V. E., and Holland, P. B. (1993). *Catholic Schools and the Common Good*. Cambridge, MA: Harvard University Press.

Burke, R. J., Greenglass, E. R., and Schwarzer, R. (1996). Predicting teacher burnout over time: Effects of work stress, social support, and self-doubts on burnout and its consequences. *Anxiety, Stress and Coping: An International Journal* 9 (3): 1–15.

Camarota, S. A., (2012). Center for Immigration Studies. Immigrants in the United States: A profile of America's foreign-born population. http://www.cis.org/articles/2012/immigrants-in-the-united-states-2012.pdf.

Carnoy, M., Jacobsen, R., Mishel, L. R., and Rothstein, R. (2005). *The Charter School Dust-Up: Examining Evidence on Enrollment and Achievement*. Washington, DC, Economic Policy Institute. New York: Teachers College Press.

Clifton, R. A., Perry, R., Parsonson, K., and Hryniuk, S. (1986). Effects of ethnicity and sex on teachers' expectations of junior high school students. *Sociology of Education* 59: 58–67.

Cohen, E. G., and Lotan, R. A. (1997). *Working for Equity in Heterogeneous Classrooms: Sociological Theory in Practice*. New York: Teachers College Press.

Cohen, G. L., Garcia, J., Apfel, N., and Master, A. (2006). Reducing the racial achievement gap: A social-psychological intervention. *Science* 313 (5791): 1307–1310. doi: DOI 10.1126/science.1128317.

Coleman, J. S. (1988). Social capital in the creation of human capital. *The American Journal of Sociology*, Vol. 94, Supplement: Organizations and Institutions: Sociological and Economic Approaches to the Analysis of Social Structure, S95–S120.

Coleman, J. S., and Hoffer, T. (1987). *Public and Private High Schools: The Impact of Communities*. New York: Basic Books.

Coleman, J. S., Campbell, E. Q., Hobson, C. J., McPartland, J., Mood, A. M., and Weinfeld, F. D. (1966). *Equality of Educational Opportunity*. Washington, DC: US Government Printing Office.

Coleman, J. S., Hoffer, T., and Kilgore, S. (1982). *High School Achievement: Public, Catholic, and Private Schools Compared*. New York: Basic Books.

Cooper, H. M. (1979) Pygmalion grows up: A model for teacher expectation communications and performance influence. *Review of Educational Research* 49: 389–410.

Condron, D. J. (2009). Social class, school and non-school environments, and black/white inequalities in children's learning. *American Sociological Review* 74 (5): 683–708.

Cooper, H., Nye, B., Charlton, K., Lindsay, J., and Greathouse, S. (1996). The effects of summer vacation on achievement test scores: A narrative and meta-analytic review. *Review of Educational Research* 66: 227–268.

Crosnoe, R. (2005). Double disadvantage or signs of resilience? The elementary school contexts of children from Mexican immigrant families. *American Educational Research Journal* 42 (2): 269–303.

Crosnoe, R., and Turley, R. N. L. (2011). K-12 Educational Outcomes of Immigrant Youth. *The Future of Children* 21 (1): 129–152.

Day, C., Elliot, B., Kington, A. (2005). Reform, standards, and teacher identity: Challenges of commitment. *Teaching and Teacher Education* 21 (5): 563–577.

Downey, D. (1995). When bigger is not better: Family size, parental resources, and children's educational performance. *American Sociological Review* 60: 746–761.

Downey, D., von Hippel, P. T., and Broh, B. A. (2004). Are schools the great equalizer? Cognitive inequality during the summer months and the school year. *American Sociological Review* 69: 613–635.

Duncan, K. C., and Sandy, J. (2007). Explaining the performance gap between public and private school students. *Eastern Economic Journal* 33 (2): 177–191.

Dusek, J. B. (1975). Do teachers bias children's learning? *Review of Educational Research* 45: 661–684.

Dusek, J. B. (1985). *Teacher Expectancies*. Hillsdale, NJ: Lawrence Erlbaum Associates, Publishers.

Dworkin, A. G. (1980). The changing demography of public school teachers: Some implications for faculty turnover in urban areas. *Sociology of Education* 53: 65–73.

Dworkin, A. G. (1987). *Teacher Burnout in the Public Schools: Structural Causes and Consequences for Children*. Albany, NY: State University of New York Press.

Dworkin, A. G. (1997). Coping with reform: The intermix of teacher morale, teacher burnout, and teacher accountability. pp. 459–498 in B. J. Biddle, T. L. Good, & I. F. Goodson (Eds), *International Handbook of Teachers and Teaching*, Dordrecht/Boston/London: Kluwer Academic Publishers.

Dworkin, A. G. (2001). Perspectives on teacher burnout and school reform. *International Education Journal* 4(2): 689–678.

Dworkin, A. G. (2005). The No Child Left Behind Act: Accountability, high-stakes, testing, and roles for sociologists. *Sociology Education* 78 (April): 170–174.

Dworkin, A. G. (2008a). School accountability and the standards-based reform movement: Some unintended consequences of education policies. *International Journal of Contemporary Sociology* 45 (October): 11–31.

Dworkin, A. G. (2008b). Dropping out of high school: Another American dilemma. *The Latino Black Education Initiative*. Atlanta, GA: Southern Education Foundation.

Dworkin, A. G. (2009). Teacher burnout and teacher resilience: Assessing the impacts of the school accountability movement. pp. 491–509 in L. J. Saha and A. G. Dworkin (Eds), *New International Handbook of Teachers and Teaching*. NY: Springer Publications.

Dworkin, A. G., and Dworkin, R. J. (1999). *The Minority Report: An Introduction to Race, Ethnic, Gender Relations*. New York: Harcourt, Brace.

Dworkin, A. G., and Lorence, J. (2007). Gaming No Child Left Behind: The effects of tokenism on the achievement of students in Texas schools. In A. R. Sadovnik, J. A. O'Day, G. W. Bohrnstedt, and K. M. Borman (Eds), *No Child Left Behind and the*

Reduction of the Achievement Gap: Sociological Perspectives on Federal Education Policy. New York: Routledge.

Dworkin, A. G., Saha, L. J., and Hill, A. N. (2003). Teacher burnout and perceptions of a democratic school environment, *International Education Journal* 4 (2): 108–120.

Dworkin, A. G., and Tobe, P. F. (2012). Politics and education in the United States. pp. 52–73 in C. Kassimeris and M. Vryodines (Eds), *The Politics of Education: The Challenge of Multiculturalism.* London/New York: Routledge, Taylor and Francis Group.

Entwisle, D. R., and Alexander, K. L. (1992). Summer setback – race, poverty, school composition, and mathematics achievement in the 1st 2 years of school. *American Sociological Review* 57: 72–84.

Epstein, J. L. (2005). Attainable goals? The spirit and the letter of the No Child Left Behind Act on parental involvement. *Sociology of Education* 78 (April): 179–182.

Flynn, J. R. (1984). The mean IQ of Americans: Massive gains 1932–1978. *Psychological Bulletin* 95: 29–51.

Fordham, S., and Ogbu, J. U. (1986). Black students' school success: Coping with the 'burden' of 'acting white'. *Urban Review* 18: 176–206.

Freudenberger, H. J. (1974). Staff burn-out. *Journal of Social Issues* 30: 159–165.

Friedman, I. A. (1991) High- and low-burnout schools: School culture aspects of teacher burnout. *Journal of Educational Research* 84 (6): 325–333.

Friedman, I. A. (1995) Student behavior patterns contributing to teacher burnout. *The Journal of Educational Research* 88 (5): 281–289.

Friedman, I. A. (2003). Self-efficacy and burnout in teaching: The importance of interpersonal-relations efficacy. *Social Psychology of Education* 6: 191–215.

Fry, R. (2007). *How Far Behind in Math and Reading are English Language Learners?* Washington, DC: Pew Hispanic Center.www.pewhispanic.org/topics/?TopicID=4.

Fry, R. (2008). *The Role of Schools in the English Language Learner Achievement Gap.* Washington, DC: Pew Hispanic Center. http://www.pewhispanic.org/files/reports/89.pdf.

Gamoran, A. (1992). The variable effects of high school tracking. *American Sociological Review* 57: 812–828.

Gamoran, A. (2001). American schooling and educational inequality: Forecast for the 21st century. *Sociology of Education* 34 (Extra Issue): 135–153.

Gibson, C. J., and Lennon, E. (1999). Historical census statistics on the foreign-born population of the United States: 1850–1990. *Population Division Working Paper No. 29.* Washington, DC: Population Division, US Bureau of the Census.

Goldberg, M., and Harvey, J. (1983). A nation at risk: The report of the national commission on excellence in education. *The Phi Delta Kappan* 65 (1): 14–18.

Gordon, M. J. (1964). *Assimilation in American Life: The Role of Race, Religion, and National Origins.* New York: Oxford University Press.

Gordon, M. J. (1978). *Human Nature, Class and Ethnicity.* New York: Oxford University Press.

Glazer, N., and Moynihan, D. P. (1963). *Beyond the Melting Pot.* Cambridge, MA: MIT Press.

Grissmer, D., Flanagan, A., and Williamson, S. (1998). The impact of schools and culture. Does the black-white test score gap widen after children enter school? In Jencks, C. and Phillips, M. *The Black-White Test Score Gap.* Washington, DC: Brookings Institution Press.

Hammond, C., Linton, D., Smink, J., and Drew, J. (2007). *Dropout Risk Factors and Exemplary Programs: AS Technical Report.* Clemson, SC: National Dropout Center/Network, Communities in Schools, Inc.

Haney, W. (2000). The myth of the Texas miracle in education. *Education Policy Analysis Archives* 8 (41): 1–126.

Hanushek, E. A., and Kain, J. (1972). On the value of the equality of educational opportunity as a guide to public policy. pp. 116–145 in F. Mosteller and D. P. Moynihan (Eds), *On Equality of Educational Opportunity: Papers Deriving from the Harvard University Faculty Seminar on the Coleman Report*. New York: Vintage Books.

Hanushek, E. A., and Rivkin, S. G. (2010). Using value-added measures of teacher quality. National Center for Analysis of Longitudinal Data in Education Research, The UrbanInstitute, Brief no. 9. http://www.urban.org.

Haskins, R., and Tienda, M. (2011). The future of immigrant children. *Policy Brief* (Spring 2011). Princeton, New Jersey: The Future of Children, Princeton-Brookings.

Hauser, R. M. (2001). Should we end social promotion? Truth and consequences. pp. 151–178 in G. Orfield and M. L. Kornhaber (Eds), *Raising Standards or Raising Barriers? Inequality and High-stakes Testing in Public Education*. New York, NY: The Century Foundation Press.

Hauser, R. M., Taylor, R. M., and Duster, T. (1995). Reviews of *The Bell Curve*. *Contemporary Sociology: A Journal of Reviews* 24 (2):149–161.

Hedges, L. V., and Nowell, A. (1998). Changes in the black-white gap in achievement test scores. *Sociology of Education* 72 (April): 111–135.

Herrnstein, R. J. and Murray, C. (1994). *The Bell Curve: Intelligence and Class in American Life*. New York: The Free Press.

Heyns, B. (1978). *Summer Learning and the Effects of Schooling*. New York: Academic.

Heyns, B. (1987). Schooling and cognitive development: Is there a season for learning? *Child Development* 58: 1151–1160.

Heubert, J. P., and Hauser, R. M. (1999). *High Stakes: Testing for Tracking, Promotion, and Graduation*. Washington, DC: National Academy Press.

Ingersoll, R. M. (1999). The problem of underqualified teachers in American secondary schools. *Educational Researcher* 28: 26–37.

Ingersoll, R. M. (2005). The problem of underqualified teachers: A sociological perspective. *Sociology of Education* 78 (April): 175–178.

Jencks, C. S. (1972). The quality of the data collected by *The Equality of Educational Opportunity*. pp. 437–512 in F. Mosteller and D. P. Moynihan (Eds), *On Equality of Educational Opportunity: Papers Deriving from the Harvard University Faculty Seminar on the Coleman Report*. New York: Vintage Books.

Jencks, C. S., Crouse, J., and Mueser, P. (1983). The Wisconsin model of status attainment: A national replication with improved measures of ability and aspiration. *Sociology of Education* 56 (1): 3–19.

Jencks, C. S., and Phillips, M. (1998). *The Black-White Test Score Gap*. Washington, DC: Brookings Institution Press.

Jimerson, S. (1999). On the failure of failure: Examining the association between early grade retention and education and employment outcomes during late adolescence. *Journal of School Psychology* 37 (3): 243–272.

Jimerson, S., Anderson, G. E., and Whipple, A. D. (2002) Winning the battle and losing the war: Examining the relationship between grade retention and dropping out of high school. *Psychology in the Schools* 39 (4): 441–457.

Kane, T. J., Rockoff, J. E., and Staiger, D. O. (2008). What does certification tell us about teacher effectiveness? Evidence from New York City. *Economics of Education Review* 27: 615–631.

Kane, T. J., and Staiger, D. O. (2002). Volatility in test scores: Implications for test-based accountability systems. pp. 235–283 in D. Ravitch (Ed.), *Brookings Papers on Education Policy*. Washington, DC: The Brookings Institution.

Kao, G. (2004). Social capital and its relevance to minority and immigrant populations. *Sociology of Education* 77 (April): 172–183.

Karen, D. (2005). No Child Left Behind? Sociology ignored. *Sociology of Education* 78 (April): 165–169.

Kelly, S., and Carbonaro, W. (2012). Curriculum tracking and teacher expectations: Evidence from discrepant course taking models. *Social Psychology of Education* 15: 271–294.

Kerckhoff, A. C. (1976). The status attainment process: Socialization or allocation? *Social Forces* 52: 368–81.

Kornhaber, M. L., and Orfield, G. (2001). High-stakes testing policies: Examining their assumptions and consequences. pp. 1–18 in G. Orfield and M. L. Kornhaber (Eds), *Raising Standards or Raising Barriers? Inequality and High-stakes Testing in Public Education*. NY: The Century Foundation Press.

Kroneberg, C. (2008). Ethnic communities and school performance among the new second generation in the United States: Testing the theory of segmented assimilation. *Annals of the American Academy of Political and Social Sciences* 620 (November): 138–160.

Lareau, A. (1987). Social class differences in family-school relationships: The importance of cultural capital. *Sociology of Education* 60: 73–85.

Lareau, A. (2000). *Home Advantage: Social Class and Parental Intervention in Education*, 2nd ed. Lantham, MD: Roman Littlefield.

Lareau, A. (2002). Invisible inequality: Social class and childrearing in black families and white families. *American Sociological Review* 67: 747–776.

LeCompte, M. D., and Dworkin, A. G. (1991). *Giving Up on School: Student Dropouts and Teacher Burnouts*. Newbury Park, CA: Corwin.

Lee, S. (1998). *Unraveling the Model Minority Stereotype*. NY: Teachers College Press.

Leithwood, K., Menzies, T., Jantzi, D., and Leithwood, J. (1996). School restructuring, transformational leadership, and the amelioration of teacher burnout. *Anxiety, Stress, and Coping: An International Journal* 9: 199–215.

Lewis, S., Simon, C., Uzzell, R., Horwitz, A., and Casserly, M. (2010). *A Call for Change: The Social and Educational Factors Contributing to the Outcomes of Black Males in Urban Schools*. New York: Council of Great City Schools.

Lorence, J. (2006). Retention and academic achievement research revisited from a United States perspective. *International Education Journal* 7 (5): 731–777.

Lorence, J., Dworkin, A. G., Toenjes, L. A., and Hill, A. N. (2002). Grade retention and social promotion in Texas: An assessment of academic achievement among elementary school students. pp. 13–68 in D. Ravitch (Ed.), *Brookings Papers on Education Policy, 2002: The Policy of Ending Social Promotion*. Washington, DC: The Brookings Institution.

Lucas, S. R. (1999). *Tracking Inequality: Stratification and Mobility in American High Schools*. NY: Teachers College Press.

Lucas, S. R., and Gamoran, A. (2002). Tracking and the achievement gap. pp. 171–198 in J. E. Chubb and T. Loveless (Eds), *Bridging the Achievement Gap*. Washington, DC: Brookings Institution Press.

Luce, S. R., and Hoge, R. D. (1978). Relations among teacher rankings, pupil-teacher interactions, and academic achievement: A test of the teacher expectancy hypothesis. *American Educational Research Journal* 15: 489–500.

Mack, R. W. (1968). *Our Children's Burden: Studies of Desegregation in Nine American Communities*. New York: Random House.

Madaus, G. F. and Clarke, M. (2001). The adverse impact of high-stakes testing on minority students: evidence from 100 years of test data. pp. 85–106 in G. Orfield and

M. L. Kornhaber, (Eds), *Raising Standards or Raising Barriers? Inequality and High-Stakes Testing in Public Education.* New York, NY: Century Foundation Press.

Marrett, C. B. (1990). The changing composition of schools: Implications for school organization. pp. 71–90 in M. T. Hallinan, D. M. Klein and J. Glass (Eds), *Change in Social Institutions.* New York, NY: Plenum.

Maslach, C. (1978). Job burnout: How people cope. *Public Welfare* 36: 56–58.

Maslach, C. (1993). Burnout, a multidimensional perspective. pp. 19–32 in W. B. Schaufeli, C. Maslach and T. Marek (Eds), *Professional Burnout, Recent Developments in Theory and Research.* Washington, DC: Taylor and Francis.

Maslach, C., and Jackson, S. E. (1981). The measurement of experienced burnout. *The Journal of Occupational Behaviour* 2: 99–113.

McNeil, L. M. (2000). *Contradictions of School Reform: Education Costs of Standardized Testing.* New York: Routledge.

McNeil, L. M. (2005). Faking equity: High-stakes testing and the education of Latino youth. pp. 57–111 in A. Valenzuela (Ed.), *Leaving Children Behind: How 'Texas-style' Accountability Fails Latino Youth.* Albany, NY: SUNY Press.

McNeil, L. M., Coppola, E., Radigan, J., and Vasquez Heilig, J. (2008). Avoidable losses: High-stakes accountability and the dropout crisis. *Education Policy Analysis Archives* 76 (3). Retrieved from http://epaa.asu.edu.ezproxy.lib.uh.edu/epaa/v16n3/.

Mehta, J. (2013). How paradigms create politics: The transformation of American educational policy, 1980–2001. *American Educational Research Journal* 50 (2): 285–324.

Michell, J. B. (1999). *Measurement in Psychology.* Cambridge: Cambridge University Press.

Mickelson, R. A. (1990). The attitude-achievement paradox among Black adolescents. *Sociology of Education* 63 (January): 44–61.

Mickelson, R. G. (2001). Subverting Swann: First- and second-generation segregation in Charlotte-Mecklenburg schools. *American Educational Research Journal* 38: 215–252.

Mickelson, R. G. (2003). The academic consequences of desegregation and segregation: Evidence from the Charlotte-Mecklenburg schools. *North Carolina Law Review* 81: 1513–1562.

Mosteller, F., and Moynihan, D. P. (1972). A path-breaking report. pp. 3–66 in F. Mosteller and D. P. Moynihan (Eds), *On Equality of Educational Opportunity: Papers Deriving from the Harvard University Faculty Seminar on the Coleman Report.* New York: Vintage Books.

Mulkey, L. M., Catsambis, S., Steelman, L. C., and Hanes-Ramos, M. (2009). Keeping track or getting offtrack: Issues in the tracking of students. pp. 1081–1100 in L. J. Saha and A. G. Dworkin (Eds), *International Handbook of Research on Teachers and Teaching.* NY: Springer.

Myerson, J., Rank, M. R., Raines, F. Q., and Schnitzler, M. A. (1998). Race and general cognitive ability: The myth of diminishing returns to education. *Psychological Science* 9: 139–142.

National Commission on Excellence in Education. (1983). *A Nation at Risk: The Imperative for Educational Reform.* Washington, DC: US Government Printing Office.

Nichols, S. L., and Berliner, D. C. (2007), *Collateral Damage: How High-Stakes Testing Corrupts America's Schools,* Cambridge, MA: Harvard University Press.

Noguera, P. A. (2004). Social capital and the education of immigrant students: Categories and generalizations. *Sociology of Education* 77 (April): 180–183.

Oakes, J. (1985). *Keeping Track: How Schools Structure Inequality.* New Haven: Yale University Press.

OECD. (2011). Lessons from PISA for the United States, Strong Performers and Successful Reformers in Education, OECD Publishing.

Ogbu, J. (1978). *Minority Education and Caste.* New York: Academic Press.

Orfield, G. (2002/3). The resurgence of school segregation. *Educational Leadership* 60(4): 16–20.

Orfield, G. (2009). Reviving the goal of an integrated society: A 21st century challenge *The Civil Rights Project/Proyecto Derechos Civiles at UCLA*. Los Angeles, CA: UCLA.

Phillips, M., Crouse, J., and Ralph, J. (1998) Does the black-white test score gap widen after children enter school? pp. 229–272 in C. Jencks and M. Phillips (Eds), *The Black-White Test Score Gap*, Washington, DC: Brookings Institution Press.

Planty, M., Hussar, W., Snyder, T., Provasnik, S., Kena, G., Dinkes, R., and Kewal Ramani, A. (2008). *The Condition of Education 2008*. National Center for Education Statistics. Institute of Education Sciences, US Department of Education. Washington, DC.

Plessy v. Ferguson (1896). 163 U.S. 537.

Portes, A., and Zhou, M. (1993). The new second generation: Segmented assimilation and its variants. *The Annals of the American Academy of Political and Social Science* 530: 74–96.

Rampey, B. D., Dion, G. S., and Donahue, P. I. (2009). *NAEP 2008 Trends in Academic Progress* (NCES 2009–479). National Center for Education Statistics, Institute of Education Sciences, US Department of Education, Washington, DC.

Reardon, S. F. (2011). The widening academic achievement gap between the rich and the poor: New evidence and possible explanations. pp. 91–116 in G. J. Duncan and R. J. Murnane (Eds), *Whither Opportunity? Rising Inequality, Schools, and Children's Life Chances*. New York: Russell Sage Foundation.

Reardon, S. F., and Bischoff, K. (2011). Income inequality and income segregation. *American Journal of Sociology* 116 (4): 1092–1153.

Reardon, S. F. (2013). No rich child left behind. (Except from *The Great Divide*, a series on inequality, at nytimes.com/opinionator) *New York Times*, 26 April 2013.

Reininger, M. (2013). Hometown disadvantage? It depends on where you're from: Teacher location preferences and the implications for staffing schools. *Education Evaluation and Policy Analysis* 34 (2): 127–145.

Rist, R. C. (1970). Social class and teacher expectations: The self-fulfilling prophecy in ghetto education. *Harvard Educational Review* 40: 411–451.

Roscigno, V. J. (1998). Race and the reproduction of educational disadvantage. *Social Forces* 76: 1033–1061.

Roscigno, V. J. (1999). The black-white achievement gap, family-school links, and the importance of place. *Sociological Inquiry* 69 (Spring): 159–186.

Rosenthal, R. and Jacobson, L. (1968). *Pygmalion in the Classroom*. New York, NY: Holt, Rinehart, and Winston.

Rumbaut, R. G. (1997). 'Assimilation and its discontents: Between rhetoric and reality'. *The International Migration Review* 31(4): 923–960.

Sadovnik, A. R., Dworkin, A. G., Gamoran, A., Hallinan, M., and Scott, J. (2007). Sociological perspectives on NCLB and federal involvement in education. pp. 359–373 in A. R. Sadovnik, J. A. O'Day, G. W. Bohrnstedt, & K. M. Borman (Eds), *No Child Left behind and the Reduction of the Achievement Gap*. New York: Routledge.

Saha, L. J., and Keeves, J. P. (2003). Leading the way: The development of analytical techniques in the sociology of education. pp. 160–179 in C. A. Torres and A. Antikainen (Eds), *The International Handbook on the Sociology of Education*. Lanham: Roman & Littlefield Publishers, Inc.

Sewell, W. H., Haller, A. O., and Portes, A. (1969). The educational and early occupational attainment process. *American Sociological Review* 34 (1): 82–92.

Sheldon, K. M., and Biddle, B. J. (1998). Standards, accountability, and school reforms: Perils and pitfalls. *Teachers College Record* 100: 164–180.

Shepard, L., and Smith, M. L. (1989). *Flunking Grades: Research and Policies on Retention.* Philadelphia: Falmer/Taylor & Francis.

Snyder, T. D., and Dillow, S. A. (2011). *Digest of Education Statistics 2010* (NCES 2011–015). National Center for Education Statistics, Institute of Education Sciences, U. S. Department of Education, Washington, DC.

Snyder, T. D., Tan, A. G., and Hoffman, C. M. (2006). *Digest of Education Statistics 2005* (NCES 2006–030). US Department of Education, National Center for Education Statistics, Washington, DC: US Government Printing Office.

Steele, C., and Aaronson, J. (1995). Stereotype threat and the intellectual test performance of African Americans. *Journal of Personality and Social Psychology* 69 (5): 797–811.

Stevens, P. (2007). Researching race/ethnicity and educational inequality in English secondary schools: A critical review of the research literature between 1980 and 2005. *Review of Educational Research* 77 (2): 147–185.

Tedesco, J. C. (1997). *The New Educational Pact: Education, Competitiveness, and Citizenship in Modern Society.* Paris: UNESCO, International Bureau of Education.

Tobe, Pamela. (2009). Value-added models of teacher effects. In L. J. Saha and A. G. Dworkin (Eds), *New International Handbook of Teachers and Teaching.* NY: Springer Publications, 1113–1134.

Toenjes, L. A., and Dworkin, A. G. (2002). Are increasing test scores in Texas really a myth, or is Haney's myth a myth? *Educational Policy Analysis Archives* 10, No. 17, March.

Toenjes, L. A., Dworkin, A. G., Lorence, J., and Hill, A. N. (2002). High-stakes testing, accountability, and student achievement in Texas and Houston. pp. 109–130 in J. E. Chubb and T. Loveless (Eds), *Bridging the Achievement Gap.* Washington, DC: The Brookings Institution.

US Census. (2010). American Community Survey. http://www.census.gov/acs/.

US Census. (2010). Current Population Trends. www/.census.gov/popest/data/index.html.

US Department of Education, National Center for Education Statistics. (2005). Annual Reports Program. http://nces.ed.gov/program/digest/d05/figures/fig_01.asp.

US Department of Education, National Center for Education Statistics. (2009). Achievement Gaps: How Hispanic and White Students in Public Schools Perform in Mathematics and Reading on the National Assessment of Educational Progress. Statistical Analysis Report. US Department of Education.

US Department of Education, National Center for Education Statistics. (2011). Achievement Gaps: How Black and White Students in Public Schools Perform in Mathematics and Reading on the National Assessment of Educational Progress. Statistical Analysis Report. US Department of Education.

US Department of Education, National Center for Education Statistics. (2004). *The Condition of Education 2004.* Washington, DC: US Government Printing Office.

Urban Institute. (2006). Children of immigrants: Facts and figures. (May, 2006).

Valenzuela, A. (1999). *Subtractive Schooling: U.S.-Mexican Youth and the Politics of Caring.* Albany, NY: SUNY Press.

Wenglinsky, H. (2007). *Are Private High Schools Better Academically than Public High Schools?* Washington, DC: Center on Education Policy. http://www.cep-dc.org.

White, K. W. and Rosenbaum, J. E. (2007). Inside the black box of accountability: How high-stakes accountability alters school culture and the classification and treatment of students and teachers. pp. 97–114 in A. R. Sadovnik, J. A. O'Day, G. W. Bohrnstedt, & K. M. Borman (Eds), *No Child Left behind and the Reduction of the Achievement Gap.* New York, NY: Routledge.

Wilde, J. (2010). Comparing results of the NAEP long-term trend assessment: ELLs, former ELLs, and English-proficient students. http://www.ncela.gwu.edu/files/uploads/16/AERA_2010_Wilde.pdf.

Wilson, W. J. (1980). *The Declining Significance of Race: Blacks and Changing American Institutions,* 2nd Edition. Chicago: University of Chicago Press.

Wilson, W. J. (1987). *The Truly Disadvantaged: The Inner City, the Underclass, and Public Policy.* Chicago: University of Chicago Press.

Wilson, W. J. (1996). *When Work Disappears.* New York, NY: Knopf.

Witty, P., and Theman, V. (1943). A follow-up study of educational attainment of gifted Negroes. *Journal of Educational Psychology* 34: 35–47. doi: 10.1037/h0055003.

Wojtkiewicz, R. A., and Holtzman, M. (2011). Family structure and college graduation: Is the stepparent effect more negative than the single parent effect? *Sociological Spectrum* 31 (4): 498–521. doi: Pii 938496031 Doi 10.1080/02732173.2011.574048.

Zhou, M. (1997). Segmented assimilation: Issues, controversies, and recent research on the new second generation. *International Migration Review* 31 (4): 975–1008.

20

Researching Race and
Ethnic Inequalities in Education
Key Findings and Future Directions

Peter A. J. Stevens and A. Gary Dworkin

As pointed out in the introduction, the sheer scope of the research discussed in this Handbook does not allow us critically to integrate all the findings that emerged out of these studies into a single concluding chapter that advises on future directions for research in each of the key research traditions and national and regional contexts. Instead in this concluding chapter we aim to realize three goals. First, we summarize and discuss some of the key characteristics of each national/regional review presented in an overview grid, which includes information on the: (1) research traditions, (2) research goals, (3) dominant research designs, (4) focus on racialized or ethnicized groups, (5) relationship between policy-makers and the research community, (6) key policy characteristics and developments over time, and (7) main language(s) of publication. This overview grid is used both as a tool to summarize research conducted in this area and as a reference guide that can be used by readers to identify particular areas of research and information and as a result assist in developing more specific, integrative reviews.

A second goal is to provide a cursory theoretical context with which readers of this Handbook might examine the national research literature on educational inequality among racial, ethnic, and other groups. This context acknowledges that the content of any national research literature on educational inequality is likely to reflect salient issues that a particular nation confronts in educating its populace, and especially members of groups who are not part of the society's dominant population or who do not participate in the core culture of that society. This concluding section will not attempt to analyze the studies central to the research traditions of each nation, but instead will only suggest that, (1) research in the sociology of education tends to focus on the social facts prevalent in a society, asking about the extent to which they are factual, and assessing their causes and implications for individuals and groups, and (2) the context of educational inequality is vested in the history of intergroup relations in the particular country. It therefore matters whether the disadvantaged groups are members of an indigenous and/or aboriginal population that have faced colonization, attempts at extermination, or historically been excluded from the mainstream of the nation. Somewhat different experiences and outcomes might exist if the disadvantaged group were conquered peoples as a result of warfare between nations. Here they may not be aborigines or even indigenous peoples, but rather those whose nation lost a war against the current dominant population. It further matters whether the group is composed of recent immigrants to the society, who arrived as guest workers or as refugees from political oppression in their homelands.

Finally, a third goal of this concluding chapter is to highlight several gaps in the literature and suggest directions through which research on race and ethnic inequalities can further develop.

20.1 Key characteristics of research on ethnic and racial inequalities in education

Table 20.1 summarizes some of the key characteristics of research on ethnic and racial inequalities as it developed in each of the 18 national and regional contexts included in this Handbook.

Observing this comparative summary table and a close reading of the chapters included in this Handbook allow us to draw some general conclusions regarding the development of research on ethnicity, race, and educational inequality worldwide. First, the chapters included in this review testify to the wealth of research carried out on ethnic and racial inequalities worldwide. Second, although researchers appear increasingly more likely to publish their work in English and consider research developed abroad, most of the research carried out on this topic is 'inward looking', with scholars developing research traditions mainly in interaction with local developments in terms of policy and intellectual thought, and generally neglecting research conducted abroad. Additionally, a fully comprehensive cross-national review is a challenge because a considerable amount of published research on the ethnic and racial inequalities in education is written in the native language of the country studied (see chapters on Argentina, Austria, Brazil, Canada, China, France, Germany, Japan, Russia, and the Netherlands). This tendency makes some significant portion of the published research less accessible to a global research community and less likely to be included in the more popular and authoritative, academic electronic databases (such as ERIC, Sociological Abstracts, and Web of Science).

Sometimes, the language in which research is written can indicate particular ideological preferences or assumptions on the part of researchers. This is perhaps best illustrated by the context of China, which has produced both a Chinese and an English body of literature on ethnic and racial inequalities. While there is considerable overlap between these bodies of research in terms

Table 20.1 Key characteristics of research on ethnicity, race, and educational inequality in different national contexts, 1980–2012

Country	Research traditions	Main research goal(s)	Dominant research designs	Focus on which racialized or ethnicized groups	Relationship between researchers and policy-makers, 1980–2012	Policy towards ethnic or racial minorities, 1980–2012	Main language of publication
Argentina	(1) Mapping educational access; (2) **Intercultural educational policies;** (3) Language conflict and schooling; (4) **Difference and diversity;** (5) School texts as a means of othering.	Analyzing how social, policy and educational discourses contribute to disadvantage some minority ethnic groups' educational experiences and schooling.	Qualitative	Indigenous minority groups: • Mapuche • Toba • Kolla • Wichí • Bordered immigrants and their descendants.	Researchers take a more critical relationship to social policy-makers and rely on diverse funding sources (including NGOs, universities, and governmental research agencies).	A shift from more assimilation oriented policies to policies that emphasize the reality and importance of cultural differences and diversity.	Spanish
Australia	(1) **Family (structural and cultural) characteristics;** (2) Political arithmetic; (3) Bilingual education; (4) **English deficit;** preparation for migrant and	Explaining education and occupation ambitions; education under-achievement; teacher preparation for migrant and	Quantitative, qualitative, case-studies, and mixed methods.	• European immigrants • Turkish immigrants • Asian immigrants • African humanitarian refugees	Researchers can be critical of, but have also a collaborative relationship with social policy-makers; government funding for research.	Pro-multiculturalism and integration, but periods of laissez-faire attitudes, and occasional criticism of the policy.	English

Country						
	(5) Teacher preparation and classroom interaction; (6) Racism and discrimination.	indigenous students		• 'boat people' • Indigenous Aboriginals and Indigenous Torres Strait Islanders		
Austria	(1) Political arithmetic; (2) Family background; (3) Structures of educational systems; (4) Intercultural education and discrimination; (5) Multilinguality.	Explaining underachievement of ethnic minorities.	Since 2000 quantitative, before qualitative and critical theory	Descendants of immigrants from: • Turkey • Former Yugoslavia Autochthonous minorities such as Carinthian Slovenes.	Shift from a critical attitude towards social policy to a more collaborative relationship and an increase in policy-funded and oriented research.	Contradicting policies emphasizing both multiculturalism and assimilation.	German
Belgium	(1) **Political arithmetic;** (2) Cultural and educational outcomes; (3) Language proficiency; (4) Racial and racial discrimination in school; (5) **School effectiveness.**	Explaining underachievement of ethnic minorities.	Quantitative	Descendants of immigrants in general ('allochtons') and in particular from: • Turkey • Morocco	Collaborative and critical relationship with government and increasingly more research funded through government-independent channels.	Contradicting policies emphasizing both multiculturalism and assimilation.	Initially in Dutch but increasingly more in English

(continued)

Table 20.1 Continued

Country	Research traditions	Main research goal(s)	Dominant research designs	Focus on which racialized or ethnicized groups	Relationship between researchers and policy-makers, 1980–2012	Policy towards ethnic or racial minorities, 1980–2012	Main language of publication
Brazil	(1) **Charting ethnic/racial inequalities in education;** (2) Race and school effectiveness; (3) **Racism and discrimination in schools.**	Describing inequalities in access, survival, and achievement, and experiences of racism.	Quantitative and qualitative	Indigenous (Indian) minorities and African Brazilian minorities	Collaborative relationship with considerable policy-funded and oriented research.	Pro-multiculturalism and affirmative policies.	Portuguese
Canada	(1) **Mobility / Meritocracy;** (2) Individual discrimination/ prejudice/ racism; (3) Identity/values; (4) Aboriginal education; (5) **Institutional processes.**	Explaining underachievement of visible minority students and highlighting the production and negotiation of racialized identities and hierarchies through schooling processes.	Quantitative and qualitative, with the latter more dominant in recent years.	Aboriginal and non-white, visible minority students.	A detached relationship between the research community and government.	Increased emphasis on pro-multicultural policies (and intercultural policies in Québec).	English and French

China	**Chinese literature:** (1) Marxism and ethnic minority education; (2) Patriotism and national unity in education for ethnic minority students; (3) Multicultural education; (4) **Determinants of ethnic differences in education;** (5) School facilities and teacher quality; (6) Preferential/ affirmative action policies. **English literature:** (1) **Policy overviews;** (2) Education and ethnic identity; (3) Incentives and disincentives for buy-in to the education system; (4) Educational stratification.	Describing the complex interrelationships of ethnicity with cultural, policy, development, and language issues.	Quantitative and qualitative designs, particular qualitative analyses of (policy) texts.	Indigenous minority groups.	Chinese literature is mainly collaborative while English literature is more critical of social policy.	The Chinese government adopts an integrationist perspective towards ethnic minorities, which is realized and in turn fosters patriotism and economic development.	Chinese and English

(continued)

Table 20.1 Continued

Country	Research traditions	Main research goal(s)	Dominant research designs	Focus on which racialized or ethnicized groups	Relationship between researchers and policy-makers, 1980–2012	Policy towards ethnic or racial minorities, 1980–2012	Main language of publication
Cyprus	(1) School ethnographies of national identity construction; (2) **School ethnographies of racism;** (3) Critical studies of curricula and textbooks; (4) Studies of teachers and intercultural education.	Explaining Greek Cypriot ethnocentric identity construction in relation to 'others'	Qualitative	• Turks • Turkish Cypriots • Immigrants from Russia and Eastern European countries. • Asian countries like China, Sri Lanka, and Vietnam.	Researchers take a more critical approach to social policy-makers and rely on self-funding and/ or funding sources that are independent of the government.	From assimilation-oriented policies to more pro-multicultural policies.	Greek and English
England	(1) Political arithmetic; (2) **Racism and racial discrimination;** (3) school effectiveness and inclusion;	Identifying inequality in educational experiences and outcomes of racial and ethnic minorities.	Qualitative	Descendants of immigrants from: • Caribbean • Africa • Pakistan • India • Bangladesh • China	Critical approach to government policies.	Pro-multiculturalism-oriented policies with a less visible, more assimilation-oriented agenda.	English

Country						
France	(4) Culture and educational outcomes; (5) Educational markets and educational outcomes. (1) Structures, curriculum and policies for minority students; (2) Family background and ethnic inequalities in education; (3) Limited educational resources of ethnic minority families; (4) Ethnic school segregation; (5) Ethnic relations in classrooms and schools.	Analyzing the gaps between official color-blindness and concrete evidence of ethnic differences and inequalities	From a focus on mainly qualitative research to more quantitative research designs.	Mainly descendants from immigrants from North African and sub-Saharan countries. • Gypsy/Traveller/Roma' children.	A critical approach to social policies with little research being policy orientated and funded.	Traditional French integration (assimilation) policies with some limited departure from the assimilationist model in educational policy.	French

(continued)

Table 20.1 Continued

Country	Research traditions	Main research goal(s)	Dominant research designs	Focus on which racialized or ethnicized groups	Relationship between researchers and policy-makers, 1980–2012	Policy towards ethnic or racial minorities, 1980–2012	Main language of publication
Finland	(1) Non-Finnish backgrounds of students as a pedagogical and didactic problem; (2) Minority students' educational paths as parts of marginalized life-courses; (3) Ethnic discrimination in secondary education.	Explaining how cultural differences and poor Finnish language skills lead to educational drop-outs of minority youth.	Qualitative	Immigrants (and their descendants) from: • Russia • Somalia • Roma/Traveller background	A collaborative relationship with few critical studies on government policies.	Contradicting policies emphasizing both multiculturalism and assimilation.	Finnish and more recently English.
Germany	(1) **Family background and inequality**; (2) Characteristics of the education system and inequality; (3) Linguistic diversity and inequality. (4) Discrimination.	Explaining underachievement of ethnic minority groups.	Quantitative and qualitative, often mixed methods	• Turkish immigrants • Russian-speaking (Eastern European) immigrants.	Critical and collaborative.	From multiculturalism to super diversity	German and more recently English

Ireland	(1) Charting ethnic inequalities and policy issues; (2) Racism and education; (3) **Developing newer and more critical research agendas.**	Focusing on gaps between progressive policy rhetoric and practices drawing mainly on Bourdieu.	Qualitative research through analysis of (policy) texts.	Focused more on policies than immigrants (most of which are very recent migrants of Polish and Lithuanian background and to a lesser extent of Indian, Chinese, and Nigerian background).	A widening relationship between educational sociologists and policy-makers, and practice in the field.	A development towards more pro-multicultural policies.	English
Japan	(1) Quantitative descriptions of minority students' educational achievements; (2) **Schooling processes in relation to discrimination, school interventions, and identity formation;** (3) Home cultures.	Explaining underachievement of ethnic minorities.	Qualitative	Indigenous minority groups, and descendants of former colonial subjects and migrants such as: • *Ainu* people • *buraku* people • *zainichi* Koreans • new migrants	A collaborative relationship between educational anthropologists and local governments.	A policy that emphasizes human rights over cultural diversity.	Japanese

(*continued*)

Table 20.1 Continued

Country	Research traditions	Main research goal(s)	Dominant research designs	Focus on which racialized or ethnicized groups	Relationship between researchers and policy-makers, 1980–2012	Policy towards ethnic or racial minorities, 1980–2012	Main language of publication
The Netherlands	(1) **Political arithmetic;** (2) Racism and ethnic discrimination; (3) School characteristics; (4) School choice; (5) **Family background;** (6) Institutional approach.	Explaining underachievement of ethnic minorities.	Quantitative	Descendants of immigrants from: • Turkey • Morocco • Suriname	Collaborative relationship with considerable policy-funded and oriented research.	From pro-multicultural to more assimilation-oriented policies.	Initially in Dutch but increasingly more in English
Russia	(1) Languages of school education; (2) **School quality and ethnic background;** (3) Socio-cultural differences and education; (4) Problems of migrants and receiving society; (5) Students' inter-ethnic relations	Describing the educational problems experienced by various ethnic minority indigenous populations and migrants.	Quantitative	Indigenous (national) minority groups such as: • Tatars • Yakuts • Bashkirs • Chuvashs • Buriats • Armenians • Georgians.	Collaborative relationship with considerable policy-funded and oriented research.	A post-USSR context that is characterized by political tension conditioned by demands for cultural autonomy of various sub-national regions and ethnic minority groups.	Russian

| South Africa | (1) From oligarchy to democracy;
 (2) **Policy development – state versus resistance movements;**
 (3) The impact of the removal of race-based policies;
 (4) **Racial (de)segregation: causes and consequences;**
 (5) **(de)Segregation and school resources;**
 (6) Curriculum studies;
 (7) Teacher training and pedagogy;
 (8) Charting inequalities in student outcomes. | The development of social policy and the systematic educational inequalities between the majority black and minority white learners, in particular in relationship to achievement and school resources. | Quantitative | Black majority population. | Close collaborative ties with government as most research is government funded and aimed at evaluating and guiding social policy interventions. | From apartheid to post-apartheid regime. | English |

(continued)

Table 20.1 Continued

Country	Research traditions	Main research goal(s)	Dominant research designs	Focus on which racialized or ethnicized groups	Relationship between researchers and policy-makers, 1980–2012	Policy towards ethnic or racial minorities, 1980–2012	Main language of publication
United States of America	(1) **Emphasis on students;** (2) **Emphasis on families;** (3) **Emphasis on schools.**	Measuring and accounting for the race/ethnic-based test-score gaps; assessing the magnitude and effects of school desegregation and re-segregation; explaining the effects of the accountability movement on students and school staff.	Quantitative in assessing the magnitude and nature of the test-score gap; Quantitative and qualitative in examining the causes of the gap.	Racial and ethnic minorities and immigrant groups, especially native-born: • African Americans • Hispanics • Native Americans (Indians) • Asian Americans Immigrants from • Latin American • – Asia	A considerable amount of the research is either policy research or policy-relevant research; Many of the large studies have been funded by the US Department of Education or by state education agencies.	A combination of policies that encourage multiculturalism as well as assimilation, promote educational opportunities across racial/ ethnic and social class groups, but also address the threats by elites who seek to continue affluent and middle-class hegemony over educational advantages.	English

Note: Research traditions printed in bold are the most dominant traditions of research within this particular country.

of focus and employed methods, they often draw on different ideological start-ing points: while the Chinese literature draws more on a Marxist ideology of ethnic minority education which emphasizes the role of the state in creating national unity and patriotism, English research is much more critical of such a view and emphasizes much more the importance (and lack of) multicultural policies in education.

Third, the chapters included in this Handbook show that research on eth-nic and racial inequalities in education is strongly influenced by nationally specific political, economic, and demographic processes. For example, most of the research carried out in Northern Europe focuses on the underachievement of second- and third-generation immigrant children, whose parents migrated from Southern Europe, North Africa, Turkey, and former colonies, particularly between the 1960s and 1970s due to labor shortages in Northern European countries. In sharp contrast, research in **South Africa** is more focused on the educational inequality between the white minority and black majority population in South Africa and the importance of the apartheid legacy and post-apartheid policies in sustaining or changing these inequalities. While a vast amount of research has been conducted on ethnic and racial inequali-ties in the **USA**, focusing on large immigrant groups such as (children of) Spanish speaking migrants and descendants of the Spanish conquest of the New World, as well as Asian migrants, the most dominant tradition of research focuses on the persistent 'achievement gap' between the large and historically important (due to the legacy of slavery) black minority population and the white majority population. Finally, in **Russia**, research on multilingualism sharply increased after the collapse of the USSR and the subsequent regional developments of national and ethnic movements; as the politics of language became both related to a discourse on socio-economic inequality and cultural self-governance.

However, historical, political processes do not only influence the focus of research in terms of what are legitimate research questions and populations that need to be involved in research on ethnic and racial inequalities, but also how such research is framed. For instance, while there is considerable research on racial discrimination of ethnic minority groups and educational inequal-ity in **Germany**, this research is rarely framed as such but instead linked to research on the role of families, school structures and processes, and multilin-gualism. The reasons why this body of research rarely explicitly refers to racism (or racialized groups) is that the concept of racism in Germany is heavily linked to and used in the context of studying the racist ideologies and practices of Nazi Germany.

The chapters in this Handbook also show that it is important to study the process of how particular ethnic and racial inequalities (do not) become a legitimate social problem that requires attention from social policy-makers and educationalists. For example, the lack of large-scale nationally representative data and related studies on ethnic and racial inequalities is most pronounced in those countries and regions (e.g. **China**, **France**, **Japan**) where national policies prefer to downplay the importance of 'ethnic' or 'racial' background in developing educational inequalities (by, for instance, focusing instead on social class or poverty, or, as in the case of **Argentina**, where persons of non-European descent are categorized as 'the Other'). In contrast, in countries where governments have taken ethnic and racial inequalities in education on board as a policy concern, research on this topic, and particularly large-scale, quantitative research has flourished (e.g. **Belgium**, **Germany**, **The Netherlands**, **South Africa** and **the USA**), sometimes through direct funding of nationally specific policy-orientated research projects or through the participation in international comparative research projects (for the latter see, for instance, the chapter on **Austria**).

While, the (in)dependence of (particular types of) research on government funding poses important questions on how this relationship impacts on the production of knowledge and policy in this area, the chapters included on this Handbook suggest that there is considerable variability in terms of this relationship and its potential consequences. For example, research in **Argentina** and **Cyprus** is primarily qualitative, with strong roots in anthropology, and in both countries researchers adopt a more critical approach to social policy initiatives and educational processes, which are criticized for failing (often implicitly) to recognize ethnic minority interests and needs, and adopting a more assimilationist approach to diversity. However, while research in Cyprus has largely failed to make an impact on social policy and is – in terms of funding – largely independent from the government, researchers and social policy-makers in Argentina (and also in **Brazil**) seem to depend more on government funding and appear to have a more collaborative relationship in which critical research seems to lead to the adoption of more multicultural policy initiatives and practices in schools, which in turns spurs further research on these issues.

Fourth, in terms of focus on particular research traditions seven key traditions seem to dominate the field of ethnic and racial inequalities in education:

(1) Large-scale, mainly descriptive studies of (developments in) inequality in outcomes between ethnic and racial groups, particularly between the dominant (largest and/or most powerful) ethnic or racial group and various ethnic or racial minority groups;
(2) Racism in education, including a focus on policy, curriculum, pedagogy, and inter-ethnic or racial relationships and attitudes;
(3) The importance of family (and social class) background in accounting for differences in educational outcomes between majority and minority ethnic and racial groups;

(4) The importance of (structural) school characteristics in explaining variability in educational outcomes between majority and minority ethnic and racial groups;
(5) The development of students' ethnic/racial and national identities;
(6) Multilingualism;
(7) Teacher training.

Although most of these traditions feature in all the countries/regions included in this volume, the first four traditions tend to be the most dominant research traditions in the selected countries/regions. Whilst these seven research traditions are characterized by a different focus, there is considerable variability within each of these traditions and overlap between them. For instance, researchers working in the 'multilingualism' tradition often focus on issues related to racism, but also on the effectiveness and development of policy and school interventions, and the role of families in developing language and educational outcomes more generally (see, for instance, the reviews on **Argentina, Austria, Belgium, China, Finland, Germany** and **Russia**). Furthermore, some research traditions overlap in terms of their approach and focus, with studies producing findings that are relevant to different research traditions at the same time. This is particularly the case for quantitative research that aims to map inequalities in educational achievement between ethnic or racial groups and assess the importance of school and family characteristics in explaining these differences (see, for example, the chapter on **Austria**). Finally, cross-cutting these research traditions is a more basic philosophical and to some extent methodological divide with, on the one hand, researchers adopting more critical, relativistic and/or postmodern philosophical assumptions and qualitative research approaches (see, for example, research in **Argentina, Cyprus, England**) and, on the other hand, researchers working from a more post-positivistic and usually more quantitative research approach (see, for example, research in **Belgium, Russia** and **The Netherlands**). While the former are more focused on critically examining how the educational system and school processes disadvantage particular ethnic and racial groups and as a result perpetuate existing social, ethnic and racial inequalities in education, the latter are more concerned with charting and explaining variability in underachievement of ethnic and racial minority groups. This shows that the demarcation of specific research traditions is to some extent arbitrary, and that the research traditions identified in this Handbook should be conceptualized more as different and relatively loose sets of research that overlap in varying degrees.

However, the seven research traditions identified are different in terms of their general focus and often in terms of their adopted research methods, with quantitative research used predominantly by researchers working in traditions one, three and four and qualitative research methods mainly in traditions two, five and seven.

20.2   Conceptualizing minority group outcomes across nations

The second goal of this concluding chapter is to provide the reader with a conceptual framework with which to read the individual national chapters. In the broadest sense each of the disadvantaged racial, ethnic, and economic groups subject to differential and pejorative educational outcomes is a minority group (Dworkin and Dworkin, 1999). According to that perspective, minority group status is a process involving four linked components. Thus, we view minorities as groups that are (1) identifiable, (2) have differential (less) power, and consequently are (3) subjected to differential and pejorative treatment, and (4) ultimately develop a sense of group awareness or consciousness of kind. The conjoined effects of identifiability and differential power generally lead to pejorative treatment, which eventually facilitates group awareness. This definition of minority avoids the problems associated with 'trait definitions' (see also below) in which specific phenotypic or genotypic characteristics or cultural patterns are specified, thereby requiring a continuous updating of the definition whenever a new disadvantaged group arrives.

Theoretical work by two groups of scholars can provide the basis for the present conceptual argument. First, Pierre van den Bergh (1967) noted that the relationships between the dominant group and the minority group often was influenced by the extent to which race relations in the society was 'paternalistic' or 'competitive'. The nature of initial contact and the history of conflict among the groups will affect the extent to which the minorities are stereotyped as 'intellectually and biologically inferior' and hence relatively uneducable, as seen in paternalistic systems. Such presumptions may focus research agendas on accounts for present academic outcomes and attainments. By contrast, when minorities are seen as competitors, restrictions of educational opportunities may occur in order to prevent the minority from gaining an advantage at the expense of the majority. Sometimes societies move from paternalistic to competitive race relations in the course of this history. Thus, in the USA relations between whites and African Americans were initially paternalistic, during the era of slavery and following racial segregation. Opposition to affirmative action and the emergence of the Standards-based School Accountability movement in the 1980s and beyond reflect white middle-class concerns that white hegemony and privilege had ebbed. Relations between groups in **South Africa** are also undergoing such a transition under black rule, while the treatment of South Asians in **South Africa** reflected a combination of paternalistic and competitive forces. Asian Indians were brought to South Africa by whites because it was assumed that they were more capable of low-level management activities than were the native population, but there were concerns about the extent to which Asian Indians might gain too many advantages because of their hard work. By contrast, the relations between the dominant populations in most of the European countries in this Handbook and other European and Turkish minorities reflect issues of concerns about competition, including fears that the guest workers and political refugees who do not leave will alter the nature of the society to which they emigrated. In fact, educational issues associated with the children of guest workers may include condoning educational inequalities on the assumption that the children will leave shortly, while the education of children of political refugees who are culturally quite different from the dominant population may create longer-term strains that raise research questions about pressures toward assimilation as seen in **Finland, Austria, Germany, France, Belgium** and **The Netherlands**, and **China's** treatment of some of its population in the western portion of the nation. In the case of **France**, the assumption has been that all people in France are de facto 'French'.

Michael Banton (1967) in his analysis of possible outcomes of intergroup relations held that different forms of initial contact between groups affect future outcomes. Thus, the long-term outcome of domination, whereby the minority group is conquered and oppressed may result in a pluralistic society with the minority retaining its distinctive culture. Paternalism and acculturation, Banton notes, will lead to integration and the incorporation of the minority into the core society. However, Aboriginal peoples in Australia and Native American groups in the USA have experienced both domination and paternalism, and some have remained excluded (or protected) from assimilation into the dominant society. The same has been the condition of some tribal groups in **South Africa, Brazil**, and to some extent in **Argentina**.

Another useful theoretical orientation incorporates work on the nature of economic systems and the obligations nations owe their people. Green, Preston, and Janmaat (2006) examined the interplay between educational and employment opportunities, social capital, and social cohesion. They described three models, each with different consequences for social cohesion and for minority populations. The Social Democratic and Nordic model, exemplified in the Handbook by the chapter on **Finland**, has high levels of economic productivity, high employment, life-long learning that promotes continuous job-skill improvements, a strong social welfare policy, but tends to reserve these benefits to citizens, especially those who are from the dominant population. Culturally different minorities are a concern for the educational system, especially for non-standard language learners. Thus, research in educational inequality will explore the extent to which such societies encourage the assimilation of immigrant minority groups as a prerequisite for equity. The Social Market model, as found in **France, Germany**, and **Austria** maintains high productivity due to the reliance on technology, but labor agreements lead to shorter working hours and lower employment rates. Domination by high-priced labor presents barriers to immigrant and minority workers. Research in social market countries will more often focus on the extent to which minorities are considered to be sojourners with less attention paid to societal efforts to produce cohesion and assimilation of immigrant groups. Finally, the Liberal Anglo-Saxon model as seen in the **UK**, **USA**, **Canada**, and **Australia** has high employment and somewhat longer working hours, with more diversity in the better-paid labor force. Additionally, more restricted welfare policies than in the Nordic countries results in less social cohesion. Research on educational inequality will tend to focus on how meritocratic policies and restrictions on access to educational resources have produced such inequalities.

20.3   Directions for future research

A final goal of this concluding chapter is to identify particular gaps in or issues with the literature that can stimulate researchers in developing more innovative research questions that build on this rich area of research. These suggestions are based on our reading of the various chapters and are by no means comprehensive. Hence, readers might not (fully) agree with our analysis of the research literature or consider additional issues to be more important. Nevertheless we feel that innovation in this rich area of research is possible by considering (some of) these suggestions.

20.3.1   Further integration of qualitative and quantitative research on the importance of educational systems in developing inequality

In focusing on the role of schools and educational systems more generally researchers tend to either opt for large-scale quantitative studies to investigate how school structural characteristics (such as composition of student population, school resources) impact on educational outcomes, or for qualitative case-studies to investigate processes of racism and discrimination in education. A notable exception concerns research on ability grouping (or processes of tracking, streaming, or setting), which covers a long tradition of both qualitative and quantitative studies that build on each other but only indirectly focus on ethnic and racial inequalities in education (for reviews see, for instance, Gamoran and Berends, 1987; Van Houtte, 2004). However, quantitative research in the 'school effectiveness' tradition and qualitative research on racism in education could develop more comprehensive models and expand our knowledge of how schools and educational systems more generally influence ethnic and racial inequalities in education by incorporating each other's findings and methodological approaches.

For example, while there is a very rich tradition of qualitative research that describes in detail the complex nature of racism in education, as expressed in policies, pedagogy, the curriculum, and the experiences of ethnic minorities in education, there is virtually no research that aims to test the occurrence and impact of different forms of racism on a broad range of educational and wider outcomes (for an exception, see Chapter 18 on **the Netherlands**), with qualitative research either assuming such effects or establishing them in relationship to small groups or by focusing mainly on racism as a negative outcome that needs to be addressed. Quantitative research could add to our understanding of how racism impacts on outcomes by testing some of the key hypotheses developed in qualitative research in relationship to racism. A key challenge in doing this concerns the measurement of (anti-)racism, and related to this, the development of large-scale quantitative research projects that are specifically designed to test the development and effects of (anti-)racism in education by using a broad range of existing and validated indicators of (anti-)racism (Quillian, 2006) and, by developing new measurement tools that are sensitive to the complex and hidden nature of how (anti-)racism operates in schools and society more general (for example. Pinterits et al., 2009).

20.3.2 More international, comparative research on the influence of institutional processes

One of the key findings of this Handbook is that research on race/ethnic inequalities is primarily focused on particular (national/regional) educational systems, instead of examining how differences between educational systems impact on ethnic and racial inequalities in education.

While there is a developing body of cross-national, comparative research on the performance of students on standardized tests and the importance of key school and family background characteristics in explaining differences between countries in terms of differential student achievement (see, for instance, Chapter 19 on **USA** for more information), there is a lack of research that investigates how specific education and school selection, evaluation, and support systems impact on ethnic minority and majority students' educational outcomes, particularly in relationship to key transition points in students' school careers (e.g. the transition from primary to secondary education). Crul and Schneider rightly emphasize the fruitfulness of adopting what they call an 'institutional approach' (see Chapter 18), which relies on both quantitative and qualitative international comparative research to investigate how minorities' educational trajectories differ between countries, and how this variability can be explained by pointing to specific characteristics of educational systems. They conclude that such research does not lead to particular judgments of educational systems as either 'bad' or 'good' but as having different consequences for different groups of students.

In addition, international comparative research is not synonymous with choosing large (random) and more representative samples, in that researchers should consider the benefits from doing research in particular national contexts that are theoretically interesting to compare. The case of **Belgium** illustrates both the importance of conducting comparative case-study research on ethnic and racial inequalities in education between regions and how strongly the development of research in this area depends on cultural traditions and political structures. Belgium is divided into three main regions, with the mainly Dutch-speaking northern (Flanders) and French-speaking southern regions (Wallonia) the largest; regions that (since 1989) are also responsible for the organization of their respective educational systems. Analysis of PISA data suggests that Flemish secondary students obtain on average much higher scores on standardized tests compared to their peers from Wallonia, even after controlling for students' social background characteristics (Prokic-Breuer and Dronkers, 2011). In addition, while the same PISA data shows that inequalities between ethnic majority and minority students in both regions are amongst the highest of all EU countries (Jacobs et al., 2009), there are important differences between the achievement patterns of ethnic minorities, as ethnic minority students are more likely to obtain a secondary school diploma in Flanders, but less likely to obtain a university diploma compared to their peers in Wallonia (see Chapter 5 on **Flanders** for more information). Despite these theoretically interesting differences between these two regions, researchers in Flanders pay almost no attention to the context of and research carried out in Wallonia and vice versa (but see Chapter 7 on **Canada** for closer links between researchers working in different institutional and cultural regions). Similarly, the reviews on Brazil, South Africa and the USA show how these countries differ in terms of the historical development and (perceived) contemporary nature of race-relations. A similar observation has encouraged Lareau and colleagues (Lamont and Mizrachi, 2012) to investigate how country-specific historical processes inform the discourses that are available and used by racial minorities in responding to experiences of racism. In addition, researchers could, for instance, explore how different models of multiculturalism and assimilation as applied in particular countries (with France and the UK as obvious examples in an EU context) impact on the development of race and ethnic inequalities in education. Finally, Stevens and Van Houtte compare how teachers' perceptions and interactions with ethnic minority students are informed by a market-driven (school accountability) educational context (i.e. England) and a system where teachers and schools have much more freedom and power to determine the careers of students (i.e. Belgium). These examples suggests the importance of future qualitative and quantitative case-studies conducted in carefully selected national and/or regional contexts.

20.3.3   More research on how actors negotiate structural and cultural opportunities and constraints

Most sociological research on race and ethnic inequalities in education investigates how the social organization of educational settings or the social background characteristics of ethnic minority families facilitate or constrain the opportunities of minority students, without paying much attention to how young people manage these structural and cultural characteristics. While a rich line of research developed in **England** focuses on how (particularly) Muslim girls and parents of different social classes negotiate various structural and cultural constraints and opportunities in making educational choices, several fruitful lines of analysis could be further developed in this respect. For instance, research on racism could further develop by focusing more on the variability in actors' strategies in response to racism (Mellor, 2004), both in terms of how the social context informs students' choices for responding to racism in particular ways, and the impact of such strategies on their educational and wider outcomes (Brondolo et al., 2009). In addition, while there is considerable research that critically analyzes the development and content of educational policies, there is far less research that investigates how teachers in schools enact or translate such policies in their everyday interactions with their social environment in schools, and how this impacts on race and ethnic inequalities in education (Ball et al., 2012). In a way, this calls for a revaluation and contemporary application of classic ethnographic and symbolic interactionist studies that developed mainly in the UK in the 1970s and 1980s, and which highlight the importance of considering students, parents, and school staff as active (re)creators of their own social environment (Delamont, 1977; Hammersley and Woods, 1984; Hargreaves and Woods, 1984; Woods, 1990; Woods and Hammersley, 1977). Research with a stronger focus on the role of 'agency' would help not only to develop more comprehensive and less deterministic theories for race and ethnic inequalities in education, but also to deconstruct prevailing stereotypes of certain racial and ethnic groups in popular discourse.

20.3.4   Interrogating notions of (in)equality and ethnicity/race

In line with Foster, Gomm and Hammersley (1996), we call for a more critical approach to how researchers conceptualize and measure notions of 'equality' and 'equity'. Whilst a concern for more equal opportunities and outcomes for racial and ethnic minorities drives almost all research written in this area, there is virtually no consideration of or critical reflection on what is actually meant by these concepts, and why certain indicators and/or (often implicit) definitions of what constitutes 'inequality' should be favored over others. In line with the contributors' observation in relationship to research carried out in **Canada**, we find that in most countries two general, almost oppositional views in relationship to equality emerge. While the first view equates inequality with academic underachievement, linked to (lack of) social mobility, a second view perceives inequality more in terms of an equal, accurate, or representative portrayal of cultural knowledge, history, and difference. While the first view appears to be more dominant in research on ethnic and racial inequalities in education (see overview grid), there is little consideration given to why and how certain conceptualizations and measurements of 'underachievement' are preferred over others (and preferred over 'educational success') and how actors develop particular definitions (including those of minority students themselves) of these concepts and the processes and contexts underlying their views. A very interesting exception in this respect constitutes the debate that developed in **England** over the measurement of educational outcomes between racial and ethnic minorities over time (see Chapter 10), which shows that very different conclusions can be drawn regarding the 'underachievement' of particular groups depending on how this is measured and interpreted.

Similarly, future research should adopt a more careful approach to the use of 'ethnicity' and 'race' as explanatory concepts. Typically, research tends to focus on ethnic and racial groups that are considered to be sufficiently large and/ or visible and/or politically recognized and/or underachieving in a particular national or regional context. This often leads to the construction and use of particular ethnic or racial classifications which are subject to change and contested in terms of their validity (see for instance the chapter on **Brazil** which describes ongoing debates on the validity of the classification system proposed by the government). In line with more contemporary criticism leveled at much sociological research that uses ethnic and racial groups as structural (ontological) determining forces (Brubaker, 2004; Carter and Fenton, 2009), researchers should focus more on how people develop particular in-group identifications and out-group categorizations in relationship to educational inequality, and how such ethnicized and racialized notions of collective belonging and positioning are mobilized as a resource, rather than assigning any determining force or constitutive properties *a priori* to such groups. As a result, instead of 'explaining Turkish underachievement', researchers could focus more on the processes and factors that are shared by people who 'underachieve', which might highlight the importance of experienced discrimination, collective identifications, and availability and strategic use of particular social and cultural resources that do not necessarily overlap with the experiences and characteristics of a group of 'students whose mother or grandmother was born in Turkey' or other (often implicit) measurements of 'ethnicity' or 'race'. In so doing the underlying processes and factors that result in particular educational outcomes become detached from any *a priori* assumptions about so-called ethnic or racial groups. In some national contexts, the different ways in which ethnicity and race are used as concepts in research has resulted in the development of very different, almost oppositional traditions of research that focus on different research questions and findings, even when focusing on similar issues (see for example the discussion in the chapters on **Canada** or the **USA** on research analyzing the impact of teacher expectations on students).

In the course of this Handbook the contributors and the editors have attempted to emphasize that the research traditions found in each country reflect the particular salient social issues present in that country. Because sociological research often has substantial policy implications, and in fact, is frequently undertaken to inform and influence educational decision-makers, the watchword for much of the research discussed in this Handbook is 'relevance'. Our purpose in organizing this Handbook has been two-fold. First, we wanted to portray the rich diversity of research traditions, existing cross-nationally, that address educational inequalities in our globalizing world. Second, we wanted to develop a framework by which educational researchers from many parts of the world can come to recognize that in this diversity of research traditions there are also numerous commonalities, albeit influenced by the particular nature of a society's history of intergroup contacts. In a world in which education is increasingly being globalized and in which standards and measurement of academic achievement have ramifications for the competitiveness of national labor forces (Pigozzi, 2006), we think that both diversity and commonality of research themes and traditions can be most informative.

References

Ball, S. J., Maguire, M. and Braun, A. 2012. *How Schools do Policy: Policy Enactments in Secondary Schools*, London: Routledge.

Banton, M. 1967. *Race Relations*, New York: Basic Books.

Brondolo, E., Brady Ver Halen, N., Pencille, M., Beatty, D. and Contrada, R. J. 2009. Coping with Racism: A Selective Review of the Literature and a Theoretical and Methodological Critique. *Journal of Behavioral Medicine*, 32: 64–88.

Brubaker, R. 2004. *Ethnicity Without Groups*, Cambridge, MA, Harvard University Press.

Carter, B. and Fenton, S. 2009. Not Thinking Ethnicity: A Critique of the Ethnicity Paradigm in an Over-Ethnicised Sociology. *Journal for the Theory of Social Behaviour*, 40: 1–18.

Delamont, S. (ed.) 1977. *Readings on Interactionism in the Classroom: Contemporary Sociology of the School*, London/New York: Methuen.

Dworkin, A. G. and Dworkin, R. J. 1999. *The Minority Report*, New York: Harcourt Brace Publishers.

Foster, P., Gomm, R. and Hammersley, M. 1996. *Constructing Educational Inequality: An Assessment of Research on School Processes*, London: Falmer.

Gamoran, A. and Berends, M. 1987. The Effects of Stratification in Secondary Schools: Synthesis of Survey and Ethnographic Research. *Review of Educational Research*, 57: 415–435.

Green, A., Preston, J., and Janmaat, J. G. 2006. *Education, Equality, and Social Cohesion: A Comparative Analysis*, Basingstoke: Palgrave Macmillan.

Hammersley, M. and Woods, P. 1984. *Life in School: The Sociology of Pupil Culture*, Milton Keynes: Open University Press.

Hargreaves, A. and Woods, P. 1984. *Classrooms and Staffrooms: The Sociology of Teachers and Teaching*, Milton Keynes: Open University Press.

Jacobs, D., Rea, A., Teney, C., Callier, L. and Lothaire, S. 2009. *De sociale lift blijft steken. De prestaties van allochtone leerlingen in de Vlaamse Gemeenschap en de Franse Gemeenschap*, Brussels: De Koning Boudewijnstichting.

Lamont, M. and Mizrachi, N. 2012. Ordinary People doing Extraordinary Things: Responses to Stigmatization in Comparative Perspective. *Ethnic and Racial Studies,* 35: 365–381.

Mellor, D. 2004. Responses to Racism: A Taxonomy of Coping Styles Used by Aboriginal Australians. *American Journal of Orthopsychiatry,* 74: 56–71.

Pigozzi, M. J. 2006. 'What Is the Quality of Education?' A UNESCO Perspective. pp. 39–50 in K. N. Ross and. I. J. Genevois. *Cross-national Studies of the Quality of Education: Planning Their Design and Managing Their Impact.* Paris: UNESCO: International Institute for Educational Planning (http://www.unesco.org/iiep).

Pinterits, E. J., Spanierman, L. B. and Poteat, P. V. 2009. The White Privilege Attitudes Scale: Development and Initial Validation. *Journal of Clinical Psychology,* 56: 417–429.

Prokic-Breuer, T. and Dronkers, J. 2011. Highly Differentiated but Still Not the Same Results: Explaining Differences in Educational Achievement Between Highly Differentiated Educational Systems with General and Vocational Training. *Onderwijsresearchdagen.* University of Maastricht (Netherlands).

Quillian, L. 2006. New Approaches to Understanding Racial Prejudice and Discrimination. *Annual Review of Sociology,* 32: 299–328.

Van Den Berghe, P. 1967. *Race and Racism: A Comparative Perspective,* New York: Wiley.

Van Houtte, M. 2004. Tracking Effects on School Achievement: A Quantitative Explanation in Terms of the Academic Culture of School Staff. *American Journal of Education,* 110: 354–388.

Woods, P. 1990. *The Happiest Days? How Pupils Cope with School,* London/New York: The Falmer Press.

Woods, P. and Hammersley, M. (eds) 1977. *School Experience. Explorations in the Sociology of Education,* New York: St Martin's Press.

Index

Printed and bound by CPI Group (UK) Ltd, Croydon, CR0 4YY